PRAISE FOR THE *NEW YORK TIMES* BESTSELLER

Ladies of Liberty

"What women these were! . . . [Roberts] is perfectly placed to observe the ins and outs of Washington women. . . . If you love gossipy history, with lively quotes from primary sources (these ladies
were fabulous correspondents!), then you'll enjoy this book."
—*Washington Post*

"Entertaining. . . . Surprising. . . . Intriguing. . . . With a little-seen
perspective and fascinating insight into the culture of the day, this
is popular history done right." —*Publishers Weekly* (starred review)

"Total immersion in the period. . . . [Roberts] knows how to create the rich surround of a woman's life—from what women were
reading and writing, to what they were wearing, what recipes they
made, what they were thinking. . . . Here is a parade of history, a
krewe of powerful women and presidents' wives. . . . A collective
portrait of female solidarity." —*Times-Picayune* (New Orleans)

"*Ladies of Liberty* is both scholarly and accessible, deftly organizing
a great deal of information—in a humorous, confiding, and unpre-
tentious style that her fans will recognize."
—*Pittsburgh Post-Gazette*

"Roberts weaves a colorful story of the trials and triumphs of the
women of the post-Revolution by quoting letters, journals, and
other documents written by and about women. . . . *Ladies of Liberty*
is not only informative but entertaining, thanks to Roberts. . . .
She's a keen political observer, as well as a feminist, whose remarks
enliven the text." —*Denver Post*

© Lynn Goldsmith

About the Author

COKIE ROBERTS is a political commentator for ABC News and a senior news analyst for National Public Radio. From 1996 to 2002, she and Sam Donaldson coanchored the weekly ABC interview program *This Week*.

In addition to broadcasting, Roberts, along with her husband, Steven V. Roberts, writes a weekly column syndicated in newspapers around the country by United Media. Both are also contributing editors to *USA Weekend*, and together they wrote *From This Day Forward*, an account of their now more than forty-year marriage and other marriages in American history. The book immediately went onto the *New York Times* bestseller list, following a six-month run on the list by Roberts's first book on women in American history, *We Are Our Mothers' Daughters*. Roberts is also the author of the bestselling *Founding Mothers*, the companion volume to *Ladies of Liberty*. A mother of two and grandmother of six, she lives with her husband in Bethesda, Maryland.

Ladies of Liberty

Also by Cokie Roberts

From This Day Forward
with Steve Roberts

We Are Our Mothers' Daughters

Founding Mothers

Ladies of Liberty

THE WOMEN WHO SHAPED OUR NATION

Cokie Roberts

HARPER PERENNIAL

NEW YORK • LONDON • TORONTO • SYDNEY • NEW DELHI • AUCKLAND

HARPER ● PERENNIAL

A hardcover edition of this book was published in 2008 by William Morrow, an imprint of HarperCollins Publishers.

HarperCollins books may be purchased for educational, business, or sales promotional use. For information please write: Special Markets Department, HarperCollins Publishers, 10 East 53rd Street, New York, NY 10022.

FIRST HARPER PERENNIAL EDITION PUBLISHED 2009.

Designed by Gretchen Achilles

Library of Congress Cataloging-in-Publication Data is available upon request.

ISBN 978-0-06-078235-1 (pbk.)

09 10 11 12 13 WBC/RRD 10 9 8 7 6 5 4 3 2 1

To my sister, Barbara Boggs Sigmund, my toughest teacher, who always wanted to write history.

And to my sisterhood, my wonderful women friends—including relatives—who share my prayers, works, joys and sufferings.

CONTENTS

Contents

Acknowledgments and Author's Note

First a word about what this book is and what it isn't. It is the story, told as much as possible in their own words, of the influential women in the period between the inauguration of John Adams in 1797 and his son, John Quincy Adams in 1825. It is not the story of everyday women in the late eighteenth and early nineteenth centuries, many of whom had much harder lives than the elite women who had the ears of the Founding Fathers. Because I wanted to focus on the story, not the writings, I have modernized and corrected the spelling and punctuation to make the letters and journals easier to read.

This book turned out to be a much bigger undertaking than I expected for happy reasons. After I wrote *Founding Mothers,* the librarians and custodians of collections, historical societies, and historic homes saw that their troves of papers would be of use, and they have been steadfast about finding unpublished treasures for this project. For a couple of years now, I've waited with anticipation for some packet of letters to arrive in the mail, providing fresh insights. Once the packets showed up, they were often tough-going—Xeroxed eighteenth century handwriting can be very rough to read—but they were thrilling. Seeing Abigail Adams's handwriting is a treat all unto itself. And then there were the unexpected pleasures. Sitting in the beautiful reading room of the Huntington Library, coming across the invitations from members of the Napoleonic court to Ruth and Joel Barlow was truly exciting. It was all I could do not to let out a whoop that would not have pleased my fellow researchers. There were some disappointments along the way as well. I had hoped to find information about my own family. An ancestor, William Charles

Cole Claiborne, the first governor of Louisiana, is a character in this book and I thought someone might have letters from at least one of his three wives, but I couldn't find any female Claiborne papers. That was too bad, but there was so much I did find, and that others found for me, that I was able to get to these wonderful women and enable them to speak to us over the centuries. So there are many people to thank.

Ann Charnley, intrepid researcher and friend, has been working with me on books for more than ten years now (she won't let me say how long we've been friends) and this one was by far the most challenging. Knowing what we know now about the need to locate, preserve and publish women's letters, she is launching a fundraising drive to build the Founding Mothers Digital Archive, a website for women's papers, so that posterity will have access to the other half of history. Annie Downing not only did all of the many, many footnotes in this book, she also keeps the rest of my working life on track, with humor and good sense. Heather Gilbert rode in to save me at the last minute by transcribing the letters of Louisa Catherine and John Quincy Adams. My friend and lawyer Bob Barnett shepherded this project as he does all of my work, with my interest at heart. Without Claire Wachtel, my editor and coconspirator, this book wouldn't exist, nor would any of the earlier ones—a huge thanks to her for her guidance in many ways, not to mention the laughs. At William Morrow, Barbara Levine found the women's portraits for the cover and chapter heads; Kim Lewis somehow managed to get this book printed with grace under pressure; Joyce Wong, the production editor, had to work super-fast; the phenomenal DeeDee DeBartlo is the best publicist in the business; and thanks to publisher, Lisa Gallagher. And at the "parent," HarperCollins: Claire's able-assistant Julia Novitch; the talented and kind Michael Morrison, and the woman much like those in this book, the woman who shaped the publishing world, Jane Friedman.

The Massachusetts Historical Society, which has the most amazing website where John Quincy Adams's Diary is available online, was particularly helpful as I kept asking for more and more information about the fascinating Louisa Catherine Adams. I'm happy to say that MHS will be publishing her papers soon. Dennis Fiori, the president of the society has been especially supportive, along with Peter Drummey, Judith Graham, Jeremy Dibbell, Laura Lowell, and Kim Nusco. Also, everyone connected with Louise Livingston was a big help. I started with Bonnie Livingston who sent me to Mary Ann Fish who sent me to Wint Aldrich and Joey Delafield, who reproduced the book about Louise for me. At Historic Hudson Valley Kathleen Eagan Johnson and Catalina Hannan were terrific. Thanks to Olga Tsapina and Kate Henningsen for the Ruth Barlow letters at the Huntington Library. Holly Cowan Shulman has created the Dolley Madison Digital Edition, a remarkable resource. Thanks to her and to Jason Coleman for access to it. Dan Preston at the University of Mary Washington, Jim Wootten at Virginia's Capitol Square Preservation Council, and Doris Delk at the Virginia Historical Society, aided with the elusive Elizabeth Kortright Monroe. And Fredricka Teute, on a fellowship this year at Washington College, filled in the blanks on Margaret Bayard Smith. Jane Aldrich at the South Carolina Historical Society did the same for Mary Stead Pinckney, along with Henry Fulmer at the University of South Carolina. And to all the following a big thank-you: Dan Jordan, Susan Stein, Sue Purdue, and Jeff Looney at Monticello and Anna Berkes at the Jefferson Library; Jennifer Kittlaus at Mount Vernon; Barbara Bair and Janice Ruth at the Library of Congress; Ellen Dunlap at the American Antiquarian Society; the Historical Society of Washington, D.C.; the New York Historical Society, which is enjoying a grand revival; the New York Public Library; and the Boston Public Library. The *Legacy Reprint Series* has made access to old books much more available and affordable by reproducing them in inexpensive formats. And Google, the internet search engine, has made research about ten thousand times easier than it was even four years ago. To sit at home and type in the names of the people inviting Ruth Barlow to tea in early nineteenth century Paris and find out who they are in seconds is a blessing. The American Association for State and Local History is the organization representing the custodians of much of this information. Its New Century Endowment Campaign is well worth supporting.

It would be impossible to even contemplate an enterprise of this magnitude without the care of my friends and family. My great "girl bosses" at NPR and ABC, Ellen McDonnell and Robin Sproul, were understanding as always. Kim Roellig, who has become a good friend over many years, makes it possible for me to continue to be a human being while off on a project like this—she does what I should be doing but better. My wonderful daughter-in-law, Liza Roberts, offered support above and beyond the ordinary, taking time out from her own busy writing schedule and the raising of my three adorable grandchildren to edit carefully every word. My delightful daughter Rebecca Roberts also added to her already heavy load as radio host and mother of the other three adorable grandchildren to give the book a read and cheer me on. And there's no way to say enough about my husband, Steven. He has picked up the load of much of my over-booked life—not just by writing our weekly newspaper column and doing a good many household chores, but by sharing the caretaking and concern for our mothers, usually a task left to the women of the family. He is my biggest fan and best friend. He is my love. And finally, my smelly old Basset hound, Rupert, who kept me constant company through the writing process. He is very happy that the alarm is no longer going off at five A.M.

INTRODUCTION

THE NEW AMERICAN NATION bristled with expectation and exploration at the end of the eighteenth and beginning of the nineteenth centuries. But the Old World looked with such skepticism at the upstart across the sea that the country was forced to fight what amounted to a second war of independence. In this unsettled, still self-defining time women were in the middle of everything—contributing to the culture as writers and educators, shaping the society as reformers and religious, expanding the nation as settlers and seekers. And though they possessed no official power—not only were women denied the right to vote, married women could not even own property—their considerable political influence is evident in their own words and those of the men in their lives. Take, for example, the great trader John Jacob Astor's letter to Dolley Madison in 1812, after war had been declared, thanking her for following through on a promise: "He well remembers Mrs. Madison's assurances that all Mr. Astor's ships should arrive and he is happy to say that they have arrived from Canton with valuable cargos." The First Lady had been the one to guarantee his ships' safe passage. Everyone seemed to take it for granted that these elite women would be called upon to play essential parts. Soon after Elizabeth Pinckney married William Lowndes, her father, statesman and General Thomas Pinckney, charged her with studying her husband's plantation books because public life would soon call him: "Lowndes cannot escape it, for the country will demand it, and you must learn to manage his business for him."

As central as they were to the survival of the country, the women have been almost completely obscured by America's best-known politicians—the men we call the Founding Fathers. Not only have there been countless volumes analyzing their actions, they remain a daily part of American political life, invoked in legislative chambers, consulted in courtrooms, lauded in political campaigns. I have written about politics and Congress for more than three decades, and the men who wrote the Declaration of Independence and the Constitution have become my close acquaintances. That's one of the reasons why I wrote *Founding Mothers* a few years ago. I wanted to know what the women were up to while the men were thinking their great thoughts. Unsurprisingly, it turned out that the women were heroic in a time when heroic acts were called for in resisting the British, enforcing boycotts, enduring war, sacrificing for the cause. I had expected that book to end with the election of John Quincy Adams—when the torch of the American presidency passed to a new generation. But it was getting to be much too big a book, and I would never have made the deadline. I stopped with the inauguration of his father instead, after the first contested presidential election testing the new Constitution.

Now that I've learned about the women of this next period—from Adams to Adams—I'm so glad I didn't give them short shrift by jamming them into the end of that book. The years from the presidency of John Adams to the election of his son are not as dramatic as the Revolutionary period, but in many ways they're more important. It's much easier to band together, as the Founding Fathers did, to fight against an outside enemy than to hold together while differing philosophically and politically on ends as well as means—on what kind of country would and should emerge from this American experiment. At various points over these years fierce partisanship and regional jealousies threatened our nationhood when it was too young and fragile to withstand the blows easily. But even as the men were literally ready to kill each other, to fight duels over political arguments—the women continually tried to provide wise counsel and cool the passions. Exception: Abigail Adams, who was considerably more partisan than her husband. But she is the exception who proves the rule—with her intemperate advice and her failure to act as an ameliorator, her husband lost reelection.

Washington women used the world of society, from formal receptions to casual card parties, to bring men together to effect political ends. In the fledgling federal city everything was still evolving in terms of who played what role. In that fluid situation, the worlds of state and society overlapped so thoroughly that it was impossible to tell where one left off and the other began. As a reporter, I went digging for the best sources on all of this activity and found them to be the women themselves plus their friends and relatives. With only a handful of exceptions, every quotation in this book is either written by a woman, to a woman, or about a woman. It turns out that the men consulted the women constantly. Aaron Burr sought his daughter's guidance about his amours; Rosalie Calvert's father needed her business acumen for his investments. In fact, the way fathers benefited from their daughters' wisdom turned out to be one of the many happy surprises of this book.

Surprises, because history looks very different when seen through the eyes of women. I would argue that the view is much broader, not only because it includes the other half of the human race but also because the men become more three-dimensional when they correspond with women, and especially when women correspond *about* them. The marble and bronze deities we know as the Founding Fathers become flesh-and-blood fathers, husbands, lovers, sons, and friends with all the passion and playfulness, flaws and feelings that go with those roles. When these men addressed each other it was usually with great seriousness (often well over the line into pomposity); they assumed their correspondence would be preserved and with all probability published and pored over. Those letters carry the weight of posterity. When the same men wrote to women, they showed much more of themselves. Even the dour John Quincy Adams could be delightful when writing to his wife. On his way to Ghent to negotiate the treaty ending the War of 1812, he gave a running commentary to Louisa back in St. Petersburg on the people and places along the way: "There is so much gossiping in my letters to you, that if the inspectors of the post office at the Capital take the trouble of opening and reporting them to the government, my diplomatic gravity and dignity will be 'furiousemant compromise.'"

And who else but his wife would learn that the great jurist John Marshall went riding the circuit without any breeches! When Marshall discovered his predicament "I immediately set out to get a pair made. I thought I should be a sans culotte only one day," but he found all the tailors in the town of Raleigh, North Carolina, too busy to help him, and "I have the extreme mortification to pass the whole term without that important article of dress I have mentioned." What a mental image!

When writing to women the men were not just less guarded about their personal foibles, they were also more honest about their political judgments. In 1814, Congressman William Lowndes believed that the peace negotiators would soon end the War of 1812 but he wouldn't say so in public: "It is indeed, very important that our exertions should not be weakened by the opinion that they may be unnecessary. Yet the hope in which I sometimes indulge myself I cannot refuse to communicate to you." That communication assumed discretion on the part of Elizabeth Lowndes and, in fact, she was so discreet that her friends thought her husband refused to share confidences with her. She finally asked him to tell her when "facts or opinions were to be kept to herself." Hannah Gallatin, on the other hand, almost wrecked the country's borrowing ability because she couldn't keep her mouth shut. Her husband, longtime Treasury Secretary Albert Gallatin, was one of the commissioners negotiating an end to the War of 1812. When she spread it about that he had written a gloomy assessment of the peace prospects, the news came close to causing a calamity. Her friend Dolley Madison warned Hannah that her reports "had a distressing effect on our loan & threw many into consternation for a while but we were able to contradict and soften consequences." Message delivered, Dolley then went on to talk about mutual friends.

And that's the way it works with these women's letters. What a treat! In one often dashed-off page we find out about the issues of the day, and how the writer thinks they should be handled; who is having babies, and all too often losing them; what business transactions she's conducted; what's in fashion, who's in town, and just generally good gossip. Most are lively and fun and, especially, frank. We hear from these women on everything from politics to pregnancy and we see this period of history from their perspective.

My interest in the power of political wives comes from my own experiences growing up in politics. My own mother, Lindy Boggs, whose family was always in public office, found herself a congressional wife at the age of twenty-four, a Member of Congress herself at the age of fifty-seven, and ambassador to the Vatican at the age of eighty-one. She would be the first to say that a woman should be in any room where powerful decisions are made, but she is very interesting about power behind-the-scenes versus the onstage role. Her decades of backstage experience swaying extremely powerful men—congressional leaders and presidents—made her much more successful once *she* was the player on the scene. Her biggest problem when she was actually elected to Congress, as my politician sister had warned her, was that she had to vote—to say yes or no—instead of seeming to side with everyone, cajoling them until they came to the conclusion she wanted. She was in a direct line of descendants from Dolley Madison, a brilliant people-person. When Dolley's husband was running for reelection, a member of the opposition party complimented the First Lady: "By her deportment in her own house you cannot discover who is her husband's friends or foes."

In the 1950s and '60s I watched my mother and the other political wives, along with the local African-American women who were their allies, run all the social services in Washington—family and child services, homes for unwed mothers, for the homeless, for victims of domestic violence, hospitals, food banks, you name it. They also ran their husbands' campaigns, the national political conventions, the voter registration drives, the presidential inaugurations, and all of the social events where many of the deals were struck that later became law. And of course they managed us kids as well, as we moved back and forth from our fathers' states to the federal city.

With my mother in mind, much seemed familiar to me as I learned about the women of the earliest days of Washington. Take the question of where to live—congressional families constantly struggle with the choice of settling in the District of Columbia or staying in the home district, and now I know they've always struggled with that question. As little children, our family lived in Washington when Congress was in session, in Louisiana when it was not. My sister and brother and I went to school half-year in each place. As we grew older and started going to school year-round in Washington, spending the summers and Christmas in Louisiana, we were often separated from our father—there was never a perfect solution to the two-city problem. When Senator John Quincy Adams and his wife, Louisa, tried moving their small boys back and forth between Washington and Boston, they found it expensive and difficult. Much to Louisa's dismay her husband sided with his mother, Abigail Adams, and left the children with her in Massachusetts when they went to Washington for the congressional term in 1805. Louisa's complaints about the situation elicited a sharp rebuke from her mother-in-law: "There cannot be anything more disagreeable than transporting young children twice a year, either by water, or in crowded stages at such a distance, and however reluctant you might feel, at being separated from them, I should suppose that your own judgment, experience and good sense would have convinced you of the propriety of the measure."

Abigail Adams's letter points up both the similarities and the differences between the women in this book and the ones I grew up with. My mother and her cohorts had much in common with Louisa Adams and Dolley Madison and the rest. The men of both eras used the women as gatherers and disseminators of information, as softeners of blows, as intermediaries between factions, as the diplomats they themselves often were not. And periodically some long-suffering wife, like Eliza Hamilton, would be called on to stand by, or slightly behind her man, smile fixed firmly on her face, trying to salvage his political career as he confessed to some scandalous behavior. But as Abigail's curt missive makes clear, the times were also very different. Though my mother would probably agree that it was "disagreeable to transport young children," at least we weren't going by stagecoach. And the rotten two-lane state roads we traveled between New Orleans and Washington were good enough that we weren't forced to take to the waterways for transportation. Our separations were for days, or at most weeks, at a time, not the years these women sometimes went without seeing their husbands or children or parents. Those are just small examples of how much harder life was in this period, even for wealthy women who hired servants or, sadly, owned slaves. Just getting through the day at the end of the eighteenth and the beginning of the nineteenth century could be challenging. Death was everywhere. The losses these women suffered are almost overwhelming. Every illness, every pregnancy—and they were perennially pregnant—every journey held the prospect of disaster. Still these ladies soldiered on with remarkable resiliency.

To understand just how remarkable, take a look at what life was like for women at the time this book begins. The first census in 1790 put the population at close to four million people. With immigrants trickling in from Europe and American women producing large families, the nation was rapidly growing. About fifty white babies were born for every thousand people before 1800 (the number was just over fourteen in 2000), but those babies' mothers could only expect to live to age forty, half as long as white women today. Only about one-fifth of the households were without children according to the first census, more than two-thirds were childless in the last one. The average household held seven people then, now it's less than three. In 2000, more than twenty-five percent of Americans lived alone, compared to fewer than four percent in 1790. And the first accounting of the nation revealed that almost one-quarter of the population—twenty-four percent—was held in bondage.

With all those people crowding the house and all those children to care for, most women were probably much too busy to worry about the fact that they held no legal or political rights. Not only were married women barred from owning property, the very clothes and jewelry on their bodies belonged to their husbands, and only property owners could vote. But even as the franchise spread to nonproperty-holding white men, women weren't on the political radar screen. The one exception: New Jersey, where unmarried women briefly could cast ballots, along with free blacks, until the powers-that-were decided they didn't like the way politicians were appealing to the women's vote, so passed a law revoking their franchise. When the New Jersey women did go to the polls they were ridiculed for taking on a man's role:

> *To Congress, lo! Widows shall go,*
> *Like metamorphosed witches!*
> *Clothed in the dignity of state,*
> *And eke! In coat and breeches!*

New Jersey legislators revoked free blacks' right to vote at the same time they disenfranchised women. The numbers of free blacks in the North kept growing during the years after the Revolutionary War when states above the Mason-Dixon line passed laws abolishing slavery. In the South too the "peculiar institution" was dwindling until after 1793, when Eli Whitney invented the cotton gin (with the help of Catherine Littlefield Greene, but that's another story). With a free labor pool, the planting of short-staple cotton became enormously profitable, leading to a giant leap in the numbers of slaves.

Other inventions also affected the economy and the way families lived their lives. Almost all Americans—ninety percent—worked on farms in 1790. But that was changing rapidly. Sam Slater's water-powered textile mill opened in Pawtucket, Rhode Island, in 1793, essentially starting the Industrial Revolution in this country. It wouldn't take long before men and women no longer worked together at home manufacturing goods. Men went out to work, so did many single women. Married women, still burdened with onerous household duties, lost the help of the men and sometimes of their older daughters as well. These overworked "Republican mothers" were also assigned the task of raising virtuous citizens to rule the new republic.

And that republic was ever expanding. From the first census in 1790 to the last census in this time frame, in 1820, the population had more than doubled to more than nine and a half million. The center of population had moved from the Atlantic seaboard, around Chestertown, Maryland, to what's now West Virginia. Over horrible roads and in dreadful conditions the westward movement over those thirty years was about the same as it has been in the thirty years between the 1970 and 2000 head counts. And as the country moved, bursting with basically unfettered capitalism, it was the women who realized that there were some people left out of this energetic expansion. So women set up the social-service networks to protect the less fortunate. And as they came to understand the conditions of the poor, the women became reformers. The benevolent societies started in the early nineteenth century turned in many cases into associations arguing for the abolition of slavery and then, eventually, to expanding the suffrage. Women ever so slowly came to understand that they needed the power of the vote in order to achieve their social ends.

How could it have taken so long? It's almost impossible for me to wrap my mind around the fact that my mother was born before women had the right to vote. And it's almost equally impossible for my daughter, despite her well-internalized indoctrination by her foremothers, to comprehend completely that I had graduated from college before employment discrimination against women was outlawed. And I am confident that my granddaughters will be amazed that their mother was a grown woman before America elected a female president. There are generations of women, and their male champions, to thank for those changes, starting with these ladies of liberty who truly did shape our nation.

Ladies of Liberty

CHAPTER ONE

THE PRESIDENCY OF JOHN AND ABIGAIL ADAMS
1797~1801

ABIGAIL SMITH ADAMS
The Granger Collection, New York

FOR THE FIRST TIME, Americans mourned as one. Again and again over the centuries the country would come together in grief or shock—the assassinations of Abraham Lincoln and John F. Kennedy, the attacks on Pearl Harbor and the World Trade Center, the death of Franklin Roosevelt. The first of those nation-binding tragedies rocked the public in the last days of the eighteenth century. On December 14, 1799, George Washington died.

Of course on that day no stentorian-voiced anchormen broke into regular programming to announce the sudden and unexpected death; no dramatic stop-the-presses moment marked the passing of the "Father of the Country." It took some time for the news from

Mount Vernon, where Martha Washington had been keeping watch over her husband of almost forty-one years, to reach the rest of the world. First family and friends nearby, then the Congress, still meeting over Christmas in the temporary capital of Philadelphia, received the report of the sudden loss of the sixty-seven-year-old man who had been leader since soon after the first shots of the Revolution were fired almost twenty-five years earlier. Congress set the official memorial service for the day after Christmas. A Philadelphia woman the next day estimated that four thousand people attended that service—led by President John Adams and "his Lady," the indomitable Abigail Adams. Her husband's chief adviser, the First Lady knew that this public display would help John Adams politically, and she was nothing if not politically savvy. An important election was in the offing, or as Abigail Adams put it, "a time for intrigue is approaching," and it couldn't hurt the embattled incumbent president to remind the voters of his ties to the Federalist "fallen hero"—of the fact that Adams had served loyally as vice president to President George Washington—going into a tough campaign against his own vice president, Republican Thomas Jefferson. Abigail, always on the lookout for what she saw as her husband's best interests, would get out front on this tragedy to milk it for all it was worth politically.

And it soon became clear that the political impact could be huge. The demise of Washington seemed to hold the country spellbound; especially affected were the women who documented the death in dire accounts. During the Adams presidency, women were beginning to bring their private political views into the public sphere and to publish under their own names. One of them, Judith Sargent Murray, described the scene when the news of the death reached Boston. "The calamitous tidings reached us this morning," the feminist writer informed her sister on December 23. "The bells commenced their agonizing peels, the theatre, and museum were shut, balls, festive assemblies and amusements of every description are suspended, ships in the harbor display the insignia of mourning, and a day of solemn humiliation, and prayer, in every place of public worship in this Town is contemplated."

Instead of huddling around the television, saddened citizens congregated in churches, paraded in processions, printed poems, offered orations, sought mementos, and fashioned souvenirs of the man who seemed to symbolize the young country. No one was sure that the nation would survive the loss of its first leader. With the perspective of a foreign observer, Henrietta Liston, the wife of the British ambassador, pondered the political repercussions: "It is difficult to say what may be the consequences of his death to this country," she wrote to her uncle. "He stood the barrier betwixt the northernmost and southernmost states, he was the unenvied Head of the Army, and such was the magic of his name that his opinion was a sanction equal to law."

As Henrietta Liston suspected, and as Abigail Adams quickly learned, America found Washington's death unsettling. One of New York's great social reformers, Isabella Graham, chronicled the impact to her brother abroad: "The city, indeed the United States, have been swallowed up in the loss of Washington," Graham wrote soon after the official day of mourning, February 22, Washington's birthday. By then in hundreds of cities the general had been praised in speech and song at ceremonies and commemorations. Nothing was too outlandish, too over-the-top for a country steeped in public shows of sorrow. Famed novelist Susanna Rowson, always ready to draw attention to herself, composed one of many dirges droned out at the mock funerals:

> *For him the afflicted melts in woe,*
> *For him the widow's tears will flow,*
> *For him the orphan's prayer shall rise,*
> *And waft his spirit to the skies.*

Since no one had ever mourned an American head of state before, everyone was making up the rituals as they went along, with

Federalist politicians determined that they last as long as possible. One of those Federalists, Congressman Harrison Gray Otis, knowing that his wife Sally, home in Boston, would be dying to know every detail of what was happening in Philadelphia, described the official memorial service in a letter written from the chamber of the House of Representatives: "Before my eyes and in front of the speaker's chair lies a coffin covered with a black pall, bearing a military hat and sword," he told her. "In about one hour we shall march attended by the military in grand procession to the German Lutheran Church."

Years later John Adams admitted that there was more than a little politics underpinning the paeans: "Orations, prayers, sermons, mock funerals" were used by the extremists in Adams's own party, to promote Federalist issues and to "cast into the background and the shade all others who had been concerned in the service of their country in the Revolution." The hoopla might have gotten out of hand in Adams's view, but in fact he and his wife had set the tone for the marathon of mourning. As soon as the news reached the temporary capital and Abigail Adams saw the response: "All business in Congress has been suspended in great measure and a universal melancholy has pervaded all classes of people," she told her nephew; the First Lady made sure that she occupied a prominent position in the melancholy. She announced in the newspapers that women visitors would not be welcome at her receptions unless they donned mourning clothes. Congress had tried to establish the national garb with its resolution that "the president by proclamation, recommend to the citizens, the wearing of crape around the arms for 30 days." Abigail Adams was one-upping the lawmakers, assigning herself and the president the jobs as mourners-in-chief.

Just about the only person not caught up in the public demonstrations of dolor was the deeply affected Martha Washington. Too grief-stricken to attend the funeral services held at Mount Vernon a few days after Washington's death, the widow moved to an attic room and directed others to answer the volumes of mail coming in from around the country and the world. From Rhode Island, for instance, a "Society of Females" whose fathers fought in the Revolution requested a lock of the general's hair so they could honor him as the man who "defended our mothers from the tomahawk of the savage." The always-prepared Martha had arranged that some of the general's hair be cut before burial for just such requests. (The volume of mail became so onerous that a few months later, Congress, in recognition of her role as a public person, granted the Widow Washington the franking privilege, the right to send mail for free.) Dry-eyed, she fulfilled her duties, but one request proved particularly difficult. It came at the end of December, when Abigail and John Adams sent the president's personal assistant to Mount Vernon with their letters of condolence, and a communication from the Congress. After the visit, Abigail told her sister that Martha "had not been able to shed a tear since the general's death until she received the president's and my letters." What probably caused the widow's tears were not the sympathetic words of her successor as First Lady but the ham-handed letter from the president asking her to "assent to the interment of the remains of the general under the marble monument to be erected in the Capitol, at the City of Washington."

Almost all of her adult life Martha Washington had put her country first. Now she was being asked to do it again—to take her husband's body out of the grave at Mount Vernon and bury it in what was then a muddy construction site. And, as always, she was ready to comply, because she had learned "never to oppose my private wishes to the public will," but she added, "I cannot say what a sacrifice of individual feeling I make to a sense of public duty." Again. One of Martha's friends, Anna Thornton, tried to soften the blow by lobbying Congress to "pass a secret vote that Mrs. Washington at her decease might be laid in the same tomb with the general." As the wife of William Thornton, the original designer of the United States Capitol, Anna knew she had some clout with Congress, particularly on a matter like this one, and she didn't hesitate to use her influence. (In the end, Congress never coughed up the money for the mausoleum and both George and Martha stayed peacefully buried at Mount Vernon. But there's a wonderfully spooky vaulted room under the Capitol where the bones of the First among the Founding Fathers were supposed to rest. What's there instead is the catafalque used to support the coffins of those who lie in state in the Rotunda two stories above. Not until 1848 was the cornerstone laid for a monument to Washington. Dolley Madison, who had helped raise money for the project along with Eliza Hamilton and Louisa Catherine Adams, was in attendance. It took forty years more for the obelisk known as the Washington Monument to open to the public.)

Even though the encomiums to Washington had the potential to help her husband's chances in the coming election, they finally got to be too much for Abigail Adams. "To no one man in America belongs the epithet of *Savior* of his country," she huffed to her sister, "at no time did the fate of America rest upon the breath of even a Washington." The First Lady was taking umbrage at the notion that *her* husband was not accorded the honor she thought *his* due as a Founding Father, and she was worried, with good reason, that after one term his presidential career was coming to an end. She should know: taking the political pulse came as second nature to Abigail Adams, who had acted as John's most-valued adviser since he first held public office. For twenty years, starting before the Revolution when he was off in Philadelphia helping draft the Declaration of Independence in 1776, up through his successful run for president in 1796, Abigail kept her husband apprised of what was brewing politically. Trusting her judgment entirely, John used his wife as a source of information and a sounding board during his long years in public service.

Growing up near Boston in Weymouth, Massachusetts, as the daughter of a minister, Abigail Smith and her two sisters were far better educated than most girls of their day by their father and his students. The three women read everything they could get their hands on and had opinions on all the events of the era. Abigail met John as a teenager and struck up a correspondence with him that lasted for decades and that happily survives. The couple married in 1764, when Abigail was twenty and John, almost ten years older, was an ambitious young lawyer in Boston. Drawn away from home by the cause of rebellion against the British, John counted on Abigail to function as his eyes and ears on the home front when he toiled first in the Continental Congress, then as a diplomat in France, Holland, and England, where she eventually met up with him. At that point John and Abigail Adams had not seen each other for five years.

Throughout those years Adams depended on his wife to support the family by running the farm and selling goods he sent from abroad. Of course she was also expected to raise the children and take care of elderly relatives. Plus . . . the British might be coming, at least in the early days of the Revolutionary War. Her son, John Quincy, later wrote about that time, "My mother with her infant children dwelt, liable every hour of the day and night to be butchered in cold blood, or taken and carried to Boston as hostages." Through it all Abigail Adams had managed admirably, protesting from time to time that women were the best Patriots because they were handling all of the hardships and suffering all the sacrifices for the American cause, but they would not hold high office or even be able to vote if they won. It wasn't the hardships, however, that she complained about during those years—it was her husband's letters, they lacked "sentiment." If she was going to be on her own, the least he could do was tell her he loved her.

When Abigail Adams finally joined John in Europe in 1784, the family spent some pleasant and productive years in Paris and London, but by 1788 it was time to come home where Adams would serve two terms as vice president under George Washington. As the first person to play the role of Second Lady, Abigail enjoyed her time in the temporary capitals—New York, then Philadelphia—but found that the constant entertaining was taking its toll on the family finances, which she had so carefully husbanded for many years. She spent most of Adams's second term as vice president at home in Quincy, Massachusetts, where she was socking away some of his salary for their old age, while conducting a constant correspondence as political consultant to presidential candidate John Adams, who sought her advice as he ran in what was the nation's first contested election. George Washington had declined a third term, having twice been chosen for president without opposition. The former commander of the Continental army was a unique political figure, as the later ceremonies surrounding his death showed, and in 1796 when he made it clear he would not run again, the starting gun sounded for the kind of hard-fought campaign Americans have seen almost every four years since: the election of John Adams versus Thomas Jefferson.

Political parties emerged in this country soon after the men who had fought together in the Revolution and struggled to ratify the Constitution formed the first federal government. With each side claiming to carry the banner of the Spirit of Seventy-Six, John Adams's Federalist Party—which advocated a strong central government—was derided as pro-British and monarchical while Thomas Jefferson's Republican Party—more inclined to support states' rights—was attacked as pro-French and anarchical. Since it was considered unseemly to seek the job of president openly, surrogates waged this first presidential campaign through the bitterly partisan newspapers, with intraparty shenanigans making the outcome unknown. When the ballots were counted the results proved interesting indeed. Under the system at the time, the man with the most Electoral College votes became president, the number two in the tally, vice president. As president of the Senate, John Adams announced the totals on February 9, 1797: John Adams 71, Thomas Jefferson 68, Thomas Pinckney (running for vice president as a Federalist) 59, Aaron Burr (running for vice president as a Republican) 30. Not only was it a hair-thin victory for Adams, but the president and vice president for the first—and last—time would hail from opposing parties.

Though political enemies, Adams and Jefferson had formed a close personal relationship when both men represented America in Europe. And it was not only John Adams who was Thomas Jefferson's colleague and correspondent—Abigail Adams had struck up her own friendship and shopping alliance across the English Channel with the man who would now be her husband's number two. And Jefferson's young daughter, Maria, had stayed with Abigail in London on her way from Virginia to Paris. Because of their history together, Abigail, though usually highly suspicious of possible rivals, seemed sanguine about Jefferson's election, "Though wrong in politics, though formerly an advocate for Tom Paine's *Rights of Man* and though frequently mistaken in men and measures, I do not think him an insincere or a corruptible man. My friendship for him has ever been unshaken." Not exactly a ringing endorsement, but far higher praise than she sang for many politicians of the day, especially the man she called a dangerous "subtle intriguer," fellow Federalist Alexander Hamilton.

If she professed to be unconcerned with Jefferson, Abigail felt true trepidation about her own role. She worried that her outspokenness would get her in trouble, that she wouldn't be able to "look at every word before I utter it, and to impose a silence on myself when I long to talk." John assured her, "A woman *can* be silent when she will." He certainly knew that the strong-minded Abigail was unlikely to stifle her opinions. He didn't care. In fact he wanted to hear her opinions. Now that he was president, John Adams desperately needed Abigail by his side. "I never wanted your advice and assistance more in my life," he told her a couple of weeks after his inauguration. "I must entreat you to come on as soon as you can," he begged a few days later and then a couple of days after that, "I pray you to come on." He kept it up in almost daily letters. "I will not live in a state of separation," complained the man who had been separated from his wife for years at a time, "You, I must and will have." He appealed to her patriotism: "The times are critical and dangerous, and I must have you here to assist me." He became more and more adamant: "I can do nothing without you. We must resign everything but our public duties." Forget about the farm, John insisted, let other people worry about it.

Abigail wasn't about to abandon the property she had worked so hard to preserve and make prosper. She would go to Philadelphia only after she found someone to run the farm in Quincy, and meanwhile would continue as always to ply the president with political news from home. Besides, her nursing skills were needed because his mother was sick, as well as one of Abigail's nieces. Even after learning of his mother's illness John didn't stop badgering his wife: "It seems to me that the Mother and the Daughter ought to think a little of the President as well as the Husband. His Cares! His Anxieties! His Health! Don't laugh." Right. Then both his mother and Abigail's niece died, with the news reaching John after Abigail was already on the road to Philadelphia. "You and I are now entering on a new scene which will be the most difficult and least agreeable of any in our lives," he warned her. "I hope the burden will be lighter to both of us when we come together."

The burden Adams feared he could not carry alone was the threat of war with France. This country's first ally, France had taken to seizing American ships in response to what the French government saw as a hostile commercial agreement signed between the U.S. and Britain. The fledgling American states needed trade with England to survive, but Britain and France were embroiled in nonstop skirmishes, in what came to be called the Napoleonic Wars, and any accommodation with one country was seen as treachery by the other. U.S. political parties split their allegiances—Jefferson's Republicans favored France, Adams's Federalists supported England. George Washington fortuitously left office just as the tinderbox of war with France seemed ready to ignite. No wonder John Adams wanted his wife at his side.

Hoping "that I may discharge my part with honor and give satisfaction," Abigail finally set out for Philadelphia in late April with an entourage of relatives and servants. Along the way she visited her daughter Abigail, called Nabby, in New Jersey and her son Charles in New York. She fretted to her sister Mary Cranch about Nabby's ne'er-do-well husband, William Smith, but thought Charles and his wife, William's sister, had a "lovely babe." The other Adams off-spring, John Quincy and Thomas, were abroad. In one of his last communications as president, George Washington had gone out of his way to praise the young diplomat, John Quincy Adams, who was representing the country in the Netherlands. Calling him "the most valuable public character we have abroad," Washington said he had no doubt that John Quincy Adams would "prove himself to be the ablest of all our diplomatic corps." His brother Thomas was also in Holland, acting as John Quincy's secretary.

No sooner did the second First Lady take up her post than the entertaining began. "Yesterday being Monday, from 12 to half past two I received visits, 32 ladies and near as many gentlemen," she re-counted in the first letter to her sister from Philadelphia, "I shall have the same ceremony to pass through today, and the rest of the week." Agreeing with a friend that her situation was one of "splen-did misery," Abigail added a P.S.: "The ladies of Foreign Ministers and the Ministers, with our own Secretaries and ladies have visited me today, and add to them the whole levee today of Senate and House. Strangers, etc. making near one hundred asked permission to visit me so that from half past 12 till near 4, I was rising up and sitting down." Not a whole lot of fun, but as hostess for the nation, Abigail Adams followed in the footsteps of Martha Washington, holding regular receptions, or levees, where diplomats, politicians, plus the distinguished and not so distinguished folk of Philadelphia could meet and greet. Not everyone appreciated the efforts of the new First Lady; the Republican press criticized her formality and accused the starchy Adams couple of monarchical aspirations. Some of the same grumblings surrounded Martha Washington's enter-tainments when she created the role of First Lady by consciously setting a tone elegant enough to be taken seriously by emissaries from the courts of Europe, yet open enough to satisfy the constitu-ents of the new republic. But Martha Washington, like her hus-band, occupied a place in American society above common criticism. Having camped with the American army every winter of the eight-year-long Revolutionary War, "Lady" Washington was beloved by the troops, as her husband was revered, and veterans often called on her in her years as the wife of the president. And her gracious southern ways, aided by great wealth left to her by her first husband, welcomed all who crossed her path.

The blunt-spoken New Englander Abigail Adams had none of those advantages. She also didn't have with her the beautiful and fun-loving Nelly Custis, Martha's granddaughter, who grew up in the president's house and made fast friends in Philadelphia. Young Sally McKean, daughter of a Republican politician, viciously described Abigail's "hawks eyes" and guessed that she had brought her niece, Louisa Smith, to live in the executive mansion to "set up for a Miss Custis of the place." But Louisa would never match Nelly, Sally nastily added, "for she is not young, and confounded ugly." Glitzy society in the City of Brotherly Love would never fully accept the Boston Puritan Abigail Adams, who would have as hard a time living up to Martha Washington as the president would to George.

But the First Lady was too consumed with affairs of government to care much about Philadelphia parties. The president had summoned a special session of Congress to deal with the crisis created by the French government sanctioning attacks on U.S. ships and refusing to receive the American envoy, Charles Pinckney. In a letter to her sister Mary soliciting her comments, Abigail enclosed a copy of her husband's address, which called for renewed attempts at negotiation and "effectual measures of defense." These women lived and breathed politics. And Abigail harbored a take-no-prisoners attitude toward John's opponents, particularly in the press. Her most despised nemesis: Benjamin Franklin Bache, the grandson of the great Doctor Franklin, called "Lightning Rod Junior" by his enemies. With the printing presses left to him by his grandfather, Bache was the publisher of a radical Republican Philadelphia newspaper, *Aurora*. After Adams's speech to Congress, Abigail ranted, "Bache opened his batteries of abuse and scurrility the very next day." Still, she was happy to report that the Senate was backing the president, while the House still debated the matter. Then, in typical Abigail Adams fashion, she went on to ask Mary to send her a bonnet she left behind and to make sure that the woman running the family farm added some aniseed to the cheese to make it saltier. No matter that an international crisis was brewing and "tomorrow we are to dine the Secretaries of State, etc. with the whole Senate," there was still a farm and fashion to worry about. Not to mention meddling in her children's lives.

John Quincy Adams, the oldest of the siblings, was turning thirty and still unmarried. Increasingly, his letters from Europe hinted that his bachelor days might soon be ending. However, his mother wasn't sure she approved of the bride-to-be. Would she be sufficiently American for the son his mother saw as the political successor to his father? Abigail implied that it would be downright unpatriotic of her son to marry a European, hoping instead, "For the love I bear my country that the siren is at least half blood." In fact, the woman in question—Louisa Catherine Johnson—was the daughter of the U.S. consul in London, an American businessman married to an Englishwoman, so she qualified as the "half blood" that her mother-in-law-to-be demanded. Instead of taking umbrage at his mother's unsolicited advice from abroad, John Quincy tried to ease her concerns. While conceding that it was "perfectly natural" for her to fear that "the tastes and sentiments of my friend . . . may be anti-American," John Quincy assured Abigail that his intended had "goodness of heart and gentleness of disposition as well as spirit and discretion and with those qualities I will venture upon the chances of success." John Quincy Adams and Louisa Catherine Johnson married in London on July 26, 1797, in the Church of All Hallows, Barking. One of the few guests, younger brother Thomas Adams, soothed his mother with the judgment that his brother had given him "an amiable and accomplished sister."

Thomas also reluctantly agreed to go with John Quincy to his new assignment in Berlin, but he begged Abigail to "negotiate a successor for me." He was ready to come home and figured his powerful mother was the person who could make that happen. Having a son in the diplomatic service proved problematic for President Adams, since John Quincy's salary created fodder for the Republican press. "These salaries are all set by law," Abigail erupted to her sister. "The mischief of these publications arises from their circulating amongst persons and in places where no inquiry is made into facts." The Adams family, like most who have occupied the executive mansion, found more and more fault with the newspapers as the administration moved forward. Abigail's intense hatred of the popular press, however, would harm her husband in the long run.

Other, more critical diplomatic assignments caused considerably more controversy than the posting of the president's son. French attacks on U.S. ships were growing more frequent—some three hundred had been seized—terrorizing American sailors and wreaking havoc with commerce. As part of the promise to ratchet up negotiations with France, President Adams appointed two distinguished politicians to join Pinckney, who had decamped to Holland after being refused recognition in Paris. In an effort to include different regions and parties, the president named Virginia Federalist John Marshall and a pro-French Massachusetts independent, Elbridge Gerry, to the team of negotiators. Though she didn't always agree with him politically, Gerry was an old friend of Abigail's who called him "an honest man and a friend to his country, who will neither be deceived or warped." Somewhat plaintively, she added, "The task of the president is very arduous, very perplexing and very hazardous." She had always been ambitious for John, had been eager for him to hold the highest office, but this was a tougher job at a tougher time than Abigail had had any reason to expect. Writing to Mary she did not hide her concern, "We know not what a day will bring forth. From every side we are in danger." The danger heightened as Napoleon marched across Europe and rattled sabers against England. "The threatened invasion of England I do not much credit," wrote the First Lady, acting in her accustomed role as political analyst, but she was worried because the envoys sent to try to make peace with France had not been heard from.

JOHN MARSHALL AND ELBRIDGE GERRY sailed separately to Europe in the summer of 1797. Marshall went first to The Hague, collected Charles Pinckney, and headed for Paris, where Gerry joined them. Pinckney had reason to be skeptical whether the three would be successful in their attempt to stop the wholesale attacks on American ships. The French government had rejected the South Carolinian as an envoy earlier that year and expelled him along with his wife and young daughter. Pinckney, a prominent lawyer and politician, was the son of one of the most remarkable women of early American history—Eliza Lucas Pinckney. As a teenager she had introduced the planting of South Carolina's biggest cash crop, indigo, into the colony. Both of her sons, Charles and Thomas, fought under Washington during the Revolution and then held high positions in the new American government. As president, Washington made a point of visiting Eliza Pinckney in 1791 on his tour through the South, and then in 1793 insisted on serving as a pallbearer at her funeral in Philadelphia, where she died after traveling there for breast cancer treatments. Charles, her older son, helped craft the Constitution, but then pursued his legal career rather than joining the administration of his friend George Washington. Pinckney's first wife, the mother of his three daughters, died in 1784 and he married Mary Stead, a spinster of thirty-four with a handsome inheritance, a couple of years later. Mary accompanied Charles to Philadelphia for the 1787 Constitutional Convention, and in 1796 went along on the assignment to Paris, where she had lived as a young woman. A frequent and lively correspondent, her letters home offered political commentary on the diplomatic scene while delivering some delightful glimpses of European life.

At that time, Charles Pinckney was the rare American politician, one committed to neither political party, but France's man in

Philadelphia had poisoned the well against him by telling the government in Paris that the new envoy was an anti-French Federalist. The fact that Pinckney was coming to replace James Monroe, who was being removed for his pro-French sentiments, didn't help matters; neither did his brother Thomas's affiliation with the Federalist Party as candidate for vice president. Before they even left the United States, Mary Pinckney predicted that she was not headed to a nation eager to make peace. "French and English determined to fight it out," she wrote to her cousin Margaret Manigault.

Nothing augured well for this mission. The arduous trip across the ocean was still in the offing when the journey from Charleston to Philadelphia proved rough enough to discourage the travelers. Since roads were so terrible at the end of the eighteenth century, almost all travel was by boat, and on their voyage north the Pinckneys encountered first "a violent Northeast wind rolling us about at a furious rate in the Gulf Stream, then came a violent Southeaster, afterwards calms, and lastly a steady Southwest gale," all prompting Mary to "bid the future stand still." But soon she was off to Europe on a terrifying Atlantic crossing featuring tiller-breaking storms followed by near shipwreck because the captain of the *Liberty*, "a man of a rough, violent, obstinate and at the same time contradictory temper was quite drunk." Only a mutinous mate saved the ship. The landing at Bordeaux brought only more bad news: the American consul there warned that the French government's reception of Pinckney "would be as cool as it was possible." Not at all an auspicious beginning.

Despite the disheartening political prospects, Mary Pinckney decided to have some fun in Bordeaux. She went to the theater one night, where she sat next to "two ladies of pleasure," and then discovered that most of the theatergoers shared the ladies' occupation. French fashions also fascinated the wife of the would-be diplomat, especially the caps, which were "immense," and some of the ladies wore "still more immense hats over those caps, clapped right on the back of the head and standing up and down in a perpendicular line, with a hole for an enormous chignon." Mary determined to buy a hat immediately. Despite the diversions, she was well aware of the ominous reports from the battlefields of Europe: "The successes of the French in Italy have latterly been more rapid than ever. Mantua is besieged and most of the Italian States have sued for peace. . . . The Pope has been under the necessity of paying large sums. . . . Corsica is evacuated, and the retreat of the English made with so much precipitation that there are many made prisoners." With the pope forced to pay tribute and the English running in retreat, what chance did fledgling America have of wringing concessions out of the French government?

After a harrowing eleven-day trip over rocky roads, always on the lookout for robbers, the Pinckneys arrived in Paris in December to learn that their concerns were justified. James Monroe, the current ambassador, brought the news that the government "will not receive any minister from the United States" until grievances raised by the treaty with the English were redressed. Mary thought it was "prudent" to refrain from writing any real political news for fear that her letters would be intercepted and she "should unintentionally give offence," so she entertained her sister with sketches of the theaters and shops of Paris where she and her stepdaughter, Eliza, were made to feel like the country cousins. On their first trip to the stores they found "our dress and appearance so much the objects of merriment to the gazing crowd that Eliza almost swore she would never go again." What to do with young Eliza was perplexing. Mary had planned to enroll her in the school run by Marie Antoinette's former lady-in-waiting, which had been "strongly recommended" by James and Elizabeth Monroe, "who have both been very obliging." But the Pinckneys' uncertain situation made their stay precarious at best and having just arrived in Paris, they were already planning to move on to The Hague or Amsterdam "if chased." Meantime they were "living in the most uncomfortable manner, at a great expense, in cold smoky apartments, and unable to entertain any of our country people." Even so, the family would "leave Paris with regret."

Paris was Paris even if Charles couldn't work and Eliza couldn't go to school. "Very gay and brilliant, independent of its 13 spectacles a night and its public balls," the city had much to "engage and amuse a stranger" and it was a source of such good gossip. Mary spotted the infamous Madame Tallien at a concert. Loved by the public for her opposition to the terrorist Robespierre but not loved by her husband for her attachments to other men, Madame had been seen going "into public à la grecque, with drawers, and a gauze petticoat," and "sometimes she actually wears breeches." And Thomas Paine, the propagandist who had stirred the American Revolution with his *Common Sense*, but whose distrust of a forceful federal government turned him against George Washington in later years, was "almost continually in liquor." More flattering, "Mrs. Monroe dresses her own hair (for she told me she was tired of wigs)," and "I think it is very pretty."

Pinckney's arrival signaled James Monroe's ouster, but the Monroes were cordial—Elizabeth Monroe, a New York beauty, showed Mary the ropes in Paris. But the Jefferson forces in America were telling French officials that public opinion in the U.S. was on their side, there was no need to accept Pinckney as minister of a Federalist administration. Despite her pledge not to cover politics in her letters home, Mary couldn't contain her outrage at the actions of the French government. Not only was the foreign minister denying her husband diplomatic status, he was treating Charles Pinckney like any foreigner in France without the proper papers. And the man soon to become foreign minister, Charles Maurice Talleyrand, was advising the government against negotiating with a third-rate power like the United States, where he had spent a couple of years in exile during the tumult in Paris after the French Revolution. Mary angrily recounted what Talleyrand had told his government about her country: "There are no men of ability in it—that the male part of the community do nothing but drink Madeira wine, and the women are only employed in suckling their children—that America possesses only three millions of inhabitants scattered along an extensive coast," and worst of all, "The French nation may treat America just as it does Genoa and Geneva." She added, fuming, "I am extremely vexed with Mr. Talleyrand." The situation was not only humiliating, it was lonely: "The French I believe dare not come to visit us and the foreign ministers have nothing to do with us as we are not received." Only the Monroes and various friends and family members from South Carolina who were in France kept them company. And they had been gone four months and heard not one word from home.

Still in Paris as the city rang in the New Year of 1797, Mary did not "venture to foretell where we shall finish it." She admitted to her cousin, "I wish I had never left Carolina," though she was spending her mornings "very pleasantly" sightseeing and the evenings "with my family round the fire, reading, writing, talking American politics, and of our dear Carolina." And finally letters from dear Carolina arrived, bringing the good news that "the fatal month of September," when yellow fever annually threatened Charleston, had left all well. Whatever homesickness the Pinckneys were feeling was exacerbated by their uncertain status in Paris, where an unrecognized diplomat was "kind of a scare crow." So it might have come as some relief when five days later they were expelled from France. On seeing the orders from the government, Mary's "first thought, my first sigh I hope and believe was for my country, thus threatened with the horrors of war." But her next thoughts, she wrote from Antwerp in February, were for her family. She felt sorry for Eliza, who had finally started school and was eager to improve her French; much worse was "to see my respectable husband, beloved and esteemed by his country, to see him at his time of life driven from post to pillar!" And she was nowhere near done shopping. "I thought if we remained in Paris I should get better acquainted with the prices," she sighed.

Settling briefly in Amsterdam, the Pinckneys found the Dutch city sleepy after the excitement of Paris: "There does not seem to be any bustle in this great city; it is as quiet as Charleston." But Mary was ready to admit that she might not be giving Amsterdam a chance. "Perhaps my mind is too much engaged by what passes in the political world, in which our dear country is so much interested to receive much amusement from sights." This was not just a somewhat bored wife worried about her husband and stepdaughter. This was a true Patriot, concerned for her nation. As the family moved from Amsterdam to The Hague, taking pleasant side trips to Haarlem and Rotterdam, news of Napoleon's victories added to their fears, particularly as the French general advanced to "within 8 posts of Vienna." One city after another fell to the advancing French army, causing Mary ruefully to marvel, "The splendor of their victories almost dazzles one." Charles waited for his marching orders, unaware that John Adams had gone to Congress and called for one more attempt at diplomacy in an effort to avoid war with the French, who continued to seize American ships.

The Pinckney family tried to stay occupied. They went to the theater (where one night the leading actress produced a scream that "though we had been prepared for it, thrilled through our hearts and shook every nerve") and to the debates over the Constitution for the Batavian Republic (which lasted for three years). Even so, their state of suspended animation was unsettling, especially for young Eliza, who was "weary of being without a companion in Holland." There was much more to cause concern than a peevish teenager. Congress had not yet told Pinckney "whether a new trial is to be made to soothe the French, whether he is to make it, or whether war, dreadful war is again to desolate our country." If America were to go to war with France, Mary had reason to dread the outcome, "What part is France now playing on this globe! All of Europe is at her feet."

After two months in The Hague waiting for "further directions," Mary was grateful when the new American ambassador to the Netherlands, William Vans Murray, and his wife arrived to replace John Quincy Adams. A fresh diplomat on the scene meant a round of dinner parties for diversion. And Mrs. Pinckney guessed the folks at home might be interested in the menu. "Two large dishes of fish, one a turbot, the other soles—two plates of potatoes, fish sauce and a soup constituted the first course. The second was a large piece of cold smoked Dutch beef, and four small dishes of vegetables. The third had a goose at top, four partridges at bottom, stewed pigeons in a tureen in the middle and at the four corners a baked pudding, burnt cream, puffs and sweetmeats. The dessert was pretty, and an excellent rock melon and indifferent peaches, both from the hot-house made part of it." All that for just over a dozen people! Word of President Adams's speech to Congress arrived at the end of June, so the Pinckneys were hoping to discover their next move soon. When they did it was in the newspapers, which reported that John Marshall and Elbridge Gerry would be joining Charles Pinckney in a three-man commission to France. The wife of Commissioner Pinckney was wary, "I have heard and read enough to be convinced that submission will not avail a nation with the French Republic."

Now that they knew they were heading back to Paris, the Pinckneys were eager to get going. In August, Mary lamented, "the westerly wind blows and blows, but no commissioners arrive." Later in the month, she was still looking for Marshall and Gerry, complaining to a niece, "I believe these commissioners will never arrive." Living in limbo at The Hague was becoming tiresome, especially for young Eliza, who had no friends her age; Mary joked that her stepdaughter reminded her of "our poor Rhode Island cow, shut up in the yard at Charleston and wondering to what new and uninhabited . . . country she was transported." Quickly the stepmother added, "You must not tell Eliza that I have made this elegant comparison between her and the cow." Finally, in early September, Mrs. Pinckney was able to announce, "General Marshall arrived here last Sunday."

After his service in the Revolutionary War, John Marshall had returned to Virginia to practice law and pursue local politics. When the rest of the state was following favorite sons Jefferson and Madison into the Republican Party, Marshall stayed stalwartly behind First Statesman George Washington. In return, Washington offered Marshall a number of jobs in his administration, but the father of an ever-growing family turned the president down. When Adams asked him to accept the job as envoy, war was imminent and Marshall accepted the appointment. Though none of his wife's letters have survived the centuries, it's clear from Marshall's letters to her that Polly Marshall was none too pleased about his decision. Her life as the long-suffering helpmeet on the home front was far more common than Mary Pinckney's place at her diplomatic husband's side.

Mary Ambler, called Polly, had married John fourteen years earlier, when she was only sixteen years old. Marshall family lore has it that she first refused his proposal and then quickly changed her mind, sending a cousin out after the spurned Romeo with a lock of her hair. As the story goes, John wrapped a piece of his own hair around Polly's and sent it back to her. She wore a locket encircling the entwined hairs until she died. With babies coming in rapid succession, and half of them dying—in 1792 the Marshalls lost two children within a couple of weeks—Polly was frequently depressed and often kept to her home, where John valued her "sound and safe" opinion, writing that he "never regretted the adoption" of it and "sometimes regretted its rejection."

But apparently Marshall did reject Polly's advice when he accepted the assignment to France. Leaving his pregnant wife at home with their three surviving children (three had died), John stopped at Mount Vernon in June 1797 on his way to Philadelphia to receive instructions. He wrote from nearby Alexandria, "Do tell me and tell me truly that the bitterness of parting is over and your mind at rest . . . and that you will permit nothing to distress you while I am gone." Typically wanting to have it all—to go, and for her to like it, he signed off, "Farewell—I never was peremptory but I must now give you one positive order. It is be happy." In Philadelphia, John himself seemed perfectly happy as he took in the sights of the capital city and was wined and dined by President Adams, members of Congress, and chic society. Still, he kept after his wife to cheer up, hoping her next letter would bring "the delight of receiving assurance that your mind has become tranquil and as sprightly as usual." But then he gave her news likely to depress her more: he had no idea when he would be home, but he would probably be gone longer than "we contemplated." As it turned out, Polly Marshall would not see her husband for more than a year.

From the ship John wrote somewhat bullying letters, trying to rally his wife's spirits, but when he reached The Hague, he had to admit that he would probably not "return until the spring and that fear excites very much uneasiness and even regret at my having ever consented to cross the Atlantic." So much for happiness. The news from France was all bad and war seemed more and more likely, especially when Talleyrand, the man who had been so dismissive of America, was appointed foreign minister. Waiting for Gerry to arrive, Marshall shared the Pinckneys' impatience. It was time to go to France to make the hard case for peace.

The three envoys, along with Mary and Eliza, finally met up in the French capital, where the men presented their credentials to Talleyrand, who basically brushed them off. Instead of granting them diplomatic standing, the foreign minister issued the equivalent of police passes that simply allowed them to stay in Paris. The Pinckneys had landed right back where they were a year before, except this time they shared their frustration with the other commissioners. When Mary reported the situation to the folks at home she asked them to keep quiet about it because "General P. and his colleagues are here to conciliate." She didn't want her letters to ruffle any feathers and France was in such turmoil almost anything could happen. The government had been debating a law to expel everyone of nobility from the country, much to Mary's amusement: "Numbers of ladies had determined to marry their footmen, or in default of them, any person they could pick up on the streets, to put themselves out of reach of the law. Was this love of their country, or an impossibility to relinquish the remainder of their fortunes and the few comforts of life which they still enjoy?" Fortunately for the ladies, the law didn't pass.

By November Mary Pinckney had concluded, "there are but faint hopes of a favorable termination of our differences with this republic." And John Marshall was sorry he had ever said yes to the president. "How much time and how much happiness have I thrown away!" he sighed to Polly. But then, "Paris presents one incessant round of amusement and dissipation," he told his wife, who was trying to cope with a bunch of kids in Virginia. "I now have rooms in the house of a very accomplished, a very sensible and I believe a very amiable lady." Just what she wanted to read. Polly received the letter not long after she had given birth to their seventh child. The amiable lady, Madame Villette, visited with her American tenants in the afternoons. At night the envoys received visits of a less savory sort. Three henchmen of Talleyrand's came around regularly to demand payment in exchange for recognizing the U.S. diplomats. The foreign minister's agents, characterized in the communications to Philadelphia as X, Y, and Z, laid out the terms: an American loan of ten million dollars to the French government plus a quarter million dollars for Talleyrand's personal pocket. The envoys angrily rejected the demand, with Pinckney famously replying, "No! No! Not a sixpence." In the retelling, Pinckney's refusal evolved into the more American aphorism "Millions for defense, but not one cent for tribute."

"I love my country a thousand times more than ever I did, since it has been ill treated," Mary Pinckney wrote in January 1798, when the impasse between the two governments seemed insurmountable and she was convinced there would be war. "We dread the future," she gloomily concluded in February. In Virginia, the present was posing a harder time for Polly Marshall. Her father died, sending her into a "deep melancholy from which no one could relieve her," sympathized her sister who was left to care for the new baby. And in Philadelphia, Abigail Adams fretted, "Our envoys have been near six months in Paris but to this hour not a line has been received." Rumors circulated through the capital city that the envoys had "not been permitted to hold any society or converse with any citizen. In short they have been in a mere Bastille." Abigail was in a state of constant fury. She was mad at the voters for sending Republicans to Congress, mad at the Congress for its pro-French sympathies, mad at Jefferson for undermining the president, mad at the press for its attacks on her husband, and mad at the people of Philadelphia for throwing a party for George Washington's birthday. She was affronted by the invitation to the First Couple, "The president of the United States to attend the celebration of the birthday in his public character of a private citizen!" It was one thing for Virginians to honor Washington. "But the propriety of doing it in the capital in the *metropolis* of America as these Proud Philadelphians have publicly named it, and inviting the Head of the Nation to come and do it too, in my view is ludicrous beyond compare." Given the way members of the political opposition and their press treated Adams, Abigail's readiness to read insult into almost anything was understandable. Even so, refusing to celebrate George Washington's birthday was pushing the parameters of propriety. But the First Lady stayed constantly on watch, wondering why people didn't understand that "they now have a Head, who will not knowingly prostrate their dignity and character, neither to foreign nations, nor the American people."

On the other side of the Atlantic, Mary Pinckney was witnessing just how hard it could be to avoid prostrating the dignity of the United States to a foreign nation. "The difficulties of our negotiations increase daily," she announced in March. By then the U.S. government had heard the bad news of the French demands for bribery from the commissioners. "I fear we shall be driven to war," Abigail informed her sister. Declaring the Pinckney/Marshall/Gerry mission a failure, President Adams called on Congress to enact a defense buildup in case of attack, including the outfitting and arming of a navy to defend American interests at sea. Pro-French Republicans, suspicious that the president was overstating the threat, insisted that the reports from Paris be made public.

It was a dicey situation, Abigail explained, "Ministers can never be safe, or they will cease to be useful abroad, if their communications are all to be communicated." The president had to consider the commissioners before he revealed the documents, but the Congress and the columnists kept up the clamor to release them. Abigail was convinced that Jefferson's political allies and the press meant to hound her husband out of office, "to calumniate the president, his family, his administration, until they oblige him to resign, and then they will reign triumphant, *headed by a man of the people*." Amid great uproar, the House of Representatives passed a resolution requiring the president to present the dispatches from France. The next day Adams did just that. When House members, meeting in closed session, read the sordid tale of attempted bribery, they were "struck dumb, and opened not their mouths," gloated Abigail. Leaks to the press took no time at all once the Senate voted to print the documents for internal use.

After newspaper stories appeared describing the XYZ affair, the public railed against both the French government and the Republican press and rallied round the president. With more than a little satisfaction, Abigail reported, "The common people say if Jefferson had been our president and Madison and Burr our negotiators, we should all have been sold to the French." War fever filled the air as a stirring new song, *Hail Columbia*, greeted Adams when he attended public events. The lyrics were far from subtle:

> *Immortal patriots rise once more*
> *Defend your rights—defend your shore*

Abigail too received her share of attention on the streets of Philadelphia; only the Republican newspaper run by Benjamin Franklin Bache continued to criticize Adams, "Wherever I passed, I received a marked notice of bows . . . in short we are now wonderfully popular except with Bache & Co. who in his paper calls the president old, querulous, bald, blind, crippled, toothless Adams." Even that outlandish ridicule couldn't suppress Abigail's good humor. She was more than ready for her husband to request a declaration of war. Instead, Adams announced a day of fasting, putting religion on his side. He was following in the footsteps of Washington, whose

Thanksgiving proclamations had caused one clergyman to voice a complaint echoed so many times in the centuries since, "I feel ministers have stepped out of line and preached politics instead of the Gospel." It was Thomas Jefferson's turn to sulk in his tent, telling his daughter Martha, "Politics and party hatreds destroy the happiness of every being here."

Unaware of the reaction to the XYZ affair at home, John Marshall and Charles Pinckney demanded diplomatic passports for their departure from Paris. Elbridge Gerry, at the invitation of Talleyrand, decided to stay behind. "He has been false to his colleagues and wanting to his country," Mary Pinckney judged Gerry. "If he is not lost to all sense of feeling, his duplicity must have planted a thorn in his breast." Gerry had been secretly negotiating with Talleyrand, who thought the pro-French American could convince the U.S. government to come up with his bribe. When she heard the news, Abigail Adams was dismayed to think that her old friend Gerry could turn on her husband, "You may easily suppose how distressed the president is at this conduct, and the more so because he thought Gerry would certainly not go wrong, and he *acted* his own judgment, *against his counselors.*"

Since the sentiment in the U.S. had turned against France unbeknownst to him, Gerry thought Marshall and Pinckney would be vilified when they returned home. Instead, "an immense concourse of citizens" of Philadelphia greeted John Marshall as a conquering hero when he arrived in June. Here was the man who had refused to allow his country to be humiliated. Marshall told the president that Gerry's decision to stay behind wasn't an act of treachery—that he had accepted Talleyrand's invitation because he thought war was certain if he left. Peace was still possible but preparations for war were going forward. Congress had not yet adjourned. "I believe they will declare war against the French first," Abigail observed hopefully. "France can pour in her armies upon us," she warned, and spread "her depravity of manners, her Atheism in every part of the United States." It was unfathomable to her that the lawmakers did not call the country to arms: "Congress would not proceed to a declaration of war, they must be answerable for the consequences." The First Lady's views became so well known that a Republican politician referred to her as "Mrs. President, not of the United States but of a faction."

In fact, despite his wife's lobbying, John Adams did not ask Congress to declare war before the members headed home in early July. John Marshall went home as well, where he met his six-month-old son, and tried to coax his wife back to good health. And in October, after two years of unfulfilled efforts to make peace, Charles Pinckney with his wife and daughter arrived in America. "My tears flowed on landing," Mary wrote from Newark, New Jersey. She didn't know when they would leave for Charleston, but knew "it will not be as soon as I wish." There would still be duties to country to perform, and Mary Pinckney would remain away from home for a while longer.

WHEN MARY PINCKNEY RETURNED in 1798, the country had grown even more virulently partisan. Federalists pushing for war with France believed in a strong central government and feared the "rabble," the lower-class voter. Republicans, siding with France against England, denounced the "monarchical" tendencies of their opponents and championed states' rights. While serving as vice president, Thomas Jefferson took on the role of leader of the opposition as well. Though he had been one of the main instigators of the discord between the parties, Jefferson complained from Philadelphia to his daughter in Virginia, "You should know the rancorous passions which tear every breast here, even of the sex which should be a stranger to them." Jefferson disapproved of women participating in politics, but "the sex" was joining the fray. From Virginia, Martha Washington's granddaughter, young Nelly Custis, informed a friend in Philadelphia, "I am becoming an outrageous politician, perfectly *federal*." Women like Nelly were expected to show up at patriotic events decked out in their party colors to encourage the men to rally round the Federalist flag. At elaborate ceremonies throughout the summer of 1798, as men formed militias to protect the homeland, female Patriots presented flags emblazoned with the company insignia, often embroidered by one of the women. Along with the flags came speeches, later reprinted in the newspapers, bullying the men into battle. "Our love can only be obtained by bravely defending our liberties, the Independence, and the Religion of our Country," one young woman threatened in a public ceremony.

When women went into the political kitchen, they had to be ready to take the heat. As acerbic newspaperman William Cobbett could be counted on to say, he would go after anyone who disagreed with the Federalist cause, "bearded or unbearded, whether dressed in breeches or petticoats." But their party's press had only praise for the Federalist females who urged men into uniform: "What more liberal encouragement can the cause of Columbia have than the sanction of her fair daughters. Even they are roused to expressions of political sentiment, which bear the plausible stamp of Federalism." Women in Philadelphia honored the president by joining the militia men in singing the stirring song "Adams and Liberty." It was music to Abigail Adams's ears.

The Fifth Congress had recessed in July 1798 without declaring war against France, but in the last days before adjourning it did approve other measures championed by Abigail Adams that aided in the undoing of her husband—the Alien and Sedition Acts. Worried about French agents in their midst, the lawmakers passed punitive measures changing the rules for naturalized citizenship and making it legal for the U.S. to round up and detain as "alien enemies" any men over the age of fourteen from an enemy nation after a declaration of war. Abigail heartily approved. But it was the Sedition Act that she especially cheered. It imposed fines and imprisonment for any person who "shall write, print, utter, or publish . . . any false, scandalous and malicious writing or writings against the government of the United States, or either house of the Congress of the

United States, or the President of the United States" with the intent to defame them. Finally! The hated press would be punished.

To Abigail's way of thinking, the law was long overdue. (Of course she was ready to use the press when it served her purposes, regularly sending information to relatives and asking them to get it published in friendly gazettes.) Back in April she had predicted to her sister Mary that the journalists "will provoke measures that will silence them e'er long." Abigail kept up her drumbeat against newspapers in letter after letter, grumbling, "Nothing will have an effect until Congress pass a Sedition Bill, which I presume they will do before they rise." Congress could not act fast enough for the First Lady: "I wish the laws of our country were competent to punish the stirrer up of sedition, the writer and printer of base and unfounded calumny." She accused Congress of "dilly dallying" about the Alien Acts as well. If she had had her way, every newspaperman who criticized her husband would be thrown in jail, so when the Alien and Sedition Acts were passed and signed, Abigail still wasn't satisfied. Grumping that they "were shaved and pared to almost nothing," she told John Quincy that "weak as they are" they were still better than nothing. They would prove to be a great deal worse than nothing for John Adams's political future, but the damage was done. Congress went home. So did Abigail and John Adams.

By July 1798, Abigail had been preparing a surprise for her husband for months. She decided to build a major addition to the house in Quincy without telling him! She cooked up the scheme with her cousin Cotton Tufts, who was overseeing the construction. He would enclose his updates and bills in Mary Cranch's letters, because when Abigail had found John opening a missive from her sister, she testily made him promise not to do it again. She let Mary in on the secret that she was doubling the size of the house, adding that she planned to have the whole thing done "without Mr. Adams knowing any thing of the accommodation until he sees it." Abigail had become so used to making decisions on her own during the long years that John was away, that she was not interested in second opinions. But in early

July a visitor from Massachusetts, unaware that the "master of the house" was ignorant of the project, let the cat out of the bag. "The President had a hearty laugh," his wife reported with some relief. Adams was only sorry the addition wasn't finished before he went home.

No sooner did the couple return to Quincy than Abigail fell gravely ill and remained so for many weeks. Her daughter Nabby came to help care for her, and John stayed as long as he could, writing to George Washington in October, "Her destiny is still very precarious and mine in consequence of it." Philadelphia's destiny was precarious as well, with yellow fever ravaging the city, claiming the lives of three thousand people, including Abigail's nemesis, the newspaperman Benjamin Franklin Bache, who had been arrested under the Sedition Act. When the First Couple learned that fifty children had been left without parents, they anonymously sent five hundred dollars for the orphans' care. By November, with the city declared safe for habitation, John finally set out for the capital. From the road he wrote to his wife, "If I had less anxiety about your health, I should have more about public affairs, I suppose."

He had plenty to be worried about in public affairs. In response to the Alien and Sedition Acts, Vice President Thomas Jefferson and his fellow Republican James Madison had drafted resolutions asserting that a state could nullify a federal law. "The House of Representatives will dispute about the Alien and Sedition Laws all winter," John told Abigail after Congress convened, adding, "The dangerous Vice is not arrived." Abigail thought she knew why Jefferson—the dangerous Vice—wasn't there: "It is thought the VP stays away for very bad motives. I am told he is considered here as the head of the Opposition." When Jefferson did show up in Philadelphia, he sensed a change in mood since the pro-Federalist fervor following the XYZ affair. With the Alien and Sedition Acts, the Federalists had committed the perennial political sin of overreaching. To his daughter at home at Monticello, the vice president said with some satisfaction, "The republican gentlemen whom I have seen consider the state of the public mind to be fast advancing in their favor." Exiled in Quincy by her illness, Abigail was antsy: "I want to know how the world passes, though I cannot gain admittance now into the Cabinet." It seems she was privy to what the cabinet was up to when she was in the capital. Even from out of town she could read what the Congress was up to, and she didn't like it. How dare the opposition try to undo the Alien and Sedition Acts, "the two strongest barriers which the friends of the government have erected for their security and that of the public." Abigail fundamentally did not understand the American impulse toward free expression. She believed that good men (and women if she had her way) should be left to run the government without the interference of carping critics. If journalists, often paid by the political parties, would not cooperate, then in her view the only sensible thing to do was silence them. She never fully realized that the passage of the Alien and Sedition Acts would expose her husband to charges of tyranny and eventually lead to his defeat.

While Abigail fussed from Quincy, John spent his time alone in Philadelphia fretting about his children. Though John Quincy was ably representing the country as ambassador to Prussia, with the assistance of his brother Thomas, Charles was an alcoholic; Nabby's husband, a phony and a failure. Maybe he should never have gone into public life, moaned this quintessential public servant, "With my family and my children ought I not to have stayed at home." The age-old lament of busy men later in life. Abigail wisely replied, "You have the satisfaction of knowing that you have faithfully served your generation, that you have done it at the expense of all private considerations and you do not know whether you would have been a happier man in private than you have been in public life." He was morose, she told him with some irony, because he didn't have the distraction of a "talkative wife."

Abigail had other sources of anxiety as well. The word in Boston, she told her husband, was that Alexander Hamilton would really run the army assembling under George Washington in case of war with France. The former president would be the commander in name only. The thought of Hamilton in that high position outraged Abigail. She had never trusted him, and her convictions about his lack of character had been confirmed in a widely reported story only a year earlier. While Treasury Secretary, Hamilton had been forced by a Republican newspaperman to reveal that he had been paying blackmail to the husband of a woman with whom he had an affair. Hamilton had to go public in the matter to prove that the blackmail was over personal matters, not the misuse of government securities. The infidelity confirmed Abigail's worst suspicions: "I have not any confidence in the honor, integrity or patriotism of any man who does not believe that thou shalt not commit adultery is a positive prohibition of God." Why, she sardonically added, would anyone believe the reasoning that "I would not upon any consideration do a public wrong or injury, but I can be guilty of breaking the most solemn private engagement and that to one to whom I am bound by affection, and by honor to protect, to love and respect"? As it turned out, Abigail Adams had every reason to mistrust Alexander Hamilton.

From Philadelphia, her husband, the president, wasn't providing enough news for the First Lady at home in Massachusetts. "You used to write much more freely," she complained to him. But Abigail had another source of information, Hannah Cushing, the wife of Supreme Court Justice William Cushing. "I shall get more political intelligence from her, than from all the Members of Congress and the Senate added to them." Abigail understood why this was so. She told her nephew William Shaw, now working as secretary to her husband, that women were "entitled to a greater latitude of speech than men," because they were free of the bonds of some pledge of secrecy. Mrs. Adams certainly exercised that latitude, and soon she reported some intelligence of her own—when Elbridge Gerry, back from France, came to call. He brought word that he had been negotiating in good faith with the French, and he believed their government wanted peace. Abigail was greatly relieved that her confidence in her old friend had not been misplaced: "Whoever questions the integrity of Mr. Gerry's heart does him an injury," she insisted, while still slipping in one of her acerbic observations, "though I thought yesterday from his slowness of speech and his round about and about manner of conveying his ideas, I would as soon vote for a voluble old woman to an embassy, as for him." Her husband diplomatically responded, "I agree with you that voluble old women or handsome young ones are the best ambassadors to some Courts and governments. I wish some power or other would send you to me."

Abigail was still not well enough for the difficult trip to Philadelphia, but John soon sent the good news that their son Thomas was back in the United States after four and a half years abroad. And the diplomats he had worked with in Europe, his brother John Quincy, and William Vans Murray at The Hague, agreed with Gerry that the French were ready to negotiate. Without consulting anyone, and much to the distress of the war hawks in his party, Adams appointed Murray as a new emissary to Paris, trying once again to make peace. "Oh how they lament Mrs. Adams absence!" John wrote of the reactions among Federalists. Knowing that Abigail had lobbied for a declaration of war with France, her fellow hawks thought the president's wife would have dissuaded him from suing for peace. Adams quoted the mutterings to his wife, "If she had been here, Murray would never have been named nor this mission instituted." John teased Abigail. "That ought to gratify your vanity enough to cure you." She replied that Thomas had heard the same thing when he made his rounds on returning to Boston: "Some of the Feds who did not like being taken so by surprise, said they wished the old woman had been there; they did not believe it would have taken place. This was pretty saucy, but the old woman can tell them they are mistaken, for she considers the measure a master-stroke of policy." It showed, she said, that Adams was "pacific" and it tested the sincerity of the French government, plus it surprised and silenced the Republicans. "Pray am I a good politician?" she concluded. Yet again.

Though she had conceded to her husband the brilliance of his latest diplomatic effort, Abigail clearly was having second thoughts about whether the Murray mission was in fact a good idea, "I have not any very sanguine expectation of success." She wanted to know what the Senate was doing about the nomination, "which has agitated the public much more than a declaration of war could have done." Federalist New England was ready to go to war and wanted nothing to do with diplomacy. Whatever her own misgivings, Abigail would support her husband and was in high dudgeon over senators dragging their feet. As members of an independent branch, the senators complained—as senators would for centuries to come—they hadn't been consulted before the president made his move. Making fun of their insistence that they were supposed to advise before they consented, Abigail mockingly asked, "Are there any others whom he is obliged to consult?"

In truth, Adams had no one he *could* consult. His cabinet, held over from George Washington, was in the camp of the girded-up and ready-to-fight Alexander Hamilton. Only his family could be trusted to support the president, and his war-hawk wife assured him that she was on his team. She was not pleased "to have the public imagine that I am not equally pacific with my husband" or that she would not agree with him "if I had been admitted a partner in the counsel. I never pretended to the weight they ascribe to me." Right. To try to calm the critics, Adams appointed Chief Justice Oliver Ellsworth and North Carolina Governor William Davie to serve with Murray, once again hoping the French would receive a triumvirate of prominent Americans. And then John traveled home to Quincy, where his wife's counsels would be welcome.

He stayed too long. While John and Abigail tarried on the farm over the spring and summer of 1799, the president's enemies inside his own Federalist Party took the opportunity to plot against him, while the Republican opposition, as the opposition party has during almost every presidential vacation since, accused him of neglecting the country's business. Though he was corresponding with his department heads and receiving diplomatic dispatches, the president was often so irritated by politics that Abigail took to hiding state papers from him, for fear that he would act impetuously. John Adams's trip back to Philadelphia in the fall did nothing to improve his state of mind. He visited in New York with his daughter Nabby, and found his son Charles's wife and children there as well. They didn't know where the debauched Charles might be. Condemning his son as a "rake, buck, blood and beast," John told Charles's mother, "I renounce him." After dealing that blow, Adams continued, "To go from a private calamity to a public—the fever in Philadelphia is still bad." Every day, the president reported, another yellow fever epidemic was claiming the lives of ten to fourteen Philadelphians.

Settling in Trenton, New Jersey, to wait for the first frost to kill the fever, John listened to reports from his fellow Federalists. What he heard made him realize what he was up against. Not only would the Republicans oppose him in the coming election, he would be under siege from some Federalists as well, with Alexander Hamilton and members of his own cabinet spearheading the charge against him. To Abigail, who was on the road to meet him, he predicted, "An election is approaching which will set us at liberty from these uncomfortable journeys." Not that he wanted to be set free. Under any circumstances, with the new Washington City expected to be ready for the government by the next year, he could be fairly certain that "the next winter will be the last we shall ever spend in Philadelphia." And what a winter it was.

Everyone knew the capital would soon be moving and Philadelphia society scurried to make the most of the closing months of the century—the city's last season in the sun. When Abigail arrived in mid-November, with her daughter Nabby, son Thomas, and Nabby's not quite five-year-old daughter Caroline in tow, she expected the social season to begin as soon as Congress convened in December and the ladies had figured out the latest fashions, "adjusting for some late importations." Though she was looking forward to seeing her Philadelphia friends, Abigail was nervous about the coming Congress, telling her sister, "I expect it to be a stormy session. Electioneering is already begun." And on the day President Adams addressed a joint session to explain the mission to France, she chafed that a large number of ladies went to watch, "but it would not have been proper" for her to attend. Abigail predicted that both parties would find fault with the speech, whose contents she knew well, and she was right about the Senate. But she was pleasantly surprised to learn that the House of Representatives had responded with "full and un-qualified" approval of the peace overture in a message crafted by freshman Congressman John Marshall.

Marshall had been drafted as a congressional candidate by none other than George Washington. The old general summoned his fellow Virginian to Mount Vernon and hammered at him for three days until Marshall finally succumbed. When he left home this time John Marshall, who had left the emotionally fragile Polly behind with a brood of children while he was in France, took his wife with him to the capital city. Stopping in Philadelphia two years earlier, John had regaled Polly with tales of the salons of Mrs. Morris and Mrs. Bingham, with elaborate descriptions of how the tables were set and what the women were wearing, gabbing to his pregnant wife at home, "Mrs. Bingham is a very elegant woman who dresses at the height of fashion." The daughter of one wealthy merchant and the wife of another, the glamorous Anne Willing Bingham had dominated the political and social scene in the nation's largest city for more than a decade.

In this last year of Philadelphia's governmental glory, Anne Bingham wasn't about to let anything dethrone her—even her fifteen-year-old daughter Maria's scandalous elopement with a Frenchman. The Binghams paid off the Frenchman, successfully lobbied the legislature—which was the only entity that could dissolve a marriage—for a bill of divorce, and brazenly brought Maria into society. It was a delicious scandal for the gossipmongers. While the divorce was pending, Maria "was everyday walking with her mother," Harrison Gray Otis told his wife, Sally. "I have been regaled with the sight of her whole legs for five minutes together." When the young woman came calling at the Executive Mansion, the First Lady was shocked. "She has all the appearance and dress of a real French woman, rouged up to the ears; Mrs. Bingham did not appear to feel any embarrassment at introducing her." Maria's mother and sister might be "fine women" and "leaders of the fashion, but they show more of the bosom than the decent matron, or the modest woman," Mrs. Adams sniffed, adding that many of the young women dressed so skimpily they looked like "nursing mothers." Abigail could be predictably Puritan, but she did love fashion and was delighted that "red cloth cloaks are all the mode, trimmed with white furs. This is much more rational than to wear only a shawl in winter." Soon the women would have to put away their red and don mourning clothes. The hero of the nation was dead. (Probably killed by excessive "bleeding" by doctors trying to cure a throat ailment.) It fell to John Marshall to make the official announcement, "Our Washington is no more!"

Though the country was shrouded in sadness, the situation with France still occupied the administration and the round of social events still occupied the ladies of Philadelphia. After the jammed memorial service for the late president, Abigail hosted the most crowded reception she had ever held, with close to two hundred people, "all in mourning. The ladies' grief did not deprive them of taste in ornamenting their white dresses," she drolly recounted. "Their caps were crape with black plumes or black flowers." How long, the women all wanted to know, would they have to wear mourning attire, since it would be their last winter in Philadelphia and "they intended shining"? More "Congress Ladies" had joined their husbands than usual because "they do not expect any accommodations at the new city for them, and they seem determined to take their turn now." Only Vice President Jefferson, who hadn't arrived in town until after the service for Washington, was avoiding the soirees. "Politics are such a torment that I would advise every one I love not to mix with them. I have changed my circle here according to my wish," he informed his daughter Martha, "abandoning the rich and declining their dinners and parties, and associating entirely with the class of science."

New Year's Day 1800 rang in a new century and the prospects of a new government—a presidential election would take place before it was over. Fearing that her husband would lose, Abigail dismissed the whole idea of "frequent popular elections" as engines to "corrupt and destroy the morals of the people." She knew the campaign was going to get nasty, "A whole year we shall hear nothing else, but abuse and scandal." Recognizing that much of the abuse was coming from inside his cabinet, Adams finally ousted his enemies, replacing the perfidious secretary of state, Timothy Pickering, with the new man in town, John Marshall, and setting off a fresh round of Federalist furor led by Alexander Hamilton, who was still highly influential in politics though no longer in government.

For Adams the dismissal of his advisers came as too little, too late. Congress grumpily adjourned in May, with each party caucus having nominated its presidential ticket: John Adams and Charles Cotesworth Pinckney for the Federalists, Thomas Jefferson and Aaron Burr for the Republicans. The battle was on. And Abigail was right—it was nasty. James Callendar, the Republican journalist who had broken the story of Alexander Hamilton's blackmail, went after Adams with everything he had. Thomas Jefferson secretly paid Callendar a retainer to assure a steady stream of anti-Adams propaganda. Callendar did not disappoint, deeming the election a choice "between Adams, war and beggary and Jefferson, peace and competency." Under the Sedition Act, Callendar went to jail and became a hero, something his patron, Jefferson, would come to regret.

Though Abigail was furious with Callendar, and disgusted with the political campaign, she was sorry to say goodbye to her life in Philadelphia. "There is something always melancholy, in the idea of leaving a place for the last time. It is like burying a friend," she sadly said to her sister Mary, and she questioned the move to Washington, "a place so little at present, and probably for years to come, so ill calculated for the residence of such a body as Congress. The houses which are built are so distant, the streets so miry, and the markets so ill supplied." As usual, Abigail had that right. With her days in Philadelphia numbered, the First Lady loosened up a little. During one of her stuffy dinner parties her son Thomas "came round and whispered to me, have you any objection to my having a dance this evening?" "None in the world," she answered, as long as it seemed spontaneous. When the party broke up at midnight, the hostess judged it a great success, "More pleasure ease and enjoyment I have rarely witnessed."

Then it truly was time to say goodbye to Philadelphia. The First Lady held her last "drawing room" reception on May 2, 1800. On May 13, Congress adjourned. The Adams family furniture was shipped to the unfinished federal city, and Abigail headed home to Massachusetts. On the way, she stopped to see Nabby and little Caroline; they were with Nabby's husband, William Smith, who had joined the army and was stationed in New Jersey. During her visit Abigail was called on to review the troops. "I acted," she boasted to John, "as your proxy—praised and admired, and regretted, etc." With peace envoys meeting in France, the army would soon be disbanded, leaving son-in-law William Smith once more out of a job. Smith's career prospects were a constant source of concern and embarrassment to the Adams family, as was Charles Adams's alcoholism. Finding his family so forlorn when she arrived for a visit, Abigail brought Charles's oldest child, a four-year-old girl named Susan, home to live with her. Aside from the family troubles, the First Lady filled her letters from the road with the latest rumors, gossip, and political intelligence, including the mixed reaction to the firing of the cabinet officers. As Abigail traveled north, John headed south for his first look at Washington, D.C.

The president arrived in the new capital on June 3, 1800, and reported to his wife ten days later, "The establishment of the public officers in this place has given it the air of the Seat of Government and all things seem to go well." Construction was going on all around Adams, and the few souls who had been in town trying to mold a capital out of a swamp were eager to see the president. Anna Thornton, wife of the architect of the Capitol, wrote in her diary, "The

President intends staying to receive an address from the inhabitants of George Town tomorrow." Adams was entertained by two of Martha Washington's granddaughters who had married local men, and he visited Mrs. Washington herself on a pilgrimage to Mount Vernon. She sent her regards to Abigail and the children—that was the good news. The bad news was that the presidential campaign was growing more and more vicious. And it would only get worse over the summer, which John Adams spent back home in Quincy with Abigail.

The new secretary of state, John Marshall, was left to keep his eye on the government, hoping to hear from the commissioners in Paris. Polly Marshall, with yet another new baby, had gone home to Richmond, where her husband wrote to her after *his* visit with Martha Washington. According to Marshall, Martha appeared "tolerable cheerful but not to possess the same sort of cheerfulness as formerly. You as a widow would I hope show more firmness." Such sympathy! Politically, Martha Washington showed quite frank firmness, telling another visitor that Thomas Jefferson, the opponent of her husband's handpicked successor, was "one of the most detestable of mankind."

Martha Washington's devastating assessment was the least of the attacks. According to the press and the pamphlets, Jefferson was a French-loving, atheistic libertine. Adams was a warmongering, monarchical madman. Jefferson supporters rebutted a whispering campaign about a liaison between their candidate and a slave woman with the charge that Charles Cotesworth Pinckney, the Federalist vice-presidential candidate, had picked up four women in London—two for him, two for Adams. "If this is true," Adams chuckled to a friend, "General Pinckney has kept them all for himself and cheated me out of my two." But the newspapers weren't Adams's biggest problem—Alexander Hamilton was.

Abigail had been right to distrust the man she once called as ambitious as Julius Caesar. In October, Hamilton—who resented the fact that Adams never accorded him the prominence or appointed him to the positions he sought—sent out a blistering, venomous attack on the president of his party. The fifty-four-page *Letter from Alexander Hamilton, Concerning the Public Conduct and Character of John Adams, Esq., President of the United States,* lashed out at Adams for "great intrinsic defects of character." John Adams's goose was cooked and he knew it. He told Abigail that Hamilton's diatribe would "ensure the choice of the man whom he dreads, or pretends to dread more than me." If that was true, if Hamilton had ensured the election of a Republican president, Abigail feared for her son John Quincy's future as a diplomat. It was time to come home, she told him, where people could see what he was up to, because "services to a country in a diplomatic line can be known only to a few." Her children were never too old or too important for Abigail Adams to try to run their lives.

In the heat of the campaign, President Adams returned to the new capital city, arriving on November 1, 1800. He spent the night in the building that would come to be called the White House and wrote to Abigail the next day: "I pray heaven to bestow the best of blessings on this House and all that shall hereafter inhabit it. May none but honest and wise men ever rule under this roof." Those words are inscribed above the fireplace of the State Dining Room in the White House today. Adams had reason to believe that it would not be long before another man ruled under the roof of the executive mansion, and he was glad that his wife would soon join him, because it was "fit and proper that you and I should retire together." Abigail was already on her way. She stopped in New York to see Charles, whose dissipation had landed him on his deathbed. "Sally was with him but his physician says he is past recovery," his mother despondently told her sister. A few days' stay in Philadelphia made her dread the fact that she had to leave that friendly and familiar city for "an unknown and unseen abode." But Abigail soldiered on to Washington, getting lost in the woods outside of Baltimore, astonished that she saw "nothing but a forest and woods on the way, for 16 and 18 miles not a village."

The brand-new "city" turned out to be just what the First Lady expected: "a new country, with houses scattered over a space of ten miles, and trees and stumps in plenty." She judged Georgetown "the very dirtiest hole I ever saw." Looking for something good to say, Abigail found the president's house "in a beautiful situation in front of which is the Potomac with a view of Alexandria." But the house was huge, expensive, requiring thirteen fires to keep it warm, and unfinished—not one room was completely done, and there was famously no place to hang the laundry but "the great unfinished audience room," now known as the East Room, where presidents hold receptions and press conferences. "I had much rather live in the house in Philadelphia," Abigail complained to her sister Mary, but promised to confine her criticism within the bosom of the family. "I am determined to be satisfied and content, to say nothing of the inconvenience, etc." If anyone asked her daughter Nabby what her mother thought of Washington, she should say the "situation is beautiful, which is true."

Unfinished house or not, Abigail would have to expect callers. "The ladies from Georgetown and in the city have many of them visited me," she told Nabby soon after she arrived. The First Lady had been there just three days when Anna Thornton went to get a look. "Mrs. A. is a short lady; in person something like Mrs. Washington—has a sensible look." Abigail returned the call the day her husband addressed a joint session of Congress at the unfinished Capitol. She was able to get an immediate report from Anna Thornton: "There were a great many people, the galleries were full—the ladies sat and stood below on the same floor as the Senate, etc." Congressional sessions provided the chief entertainment for the citizens of this humble hamlet, so it was no wonder that soon Nabby heard from her harassed mother, "The ladies are impatient for a drawing room." A reception at the executive mansion, whatever its condition, was expected. But settling into life in Washington proved the least of the First Family's problems. Personal and political tragedy soon overcame any concerns about hanging out the laundry.

On December 3, as members of the Electoral College cast their votes for president, John and Abigail Adams learned that their thirty-one-year-old son, Charles, was dead. "He was no man's enemy but his own," his mother mourned. There was, however, some good news: a treaty with France had been signed. The crisis that had occupied the entire Adams presidency—known by history as the Quasi-War with France—was finally over. But the president had not yet received official word from his ministers, so he had to keep the news of his success under wraps until after the election. Who knows whether it would have made a difference?

As it was, John Adams lost. Abigail, as usual, was ready with perceptive political analysis. The election pivoted on the votes of New York City, organized by Aaron Burr and the Republican Party "with more skill than their opponents," she told her son Thomas. And South Carolina's decision to abandon its favorite son, Charles Pinckney, in favor of Thomas Jefferson sealed the Federalists' fate, confirming Abigail's belief that southern promises to "northern men" had no more weight than "lover's vows." Still, her fundamental patriotism emerged in a letter to Mary: "I wish for the preservation of the government and a wise administration of it." There were times she said when John had thought about retiring, but she had thought it better to leave that decision to the people. "I do not regret that he has done so." Adams had lost, but who had won? That would not be clear for weeks to come.

Candidates for president and vice president did not run as a ticket. Members of the Electoral College could each cast two votes, presumably one for president, one for vice president. The man with the highest number of votes would be president, the runner-up, vice president. Even though the party's nominating caucus had made it clear that Thomas Jefferson was intended for the first position, Aaron Burr for the second, no Republican elector withheld a ballot for Burr in order to give Jefferson the most votes. The country learned the results in late December when newspapers printed the tally: Jefferson 73, Burr 73, Adams 65, Pinckney 64, plus one vote for Federalist John Jay. The election had officially ended in a tie. The outcome would be decided by the House of Representatives. (The Twelfth Amendment to the Constitution, ratified in 1804, fixed the problem by designating the votes. Each elector casts one vote for president, one for vice president.)

Republicans had won the congressional elections as well as the presidency, but it was the still-sitting lame-duck Federalist Congress that would break the tie between Jefferson and Burr. The politicking was fierce, with Hamilton again in the thick of it, when the Adamses held the first New Year's reception at the White House. But according to one chronicler, Abigail Adams handled that potentially dicey occasion with her usual aplomb: "No one would have guessed that the house was half finished, the principal stairs still lacking, her china stolen and her husband defeated. She was mistress not only of the White House but of the situation." Two days later the Adamses graciously invited Thomas Jefferson to dinner with a group of congressmen. When Jefferson asked his hostess what she thought the Congress would do in the election, she replied that it was a subject she didn't "choose to converse upon." Though Abigail could be civil with her old friend, she was understandably upset by the prospect of Jefferson as president. She didn't think the Republican standard-bearer was an atheist, "but he believes religion only useful as it may be made a political engine." And Burr, a well-known womanizer, was even worse. "What a lesson upon elective governments have we in our young republic of 12 years old?" asked the woman who had been wary of "frequent elections" from the beginning. Even so, Abigail was dying to see how it all came out. She stayed in Washington waiting for the House of Representatives to meet to determine "the fate of our country."

Thomas Jefferson really did not know what the Congress would do. The Federalists could make or break him, and some of his worst enemies among them were scheming to elect Aaron Burr, with one prominent exception: Alexander Hamilton, who despised Burr even more than he disagreed with Jefferson. Perhaps to curry favor with the opposition party, Jefferson trekked to Mount Vernon to pay homage to Martha Washington on the same day he dined with Abigail Adams. (Presumably he didn't know what Mrs. Washington had been saying about him.) Abigail had earlier also paid a farewell call on her mentor as First Lady. Martha told her successor that she didn't feel safe at home with her some three hundred slaves, because George Washington's will stipulated that they would be given their freedom when she died. According to Abigail, the former First Lady fearfully confided that many of the slaves "told her that it was in their interest to get rid of her. She therefore was advised to set them all free at the close of the year." For the longtime abolitionist Abigail Adams, it was just one more argument against slavery in her quiver. Even after she freed her slaves, Martha needed them to run the large estate that her husband had once described as a "well resorted tavern."

Poor Mrs. Washington—everyone seemed to show up on her doorstep. Sally Otis, wife of Massachusetts Congressman Harrison Gray Otis, traveled with a party that spent the night at Mount Vernon, where Martha "received us with the most gracious cordiality, in her deportment is that mild benevolence that serene resignation which characterizes the saint." Resignation probably was the best Martha could muster with the constant stream of strangers. Fortunately she and George had managed to hang on to the money she had brought into their marriage as a very wealthy widow.

Trying to puzzle out what Congress was up to, Jefferson regularly wrote about the political machinations to his two daughters in Virginia—Maria Eppes and Martha Randolph. He knew the Federalists were plotting to elect Aaron Burr as president, but he believed Burr was acting honorably by not encouraging the opposing party. As February 11, the day the House would vote, drew closer, Jefferson hoped he would be able to report the results to his older daughter, Martha, in his next letter, "I believe it will be as the people have wished, but this depends upon the will of a few moderate men; and they may be controlled by their party." It's a lament heard in Washington ever since.

The public was desperate to know the goings-on in the House chamber, which was locked and sealed as the members met in secret. Margaret Bayard Smith, the wife of a Republican newspaperman, who later became a reporter herself, described the scene as the House of Representatives prepared to vote: "Crowds of anxious spirits from the adjacent county and cities thronged to the seat of government and hung like a thundercloud over the Capitol, their indignation ready to burst on any individual who might be designated as president in opposition to the people's known choice." Washington locals tried to put together some semblance of social life to break the tension. After one evening out, Congressman Otis complained to his wife (who had scurried off to Philadelphia after a brief stay in the primitive capital) that the supper "was shabby beyond all former precedent. A sideboard with a round of cold beef and a ham which the dear ladies were obliged to eat on their knees, presented the sum total" of the meal.

It would be a while before "the People's Choice" would know if he had won. Jefferson told Maria, "After 4 days of balloting, they are exactly where they were on the first." There was no majority in the House of Representatives for either Jefferson or Burr. "The balloting took place every hour," Margaret Smith wrote, and then the results were brought to her husband at the newspaper. One ailing congressman, Joseph Nicholson of Maryland, had been carried to the Capitol in a snowstorm with his wife in attendance. "In a room adjacent to the Hall of R. he lay on a bed beside which she knelt supporting his head on her arm, while with her hand she guided his, in writing the name of the man of his choice." His choice was Jefferson. Without Nicholson, Maryland could have easily gone for Burr, and history might be quite different. Mrs. Nicholson, Margaret Smith dramatically recounted, had been told the trip to the Capitol could kill her husband; still she didn't dissuade him. Why? "It was for her country!"

In the middle of all of this excitement, Abigail Adams was forced to leave town before the winter weather made the roads too

treacherous to travel. Shortly before she left, somewhat to her surprise, Jefferson stopped by for tea and to "wish me a good journey."
Two days into the balloting, the First Lady left the capital city she
had braved for a few long months, arriving in Baltimore in a "violent
snow storm . . . not so weary however as to have lost my curiosity
about the fate of the election." She couldn't wait to learn what had
happened. Three days later Adams wrote that in his judgment: "The
election will be decided this day in favor of Mr. Jefferson." He added
that he was hosting "Indian Kings and aristocrats" at his last official
dinner that night. In fact, it took one day more before the deadlock
between Thomas Jefferson and the man who would become his vice
president, Aaron Burr, was broken on the thirty-sixth ballot. "The
assembled crowds without the Capitol rent the air with their acclamations and gratulations," Margaret Smith exulted.

While the intrigue in the House played out, Adams was busy
with a judiciary bill that vastly expanded the third branch of government and allowed the lame-duck president to appoint a group of
last-minute judges, including John Marshall as chief justice of the
Supreme Court. The so-called "midnight judges" infuriated Jefferson and made for more bad blood between him and his old friend,
Adams. Abigail's reaction when she heard of the appointments: "I
want to see the list of judges." She had some lists of her own, and the
president spent his final days in office naming friends and relatives
to patronage positions. He also recalled John Quincy Adams from
the embassy in Berlin, depriving Jefferson of the chance to hurl that
particular insult. Traveling home, Abigail reached Philadelphia,
where she was called on by "throngs" of people but was appalled at
the church bells tolling for "an *Infidel* President."

She was lucky to have made it to Philadelphia at all. The journey
had been hazardous, especially when it came time to cross the frozen
Susquehanna River. The ice wasn't strong enough to hold a carriage,
but there were no coaches available on the other side, so Abigail's
traveling party experimented to see how much weight the ice could
bear. First they sent a horse over safely, then put wooden slats under

the carriage and dragged it over. "Having effected this, the horses were all led over, and then they put us in a boat, and drew us over the same way; the ice however breaking near the shore and letting the men in above their boots." Louisa Smith, Abigail's niece, pleaded with her to turn around, to wait to make a trip until a gentleman could accompany them. Though it might have been "agreeable" to have a man along, Abigail retorted, she could handle the situation, since she was "accustomed to get through many a trying scene and combat many difficulties alone." As unhappy as she might have been about her husband's defeat and however much she might miss the power of "Mrs. President," Abigail Adams would, for the first time in her long marriage, no longer be alone. She would soon have her husband with her for the rest of her life.

DURING ABIGAIL ADAMS'S FOUR YEARS as First Lady, the United States saw some marked changes in women's roles as educators, writers, and activists. Abigail had militated mightily for women's education all through the years of the Revolution. In 1778, when John Adams was dispatched to France as a representative of the rebellious Americans, he had the bad sense to write home about how much he admired the French women. Abigail, struggling on her own to make ends meet in Massachusetts, shot back that American women would be just as accomplished if they had access to a better education. Partly because of the varied roles women were called on to play while the men were off during the war, and partly because of the perceived need for mothers to raise "virtuous citizens" for the new republic, women's education took off in the years following the Revolution.

Female academies cropped up around the country, including one in New York where Martha Washington sent her granddaughter, Nelly Custis, when she was First Lady. Run by Isabella Graham, a Scottish widow, the school opened its doors in 1789 for the purpose of educating the daughters of wealthy Manhattanites who didn't want to send their girls away to one of the several recently established female boarding schools. By the time Abigail Adams became First Lady in 1797, Graham's school was so well regarded by rich families that she was able to shift her considerable energies into what was to become her lifelong vocation—social activism on behalf of the poor. "Invitations in the form of circular letters were sent to the ladies of New York, and a very respectable number assembled at the house of Mrs. Graham," remembered Isabella's daughter, Joanna Bethune, who wrote an account of her mother's life that sold briskly in the nineteenth century. The meeting gave birth to the Society for the Relief of Poor Widows with Small Children, the brainchild of Isabella, Joanna, and Joanna's friend Elizabeth Bayley Seton, then a married Protestant woman, later a canonized Catholic nun.

The organization was one of the first examples of what soon became a countrywide phenomenon—social safety-net societies run by women to benefit those left behind by the rollicking capitalism of the time. These benevolent associations required women to organize, fund-raise, assume positions of leadership, and engage in politics. The Widows' Society, for instance, was incorporated by the state legislature, which also allocated some funds for the endeavor. The women bought a building and opened a school, along with training "some of the widows best qualified for the task" to teach children of other widows in "distant parts of the city." Running soup kitchens became the job of other clients.

Soon providing food, fuel, and clothes to about 150 widows and more than 400 children, the welfare organization stood as the first of several charities Graham and her colleagues created, including the Society for the Promotion of Industry among the Poor. After enlisting thirty women to sign a petition to the mayor and city council in support of that organization, Isabella successfully lobbied the state legislature to pony up five hundred dollars a year to employ women as seamstresses, weavers, and tailors. Still, she found it hard to keep up with the need. "The poor increase fast: Immigrants from all quarters flock to us and when they come they must not be allowed to die for want." None of this work was easy, especially for a woman. At one point, when addressing a group of young matrons who were volunteering to open a school for "street kids," Isabella Graham gave a glimpse of the difficulties she had encountered. The Widows' Society had been "the jest of most, the ridicule of many and it met the opposition of not a few. The men could not allow our sex the steadiness and perseverance necessary to establish such an undertaking." She warned the young women that they should expect similar "painful banter," but encouraged them with the success of her society. "Its fame is spread over the United States and celebrated in foreign countries. It has been a precedent to many cities who have followed the laudable example."

It was remarkable enough that any woman in the eighteenth century had started what essentially became a nationwide relief movement. The fact that the woman who had done it was Isabella Graham was even more remarkable. Decades earlier, as the new bride of a British army doctor, she went with her husband to Canada, where he was posted in 1767. The next assignment, at Fort Niagara, convinced the couple that they wanted to stay in the United States with their rapidly increasing family. Before John Graham could buy land, however, the stirrings of rebellion in America caused the British government to redeploy his regiment to Antigua. About a year after arriving there, John died, leaving the pregnant Isabella virtually penniless in a strange land with three little girls under the age of five. Her husband's army buddies helped pay her fare home to Scotland, but she soon learned that living off her widow's pension meant living in poverty. With the encouragement of wealthy friends, she eventually landed the job of running a boarding school in Edinburgh. But she always harbored the hope of returning to America and was encouraged in that dream by the president of Princeton University, the Reverend John Witherspoon.

A native of Scotland, Witherspoon met Isabella on a trip home, where she impressed him both as a rigorous educator and a religious example. He helped connect her with prominent families in the

United States so that when she arrived in New York in 1789, she was able to capitalize on those connections. As luck would have it, Isabella's timing was perfect. A growing port city, New York was fast recovering from the ravages of British occupation during the Revolution and serving as the temporary capital of the new U.S. government. There was a ready supply of young ladies to populate Mrs. Graham's school, which she opened a month after her arrival. Within a few weeks she had enrolled fifty students and soon found the granddaughter of the president of the United States among her pupils. Nelly Custis, daughter of Martha Washington's only son, Jack, had been adopted by her grandparents when her father died and was still a young girl when the Washingtons moved to New York. Martha considered Nelly's superior education one of the few bright spots of her sentence as a "state prisoner"—her definition of the role of First Lady. As headmistress of the city's chic girls' school, Isabella could cultivate the contacts, and collect the cash, that allowed her to begin her work of benevolence, which "prospered beyond the most sanguine expectations of its propagators."

Though Isabella Graham usually worked with the white Protestant "society women" who were her former pupils or their mothers, one of her coworkers was an African American credited with founding the first Sunday school in New York. Catherine Ferguson's biography is sketchy, but shortly before she died she told her life story to Lewis Tappan, who published it as an obituary in the *New York Daily Tribune*. Born a slave, when she was still a small child her owner "sold my mother away, but I remember that before we were torn asunder, she knelt down, laid her hand on my head, and gave me to God." It's possible that as a teenager Katy worked for Isabella Graham, who may have been the person who set the young slave free. The obituary revealed only "a benevolent lady purchased Katy's freedom for two hundred dollars, when she was sixteen years of age." Since some of the money was supplied by Graham's son-in-law, Divie Bethune, it's likely that Isabella played a role in the manumission. At eighteen, Catherine married and had children, but according to a religious tract about her life, they "did not live long."

Supporting herself as a cake-maker who supervised the "nicer provisions of the table" at fashionable weddings, Katy Ferguson lived in a New York neighborhood where children roamed the streets with "none to care for their bodies or souls." Somehow the former slave took charge of forty-eight kids, both black and white, either placing them with other people or taking them in herself. In about 1793, when she realized how little the children knew about religion, she set up Katy Ferguson's School for the Poor in New York City. But because the mistress of the "Sabbath school" was herself illiterate, "sometimes the sainted Isabella Graham would invite Katy and her scholars to her house and there hear their catechism and give them instruction." And it might have been Isabella who told Dr. John Mason, the pastor of the Presbyterian church both women attended, about the school in Catherine Ferguson's parlor. At any rate, he showed up at Katy's house, offered to help, and moved the operation to the Murray Street church, effectively launching the Sunday school movement in New York, which provided poor kids with at least some rudimentary education.

Then, as now, women writers often did double duty as teachers, and the number of published women writers was growing in the early years of the new nation. Hannah Adams, a distant cousin of John Adams, published a couple of texts about religion in order to earn a living, making her the first woman in the country to live off her writing income. Most others, including such popular novelists as Susanna Rowson, found other ways to supplement whatever they could bring in by their way with words. In Rowson's case it was acting and teaching. Wealthy young women in New England matriculated at Mrs. Rowson's Young Ladies Academy under the tutelage of the famous author of the first best-selling novel in America. Though that novel, *Charlotte Temple: A Tale of Truth,* is Susanna Haswell Rowson's most widely known work—it's been printed in almost two hundred editions—it was just one of many of this amazing woman's accomplishments.

As well as running her school, working with *Boston Weekly Magazine*, and engaging in social activism, Rowson published prolifically—eight novels, seven plays, six textbooks, two poetry collections, magazine pieces, and song lyrics. (She composed songs and poems for special occasions. Among them: the dirge for George Washington's funeral and a celebratory rhyme for John Adams's birthday. Only Federalists were honored by Susanna's pen, she had no words of praise for Thomas Jefferson.) In her work she found ways to look at the role of women in the world and the role of the world toward women. Rowson's geography textbooks, for instance, rebuked some countries—Egypt, Turkey, Tibet—for their treatment of females. And her plays directly addressed women in the audience about their position in society. In the epilogue to her popular production *Slaves in Algiers,* the lead actress-playwright came onstage to ask the Philadelphia audience, "Well, Ladies, tell me—how d'ye like my play?"

Did they think:

> *Women were born for universal sway,*
> *Men to adore, be silent and obey.*

Or:

> *To bind the truant, that's inclined to roam,*
> *Good humor makes a paradise at home.*
> *To raise the fall'n—to pity and forgive,*
> *This is our noblest, best prerogative.*
> *By these pursuing nature's gentle plan,*
> *We hold in silken chains the lordly tyrant man.*

Her boldness earned Rowson the contempt of Federalist newspaperman William Cobbett, who lambasted her feminist sentiments along with the "whole tribe of female scribblers and politicians."

This particular "female scribbler" had grown up in Massachusetts, which produced more than its share of women writers. Susanna moved across the ocean when her father, an English soldier, was sent back to Britain in bad health as part of a prisoner exchange during the Revolutionary War. To support the family, the young woman took a job as a governess to the daughters of the Duchess of Devonshire, who became her literary patron. In 1786, when she had already published one novel, Susanna married Royal Horse guardsman William Rowson, owner of a failing hardware enterprise. After the business went under, the couple, along with William's sister, tried their hands as actors, appearing in venues around England. Though the little troupe was never very successful, an American impresario caught their act in 1792 and booked them in his New Theater in Philadelphia. By that time Susanna had successfully published short stories, poetry, dramatic criticism, and four novels, including the popular *Charlotte: A Tale of Truth*. All dealt in one way or another with the status of women.

In Philadelphia, Susanna Rowson, as the playwright of dramas and musical comedies, became an instant hit with the city's political and social elites. Soon she published an American edition of her English novel with the title *Charlotte Temple,* which reigned as the bestselling book in this country until Harriet Beecher Stowe wrote *Uncle Tom's Cabin* more than fifty years later, giving it the longest popular run of any American novel. Because she didn't own the copyright to her work, its huge success didn't do much for the Rowson family pocketbook, so gambling that the 1796 opening of a new theater in Boston—where plays had been banned by the Puritans until 1793—would allow for some financial stability, the couple moved back to the state where Susanna had grown up, hoping for receptive audiences. It didn't take long, however, for Susanna to realize that she could do better appearing in front of a classroom than onstage and in 1797, somewhat improbably for a woman in the not-very-genteel acting profession, she started her school for proper young ladies.

Mrs. Rowson's students found her an "amiable lady" who treated "all her scholars with such a tenderness as would win the affection of the most savage brute," but the schoolmistress was a tough taskmaster. She wrote her textbooks because she couldn't find any that met her exacting standards, and her exams were exhaustive. "This morning I was up at 4 o'clock sitting by the lamp studying & every night I have 3 or 4 books under my head," one terrified student wrote home. Along with geography, history, literature, music, and religion, Mrs. Rowson dispensed a light-touched dose of feminism. She compiled her own poetry and prose in *A Present for Young Ladies,* with selections recited by her students in their exhibitions for friends and family.

"It would be absurd to imagine that talents or virtue were confined to sex or station," she radically proclaimed in that work, which also included a section called "Female Biography" with sketches of powerful women in history, like Elizabeth I. In it she addressed the question of whether women are the "weaker sex" and concluded, "perhaps through constitution, habit, and education in some degree they are so; but there have been numberless instances of women who have proved themselves adequate to every trial that proves their attachment to their husbands, children, parents or country." One student wrote to a friend that she learned in the Biographical Class about "the doctrine of the equality of women with the other sex." When the class performed a recital, she reported, "although by sedulously ransacking ancient and modern history Mrs. Rowson could not find a sufficient number of honorable examples of female excellence to reach 3 times around the class," even so they were to make "a pretty formidable show by showing the assembly how several virago queens and blustering heroines" had achieved fame by killing themselves or others! Still, despite her fame as an actress and influence as a schoolmistress who passed on the histories of powerful women, it was not Susanna Rowson's story most Americans knew, it was Charlotte Temple's.

It's a sad tale of the seduction of a young English girl by a United States soldier who, with the help of Charlotte's perfidious French teacher, lures her away from her boarding school, packs her onto a ship to America, and sets her up as his mistress while he goes off to marry a wealthy woman. Lonely, pregnant, dependent on a cad for her bread and butter, Charlotte is miserable. And the author feels for her, even though she's a "fallen woman." In one of her many asides to the reader, Susanna justifies her sympathy: "Surely when we reflect on how many errors we are ourselves subject to, how many secret faults lie hid in the recesses of our hearts," Susanna lectures, "I say, dear Madam, when we consider this, we surely may pity the faults of others." Charlotte is brought down not only by her evil seducer but also by her own lack of resources. She has neither the money nor the training to make it on her own. Abandoned and alone, Charlotte dies soon after giving birth in a kind servant's hut. Her father dramatically shows up minutes before she expires, forgives her, and promises to raise the baby.

Knowing a good thing when she saw it, Susanna Rowson later produced another well-read novel, *Charlotte's Daughter.* But nothing could compare to the popularity of the original. *Everybody* read the book. Susanna's American publisher told her that the "sales exceed those of any of the most celebrated novels that ever appeared in England." The *Washington Household Account* books include an entry of a payment "for a book called Charlotte (by Mrs. Rowson) for Mrs. Washington." As the novel became an integral part of the nation's culture, a cult grew up about the title character, with readers coloring in her illustrations in the book, and visiting the grave of a woman they believed to be the real Charlotte. A headstone in New York's Trinity churchyard does bear the name "Charlotte Temple," but various versions have evolved over time of how that marker came to be. Since the church burned during the Revolution, the period of the novel, there's no way of knowing if the grave is really that of the woman whose story so affected thousands of early Americans, or even if the Charlotte Temple of the novel ever existed.

No such mystery surrounds Hannah Foster's *The Coquette,* the next widely read novel about a seduced woman in saddened straits. The plot was already well known when the novel, based on a true story that served as a cautionary tale to flirtatious young women, hit the burgeoning bookstores in 1797. Nine years earlier the *Salem Mercury* had printed a titillating item about a "female stranger" who died at the Bell Tavern in Danvers, Massachusetts, under circumstances that "excite curiosity and interest our feelings." Soon it was known throughout the state that the woman in question was Elizabeth Whitman, a well-bred minister's daughter, that she had arrived at the tavern very pregnant and without a husband, and that she died soon after the delivery of her stillborn baby. The story was picked up and repeated, with suitable warnings to young women not to follow in Elizabeth Whitman's wanton ways. She had been too given to flights of fancy and reading romantic novels, too unwilling to settle for an appropriate husband, too willing to play "the coquette" flirting with two men, choosing neither. Eventually she was left with no one, a fate worse than death for a proper eighteenth-century woman, and, unmarried, took up with one of the spurned lovers only to end her life in disgrace. The moral: marry respectably even if the man's an insufferable bore.

A somewhat different message comes through in Hannah Foster's fictional version of the story, which challenges the crusty sexual double standard. Written as letters among the cast of characters, from them we learn that Eliza Wharton, a thinly veiled Elizabeth Whitman, finds neither suitor acceptable and the reader can easily see why—one's a pompous prig, the other an unreliable rascal. Though beautiful, Eliza is not rich. These are the men available and since she's trained for nothing but marriage, she needs to choose a mate before the bloom is off her rose. The fact that she does not settle leads to her tragic end. But Foster urges her readers to ask why it should be so. At a time when women were being encouraged into motherhood in order to raise good republican sons, the dialogue in *The Coquette* hints at the idea that the women themselves are capable of concerned citizenship. Rebuffing a silly character who argues that ladies should not meddle in politics, the noble woman of the story retorts that she and Eliza "think ourselves interested in the welfare and prosperity of our country; and consequently claim the right of inquiring into those affairs, which may conduce to or interfere with the commonweal." Women might not be called to the Senate, she continued, but, "If the community flourish and enjoy health and freedom, shall we not share in the happy effects? If it be oppressed and disturbed, shall we not endure our proportion of the evil? Why then should the love of our country be a masculine passion only?"

It was a question more and more women were beginning to pose in the years that Abigail Adams served as First Lady. It was a question she had asked as early as the days of the Continental Congress, when she had famously scolded John that he must "remember the ladies" in the formation of a new government. As the eighteenth century closed, the rapid spread of publishing was making it possible for women to present questions about their rights before a wide audience. More publishing meant not only more bookstores but the birth of lending libraries—making books, newspapers, and, especially, magazines available to all comers. The 1790 population of four million people could choose from fewer than one hundred newspapers; twenty years later the number of newspapers had more than tripled as the population doubled. And magazines designed explicitly for women, with articles often written by women, started filling the stacks in the 1790s. (The first American cookbook was also published. In 1796, *American Cookery,* by Amelia Simmons, An American Orphan, finally provided U.S. cooks with recipes using New World ingredients like cornmeal. The word "cookie," taken from the Dutch *koekje,* appeared for the first time in Amelia Simmons's book.) Recognizable to readers of women's magazines today, the eighteenth-century versions featured fiction, poems, and advice on such subjects as how to have a happy marriage, but they also served as platforms for and against women's rights.

Stepping full frontally into that fight was America's foremost feminist of the late eighteenth century—Judith Sargent Murray. Articles about girls' lack of self-esteem have become staple fare in female periodicals over the last couple of decades, but Murray first broached the subject in 1784 in her essay "Desultory Thoughts upon the Utility of Encouraging a Degree of Self-Complacency, Especially in Female Bosoms." Writing as "Constantia" in *The Gentleman and Lady's Town and Country Magazine*, she argued "to teach young minds to aspire ought to be the ground work of education." A girl who didn't value herself, Murray insisted, would "throw herself away upon the first who approaches her with tenders of love, however indifferent may be her chance for happiness." It took six years for her to publish again as she suffered through the bankruptcy and then death of her first husband. In 1790, after she married John Murray, the founder of the Unitarian Universalist Church in the United States, her bombshell "On the Equality of the Sexes" appeared in *Massachusetts Magazine*. Remarkably, Murray had actually written the piece in 1774, before the Revolution had produced its consciousness-raising effects.

With "Constantia" again her byline, she sarcastically queried whether anyone thought a two-year-old boy smarter than a two-year-old girl. Murray made the case that it was a lack of education, rather than intellect, holding women back. "As their years increase, the sister must be wholly domesticated, while the brother is led by the hand through all the flowery paths of science." Women should have equal opportunity to learn, she insisted, and for those who feared women's education would lead them to abandon their "domestic duties," Murray assured them "while we are pursuing the needle, or the superintendency of the family, I repeat, that our minds are at full liberty for reflection." What a concept, women could do housework and think at the same time! Did it make sense, she asked, "that a candidate for immortality, for the joys of heaven, an intelligent being, who is to spend an eternity in contemplating the works of Deity, should at present be so degraded, as to be allowed no other ideas, than those which are suggested by the mechanism of a pudding, or the sewing the seams of a garment?" This a full two years before the Englishwoman Mary Wollstonecraft's *A Vindication of the Rights of Women* rocketed across the ocean where magazines up and down the U.S. excerpted it, contributing to a national debate about a woman's place.

It was common for women at the time to sign pseudonyms to their writing. In addition to "Constantia," Judith Murray disguised her work as that of a man called "The Gleaner," because she wanted to avoid "the indifference, not to say contempt, with which female productions are regarded." Murray had run into a good deal of criticism for her plays and newspaper articles written in her own name. As a "man," the public was much more accepting of her columns about politics, education, and marriage. ("Mutual esteem, mutual friendship, mutual confidence, *begirt about with mutual forebearance*— these are the necessary requisites of the matrimonial career.") No one knew who "The Gleaner" was—not even Judith's husband. But the anonymous writer was popular, attracting quite a following. Eventually Murray wanted to claim the credit. She decided to "come out," to publish her "Gleaner" collection as a book, partly because she needed the money, partly because she wanted to "distinguish myself." It was quite an admission of ambition for a woman at the time, as it still would be today.

In order to pay for publishing, she needed to solicit subscribers, so she started at the top. Judith and John Murray had met John and Abigail Adams in Massachusetts, and then visited them on a trip to New York, where the Murrays also met George and Martha Washington. To launch her book, Judith first contacted Vice President Adams to ask his permission to dedicate it to him. She knew it was a presumptuous request, but she was willing to take the chance because "we entered your hospitable mansion, you smiled benignly on me, and grateful admiration absorbed every lesser consideration." Another letter—this one to President Washington—followed. After the usual flattery she made the pitch, "Deign, honored Sire, to set your name to the enclosed proposals and thus give éclat to the production they announce." Judith got what she wanted. "Our illustrious President wrote me with his own hand, a very pleasing letter, that he has honored me with his signature, and that Mrs. Washington has also joined hers," she told a friend; then Murray used the endorsements of Washington and Adams to hound other notables into subscribing. Her dozens of letters and ads in the newspapers elicited 730 responses, including Susanna Rowson's, which read like a Who's Who of early America.

When the book came out in three volumes in 1798, Murray hammered home her call for equality of the sexes. Assuming that younger women had been inspired by Wollstonecraft, she exulted, "I may be accused of enthusiasm; but such is my confidence in THE SEX, that I expect to see our young women forming a new era in female history." Once *The Gleaner* was published, Murray had the nerve to go back to George Washington to make sure he had received his copies. She was fishing for a thank-you letter that she could use for promotional purposes. When she didn't hear from him, she wrote again! The former president finally responded, saying her book had given him "an enjoyment so richly zested." She was thrilled: "Accept, illustrious Chief, my utmost gratitude for the dignity and importance you have conferred upon my publication." Judith Sargent Murray had achieved her goal of distinguishing herself.

Murray also helped stoke the discussion about women's rights that crackled through the last decade of the eighteenth century, when the much later move for women's political rights found its embryonic beginnings. "Had the new theory of the *Rights of Women* enlightened the world at the period of the formation of the Constitution," conceded Harvard President John Thornton Kirkland in 1798, "it is possible that the framers, convinced of its arguments might have set aside the old system of exclusion, upon which the world has always proceeded till this reforming age, as illiberal and tyrannical." Other men refused to entertain such thoughts. "Every man, by the Constitution, is born with an equal right to be elected to the highest office. And every woman, is born with an equal right to be the wife of the most eminent man," smugly summed up a New Hampshire gentleman. But women's rights were clearly on the minds of American men and women as the country entered the nineteenth century, and even if women couldn't vote they could still participate in politics, with Abigail Adams serving as the prime example. She would no longer be at the forefront of the political scene, but she continued to hold passionate views. She wasn't the only one: in private letters, in public meetings, and in the parlors of society American women were expressing their political opinions. And in the new century there would be a new stage where those views could play out—the new capital city of Washington under a new president and a new party.

CHAPTER TWO

The First Term of Thomas Jefferson and the Ladies of the Place

1801~1805

Elizabeth Patterson Bonaparte

*The Metropolitan Museum of Art, Dodge Fund and funds from various
donors, 2000 (2000.359) image © The Metropolitan Museum of Art*

UNCEREMONIOUSLY, Thomas Jefferson strode from his boarding-house to the partially erected Capitol to take the oath as third president of the United States. George Washington and John Adams might have chosen to arrive by carriage at their inaugurations—not so this "man of the people." Jefferson was making a statement, much the same as the one made by Jimmy Carter 176 years later, when the newly inaugurated thirty-ninth president and his wife, Rosalyn, clambered out of their car and proceeded to grab hands and greet well-wishers on their way down Pennsylvania Avenue. In each case the message was clear: the imperial presidency was over. A widower, Jefferson had no wife at his side as he made his entrance at the Capitol, and no sitting president waiting to hand over the office; earlier that day John Adams had stolen out of town on a predawn coach, unwilling to make the gracious gesture of attending his successor's inauguration that we have come to expect as the symbol of a seamless transfer of power. No rules had been established for this first ever peaceful hand-off from one political ideology to another. And the throngs crowding the Senate chamber, where senators sat on one side, the other assigned "by the representatives to the ladies," knew they were witnessing something remarkable. Seismic shifts of this kind, the political observer Margaret Bayard Smith marveled to her sister-in-law, "in every government and in every age have most generally been epochs of confusion, villainy and bloodshed, in this our happy country take place without any species of distraction, or disorder."

It was a stretch to claim there had been no disorder. It took thirty-six ballots for the House of Representatives to break the tie between Thomas Jefferson and the man sharing his inaugural ceremony, Vice President Aaron Burr. As the country teetered on the brink of constitutional crisis, Jefferson came to suspect that Burr had encouraged the Federalist scheme to make him president. Burr could have cleared up the confusion by announcing that he would not take the job, that he had run as vice president. Jefferson's supporters found Burr's silence telling, and relations between the two men would never recover. But on Inauguration Day, hostilities were temporarily put aside as the vice president joined the new president in the Senate chamber where another Jefferson foe—his cousin Chief Justice John Marshall—administered the oath of office. Appointed by Adams to head the third branch of government, Marshall stood as a reminder that the "Revolution of 1800," as Jefferson came to call his election, could not undo everything that had gone before it. And the about-to-be-sworn-in president used his inaugural address, "delivered," said Margaret Smith, "in so low a tone that few heard it," to assure his skeptical opponents that he would represent the whole country—"We are all republicans, we are all federalists"—and then Jefferson ambled back to his boardinghouse and pulled up to the foot of the crowded dinner table. Mrs. Brown, the wife of a senator from Kentucky, indignant that no one offered the chief executive the *best* seat "for a moment almost hated the leveling principle of democracy, though her husband was a zealous democrat." Jefferson had made his anti-imperial point, but unlike Abigail Adams and her husband, the man who had put on a showy spectacle of down-home democracy would wait until the Executive Mansion was a little more comfortable before he moved in.

With the election finally settled and the president inaugurated, the federal city witnessed the first big upheaval of its temporary residents. Margaret Bayard Smith spent the afternoon of Inauguration Day saying goodbye to departing members of Congress. One in particular she was sorry to see go: "Mr. Claiborne, a most amiable and agreeable man, called the moment before his departure and there is no one whose society I shall more regret the loss of." William Charles Cole Claiborne and his wife, Eliza, were off on an adventure. As a reward for sticking stalwartly with Jefferson through the thirty-six ballots, though the Federalists had tried to woo him away by appealing to his youthful vanity, Claiborne had been named governor of the Mississippi Territory. The sole representative from Tennessee, his vote counted for as much as all of the Virginians combined, since the House of Representatives votes by state in a presidential contest. Alexander Hamilton was convinced the twenty-five-year-old congressman could be turned, but he was wrong. Claiborne never wavered from his commitment to Jefferson, and now he would hold high office, albeit in an unsettled part of the country.

As after every election since, some politicians left Washington, some new ones arrived. But when Thomas Jefferson took office, the city still glimmered more as a vision than a reality. The first national capital created from scratch, or, as the men of the time more elegantly put it, carved out of the wilderness, the small government town struggled to catch on as a place for people to purchase property and establish enterprise. George Washington, whose Mount Vernon home sat close to what were to be the original boundaries of the District of Columbia, promoted the project relentlessly. Assuming that the city would soon attract buyers eager to do business with the federal government, he bought a good bit of property himself and helped sponsor events aimed at auctioning off tracts of what he considered prime real estate. But few buyers took the bait—the government was too small and insignificant to bother with, a far cry from today when the influence peddling of more than twenty thousand lobbyists makes up a major part of the Washington economy.

As Abigail Adams had noted, at the time the federal government actually set up shop in Washington, or, in the lingo of the day, "removed" to the capital, the wilderness was in want of a good deal more carving. One hundred and nine buildings of brick or stone were considered "permanent," ready to house the three hundred government employees who settled there, joining the population of some three thousand already scattered about the neighborhood. Members of Congress—138 strong—clustered on the newly christened Capitol Hill, crammed in boardinghouses with like-minded politicians. Executive branch appointees huddled in homes around the presidential mansion across the grandly named Tiber Creek, a stream that ran down the middle of the "city" from the Capitol.

On either side of the construction site called Washington, D.C., longtime residents of the colonial towns of Georgetown and Alexandria looked bemusedly on the newcomers mired in the mud between them. A carriage ride from Georgetown to the Capitol, with a stop at the White House in between, took three hours round-trip. Given the condition of the roads, it wasn't a trip anyone would want to make regularly, either to shop or to worship. So a few entrepreneurial and ecclesiastical souls opened businesses on "The Hill" and started holding church services in the Capitol building. Those Sabbath gatherings soon grew into more social occasions than religious ones, with "ladies in the gayest costume" flirting through services conducted by "preachers of every sect and denomination of Christians . . . even women were allowed to display their pulpit eloquence in this national Hall." Still, Senator Gouverneur Morris joked to a lady friend: "We want nothing here but houses, cellars, kitchens, well-informed men, amiable women and other little trifles of the kind to make our city perfect." And the man who would become Jefferson's Treasury Secretary, Congressman Albert Gallatin, told his wife it was "far from pleasant" with only "one tailor, one shoemaker, one printer, a washingwoman, a grocery shop, a pamphlets and stationery shop, a small dry-goods shop and an oyster house." In another couple of years other "amenities" such as bookstores, taverns, and, of course, a liquor store had cropped up as well. No wonder most congressmen chose not to bring their wives with them to the brawling boardinghouses: "Without hardly any other society than ourselves, we are not likely to be either very moderate politically or to think of anything but politics," Albert Gallatin lamented to Hannah, who was at home with her family in New York.

Few women on Capitol Hill and no woman to preside at the executive mansion—the president and vice president had both been widowers for years—no women to fill the official roles as hostesses or unofficial roles as advisers played in New York and Philadelphia by the wives of men in government, led first by Martha Washington and then Abigail Adams. Querulous on the subject of women, Jefferson was on the record as objecting to any female participation in politics, though he had once maintained a correspondence with Abigail Adams where the two discussed political ideas as equals. From his perch as ambassador in Paris, observing the court intrigue of French women, Jefferson had written to Anne Bingham in Philadelphia (whose daughter later so scandalized society by eloping with a Frenchman), insisting that women should only "soothe and calm the minds of their husbands returning ruffled from political debate." To her credit, Anne shot back that the meddling of French women worked to their advantage: "They have obtained that rank of consideration in society, which the sex are entitled to."

Jefferson remained unconvinced; in fact, he considered women such a destructive force in politics that he was ready to place the entire blame for the excesses of the French Revolution, which he once supported, on the shoulders of Marie Antoinette, stating firmly, "I have ever believed that had there been no queen there would have been no revolution." As if to underline his determination to remove women from the political scene, Jefferson abolished the regular presidential receptions, or levees, suffered through by the first two First Ladies, announcing that he would receive the public only on New Year's Day and the Fourth of July. Furious, the women of Washington barged into the White House on what had formerly been levee day, daring Jefferson to throw them out. When the widower president returned from a horseback ride to find his parlors overflowing with irate females, he joined the company and managed to charm the intruders into grudging acceptance of the new rules. Even so, Jefferson knew he couldn't ignore the "ladies of the place" as he termed them—the women already in Washington when he arrived, plus the wives of his executive appointees. To deal with them he summoned the assistance of a professional—Dolley Madison.

President Jefferson's secretary of state, James Madison, had met the widow Dolley Payne Todd while serving in Congress in Philadelphia; he married her in 1794, midway through George Washington's second term. When the fifteen-year-old Dolley had moved with her family from North Carolina to Philadelphia, a friend remembered many years later, the southern girl stirred the spirits of the local Quaker community: "She came upon our comparatively cold hearts in Philadelphia, suddenly and unexpectedly with all the delightful influences of a summer sun." In 1790, Dolley married a fellow Quaker, John Todd, who, along with her newborn baby boy, died in the yellow fever epidemic three years later, leaving her with a one-year-old son and a young sister to care for, plus a battle with her brother-in-law over her inheritance from her husband. But the comely Widow Todd had connections in Philadelphia—her mother had run a boarding-house patronized by prominent men, among them Aaron Burr.

Dolley won her legal battle and soon another husband as well. Burr's colleague James Madison asked to be introduced to the delightful Dolley and soon fell head-over-heels for the woman who was seventeen years his junior. Madison poured out letters protesting his undying love until the young widow finally consented to his proposals. First she consulted her lawyer, who advised her that Madison was a good match though her counselor admitted he himself had "not been insensible to your charms."

Only a few months after the introduction, Dolley drew up documents to provide financially for her son, Payne Todd, naming Aaron Burr as his guardian, and then traveled to her sister's plantation in Virginia, where she married Madison. In a daytime letter to her dear friend and lifelong correspondent Eliza Collins Lee, the about-to-be bride signed her name, "Dolley Payne Todd," then that night, her wedding night, added a P.S., "Evening, Dolley Madison! Alas!" Who knows why? Was it marriage or Madison that caused her sigh? The Quaker meeting immediately read her out—declared her an apostate for marrying outside of the faith. There might have been more than a little tension in the family as well. Dolley's sister Lucy was married to George Steptoe Washington, nephew of the president, and at the time of the wedding James Madison had emerged as the leader of the opposition to Washington's party.

Rather than follow the Jeffersonian maxim that a wife should simply dress the wounds of her politically embattled husband, the new Mrs. Madison entered the fray in the most friendly fashion. Already popular on the Philadelphia social scene, she used her entertainments to gather facts and garner friends for Madison. When the bipartisan election of 1796 brought Thomas Jefferson to Philadelphia as vice president, after a three-year sojourn at Monticello, it was Madison's turn to head home to *his* Virginia hilltop, this one called Montpelier. Seeing how Jefferson's retreat to Monticello had buoyed his political position, John Adams ruefully assessed Madison's move in a letter to Abigail, "Madison I suppose after a retirement of a few years is to become President or V.P. It is marvelous how political plants grow in the shade." In a few years Adams would be proven right, but first Madison would serve as his fellow Virginian's top cabinet officer, and Dolley would assume the job of surrogate First Lady.

In early May 1801, the Madison entourage, which included Dolley's son Payne Todd and her sister Anna Payne, moved into the executive mansion for three weeks while house-hunting in Washington. "Mrs. Madison's stay here enabled me to begin an acquaintance with the ladies of the place, so as to have established the precedent of having them at our dinners," Jefferson told his daughter Martha, who was at home in Virginia with an ever-growing family and a husband who needed her. Without a hostess in residence, he thought it would be "awkward" to entertain ladies, but knew he courted their wrath if he did not. "It would make them as well as myself very happy could I always have yourself or your sister here," he sighed to his younger daughter, Maria, laying on the guilt. Aside from the awkwardness of mixed social events, when the Madisons moved out Jefferson and his secretary, Meriwether Lewis, missed their company. "Capt. Lewis and myself are like two mice in a church." The day after Dolley decamped, the president sent a somewhat panicked missive: "Thomas Jefferson begs that either Mrs. Madison or Miss Payne will be so good as to dine with him today, to take care of female friends expected." One of those female friends took an instant liking to Dolley after meeting her at the president's house that May: "She has good humor and sprightliness, united to the most affable and agreeable manners." Margaret Bayard Smith and Dolley Madison were to form a lifelong friendship.

Margaret Smith had only recently come to Washington herself as the twenty-two-year-old bride of Samuel Harrison Smith, a Republican newspaperman Jefferson had lured to the capital to promote his policies. Over the next forty years, Margaret occupied a front seat to history, writing extensive eyewitness accounts, at first to her family and then for newspapers and journals, reporting the goings-on and gossip of successive administrations. Her move to the makeshift federal city from the elegant metropolis of Philadelphia was more than a shock. "I look in vain for the city but see no houses," she told her family, but the shock was cushioned by the other "ladies of the place," who took her in immediately. Two of Martha Washington's granddaughters, older sisters of Nelly Custis, sat at the center of a lively group of local ladies soon augmented by the wives of Jefferson's cabinet. Foremost among them—Dolley Madison, whose house on F Street became the social center of the town, the place where political information could be obtained and exchanged. Somehow managing to make each of her guests feel like the most important person in the room, Dolley serves as the prototype of a venerable institution: the Washington hostess, a term that describes someone who can put together political deals by putting together the deal-makers. A shrewd student of popular opinion, Dolley was also a lot of fun. Along with her sisters, Anna Payne and Lucy Washington, who visited from time to time, the three became known as the Merry Wives of Windsor and were a more than welcome addition to the bleak little capital.

Despite the difficulties of living in Washington, Thomas Jefferson was enjoying a somewhat conflict-free period on the national and international stage. Peace with France, thanks to the efforts of John Adams, had been achieved; the Alien and Sedition Acts were allowed to expire and the Republicans held such a large majority in Congress that the president was able to pass just about anything he wanted. In an effort to wipe his opponents out of office, and to offer juicy jobs to his supporters, Jefferson fired scores of office holders suspected of harboring Federalist sympathies. Since the Federalists had been the party of government, the president had a hard time filling the vacancies. His Treasury Secretary, Albert Gallatin, husband of the politically savvy Hannah Nicholson Gallatin, frustrated over the inability of his agency to function, suggested that Jefferson consider hiring women for the empty slots at Treasury. The president tartly replied, "The appointment of a woman to office is an innovation for which the public is not prepared, nor am I." But soon, for all his prickliness on the subject of women, and despite his determined distance from distaff distractions, the president found himself the subject of a salacious scandal involving a female slave.

JEFFERSON FAMILY LORE has it that Thomas's wife, Martha Wayles Jefferson, extracted a promise from him on her deathbed. Family slaves passed down the story that Martha, dying from complications of childbirth, tearfully told her husband that she could not stand for her children to be raised by a stepmother. At age thirty-nine, the story goes, Jefferson swore he would never marry again. He never did. Left with three small girls (three other babies had died, and each birth had been treacherous for their mother), Martha's death sent her husband into a dramatic depression. Years later his oldest daughter recounted those devastating days: "He kept his room three weeks, and I was never a moment from his side. . . . When at last he left his room, he rode out, and from that time he was incessantly on horseback, rambling about the mountain. . . . In those melancholy rambles I was his constant companion—a solitary witness to many a burst of grief." Just turning ten years old, the motherless little girl took on the responsibility for her distraught father; Martha remained utterly committed to him for the rest of Thomas Jefferson's life. The other children, four-year-old Mary and the infant Lucy, went to live with Elizabeth Eppes, their mother's sister.

Because of his wife's poor health over the years, Thomas Jefferson had refused many calls to public service once he finished his tenure as governor of Virginia during the Revolution. But after Martha died in 1782 as the war was winding down, he ran for and was elected to the Continental Congress then meeting in Philadelphia. His oldest daughter went along. Jefferson enrolled Martha, called Patsy, in a course of study that he deemed inappropriate for a girl anyplace but in America, where mothers would need to raise virtuous sons as citizens. When Congress moved briefly to Annapolis, Maryland, Patsy stayed with friends in Philadelphia, where she received hectoring letters from her father telling her how to organize her day ("from 3 to 4 read French, From 4 to 5 exercise yourself in music . . ."), how to dress ("I do not wish you to be gaily clothed at this time of life. . . ."), and how to behave ("never to say or do a bad thing"). Then in July 1784, father and daughter set sail for France, where Jefferson would replace Benjamin Franklin as the long-standing American ambassador.

Franklin, along with John Jay and John Adams, had successfully negotiated the peace treaty ending the American Revolution and after years abroad the aging and ailing "Doctor Franklin" was ready to go home. Adams, joined by Abigail and their daughter Nabby, stayed on in Paris to help craft commercial agreements. The Jeffersons and Adamses became fast friends, though Abigail was somewhat shocked that the Protestant Jefferson would send his daughter to a Catholic convent school. Then John Adams was appointed as the first U.S. ambassador to the Court of St. James's, putting Abigail in a position to receive little Mary Jefferson when she made her voyage across the Atlantic.

A few months after Patsy and her father left America, two-year-old Lucy Jefferson, the baby whose birth caused her mother's death, died of the whooping cough, which also killed her cousin, Lucy Eppes. In the space of one week Elizabeth Eppes had lost two children—her own and the niece she was raising. "It is impossible to paint the anguish of my heart," she told her brother-in-law. "Life is scarcely supportable under such severe afflictions." Jefferson determined then to take another child away from Elizabeth; he wanted his daughter Mary, now six years old, to come live with him in Paris. Otherwise, he feared, she would become so attached to her aunt's family that he would lose her forever. Little Mary, called Polly, was having none of it. Even though her father promised her "as many dolls and playthings as you want for yourself or to send to your cousins," Polly adamantly refused her father's demands. "Dear Papa—I want to see you and sister Patsy, but you must come to Uncle Eppes house," she wrote in the fall of 1785, when she had just turned seven. Then, in the spring of

1786, "I don't want to go to France, I had rather stay with Aunt Eppes." And again, almost a year later, "Dear Papa—I should be very happy to see you, but I can not go to France."

By this time, Polly's father was growing impatient, as his letters to his wife's family make more than evident. But he did worry about the long sea voyage and hoped his brother-in-law could find some-one suitable to accompany the little girl. Elizabeth Eppes tried to dissuade Jefferson: "We have made use of every stratagem to prevail on her to consent to visit you without effect." Finally, in May 1787, the Eppes family settled for subterfuge. Clearly upset, Elizabeth explained the strategy she planned to trick her niece into sailing: "The children will spend a day or two on board the ship with her, which I hope will reconcile her to it." Thomas Jefferson would have his way. His nine-year-old daughter and her cousins boarded ship together, then, after Polly fell asleep, the cousins slipped ashore. When she woke up in the morning the little girl was out at sea with only a teenager for company—the fourteen-year-old slave, Sally Hemings.

Five weeks later they arrived in England, and this time Polly had to be tricked *off* the ship since she had developed a deep attachment to the captain. He brought Mary Jefferson and Sally Hemings to the Lon-don home of John and Abigail Adams, who immediately informed their friend Thomas Jefferson of his child's arrival. Abigail asked Jefferson to bring fourteen-year-old Patsy when he came to fetch his sad younger daughter: "It would reconcile her little sister to the thoughts of taking a journey." The next day Abigail reported to Jefferson that Polly was cheering up, but the formidable Mrs. Adams had nothing good to say about Sally Hemings. "The girl who is with her is quite a child, and Captain Ramsey is of the opinion will be of so little service that he had better carry her back with him. But of this you will be a judge." The antislavery Abigail Adams assumed that Jefferson would personally travel to London to bring his little girl to Paris, and would then decide what to do about the young slave. Instead, Thomas Jefferson sent a servant to collect Polly. Abigail decidedly disapproved: "She told me this morning, that as she had left all her friends in Virginia to come over the ocean to see you, she did think you would have taken the pains to have come here for her, and not have sent a man she cannot understand." The mother of grown children herself, Abigail had come to love little Polly, and it was mutual. The child was so afraid of being tricked again that she wouldn't let the older woman out of her sight and Abigail could see why. "The girl she has with her, wants more care than the child." Despite her dismay, Abigail sent Polly Jefferson and Sally Hemings off on the stagecoach with Jefferson's emissary. They arrived in Paris on July 15, 1787.

Polly joined her older sister at the convent and there they stayed for a couple of years until Patsy wrote to her father that she wanted to become a nun. Jefferson did not reply. Instead, a day or two later he swooped into the school and swept up his daughters—determined that they would finish their education in America. Jefferson and his girls left Paris on September 26, 1789, with the French Revolution erupting around them and a government under the new Constitution organizing in America. That same day Congress approved his appointment as the nation's first secretary of state. But that was something Thomas Jefferson had no way of knowing as he sailed out of Le Havre with his two daughters and two slaves, James Hemings and his sister Sally.

When Sally Hemings boarded that ship, one of her children told an Ohio newspaper almost eighty-four years later, she was pregnant with Thomas Jefferson's child. More than one hundred years after that, in 1998, DNA tests revealed that a Jefferson male did in fact father at least one of Sally Hemings's children. Until then most historians and Jefferson descendants had rejected and ridiculed the Hemings' family story. No more. With the scientific evidence came a rash of publicity about Thomas Jefferson and Sally Hemings. But the story had first appeared in print in 1802.

"It is well known," the *Richmond Recorder* trumpeted on September 1, 1802, "that the man, *whom it delighteth the people to honor,* keeps, and for many years past has kept, as his concubine, one of his own slaves. Her name is SALLY." The article went on to assert: "By this wench Sally, our president has had several children. There is not an individual in the neighborhood of Charlottesville who does not believe the story." That might have been so, but luckily for President Jefferson, people outside of the neighborhood were ready to dismiss the charges as the venomous retribution of a rascal reporter.

James Callendar, the article's author, was the same journalist who had broken the story of Alexander Hamilton's affair, and had been the darling of the Republican Party, receiving financial support from Jefferson himself. His anti-Federalist harangues landed Callendar in jail under the Sedition Act, along with several other Republican newspapermen. Jefferson's presidential victory meant Callendar's release and the payment of the fines of the convicted journalist. But that wasn't enough for the self-righteous Scotsman, who demanded a patronage job as Richmond postmaster. For his part, Jefferson wanted nothing more to do with this erstwhile propagandist—Callendar's drunkenness and ill-tempered tirades had turned him into an embarrassment for the president. When the reporter didn't get the postmaster job, he turned his fury on his former patron with the bombastic bulletin about the slave named Sally. The fact that the unstable Callendar was the instigator of the accusations made them easier for Jefferson to ignore and his allies to dismiss. Still, the Federalist press had a field day. Some papers accused Jefferson of dastardly deeds while others employed verse, the fun-poking tool of the day, printing irreverent ditties about the president and his "Dusky Sally." One to the tune of "Yankee Doodle" included many stanzas along the same theme:

> *When pressed by loads of state affairs*
> *I seek to sport and dally*
> *The sweetest solace of my cares*
> *Is in the lap of Sally*

The Republican press rose to Jefferson's defense and soon newspapers all over the country were flinging charges and countercharges about the president's personal life.

The randy reports never received any retort from Jefferson himself, and history will probably never know the nature of the relationship between the third president and the slave woman. What is known is that Sally Hemings was almost certainly Thomas Jefferson's wife Martha's half sister, the daughter of her father, John Wayles, and his slave, Betty Hemings. In fact, Sally had so many white ancestors that a fellow slave declared her "mighty near white," and her children had such a preponderant percentage of white blood—seven-eighths—that they would have been considered white under the Virginia laws of the time. (In an 1830 census, after he had left Monticello, the government listed the youngest Hemings son as a white man.) But white as they were, the Hemings children were legally still slaves because their mother was a slave.

According to her son's story, Jefferson bribed Sally into coming home from France with him by promising to free all of her not-yet-born children when they reached their twenty-first birthdays. Thomas Jefferson made good on that promise, but he never released Sally herself from bondage. To have done so would have meant losing her since freed slaves were forced to leave Virginia. It took Jefferson's death to set Sally Hemings free. Then his daughter Martha granted liberty to the woman who was her aunt as well as the likely mother of her half sister and brothers.

Thomas Jefferson's oldest white grandson, Thomas Jefferson Randolph, staunchly defended his grandfather's honor when historians came calling in the mid-nineteenth century. But his story has now added more credence to the claims of his Hemings kin. Sally's children, Randolph said, "resembled Mr. Jefferson so closely that it was plain that they had his blood in their veins." One slave looked so much like Randolph's grandfather that the two men could be mistaken for one another, and "a gentleman dining with Mr. Jefferson looked so startled as he raised his eyes from the latter to the servant behind him, that his discovery of the resemblance was so perfectly obvious to all." Because the Hemings children worked in the house, Randolph added, "the likeness between master and slave was blazoned to all the multitudes who visited this political mecca."

In other words, everyone who called at Monticello saw how much these slaves looked like their master. And everyone must have talked about it. What must Martha Randolph have felt? She "would have been very glad" if Jefferson's look-alikes had been sent away to another property so she wouldn't have to see the reaction of an unsuspecting guest, her son later reported. Though southern women could not help but know that the men in their families fathered slave children, it wasn't something people talked about openly, except in the case of Thomas Jefferson. Martha "took the Dusky Sally stories much to heart" and charged her sons with protecting their grandfather's good name. And Thomas Jefferson Randolph did just that—insisting there was an explanation for the remarkable resemblances. His grandfather's sister's sons had grown up at Monticello and were well-known gadabouts. *They* were the Jefferson men responsible for Sally Hemings's white children, according to Randolph. The family stuck to that story until the DNA evidence definitively ruled out the nephews' family lines.

What did Sally Hemings mean to Thomas Jefferson? He might well have been faithful to her—Sally's son Madison maintained that he and his siblings were the only children of Jefferson's by a slave—he might have even loved her. But his slave certainly wasn't his equal. Thomas Jefferson does not seem to have treated women as equals. The women he acknowledged in his life, his daughters, were by definition his inferiors as children. And they remained his admirers and acolytes throughout their lives.

Not long after she returned with her father from France in 1789, Martha Jefferson married her cousin Thomas Mann Randolph. (Thus thwarting a plan by Abigail Adams to marry off her son John Quincy to her then-friend Jefferson's daughter: "I am all in favor of a federal union.") It was to prove a long, fruitful, and disastrous marriage. Martha made it perfectly clear that the primary object of her affections was not her husband but her father. After she had been married for eight years and had borne four children, Jefferson's oldest still assured him, "The first sensations of my life were affection and respect for you and none others in the course of it have weakened or surpassed that." Martha's younger sister Polly, called Maria after her years in France, was somewhat more independent. The little girl who had stubbornly resisted her father's summons to Paris eventually settled back into her Aunt Elizabeth Eppes's family, solidifying that relationship by marrying her cousin Jack Eppes, one of Polly's childhood playmates.

In 1801, the year Jefferson was sworn in as president, each of his daughters produced a baby—it was Martha's sixth, one had died in infancy, and Maria's second, her first having died after only a few weeks. The demands of the nursery didn't dissuade their father from badgering his daughters to join him in Washington, and finally, in the fall of 1802, as the Sally Hemings scandal continued to swirl and the president needed some female family members to stand by his side, the young women agreed. Leaving the babies behind, Martha and Maria and two of Martha's older children moved into the executive mansion for a several weeks' display of filial devotion. Years of living on Virginia plantations meant neither woman was quite city ready, and the flurry of preparations included a request from Martha to her father that "Mrs. Madison who very obligingly offered to execute any little commission for us, to send to Philadelphia for 2 wigs the color of the hair enclosed and of the most fashionable shapes, that they may be at Washington when we arrive." That way they wouldn't have to do their own hair, "a business in which neither of us are adepts."

The visit finally gave the curious Washington women a good look at the president's daughters. After they had been in the capital for about a month, Margaret Bayard Smith reliably dispatched a report on the pair to her sister-in-law: "Mrs. Eppes is beautiful, simplicity and timidity personified when in company, but when alone with you of communicative and winning manners. Mrs. R. is rather homely, a delicate likeness of her father, but still more interesting than Mrs. E. She is really one of the most lovely women I have ever met with, her countenance beaming with intelligence, benevolence and sensibility, and her conversation fulfills all her countenance promises." Martha truly was her father's daughter. And another apple had fallen close to the tree—six-year-old Ellen Randolph also conquered the capital with charm.

Somewhat stern with his own children, the president was playful and indulgent with his grandchildren, writing them regularly throughout his presidency, often promising presents and delivering "numberless kisses on this letter which you are to take from it." After the slave scandal died down and his daughters and the children left Washington, the president worried about their journey over hazardous roads and "I felt my solitude too after your departure very severely," he complained to his eldest. He clearly missed his daughters' company as well as the political cover from the sex scandal that they provided, but after almost two months with their father it was time for the Jefferson women to go back to their own lives. Too bad for the president—they might have coaxed him out of a calculated insult that became a diplomatic disaster.

THOMAS JEFFERSON—the author of America's Declaration of Independence from Great Britain—never lost any love for the former "Mother Country." And the English gave him no reason to change his mind. When Jefferson had been presented by Ambassador John Adams at the Court of St. James's, George III made a point of turning his back on the American diplomat. Now it was President Jefferson's turn to play a dangerous tit for tat, where he could take out his hostilities against the powerful British nation by insulting its new envoy and, especially, the envoy's wife. In November 1803, when Anthony and Elizabeth Merry arrived in Washington, their extravagance immediately set the gossips abuzz in the rudimentary capital city. "They seem inclined to live in great style and magnificence which will enliven the society very much," Louisa Catherine Adams, the wife of now-Senator John Quincy Adams, told her mother-in-law.

Young Rosalie Stier Calvert also reported to her mother in Belgium on the new ambassador: "He has three different carriages, all of the latest fashion, an enormous amount of furniture, servants, etc., and he has rented two houses." Rosalie's family had lived for a while in America, where she met and married George Calvert, a member of the prominent Maryland family. George's sister Eleanor was Martha Washington's daughter-in-law, the mother of all of the Custis children. Rosalie was a decided Federalist who, with a wonderful wit, kept her European relatives abreast of the comings and goings in nearby Washington from the family estate in Bladensburg, Maryland. Her letters, alongside those of the Republican Margaret Bayard Smith, often read as a political point counterpoint. Rosalie hit the nail on the head when describing how Jefferson would react to the arrival of the ostentatious Merrys: "They plan on living in the most splendid style, which will not be at all agreeable to Mr. Jefferson and his Democratic party who want to introduce a system of equality and economy, thinking by that means to please the populace."

Jefferson went out of his way to offend the British ambassador. When Merry, in full dress regalia, arrived at the White House to present his credentials, the president received him in bedroom slippers and disheveled clothes. Worse by far, however, was the executive mansion dinner supposedly held in honor of the new minister and his wife. First, the Merrys were shocked to see the French ambassador also invited, since the two countries were once again at war, and then, when it came time to proceed from the drawing room to the dining room, President Jefferson rebuffed the guest of honor, Elizabeth Merry, escorting Dolley Madison instead. Dolley tried to avert what she knew would be a diplomatic incident, quietly urging the president to "take Mrs. Merry." When Jefferson ignored her, Dolley's old friend from Philadelphia, Sally McKean, now the wife of the Spanish ambassador, announced, "This will be the cause of war!" Merry's secretary later wrote that Jefferson was "playing a game for retaining the highest office in a State where manners are not a prevailing feature in the great mass of the society, being, except in the large towns, rather despised as a mark of effeminacy by the majority, who seem to glory in being only thought men of bold, strong minds and good sound judgment." Not much has changed along those lines.

Jefferson might have been scoring political points by snubbing the wife of the former enemy, but he was also courting a crisis between the United States and Britain. And the situation only grew worse a short time later, when the secretary of state entertained the English couple. Rosalie Calvert repeated the story that Madison, "instead of conducting Mrs. Merry into dinner first, gave his hand to Gallatin's wife, leaving the Ambassador to conduct his own wife. It made a huge uproar—as much as if a treaty had been broken." Merry didn't know whether this was some kind of signal to England about the state of relations between the countries, or how he should respond. He wrote home for instructions, and meanwhile decided to boycott all entertainments.

The president soon learned that it was hard to do business just during "office hours," so he tried to find a way to make up with Merry without actually apologizing. He instructed his cabinet to adopt a statement on the rules of etiquette, explicitly stating, "At public ceremonies, to which the government invites the presence of foreign ministers and their families, a convenient seat or station will be provided for them . . . each taking place as they arrive and without any precedence." This so-called "pell-mell" arrangement created chaos at social occasions, but at least made it seem as if the English had not been singled out for insult. Merry grumped that someone should have told him the "rules" before he arrived, and his wife never attended another function hosted by Jefferson. Having caused the problem in the first place, the president came up with an excuse for his rudeness in a letter to his ambassador in London, James Monroe, who was feeling the fallout of the debacle. "I had been in the habit when I invited female company (having no lady in my family) to ask one of the ladies of the four Secretaries to come and take care of my company; and as she was to do the honors of the table I handed her to dinner myself. That Mrs. Merry might not construe this as giving them a precedence over Mrs. Merry, I have discontinued it." But also to Monroe, Jefferson lashed out at the Englishwoman, calling her a "virago" who has "disturbed our harmony extremely" and that Merry's taking umbrage at the behavior toward his wife meant the couple "put themselves into Coventry."

It wouldn't have taken much for Elizabeth Merry to become the talk of the sleepy little city of Washington, but Jefferson turned the woman Margaret Smith called "large, tall, well-made" and "rather masculine" into an object of endless fascination. When Mrs. Merry finally went to a ball, "her dress attracted great attention; it was brilliant and fantastic, white satin with a long train, dark blue crape of the same length over it and white crape drapery down to her knees and open at one side, so thickly covered with silver spangles that it appeared to be a brilliant silver tissue," Margaret Smith detailed the description to her sister: "Her hair bound tight to her head with a band like her drapery, with a diamond crescent before and a diamond comb behind, diamond earrings and necklace, displayed on a bare bosom." The "bare bosom" tickled Rosalie Calvert. "Mrs. Merry, the new English Ambassadress, is very fat and covers only with fine lace two objects which could fill a fourth of a bushel!"

But it was not just Elizabeth Merry's dress that caused comment, Margaret Smith explained. "She is said to be a woman of fine understanding and she is so entirely the talker and actor in all companies, that her good husband passes quite unnoticed." A woman deemed superior to her husband—not the sort of woman that Thomas Jefferson would be comfortable with. His vice president, Aaron Burr, on the other hand, described Elizabeth Merry to his daughter as a woman "full of intelligence. An Englishwoman who has lived much in Paris, and has all that could be wished of the manners of both countries." Exactly the kind of woman Jefferson railed against in the courts of Europe.

Life wasn't easy for Elizabeth Merry, who was "always riding on horseback" and hardly associating with anyone, according to Dolley Madison. But the good-natured Dolley soon befriended the isolated Englishwoman, who was treated badly by Jeffersonians at various public events. The brouhaha caused so much stir in the press that for once the president told his daughter Martha he was glad she wasn't in Washington—otherwise she'd certainly take heat from Federalist newspapers as the hostess at her father's events. Congress, Jefferson continued, tried to circumvent criticism by holding a "dinner on the acquisition of Louisiana" where no foreign ministers would be invited, thus avoiding "questions of etiquette." Jefferson was convinced that the British government would eventually order Merry to "acquiesce in our principles of the equality of all persons meeting together in society." But a much more important event was unfolding that would quickly overshadow the Merry Affair. In the president's letter to his daughter, he alluded to the "acquisition of Louisiana," something that was nothing short of a triumph for the country. Due to a series of fortunate circumstances for the United States, Napoleon had agreed to sell the entire Louisiana Territory to America, thereby doubling the size of the country overnight and assuring Thomas Jefferson's popularity regardless of his manners.

PEOPLE IN THE UNITED STATES, European visitors commented, seemed stir crazy. They were constantly moving, exploring fresh territory, breaking new ground. Between 1790 and 1800, the populations of Kentucky and Tennessee grew by three hundred percent and Ohio followed close behind. The westward movement depended on the Mississippi River for transportation and commerce. Central to the pioneers' ability to ship their products abroad and to import the goods they needed was an open port in New Orleans. The city, founded and populated by the French in the early eighteenth century, was ceded to Spain in 1763 as one of the spoils of the Seven Years' War. In 1795, Spain had signed a treaty granting America unfettered navigation of the Mississippi plus the right of "deposit" at the port, meaning merchants could unload their cargo there and transfer it to ocean-crossing vessels. But in 1802, Spain, which had secretly determined to transfer Louisiana back to the French, rescinded the right of deposit, setting up a howl from the settlers of the western territories. Then, when the Americans got wind of the fact that France was about to retake control of the crucial port as part of Napoleon's plan to establish an empire in the New World, Jefferson feared war.

The president was already doing battle with Tripoli—present-day Libya—over shipping rights in the Mediterranean, but taking on the Barbary pirates was one thing, challenging the mighty Bonaparte something else altogether. Jefferson instructed Robert Livingston, his envoy in Paris, to see if he could convince the French to sell New Orleans. While negotiations over the sale dragged on, Napoleon's imperialistic dream collapsed: first, a slave uprising then a yellow fever epidemic decimated his troops in the Caribbean, and sent more than a thousand French refugees fleeing from Haiti (then Saint Domingue) to New Orleans. Combining those setbacks with the eminent prospect of another costly war with England, the French ruler decided to go for the money.

By the time Jefferson dispatched a second negotiator, James Monroe, to drive home the deal for New Orleans, unbeknownst to the government in Washington, Livingston had already been approached about purchasing all of the Louisiana Territory. (Federalists in Congress, getting even with Jefferson's Republicans who had refused to allow a Federalist ambassador to sail on a navy ship, denied Monroe the same privilege. To pay for the diplomat's wife and daughters to accompany him, James and Dolley Madison bought the Monroes' china and silver.) Monroe arrived in Paris, learned of the offer to sell all of Louisiana to Livingston, and nailed down an accord—fifteen million dollars for the entire territory. No one knew exactly what America had bought with the millions, it would take the Lewis and Clark and Pike expeditions to determine that, but it turned out to be the best real estate negotiation in U.S. history. In addition to land around

New Orleans, the entire states of present-day Arkansas, Missouri, Iowa, Oklahoma, Kansas, and Nebraska, plus parts of Minnesota, North and South Dakota, New Mexico, Texas, Montana, Wyoming, and Colorado came within the country's borders. And the incorporation of so many Catholic French and Spanish speakers into the nation signaled the birth of multiculturalism in the United States.

As the ink on the contract dried, Napoleon began to have second thoughts, so Jefferson moved quickly to assert control over the new territory. Concerned that the citizens of New Orleans would resist U.S. rule, he ordered the governor of the Mississippi Territory and the senior officer of the U.S. military to gather a few hundred troops in Natchez and rush down the river to take possession of Louisiana. Governor William Claiborne and General James Wilkinson presided over the lowering of the French flag and the raising of the American one on December 20, 1803, watched by "beautiful women and fashionable men." New Orleanians offered no resistance, but they were none too happy that "strangers to their laws and manners as well as language had been sent to rule over them," recorded a descendant of one of the Creole women. Especially nervous were a group of women who had been key to the development of the Mediterranean metropolis—the Ursuline nuns.

Recruited by the early colonists to run a military hospital in the new port city, the French religious order added the education of women to their portfolio as soon as they arrived in 1727, establishing the first school for women and the first Catholic school in what was to become the United States, long before the social reformers Isabella Graham and Susanna Rowson opened their schoolhouse doors in New York and Boston. In addition to teaching boarding students from wealthy French and Creole (the term for a French person born on colonial soil) families, the nuns also operated a free school for black and Indian girls, a radical concept at the time. As the city grew, they cared, as well, for other women in need—chaperoning and housing the *filles à la cassette,* the marriageable women sent by the French government as mates for the colony's large population of men and running an orphanage soon overrun by girls left homeless after an Indian raid on a European outpost in Arkansas. When control of New Orleans shifted from France to Spain, the Ursulines managed to go with the flow, bringing in Spanish nuns to augment their numbers. But the news of a return to French rule in 1803, this time under a Napoleonic regime, filled the women with fear.

Terrified by the persecution of the Church and the clergy during the French Revolution, some of the nuns chose to leave rather than risk living under Bonaparte. In November, when the French formally took possession of the city, the new governor tried to stop these highly useful women from deserting: "My ladies, the need that the colony has of you, the good that you do here, the esteem of the public which you enjoy and which is justly due you have come to the knowledge of the French government which has decreed that you will be preserved with all property." Pierre Clement Laussat clearly didn't want to cross swords with these women. Still, sixteen Ursuline religious decided not to take their chances with Napoleon, opting instead to sail to Havana, where they would remain under the domain of "His Catholic Majesty" of Spain. The city turned out to say farewell: former students and slaves assembled at the convent; a crowd including city officials escorted them mournfully to the dock. For the eleven women who chose to brave it out in New Orleans, another, more dramatic change was in store—in a few short weeks the Americans were coming.

Rumors about what would happen to the nuns spread as far as Paris, where one newspaper printed the fiction that the U.S. had announced that the state would eventually seize Ursuline property. To the contrary, when Governor Claiborne arrived from Natchez, he wasted no time in visiting the Ursuline convent and assuring the religious "that they would be protected in their persons, their property, and the Religion of their choice." Claiborne had been impressed by the scope of the educational establishment, "*seventy three boarders* and a hundred day scholars," and the fact that tuition was based on parents' ability to pay. Even so, the nuns worried what their place would be in the new secular society, writing twice to President Jefferson to enlist him in an effort guaranteeing their property rights. The president replied that the nuns could rest assured that the Constitution protected them, adding that their institution furthered "the wholesome purposes of society, by training up its younger members in the way they should go . . . it will meet all the protection which my office can give it." Jefferson's daughters, after all, had attended a Catholic convent in Paris; he was not about to interfere with the good sisters. Still the Mother Superior covered her bases, staying in touch with Governor Claiborne, writing to commiserate when his wife and child died on the same day in a yellow fever epidemic less than a year after his move to New Orleans. In his thank-you letter, Claiborne reiterated that "you Sister and the very respectable community over whom you preside, shall continue to receive all the protection which my authority can afford." And so the Ursulines, and much of the rest of the city, kept functioning as they always had in their Latin redoubt of the United States, either welcoming or ignoring the new American arrivals. One of them, Edward Livingston, brother of the man who negotiated the purchase, soon met and married a ravishing young refugee from the Caribbean. Louise D'Avezac Livingston and her daughter Cora would eventually join the political women of Washington, where they would shine.

IF THE RESIDENTS OF NEW ORLEANS were less than thrilled with their newfound status as Americans, most of the rest of the country was delighted to annex the vast Louisiana Territory. The one exception: New England Federalists who correctly saw the addition of so many potential new states as the death knell for the influence of their region. Outnumbered in the Republican Congress, a hastily called special session in the fall of 1803 rolled over Federalist objections, readily ratified the treaty, and rendered implementation money. When word reached Washington that the transfer in New Orleans had gone without a hitch, the capital city started celebrating. More than a hundred congressmen gathered at Steele's Hotel, their cheering accompanied by the firing of cannons from the Navy Yard. A Georgetown ball drew even more happy revelers assembled to praise the president for his remarkable coup. And though the Federalists had opposed the Purchase, Rosalie Calvert noticed that, despite the fierce partisanship, they joined the Republicans and "dined and danced together." In the midst of all this gaiety the city welcomed a new couple into the social circle. On Christmas Eve 1803, Napoleon's youngest brother, Jerome, had married a young, headstrong Baltimore beauty, Elizabeth, known as Betsy, Patterson. This somewhat shocking pair enjoyed grinding grist for the gossip mill as politicians vied to entertain the brother of the most powerful man in Europe and his rich American wife.

The marriage occupied at least as much public attention as the doubling of the nation's size. Betsy "was followed as persons are who have attracted public attention by any extraordinary act," Louisa Adams recorded. "Jerome Bonaparte, wife, maids of honor . . . will be here tomorrow," wrote Vice President Aaron Burr to his daughter Theodosia. "There are various opinions about the expediency, policy, decency, propriety, and future prospects of this match." Spoiled and impetuous, nineteen-year-old Jerome had defied the French minister in Washington by marrying eighteen-year-old Betsy, whose wealthy Baltimore family also opposed the union. Eager to escape Baltimore, Betsy saw Jerome as her ticket out of town. (Years later when her own son married a woman from Baltimore, Betsy fumed to her father, "I hated and loathed a residence in Baltimore so much, that when I thought I was to spend my life there I tried to screw my courage up to the point of committing suicide. My cowardice, and *only* my cowardice, prevented my exchanging Baltimore for the grave.") Realizing that he couldn't shake his daughter's determination to wed the dashing young Frenchman, William Patterson arranged for the bishop of Baltimore, John Carroll, to preside over the nuptials, making it legal in the eyes of the Catholic Church. Bishop or no, Betsy donned one of her trademark scanty dresses for the ceremony, causing one guest to comment, "Whatever clothes worn by the bride could have been put in my pocket."

Betsy's clothes, or the lack of them, were the talk of the town. Rosalie Calvert told her mother that Madame Bonaparte "wears dresses so transparent and tight that you can see her skin through them, no chemise at all." Especially shocking, said Rosalie, was a dress Betsy wore to a recent dance "so transparent that you could see the color and shape of her thighs, and even more!" Margaret Smith described the same scene with reportorial relish: "Mobs of boys have crowded round her splendid equipage to see what I hope will not often be seen in this country, an almost naked woman," she clucked to her sister. "No one dared to look at her except by stealth; the window shutters being left open, a crowd assembled round the windows to get a look at this beautiful little creature, for every one allows she is extremely beautiful. . . . Her back, her bosom, part of her waist and her arms were uncovered and the rest of her form visible." For the next night's gathering, Margaret crowed, the women of Washington sent word to the new Mrs. Bonaparte, "If she wished to meet them there, she must promise to have more clothes on. I was highly pleased with this becoming spirit in our ladies." This at a time when Aaron Burr told his daughter that Washington was under a foot of snow! Always the contrarian, Vice President Burr thought Betsy dressed "with taste and simplicity (by some thought a little too free.)" For once Jefferson and his number two seemed to agree; the president, still smarting over the Merrys' refusal to return to the White House, escorted Betsy Bonaparte to his dinner table, setting more tongues wagging. And despite "the spirit of our ladies" in trying to change Betsy's sartorial habits, she continued to appear at social events "almost naked," according to Louisa Catherine Adams, who snarkily told her mother-in-law, Abigail, that "Madame Bonaparte . . . makes a great noise here."

After the couple was feted at "balls, suppers and parties of every kind" so that Mrs. Adams griped, "we lived in a perpetual round of dissipation," the Bonapartes made a grand tour, traveling to New

York in May where the rich and powerful competed to wine and dine them. Betsy and Jerome accepted the invitation to the country estate of Alexander and Eliza Hamilton, but snubbed Hamilton's enemy, Aaron Burr, who was at home in New York. Burr complained to Theodosia: "Madame Bonaparte and husband are here. I have just seen them and no more. For reasons unknown to me (doubtless some state policy), we are suddenly become strangers." If Betsy Bonaparte was ignoring him, Burr knew that he was being politically and socially isolated.

Undoubtedly rubbing salt in Burr's wounds was the fact that the Bonaparte couple received prominent play in newspapers from Washington to New York, but Jerome's older brother in Paris was not amused. Having declared himself emperor in May 1804, persuading Pope Pius VII to preside over his December coronation, Napoleon denounced the American marriage and ordered his baby brother to return to Paris alone. Everyone knew that the celebrated couple was in trouble. Louisa Adams had heard that Napoleon "does not *choose* to know that his brother is married." Word was that the "Tyrant" had ordered Jerome to "return to France immediately in the frigate sent for him. She has chosen to go and her fate seems very doubtful." Mrs. Adams had that right. After several false starts, Jerome and five-months-pregnant Betsy finally set sail in March 1805, with the young mother-to-be convinced that she could charm the emperor into accepting her. She was wrong. As their ship approached Lisbon, a French guard surrounded it and refused to allow Betsy to disembark. When Napoleon's emissary offered to provide some sort of assistance to "Miss Patterson," Betsy replied in a huff, "Tell your master that *Madame Bonaparte* is ambitious, and demands her rights as a member of the imperial family."

Jerome left his wife at sea and set off for Paris to plead his case before his brother, the emperor. He never spoke to Betsy again. Looking for a friendly harbor as she awaited the birth of the baby, when she attempted to land in Amsterdam, Betsy discovered that Napoleon had closed all the ports of Europe to her. Eventually she opted for England, France's enemy, as the only place that would allow her to set up housekeeping while she hoped for her husband to summon her. When the beautiful Madame Bonaparte docked at Dover in May 1805, she was treated like a modern-day celebrity. Prime Minister Pitt dispatched a military escort to protect the famous bride of the emperor's brother from the curious crowd. The next day's London newspapers blazoned the story of her arrival. But, too pregnant to enjoy English social life, Betsy moved to the countryside. Her baby, Jerome Napoleon Bonaparte, arrived less than two months later.

Meanwhile her husband had heard nothing encouraging from Napoleon, who steadfastly refused to recognize the marriage or have any dealings with Jerome on the subject. Despite his regular letters pledging undying love, Betsy knew that the pressure was on to renounce her. She warned her father that the French minister in Washington was likely to "try and sound you with respect to my consenting to a separation from Bonaparte on certain conditions; but as we have no reason to suppose that he will ever consent to give me up, we must certainly act as if we supposed him possessed of some principle and honor." Betsy knew her flighty young husband was lacking in both. Her father, always doubting the young man's trustworthiness, had drawn up a prenuptial agreement stipulating that his daughter would have a right to one-third of Jerome's property if he or "any member of his family" should demand that the marriage be annulled. Napoleon did pay Betsy a pension, but he demanded that she drop the Bonaparte name. She never did. And the emperor failed in his attempts to persuade the pope (with arguments augmented by the gift of a gold tiara) to annul the marriage. Pius VII, with some trepidation, refused. So she and her child carried the name "Bonaparte" as Betsy spent the rest of her life on both continents being courted by and courting the high and mighty, promoting the interests of her son, and breaking the hearts of her suitors. Jerome soon bowed to his brother's wishes, married the Princess of Württemberg, and assumed the title of King of Westphalia. Years later, on a tour of the Pitti

Palace in Florence, Jerome and his European wife spotted Betsy across the gallery; the royal couple went unnoticed by the proud American beauty.

IN THE WINTER of 1803–1804, while the capital city babbled about Betsy Bonaparte and lauded the Louisiana Purchase, Thomas Jefferson was trying to hurry the Congress out of town so he could go home to see about his daughter Maria. The president's younger child, so like her mother in appearance, also inherited Martha Jefferson's difficulties with pregnancy and childbirth. Maria's husband, John Eppes, had been elected to Congress, along with her sister Martha's husband, Thomas Randolph. Jefferson's sons-in-law bunked with him for the congressional session, leaving Martha, who had just produced her sixth child, to take care of her pregnant and depressed little sister. From Washington, the president complained about the "dilatoriness of business" keeping Congress in session as he tried to jolly Maria into "good spirits."

While the lawmakers waited for news of "the delivery of New Orleans" they did nothing "but meet and adjourn" leaving Jefferson with time to fret. "I am anxious on your account," he confessed to Maria even as he tried to make light of her concerns about childbirth, "Some female friend of your Mama's (I forget whom) used to say it was no more than a knock of the elbow." This to the daughter of a woman who had died from the complications of childbirth! But then he advised that she have "scientific aid in readiness, that if anything uncommon takes place, it may be redressed on the spot and not made serious by delay." Martha, writing "amidst the noises and confusion of six children interrupted every moment by their questions," told her father: "Maria's spirits are bad, partly occasioned by her situation which precludes every thing like comfort or cheerfulness, and partly from the prospect of congress not rising till April." That meant Jack Eppes was unlikely to join his wife any time soon, though "her mind would be more at ease could he be with her."

Eppes was still in Washington when Jefferson got the news that Maria delivered a baby girl on February 15 and that both mother and child seemed fine. "A thousand joys to you, my dear Maria, on the happy accession to your family," her father exuberantly declared. "I rejoice indeed that all is so well." But soon the reports turned gloomy, and Maria's husband abandoned his post in Congress to rush to his wife's bedside while Jefferson waited with "terrible anxiety" to hear how his youngest fared. "God bless you my ever dear daughter," he prayed, "and preserve you safe to be the blessing of us all." Once home, Eppes tried to be upbeat about Maria's condition, unable to deal with the fact that he was losing the woman who was not only his wife but also his cousin and life-long friend. At the end of March he assured his father-in-law, "She is extremely thin, a mere shadow, but as debility is now her only complaint, I have the pleasure of feeling that the recovery of her health, although slow is absolutely certain." Jefferson kept urging his own remedy: sweet wine, "the sherry at Monticello is old and genuine," he insisted.

Slaves carried the twenty-five-year-old dying woman across four miles on a stretcher from her own home to Monticello, where she could partake of the sherry and await her father's ministrations. Finally, the Congress adjourned and the president was able to leave Washington on April 4. He arrived at his mountaintop retreat, encouraged that he had bolstered his daughter's "spirits and confidence." Before long, however, he confided to his secretary of state, Madison, "my daughter exhibits little change." On April 17, 1804, he recorded in his diary, "This morning between eight and nine o'clock my dear daughter Maria Eppes died." Once again, as she did after her mother's death, Martha was left to console her father. Martha, who had just lost her sister, who was breast-feeding Maria's child along with her own, was summoned to her father's side. She found a man "with a Bible in his hands," who weepingly confessed when she joined him, "Oh my daughter, I did not send for you to witness my weakness, for I thought I could control myself, but to comfort me with your presence." And so Martha, as she had as a young girl, buried her own grief in order to nurse her father's.

Maria's death caused distress in the president's political family as well as his personal one. "This is among the many proofs my dear sister of the uncertainty of life!" Dolley Madison lamented to her sister Anna. "A girl so young, so lovely—all the efforts of her father, doctors and friends availed nothing." From Washington, Louisa Adams provided the details to her husband, John Quincy, home in Massachusetts: "Mrs. Eppes dies of an abscess in her breast produced by a cold taken during her confinement. She was removed in a litter to Monticello where for a day or two she appeared to recover which raised her father's hopes and rendered the shock more bitter. Mrs. Madison says this stroke has been almost too severe for him. She was his favorite child." Louisa's mother-in-law, Abigail Adams, who had so resented Jefferson's victory over her husband and had furiously followed the reports of the Republican presidency, was moved by the memory of the little girl who had stayed with her in London so many years before. Abigail's "sorrow over the departed remains of your beloved and deserving daughter" caused her to cast aside her concerns for what may have been considered an improper correspondence between the president and the wife of the man he defeated. She sent off a sympathy note to Maria's father. Conceding that it had been some time since she and Jefferson shared "feelings of mutual sympathy," Abigail said she knew how he was suffering, since she too had "tasted the bitter cup" of losing a child. Her letter, signed by one "who once took pleasure in subscribing herself your friend," started a remarkable, though short-lived, correspondence.

Jefferson readily renewed the discourse, responding to Abigail that he had always considered her and her husband as his friends, that the differences between their parties did not "lessen mutual esteem" and, he soothingly stated, he and Adams "never stood in one another's way" because each of their supporters would have never chosen the other one but rather "some one of homogeneous opinions." That meant, he blithely asserted, he and Adams were able to "keep down all jealousy between us, and to guard our friendship from any disturbance by sentiments of rivalship." Abigail might have swallowed that version of the truth, even if she found it unrecognizable, but then Jefferson continued: "I can say with truth that one act of Mr. Adams's life, and one only, ever gave me a moment's personal displeasure. I did consider his last appointments to office as personally unkind." Jefferson objected to the so-called "midnight judges," President Adams's eleventh-hour appointment of members of the judiciary, including the new president's old nemesis, John Marshall. "They were from among my most ardent political enemies, from whom no faithful cooperation could ever be expected."

That did it. Jefferson had opened the door to political debate and Abigail marched right through it. "The Constitution empowers the president to fill up offices as they become vacant," she lectured the president, reminding him that Washington had also made appointments "in the last days of his administration so that not an office remained vacant for his successor to fill upon his coming into the office." How could Jefferson consider Adams's actions personally unkind when "at the time these appointments were made, there was not any certainty that the presidency would devolve upon you." (Abigail was wrong about that. Jefferson's election was solidified in February; Adams made the appointments in March. Either through faulty memory or intentionally, she pressed the president on the question.) How could Jefferson take *personal* umbrage, she disingenuously asked, when he was still in a contested race? But if her old friend wanted to cite slights, she could match and trump him. "One of the first acts of your administration was to liberate a wretch who was suffering the just punishment of the law." Still livid over Jefferson's pardoning of the scandalmongering newspaperman James Callendar and the payment of his fine, Abigail wondered how Jefferson could profess friendship while approving of a man who wrote "the lowest and vilest slander which malice could invent or calumny exhibit against the character and reputation of your predecessor." That was what had wrecked their friendship, she insisted, as she reflected with some satisfaction that "the serpent you cherished and warmed, bit the hand that nourished him." Abigail was, of course, not so subtly referring to Callendar's stories about Jefferson and Sally Hemings. More subtly, in fact so subtly, that the president didn't know what she was talking about, Abigail continued, "There is one other act of your administration which I considered as personally unkind, and which your own mind will readily suggest to you, but as it neither affected character, or reputation, I forbear to state it." Then she signed off, assuring her correspondent that her letter was confidential, seen by "no eye but my own."

Jefferson couldn't let her arguments lie. He soon sent off a point-by-point rebuttal. He had supported Callendar's work in England, the president explained, and when the pamphleteer came to America he at first "told some useful truths in a coarse way." Paying his fine was no more an endorsement of Callendar's character than charities "to a beggar at my door are meant as rewards for the vices of his life." And there was one action in the Callendar saga that Jefferson was not the least defensive about—releasing him from jail. "I discharged every person under punishment or prosecution under the Sedition law, because I considered and now consider that law to be a nullity as absolute and as palpable as if Congress had ordered us to fall down and worship a golden image." The president knew he was waving a red flag in front of one of the law's most ardent advocates, but he felt strongly about the Alien and Sedition Acts, the unpopular laws that had brought down the Adams presidency, and he was happy to have the opportunity to denounce them even after they were gone from the books. The other matter of personal unkindness Abigail had written of truly puzzled Jefferson: "I declare on my honor, Madam, I have not the least conception what act is alluded to. I never did a single one with an unkind intention."

Now Abigail had a real reason to respond. She could tell the president the cause of her pique. But first there was the Sedition

Act to defend, both in terms of process and policy. As to the process by which Jefferson released all those convicted under the law, "If a Chief Magistrate can by his will annul a law, where is the difference between a republican and a despotic government?" And the policy? "That some restraint should be laid upon the assassin who stabs reputation, all civilized nations have assented to." Otherwise people would take the law into their own hands and defend their reputations with "the sword and the pistol." Given the vituperativeness of both political parties, she continued to believe a check on "calumnies" in the press was essential to a civilized society. Abigail never would give up on the Sedition Act even though its unpopularity had sunk her husband politically, giving Jefferson the upper hand in the election. As to the other matter: "Soon after my eldest son's return from Europe, he was appointed by the district judge to an office into which no political concerns entered," the mother of former diplomat John Quincy Adams pouted. "As soon as Congress gave the appointments to the president you removed him." Careful to protect the political future of her son, who was then serving in the Senate, she added quickly that John Quincy himself had never said anything disrespectful about Jefferson. "With pleasure I say he is not a blind follower of any party." Recognizing the extraordinary nature of this very frank conversation between a woman and a sitting president, Abigail acknowledged that she had "written to you with the freedom and unreserve of former friendship to which I would gladly return could all causes but mere difference of opinion be removed."

This time Jefferson did not have to summon specious arguments to his defense. He really *didn't* know that John Quincy Adams was one of a group of bankruptcy commissioners that he had replaced. Had he known, "it would have been a real pleasure to me to have preferred him to some who were named in Boston in what were deemed the same line of politics." So *that* fracture of the friendship could now be healed. But the president couldn't help himself; he had to hammer away at the constitutional argument over the Sedition

Act. First he defended his own actions: "The Executive, believing the law to be unconstitutional, was bound to remit the execution of it; because that power has been confided to him by the constitution." Then he answered the accusation that, without the law, liars and slanderers would be able to run rampant: "While we deny that Congress have a right to control the freedom of the press, we have ever asserted the right of the states, and their exclusive right, to do so." But he offered an olive branch—"I hope you will see these intrusions on your time to be, what they really are, proofs of my great respect for you." People of good will in both parties, he averred, had the interests of the country at heart. It would be history's role to judge which party's method of serving those interests would turn out to be right.

Abigail decided it was time to let it lie. She still smarted too much from the last election to forgive and forget. She was ready to accept Jefferson's explanation for the removal of John Quincy from office, but she tartly questioned the wisdom of Jefferson's wholesale firings of Federalists, asking, "whether in your ardent zeal and desire to rectify the mistakes and abuses as you may consider them of the former administrations, you are not led into measures still more fatal to the constitution, and more derogatory to your honor and independence of character? Pardon me Sir if I say that I fear you are." Ouch. And she was determined to have the last word on the Sedition Act, declaring firmly that it could not "be considered an infringement of the liberty of the press to punish the licentiousness of it." Then Abigail Adams called a halt to continued communication with the president of the United States: "I will not sir any further intrude upon your time, but close this correspondence, by my sincere wishes that you may be directed to that path which may terminate in the prosperity and happiness of the people over whom you are placed by administering the government with a just and impartial hand." A few weeks later Abigail, for the first time, showed her husband the letters to and from Thomas Jefferson. John Adams added a note for posterity revealing that he knew nothing of the correspondence, wisely concluding, "I have no remarks to make upon it at this time and in this place."

SINCE THEIR RETURN to the small town of Quincy, Massachusetts, John and Abigail Adams had retreated from the public eye, but had kept up an active political correspondence with friends and family, Abigail's often interrupted by her bouts of illness. But they didn't lead a retired life—their house bustled with family members—nieces, nephews, children, and grandchildren who lived with them either permanently or occasionally. John Adams, so accustomed to having Abigail run everything, took to reading romance novels, much to his wife's amazement, and continued to rely on her to manage their finances. Abigail also tried to manage her son's family after John Quincy and his wife, Louisa, with their baby, George Washington Adams, arrived in America not long after Thomas Jefferson assumed the presidency.

Louisa Catherine Adams had had a tough time in her marriage. Soon after the wedding between the son of the president of the United States and the daughter of a prominent London mercantile agent, her father's business failed, leaving Louisa with no dowry and creating a taint of scandal around her family. She was mortified, convinced that her husband and her illustrious in-laws would think that she had lured John Quincy into a rushed marriage under false pretenses. Two accounts of her life that she wrote as an older woman show Louisa's continued distress decades after her father's disgrace about her suddenly changed circumstances. Recounting for her children "My Story," when she was fifty years old, Louisa agonized still about the financial reversals: "Conceive my dear sons the shock I underwent, every appearance was against me; actions proceeding from the most innocent causes looked the deliberate plans to deceive, and I felt that all the honest pride of my soul was laid low forever." She believed she had "forfeited all that could give me consequence in my husband's esteem or in my own mind." When she wrote those words she was the First Lady of the land. And then again, fifteen years later in her autobiographical "Adventures of a Nobody," Louisa bitterly penned, "It is forty three years since I became a Wife and yet the rankling sore is not healed which then broke upon my heart of hearts, it was the blight of every future prospect and has hung like an incubus upon my Spirit." This was a woman who clearly saw every ounce of pride slip down the drain with her father's fortunes.

By her telling, Louisa's family led an idyllic life until Joshua Johnson's financial collapse. The second of seven daughters and one son of the American businessman and his British wife, Louisa was born in England only a few months before the first shots of the American Revolution were fired. As an advocate of independence, Johnson deemed it "no longer sage" to live in England during the Revolution, so the family took up residence in France for the duration. Returning to London after the Peace Treaty in 1783, Johnson was appointed by George Washington as American consul. Louisa's recollections are typical for a child starting school in a strange place. She remembered other girls teasing her and her sisters for their French clothes and "utter ignorance of English." But the middle-aged Louisa ascribed some of the problems she later encountered in the world of politics to that time. "I became serious melancholy and almost gloomy, which caused me to be called Miss Proud by my schoolfellows." It was an epithet whose meaning would follow her into adulthood. So would the periods of melancholy and gloom.

Still, Louisa's memory of her life at home was nothing short of rapturous: "My father was the handsomest man I ever beheld"; "My mother's conversation was brilliant. . . . My father seemed to hang on every word she uttered and gazed on her with looks of love and admiration." A woman who often felt slighted by her own husband, Louisa saw perfection in her parents' marriage: "Never did man love woman with devotion so perfect." And the children were all good and beautiful. As the daughters of this wealthy American grew up, suitors came calling. John Adams was the American ambassador at the time, and his daughter Nabby married her father's secretary, William Smith, in London. The Johnson family became so friendly with Nabby and her husband that the two families rented adjoining houses at the seashore one summer. As his children grew older, Joshua Johnson strived to make Americans out of his brood, insisting that the girls only consider fellow countrymen as husbands, and sending his son to "live among republicans, a thing very difficult to people who have lived in the European cities as I have found to my cost," his sister later recounted.

Americans traveling through London enjoyed dinners at the Johnson household, where they were entertained by the bevy of daughters. When John Quincy Adams came to call in the spring of 1795, he was especially welcome as the brother of their friend Nabby Smith, who by that time had returned to the U.S. with her husband and children. Soon Adams, who was visiting England from his post in Holland on a diplomatic errand, became a regular caller. "His devotions were supposed by everybody to be paid to my Sister Nancy," the eldest of the girls, so Louisa treated her sister's caller with teasing camaraderie. John Quincy "was a great favorite of my mother's but I do not think my father admired him so much." Marylander Joshua Johnson "had a prejudice towards the Yankees and insisted that they never made good husbands." It came as a great surprise when Louisa realized that *she* was the object of young Mr. Adams's affections. When they became engaged, her sister Nancy was none too pleased. Smarting from her sister's silence, but decidedly in love, Louisa said a sad goodbye as John Quincy departed for Holland, telling her he had no idea when they would get married. "He recommended to me during his absence to attend to the improvement of my mind, and laid down a course of study for me until we met which might be in one year or in seven." Imagine—they are engaged but he doesn't know when he'll see her again, maybe not for seven years, and she's supposed to study what he assigns in the interim! Louisa was nervous about writing to him, convinced that she couldn't measure up to his standards; his letters did nothing to alleviate her fears. "Consider untoward events as a test of character," he instructed her, adding, "a large portion of all human merit consists in *suffering* with dignity." What fun.

A year later, in the spring of 1797, John Quincy Adams announced to the twenty-two-year-old Louisa that he was to be posted to Lisbon and that he would come through London, where "our nuptials must take place immediately after his arrival as he could only spare a few days to me and my family." Despite this peremptory demand, the Johnsons cheerily prepared for the wedding and then heard nothing more from the presumptive groom. Thinking he had backed out, the wedding finery was "concealed with as much care as if I had committed some crime." But then in July, John Quincy wrote again asking Joshua Johnson to "procure him a passage on board some vessel bound to Lisbon," once again stating that he didn't want to dally in England. These were important facts, Louisa insisted to her sons so many years later, because they showed why the wedding happened so soon after Adams's arrival. She was simply following his orders. And she had no reason to think that anyone would look askance on these arrangements. "At this moment everything seemed to combine to make my prospects brilliant." Her father, she believed, had settled with his creditors and expected "to give each of his children a small fortune."

The couple married on July 26 and planned to sail for Lisbon, where John Quincy had already sent his belongings, when President Adams changed his son's orders. The two-week honeymoon the newlyweds enjoyed while waiting to learn of the groom's next assignment was swiftly shattered by the news that Louisa's father was ruined. Immediately, the rumors started that she had tricked Adams into marrying her. Her family, which had been the source of so much joy, left surreptitiously for America to escape their debts. "When I arose and found them gone I was the most forlorn miserable wretch that the sun ever smiled upon." Louisa Adams never really recovered from the blow.

After some months of fending off her father's creditors, Louisa, already pregnant, sailed off to her new home in Germany along with her husband, John Quincy, and his brother Thomas. A few days after they arrived she suffered the first of what would turn out to be seven miscarriages. This one almost killed her. There she was, "without a female friend," with her husband's time "entirely occupied by his public avocations," feeling more and more like a failure in her marriage, bereft of family, friends, and good health. Soon it became apparent that she would be stripped of her good name as well, if she didn't do something about it. Gossip was circulating that she hadn't been presented at court because she and John Quincy weren't really married. The couple swung into action, enlisting the help of a member of the royal family, borrowing a dress for Louisa, and arranging her debut before the queen. She succeeded brilliantly and became something of a court darling, a decided asset to her husband's service in Berlin. And though Louisa was always self-deprecating to a fault, she realized that she had become "a Belle." "Remember I was the *wife* of a Foreign Minister, and daughter-in-law to the President of the United States, always addressed as your Excellency, and sometimes called *Princess Royal*." Good thing the voters of America didn't know that; John Adams was already under attack for his "monarchical" views.

Despite her triumphant forays in court circles, interrupted by repeated miscarriages, John Quincy worried that Louisa might make some mistake that would reflect badly on him. Disputes between the couple came to a head over the question of rouge. The queen herself told Louisa that she looked pale—no wonder, with the number of miscarriages she endured—and promised to "make me a present of a box of rouge." When Louisa responded that her husband would never let her wear it, the queen "smiled at my simplicity and observed that if she presented me the box he must not refuse it, and told me to tell him so." When Louisa recounted the conversation to John Quincy, "he said I must refuse the box, as he should never permit me to accept it." It took a year for Louisa to work up her courage. Before going to a party, "being more than usually pale I ventured to put on a little rouge," which Louisa thought made her "look quite beautiful." She tried to trick her husband by rushing through the room, telling him to put out the lights as she headed to the carriage. John Quincy became curious, took one look at her, and told her that "unless I allowed him to wash my face, he would not go. He took a towel and drew me on his knee, and all my beauty was washed away." A well-timed kiss made peace.

It took another year and "everlasting teasing about my pale *face*" from the other women at court for Louisa to try again. This time, "I walked boldly forward to meet Mr. Adams. As soon as he saw me, he requested me to wash it off, while I with some temper refused." John Quincy turned on his heel, and left without her. Louisa, rather than collapsing in a puddle, as she might have a year or two before, simply changed clothes into something simpler and went to dinner with friends. When her husband came to fetch her at the end of the evening, "we returned home as good friends as ever." After more than three years of marriage, Louisa was beginning to stand up to her husband. She was also pregnant for the fifth time. And this time, finally, she carried the baby to term.

On April 12, 1801, attended by a drunken midwife who almost killed her, Louisa gave birth to a healthy baby boy. When John Quincy Adams had learned of the death of George Washington, he had been "much affected by it," so the baby was named in honor of the first president of the United States. By then the second president, John Adams, had been defeated for reelection. The opposition party was in power and it was time for Louisa and John Quincy Adams to go home. First, she would have to recover from the botched childbirth, which had resulted in paralysis of her left leg. Louisa had become such a favorite of the king that he closed off the streets around her house, so she wouldn't be disturbed during her recuperation. Sick as she was, Louisa was ecstatic. "I was a *Mother*. God had heard my prayer." Three months later Louisa Adams sailed with her husband and son for America, a country she had never seen.

John Quincy chose to spend some of the time on the fifty-eight-day voyage telling Louisa about his lost love. As a younger man, he had wooed a woman named Mary Frazer, but his family discouraged him from marrying her because he wasn't well enough established professionally or financially. Here's the still ailing Louisa, "poor faded thing that I was," hearing her husband go on and on about another woman's "extreme beauty, her great attainments, the elegance of her letters," etc., etc. "My only consolation was that at any rate I had a *Son*." The little son's life at sea was threatened by a bout of dysentery, but George Washington Adams recovered and arrived with his parents in Philadelphia on September 4, 1801.

The couple then went their separate ways—John Quincy traveled north to see his mother and father after seven years abroad, Louisa headed south with the baby to her family in Washington. If the young mother was also postponing the inevitable meeting with her in-laws, it would have been completely understandable. John Quincy had told Louisa all about his old girlfriend; he might have also recounted his mother's letters where she fretted that "Mrs. Adams is going to a place, different from all she has ever yet visited, where it is impossible for her to be too guarded." As it was, Louisa dreaded the trip alone: "We had never parted before, and though this country was to be my home, I was yet a forlorn stranger in the land of my Fathers." Worse, when she reached Washington, Louisa's father didn't recognize her, she was so drawn and sickly. Though her mother and sisters soon revived her spirits, Louisa's father was "fearfully changed." President Adams had given the ruined Joshua Johnson a government job that paid a couple of thousand dollars a year, but he lost even that with the advent of the new administration. A broken man, Johnson died not long after his daughter's visit.

Louisa insisted that John Quincy come to Washington to collect her for the difficult ride to Boston. While he was there, President Jefferson entertained the couple; so did James and Dolley Madison and Samuel and Margaret Bayard Smith. Best was a visit to Mount Vernon, where Louisa met "the celebrated Nelly Custis, a beautiful woman." Martha Washington was still entertaining curious visitors, though she was frail and getting older. The mistress of Mount Vernon was probably actually glad to have the Adams couple come by, a pair she could count on to share her political views. "We were all Federalists, which evidently gave her particular pleasure," another visitor about that time remembered, quoting Martha as thinking Jefferson's election was "the greatest misfortune our country had ever experienced."

The former First Lady's passion about politics had not diminished, but her health had. Only a few months after Louisa and John Quincy Adams visited, Martha Washington, always aware of appearances, set aside a white satin dress for her burial, and died on May 22, 1802, at the age of seventy-one. Newspapers throughout the country took respectful but brief notice of the woman who had spent every winter of the Revolutionary War at camp with the American troops, starving and freezing alongside them, leading other officers' wives as they cooked and sewed for the soldiers, alternately nursing and entertaining the men who were deeply devoted to "Lady Washington." The woman who had created the role of First Lady and understood its obligations all too well received scant praise: "She was the worthy partner of the worthiest of men," eulogized the *New England Pledium,* "They lived an honor and a pattern to their country."

Before winter made travel impossible, John Quincy Adams insisted it was time to get on the road to Massachusetts. Reluctantly, Louisa bid goodbye to her family, climbed into a carriage with her husband and child, and left for the dreaded meeting with her mother-in-law. Cold wet weather along the way and bouts of illness plus a "constantly shrieking" baby did nothing to soothe her anxiety: "Suffering and sorrow, sickness and exhaustion, with anguish of mind, all combined to harass me," she lamented almost forty years later. "Under such circumstances could I appear amiable?" Apparently not. Louisa herself admits to having been "completely disagreeable," and Abigail was so alarmed at the state of her daughter-in-law's health that she told her son Thomas, "I have many fears that she will be of short duration." As for her son John Quincy, caring for his ailing wife had "added a weight of years to his brow." It was not a beginning that boded well. Years later, Louisa, the self-described "spoilt child of indulgence," grouched that in her husband's family she was "gazed at with surprise, if not contempt." The more her mother-in-law tried to pamper her, "the more particular the attentions that they thought it necessary to show me, the less I felt at *home*." This young woman who "was literally and without knowing it a *fine* lady," who had "lived in the City of London, in Berlin at Court," found nothing in the Puritan New England world familiar or fun: "Had I stepped into Noah's Ark I do not think I could have been more utterly astonished. Dr. Tufts, Deacon French! Mr. Cranch! Old Uncle Peter! Capt. Beale!!! It was lucky for me that I was so much depressed, and so ill, or I should certainly have given mortal offence." Louisa did find one Adams in her corner. "The old gentleman took a fancy to me." John Adams would be an ally for life.

As Louisa struggled to adapt to a strange, and to her mind primitive, continent, though filled with extraordinary women of "masculine minds," John Quincy, the quintessential public servant, had to find work. He set up law practice in Boston, but soon eagerly jumped into the political arena; he went to the state senate, was defeated in a run for the House of Representatives, and then, in February 1803, accepted an appointment to fill a vacant seat in the U.S. Senate. Little George was not quite two and his mother was pregnant again, soon to give birth to her second boy, John Adams II. In looking for a baby nurse, Louisa discovered that the proper façade exhibited by the puritanical Bostonians concealed a seamier side. All twenty of the women she interviewed revealed that they were mothers of an out-of-wedlock child. Soon, however, Louisa was able to leave Boston behind.

In October the family headed to Washington, starting the journey by ship with all of them seasick and three-month-old baby John refusing to "leave the breast one moment." When two-year-old George started feeling better, Louisa didn't notice him playing near a window "open just wide enough to put his hand through, but when about to land he told me he had thrown the keys of all our trunks and his shoes out of the window, and they of course had fallen in the sea." Nothing would be easy for Mrs. Adams, who knew her husband had set as his goal the achievement of "the highest honors your country admits to." There was no place she and John Quincy could afford to stay in the capital city, so they moved in with her sister Nancy and husband to a "lonely and dreary" country house far away from anything in the city "of magnificent distances." After the courts of Berlin or even the settled city of Boston, Washington was a shock. "We frequented the parties, the dinners, the assemblies . . . almost at the risk of life . . . the city not being laid out, the streets not graduated, the bridges consisting of mere loose planks, and huge stumps of trees recently cut down intercepting every path, and the roads intersected by deep ravines continually enlarged by rain."

But an evening at the executive mansion with its "French servants in livery, a French butler, a French cuisine" was almost like being in Europe. It also gave Louisa a chance to observe the major figures of government: "Mr. Jefferson was the president of the day—the ruling demagogue of the hour. Everything about him was *aristocratic except* his person which was ungainly ugly and common. His manner was awkward, and excessively inelegant; and until he fairly entered into conversation, there was a sort of peering restlessness about him, which betrayed a fear of being scanned more closely by his visitors, than was altogether *agreeable* to his self complacency. While conversing he was very agreeable, and possessed the art of *drawing* out *others* and at the same time attracting attention to himself." Then there was Virginian John Randolph, "who gave us a specimen of his wonted rudeness" by criticizing the wine. "Mr. Madison was a *very* small man in his *person,* with a *very* large *head*—his manners were peculiarly unassuming, and his conversation lively, often playful, with a mixture of wit and seriousness so happily blended as to excite admiration and respect." When Louisa was writing this years later, she still had not forgiven Jefferson for removing her father from some low-level job in government, whereas Madison had appointed her husband to high office. "Mrs. Madison was tall, large and rather masculine in personal dimensions; her complexion was so fair and brilliant as to redeem this objection, in its perfectly feminine beauty." Dolley, judged Louisa, "won golden opinions from all, and she possessed an influence so decided with her little Man that She was the worshiped of all the idol mongers."

As a senator whose father had been defeated by the sitting president, the thirty-six-year-old Adams attracted considerable attention, particularly when he broke with his party and his region as the only Federalist to support Thomas Jefferson's Louisiana Purchase. And though his mother was proud of him as a man of country, not of party, Abigail also offered a steady stream of advice to both her son and his wife. John Quincy was too stiff, she told him, and showed "a coldness of address upon entering company" and he dressed badly. Get a good coat, she nagged, and shave often, don't look like a fop but dress fashionably enough so no one would "ask what kind of Mother he had? Or to charge upon a Wife negligence and inattention when she is guiltless." Louisa was instructed to send her husband to Congress with "a cracker in his jacket" and to try to do something about "the cut of his coat, the strangeness of his wigs."

Abigail's badgering might have been intrusive, but Louisa Adams was anxious for some guidelines in this peculiar capital city. "At the courts of princes you get written instructions to teach you the forms and etiquettes; you are therefore seldom liable to give offence by erring," she wisely observed. "In a democratic government where all are monarchs . . . there is a perpetual struggle for a *position,* which gives rise to constant feuds." Protestations of equality notwithstanding, "only the *elite* of Congress entered into what was termed the best society." The one exception—New Year's Day, when the president opened his house to "an unruly crowd of indiscriminate persons from every class." To the "Corps Diplomatique" the scene was "exceedingly trying and unpleasant," but Louisa did derive some satisfaction from the president's discomfort; "Tom Jefferson as the founder of democracy" had to allow the rabble to ransack his wardrobe "that the People might admire his *red breeches* etc, etc and amuse themselves at his expense and *not a little* annoyance."

When the Congress recessed that spring, John Quincy went home to Massachusetts without his wife and children, leaving them at Nancy's house. He had told Louisa that they couldn't afford to live in two places and he expected her to return with him to Quincy and stay there. When she chose instead to stay in Washington year-round, he was more than miffed, and she was mortified at his reaction. It was *he*, she insisted, who had repeatedly told her that they would "be separated one half of the year for six years. The only thing left for me was to endeavor to make our separation as easy to myself as possible and preferred passing the summer months with my family to living alone at Quincy through five dreary winters. I do not think my beloved friend you do me justice when you say I 'prefer a separation from you rather than separation from them.'" Political marriages have never been easy. And the separation was hard on the children. Three-year-old George "is very angry with you. He says you are very naughty to go away and leave him." Mrs. Merry, who seems to have become quite friendly with many American women, joked that George would be a politician: "He understands the art of *twisting* a subject better than any child she ever saw." Like congressional wives ever since, Louisa complained that the children missed their father: "George talks of Papa incessantly though he has never forgiven you for your desertion. John calls every body papa he sees. Poor little fellow he was too young when you left us to remember you."

Louisa Adams clearly missed her husband, dramatically declaring that "Life is not worth having on such terms," and hoping "something will arise to induce you to shorten the period of your absence that we may at least enjoy a few weeks before *Congress* takes you from me," still she provided a steady stream of chatter about goings-on in Washington. On the fourth of July she "followed the multitude today and went to pay my respects to the President. Everybody attended that remained in town and we had as much ice cream and cake as we could eat. The president is so altered I scarcely knew him. He is grown very thin and looks old." Jefferson was sorely suffering the loss of his daughter. When September rolled around, Louisa and her sisters enjoyed "a company of comedians in town from Philadelphia." Also expected in town—new members of Congress, called by Jefferson. "This is however mere talk for there is nobody here who can know anything about it. Even the *clerks* are out of town." Washington hasn't changed in summer with Congress in recess. Still, Louisa was happy to report: "The City is so much improved you will be surprised on your arrival. The theatre is almost completed. It is to be played in the first three nights of the races which begin the thirteenth of next month. The Philadelphia Company are engaged." Also two big hotels were going up "for the accommodation of the Members," and work on the Capitol building had "advanced considerably," plus "the president has had his House improved." Things were looking up in the federal city, and her husband was heading her way.

From Quincy, Louisa had received letters from her mother-in-law grumbling over missing her grandchildren and chiding Louisa about John Quincy's poor health. With her husband back in her clutches, the wife was able to scold in return: "I was much surprised and grieved to see him look so ill when he returned." Daughter-in-law and mother-in-law might bicker, but they could agree about one thing—John Quincy was a star: "His talents are so superior and he is so perfectly calculated for the station in which he is placed. His manners are so perfectly pleasing and conciliating and his understanding is so refined even his enemies envy and admire him." Both his wife and his mother were ready to push John Quincy Adams to the top.

WHEN ADAMS RETURNED to take his seat in the Senate in the fall of 1804, the man presiding, the vice president of the United States, was under indictment for murder. That summer Aaron Burr had shot and killed his old political nemesis, former Treasury Secretary Alexander Hamilton, in a duel.

Burr had never recovered politically from the shenanigans surrounding the tied election of 1800. Jefferson, who didn't trust him, shut Burr out of his councils and in February 1804, the Republican Party caucus unanimously rejected the sitting vice president as the candidate to run with Jefferson for a second term; old George Clinton, the longtime governor of New York, was picked instead. So Burr decided to go after Clinton's job, a tall order given the fact that the Clinton and Livingston families held a lock on New York politics, with Alexander Hamilton always trying to pick it for his purposes. "The Clintons, Livingstons, etc, had not, at the last advice from Albany, decided on their candidate," Burr told his daughter Theodosia in February, adding "Hamilton is intriguing for any candidate who can have a chance of success against A[aron].B[urr]."

Alexander Hamilton and Aaron Burr had long been rivals in N.Y. legal and political circles, and twelve years earlier Burr had ousted Hamilton's father-in-law, Philip Schuyler, in a U.S. Senate race. (Schuyler then defeated Burr in the next election.) Hamilton, horrified when Federalist politicians plotted to elect Burr over Jefferson when breaking the tie in the 1800 election, went on a frantic letter-writing campaign to convince his partisans that even the enemy Jefferson was preferable to a man who was "wicked enough to scruple nothing." Once the 1804 gubernatorial campaign began, it was clear that the New York newspapers would "scruple nothing." Even by the standards of the day, the outlandish articles about Burr's purported debauchery with both sexes went well beyond the pale. And they had their effect. "The election is lost by a great majority," the vice president reported to his daughter after the April balloting. What was Burr to do? He had no role in the Jefferson administration and no future in New York politics. It was a question Alexander Hamilton had been grappling with for years—ever since his champion, George Washington, had left office and John Adams gave him the cold shoulder.

Hamilton's political disappointments had been more than matched by personal tragedy. His talented firstborn son, Philip, had been killed in a duel in November 1801, the result of a dispute over a political speech attacking the elder Hamilton. As the young Philip lay dying at his aunt and uncle's house, his mother, pregnant with her eighth child, joined Alexander there. The scene, wrote a friend who was present, "when she met her husband and son in one room beggars all description." Philip's death killed the spirit of another child of Elizabeth and Alexander Hamilton—seventeen-year-old Angelica suffered such a severe mental breakdown that she never recovered. So the Hamiltons effectively lost two children on the New Jersey dueling grounds. A much-saddened Alexander retreated to his home in the country and to the practice of law, leaving politics aside until Aaron Burr declared for governor.

Then Hamilton reentered the fray, denouncing Burr vociferously both in public and in private. One of those private conversations—where Hamilton was alleged to have called Burr a dangerous man and then expressed "a still more despicable opinion" of his old rival—ended up in the newspapers. By the time Aaron Burr read the account, the election for governor was over and he was an angry and defeated man. He demanded that Hamilton explain what this "despicable" opinion might be. A series of letters back and forth between the two men failed to settle the matter; instead, each dug in to an intractable position, which led inexorably to the encounter in Weehawken, New Jersey, on July 11, 1804.

Both men bade their adieus to the women in their lives. The widower, Aaron Burr, instructed his only child, his daughter Theodosia, to burn any of his letters that would "injure any person," particularly the letters "of my female correspondents," of which there were quite a few, and he warned her that "my estate will just about pay my debts and no more." Since Theodosia was married to wealthy South Carolina planter Joseph Alston, her father knew that money would not be a problem. He signed off with affection and advice: "I am indebted to you, my dearest Theodosia, for a very great portion of the happiness which I have enjoyed in this life. You have completely satisfied all that my heart and affections had hoped or even wished. With a little more perseverance, determination, and industry, you will obtain all that my ambition or vanity had fondly imagined. Let your son have occasion to be proud that he had a mother. Adieu. Adieu."

To his wife, Eliza, the mother of his seven living children, Alexander Hamilton tried to justify the duel. Knowing that he might be leaving her to fend for herself, he insisted that he had no choice but to defend his honor despite "my love for you and my precious children." Hamilton could not avoid the duel "without sacrifices which would have rendered me unworthy of your esteem. I need not tell you of the pangs I feel from quitting you, and exposing you to the anguish I know you will feel. Nor can I dwell on the topic, lest it unman me." He commended her to seek solace in religion; and then his farewell: "Adieu, best of wives, best of women. Embrace all my darling children for me." Eliza Hamilton, called Betsey in her youth, probably felt that she would have no problem holding her husband "in esteem" if he failed to answer the challenge to a duel. After all, he was on the record as opposing dueling, which was against the law in New York, plus she had already lost one family member who chose to settle an argument by this primitive practice. And Betsey Hamilton had stood by her man, continued to consider him "worthy of her esteem" through her public humiliation when he confessed to his affair with Maria Reynolds. Now she would not only be left to raise the children alone, she would have to struggle financially to do it, since her husband would be leaving large debts behind.

In his face-off with Aaron Burr, using his brother-in-law's dueling pistols, the same weapons that had gunned down his son, Alexander Hamilton fell in the first round of firing. Only later did Burr learn that Hamilton had decided to hold his fire on the first shot as a symbol of his disapproval of dueling. The mortally wounded former general was taken back across the Hudson to the home of a friend, where Eliza was summoned with the news that her husband was having "spasms." When she arrived at his bedside and saw the truth, she erupted in "frantic grief," according to the doctor at the scene. Eliza's sister Angelica also rushed to the deathbed, where she started "weeping her heart out." For years the relationship between Angelica and Alexander had been the subject of speculation. Was Eliza's husband having an affair with her sister? At the very least, the two were soul mates. "I have the painful task to inform you that Gen. Hamilton was this morning wounded by that wretch Burr," Angelica hurriedly told her brother Philip Schuyler. "My dear sister bears with saintlike fortitude this affliction. The town is in consternation and there exists only the expression of grief and indignation." After Hamilton lingered for a day, his wife brought their children in to say goodbye, lifting baby Philip, named for his dead brother, for a farewell kiss. With friends and family surrounding him convulsed by sorrow, Alexander Hamilton died at the age of forty-nine. Eliza cut a lock of his hair and prepared for what would be the equivalent of a state funeral, with crowds filling the streets, businesses shuttering their doors, ships in the harbor firing their guns in salute.

"You have heard no doubt of the terrible duel and the end of poor Hamilton," Dolley Madison wrote to her sister Anna a few days later. It would have been hard not to hear of the duel. Much of the country was mourning "the dreadful fate of General Hamilton which seems to spread a general gloom," observed Louisa Catherine Adams, daughter-in-law of the man Hamilton had helped defeat. "His loss must be severely felt by his country and friends and foes here unite in lamenting his untimely death," Louisa informed her husband. Friends and foes also united in identifying the villain in the piece: the vice president of the United States. "America has just had a great loss in the person of Alexander Hamilton who was killed in a duel with Colonel Burr, the vice-president," Rosalie Calvert recounted to her mother in Belgium. "Even General Washington's death did not produce such a sensation. The city of New York is in an uproar, and if Burr had not fled, they would have made him pay dearly for his vengeance."

"Hang Burr!" shouted the handbills posted around New York.

Though dueling was a well-accepted tradition, it was illegal in New York, where a grand jury indicted Burr. And in New Jersey, where dueling was legal, the unpopular politician was charged with murder. Amazed at the public outcry and still trying to sound sanguine about his situation a week after Hamilton's death, the vice president did indeed flee, telling Theodosia, "I shall journey somewhere within a few days, but whither is not yet decided." Burr snuck out of New York and landed in Philadelphia saying, "I absent myself from home merely to give a little time for passions to subside, not from any apprehension of the final effects of proceedings in courts of law." Trying to allay any concerns of his daughter, Burr added, "You will find the papers filled with all manner of nonsense and lies. Among other things, accounts of attempts to assassinate me. These, I assure you, are mere fables. Those who wish me dead prefer to keep at a very respectful distance." Despite the danger, Burr kept up his teasing tone, regaling Theodosia, as he often did, with his romantic exploits, wryly observing, "If any male friend of yours should be dying of ennui, recommend to him to engage in a duel and a courtship at the same time." Still, Aaron Burr deemed it the better part of wisdom to move farther away from the scene of the crime, so he traveled on to a friend's plantation in Georgia to lie low for a couple of months, asking his daughter to address his mail to a "Mr. R. King" so no one would be alerted to his whereabouts.

In the fall, the fugitive determined that it was safe to travel north and resume his duties presiding over the United States Senate, where Burr wielded the gavel while still facing murder charges in New York and New Jersey. The two states, he told Theodosia, were arguing over "which shall have the honor of hanging the vice president." He managed to turn the prospect of his "hanging" into a joke: "You shall have due notice of the time and place. Whenever it may be, you may rely on a great concourse of company, much gaiety, and many rare sights; such as the lion, the elephant, etc." The day he wrote that letter, Burr's successor as vice president was chosen: on December 4, 1804, Thomas Jefferson was elected for a second term as president of the United States, with George Clinton as his vice president. A new amendment to the Constitution had mandated separate ballots for the offices of president and vice president, so there was no confusion as there had been four years earlier, and no mixture of parties as there had been four years before that. Thomas Jefferson and his Republican Party were clearly in charge, having whipped the opposition Federalist candidates—Charles Cotesworth Pinckney for president and Rufus King for vice president by a whopping Electoral College vote of 162–14.

Burr might have been the lamest of lame-duck vice presidents, but he still had one more constitutional duty to perform: presiding over the Senate for the impeachment trial of Supreme Court Justice Samuel Chase. By his blatantly political decisions and partisan statements from the bench, Federalist Chase had aroused the ire of the Republican majority, including the president. Eager to be rid of the old man, and to exert authority over the courts, Jefferson hoped Burr would help convict Chase. So, despite the murder charges, the vice president suddenly found himself the darling of the Jefferson administration—not only was the former outcast invited to the executive mansion, Burr's friends and relatives were rewarded with government jobs.

"Everybody is flocking to Washington on account of a proceeding against the Justice Chase by the Democratic party," Rosalie Calvert told her sister. "All the most important attorneys in the United States are there and many foreigners have come to hear them." Louisa Adams agreed that "everybody seemed to take great interest in the proceedings." It was quite a spectacle, "attended by so many ladies that it partook of the nature of a social event," concluding with the acquittal of the justice just three days before the end of Burr's term as vice president. "Mr. Burr took his leave of the Senate in a most elegant and even pathetic address delivered in the most graceful and touching manner," Louisa Adams recounted. "Oh how winning is refinement and polished decorum. I fear it will ever white wash many sins which morality must condemn." And then Aaron

Burr left town. On the stagecoach to Baltimore, Louisa Adams was distressed to learn that the former vice president was a fellow passenger; she "felt a sort of loathing for this Col. Burr who had recently killed Gen. Hamilton in a duel." But once she was introduced to him on board the ship she and her family had boarded to Philadelphia, Louisa, like many women before her, changed her mind: "In spite of myself I was pleased with him." The charming colonel helped her children "with so much ease and good nature that I was perfectly confounded." By the time they reached Philadelphia "we were quite intimate." Aaron Burr's "refinement and polished decorum" would continue to serve him well as he headed west for a prolonged tour, telling his daughter that he expected the trip to be "both useful and agreeable," and that she would "hear of me occasionally on my route." Before long the whole country was to hear of what Aaron Burr had in mind for himself and his daughter Theodosia.

CHAPTER THREE

THE SECOND TERM OF THOMAS JEFFERSON AND WOMEN TALKING POLITICS

1805~1809

ROSALIE STIER CALVERT
Courtesy of the Maryland Historical Society

"*I SEE BY YOUR LETTERS* and the newspapers that talking about politics or government is not fashionable in your country," the young matron Rosalie Calvert mused to her father in Belgium in the summer of 1805. "Here we talk of practically nothing else—men, women and children—not only about what is going on in the United States, but in all the corners of the world." As America settled in for Jefferson's second term, after the first presidential *re*election since George Washington's, politics remained a preeminent occupation of the citizens, but other diversions were also developing as the seacoast cities grew more sophisticated and the frontier pushed farther west. Ohio had joined the Union as the seventeenth state in 1803, adding to the Republican majority in Congress and, along with Kentucky and Tennessee, bringing some exotic characters from the western settlements to the nation's capital. Margaret Bayard Smith tells with some amusement of two senators at her dinner table staring with "astonishment" at the first piano they had ever seen: "They looked and looked, felt all over the outside, peeped in where it was open, and seemed so curious to know how the sound was produced, or whence it came." Through the intelligent eyes of Margaret Smith and Rosalie Calvert we can peer into a window on the world of women who kept company with and often counseled the men running the country.

Ten years earlier, as a recently arrived seventeen-year-old fleeing the French Revolution with her family, Rosalie had not been so appreciative of the New World: "America displeases me more and more every day—you meet only scoundrels." Now, married to an American for five years and the mother of three children, she saw marked improvement: "There have been a great many changes since you left—luxury is increasing a good deal and European customs are becoming prevalent," she told her sister, who had returned with her husband and parents to Belgium two years earlier. "In the large cities when one is entertaining, cooks can now be hired by the day, as well as caterers and French confectioners who will come to arrange a dinner, dessert, etc."

A wealthy plantation mistress with adamantly anti-Jeffersonian views, Rosalie's letters display a deepening devotion to her adopted country. When her father observed, "The general rule in America is to spend; thrift is considered a vice there. People think only of themselves; they worry little about their families," she somewhat defensively countered: "You are mistaken in thinking that the general custom in this country is to spend all one's income and not give a thought to one's children." Americans were, she admitted, less frugal than Europeans but "I find that economy is becoming more fashionable than before," due to frequent bankruptcies. "The more I contemplate America and the more I know her, the more I realize the advantages she has over Europe," this woman who was managing her father's considerable U.S. holdings concluded. "Everything here is improving every day—land is increasing in price, society and entertainments becoming more refined, all the comforts of life easier to get, one is less subject to huge losses, and the government is stable and good, the justice impartial." The political situation in maturing America compared favorably in her mind to the turmoil in Europe: "The present ascendancy of the democratic spirit is a genuine good fortune for the country. It certainly has not caused any of the disorders which were feared," she admonished her aristocratic father, and, better yet, she paid a lot less in taxes than he did. Still, Rosalie had to admit she would be forced to educate her daughter herself, to home-school her, because "the education of girls in the schools here is so objectionable." The prospect was far from pleasing, since it would "cause me a good deal of work and trouble." And the ardent Federalist deeply disliked the man she derided as "Tommy Jeff." It was wishful thinking on Rosalie's part when she reported to her sister in 1805 that "the Democratic party weakens day by day. People make fun of Jefferson."

Though Jefferson's party (the party was called the Democratic-Republicans or the Jeffersonian Republicans; in the early days its supporters called it "Republican," its opponents called it "Democratic") was beset by internal squabbles, the president was still riding high politically off the Louisiana Purchase. Most of the country preened over the incredible expansion of the new nation and waited eagerly to hear from the men dispatched to explore the vast new territory with the goal of finding a northwest passage to the Pacific Ocean—Meriwether Lewis and William Clark. The women of Washington had so understood the importance of this mission that they supplemented the paltry congressional appropriation with a fund-raising drive, spearheaded by Dolley Madison. (The women were treated to special souvenirs from the journey when it was finally over.) In the first year of his new term, as artifacts arrived from the explorers, Jefferson delighted in the news: "We have just heard from Captain Lewis," he reported to Martha, "who wintered 1600 miles up the Missouri: all well." The two men led a few dozen others in the Corps of Discovery up the Missouri River in the spring of 1804, traveling north across the Great Plains on to what is now North Dakota, where they reached the villages of the Mandan and Hidatsa tribes in October. There they found more than 4,500 people—a bigger population than the still-struggling nation's capital—who offered hospitable, if bitterly cold, winter lodgings. It was there the explorers met the French-Canadian fur trader Toussaint Charbonneau and his Shoshone, or Snake, wife, Sacagawea.

If they were to make it all the way west, Lewis and Clark would need to convince the Shoshones, who lived at the Missouri's headwaters, to sell some horses from their famous herds. A Shoshone speaker could greatly enhance their chances of success, so the captains signed Charbonneau and his wife up for the journey. Sacagawea had no choice in the matter. The girl—she was about sixteen years old—had been captured by the Hidatsas and sold to her husband, or perhaps won by him in a card game. In February, attended by the strange American men, the Indian girl gave birth to a baby boy: "Her labor was tedious and the pain violent," Meriwether Lewis recorded in his journal, adding that one of the other members of the party swore that the rattles of a rattlesnake "never failed to produce the desired effect, that of hastening the birth of the child; having the rattle of a snake by me I gave it to him and he administered two rings of it to the woman broken in small pieces with the fingers and added to a small quantity of water." Ten minutes later the baby was born, though Lewis questioned whether the snake rattle had done any good. The exploration's captain was well versed in administering medicine, having learned it from his mother, the stalwart Lucy Meriwether Lewis Marks. During the Revolution, a rifle-toting Lucy had achieved fame running drunken British soldiers off her Virginia plantation; in peacetime her knowledge of the medical uses of wild plants made her legendary. Lewis relied on his mother through his life, writing to her regularly from his journeys.

Sacagawea's baby, Jean Baptiste Charbonneau, was certainly the youngest member of the Corps of Discovery when the expedition started the spring trek on April 7, 1805. That night, when they set up camp, most of the men slept outdoors, but the captains, Lewis and Clark, stayed cozy in a buffalo-skin tepee that was big enough for them, their interpreters, and the baby. The captains were making sure to keep the lone woman, Sacagawea, safe from their homesick men, but she quickly showed her strength as a team member. While the men secured the campsite that first night, she poked a stick in the ground, searching for wild artichokes. "Her labor soon proved successful," Lewis wrote, "and she procured a good quantity of these roots. The flavor of this root resembles the Jerusalem artichoke." With her baby on her back, the girl continued to supply the men with plants and roots to supplement their otherwise all-meat diet. Clark reported in late April that she "brought me a bush something like the currant, which she said bore a delicious fruit and that great quantities grew on the Rocky Mountains." The young woman clearly knew the territory. A few days later it was wild licorice and something called the "white apple" that she added to the list of the white men's culinary discoveries. Sacagawea's husband's one talent also came in the food department. Regularly hunting and killing buffalo, the men tired of the monotonous slabs of meat that made up the menu and were grateful when Charbonneau treated them to his trademark *boudin blanc* sausage.

For the most part Charbonneau was more trouble than he was worth. At the helm of the lead boat one day in mid-May, when the corps had reached modern-day Montana, the Frenchman panicked when a squall hit and almost lost the boat with all its provisions. Charbonneau finally righted the craft and "by 4 o'clock in the evening our instruments, medicine, merchandize provision, etc. were perfectly dried, repacked and put on board the pirogue," Lewis reported. "The Indian woman to whom I ascribe equal fortitude and resolution with any person onboard at the time of the accident, caught and preserved most of the light articles which were washed overboard." Perhaps in recognition of that fortitude, a few days later the men named a river in Montana "Sacagawea," "after our interpreter, the Snake woman." (Several of the bodies of water Lewis and Clark christened on the trip were named after women back home.)

Soon the captains found themselves forced to admit Sacagawea's contributions. As the party prepared for a punishing mountain climb, Lewis returned from a scouting mission to find "the Indian woman extremely ill and much reduced by her indisposition." Not only was he concerned for "the poor object herself, then with a young child in her arms," but Lewis was especially worried because Sacagawea was the only hope "for a friendly negotiation with the Snake Indians on whom we depend for horses to assist us in our portage from the Missouri to the Columbia River." The men needed this girl. Clark too wrote of his worry: "The Indian woman very bad and will take no medicine whatever until her husband finding her out of her senses, easily prevailed on her to take medicine." (One cringes to imagine what method Charbonneau used to convince her.) Lewis concocted a remedy that eventually worked well enough for Sacagawea to move on with the men of the expedition, who now knew they didn't want to go without her.

The way west proved even more daunting than the captains had anticipated. Buffalo tracks broke the axles of the wagons, and cactus needles cut into the feet of the weary travelers. At the end of June a storm blew up that almost washed away some of the party, including Sacagawea. William Clark "scrambled up the hill pushing the interpreter's wife (who had her child in her arms) before me, the interpreter himself making attempts to pull up his wife by the hand, much scared and nearly without motion." The hapless Charbonneau once again useless, they barely escaped the river, Clark excitedly recounted, "before it raised 10 feet deep with a torrent which is terrible to behold, and by the time I reached the top of the hill, at least 15 feet of water. I directed the party to return to the camp at the run as fast as possible to get to our lode where clothes could be got to cover the child whose clothes were all lost, and the woman who was but just recovering from a severe indisposition and was wet and cold. I was fearful of a relapse." Pelted by hail and wind, the rest of the men complained so much that Clark "refreshed them with a little grog" and shared some of the fast-depleting stock of whiskey with Sacagawea as well.

The party was growing impatient to find the Shoshone or Snake Indians. Lewis and Clark, having miscalculated the distances, feared winter would come on before they reached the tribe and their horse herds. Finally, in late July when they had reached what today is southwestern Montana, Lewis realized again Sacagawea's importance when he was able to record: "The Indian woman recognizes the country and assures us that this is the river on which her relations live, and that the three forks are at no great distance. This piece of information has cheered the spirits of the party." When the men came to the forks in the Missouri, they named the three rivers after President Jefferson and two of his cabinet secretaries—James Madison and Albert Gallatin. A few days later when the expedition had still not found the Shoshones, Lewis worried: "If we do not find them or some other nation who have horses I fear the successful issue of our voyage will be very doubtful." No Indians, no horses, no successful conclusion to the Lewis and Clark Expedition, that was it—plain and simple. So it was with great relief that Lewis was able the very next day to put to paper this truly remarkable entry: "Our present camp is precisely on the spot that the Snake Indians were encamped at the time the Minnetares [Hidatsas] of the Knife River first came in sight of them five years since. From hence they retreated about three miles up Jeffersons River and concealed themselves in the woods. The Minnetares pursued, attacked them, killed 4 men, 4 women, a number of boys and made prisoners of all the females and four boys. Sacagawea or Indian woman was one of the female prisoners taken at that time; though I cannot discover that she shows any emotion of sorrow in recollecting this event, or of joy in being again restored to her native country. If she has enough to eat and a few trinkets to wear I believe she would be perfectly content anywhere." How likely was it that this teenage Shoshone mother would let her feelings show to a party of older white men?

Meriwether Lewis does not describe Sacagawea's emotions, or lack of them, a few days later when she "recognized the point of a high plain to our right which she informed us was not very distant from the summer retreat of her nation." She was sure they would find her people any day now. The party split into two groups, and Lewis did not have Sacagawea with him when he finally did happen on an elderly Shoshone woman and two girls. He convinced them that he was friendly, gave them some presents, and "painted their tawny cheeks with some vermillion which with this nation is emblematic of peace." Using sign language he asked the old woman to lead him to the Shoshone camp. After about two miles, "we met a party of about 60 warriors mounted on excellent horses who came in nearly full speed." That must have been a heart-stopping moment. Lewis wisely put down his gun and walked ahead of the rest of his men. The chief and a couple of others also pulled out in front of their men to listen to the women, who displayed their presents and argued that Lewis was not to be feared. "Both parties now advanced and we were all caressed and besmeared with their grease and paint till I was heartily tired of the national hug." Far better than the alternative. After smoking a peace pipe, the Shoshones led the explorers back to their encampment, where "all the women and children of the camp were shortly collected about the lodge to indulge themselves with looking at us, we being the first white persons they had ever seen."

After a few days in camp learning the geography of the area, Lewis and the Shoshone chief set out to find Clark and the rest of the team. When they met up, Sacagawea recognized the Shoshone chief, Cameahwait—he was her brother! "She instantly jumped up, and ran and embraced him, throwing over him her blanket, and weeping profusely. The chief himself was moved, though not in the same degree. After some conversation between them she resumed her seat and attempted to interpret for us; but her new situation overpowered her, and she was frequently interrupted by her tears."

This time Lewis could not claim that the girl showed no emotion: "The meeting of those people was really affecting, particularly between Sacagawea and an Indian woman, who had been taken prisoner at the same time with her and who had afterwards escaped from the Minnetares and rejoined her nation." With Sacagawea translating the Shoshone language into Hidatsa to Charbonneau and Charbonneau translating the Hidatsa into French to a corpsman named Francis Labiche and Labiche translating the French into English to Lewis and Clark, and the train of translation going in the opposite direction to the chief, the captains made their pitch for horses. Sacagawea's brother, Chief Cameahwait, agreed to supply the Corps of Discovery with the animals they needed to complete their journey in exchange for some clothes, guns, and ammunition. Whether Sacagawea wanted to join the party for the rest of the trip or whether her husband forced her to go along we don't know. When Lewis and Clark left the Shoshone land to travel west, the Indian woman and her baby went with them.

So Sacagawea climbed right along with the men as they made the tortuous trip across the Rocky Mountains that left the troupe exhausted, starving, and sickly, but she did it with a baby on her back. Along the way she regularly safeguarded her fellow travelers simply by her presence, as William Clark testified on October 13: "The wife of Charbonneau our interpreter we find reconciles all the Indians as to our friendly intentions. A woman with a party of men is a token of peace." A few days after that journal entry, an encounter with another group of Indians, caused Clark to say again: "The sight of this Indian woman, wife to one of our interpreters confirmed those people of our friendly intentions, as no woman ever accompanies a war party of Indians in this quarter." With Sacagawea as their interpreter, navigator, and now protector, the expedition soldiered on until it was once again possible to travel by water, and in early November Clark was able to exult, "Great joy in camp, we are in *View of the Ocean*, this great Pacific Ocean which we have been so long anxious to see." In fact, they weren't quite there yet and they were pinned down by bad weather at the Columbia River estuary for more than a week before they actually saw the Pacific. But by mid-November they had made it—with the help of an Indian woman, they had crossed the continent.

Curious Indians came to stare at the strange white men, one wearing "a robe of 2 sea otter skins, the fur of them were more beautiful than any fur I had ever seen," Clark recounted in his journal. "Both Capt. Lewis and my self endeavored to purchase the robe with different articles. At length we procured it for a belt of blue beads which the squaw—wife of our interpreter Charbonneau wore around her waste." Poor Sacagawea had to give up her beautiful blue belt so one of the men could have the fur. She ended up with a blue cloth coat out of the deal.

Having declared "mission accomplished," it was time for the Corps of Discovery to decide where to spend the winter. Everyone voted, even Sacagawea and the slave named York who accompanied Captain Clark. Clark recorded the vote with the woman's name last, and he used his nickname for her: "Janey in favor of a place where there is plenty of potatoes." Food was on their minds, and they were sick of the dried fish they had been eating. The killing of an elk in early December "revived the spirits of my men very much," and then Sacagawea "broke two shank bones of the elk after the marrow was taken out, boiled them and extracted a pint of grease or tallow from them." The elk in the end decided where the winter camp would be—the explorers would settle where the animals were plentiful in what's now Clatsop County, Oregon. The camp was still under construction when the troupe celebrated Christmas with little food, no alcohol, and the last of their tobacco. Still, the party was "cheerful all the morning" and managed to give each other small presents. Captain Clark recorded a gift of "two dozen white weasel tails" from "the Indian woman."

In early January, Clark planned to set out "with two canoes and 12 men" looking for a whale. But Sacagawea was "very impatient to be permitted to go with me, and was therefore indulged. She observed that she had traveled a long way with us to see the great waters, and that now that a monstrous fish was also to be seen, she thought it very hard that she could not be permitted to see either." The young woman had clearly grown feistier over the course of the year! And her baby, nicknamed "Pomp" by Captain Clark, who was just turning one year old probably helped keep the men amused as they whiled away the wet winter and contemplated the long trip home.

In March, the journey east began. Along the way the expedition encountered Wallawallas and Nez-Percé Indians and in both cases the tribes held a Shoshone prisoner in their camps. So the translation train geared up again as Sacagawea forged friendships in the various tribes and discovered shortcuts for the journey. And again, as Lewis noted in May, she made it a more pleasant trip—supplying the men with interesting treats: "Sacagawea gathered a quantity of the roots of a species of fennel which we found very agreeable food." It was probably particularly agreeable given the fact that they had a couple of days before eaten, "several of our stud horses as they have been troublesome to us." Also troublesome was the baby—little Jean Baptiste was cutting teeth and "was attacked with a high fever." A swelling on the baby's neck worried both Lewis and Clark, who acted as the unofficial corps doctors. They gave the baby cream of tartar and applied poultices of boiled onions to his neck around the clock for several days until Lewis could finally declare him "free of fever." The captains had nursed this littlest explorer as though he were the most valuable member of the team.

Heading home the trail was more familiar, but no less grueling in crossing the snow-covered Bitterroot Mountains, finally arriving at Traveler's Rest Creek, near modern-day Missoula, Montana, at the end of June. Then Lewis and Clark decided to split up so they could explore a greater expanse of the area; Sacagawea and her husband and baby would go with Clark to the Yellowstone River and take it to the Missouri. It was familiar terrain to "the Indian woman," who, wrote Clark after a couple of days journey, "informed me that she had been in this plain frequently and knew it well." A week later, Captain Clark was ready to follow Sacagawea's advice: "The Indian woman who has been of great service to me as a pilot through this country recommends a gap in the mountain more south, which I shall cross." For the first time, Clark seemed to be directly consulting the native woman about her land. She instructed him in the migration patterns of the buffalo and explained that a "fort" built of logs and bark was erected by Indians as a defense from "pursuers whose superior numbers might otherwise overpower them." With Sacagawea's guidance, Clark's team moved quickly and was waiting on the Missouri River in what is now North Dakota for Lewis (who had been injured in an accident) and his men when they arrived on August 12, 1806.

Back at the Mandan villages after a year and a half, the explorers "took our leave of T. Charbonneau, his Snake Indian wife and their son child who had accompanied us on our route to the Pacific Ocean in the capacity of interpreter and interpretess." Clark paid Charbonneau $500.33 to cover his services plus the price of a horse and lodging. Sacagawea received nothing. But the captain did make an offer to Charbonneau: "to take his little son, a beautiful and promising child who is 19 months old." Clark had always had a soft spot for little "Pomp," now he was proposing to adopt him. The baby's mother pointed out that the boy was not weaned, but Charbonneau added that "in one year the boy would be sufficiently old to leave his mother and he would then take him to me if I would be so friendly as to raise the child for him in such a manner as I thought proper." Clark would not have to say goodbye. A few days later he wrote to Charbonneau: "Your woman, who accompanied you that long and dangerous and fatiguing route to the Pacific Ocean and back, deserved a greater reward for attention and service on that route than we had in our power to give her at the Mandans. As to your little son (my boy Pomp) you well know my fondness for him and my anxiety to take and raise him as my own child." Clearly Clark thought Sacagawea had not been paid her due.

The Lewis and Clark Expedition arrived in St. Louis on September 23, 1806, after two years and five months in the wilderness. The whole city lined the banks of the river, excitedly greeting the men who had been given up for dead—now they were hailed as heroes. And William Clark made good on his offer to Sacagawea. Instead of sending her baby off to be raised by the white man, the Indian woman moved with her husband and child to St. Louis, where Clark provided for Jean Baptiste's education. In 1823, when European explorer Prince Paul of Württemberg came to America, he hired the eighteen-year-old Jean Baptiste "whose mother was of the tribe of Shoshone or Snake Indians, and who had accompanied the Messrs. Lewis and Clark to the Pacific Ocean in the years 1804 to 1806 as interpretress." The prince took young Charbonneau back to Europe, where he added German, Spanish, and French to his English. When the young Charbonneau came back to the United States in 1829, he began a lifelong career of accompanying explorers and traders into the American West.

The fate of the boy's mother is the subject of some dispute. Sacagawea and Charbonneau stayed in the St. Louis area, where they bought land from Clark but then sold it back in 1811, when the Frenchman and "his wife, an Indian woman of the Snake nation, both of whom accompanied Lewis and Clark to the Pacific," were counted as passengers on a boat heading up the Missouri River. On December 20, 1812, the clerk at Fort Manuel, a fur company trading post in present-day South Dakota, recorded the death of the "wife of Charbonneau, a Snake squaw," adding that she was "the best woman in the fort" and "she left a fine infant girl." The little girl, Lizette, joined her brother as a ward of William Clark. Clark himself listed Sacagawea as "dead" when he did an accounting of members of the Corps of Discovery in the 1820s. Despite those facts, another version of Sacagawea's life gained some currency in the early twentieth century. According to that story, Sacagawea returned to the Shoshones, where she was reunited with Jean Baptiste and the son of her dead sister and lived to age one hundred in 1884. The story is based on

Shoshone oral tradition and the testimony of people claiming to be the grandchildren of her sister's son. And a marker erected by the Daughters of the American Revolution stands on the Wind River Reservation in Wyoming: "Sacajawea, Died April 9, 1884. A Guide with the Lewis and Clark Expedition, 1805–1806."

WHILE SACAGAWEA WAS HELPING LEWIS and Clark explore America's future, Mercy Otis Warren was exploiting the country's past. President Jefferson was interested in both, telling Mrs. Warren that he had urged all the "heads of departments" in Washington to subscribe to her magnum opus: *The History of the Rise, Progress and Termination of the American Revolution. Interspersed with Biographical, Political and Moral Observations.* It was the culmination of half a lifetime of effort by one of the preeminent propagandists of the American cause.

Born in Barnstable, Massachusetts, in 1728, Mercy Otis benefited from a rare advantage for a girl of her day—she was educated with her brothers until they went off to Harvard. She then married James Warren, who championed her political and literary pursuits. In the mid-eighteenth century, as the colonists chafed under British tyranny and taxes, the Warren home in Plymouth throbbed with revolutionary fervor, with Mrs. Warren key to the plotting and planning along with her friend Samuel Adams, her brother James Otis, her husband, and the other Patriots assembled in her parlor, including an up-and-coming lawyer—John Adams. Mercy Warren gave voice to the colonists' complaints through plays and pamphlets promoting American ambitions by ridiculing their English governors. Newspapers up and down the seacoast carried her satirical thrusts at the British and their Loyalist followers (always published under a pseudonym), stoking the fires of revolution several years before fellow pamphleteer Thomas Paine produced his *Common Sense*. Mercy's correspondence with some of the major players on the political scene also fomented revolutionary sentiment. John Adams regularly exchanged letters with the influential writer, and eventually his wife, Abigail, did as well, with the two women forming a close bond. Mercy Warren's outraged letters about British atrocities in Boston helped unite the Continental Congress in Philadelphia in defense of the beleaguered city to the north. And the older woman served as a sympathetic ear to Abigail Adams during John's many long absences.

Realizing that she was living through extraordinary times, Mercy Otis Warren determined to write a history of the American Revolution even as it was unfolding. She started work in 1775, with the active participation of the men she would be writing about, constantly nagging them to send her accounts of debates in Congress, copies of correspondence, and any other privileged information they could provide. At one point, Mercy asked Abigail Adams to send her own letters from her husband; Mrs. Adams ignored the request. Taking up the *History* in fits and starts over the decades, it took thirty years for Mercy Warren to finish and publish it. During that time she suffered the loss of three of her five sons, her eyesight, and her friendships with John and Abigail Adams.

Convinced that their revolutionary co-conspirators had returned in 1788 from their sojourn in England too friendly toward monarchical government, Mercy Warren and her husband no longer saw eye to eye politically with John and Abigail Adams. Like some of the other senior members of the revolutionary generation, who came to be called "Old Republicans," the Warrens were wary of the U.S. Constitution with its strong executive powers, and Mercy had emerged in 1788 from a long hiatus in pamphleteering to publish her *Observations on the Constitution* with the goal of defeating its ratification. But when the new government was established and John Adams elected vice president, his old friend tried to prevail on him for a patronage job for one of her sons. Rebuffed and rebuked by Adams, who huffily told her, "I should belie the whole course of my public and private conduct and all the maxims of my life if I should ever consider public authority entrusted to me to be made subservient to my private views, or those of my family or friends," the relationship never really recovered.

Still, Mercy Warren tried to make peace with the new government. In 1790, she dedicated her first book, and the first publication under her name, *Plays, Dramatic and Miscellaneous*, to President George Washington and received accolades for it from none other than arch-Federalist Alexander Hamilton: "Female genius in the United States has outstripped male." And she resisted the temptation to make her political views public, complaining in response to a request to do so: "Why do my friends call me out on politics?" But she and her husband were seen as Republican radicals in Federalist Boston, so it was with great relief that Mercy Otis Warren welcomed the election of fellow Republican Thomas Jefferson. The time now seemed ripe to seek subscribers to her more than thirteen-hundred-page, three-volume history.

Judith Sargent Murray, a brilliant success at hawking books, went to bat for the older woman. Having lined up more than seven hundred subscribers for her own three-volume tome, Judith was disappointed to admit that her attempts to gather signatures of people pledging to buy Mercy's book reaped only "apologies." There were a number of reasons the history was a hard sell, the feminist Murray explained: John Marshall had come out with a biography of George Washington that covered much of the same ground; Mrs. Warren's politics were not popular in Boston; and "in this Commercial Country, a taste for literature has not yet obtained the ascendancy." Whatever the reasons, and the fact that Warren was a woman was certainly one of them, publication would not be easy. Despite her politics, Mercy received some assistance from her nephew, Federalist congressman Harrison Gray Otis. Dutiful in his effort to sign up buyers, Otis hedged his endorsement of his aunt's work by warning that she was too much under the influence of her "disappointed patriot" of a husband, "although vastly his superior in every sort of literary attainment. She assures me however that she has been strictly impartial." An assurance that turned out not to be true. The solicitations finally collected enough cash to publish and the first volume of the *History* appeared in 1805. Unlike her earlier book, which had been widely acclaimed, this one, Mercy Otis Warren's life work, hit the market with a thud. The only review sneered that she "had not yet yielded to the assertion that all political attentions lay outside the road of female life" and that her portrayal of the actors in the drama of the Revolution was something "a *gentleman* would not, perhaps, have thought prudent."

The anonymous reviewer was right—that's what makes Mercy Warren's history so interesting. No pussyfooting around personal peculiarities for Mrs. Warren; General Charles Lee, for example, was "plain in person even to ugliness, and careless in his manners to a degree of rudeness," but "a bold genius and unconquerable spirit." She was also quick to give credit where she thought it due—even to the evil English—and had no hesitation about inserting her own views as she drew on documents, debates, letters, and other histories in her research. She also treated subjects—like the effect of war on women and children—not usually touched on by male historians. In Connecticut, she wrote, when British soldiers stormed New Haven, their cruelties included the "barbarous abuse of the hapless females who fell sacrifices to their wanton and riotous appetites." Rape, though common, was not something generally documented in wartime.

Neither were women often praised. But in Warren's work the women of Charleston, South Carolina, under British occupation "gave a glorious example of female fortitude. They submitted patiently to inconveniences never before felt, to hardships they had never expected; and wept in secret the miseries of the country, and their separation from their tenderest connections, with whom they were forbidden all intercourse, and were not permitted the soft alleviation of the exchange of letters." The women had refused to participate in "the gaieties of the city"; instead, "they visited and soothed, whenever possible, the miserable victims crowded on board prison ships and thrust into jails." The British officers resented the "conduct" of the women and "exposed them to insults of every kind." This was not the stuff you would read in a history written by a man, but it was an integral part of the story. So was the fact that as the British and Americans roamed through the Carolina countryside, "attack and defeat, surprise and escape, plunder, burning, and devastation, pervaded the whole country, when the aged, the helpless, the women, and the children, alternately fell the prey of opposite partisans." It was an eight-year-long war fought in the front and backyards of America, not only on the storied battlefields recorded by the male historians. And who else was quoting from letters of *Martha* Washington in their accounts of the American Revolution? "In this lady's character," Warren gushed, "was blended that sweetness of manners, that at once engaged the partiality of the stranger, soothed the sorrows of the afflicted, and relieved the anguish of poverty." After the war, Mrs. Washington wrote to the author that she believed that no "circumstance could possibly happen to call the General into public life again."

The British, naturally, come in for a good deal of abuse from the pen of fervid Patriot Mercy Warren, but General Charles Cornwallis was "a man of understanding, discernment and military talents" better at his job than his commander-in-chief, Sir Henry Clinton, who was "indecisive in many instances of his conduct." Clinton "never discovered, either in design or execution, those traits of genius or capacity that mark the great man or hero." Ouch. American faults were also laid bare under Warren's clear-eyed gaze. Explaining the failure of Francis Dana's mission to the Russian court of Catherine the Great, Warren asserted that it "was doubted by many at the time, whether Mr. Dana was qualified to act as envoy at the court of Russia, and to negotiate with such a potent state." He lacked "the address, the penetration the knowledge of courts, or of despotic female, at the head of a nation of machines, under absolute control of herself and her favorites." Dana was still alive and living in Boston when that damning assessment appeared in print.

Most offended by Mercy Warren was her erstwhile friend John

Adams. He had cause: "Mr. Adams was undoubtedly a statesman of penetration and ability; but his prejudices and his passions were sometimes too strong for his sagacity and judgment." Among those "prejudices" acquired while Adams was in England: "A partiality for monarchy appeared, which was inconsistent with his former professions of republicanism." The historian charged that "a large portion of his countrymen" believed that Adams had "forgotten the principles of the American revolution," and that a "pride of talents and much ambition" besmirched the former president's character. Though he was "endowed with a comprehensive genius, well acquainted with the history of men and nations," his former compatriot judged that "honest indignation at the ideas of despotism" were "beclouded by a partiality for monarchy." After several more stabs into John Adams's heart, Mercy Warren claimed that "with more pleasure" she could attest that "notwithstanding any mistakes or changes in political opinion, or errors in public conduct, Mr. Adams in private life, supported an unimpeachable character; his habits of morality, decency and religion, rendered him amiable in his family, and beloved by his neighbors." He might not be a Republican in her view, but at least he wasn't a reprobate. John Adams was furious.

Both members of the Adams couple had early on encouraged Mercy Warren in writing the history and John had urged her to be frank: "The faithful historian delineates characters truly, let the censure fall where it is." Over the years, Adams called to her attention incidents he wanted her to include: "I hope Mrs. Warren will give my Dutch negotiation a place in her History, it is one of the most extraordinary in all the diplomatic records," giving some credence to her condemnation of him as prideful. Though politics had pushed the Adams and Warren couples apart, the two women had renewed their correspondence shortly before John Adams read the *History*. At the end of 1806, Mercy wrote to Abigail reminiscing about the times they had spent together: "The recollection of those visits calls back a thousand ideas that may lay dormant but that can never be erased." Mrs. Warren didn't try to sweep their differences under the rug: "I may censure your politics, yet love you as ever,—you may renounce mine without losing your esteem and affection;—men nor women were not made to think alike on all subjects—it cannot be." Mercy reflected on the past and wondered what her old political colleague John Adams thought of the present: "One half of our time has been a period of the most remarkable revolutions that time has recorded—Should I ask Mr. Adams what he thinks the Emperor Napoleon was made for?" Mercy was still at it; trying to find out everything she could from men in power or, at this stage of her life, from men who had been in power.

In Abigail's reply, agreeing, "If we were to count our years by the revolutions we have witnessed, we might number them with the antediluvians," she supplied her husband's response to the question about Napoleon. Spewing forth anti-European sentiments, Adams sputtered that the emperor was permitted by his Maker "for a cat'-o'nine tail to inflict ten thousand lashes upon the back of Europe as divine vengeance for the atheism, infidelity, fornications, adulteries, incests and sodomies, as well as briberies, robberies, murders, thefts, intrigues and fraudulent speculations of her inhabitants." John Adams was clearly in a sour frame of mind as he turned the question to one of Mercy's fellow Republicans: "May I ask Mrs. Warren in my turn, what was Col. Burr made for? And what can you make of him or his projects?" Adams was needling his old friend about the perfidy of a partisan, but he still said nothing about her *History*. In July 1807, a letter to Abigail was the vehicle for Mercy's reply to John that Burr was "*permitted by his Maker* to exhibit to the world another instance of the abuse of superior talents. . . . He is now arraigned at the bar of justice and of law where the intricacies of his intrigues will doubtless have a clear development."

No response would come from Abigail Adams this time. By then John Adams had read Mercy Otis Warren's *History of the Revolution* and he exploded in a series of letters defending himself and denouncing her. She was unfair to him, he truthfully argued, and she didn't give him enough credit for his many accomplishments, which he proceeded to document, deluging her with copies of government papers to bolster his case. Knowing that he was only adding fuel to the fire, he couldn't stop himself: "All these little anecdotes, you will say are proofs of my 'pride of talent.' Be it so: make the most you can of them, Mrs. Warren." Adams claimed that he was writing "in the spirit of friendship" and wanted to correct her "inaccuracies." Mercy Warren knew better. She was ready to "confute the unfounded charges . . . that my pen has been guided by a malignant heart." Adams's letters were so "angry and indigested" that she protested she scarcely knew where to begin to answer them and Warren managed to find her antagonist's sorest spot and rub it with salt. She had not dealt in her history with the period of the Adams presidency, she contended, because she didn't want to discuss "an Administration that rendered you unpopular indeed. This may be done by some one of that large majority of the people whose suffrages removed you from the presidential rank and placed another in the chair." If she was wrong about him, in other words, why did the voters throw him out of office? She then cited chapter and verse of his promonarchical statements, chided him for his lack of courtesy, and cautioned him somewhat menacingly that she still had on hand all of his old letters and would keep his new ones as well.

Nothing worked. Adams became more and more exercised; he upbraided the whole Warren family, hurling untruths that they conspired with his enemies to defeat him, and he thundered to Mercy that he should "enroll her name with a list of liars and libelers." The history writer's attempts at the cool put-down just goaded him on. In his tenth and, he promised, his last letter, Adams snarled that if he had not known the author of the *History* he would have quoted Pope when reading the parts about himself:

> *"Like a cursed cur, malice before her clatters,*
> *And, vexing every wight, tears clothes and all to tatters."*

"But Mrs. Warren's egregious errors must be corrected, though I cannot, and will not, apply these lines to her. John Adams." It was too much for Mercy: "The lines with which you concluded your late correspondence cap the climax of rancor, indecency, and vulgarism. Yet, as an old friend, I pity you; as a Christian, I forgive you; but there must be some acknowledgement of your injurious treatment or some advances to conciliation, to which my mind is ever open, before I can again feel that respect and affection towards Mr. Adams which once existed in the bosom of Mercy Warren." And so, for a period of more than five years, ended a correspondence that had once been one of the yeastiest in U.S. history.

Four years after demanding an apology from John Adams and hearing nothing from him, the eighty-three-year-old Mercy Warren, by then a widow, was ready to make peace. In the fall of 1811, she asked a mutual friend, Elbridge Gerry, to help mend the rift by delivering a note to her former comrade-in-arms and Adams accepted it. Abigail Adams immediately renewed the relationship, exchanging visits and gifts with the elderly woman who had once been her mentor; it took John a couple of years more before he took up his pen to write again. Still rankled, he told Gerry, "History is not the province of the ladies." It was a far cry from the time after the Boston Tea Party when John Adams insisted the event should be "celebrated by a certain poetical pen, which has no equal that I know of in the country." Back in the early days of resistance to the British, Adams hailed the influential Patriot women, telling Mercy's husband, James Warren, that their two wives had "a share, and no small one either, in the conduct of our American affairs."

In the end, though still grumbling about the history, shortly before Mercy Warren's death, Adams was willing to go on the record about her importance in American affairs. Her play *The Group* was published in several newspapers in the colonies in April 1775, not long before the battles of Lexington and Concord. Poking fun at the British loyalists in Boston, and taking sharp aim at the royal governor, the work had served as powerful propaganda for the Patriots, rallying the rebels against England at a key moment. Because she had written it anonymously, decades later there was a dispute over the play's authorship. Mercy Otis Warren asked John Adams to testify that she, in fact, had written the now-celebrated play. He readily complied.

WHILE OLD FRIENDS John Adams and Mercy Otis Warren were privately accusing each other of treachery, President Thomas Jefferson publicly charged his former vice president, Aaron Burr, with treason against the United States of America. As Mercy Warren noted in her letter to Abigail, Burr would be brought to trial in what would be a national spectacle. At her father's side through much of the long summer of 1807 in the country's first "trial of the century" would be his only child, Theodosia Burr Alston—a prominent figure in the alleged plot. Over the centuries the extent and reality of the Burr conspiracy have never been completely clear, since the disaffected former vice president plotted different scenarios with different people. The basic outline of the allegations: he had enlisted troops to break off U.S. territory west of the Alleghenies, conquer part of Mexico, and form a new nation with himself as emperor and his daughter as empress. Some witnesses charged that he had also vowed to march on Washington, assassinate Thomas Jefferson, and overthrow the Congress. What is clear is that Aaron Burr would have certainly included his daughter, considered "by far the best-educated woman of her time and country," in any grandiose plans for a glorious future.

Even before her mother died when Theodosia was not quite eleven, father and daughter had been extremely close. Like Thomas Jefferson with his daughter Martha, Aaron Burr paid close attention to his little girl's education, outlining a rigorous course of study for her to follow. But unlike Jefferson, Burr had no hesitation about educating a girl in what were considered masculine subjects; in fact, he was inspired to treat the sexes equally by Mary Wollstonecraft's radical *Vindication of the Rights of Women,* first published in 1792. After staying up most of the night reading Wollstonecraft, Burr told his wife that "your sex has in her an able advocate. It is, in my opinion, a work of genius." Why hadn't anyone else recognized the book's brilliance, he wanted to know, "Is it owing to ignorance or prejudice that I have not yet met a single person who had discovered or would allow the merit of this work?" Aaron Burr kept a portrait of Mary Wollstonecraft with him throughout his life, giving it away on his deathbed as a precious token to a friend.

When he was in the Senate in the early 1790s, boarding at the house in Philadelphia run by Dolley Madison's mother, Burr regularly wrote to his daughter in New York with endless instructions: keep a journal, inform me of your mother's health, learn Greek—this last when she was just ten years old. By then Theodosia already knew French. She was also nursing her dying mother under her father's tutelage. As he relied on the ten-year-old to medicate her mother, sending her various remedies to try, including hemlock (!), prescribed by Philadelphia's eminent Doctor, Benjamin Rush, Burr couldn't refrain from also correcting her spelling. Theodosia dutifully cataloged all the "cures" she administered (the little girl didn't know where to get the laudanum her mother was desperate for) while demonstrating her progress in Greek and composing stories for the amusement of her demanding father. Though he was tough to please, Burr did take delight in his daughter and periodically praised her for "performance above your years." Then, in the summer of 1794 with her father off in Congress, Theodosia's mother died. "My little daughter though much afflicted and distressed, bears the stroke with more reason and firmness than could have been expected for her years," this man whose own mother had died when he was only two sadly told his uncle.

Only a couple of weeks after his wife's death, Aaron Burr was back in Philadelphia ordering his grieving child to translate the Roman writer Terence. A few short months later, Burr traveled to Albany to argue a court case, leaving Theodosia in the care of a family of French émigrés, telling her that she could not accompany him because "your manners are not yet quite sufficiently formed to enable you to do justice to your own character." He never let up on the little girl: practice Greek verbs, play the harp, study arithmetic, pay the help, date your letters, stand up straight, don't eat dessert. At the age of eleven, Theodosia fulfilled his every assignment. And her father occasionally rewarded her with plaudits for the "wit, sprightliness and good sense" of her letters. But the parental pressure could not have been greater: "The happiness of my life depends on your exertions; for what else, for whom else do I live?" he hectored her when she was fifteen, warning that if she should "relax your endeavors, it would indicate a feebleness of character which would dishearten me exceedingly. It is for my sake that you now labor." While Burr berated his daughter to keep her nose to the grindstone he also began what was to become a lifetime of regaling her with tales of his own romantic amusements. Hardly fair.

A beautiful as well as accomplished young woman, Theodosia assumed the duties as her father's official hostess at his New York mansion, Richmond Hill. Burr lost his Senate seat in 1796 to the man he had defeated in the last election, Alexander Hamilton's father-in-law, Philip Schuyler, but he remained one of the most prominent and brilliant lawyers in New York and an active participant in politics there as a member of the state assembly. Gracing Theodosia's parlor were the men we know as the Founding Fathers—Washington, Adams, Jefferson, Madison, and even Hamilton. Another caller: New York Mayor Edward Livingston, who brought the young beauty onto a French warship in the city's harbor. "You must bring none of your sparks on board, Theodosia," the mayor joked, because of the gunpowder on the ship, "we shall all be blown up." Even when her father was away Theodosia entertained illustrious guests, including a then-famous Mohawk chieftain, William Brant Thayendanegea, who was much taken with the young woman's ministrations. Another guest, who described Burr's daughter as "elegant without ostentation, and learned without pedantry," declared that she "dances with more grace than any young lady of New York." The occasional curmudgeon grumped that "her reading has been wholly masculine . . . she is an utter stranger to the use of the needle and quite unskilled in the different branches of domestic economy." One visitor in the summer of 1800, who must not have minded Theodosia's lack of skill in the womanly arts, was young Joseph Alston, a wealthy rice planter from South Carolina.

Theodosia turned seventeen on July 2, 1800, as her father was strategizing a Republican victory in the coming presidential election. Alston was a good party man and Burr used him to transmit information to southern Republicans when the young man returned to Charleston. But Joseph Alston, smitten with Theodosia, couldn't stay away for long. By the time the election results were known and the tie between Jefferson and Burr a conundrum facing the country, Alston was pleading with Theodosia to marry him. She told the twenty-one-year-old that Aristotle judged a man too immature for marriage before age thirty-six. Joseph somewhat petulantly replied that he never adopted "the opinion of anyone, however respectable his authority, unless thoroughly convinced by his arguments." He then went on for pages refuting Aristotle and the philosopher's acolyte, Theodosia: "I give you full credit for your talents, but there are some causes so bad that even you cannot support them." To his northern love, Alston talked up his native South Carolina and its women: "No Charleston belle ever felt 'ennui' in her life." Alston then put pen aside and set sail for New York City. In the snows of January, the smitten southern man had to travel on upstate to Albany to find the peripatetic Burrs. There, on February 2, 1801, as the House of Representatives was assembling in order to break the tie between Thomas Jefferson and Aaron Burr, Theodosia married Joseph Alston. Burr's enemies spread the rumor that he had forced the match in order to gain South Carolina's electoral votes, and get his hands on Alston's money. But the young woman seemed happy with her choice and deserted her doting father to take up residence on a plantation in the sultry South Carolina low country, a far cry from the bustle of New York City. The couple stopped in Washington for the inauguration in March and then journeyed south by carriage for twenty days to Theodosia's new home.

"The only solid consolation is the belief that you will be happy," the disconsolate vice president wrote a few days after his swearing in, "and the certainty that we shall often meet." Burr immediately began planning a trip south, protesting that "nothing but *matrimony*" could interfere. As the spring wore on, it wasn't marriage to one woman but trysts with many that caused the vice president repeatedly to postpone his voyage. He never mentioned his lady friends by name in his letters to his daughter, but found ways to let her know which women were the latest objects of his desires: "I have had a most amiable overture from a lady 'who is always employed in something useful.' She was, you know, a few months past, engaged to another; that other is suspended, if not quite dismissed." He counted on his daughter as a confidante: "I want your counsel and your exertions in an important negotiation, actually commenced but not advancing," he told her as Theodosia planned to return to New York for a visit and sightseeing expedition to Niagara Falls. Undertaking another long journey just a couple of months after her trek to South Carolina must have seemed daunting to the teenage bride, but it would be nice to escape her duties as mistress of "The Oaks," a large plantation with an unfinished main house, which had "absorbed all my soul. My only friends and companions of late have been masons and painters, etc." Plantations not only made for hard work—they were isolated and lonely. No wonder Theodosia went running back to New York. It was also summertime, a time when heat and malaria sent the white owners of the rice plantations on the Waccamaw River off to the seaside or the mountains, leaving the slaves to tend their fields and fend off the mosquitoes. Two hundred men and women in bondage worked for Joseph Alston; Theodosia, the daughter of an abolitionist, would be responsible for their clothing and medical care. Her new situation and new obligations must have come as a shock to this woman who knew how to conjugate Greek verbs but was useless with a needle. How beckoning the familiar rooms of

Richmond Hill, where her father hypocritically kept some slaves himself, must have seemed. And how exotic the trip to Niagara Falls and the backwoods of New York. While touring in the north Theodosia and Joseph called on the Mohawk "King" who had dined at Richmond Hill a few years before. After the visit, a letter from the chieftain singing Theodosia's praises evoked a teasing response from her father: "It would have been quite in style if he had scalped your husband and made you Queen of the Mohawks." The joke later seemed a harbinger of things to come.

The happy couple then traveled south to be feted by friends. As the daughter of the vice president, Theodosia and her husband were invited to dinner at the executive mansion. "My friend Mrs. Madison was there," presiding as hostess and making the bachelor president's invitation to a woman "lawful." Casting a critical eye, Mrs. Alston reported, "The house is really superb; it is built with a white stone which gives it an elegant appearance outside, inside it is well divided, but not as elegantly furnished as it ought to be." Then it was back to South Carolina, to the grand Alston city house in Charleston, and more letters of instruction and information from her father (Read the newspapers! Did you hear Philip Hamilton was killed in a duel?), with the admonitions increasing once he learned that she was pregnant. "You must walk a great deal," Burr lectured, beginning what would become an intense interest in his as yet unborn grandchild. "Get a very stout pair of over shoes, or short boots, to draw on over your shoes. But shoes to come up to the ankle bone, with one button to keep them on, will be best." She was old enough to advise him about the women in his life and to argue politics and Pliny but not to pick out her own boots!

Determined to be in South Carolina for the birth of the baby, Burr's letters through the winter and spring evidence his frustration with the slow pace of congressional business ("The judiciary bill debating in the House of Representatives . . . it may and it may not be finished next week"), interspersed with some gossip from the capital city ("Anna Payne is a great belle. Miss Nicholson ditto, but more retired, frequently, however at Mrs. Law's"). Finally, unable to wait out the Congress, the vice president left town for his southern sojourn before the lawmakers adjourned. At the beginning of May, Burr reached Clifton Plantation, Joseph's father's place, and there learned that his daughter had gone on to Charleston to await the birth. Failing to land a spot on the stagecoach—"The stage was full—not even a vacant seat for the vice-president"—he opted to stay with Joseph's father, who would bring him to Charleston in a couple of days. On the way, Burr told Theodosia, they would stop at the plantation of the dauntless Rebecca Motte, a renowned Revolutionary heroine who had aided America in defeating the British in South Carolina. Playfully, Burr added to his nine-month pregnant daughter that he had heard "you are *well,* and your husband *ill.* This is exactly wrong, unless he means to take the whole trouble off your hands, as some good husbands have heretofore done; so at least Darwin records." It was, to say the least, an unusual father-daughter relationship.

Aaron Burr's mission might have been entirely familial, but he was still the vice president of the United States. The newspaper announcement of his arrival created a stir: the citizens of Charleston threw a banquet in his honor and used him as a draw at a benefit theater performance. The triumphant Burr proceeded on to Savannah for more tributes before returning to Charleston to greet the object of his odyssey—Aaron Burr Alston, born May 22, 1802. Within weeks his grandfather whisked the baby and his ailing mother off to New York. Joseph Alston, busy campaigning for a seat in the state legislature, stayed in South Carolina. Though Theodosia missed her husband, she was thrilled to be back in New York: "Every woman cannot fail to prefer the style of society, whatever she may say." New York, however, was more than a diversion for the new mother; it was a place to seek medical help for the terrible pain she suffered following childbirth. No doctor of the time was ever able to relieve her of the agony she often experienced for the rest of her life. But the baby was a joy, his smiles "possess a magic which you cannot conceive until you see him," she told little Aaron's absent father. She wondered, "How does your election advance? I am anxious to know something of it; not from patriotism, however. It little concerns me which party succeeds." This was no partisan Abigail Adams, but this *was* a woman concerned about her husband's political fate even though she had chosen to spend months away from him. And she wanted him to miss her: "I am very happy you have chosen chess for your amusement. It keeps you constantly in mind how poor kings fare without their queens." But, Theodosia warned, Joseph Alston's queen would never be well. "You must summon your fortitude to bear with a sick wife the rest of her life." Unfortunately for her, she was right.

Back in South Carolina for the winter of 1802–1803, Theodosia Alston almost died, but she rallied and wisecracked to her father that she was able to spare her family "the trouble of burying, mourning, etc." Burr, meanwhile, was wooing and failing to win a woman in Philadelphia. He wrote his daughter every detail of the intricate intimacies, moaning, "You could unravel this thing in five minutes. Would to God you were here." Without the advice of his daughter Burr lost his love. By summer Theodosia had recovered and was ready, this time with her husband along, to make the trip north again. The couple stopped in Washington as well as New York and found Aaron Burr's old friend Dolley Madison, "still pretty, but oh that unfortunate propensity to snuff-taking." Mrs. Madison would in later years use her "unfortunate" habit to her advantage. The Alstons also "drank tea with Mr. and Mrs. Gallatin by invitation." Official Washington stood ready to entertain the vice president's daughter, no matter how unpopular her father was with members of his party.

The trip back home with a seventeen-month-old was like all trips with seventeen-month-olds: "Mr. Alston appears so distressed and worn out with the child's fretting, that it returns on me with redoubled force." Baby fusses, Dad gets mad, takes it out on Mom. Some things *really* don't change. Eight long cramped-in-a-carriage days later, she wrote that it was an "unpleasant" journey that "frets the boy, who has acquired two jaw teeth since he left you." A teething baby and her in-laws on board had tested the limits of Theodosia's patience: "We travel in company with the two Alstons. Pray teach me how to write two *A's* without producing something like *Ass*." But Mrs. Alston would not be soon relieved of her in-laws; she lived with them while workmen on the house at The Oaks dawdled on with her husband off at the state capital, Columbia, for the legislative session. And her own father reverted to taskmaster mode, this time insisting that her baby boy should be learning his letters at age eighteen months: "He may read and write before he is three years old," and speaking French! Burr was besotted with the little boy.

Throughout the winter and spring of 1804, Aaron Burr interrupted his instructions for his namesake with Washington gossip about the Bonapartes and the Merrys and then news of his campaign for governor of New York. As the three days of voting were under way, Burr reported: "Both parties claim majorities, and there never was, in my opinion, an election, of the result of which so little judgment could be formed." But soon the results were all too clear; he had "lost by a great majority." For the next couple of months Burr barraged his daughter with anecdotes about his latest amorous affair and badgered her for news of his adored grandson with no hint of his increasingly hostile exchanges with Alexander Hamilton. While the intermediaries between the enemies were delivering what would be deadly missives, Burr celebrated Theodosia's birthday by hanging her picture in the dining room, where he and some friends "laughed an hour and danced an hour."

Not until the night before the duel, when he declared his last will and testament and composed his farewell letters, was there any indication to his only child and confidante that Aaron Burr was about to pick up a gun and aim it at Alexander Hamilton. Even then, he never explicitly told her what he was up to. Instead, it was to his son-in-law that Burr revealed, "I have called out General Hamilton and we will meet tomorrow morning." Alston would be left with "all that is most dear to me—my reputation and my daughter." As he faced death, his daughter was foremost in her father's thoughts, or more precisely, his daughter's mind was foremost in his thoughts: "Let me entreat you to stimulate and aid Theodosia in the cultivation of her mind. It is indispensable to her happiness and essential to yours." Burr would, if he could, lecture from the grave. "If you would differ with me as to the importance of this measure, suffer me to ask it of you as a last favor." In the end Burr outlived both his daughter and son-in-law.

When the duel turned Aaron Burr into a fugitive from the law, he started acting on his monomaniacal dream of empire. The only indication he gave Theodosia of what he was hatching was a brief mention of his foray into Florida, with the report, "It is a fact that the Spanish ladies smoke cigars." Moving north to Savannah the disgraced vice president found that southerners, no friends of staunch Federalist Alexander Hamilton, still revered him: "I have invitations which it would require weeks to satisfy." The attention probably helped convince Burr that he could easily assemble a band of loyal followers. After a quick visit with Theodosia and her family, the vice president bravely headed back to Washington, a city where politicians of his own party had roundly rejected him. All along the way he was greeted by admiring crowds.

It turns out that the trip south was something of a reconnaissance mission. Before he had started his journey, the vice president of the United States had contacted the British ambassador with a shocking proposition: hire Burr and he would help His Majesty's Government "effect a separation of the western part of the United States from that which lies between the Atlantic and the mountains." Ambassador Anthony Merry transmitted that information to the foreign secretary with the warning that Burr's character was wanting and his person reviled by both political parties, but that he still had good connections and that his "great ambition and spirit of revenge against the present administration" could make him most useful. Aaron Burr, who had fought the British in the Revolution, and sworn as the nation's second-highest-ranking official to support and defend the Constitution of the United States, was proposing to a foreign power a plan to rip the country apart. When his term as vice president came to an end, he immediately headed west to enlist recruits for his outrageous undertaking. His letter to Theodosia that she would "hear of me occasionally on my route" when he left Washington also hinted at what was afoot: he would proceed to Pittsburgh, on to St. Louis, through Tennessee, then to New Orleans, and along the way he would meet with his old comrade General Wilkinson, now the governor of the Louisiana Territory, for enjoyment and "other particulars." He would end his journey with a visit to his daughter's family, and presumably an explanation of what he was up to.

From Pittsburgh, then the gateway to the West, in April 1805, Burr told Theodosia that he would be boarding a boat that was "properly speaking, a floating house . . . containing dining room, kitchen with fireplace, and two bedrooms" so he would arrive in style in the backwoods towns of the West. Stopping in Nashville, Burr was hailed as a visiting luminary, the cannon salute underlining his conviction that he would be able to sign up men eager to follow him. After being entertained by Andrew Jackson, Burr moved on down the Cumberland River, met up with Wilkinson, traveled south to Natchez, and finally to New Orleans. All along the way he stopped at the "house of some gentleman on shore" where the former vice president "always met a most cordial reception." Whether he was also conspiring with these gentlemen to join a secession movement is even today an open question.

In New Orleans, Burr was reunited with his old New York friend Edward Livingston, who had just married a woman "rich in beauty and accomplishments." Livingston had moved to Louisiana after a scandal on his watch as mayor of New York, and his Creole bride captivated the ladies' man Burr: "Fair, pale, with jet black hair and eyes—little sparkling black eyes, which seem to be made for far other purposes than those of mere vision." Louise D'Avezac and Edward Livingston had married at the Ursuline convent on June 3, 1805, at midnight. The Ursulines might have been cloistered but they managed to stay at the center of action. When the nuns heard that the famous Aaron Burr was in town, they sent him a letter "congratulating me on my arrival." He was informed that "the saints had a desire to see me. The bishop conducted me to the cloister. We conversed at first through the grates; but presently I was admitted within." There stood the unholy Burr inside the Ursuline cloister! He found "none of that calm monotony which I expected. All was gaiety, *wit,* and sprightliness." The nuns gave him a tour of the building, served him a "repast of wine, fruit, and cakes," and promised to pray for him. The Ursulines didn't miss an opportunity to woo a politician who might someday be helpful.

Though Burr was quite taken with New Orleans, where he was "received with distinction," he had work to do organizing his ambitious designs. So it was back through the wilderness along the border with Spanish Florida, up to Natchez, and on to Nashville. He sent Theodosia a map so she could trace his route but advised: "On the map you will see laid down a road from Nashville to Natchez . . . this is imaginary; there is no such road." It was a tough trip but a useful one for Burr's purposes. A week with General Jackson at the Hermitage in Nashville, on into Kentucky, Missouri, Ohio, Burr was treated as a great eminence who was all the while talking of grand plans, but always different plans to different people. To those disaffected with Washington, he talked of secession for the West; to expansionists like Andrew Jackson, he talked of seizing Spanish territory; to Jefferson haters, he talked of overthrowing the government. At the time, Burr shared none of his schemes with Theodosia, who, unbeknownst to her father, lay so sick she was sure she was dying. "Something whispers me my end approaches," the just turned twenty-two-year-old wrote to her husband in a letter intended as her will. She told Joseph how to dispose of her few personal possessions and how to bring up their son, and then offered her heartbreaking farewell: "Death is not welcome to me. I confess it is ever dreaded. You have made me too fond of life. Adieu then, thou kind, thou tender husband. Adieu, friend of my heart. May heaven prosper you, and may we meet hereafter." Thinking these might be her last words, Theodosia added a postscript: "Let my father see my son sometimes. Do not be unkind towards him whom I have loved so much, I beseech you." Apparently all was not copasetic between husband and father. The postduel Aaron Burr could draw crowds of gun-toting backwoodsmen in the West, where no love had been lost for Alexander Hamilton, but east of the Appalachians, the former vice president wore the whiff of scandal. And Theodosia Alston knew her husband had a political career to consider.

Transportation and communication might have been primitive in the early nineteenth century, but news traveled fast. By August 1805, at the same time Theodosia contemplated her demise, the Federalist newspaper *Gazette of the United States* considered the question of how long it would be "before we shall hear of Col. Burr being at the head of a revolution party of the Western Waters." How soon, the paper demanded to know "will Col. Burr engage in the reduction of Mexico, by granting liberty to its inhabitants and seizing on its treasures, aided by British ships and forces?" Burr hoped the answer would be very soon; he kept badgering Ambassador Merry for British support, threatening to go to England's enemy, France, for backing if Britain didn't come through. But the Court of St. James's had enough on its hands dealing with Napoleon. Burr needed manpower, munitions, and money. He amassed the first two throughout 1806, with the help of military men Wilkinson and Jackson; for cash, when he received no answer from the British, he turned to his wealthy son-in-law and to a rich Irishman he had befriended, Harman Blennerhassett and his wife, Margaret. Once Burr's daughter was brought in on the plot, she enthusiastically endorsed it. In September, along with her husband and son, Theodosia and her father joined forces with the Blennerhassetts in Ohio, and, with dreams of noble titles dancing in their heads, they contrived to conquer Mexico. At a social gathering, Mrs. Blennerhassett "interrupted the dancing and entertainments to make a speech urging the young men present to seize the opportunity to go south with Burr and his men."

As long as they thought the plan only involved invading Mexico and "seizing its treasures," men were ready to sign on. But what Burr didn't know as he conspired with General Wilkinson to raise an army of invasion against a Spanish possession was that Wilkinson was a Spanish spy. He had been on Madrid's payroll as Secret Agent Number 13 for decades. This traitor to his country, fearful that he would be implicated in the plot by either the Americans or the Spanish, turned traitor to his friend Burr as well. In November 1806, Wilkinson reported to President Jefferson that his former vice president was preparing to capture New Orleans and move on from there to Mexico. Jefferson, who had been hearing rumors and receiving reports of Burr's empire-building schemes for months, finally acted. He summoned his cabinet and issued a proclamation declaring that western insurgents plotting to invade Mexico were in violation of the law and must be stopped. Everyone was enlisted to seize the conspirators—the army, state militias, public officials, private citizens should all be on the alert to arrest anyone associated with an attack on Mexico.

The proclamation set the whole country abuzz. Rosalie Calvert suspected that word had even reached her father in Belgium and that he would be worried about his American investments: "I hope you are not alarmed by what is said about the separation of the western states. No one knows yet what Colonel Burr's real plan is, but whatever way it goes, we have nothing to fear here. Nor does it appear likely that bonds will be affected." With an arrest warrant hovering over their heads, Burr's would-be followers dispersed; his dream was dead and Aaron Burr was once again on the run as a fugitive from justice. Despite a disguise, he was recognized and captured in the wilds of what is now Alabama. A passel of soldiers then undertook to escort him, with a few attempted escapes along the way, to Richmond, Virginia, where the former vice president would stand trial for treason. Word of his journey spread rapidly: "I suppose you have heard that Col. Burr is retaken and on his way to Richmond for trial," Dolley Madison told her sister. Adding about the man she had once named guardian for her son, "That is all I know about him." The day after he arrived in Richmond, March 27, 1807, under guard at the Eagle Tavern, Burr was finally able to write his whereabouts to his daughter, with the news: "I am to be surrendered to the civil authority tomorrow."

The arraignment of Aaron Burr kicked off what President Jefferson hoped would be a show trial ending in the conviction of his former vice president for treason against the United States of America. The president had already declared Burr guilty, and the grand jury, filled with political opponents, expected a hanging. His cocky self-confidence temporarily jolted, Burr was feeling sorry for himself when he rhetorically asked Theodosia: "Was there in Greece or Rome a man of virtue and independence, and supposed to possess great talents, who was not the object of vindictive and unrelenting persecution?" He then assigned her to research such persecutions and write him an essay about them! Despite the rigged grand jury, Burr had an ace in his hole: Chief Justice John Marshall had assigned himself the case. The fact that Jefferson's old enemy would be in charge caused an outcry among Republicans: "The democratic papers teem with abuse against me and my counsel, and even against the chief justice," Burr railed to his daughter. "Nothing is left undone or unsaid which can tend to prejudice the public mind, and produce a conviction without evidence."

The newspapers had "greatly exaggerated" Burr's activities as far as Federalist Rosalie Calvert was concerned. While the grand jury waited to hear testimony from the chief witness, James Wilkinson, she had already judged Burr: "From all appearances, he is not guilty, but he is a dangerous and devious man." General Wilkinson, another such man, finally showed up in Richmond in mid-June to testify against his former friend. So did several other old allies. And though Burr was fighting back, "It is the general opinion that he will be convicted," Dolley Madison told her sister. The testimony produced the prosecution's desired effect—the grand jury proceeded to indict Aaron Burr and his accomplice, Harman Blennerhassett, for treason, a hanging offense. The jury also handed down a misdemeanor indictment for the alleged plan to attack another country. Reporting the charges to Theodosia, Burr commanded: "I beg and expect it of you that you will conduct yourself as becomes my daughter, and that you manifest no signs of weakness or alarm." It was off to prison for Aaron Burr while he awaited his trial.

If Theodosia was worried about her father's imprisonment as she prepared to join him in Richmond, Burr was quickly able to put her mind at ease. He had been allotted a three-room apartment in the new penitentiary and his jailer was "quite a polite and civil man." He recounted their exchange on his first night in jail:

"*Jailer,* I hope, sir, it would not be disagreeable to you if I should lock this door after dark.

"*Burr,* By no means sir: I should prefer it, to keep out intruders.

"*Jailer,* It is our custom, sir, to extinguish all lights at nine o'clock; I hope, sir, you will have no objection to conform to that.

"*Burr,* That, sir, I am sorry to say, is impossible; for I never go to bed till twelve, and always burn two candles.

"*Jailer,* Very well, sir, just as you please. I should have been glad if it had been otherwise; but, as you please, sir."

Prisoner or not, Burr was still considered a personage, and one with such magnetism that he could almost always get by on his charm. He was permitted visitors of both sexes and there was room as well for Theodosia: "If you come I can give you a bedroom and parlor on this floor." But again he warned, "Remember, no agitations, no complaints, no fears or anxieties on the road, or I renounce thee." Only brave faces for the Burrs. When Aaron Burr's trial for treason began on August 10, 1807, Theodosia Alston and her five-year-old son were in the room along with her husband, who had protested mightily that he had no involvement in the plot.

The city of Richmond was so overrun with reporters and on-lookers the trial was conducted in the House of Delegates chamber to accommodate the crowds. All eyes were on Theodosia, according to one historian: "Beautiful, intelligent far beyond the average women of her time, she was the center of admiration throughout the entire trial." Particularly taken with her was a member of Burr's defense team whose "idolatrous admiration of Mrs. Alston" made him blind to Burr's faults, according to co-defendant Blennerhassett. "Nor can he see a speck in the character of Alston, for the best of all reasons with him,—namely, that Alston has such a wife." Burr's defense team—including the defendant himself—was composed of some of the best lawyers in the country, who were able to poke holes in the damning testimony from people the would-be conspirators had confided in. The Blennerhassetts' gardener, for one, swore he had been told, "Colonel Burr would be the King of Mexico, and Mrs. Alston, daughter of Colonel Burr, was to be the queen, whenever Colonel Burr died," but no witness ever pointed to Burr committing an "overt act" of treason. He might have *planned* to raise an army, *talked* about invasions, but no witness actually saw him *doing* what he plotted. No overt act, ruled Marshall, no treason. Though the jurors clearly thought the defendant guilty, the judge's unwelcome instructions tied their hands. On September 1, somewhat testily the jury declared: "Aaron Burr is not proved to be guilty under this indictment by any evidence submitted to us. We therefore find him not guilty." Theodosia's brave face had been justified: "The knowledge of my father's innocence, my ineffable contempt for his enemies, and the elevation of his mind have kept me above any sensations bordering upon depression," she wrote after the acquittal. "Since my residence here, of which some days, and a night, were passed in the penitentiary, our little family circle has been a scene of uninterrupted gaiety."

The Alston family returned to South Carolina so Joseph could pursue his political career. Aaron Burr was also found not guilty in the misdemeanor trial, but ordered to Ohio to face more charges there. Instead, he went underground, running from both the law and his creditors. He gave Theodosia various aliases to use in writing to him and advised: "My letters to you will be often in a strange handwriting, and with various signatures. Sometimes feminine." With only the slightest bit of encouragement from a British friend, Burr decided to sail to England to try again for endorsement of his secessionist scheme and dream of Mexican empire. On June 7, 1808, the night before he left New York, under the alias of G. H. Edwards, Theodosia, or "Mary Ann Edwards," secretly met with her father for the last time. She was to tell the New York newspapers that he had headed by land to Canada. A little more than a month later he was writing to her from London.

The English were ready to entertain Burr in fine style; he particularly enjoyed the attentions of famed philosopher Jeremy Bentham and prevailed on him to send his works to Theodosia, who eagerly devoured the tomes: "Jeremy Bentham has opened a new and deeper vein of political and moral science." On her side of the Atlantic, the ailing Mrs. Alston was finding life as the daughter of a fugitive one of solitude: "The world begins to cool terribly around me." And then the news came that the British would not be backing Burr's Mexican plan. Theodosia was distressed: "I cannot part with what has so long lain near my heart, and not feel some regret, some sorrow. No doubt there are many other roads to happiness, but this appeared so perfectly suitable to you, so complete a remuneration for all the past." She had bought into the fantasy. Thoughts of what her unstable parent might do next tormented her: "Where are you going, what will occupy you, how this will terminate, employ me continually . . . tell me that you are engaged in some pursuit worthy of you." Theodosia not only worried about her father, she missed him: "Everything is gayer, more elegant, more pleasant where you are . . . I would to heaven I could be with you." But that was not to be, she was too sick to travel to Europe, and troubles between the United States and Great Britain were heating up, causing Theodosia to reflect, "Thank God, I am not near my subjects; all my care and real tenderness might be forgotten in the strife." The American woman had not given up the dream of reigning over her "subjects" in Mexico.

WHILE THEODOSIA ALSTON fed her father's fantasies of building an empire, the other woman whose life was upended by Aaron Burr was busy establishing something real and lasting—an institution for the poor children of New York. In 1806, Alexander Hamilton's widow helped the still socially active Isabella Graham found the Orphan Asylum Society of New York, designed to serve the growing number of children left homeless in the ever-expanding commercial city. Eliza Hamilton's good deeds would have been memorable even if she were a wealthy woman with time and money to spare, but her husband's debts left her to fend for her seven children while also tirelessly guarding the general's reputation. Fortunately for the family, Elizabeth Schuyler Hamilton was up to all tasks.

The second daughter in a family of fifteen children produced by the union of two aristocratic New Yorkers—Revolutionary War General Philip Schuyler and his wife, the intrepid Catherine van Rensselaer Schuyler—Eliza had grown up as a witness to courage. When the British army marched on Saratoga, sending American refugees streaming south, Catherine Schuyler drove her wagon north, rushing to burn the wheat fields of her country home before the enemy could harvest the crop. And the family held its ground at the Schuyler mansion on the frontier in Albany throughout the war, though it was under constant threat by marauding British troops and their Indian allies. Despite the occasional attack, the sprightly young women of the family chafed under the dullness of hiding out at home. The oldest Schuyler sister, the daring Angelica, solved the boredom problem by jumping out of her window and eloping with British businessman John Church, who was running the commissary for George Washington's troops. The younger sisters did nothing so dramatic (though several eventually also chose the window-jumping exit to marriage), but in 1780 they did take a trip to New Jersey, visiting not far from the Continental Army winter camp at Morristown. There Eliza, then called Betsey, met the brilliant Alexander Hamilton, who had already made such a reputation as a ladies' man that Martha Washington teasingly christened her tomcat "Hamilton."

The dashing young colonel quickly wooed and won the somewhat plain but very well-connected Betsey Schuyler, who, despite her husband's wandering ways, remained deeply devoted to him throughout their marriage. Eliza Hamilton serves as the prototype for the woman we've seen so many times since—the good political wife who stands by her man as he makes an admission of guilt. The solid support of the former Miss Schuyler saved the illegitimate immigrant Alexander Hamilton's political life when he was forced to confess to his affair with Maria Reynolds. And though his friends warned him to be more discreet in his dalliances with Eliza's sister, Angelica Church, Hamilton's wife remained loving and loyal to both members of that pair. (Angelica seems to have cut quite a swath through the lives of some of the most notable men of the time. She and her rich husband moved abroad for a while after the war, living grandly in London and Paris. Thomas Jefferson appeared quite taken with Mrs. Church when he was ambassador to France, writing a lovelorn letter about his "dejection of mind" after one of her visits: "The morning you left us, all was wrong, even the sunshine was provoking, with which I never quarreled before." And Louisa Adams had her suspicions about Angelica's relationship with the recent widower Thomas Pinckney when he was ambassador to Britain: "Major Pinckney's constant visits at Mrs. Church's and the late hours at which he returned home," she remembered years later, "caused much scandal in our little world; fortunately he was sent on a mission to Spain and was for a time forgotten.")

In much the same way that Aaron Burr depended on Theodosia's husband to make up for his insolvency, Alexander Hamilton counted on Eliza's father to take care of her and the children if he died in the duel. "Probably her own patrimonial resources will preserve her from indigence," he wrote hopefully in his will. But it turned out that Philip Schuyler had already divvied up much of his wealth among his eight surviving children, and when Hamilton's executors examined the personal finances of this man who had been the architect of the nation's financial system, they found that his family would be destitute. In order not to besmirch Hamilton's memory, his friends tried to raise funds secretly for the support of Eliza and the children. But assuming that Philip Schuyler must have money, contributors were few and far between. When Schuyler died just four months after Hamilton, and Eliza's siblings generously donated to her their shares of the inheritance, the Widow Hamilton was still forced to sell her house. Sadly she left "The Grange," the country estate she and Alexander had built together, moved into New York City, and started lobbying the Congress for back pay due to her husband from his military service. It wasn't until twelve years after Hamilton's death, years when her children grew up and the older boys went to college, that she received what was her due from the federal government.

Instead of falling apart, as she might well have done—not only had she suddenly lost her husband only a few years after her son had been shot and her daughter gone crazy, her mother and one of her sisters had died in those years as well, followed soon by her father—Eliza Hamilton's strength supported others. All through her married life, even as a new offspring showed up every couple of years, she and her husband had taken in the needy children of friends and relatives. Now she was ready to offer her assistance on a wider scale. Not quite two years after Alexander Hamilton's death, Eliza banded with some of the other socially conscious women of New York to form the Orphan Asylum Society, the forerunner of orphanages founded by concerned women in other cities around the country.

Though Isabella Graham's Society for the Relief of Poor Widows with Small Children was still going strong in 1806, it didn't fill the needs of motherless children, as Mrs. Graham noted in her memoir: "It had long before that time been discovered by the ladies of the

Widows' Society that some systematic provision should be made for the orphan children of the deceased widows, as it was not within the scope of their society to assist them after the mothers had been taken away." If the mothers died, the children were likely to end up on the streets, or be thrown into the poorhouse with unsavory adults. According to the official history of the Orphan Asylum Society, written in 1893, some of the orphans had been taken care of by individual trustees of the Widows' Society and "the young daughters of these ladies undertook to teach them to read and sew" but "before many years had passed, the number of orphan children had increased beyond the provision which private generosity could make for them, and these ladies resolved that a public appeal should be made."

The women now had the experience to know what was needed—a wide-scale public fund-raising drive and a full-on lobbying campaign in the legislature—it was just a question of doing the hard work. They held their first organizational meeting on March 15, 1806, at the City Hotel on Broadway. "Mrs. Hamilton, widow of Gen. Alexander Hamilton" was one of the foremost "promoters of the new organization" along with Isabella Graham and her daughter Joanna Bethune. In her role as "Second Directress," Eliza would take a leadership role—first setting up a shelter, which immediately admitted twelve children.

A few months later when the Orphan Asylum Society adopted its constitution, Eliza must have endorsed with special feeling the words in the preamble: "God himself has marked the fatherless as the peculiar subjects of his divine compassion." Her youngest fatherless child was not yet five years old, her oldest so mentally incapacitated that she would need care for the rest of her life. The constitution was quite clear on the duties of the small board of trustees—including regular inspections of the orphanage. It was also progressive in its view of the children: none would be admitted without having passed an examination by "a respectable physician," and when it was time for them to go out to work they would have a one-month trial period, "at the expiration of which, should the employer not be satisfied with the child, or the child with his place, they shall be permitted to choose again." Constitution in hand, the women then petitioned the state legislature for a charter of incorporation, which was granted slightly more than a year after the first meeting. The New York legislature decreed that all of the holdings of the corporation "shall be managed, directed, and disposed of by a Board of Trustees, to be composed of a First and Second Directress, Treasurer, Secretary, and seven Trustees," elected by the members of the society. Under the laws of the day, these women could not own property if they were married, but they could run a corporation. The legislature did make sure, however, to protect a woman's husband from liability should the corporation suffer from "any loss occasioned by the neglect or malfeasance of his wife." This was tricky new territory for property laws affecting women, and as female benevolent societies cropped up in places like Boston, Providence, and Savannah, they often placed an unmarried woman in the treasurer's seat so a married woman's husband couldn't get his hands on the organization's money.

After only a year, the New York orphanage had moved to larger quarters, but the women knew they needed a much bigger building, one that could accommodate two hundred children. On four lots in Greenwich Village donated by a trustee, they constructed a fifteen-thousand-dollar orphanage in 1807. Now they really needed money. Though Joanna Bethune's son rosily remembered her saying, "In any time of need, a few words stating that the funds of the society needed replenishing, thrown into a newspaper was sure to bring in donations equal to the need; more frequently, the money came in before the appeal was made," of course it wasn't that easy. Construction of the building plunged the society into debt; to come up with the considerable cash needed to pay it off, political action was called for. The women successfully petitioned the state legislature for five thousand dollars. Those public funds plus appeals in the churches and at benefit performances made it possible for these hardworking women to take in more and more of the burgeoning city's left-behind children. Though the society was determined to save the eternal souls of the young charges, the women who ran it also understood that the general public would benefit from their endeavors. Operating on the since much-proven theory that early-childhood intervention saves money in the long run, the women argued that without the orphanage the youngsters "might become vagrants and ultimate burdens" on the city. That convincing case kept the Orphan Asylum Society alive even in tough financial times. More than two hundred years later, under the name Graham-Windham, the institution created by Eliza Hamilton and her colleagues continues to serve New York's needy children and their families.

FROM THE TIME of his swearing-in for a second term, Thomas Jefferson started agitating for his daughter Martha Randolph to move to Washington for a sojourn at the White House, bringing along her six children: "Arrangements made up stairs since you were here, and additional furniture now providing will accommodate them all," the president insisted. Acquiescing to her father's wishes, Martha again sent some shopping requests to Dolley Madison, who was in Philadelphia where she had gone to be treated for a knee infection: "a fashionable wig of the color of the hair enclosed, a set of combs for dressing the hair, a bonnet shawl and white lace veil, for paying morning visits." For her part, Dolley was eager for her husband to fill her in on what was happening at home, including "if Mrs. Randolph is expected and all the other news you have time and patience to give me." Soon she had her answer in the form of "a commission from the president to procure several articles for Mrs. Randolph." The only problem: the president didn't send any money. But Dolley was always ready to oblige. With considerable confusion about arrangements, as James Madison told his wife with much understatement, "Mrs. Randolph is not arrived nor does the president know the precise time that she will," the Randolph brood landed at the president's house at the beginning of December 1805. Martha was seven and a half months pregnant.

"Mrs. Randolph the president's daughter is here. I am going to pay my respects this morning," Louisa Adams wrote to her mother-in-law. "The question of etiquette still occasions a great deal of trouble here and the heads of departments are very much puzzled how to act as it regards Mrs. Merry, who still keeps up her state." The Merry Wars had resumed as a result of the Randolph visitation. Elizabeth Merry, who had boycotted the White House since her initial indignity, sent a note to Martha asking if she was at the executive mansion in her capacity as the president's daughter, or as the wife of a Virginia gentleman. (It would have never occurred to Elizabeth Merry to ask if Martha were there as a Virginia gentlewoman.) In matters of protocol such distinctions mattered. Mrs. Merry would be expected to pay the first call on the president's daughter; the wife of the Virginia gentleman would call first on the wife of the British minister. Of course, in dealing with the Jeffersons, Mrs. Merry was asking for it. Martha answered that it was as the wife of a Virginia gentleman that she was there, but that she was there as a visitor and, as such, in this democracy where all were equal, the resident, Mrs. Merry, should call on her first. Thomas Jefferson's daughter was ready to joust along with her father in the battle over etiquette, though soon Martha was neither making nor receiving calls. "Mrs. Randolph is a charming woman," Louisa Adams wrote Abigail and she "expects to be confined in three weeks." James Madison Randolph arrived on January 17, 1806, the first baby born in the executive mansion. The woman who attended Martha recounted the birth to Louisa Adams: "After the baby was born she was desirous of giving her patient something like nourishment," but she couldn't find any food "nor a servant in the house of whom she could get anything—it was Bachelor Hall."

By spring, Margaret Bayard Smith could report: "Mrs. Randolph and Madison called and I promised to take tea with Mrs. R. in the evening." This follower of Jefferson found tea with her hero and his daughter and children enchanting: "While I sat looking at him playing with these infants, one standing on the sofa with its arms round his neck, the other two youngest on his knees, playing with him, I could scarcely realize that he was one of the most celebrated men now living." All the early histories of Washington cite Martha Randolph's visit as a high point in the still somewhat primitive social life of the federal city. The accounts repeat the praise of the Marquis de Yrujo, the long-serving Spanish ambassador, who deemed her "fitted to grace any court in Europe." And her father's enemy, John Randolph, who had challenged her husband to a duel, called Martha "the noblest woman in Virginia." Louisa Adams recounted years later, "Mrs. Randolph was a very amiable woman who to know was to respect." The chroniclers also repeat the story of the eldest Randolph daughter Anne's first ball. The fifteen-year-old arrived after her mother was already there; when Martha saw Anne come in the room, she turned to the woman next to her, Dolley Madison's sister Anna and asked, "Who is that beautiful young woman?" Anna laughed. "Don't you know your own child?" This story is so often told in contemporary literature that it's likely close to the truth. It's easy to imagine the scene—Martha so preoccupied with the baby and all of her other small children that she had no time to say goodbye to Anne as the dressed-up teenager left the executive mansion, Martha arriving at the ball harassed and then beholding this grown-up creature. It came as a shock that this was her daughter.

Despite her slaps in the face from President Jefferson, Elizabeth Merry soldiered on, socializing with the rest of official and unofficial Washington. After the Englishwoman had been in Washington a year, Dolley Madison confided to her sister that she and Elizabeth had become "unusually intimate" despite "Mrs. Merry's airs." Louisa Adams, who made no pretense about treating everyone equally, had an explanation for those airs: Mrs. Merry, "This *Lady* of high pretensions was said to have been a bar maid at a tavern in Norfolk who charmed a rich country squire who married her, died soon after and left her a large fortune—after which she married Merry, who was *poor,* for the sake of his rank in the corps Diplomatique." Then she appended, "This was the history told at the time—perhaps scandal."

At Mrs. Merry's dinners, Louisa cattily remembered, "she never took her seat at the table, but had her supper sent or carried up to her by some of our exalted Senators." Or, better yet, she went off "to play chess with John Randolph, who, she told him, she did not consider a *man.*" Still, Louisa later remembered, "We saw Mrs. Merry frequently." Elizabeth Merry might have boycotted the president's table, but official and social Washington flocked to hers. On her visit to her brother's, "I dined once with Mrs. Merry," Nelly Custis Lewis told an old friend. "I think her manners extremely affable and friendly." (The fact that Thomas Jefferson spurned Mrs. Merry might have influenced Nelly's judgment. She shared her grandmother Martha Washington's view that "one who knew so well the *first President*" would never "wish to be noticed by the present chief magistrate.") "Mr. Merry did me the honor of escorting me to table first, a preference which earned me the envy of all the other women present," Rosalie Calvert exulted to her sister. "In short, it was a delightful evening." By the time the Calverts returned the invitation, Anthony and Elizabeth Merry were headed home: "They have been extremely civil to us and I greatly regret that he has been recalled." The man expected to be the next British ambassador was wooing an American woman, Louisa Adams explained to her husband, causing Mrs. Merry to hope "the Americans will find the airs of one of their own country women more supportable than those of a foreigner."

Whatever they thought of Elizabeth Merry and how she had been treated by the Jefferson administration, the women in Washington were horrified by the behavior of the new French ambassador. He was a wife-beater. When Louis Marie Turreau and his wife appeared in the capital city, Dolley Madison thought they made "a vast addition to the comfort of this place." Madame Turreau was "good natured and intelligent, generous plain and curious," the enthusiastic wife of the secretary of state told her sister Anna; "I never visit her in her chamber but I crack my sides a laughing." Though the Frenchwoman spoke no English, the two understood each other "very well" and Dolley's French was improving. After such a full-throated announcement of their friendship, it must have been distressing to Dolley to learn a couple of weeks later that the ambassador "whipped his wife and abused her before all his servants." Quickly, the chief diplomat's wife warned her sister: "Don't breathe it in your country, as it will make them all so odious as *he* deserves to be." Dolley was worried that the abuser's actions would tilt public sentiment against France. But there was no way to keep Turreau's atrocities quiet; "the poor woman's cries were the scandal of the neighborhood," according to a historian of the period. Rosalie Calvert, who lost no love for the French, gave a contemporaneous account: "There has been a terrible uproar here about the Emperor's minister, General Turreau, who proposed to introduce some customs and manners for which the national character, although quite degenerate, is not yet sufficiently corrupted." He dared, she seethed to her father, "even though his wife was in the house" to bring in some naked dancing girls and "he beat Madame Turreau, who had displeased him, very cruelly . . . he then threw her out of the house. She is returning to France, which will not only damage Turreau, whom everyone spurns, but the French in general. These kinds of things are not tolerated in America." But, in fact, though "the French Minister was a brute," Louisa Adams noted with disgust, whose "poor vulgar wife was always so *beaten,* that the aid of the constabulary *force* was frequently called in to protect her in the fray," Turreau *was* tolerated because "Mr. Jefferson's admiration for the French Revolution," caused Washington society to ignore "all the scandalous scenes practiced by the man and tamely bow to his gross effrontery lest la Belle France should show her indignation."

Washington gossip, still a mainstay of the capital, of course didn't just focus on foreign visitors. There was plenty of homegrown scandal to keep tongues wagging, including the city's first divorce involving none other than Martha Washington's granddaughter, Eliza. Only the two youngest Custis children, Nelly and George Washington, had gone to live with their grandparents after their father died during the American Revolution. The two older girls— Elizabeth Parke Custis and her sister Martha—had stayed with their mother, who soon remarried. But George and Martha Washington kept close tabs on the girls, and when Eliza decided to marry British land speculator Thomas Law, Washington insisted on a prenuptial agreement for his step-granddaughter. It turned out to be a wise precaution. Nearly twice the age of his bride-to-be and the father of two "Asiatic sons" from his time in India, Law was described as an "eccentric" by society writer Anne Wharton. George Washington claimed the prenuptial contract was necessary because Law was "a stranger" but the general might have also been skeptical of Eliza's sticking power. "Since childhood Mrs. L. demonstrated a violent and romantic disposition," Rosalie Calvert, who had heard all the family stories, told her sister. Rosalie's husband was Eliza Law's uncle, and after her separation Mrs. Law spent a good deal of time at the Calvert plantation, Riversdale. "When Mrs. L. entered society, she was very pretty, rich, and quite intelligent. Her relatives and connections were the most respectable. Consequently, she was much admired and flattered. She never cared about the compliments she was given on her beauty, but she was always very vain about her mind and knowledge." The marriage was a disastrous one: "Never were two people less suited to live together, but during the life of her grandmother Mrs. Washington, to whom she was most attached, they restrained themselves in order to spare her pain."

Once Martha died, however, it was a completely different story. Rosalie was never indiscreet enough to divulge the details, but everybody knew them. Thomas Law went off to London in 1804, and, according to an account published that year, Eliza "eloped with a young dashing officer in the army. Mr. Law returned only to part with one of the most accomplished ladies in the land." To her sister, Dolley Madison fretted about her friend: "The fashionable talk here is of Mrs. Law and her affairs—she expects soon to be fixed on a farm by herself and the observations are terribly against her." To put it mildly. Capitol architect William Thornton joked to a friend that his wife would soon send an account of Eliza "in colors that even a description of Cleopatra's gala suit could not touch."

Thomas Law did not, however, charge his wife with adultery: "He has very generously declared her insanity to be the cause of his parting," Louisa Adams wrote, perhaps with irony. What shocked Louisa was the news that "the child is to be taken from her mother and placed at a boarding school. This is setting the opinion of the world at defiance." Thomas Law later affirmed that the divorce was due to "disagreement in disposition" and that "no elopement took place." He at least tried to protect the good name of his daughter's mother. Rosalie explained to her sister in Belgium that America was different from her native land: "As for what you say about the flirtations of your gentlemen and ladies, we are not yet so advanced. Quite contrary to Europe, the women of our better classes are generally the most virtuous. All of our young men have mistresses, as do some of our married men, but the latter not publicly." Eliza Law was definitely of the "better classes" and needed to reestablish her claim to virtue. She resumed her maiden name and thought she would "buy a small property in the country and dabble in agriculture," according to Rosalie, but "in her tastes and pastimes she is more man than woman and regrets that she can't wear pants." By the time Eliza Custis Law Custis moved to her new home she had been living in Rosalie and George Calvert's bustling household for a year. A proponent of large families early in her marriage, Rosalie soon tired of her constant pregnancy and childbirth. When her sister in Belgium accused George of "too much activity," Rosalie defensively replied that what she had feared was her fourth pregnancy in five years had, to her relief, turned out to be a "false alarm." Soon after she wrote that letter, however, Rosalie was pregnant again, though still nursing her baby, Louise, who was "quite frail." Louise never developed the ability to walk or talk and died at age five. Rosalie Calvert would live to bear nine children and bury four.

CHILDBEARING AND DEATH WERE CONSTANTS in the lives of early nineteenth-century women and Louisa Adams's pregnancy the spring and summer of 1806 had the effect of lengthening an already excruciating separation from her little boys, George and John. After her defiant stay in Washington with her Johnson family in the summer of 1804, she went back to Quincy with her husband the following year. When it came time to return to Washington for the congressional session that winter, the Adams family insisted that she leave her two small children behind. Louisa simply didn't have the emotional fortitude to buck both her husband and mother-in-law. Four-year-old George went off, like so many family members before him, to be educated by Abigail's sister Mary Cranch. Two-year-old John stayed with his grandparents. Louisa was miserable without them: "I hourly feel the loss of my children more sensibly," she moaned to her mother-in-law. "Kiss my darling children for me over and over again and remind them constantly of their mother whose every wish on this earth centers in them." Then Louisa gave instructions as to what to do should they suspect that George had worms. She was making a point—she was the mother and she knew best. But Louisa's moment of bravado soon faded as she waited for news of her children. "Having been compelled to leave them I cannot command my feelings and must trust to your kindness to let me hear frequently."

Abigail was not having any of it: "There cannot be anything more disagreeable than transporting young children twice a year," she lectured. "I should suppose that your own judgment, experience and good sense would have convinced you of the propriety of the measure without compulsion." She too had been separated from her children, Abigail reminded her daughter-in-law, "and know how great the sacrifice and how painful the task—but I considered it the duty of a parent to consult the interest and benefit of their children." Wanting her children with her marked Louisa as a bad mother, according to Abigail, and her failure to write to Mary Cranch made her an ungrateful niece as well. That criticism provoked Louisa's always at the ready prickliness about her family's failed finances. She hadn't written Mrs. Cranch because: "I did not feel myself authorized to write to her and feared that my addressing her unasked would betray a troublesome solicitude for the welfare of my child who I very well knew would receive every tender care and attention." Her family's situation had "given a harshness to my character which does not naturally belong to it and rendered me cold and fearful of forcing attentions where they might not prove acceptable." This was one touchy lady. But Louisa wasn't going to grovel. Even as she apologized, she admonished her mother-in-law about her handling of little John: "I fear my dear Madam you are too indulgent to his appetite." Abigail wasn't the only one who was ready to find fault.

Despite missing her children, Louisa was finding some amusement in Washington. The talk of the town was the new Tunisian ambassador, who "was a great admirer of handsome women, and always insisted upon holding them under his cloak as it possessed many *virtues.*" There were a good many exotic characters roaming the capital. On Christmas Day, with only women in the house, "a whole party of Cherokee Indians came in . . . they insisted on hearing the piano which my sister played for them and we were obliged to give them beads and ribbons and feathers before we could get rid of them." Christmas services, with "wretched" preaching, were held at the Capitol, where "you cannot think of the purity of heaven in a place so altogether worldly; where corruption faces you in every corner." Once Christmas was past, the social season began in earnest, starting with the New Year's reception at the president's house, where there was "a great crowd drawn by curiosity to see the Tunisian Ambassador." Louisa Adams really enjoyed "a party at Mrs. Madison's. She is the cynosure of all eyes. A really charming woman . . . possessing great influence in society and considerable interest in the political world which she was said to *use* with much discretion. The Foreign Ministers were at her feet and the world seemed to bow before her." A good object lesson for the wife of a future secretary of state.

When the congressional session ended, John Quincy went back to Boston to teach some courses at Harvard, leaving the pregnant Louisa in Washington because it was considered dangerous for her to travel. She looked "forward to his return with the most anxious impatience and should it please heaven to spare me and my infant anticipate with delight the moment when I shall present it to receive a father's blessing." But it was not to be. Toward the end of a truly miserable pregnancy that confined her to bed and left her feeling, she told John, "even my approaching hours of pain hold out some prospect of relief," Louisa answered an urgent summons from her sister whose child was dying. In the heat of a Washington summer, she walked "a long mile" to attend to her sister, watched the baby die, and walked back home. The next day she "gave birth to a dead child with the thermometer at a hundred and neither father nor children near me to console me for my sufferings." She managed to write the news herself to her husband five hundred miles away. John Quincy Adams recorded his receipt of the letter in his diary on June 29, 1806: "Her child (a son) was born dead. Her own danger had been very great. But she was so much recovered as to be able to write herself." The next day the saddened father admitted yielding to his grief and trying to count the blessings of his two living children. But the seemingly hardhearted John Quincy also felt for his wife: "Her letter affected me deeply by its tenderness—its resignation— and its fortitude. As soon as I was able to hold a pen I wrote to her." It was one of the kindest letters he ever sent Louisa, telling her how grateful he was to heaven "for having preserved you to me through the dangers of that heavy trial both of body and mind which it has called you to endure." He invited his wife to join him in Boston, rather than wait for him to return for winter in Washington. She couldn't wait to get well enough to go.

Even as Louisa Adams suffered through a difficult pregnancy and the devastation of a lost child, she somehow stayed interested in the political world around her. She told John of a change in U.S. ministers to England; James Monroe would be coming home, William Pinkney of Maryland would be going, but "the last dispatches which arrived from England are said to be so conciliatory it is perfectly unnecessary to send any one to settle the difference," reported the

hopeful daughter of an Englishwoman. Someone *was* needed to settle the differences right there at home where "John Randolph has
challenged T.M. Randolph for his speech in the house." Luckily for
President Jefferson the duel between his political opponent and
cousin, the firebrand congressman John Randolph, and his son-in-
law, Thomas Mann Randolph, never took place. And, as tired as she
might have been of separations from her husband and children, Louisa was determined that John Quincy stay in public office. When he
contemplated resigning from the Senate that summer, she scolded:
"Self and family comfort must sometimes be sacrificed for the general good and though I am conscious how much this sentiment must
operate against myself, still I feel irresistibly impelled to express it
from an ardent desire to see at least some men of respectability and
talents adorning public stations." Louisa Adams was not as different
from her mother-in-law as she thought.

Congressional families from that time to this have failed to solve
the dilemma faced by Louisa and John Quincy Adams—where to
live. That winter, John returned to Washington for the Senate session, leaving his wife, with her sister as a companion, in Boston where
she could be with her children, at least most of the time. "John is at
Quincy," Louisa told her husband in January, "where I think it is
probable he will stay, great part of the winter. I am reconciled, as
your Mother cannot live without him." Abigail didn't want to part
with her three-and-a-half-year-old grandson, and she and her
daughter-in-law seemed to be settling in somewhat. When the little
boy shuttled back to his mother in Boston and refused to go to
school, Louisa cited Abigail as her ally: "Your mother says it is of no
consequence and you know I am too much inclined to agree with her
in opinion." It was John Quincy Adams who was beginning to dis-
agree with his mother's opinion, not about raising the children but
about running the country. He started casting a series of votes that
eventually led to a split with his father's Federalist Party. "Your father," teased Louisa, "still cannot account for the vote of a *certain
friend* of mine."

The former president was "always kind and affectionate" to Louisa Adams, and he and Abigail made regular visits to their son and daughter-in-law's house in Boston. On one, when they found little George with a broken collarbone, an injury incurred when he was pushed out of a swing "by the Otis boys," John Adams gave the six-year-old a quarter for his bravery. The little boy gave it to a school friend and "told him to run and spend it all in gingerbread for the boys, and when *he* was *President he* would make *him* Secretary of State." Louisa was flabbergasted. She was also just about to have another baby. On August 18, 1807, when Charles Francis Adams was born, just fourteen months after her last birth, he at first appeared to be another stillborn. But the baby survived and less than two months later, nursing-mother Louisa and little Charles and a maid joined John for a harrowing ride, first by ship and then by stagecoach, to Washington. In New York, as the women were walking toward a carriage, "a man snatched my baby out of the maid's arms and ran up the street with it; myself and my nurse running and screaming after him." The man ducked into a house where they couldn't find him, but then "he brought my boy and put him into my arms, excusing himself by saying that the child was such a perfect beauty, he thought he must show him to his wife." What a scare! No wonder she griped that "Congress should not grudge mileage, nor the people when their Members thus peril life and comfort to get to their Post." The least the public could do, in her view, was pay for the trip. But the travails of travel were soon forgotten in the tumult of the congressional session.

"Mr. Randolph has commenced the Session by making a violent attack upon the administration," Louisa informed Abigail. Vituperative eruptions from John Randolph were hardly unusual, but this time he had a point. President Jefferson had failed to call Congress back to Washington after the "affair of the Leopard." On June 22, 1807, the British ship *Leopard* attacked the U.S. frigate *Chesapeake,* just off the Norfolk, Virginia, coast. The captain of the *Chesapeake* swiftly surrendered, but the British refused to recognize the white flag, killed three Americans, wounded eighteen, and boarded the ship to remove four sailors they claimed had deserted His Majesty's Navy. America demanded retaliation. "This fraças between our frigate and an English ship has produced great ferment in this country," Anglophile Rosalie Calvert warned her father. "Our rogue of a president will glory in a war with England. Good-bye then, to all American trade, to all the merchants who conduct it, to all the banks that make their fortune on it. Good-bye too to the profit from our tobacco, grain, etc." Rosalie turned out to be right about the economic effects of the "ferment," though she was wrong about the president wanting war. Cautiously, Jefferson told his daughter Martha that he thought the British fleet planned no more hostile acts but still: "We are making all the arrangements preparatory to the possible state of war, that they may be going on while we take our usual recess." And then he retired to Monticello for the summer.

Back in Washington in the fall, the president blithely declared to Martha: "The war-fever is past." But Louisa Adams begged to differ with him: "We hear of nothing but war. The P[resident] however has no idea of anything of the sort which gives me great hope that the negotiation may terminate amicably." Though Jefferson was determined to pursue peace, Britain and France were making it hard. At war with each other, each nation was trying to stop the United States from trading with the other by harassing U.S. vessels. The British practice of impressment, or boarding ships and kidnapping sailors they branded as British and forcing them to serve the Crown, was especially offensive to Americans. Jefferson, looking for a way to end the harassment while avoiding war, convinced the Republican-controlled Congress to pass the Embargo Act, forbidding international trade to and from American ports. The effect of the law was exactly what Rosalie Calvert had predicted—the American economy was crippled by it and crafty citizens circumvented it without concern for the consequences.

Eleven-year-old Ellen Randolph wrote to her grandfather, the president of the United States, that her Aunt Virginia said, "The embargo has thrown the dissipated inhabitants of Williamsburg in great confusion. The ladies say they cannot give up tea and coffee and the gentlemen wine." He responded that the ladies were wanting in patriotism "and that principle and prudence will induce us all to return to the good old plan of manufacture within our own families." And poor Martha Randolph, always eager to please her father, actually wove 157 yards of homespun. But for many Americans it wasn't imports that were the issue, it was exports. They couldn't sell their goods abroad. Even the president fretted about the fallout for his personal fortune. Jefferson, who announced in December 1807 that he would not run for a third term, was winding up his time in Washington in debt, but he hoped a good return on his crops would bail him out "if the embargo does not deprive me of the proceeds."

At least Jefferson's letters to his daughter could reach her; Rosalie Calvert's missives from Maryland had no hope of making it to her father in Belgium, but still she angrily assessed the situation: "Our good-for-nothing president does all the harm he can but dares not declare [war] against England—it migh cause a revolution if he did. There is a frightening stagnation in the towns—a number of merchants have gone bankrupt. This year is bound to produce momentous events whose outcome is impossible to foresee." Louisa Adams agreed: "The cry for war seems to redouble, and it is generally supposed impossible to avoid it," she told Abigail early in 1808, adding, "The presidential election is a subject which likewise furnishes a large proportion of our present conversation. Parties are becoming extremely violent." In that context, Louisa found "our situation here this winter is not very pleasant as it is universally believed your son has changed his party and the F[ederalists] are extremely bitter."

John Quincy Adams had been the only Federalist senator to vote for Thomas Jefferson's embargo, infuriating his fellow New Englanders whose manufacturing and shipping depended on trade with Britain. His mother tried to take his side, telling her daughter Nabby Smith that though "the embargo distresses us all" it was better than war. And the Federalist newspapers stirred Abigail Adams's blood in her son's defense: "Upon every occasion they attack your brother with a venom and spite, which shows fully how much they dread his talents." New England threatened rebellion or secession, talk of disunion was abroad in the land, and Rosalie Calvert forecast to her father concerned about his U.S. investments: "The eastern and northern states will detach themselves and we will have a king in the south." Again, her crystal ball for the future was wrong, but her assessment of the present was not: "The effects of the embargo here are quite ruinous. If it continues for much longer, all the merchants will fail. The farmers and planters can't sell their commodities— nobody pays and everything is expensive." The Jefferson administration, convinced the economic sanctions would work if it could just staunch the rampant smuggling, called on Congress to pass more and more restrictive laws against trade. John Quincy Adams voted with the Republicans for them all and in March 1808 officially switched parties. Abigail Adams was appalled, telling her son that news of him caucusing with the Republicans "staggered my belief." The Federalist-dominated Massachusetts legislature met to choose Adams's successor months before the scheduled election and in June he resigned from the Senate. His mother judged that he had acted like "a true American," though John Quincy did feel "wounded in the house of his friends."

By then, though the new president wouldn't take office for a full year, the campaign for Jefferson's successor was in full swing. Rosalie Calvert, the Federalist, announced, "Jefferson is definitely out, but it is still undecided whether we will have a Democratic president or not." James Madison, Jefferson's secretary of state, was the chosen heir, but he was closely tied to the despised embargo. Some northern Republicans were throwing their weight behind Vice President George Clinton, and some southerners, led by Jefferson's nemesis, John Randolph, were going instead for James Monroe. The Federalists once again fielded Charles Cotesworth Pinckney. Abigail Adams knew her husband's old running mate wasn't up to it. "Mr. Madison I think will be our next president," she predicted to Nabby. "Pinckney is not the man calculated to ride the storm and stem the torrent." By summertime, Jefferson reported with some confidence to Martha, "All doubt of the election of Mr. Madison has vanished, although some of the New York papers still keep up a useless fire."

It was not just the New York papers that went on the attack against Madison. "Your friend Mrs. Madison is shockingly and unfeelingly traduced in the Virginia papers," New York Congressman Samuel Mitchill wrote to his wife. Dolley Madison was lampooned as a promiscuous libertine who sold her sexual favors for votes, an uncaring wife who had abandoned her first husband on his deathbed. Somehow Dolley held her head high as she managed her husband's campaign, entertaining politicians at her F Street house in Washington during the congressional sessions and in the country at Montpelier over the summer. "The Secretary of State has a wife to aid in his pretensions," Congressman Mitchill handicapped the race. "The Vice-President has nothing of female succor on his side." (Clinton's wife had died seven years earlier.) Succor or no, Dolley had her work cut out for her if she wanted her husband to succeed: "The President and M have been greatly perplexed at the remonstrances from so many towns to remove the Embargo," she observed to her sister, "the evading it, also, by our people is a terrible thing." But opposition was only growing stronger. Abigail Adams who had been willing to give the embargo the benefit of the doubt now believed: "The embargo must be repealed, and the vessels permitted to arm. The people of the Northern States will not suffer it to continue much longer." But Madison and Jefferson turned tin ears to the voters, insisting that if only the public would comply with the law, it would have the desired effect of making Britain back down.

In August of election year, the Madisons visited Monticello, where Martha Randolph had just given birth to her eighth child ("and hopes its her last"), and preparations were under way for the wedding of the oldest of Thomas Jefferson's grandchildren, seventeen-year-old Anne. Martha was also beginning to lay the groundwork for her father's retirement from public life: "As the *period* of your labors draws near, my heart beats with inexpressible anxiety and impatience," she assured him, "that the evening of your life may pass in serene and unclouded tranquility is the daily prayer and as far as my powers will continue will be the dearest and most sacred duty of your devoted child."

By the time the Electoral College votes were cast, it was another landslide for the Jefferson wing of the Republican Party: 122 for James Madison, 47 for Charles Cotesworth Pinckney, 6 for George Clinton, who would continue to serve as vice president. After the count Pinckney concluded that he "was beaten by Mr. and Mrs. Madison. I might have had a better chance if I had faced Mr. Madison alone." The lopsided victory masked the near-universal unhappiness with the embargo, especially among Federalists like Rosalie Calvert, who had decided, "with Madison we can only go from bad to worse." The new president, with none of Jefferson's style or stature, would have some placating of the public on his plate. But James Madison had a decided advantage over the outgoing president—he had Dolley Madison.

CHAPTER FOUR

The First Term of James Madison and the Presidentess

1809–1813

DOLLEY PAYNE MADISON
The Granger Collection, New York

"MY CONGRATULATIONS AT A MOMENT when you are about to fill a character the most dignified and respectable in society," Eliza Collins Lee wrote to Dolley Payne Madison two days before the inauguration of the fourth president of the United States. Eliza knew her old friend from Philadelphia was "peculiarly fitted to the station, where hospitality and graciousness of deportment, will appear conspicuously charming and conciliating." Indeed, Dolley Madison *was* "peculiarly fitted" to the role of First Lady, which she carried off with style and strength throughout her husband's two terms in office and for decades beyond as the affectionately entitled "Queen Dolley."

"She looked a queen" at the nation's first Inaugural Ball. "She had on a pale buff colored velvet, made plain, with a very long train, but not the least trimming, and beautiful pearl necklace, earrings and bracelets. Her head dress was a turban of the same colored velvet and white satin (from Paris) with two superb plumes, the bird of paradise feathers." Margaret Bayard Smith waxed rapturous in her description of the Madison inaugural. And the ball was just the icing on quite the cake of a day. "The Capitol presented a gay scene" for the swearing-in ceremony. "Every inch of space was crowded and there being as many ladies as gentlemen, all in full dress, it gave it rather a gay than a solemn appearance." The one exception to the festive air—the new president seemed the soul of solemnity: "Mr. Madison was extremely pale and trembled excessively when he first began to speak, but soon gained confidence and spoke audibly."

From the Capitol the crowd converged on the Madison home on F Street and then moved en masse to the executive mansion, where Thomas Jefferson hosted a farewell fete. An ardent admirer of Jefferson, Margaret Smith was just one of the many ladies sorry to see the bachelor president go. Jefferson humorously remembered a similar departure when Benjamin Franklin left Paris: "The ladies smothered him with embraces and on his introducing me to them as his successor, I told him I wished he would transfer these privileges to me, but he answered, "'You are too young a man.'" Margaret felt, given the fact that Jefferson was about to turn sixty-six, "now this objection was removed," but she didn't have the nerve to say so.

Later that night at Long's Hotel, Dolley stole the show: "It would be *absolutely impossible* for any one to behave with more perfect propriety than she did. Unassuming dignity, sweetness, grace. It seems to me that such manners would disarm envy itself and conciliate even enemies." Margaret Smith wasn't exaggerating. Dolley did, at least for the evening, bring peace to warring Britain and France. She sat at the head of the crescent-shaped dinner table with the French minister on one hand and the British on the other. "She really in manners and appearance answered all my ideas of royalty," enthused

Margaret. "She was so equally gracious to both French and English, and so affable to all." That affability would serve Dolley Madison well as "Presidentess," a title conferred on her by the *National Intelligencer*'s report on the Madison inaugural.

The triumph of the inauguration must have been sweet indeed for Dolley Madison. The campaign had been particularly nasty, with newspapers printing outlandish falsehoods about her sex life. The childless Madison, small in stature, was rumored to have been "unsexed" by his "overly-sexed" wife. The eccentric Virginia congressman John Randolph claimed to have evidence of Dolley's indiscretions, which he threatened to reveal. Stories circulated that Thomas Jefferson had "pimped" Dolley and her sisters in exchange for votes in Congress. This was truly awful stuff. And it must have come as something of a shock. There had been similar stories of a tawdry nature in the early days of the Jefferson administration, but Dolley had become the belle of the Washington ball in the intervening years. At one "dance assembly" the scandalous Betsy Bonaparte showed up wearing a muslin dress dampened so it would cling to her shapely, underwear-free body revealing all, but it was Dolley Madison who received an ovation from the crowd when she sailed in perfectly attired. As wife of the secretary of state and surrogate presidential hostess, she had toiled tirelessly to calm the churning partisan waters, but none of that seemed to matter during the presidential campaign. Neither did the fact that she had recently lost her mother, a sister, and some little nieces as close to her as her own child. Now, with James Madison sworn in as president of the United States, Dolley put the attacks behind her and "was affable to all."

To put her affability to use, Dolley Madison needed a place to display her talents—she needed a stage. Her F Street home had ably performed that function for the wife of the secretary of state, but the president's house was going to take some work. Jefferson had shored up the structural soundness of the mansion (though Louisa Adams complained that the house was cold: "The president was very sparing of his fuel"), but that was about it. Members of Congress

crammed into bare-bones boardinghouses had no interest in cough-
ing up funds for the executive residence, so the president made little
attempt at décor, other than furnishing the place with his own
pieces, which he took with him back to Monticello. When Dolley
Madison saw her new home's sorry state, she launched a lobbying
effort to convince Congress of the need to turn the house into a
suitable site for the head of state. Soon after she traipsed some
congressmen through the depressing drab rooms, they quickly authorized five thousand dollars for what would become the symbol of
the United States presidency. But it wasn't the president who supervised this public project; he handed it over completely to his wife and
Benjamin Henry Latrobe, the architect who as Surveyor of Public
Buildings had worked on the house with Jefferson. It took Dolley
and Latrobe no time at all to run through that five thousand dollars
and then some.

"I bought yesterday four chimney pieces of Pennsylvania marble," Latrobe wrote to Dolley from Philadelphia a couple of weeks
after the inauguration. "They are handsome and cheap and may be
immediately put up." As unusual as it was for the woman of the house
to be the business partner in the important task of creating an elegant executive establishment, Latrobe clearly had no problem with
it, as he imparted political gossip to Dolley along with the news of
having located "2 dozen very elegant white handled knives and forks,
2 dozen dessert ditto." Though we don't have her letter, Dolley apparently responded in kind: "Thank you for the excellent political
news." Latrobe began a report explaining the details of the carriage
he had ordered for her. Luckily for Dolley, Latrobe's wife was an old
childhood friend from Philadelphia who knew that city well and
could help in the hunt for china. Included in the purchases: a "Yard-
wood" washing machine, making laundry day a little easier. The
First Lady was impatient to get everything in place so she could em-
bark on the entertaining that she found so essential to effecting her
husband's ends. The house wouldn't be ready for what would become
her legendary "drawing rooms" until the next New Year, but that

didn't stop the First Lady from squeezing callers into "Mrs. Madison's Parlor" (now the Red Room), painted her signature bright yellow just a couple of months after Madison took office.

Even before the guests started showing up downstairs, the family filled the upstairs quarters. Dolley's sister Anna had married Richard Cutts, a member of Congress, in 1804, and she and her family of three boys moved in during the congressional session. Another sister, Lucy, was widowed and appreciated the amusement Washington offered for her and her children. Payne Todd, Dolley's son, spent time there when he was on vacation from the Catholic boarding school he attended in Baltimore, and Dolley's cousin Edward Coles lived there as secretary to the president. Everyone in the family seemed to expect the First Lady to provide them with patronage jobs, and she did remarkably well in fulfilling those expectations. She saw it as her duty to help where she could, and she found that she could help indeed. Friends and total strangers as well called on Dolley Madison when they wanted something from the federal government.

Even before she moved to the executive mansion, Dolley had been the go-to person on patronage; but her elevated station obviously upped the number of requests for her assistance. When Jefferson was president, his own daughter, Martha Randolph, relied on her friend Dolley Madison rather than her father when a nephew needed "an under clerkship in one of the offices," because his ne'er-do-well father had abandoned the family. Dolley came through, much to the relief of the young man's mother, Mary Randolph: "I cannot express the gratitude I feel for your very friendly attention in procuring so eligible a situation for my son," she wrote. "I shall direct him to go immediately to Washington and place himself under your patronage." And Louisa Adams's mother, Catherine Johnson, sought similar patronage for her son: "the sole Prop of my declining Years, and his Sisters' only Protector, I have no Claim on your Philanthropy My Dear Madam, but what arises in general to the unfortunate." Dolley Madison eventually was able to place Thomas Johnson in the postmaster post in New Orleans.

His sister Louisa was eternally grateful. "My hitherto unfortunate Brother, is at length by your goodness, raised from adversity, and will at last be enabled, to render the declining years of a tenderly cherished, and highly respected Parent, easy if not happy." Not only was Dolley expected to find jobs, but also to bless projects and obtain pardons. Librarian of Congress George Watterston asked the First Lady if he could dedicate his play to her: "In expectation that under your patronage it will survive the nipping blasts of criticism and outlive the noisy storms of malignity," and then the demanding favor-seeker appended a P.S.: "An answer is expected." John Jacob Astor sent her a "muff and tippet made of silver fox skins," requesting that she wear it "from motives of patriotism and to give encouragement to the manufactures of our country." A mother of ten whose husband had spent eighteen months in jail for "the unintentional breach of the embargo laws" begged Dolley, "convinced that you, Madam, can and will sympathize with the miserable and unfortunate" to support a petition "forwarded by my husband to both houses of Congress praying for relief." Dolley did "patronize" the petition, and two months later James Madison pardoned John O'Bryan, the letter-writer's husband.

Political implications weighted down another pardon request to Mrs. Madison, "that you will, in my name, apply to the President for a removal of the prosecution now existing against Aaron Burr." It came, of course, from Theodosia Alston, who reminded Dolley that "my father, once your friend, is now in exile." Burr had indeed been the First Lady's good friend and lawyer, not to mention the man who introduced her to James Madison. Theodosia argued that her father was innocent, but that even if he had "contemplated the project for which he stands arraigned" he would not be able to carry it out given his lack of friends and money. Taking Dolley into her confidence, Theodosia asked that her petition be "treated with delicacy" because she was writing behind her husband's back—he didn't know about her request and presumably would disapprove. But, she said, she had no choice as "a daughter whose soul sinks at the prospect of a long and indefinite separation from a Father almost adored. . . . What indeed, would I not risk once more to see him, to hang upon him, to place my child on his knee, and again spend my days in the happy occupation of endeavoring to anticipate all his wishes?" There remains no evidence of a reply to the anguished Theodosia Alston. It's one of the few instances where Mrs. Madison seems to have determined that it would be wiser to stay out of the affair.

But there was not much she stayed out of. Dolley Madison seemed to be everywhere—at the Capitol, at the races, at the card table (though she cut back on her gambling once she became First Lady), at the dances and balls that passed for amusement in the federal city. Meetings of the president's cabinet gave Dolley an excuse to host "dove dinners" for the cabinet wives, where information flowed freely. When Henry Clay paid her the compliment: "Everybody loves Mrs. Madison," she replied that was because "*Mrs. Madison* loves everybody." One congressional friend christened her a "Queen of Hearts." The fun-loving, snuff-dipping First Lady managed to convince the populace that though she couldn't resist expensive French fashion, including her trademark turbans often topped with fantastic feathers, and though she shockingly "painted" her face, she was a down-home sort of girl. When Elizabeth Merry famously remarked that dinner at the Madisons was "more like a harvest home supper than the entertainment of a Secretary of State," Dolley chose to take the comment as a compliment rather than the insult it was intended to be. Continuing the "harvest home" atmosphere as First Lady, collecting recipes from around the country for presidential dinners, she reached out to all America, including children—she instituted the Easter egg roll. Mrs. Madison presided over all of this activity with "elegant ease," according to Elbridge Gerry, who had offered to assist her in her duties at the head of the table (the president sat in the middle, leaving the guiding of the conversation to his wife). Seeing his services would have been superfluous, Gerry marveled to his wife that Dolley conducted herself in a manner "as easy as if she had been born and educated at Versailles."

Dolley Madison's dinners and "drawing rooms" drew all of Washington. Everything from the food she served ("ice creams, macaroons, preserves and various cakes" were offered as a first dessert followed by "almonds, raisins, pecan-nuts, apples, pears, etc.") to the attire of the guests—some men wore dirty boots to accentuate their republicanism—was cause for comment. Everyone talked about the Wednesday-night "squeeze," as the gathering came to be called, and everybody went—Republicans, Federalists, even odd John Randolph wanted to see and be seen at the weekly receptions. And Dolley received them all with equal graciousness. One congressional wife observed: "She makes herself so agreeable and by her civil and polite expressions, puts every one in such a good humor with themselves that no one who has once seen her, can help being pleased with her." Of course, even Dolley Madison couldn't please all of the people all of the time. Abigail Adams clucked that "Dolley Madison adopted the new fashions and seemed in every way delighted with the French influenced manner;" the former First Lady judged that "I may say with safety that her predecessors left her no evil example." Dolley's drawing rooms were considered too courtly by some Republicans and too common by some Federalists. They were certainly egalitarian. "Invitations" took the form of announcements in the newspaper; all were welcome, as long they were appropriately dressed. And all went—skipping a Wednesday Night might mean missing a vital piece of political information or being left out of a crucial deal. Still, all of the First Lady's successes in bringing politicians together notwithstanding, the divisions in the country and the threat of war remained real.

Shortly before he left office Thomas Jefferson agreed to the repeal of the despised Embargo Acts, but Congress put in their place the Non-Intercourse Act, which allowed trade with all countries except Britain and France. If either nation stopped interfering with neutral shipping, the ban would be lifted. While doing little to quell public grumbling, the new law opened the door to a good deal of mischief making by the European powers. As usual, Rosalie Stier

Calvert—one of the few locals to snub Dolley's drawing rooms—could be counted on to disparage a Republican president, but her letters leading up to the War of 1812 provide a vivid description of the political situation and its effect on her business dealings, plus her life as the mother of an ever-growing family.

"The embargo is lifted at last," Rosalie informed her father soon after Madison's inauguration, "but they have substituted so many laws—all just as bad—that we are just where we were before." At Henry Stier's suggestion, Rosalie had befriended Treasury Secretary Albert Gallatin, who advised her to wait before purchasing bonds, to see what the Congress would do about issuing new ones. In the meantime, she tried her hand at buying and selling tobacco, but the trade restrictions banned its shipment abroad and prices in America were too low to make a profit. "Now let us put business affairs aside—I must tell you a little about myself," Rosalie continued. "We have lost our poor little Louise." First, her father would hear about politics and business, then about the death of her child. It was probably what she thought was expected of her. These father-daughter relationships could be complex.

To her brother, Rosalie kept up the political commentary: "We are only too well convinced that this government and the Federal Union cannot exist without a respectable navy, but our wretched President is, I fear, one of those wavering, weak characters and although in reality an honest man, he will do as much harm as his predecessor." Once again donning her Cassandra cap, Rosalie added, "This country has reached a very alarming crisis. Torn by two parties, the eastern states jealous of the South, Congress enacting laws it is unable to enforce and obliged to retract them afterwards only to substitute equally bad ones, our flag insulted at the same time by both England and France . . ." She wasn't far off the mark. The new British ambassador, David Erskine, had tried to reach a compromise with Madison over the shipping issues and for a time it looked as though the disputes with England were settled. But, as Rosalie Calvert reported to her father anxious to sell tobacco in Europe, "now comes the news that Mr. Erskine went beyond his instructions and [England] will not ratify the arrangements he made." The British government refused to rescind the so-called Orders in Council blockading ships of neutral nations in the war against France. Erskine was recalled and the United States was still unable to trade freely.

Some Americans tried to make the best of it, harking back to the days of the Revolution when Patriots boycotted British goods. "The other day my husband went to a 'sheep shearing' sponsored by Mr. Custis," Rosalie recounted with some sarcasm in June 1809. "All of the guests were asked to come dressed in American-made clothes. The wine had been made in Virginia, as were all the beverages—apple brandy, peach brandy, whiskey, etc. It was a completely patriotic fete." In fact, the embargo did have the effect of promoting some domestic industries. (Dolley Madison was full of praise for a woman named Mary Kies for her production of domestically made hats. In 1809, her design of weaving straw with silk or thread won the first patent awarded to an American female.) But the prices dropped out of American agriculture. "Commercial obstacles . . . prevent our selling our harvests and consequently leave us without income," Rosalie complained to her brother; now she would not be able to hire a tutor for her children but would have to keep teaching them herself, which "bores me insufferably." And the situation wasn't getting any better. "One day it seems we will have a war with France, another day with England. Our government is weak and the nation divided over this matter."

Since few letters could get through the naval blockades, Rosalie, a married woman who could not own property by U.S. law, found herself investing her family's substantial holdings without benefit of her father's advice. She warned that the Congress would not renew the charter of the Bank of the United States, partly because the British owned so many shares. She didn't trust many of the new banks springing up, except the Bank of Washington, where her husband was a trustee. But its shares were getting expensive: "You will note that I now have 2000 shares of Washington Bank stock for you. I don't think there will be any more available at par for the present. All the last shares I bought were from people who had the sheriff at their heels." As she gave her accounting, and asked for power of attorney to handle other investments, Rosalie knew she was on her own. "I don't know, dear Father, if I am using your money as you intend, but I always act as I think you would prefer." Not only her father, but her brother and sister were counting on Rosalie to keep them sound financially while Europe was overrun by the warring French and English. "I must confess that I do not like to have so great a responsibility resting on my shoulders as the management of such revenues entails." The responsibility was great, but Rosalie Stier Calvert in fact seemed to enjoy taking it on, in addition to all of her other responsibilities.

Money management was a concrete way of keeping in touch with her faraway clan. When her family first left America, Rosalie kept thinking that she and her husband would join them in Europe some day, at least for a visit if not permanently. But as the time grew longer, her family larger, and the prospects of crossing the Atlantic less likely, she became reconciled to the reality that she was unlikely ever to go home again. "You can imagine, dear Friend, how much it cost me to give up this project," she lamented to her brother. "It often makes me very sad." Particularly difficult was the separation from her sister. The two women tried to share intimacies over the many miles. "You write that I have enough children now and ought to close down the factory," Rosalie joked in October 1809. "I agree with you that I have just the right number, and in spite of that I plan to increase it again in the spring."

At age thirty-one, Rosalie Calvert was pregnant with her sixth child in ten years of marriage. "So you are determined not to have any more children—this method you have taken is certainly effective," Rosalie responded to a letter from Isabelle, who had apparently preached that the only way to avoid pregnancy was to abstain from sex. But soon Isabelle had to admit, with some embarrassment, that she was having trouble closing down her "factory" as well. Pledging never to take another trip because "each one unfailingly results in a baby," she revealed to her little sister that due to "a moment of folly" she was five months pregnant. "I am extremely downcast and rather ashamed. No one knows except Papa—Louise doesn't suspect a thing." Isabelle's oldest daughter, Louise, was being presented to European society, and her mother feared "that another little brother may cut down on the number of her suitors—that is always a problem for girls." Louise's debut was already somewhat dicey—since the Stier family had only recently come into favor in Napoleon's court. But Rosalie, despite her hatred for the French, argued that her sister was wise to forget any anti-Bonaparte sentiments for her daughter's sake: "As you know, we are quite passionate in our political opinions here, but I would sacrifice them all if Caroline were of an age to go out into society and I could even—I think—pay court to Queen Dolla lolla—a sobriquet given to Mrs. Madison." And, heaven knows, Queen "Dolla lolla" would have received the died-in-the-wool Federalist, along with everyone else.

It was not just at the executive mansion that Dolley Madison charmed the masses. She also used the Madison country estate, Montpelier, for political purposes. Margaret Bayard Smith gives us an engaging description of a visit to the Orange, Virginia, plantation. Mrs. Smith and her husband had decided to accept an invitation issued by the departing President Jefferson to visit him at Monticello, which they did in the summer of 1809, following that sojourn with a stop to see Jefferson's successor. Journalist that she would become, Margaret understood she was in the presence of historical figures and documented in detail her days at the two retreats.

At Monticello, still so awed by Thomas Jefferson, Margaret spent much of her time just basking in her hero's attention while trying to offer some help to the mistress of the house. Martha Randolph, though exhausted by sick children including her oldest daughter Anne who had just lost a newborn baby, took up her duties as hostess at a sumptuous dinner featuring an "immense and costly variety of French and Italian wines" that the former president lingered over in amiable conversation. The next morning's somewhat sparse spread of ham and muffins—"It was not exactly the Virginia breakfast I expected"—was a family occasion: "All Mrs. R's children eat at the family table, but are in such excellent order, that you would not know, if you did not see them, that a child was present." Then Jefferson and the other men retired to read in their studies or oversee their fields in solitude. Not Martha, of course, "excepting the hours housekeeping requires, she devotes the rest to her children, whom she instructs. As for them, they seem never to leave her for an instant, but are always beside her or on her lap." One evening, after showing Margaret all the clever features of the house he had designed, guiding her through his twenty-thousand-volume library, and displaying his closet of neatly labeled seeds, the former president ran races with his grandchildren "and seemed delighted in delighting them." The total picture so impressed Mrs. Smith that she was moved anew to defend Jefferson's character: "Oh ye whose envenomed calumny has painted him as the slave of the vilest passions, come here and contemplate this scene!" A not very veiled reference to the Sally Hemings stories. With a heavy heart Margaret Smith said goodbye, probably for the last time, to the man she so admired, "he is truly a philosopher, and truly a good man, and eminently a great one."

Margaret's melancholy mood was soon dispelled when she and her husband pulled up in their carriage at the home of the current president. Dolley Madison effusively welcomed her friend with "no restraint, no ceremony, hospitality is the residing genius of this house." While the two women stretched out like schoolgirls on Dolley's bed for a rest and some refreshment, Margaret explained that she had left her daughters at home for fear of inconveniencing the Madisons. Dolley's response? "'Oh,' said she laughing, 'I should not have known they were here, among all the rest, for at this moment we have only three and twenty in the house.'" Most of the other guests were relatives with children, "all plain country people, but frank, kind, warm-hearted Virginians." And here was the breakfast Mrs. Smith expected to be served in the Old Dominion—"a most excellent Virginia breakfast—tea, coffee, hot wheat bread, light cakes, a pone, or corn loaf, cold ham, nice hashes, chickens, etc." Margaret Smith enjoyed the whole experience, and became devoted to Dolley: "How unassuming, how kind is this woman. How can any human being be her enemy. Truly in her there is to be found no gall, but the pure milk of human kindness." But Dolley Madison and her husband did have their enemies, made more vocal by the administration's response to the pressures from Europe's great powers.

IF WAR WITHOUT END between Britain and France was taking its toll on the United States, the price to the peace of Europe was much higher. As the battles raged on, the Russian court informed Washington that an American envoy to St. Petersburg would be welcome. Word came just as the handover from Jefferson to Madison occurred, and, luckily for the new president, there was an experienced diplomat on hand ready to take the assignment—John Quincy Adams. Life as a professor at Harvard didn't quite do it for the ambitious son of a former president, and Adams was hoping to land a post in the new administration. So he managed to find a couple of court cases to argue in Washington around the time of James Madison's inauguration. Louisa, back in Boston, reported that all their friends suspected something was afoot: "The Town still rings with your appointment some say to be Secretary of State, others to Europe." Even John's students, she cautioned him, "have talked of looking out for other gentlemen to study with." So it couldn't have come as a surprise a couple of days after the inauguration when President Madison offered Adams the posting to Russia. Though in later years Louisa bitterly recounted her horror on learning that they were going abroad, at the time she wrote to Dolley Madison: "I sensibly feel the honor so lately conferred on Mr. Adams for which I return most grateful thanks."

What galled Louisa Adams when she looked back on it in the

private memoir she wrote many years later, was that her husband didn't tell her what he was planning: "Every preparation was made without the slightest consultation with me, and even the disposal of my children and my sister was fixed without my knowledge until it was too late to change." John Quincy Adams had decided that the two older boys, eight-year-old George and six-year-old John, would stay in America, only two-year-old Charles would make the trip to Russia, along with Louisa's sister Catherine as a companion and John's sister, Nabby's son, William Smith, as a secretary, plus two servants. When she went to Quincy to say goodbye to her sons, Louisa was never left alone with her father-in-law "lest I should excite his pity and he allow me to take my boys with me." The seventy-three-year-old former president was a softy who "was always very kind and affectionate" to his daughter-in-law and would have succumbed to her wishes. She either wanted to take her children with her or let her husband go to Russia alone "if domestic separation is absolutely necessary cling as a mother to those innocent and helpless creatures whom God himself has given to your charge. A man can take care of *himself*," she wrote angrily in her memoir. But John Quincy Adams was deaf to his wife's protestations; in his view the boys would be better off with his mother and aunt.

Having left his own mother to go abroad with his father at age ten, John Quincy disagreed with Louisa about child raising. One small bone of contention—dancing lessons for George: "His father scorns the idea of instilling the graces," the boy's mother fumed. "Why should a man not move well? Is it preferable to be a clown?" Though she found it hard to stand up to John, Louisa strongly felt that a mother's judgment was preeminent. "No substitute on the face of this earth can be found for the mother's attachment, or the mother's devotion if she is virtuous," said this woman whose two oldest sons barely saw her through much of their young lives. And even as her mother-in-law ridiculed Louisa's desire to keep her sons close, Abigail Adams questioned her own competence: "I begin to think grandparents not so well qualified to educate grandchildren as parents. They are apt to relax in their spirit of government, and to be too indulgent." Louisa was not the only Adams mother stinging from the departure. At age sixty-four Abigail Adams feared it was her final farewell: "This separation from a dear son, at the advanced age of your grandfather and myself, was like taking a last leave of him," she mourned to her granddaughter Caroline after the ship sailed on August 5, 1809. Louisa insisted nothing was worth this pain: "Can ambition repay such sacrifices? Never!!" She bitterly bade, "Adieu to America."

It was not just what she was leaving behind, it was what lay ahead that filled Louisa Adams with apprehension. "I had passed the age when courts are alluring," the former toast of Berlin wrote in her memoir. "Experience had taught me years before the meanness of an American Minister's position at a European court." She knew her husband's government salary wouldn't go far in St. Petersburg, and while she contemplated the difficulty of the life ahead of her aboard the *Horace*, with the "vessel rolling and pitching as if she would upset," Louisa and the baby were horribly seasick, "as usual I having the whole care of the child who suffered as much as any of us." The seas swelled with other dangers as a gunshot from a British brig reminded them in this era of harassment and impressment on the oceans. Another British ship pulled alongside, and sent men on deck to question the travelers. The menacing sailors finally agreed to let the *Horace* proceed because there was a "minister on board." The party stopped briefly in Denmark for some sightseeing at Elsinore to see the place where *Hamlet* was set, with the men detouring to Copenhagen to arrange for their safe passage on to Russia. The ship pressed on, though "dangers accumulated every moment" with the cold weather closing in "and at last provisions began to give out."

Eighty days after leaving Boston, the troupe finally arrived in St. Petersburg. And what a sight they were: "My sister and myself wore hats which had been chosen at Copenhagen that we might appear fashionable, and we could scarcely look at one another for laughing: immense brown beaver of the most vulgar imaginable;" the party was "ushered into an immense salon at the Admirals House full of elegantly dressed ladies and gentlemen staring aghast at the figures just introduced and with extreme difficulty restraining their risibility. Maid and child and all taking their place in the farce and our black servant following. It was exquisite beyond all description and too ridiculous in the first moments to be mortifying." The women got their own laugh a couple of days later when Minister Adams dressed for the ceremony where he would present his credentials "looking very handsome, all but the wig. O horrid!" (Czar Alexander soon allowed Adams to skip the wig when coming to court. Perhaps he agreed that it was horrid. Remember, Abigail Adams had commented on the "strangeness" of her son's wigs.)

The family moved into a miserable hotel "full of rats" and looked for someplace to live in this glitzy and glamorous city of palaces, while studying the intricacies of "the most magnificent court in Europe." Louisa and John would have separate audiences with the young czar and his wife, Princess Elizabeth of Baden. So Mrs. Adams was alone when "off I went with a fluttered pulse . . . dressed in a hoop with a silver tissue skirt with a train, a heavy crimson velvet robe with a very long train . . . white satin shoes, gloves, fan, etc and over all this *luggage* my fur cloak . . . and thus accoutered I appeared before the gentlemen of our party who could not refrain from laughter at my appearance." It might have made Louisa feel better as she had trouble "in the adjustment of my trappings" when she appeared at the palace if she had known that her mother-in-law had battled a hoopskirt and found her feathers brushing the carriage roof when she went off to be presented at the Court of St. James's almost twenty-five years earlier.

As it was, the American minister's wife was under the tutelage of a countess who "placed me in the center of the hall fronting a large folding door and informed me that the Empress would enter by that door and that I must stand unmoved until her Imperial Majesty walked up to me; that when she came up I must affect to kiss her hand which her Majesty would not *permit* and that I must take my glove off so as to be ready and take care in raising my head not to touch her Majesty." Whew! The court of Berlin had been nothing like this: "Two Negroes dressed a la Turque with splendid uniforms were stationed at the doors with drawn sabers with gold handles. At the opening of the doors I saw a suite of long rooms at each door of which stood two Negroes in the same style and the Grand Marshall in a splendid costume preceded the Emperor and Empress who came up together with a long train of ladies and gentlemen following. . . . I went through the forms with Empress made easy by extreme affability . . . and they withdrew as they came and I remained in the same position until the doors were re-closed. And thus ended act the first."

So began a round of fantastic balls, costume parties, theatrical performances, gambling games, magic shows, and midnight suppers that at first took Louisa Adams's breath away. At an event at the chancellor's, the emperor's table was "served on solid gold. That of the Corps Diplomatique with silver . . . The Chancellor was said to have 300 servants of different grades 150 at least wearing magnificent liveries according to their grades. . . . All this was too much like a fairy tale." Louisa, as one of only two women in the diplomatic corps, became an instant darling of the Russian aristocracy and her husband's fellow ambassadors. The French envoy told her she "was too serious for a pretty woman and that when 'we were in Rome we must do as Rome.' I told him if I should go to Rome perhaps I might." The American was ready to banter with the best of them, including the ambassador from France, her husband's chief rival for the czar's attention. Louisa's sister Kitty was "quite enchanted with all these parties," but the women needed more clothes to wear; "what would have dressed one modestly was by no means competent for two." They didn't have enough money for so many extravagant ball gowns. And the adult Adamses weren't the only ones expected to show up at all the elegant events. Their son Charles's attendance at "children's balls" was also required. At one, Louisa dressed the little boy "as an Indian Chief to gratify the taste for savages and there was a general burst of applause when he marched in at which he was much sur-

prised." The toddler led another tot in a dance "and they with the assistance of their mothers opened the ball . . . after the dance there
was an elegant supper, oceans of champagne for the little people and
the mothers all stood full dressed behind their chairs." Bacchus, the
god of wine, was Charles's costume at another ball. A far cry from the
Noah's Ark of Dr. Tufts, Deacon French, Mr. Cranch, and Old Uncle
Peter she had met with in Quincy, Massachusetts.

Russia had experienced an economic boom that was just beginning to end as royalty played on. The entertainments generally ended
around two or three in the morning and it all got to be a little much
for Louisa. When asked by the empress mother to a birthday party
for the emperor, "having but one dress in which I had already appeared several times, I declined on the plea of ill health." But Louisa
made the mistake of going out with a friend that evening, and word
got back to the empress mother, who was more than miffed. She sent
notice that Mrs. Adams better not refuse another invitation. The
young woman fretted about what this would mean for the Adams's
pocketbook, since she knew the imperious Russian had told "a lady
who had worn the same gown several times that she 'wished that *she*
(the lady) would get another for that she was tired of seeing the same
color so often.'" Louisa Adams stewed so about not having enough
clothes that she tried donning mourning garb to deflect attention
from her wardrobe, but her "motive was suspected." Everyone knew
the Americans were poor. John Quincy Adams's salary was nine thousand dollars a year, more than any American government official
other than the president, but considerably less than the French ambassador's more than three-hundred-thousand-dollar stipend.

Even so, with the first long winter behind them, the Adams
entourage was having a grand time in St. Petersburg. Young and pretty,
the Johnson sisters were popular in this country where the local
women could be scary-looking. After John Quincy met a Russian princess at dinner he described with disgust the "length and thickness of
her beard." The thirty-two-year-old emperor had taken a special liking to them, particularly to twenty-four-year-old Kitty Johnson. He

would arrange to run into Kitty and Louisa on their walks and, according to Louisa, "speak to us very politely." Alexander's attentions to Kitty, who "was a great belle among our young gentlemen . . . gave umbrage to beaux and occasioned so much teasing and questions that we left off our promenades for some time." When the women ventured out again the emperor demanded to know where they had been and commanded "that he should expect to meet *us* every day, looking at my sister, that the weather was fine." Kitty taunted the young men of her acquaintance with this information, and John Quincy "looked very *grave* but said nothing. The young gentlemen disapproved and hoped we would not do it." But Louisa, who was clearly enjoying herself, insisted diplomacy required acceding to the czar's wishes. So the women kept walking, occasionally taking along little Charles, "who always had a kind greeting from his Majesty."

It wasn't just on daytime strolls that Czar Alexander paid court to Kitty Johnson. At a ball at the French embassy, after Louisa survived the intimidating experience of dancing the polonaise with the emperor, he asked where her sister was. When Louisa offered to find her, Alexander answered he would search instead. "He sought her and took her out himself to dance and she not knowing the etiquettes began laughing and talking to him as she would have done to an American partner." The emperor was "so charmed with the novelty" that he delayed the dinner in order to keep dancing. Kitty "had never been presented at court so that this extraordinary distinction produced a buzz of astonishment." Even Abigail Adams had to admit that this was something. She knew "what weight and influence these apparently trifling circumstances have in the Courts of princes," she wrote to Catherine Johnson, the mother of the women so singled out by the czar. And the honors continued—special invitations to theater at the Hermitage, special access to the emperor's private entrance, and at the palace, said her sister, "The distinction paid Miss Johnson was a matter of wonder to all."

All the attention to Kitty started to make Louisa somewhat nervous. Out on a walk one day, she "saw the Emperor behind us hastening on with great strides. . . . I beckoned to my servants to drive up and with my sister got into the carriage and drove on. . . . the great distinction shown my sister . . . had occasioned so much talk I thought it was injudicious to encourage it." But the czar saw them hiding from him and took offense, something that could be harmful to Ambassador Adams, since the affable Alexander was all-powerful. So the ladies resumed their perambulations, the emperor continued to meet them, and it all paid off for America. The czar intervened with Denmark to free a number of U.S. ships that had been held for some time, and more and more American ships plied the Russian ports, engaging in robust trade with at least one European power.

The ships moved freely when the frozen waters melted, and with the thaw came letters from home. Louisa was shocked when some visitors one night told her that the czar was reading their mail, and had commented on some of the letters. "I observed that it was very ungenerous of his majesty after offering to send our dispatches by a private and especial courier to use this opportunity against *us*," Louisa exploded to a friend when she heard about it. "It was perfectly natural . . . that we should describe our first impressions without disguise to our friends to whom they must certainly be very interesting." Fortunately, she had been complimentary to Alexander. But she also underlined how much of a drain they were feeling from the expense of St. Petersburg. Louisa griped to her frugal mother-in-law about the effect on John Quincy when each bill "makes ruin stare him in the face. *He* has born it very patiently but *I* cannot." Still the free flow of mail meant "letters from our children and friends in America" and the news was good. "All well," Louisa Adams could contentedly say in the summer of 1810.

ALL WAS NOT WELL at home in America with the threat of war and the stranglehold on foreign trade. Even so, the country was expanding its cultural and continental borders in the first decade of the nineteenth century. The orchestra of the Boston Philharmonic Society played first in 1810, two years after the establishment of the New York Academy of Fine Arts, the opening in New Orleans of the nation's most elaborate opera house, at a cost of $100,000, and the debut in Philadelphia of an original American opera, *The Indian Princess*, based on the Pocahontas story. The nation's capital was beginning to emerge from the swamp into a pleasant city. "A splendid bridge has been built over the Potomac opposite the Capitol," Rosalie Calvert informed her sister. "It is nothing now to go from here to Alexandria." And more and more schools were springing up not only for the children of the elite but also for the poor, including free blacks.

At the same time, to the horror of many in the federal government, Washington was home to a burgeoning slave market. To win the South's support for the Constitution, the Founders included in that document a provision prohibiting the federal government from banning the slave trade for twenty years. The time period was now up and the Congress had passed the law abolishing the trade to take effect in 1808. No more slaves could be legally imported, but many more already in the country would be bought and sold. While orators declaimed about national honor inside the Capitol, in the shadow of its dome human beings stood on the auction block. But many free blacks also lived in the federal city, and some employers allowed enterprising slaves to earn money in order to buy their freedom. (One such arrangement took place between Dolley Madison and Francis Scott Key of "Star Spangled Banner" fame. The wife of Dolley's servant Joe worked for Key, who agreed to free her if Joe could find someone to advance him two hundred dollars. "He tells me that he has prevailed on you to make this advance," Key confirmed with the First Lady, "and to take his own & his wife's services to repay it.")

Some hard workers, like Alethia Browning Tanner, managed to free dozens of relatives. Tanner used a small piece of land near the Capitol to grow vegetables for sale in the central market, where legend has it that Thomas Jefferson was one of her customers. Her sister, Sophia Browning Bell, operated a similar business across the river in Alexandria. Between them the two women were able to release much of the family from slavery. After Sophia bought the freedom of her husband, George Bell, he helped establish the first school for blacks in Washington. A few years later, in 1810, Englishwoman Mary Billings opened an integrated school in Georgetown, but there was such an outcry about blacks and whites sharing a schoolroom, she was forced to shut down. When she reopened in another location, Ms. Billings limited her classes to black children only, and is credited with educating some of the most successful African Americans in early Washington.

Another school movement started at about the same time in Baltimore when Elizabeth Seton opened a free Catholic school for girls, initiating what would become the enormous and enormously successful parochial school system in the United States. To run her school, Mrs. Seton also established the first American religious order for women, the Sisters of Charity. Elizabeth Bayley Seton had traveled quite an odyssey since she had helped Isabella Graham establish the Society for the Relief of Poor Widows and Small Children in New York in 1797.

The well-educated and well-off daughter of a New York physician, Elizabeth had witnessed the evolution of American history. Though her father served as a surgeon with the British army, Elizabeth, at age fourteen, joined the cheering crowd when George Washington took his first oath of office in New York in 1789. At nineteen she happily married wealthy merchant William Seton, soon rejoicing that she had "my own home at 20 . . . quite impossible! All this and heaven too," and children too—five in eight years. Through her father and husband, Elizabeth knew all of the important men of the era and worked with their wives and daughters on worthy causes like the Widows' Society. But her life of privilege and comfort ended abruptly when her husband's import-export firm went bankrupt in 1801, the same year her father, New York's first public health officer, died from his ministrations to Irish immigrants infected with yellow fever. Just about a year later her husband, William Seton, developed tuberculosis. Thinking that his health might improve in Italy where he had good friends in the banking business, Seton along with Elizabeth and their eldest, eight-year-old Anna Maria, embarked for Europe in the fall of 1803, leaving the younger children with friends. Six weeks later they sailed into the harbor of Livorno.

An enthusiastic greeting—with a band set to play "Hail Columbia"—had been planned by Elizabeth's half brother, who was working for Seton's friends, the Filicchi family, but the Italian health officials swiftly snuffed out the celebration. Another yellow fever epidemic had engulfed New York and the local authorities wouldn't let these potential disease carriers off the ship. Instead of a grand welcome, the Setons were shuttled off to a "lazaretto," a hospital for infectious diseases, where it was so cold that when little Anna happened on a piece of rope she used it as a jump rope and "began jumping away to warm herself." Elizabeth recorded in her journal the dreariness and despair of their confinement, especially for desperately ill William: "My husband on the cold bricks without fire, shivering and groaning, lifting his dim and sorrowful eyes with a fixed gaze in my face while his tears ran on his pillow without one word." For a month the forlorn threesome stayed locked up in the hospital/prison, "at no loss to know the hour night and day, four bells strike every hour and ring every quarter." Finally released they fled to their friends, the Filicchis, in Pisa. William Seton died eight days later. His twenty-nine-year-old widow would have to find a way to support her five children.

Stuck in Italy for almost four months partly because little Anna was sick, the deeply religious Elizabeth visited the Church of San Lorenzo in Florence, where she experienced some kind of epiphany, according to her own account: "a sensation of delight struck me so forcibly." As the granddaughter of an Episcopal clergyman, Elizabeth had been a favorite of one of the prominent Protestant ministers in New York, but now she was drawn to the Catholic Church. Conversion would not be easy for a woman of her station in early nineteenth-century New York where prejudice against Catholics was commonplace. As it turned out, the battle for Elizabeth Seton's soul was almost comical. She wrote to her friends in Italy that not only were the Episcopalians and Catholics fighting for her, so were Presbyterians, Quakers, Anabaptists, and Methodists. After agonizing about the effect of her decision on her own future prospects and especially on those of her children, Elizabeth Bayley Seton joined the Catholic Church in the spring of 1805.

The impoverished widow had been right to worry about her children. Fortunately the Filicchi family back in Italy was willing to assist her financially, and she asked them to help get her boys into a Catholic school in Baltimore (presumably the same one where Dolley Madison's son went): "If you could only know the situation they are in here," she anguished, "the ridicule they are forced to hear of our holy religion and the mockery at the church and ministers." The boys ended up in Washington at the Jesuit-run Georgetown, while their mother tried and failed to make a living running a school in New York, where prospective students kept their distance due to her religion. Other attempts at earning an income met with the same resistance, so it was with great relief that Elizabeth Seton accepted an invitation from a French priest in Baltimore to open a Catholic school for girls. In June 1808, she and her three daughters, ages thirteen, eight, and six, boarded ship in New York for the bustling port city.

Maryland, founded as a Catholic colony, was a far more sympathetic setting for the now-destitute widow and her children. Mrs. Seton had the support of an influential Catholic community, still headed by America's first bishop, John Carroll, adviser to many of the Founding Fathers, and prominent families sent their girls to the school she established on Paca Street. Two of William Seton's sisters joined Elizabeth, much to their family's dismay, in what was at first an informal religious community. Soon other spiritually inclined women started showing up. At the end of 1808, the mother of five and her little band of followers took vows as Sisters of Charity of St. Joseph, the first religious order founded in the United States, making up the rules as they went along. Elizabeth, now Mother Seton, chose as a habit the widow's garb she was already wearing, changing only the cap. She negotiated her arrangement with the bishop, insisting that though she was now a nun, she was first a mother and "would prefer before all things the advantage of my children, if it happened that I had to choose between what I owe to them and other duties to which I was pledged." Her "other duties" entailed moving by covered wagon fifty miles from Baltimore to the tiny town of Emmitsburg, Maryland, where land had been donated for a mother-house for the religious order.

It was a rough existence at first, often without enough to eat, in a tumbledown farmhouse open to the elements. But more women joined the newly formed order, and in midwinter 1810 they opened St. Joseph's School, providing a free education for needy girls of the parish, creating the concept of a "parochial" school. Their second school, St. Joseph's Academy, started accepting wealthy girls as boarding students a couple of months later and produced enough income to support the free school. Despite the sorrows of burying her sisters-in-law and eventually two of her daughters as well, Mother Seton used her now considerable influence to expand her ministry—founding hospitals, establishing orphanages, adding more and more schools. History books credit her with creating the parochial school system in America, without any indication of what a struggle that entailed. But her supporters understood and carried the American woman's cause to Rome, insisting she was nothing short of a saint. In 1975, Pope Paul VI canonized her as St. Elizabeth Ann Seton.

THE WOMEN WHO JOINED Elizabeth Seton as Sisters of Charity were in a decided religious minority as Catholics, but they were part of a bigger spiritual movement sweeping the United States in the early nineteenth century—dubbed by history as the Second Great Awakening. A response to the arid intellectual deism embraced by many of the Founders and to the gloomy pessimism of traditional Calvinist teaching, an emotional religious upheaval stirred the country, with preachers—both male and female—working up their flocks with warnings of hellfire and damnation much the same way television evangelists do today. The spirited rituals excited many of the faithful into action, determined to "do unto others" godly deeds, including, eventually, fighting for the abolition of slavery. Taking its name from the Great Awakening in spiritualism that had run through Europe and America a few generations earlier, this religious revival was marked by a key difference: space. Some twenty-five thousand people poured into a camp meeting in Kentucky at the beginning of the century because there was *room* in the great expanse of what was then the American West for them to gather in such great numbers.

The nation's third census in 1810 confirmed what everyone had suspected after the Louisiana Purchase; the landmass of the country had doubled from about 800,000 square miles in 1800 to almost 1.7 million. The center of population had moved from the eastern seaboard in 1790, to an area about eighteen miles west of Baltimore in 1800, to an area forty miles west by northwest of Washington, D.C., in 1810. Those facts, though telling, give no sense of what this westward movement was like for the people who had the courage and pluck to settle the still primitive territory. With no means of transportation over land other than wagon, horse, or foot, just getting there signified triumph. To facilitate the western settlements, Congress had authorized the building of what came to be called the National Road from Cumberland, Maryland, to Wheeling in what's now West Virginia in 1806 but construction didn't start for five years; and though regular steamship service on the Hudson River following the 1807 maiden voyage of the *Clermont*, soon joined by the *Phoenix* on the Delaware, was highly beneficial to travelers on those waterways, the steamships didn't help the settlers headed west until the Erie Canal opened in 1825. Still, thousands of intrepid souls braved the journey across the mountains to seek their fates, or find their mates. Happily for us, some of those pioneers kept journals. One was Margaret Van Horn Dwight, who in 1810 at the age of nineteen made the six-week wagon ride from New Haven, Connecticut, to Warren, Ohio.

Born into one of the nation's most influential families, Margaret Dwight's story typifies the kind of movement going on in the early nineteenth century as even the most established and well-connected Americans chose to try their fortunes in the wilderness. Raised by her grandmother—who was the daughter of Jonathan Edwards, a leader of the First Great Awakening and president of Princeton University, and the mother of Timothy Dwight, a leader of the Second Great Awakening and president of Yale University—the formidable Mary Dwight could be counted on to educate Margaret as well as care for her. Mary Dwight had taught her son Timothy the Bible at age four, argued that he was capable of learning Latin at six, and pushed him to go to Yale at thirteen. Jonathan Edwards's many children and grandchildren held considerable intellectual and political power—another of his daughters was Aaron Burr's mother, and one of his sons, Pierpont Edwards, a famed if philandering legislator, lawyer, and journalist. It was this extended family that determined the future of Margaret Dwight after her grandmother died in 1807. The girl moved from Northampton, Massachusetts, to an aunt's in New Haven, Connecticut, until 1810 when it was off to other Edwards relatives in Ohio. We don't know why she decided to leave Connecticut or whether it was decided for her, but we do know the teenager promised to tell her cousin Elizabeth about everything that happened along the way, and Margaret faithfully fulfilled her pledge—recording daily journal entries that amount to an almost tactile account of what it meant to move west.

She set off on October 19, 1810, traveling with a family, Deacon and Mrs. Wolcott and their son and daughter. Four days into the trip, when they had gotten as far as Westchester County, New York, Margaret already had her regrets about the choice of companions: "I never will go . . . with a *Deacon* again, for we put up at every bye place in the country to *save expense* . . . The house is very small & very dirty—it serves for a tavern, a store & I should imagine hog's pen, stable & everything else." Margaret's sense of humor seems to have saved her on this rugged journey—while waiting for a hazardous ferry ride across the Hudson, she cracked to her cousin: "If we drown there will be an end to my journal." Moving slowly in the rickety wagon—eleven miles one day, fifteen another—after about ten days the optimistic young woman had hit her stride: "5 or 600 miles appears like a short journey to me now—indeed I feel as if I could go almost any distance—My courage & spirits & both very good."

Forced to walk any time they had to climb a hill to spare the horses, Margaret found some of the New Jersey roads rough going, but the surroundings still familiar. That changed as the party approached Pennsylvania, where everyone spoke German and treated the Sabbath much more casually than her Puritan family. "I believe at least 50 Dutchmen [German—"Deutsch"—speakers] have been here today to smoke, drink, swear, pitch cents, almost dance, laugh & talk dutch & stare at us—They come in, in droves young & old—black & white—women & children . . . I concluded they came to see us *Yankees,* as they would a learned pig." While the travelers were sleeping, with the Wolcotts and Margaret sharing a room, the strangers became more menacing: "In the middle of the night, I was awakened by the entrance of three dutchmen, who were in search of a bed—I was almost frightened to death. . . . I think *wild Indians* will be less terrible to me than these creatures." The currency in Pennsylvania was also strange—Margaret had never seen the local coins before—as well as the language and the dress, but the roads were good, and she thought the land must be as well: "as we see large fields of grain very frequently."

With great relief they stopped at an inn in Reading, Pennsylvania, where they were actually able to undress and go to sleep "for the first time in a long while" because "we are obliged to sleep every & any way at most of the inns now." But the deacon was kept awake by the other guests "in the room below us eating, drinking, talking, laughing and swearing" and he was in a bad temper in the morning. Margaret thought his wife's attempts to jolly him out of his mood absurd: "If I were going to be married I would give my *intended* a gentle emetic, or some such thing to see how he would bear being sick a little—for I could not coax a husband as I would a child, only because he was a little sick & a great deal cross." She was young and quick to judge, offended by cockfighting at an inn in Harrisburg, where they were delayed by a snowstorm, and understandably disgusted at the next stop where the floor was covered with "dirt enough to plant potatoes."

After almost three weeks on the trail, the now-weary travelers came to their most daunting challenge: crossing the Allegheny Mountains. To protect the precious horses, the younger members of the party walked over the first mountain; "it is not a little fatiguing to walk up a long mountain I find." On the other side they met a family with a two-week-old baby, born while his mother was already on the road; now she and her husband were preparing to pack up the suckling infant and get on their way again. Margaret too was on her way, crossing another mountain by foot that same day and waking the next morning "so lame I can scarcely walk," still "I have a mountain to walk over, notwithstanding." It was the most discouraging part of the journey. It rained relentlessly, the road ahead was unknown, there was no room in the inn, and "we have nothing to eat & can get nothing but some slapjacks at a baker's some distance off & so stormy we cannot get there." The teenage pioneer was growing apprehensive as well about what lay ahead, convinced that "the reason so few are willing to return from the Western country is not that the country is so good, but because the journey is so bad."

The journey could be particularly bad for a single young woman. One night when Margaret was sharing a bed with one of the older women in a crowded inn, one of the wagoners "came into the room & lay down by me on the outside of the bed—I was frightened almost to death. . . . I lay for a quarter of an hour crying & scolding & trembling, begging of him to leave me," which he finally did after telling her "he intended no harm & only wished to become acquainted with me." Through the night, drunken men harassed her and everyone else—"the landlord was so afraid of these wags that he did not dare stay in his own house."

Margaret was scared and she was starving. All of that walking with not enough to eat and nothing to read left her hungry in body and soul. She was also filthy and her "frock" was falling apart. But for all of the travails of the trek, people seeking a better life were pouring west: "From what I have seen and heard, I think the State of Ohio will be well filled before winter, wagons without number every day go on." And finally, a month after leaving Connecticut, she exulted to her cousin: "Rejoice with me my dear Elizabeth, that we are at length over the mountains." Heavy snow and sick horses were still to come, but the worst—miles and miles on foot up and down mountains—was over.

As they approached their goal, and she had "worn out my boots almost entirely, with walking," Margaret wondered what it would be like "not to run out to the wagon as soon as I have eaten my breakfast & not to have my journal in my workbag to fill it up. . . . I fear it will be worn out before you get it." At last, on December 1 she wrote: "Saturday—PM—Warren—After so long a time—" She had been deposited at "a very comfortable log house" belonging to an Edwards cousin, observing that "a cousin in this country, is not to be slighted I assure you—I would give more for one in this country, than for 20 in old Connecticut." Margaret Dwight would need her cousins to make a life in Warren, Ohio. But make a life she did, along with the thousands of others who abandoned the comforts of home to settle what was then the new territory of the American West. After a year in Ohio Margaret married an Irish immigrant, William Bell, and in 1815 they moved to Pittsburgh, then the city where the West began, where they raised thirteen children before Margaret died in 1834. The last line of her journal on December 1, 1810: "I have a great deal more to say, but no more time than just to tell you, I am ever & most

affectionately yours, MVD Let no one see this but your own family."
Fortunately, the family saved Margaret Van Horn Dwight's journal
and let others see it.

As wagonloads of people from the eastern seaboard pushed farther and farther west, clashes with Native Americans already on the
land grew more frequent. Though Thomas Jefferson professed admiration for the Indian way of life, he also tried to change it by em-
barking on a program of "civilizing" the tribes of the West and the
South. Determined to keep the British from moving down from
Canada into the American West, and the Spanish up from Florida
into the American Southeast, Jefferson encouraged trade with the
Indians in the hope that they would buy on credit and then be forced
to sell their lands to pay off the debt. The president aimed for a
peaceable transfer of native property to settlers of European descent, with the idyllic intent of both races joining hands to till the
soil. Some tribes went along with the plan—particularly in the Southeast, where they became known to whites as "The Five Civilized
Tribes." But, unsurprisingly, the sell-off of massive amounts of Indian territory spurred a resistance movement. Shawnee Chief Tecumseh and his brother "The Prophet" organized several tribes into
a confederacy ready to take up arms to protect their land and their
lifestyles.

Backed by the British, Tecumseh and company terrified the
Americans and added to the voices calling for war, voices loudly
heard in the congressional elections of 1810. Half of the sitting members of Congress were defeated by a new generation of politicians,
many of them sons of Revolutionary War notables. These were the
so-called War Hawks, mostly from the South and West, who in
1811 blew into Washington as a powerful force. One of them, Kentucky's Henry Clay, so impressed his colleagues that he was elected
Speaker of the House in his first term. Dolley Madison wasted no
time befriending him and his allies. Soon Clay was on such good

terms with the First Lady that he was sharing her snuffbox. Acutely aware of the clout of these men in the congressional Republican caucus that would decide whether to renominate Madison for president in 1812, Dolley called on the families of the newcomers, courting and complimenting them and of course including them in her entertainments at the president's house. "We have new members in abundance—their wives and daughters, etc.," she complained to a friend. "I have never felt the entertainment of company oppressive until now."

Attracted to power then as they are now, Washington insiders circled around Henry Clay and his wife. Margaret Bayard Smith soon reported, "Mrs. Clay persuaded me to go to the levee," the reception on New Year's Day 1811. The Clay nurse cared for the Smith baby while the women enjoyed Dolley Madison's punch and pastries. In 1810, when Samuel Harrison Smith sold the *National Intelligencer* to newspaperman Joseph Gales, the family settled into a country house in what was then a distant part of northeast Washington. For the congressional session, they and their now three children came back to the city, sharing a boardinghouse with "a large company"—the Clays, Vice President Clinton, "and a number of gentlemen." Margaret boasted to her sister, "I have formed habits of sociability with Mr. and Mrs. Clay only." The following summer "Mrs. Clay and her six children" visited the Smiths in the country. Though Clay was a Republican like James Madison, he and his fellow War Hawks differed with the president on his approach to foreign policy. They were ready to take up arms against England, both for impressing sailors on the seas and fortifying Indians on the frontier. And fighting England's ally, Spain, for control of its American possessions in West and East Florida would be fine with this group of politicians as well.

Madison, on the other hand, was desperately trying to keep the peace, and Napoleon had sent signals that a change in his policy toward American shipping was in the offing. If he could get the French to agree to a commercial treaty, Madison reasoned, the British would be pressured into following suit. But no one trusted Bonaparte.

When a ship from France arrived in late 1810, bringing official reports showing "nothing contradictory of the *affectionate* intentions of Napoleon," Dolley Madison was pleased though wary. Public affairs, she told her cousin in Kentucky, "are troublesome and difficult—You see the English are stubborn yet, but we anticipate their yielding before long." Instead of the English yielding, however, the French grew more intransigent. Still, Madison thought he had a better chance of getting a deal with Napoleon than with George III and, in a last-ditch effort at avoiding war, he dispatched an envoy to France with instructions to come home with a treaty. The man he picked for the mission, Joel Barlow, and his wife, Ruth, were both good friends of Dolley Madison, who was suspected of lobbying for Barlow with her husband. What's certainly the case is that she pushed for her hapless brother John Payne as secretary to the mission "at two thousand dollars per year." When she wrote to her brother-in-law about that plan, the First Lady confided she had other news as well about what was happening inside the administration, "but as *people say I have my opinions, etc, etc,* I must not trust my pen." Things were getting dicey for President Madison. He demanded the resignation of his incompetent and disloyal secretary of state, Robert Smith, and replaced him with James Monroe. Smith refused to go quietly, causing Dolley to complain about "*some very wicked and silly doings.*" Madison needed a diplomatic breakthrough with France, and the Barlows, who had lived in Paris for many years, seemed an obvious choice for what in the end would be a futile and fatal mission.

Joel Barlow was a poet of some renown and a prosperous businessman who in 1781 had secretly married Ruth Baldwin, described by a nineteenth-century historian as "one of the loveliest and best of women, to whose influence her husband always attributed his worldly success." The couple had fallen in love a few years before when Barlow was a student at Yale University and a friend of Ruth's brother. (Barlow also "kept company" with Elizabeth Whitman, the woman whose story inspired Hannah Foster's novel, *The Coquette*.) Ruth Barlow's father wanted her to have nothing to do with an aspiring poet who would likely never amount to anything. And Joel soon learned that a few lines of verse would not pay the bills, so, after studying for the ministry, he enlisted as a chaplain in George Washington's Continental Army, all the while working on an epic poem about America. After the war Barlow, with a group of his Yale classmates, including Margaret Dwight's uncle Timothy, earned the nickname "The Wicked Wits" for their contributions to journals and newspapers, making them the first homegrown school of writers in the country. Piecing together an income as a journalist, printer, and then lawyer, in 1787 Barlow published *The Vision of Columbus* to instant success, his dream fulfilled. Still, writing poetry was no way to make a living, so Joel Barlow eventually bit the bullet and went into business.

As an agent for what turned out to be a fraudulent Ohio land company, he traveled to France in 1788 to see what he could sell. His wife, Ruth, joined him two years later, and the pair became a fixture on the European intellectual scene, living in both London and Paris. Barlow became a political pamphleteer, befriending such notables as Thomas Paine and Mary Wollstonecraft along with Thomas Jefferson and the Marquis de Lafayette. It was in a homesick moment abroad in 1793 that Barlow wrote his most famous and lasting poem, *The Hasty Pudding.*

He would grow more homesick as the French Revolution devolved into the Reign of Terror, and the Barlows fled Paris for the town of Altona, then part of Denmark, where Joel could ply his new and very lucrative trade as an agent for American shipping companies based in nearby Hamburg. In 1796, the U.S. government sent Barlow, by now a wealthy and well-known expatriate, to Algiers with the assignment of ransoming more than one hundred American sailors held hostage by the Barbary pirates. In the course of the harrowing negotiation, after succeeding in freeing the long-imprisoned sailors, the Dey of Algiers kept Barlow himself in the country for almost a year until close to a million dollars in gold arrived from America. Forlornly Joel lamented to Ruth he was "the only American slave in Algiers." Once released, Barlow moved on to the other North African states, establishing a system of annual tribute payments—bribes to stop the pirates from seizing American ships. Alone in Altona, Ruth wrote to her brother Abraham Baldwin: "I cannot tell you how much it is my wish to return to peace and retirement. I have been so long tumbled about the world."

It must have been quite a life for her. First to defy her father by marrying Joel Barlow, then to sail to France on her own to meet him, then to run from their home in Paris to a strange country where she had to learn German because "it is difficult to live in this country without it." And she was so cut off from home. Having just learned that one brother had died, she told her brother Abraham that he was so distant that "I do not expect to see you more than once or twice in my life." In fact, she did see Abraham when he was a senator from Georgia and she ran the most popular salon in the nation's capital. It became home in 1805, after a few years back in France, living in grand style, where the childless couple "adopted" a young American would-be inventor, Robert Fulton. With their old friend Thomas Jefferson as president, Joel and Ruth Barlow thought it was time to heed his encouragement to move to Washington.

They bought an enormous estate and christened it "Kalorama," now a posh section of town. It soon became a center of social life for the city. Ruth Barlow's records find her one day receiving Mrs. Washington (Dolley Madison's sister), Mrs. Peters (Martha Washington's granddaughter), and Mrs. Monroe (James Monroe's wife); another day, Mrs. Lewis (Nelly Custis Lewis, another granddaughter of Martha Washington) and Mrs. Latrobe (wife of the architect). In addition to all the entertaining, Ruth devoted much attention to her younger half sister Clara, who lived with the Barlows after her husband deserted her.

In 1810, with Clara off in Connecticut taking care of her ailing mother, Ruth kept her apprised of the comings and goings in the federal city. On New Year's evening of 1810, President and Mrs. Madison attended a dance in Georgetown, and "as the chariot was returning to take them home, the coachman overset it and injured it much." The Barlows had tickets to the dances or "assemblies" in both Georgetown and Washington, held every two weeks, and the city was "uncommonly gay this winter, there have been a great many strangers, belles and beaux and five or six weddings and parties and balls without number." The social round was nonstop—so was the influx of houseguests. Robert Fulton "popped in . . . without the smallest notice. I was never more surprised—you see I had no opportunity to say no." Ruth was writing while her husband had taken Fulton and another guest off to one of Dolley Madison's drawing rooms. A few days later, the inventor went by himself: "Mme. Bonaparte was there. Fulton says she is very handsome." That winter the drawing rooms were especially popular with Betsy Bonaparte in town, "handsome and disposed to be sociable, her manners are easy unaffected, she is lively, rather witty." And, as always, "Mrs. Madison is gay and amiable."

"What do you think of the French Emperor's divorce from his Josephine?" Ruth Barlow asked her half sister Clara, adding with apparent sarcasm that the emperor would sacrifice anything for his people "and this divorcing his beloved wife to give them an heir to the throne from his own blood is giving the greatest and most convincing proof of his affection for them that ever man gave. So goes the world." Then, this wife of twenty-nine years added plaintively: "You must not be surprised if hubby should think *we* ought to be divorced" because they had no children. "I have at times wished to die that he might marry again and leave an heir. This is true. I do not know whether I could consent to be divorced from the man I love, from pure affection and regard for his happiness, this is going a great length."

Contemplating Clara's future, Ruth advised the younger woman to think hard "before you put on the shackles again. At best matrimony is a kind of bondage, enjoy a while your liberty with those who love you." The women of Washington had been chewing over the hot topic of whether Clara should change her name from that of her perfidious husband, "Kennedy," back to "Baldwin." "We think it should be Mrs. Baldwin until you choose to change that name for one you like better." Again and again the older sister who had defied her father's counsels for the sake of love cautioned against "the folly of matrimony," warning that "few men are worthy of the sacrifice of liberty." She herself had been "more fortunate in my *matrimony* than most of my sex," but still, "*love* my dear sister is a soft but delusive passion. Trust it not. I have been its votary and now know what it is, not worth the pangs it costs." Ruth would admit, however, that the new Russian ambassador had "one of the finest faces I ever saw," and she swooned, "were I in love's way might be dangerous to my heart." Despite her stern sermons, Ruth Barlow still had a romantic streak. She needn't have worried so much about her sister leaping back into the married state. It was as a single woman that Clara Baldwin accompanied Joel and Ruth Barlow when they embarked on their mission to France.

As the Barlow party boarded the U.S.S. *Constitution* in the summer of 1811 (without Dolley Madison's brother who had money problems) Rosalie Calvert was excited that an official delegation might actually be able to deliver correspondence to her family. "This will reach you through the courtesy of Mr. Barlow who is going as Ambassador to Paris," she told her sister in July. Later that year she guessed that Mr. Barlow "could manage it so that I could get the candelabra, etc., that you bought for me. A large number of articles always come in these government ships." Dolley Madison too hoped to import some French finery courtesy of the Barlows: "I will ask the favor of you to send me by safe vessels—large headdresses, a few flowers, feathers, gloves & stockings (black & white) or any other pretty thing, suitable to an economist." Ruth Barlow was the recipient of that request, but it was William Lee, the secretary to the delegation, who became chief purchasing agent for the First Lady. "Never a poor fellow worked harder or took more pains to endeavor to give satisfaction," Clara Baldwin chuckled to Dolley. "He has done nothing else this two months but waddle round Paris & cull from the magazines of fashion—he ought to thank you for it, for it has reduced him to quite a decent size." Clara was certainly exaggerating about how much time Lee spent shopping, but the Barlow mission did seem to be spinning its wheels in Paris.

Joel Barlow had been burdened with the impossible task of convincing Napoleon to act against what the emperor saw as his own self-interest. But the French monarch did not simply reject the U.S. request that he reverse his policy toward neutral shippers. Instead, Bonaparte strung Barlow along, implying that any day he might be summoned to talk shop. Knowing that he was likely to be coming under attack at home for having "produced but little effect" after three months in Paris, Barlow explained himself to *Mrs.* Madison, in the hope that she would favorably represent his case to the president. "The president may think I have been idle. If he should approve my conduct I wish you would let me know it. For you cannot realize how much I am attached to him & his administration." Napoleon kept dangling the prospect of "changing his system relative to the U States" and Barlow held up the departure of a U.S. ship, hoping to be able to convey that good news. Finally the ship sailed with no official response from the emperor, but Barlow was sure he would have it soon.

The diplomat had every reason to believe that things would go his way—he had been warmly received by the French government. In sharp contrast to the treatment of Charles and Mary Pinckney fifteen years earlier, Ruth and Joel Barlow were the toasts of the town. The invitations came from the highest quarters—from the emperor himself to the Palace of St. Cloud; from Queen Hortense, married to the King of Holland, Napoleon's brother, but living in Paris; from the Prince and Princess of Schwarzenberg, intimates of the emperor; from the Duke and Duchess of Bassano, minister of foreign affairs and his wife; from the Duchess of Montebello, widow of one of Napoleon's most revered generals. "I have got to be a prodigious fine gentlemen & perfect courtier," Barlow pouted to Dolley, but the diplomatic dance wasn't getting him any closer to a treaty with France.

The Barlows comfortably moved back into the house in Paris they had lived in a few years earlier, and Ruth kept up her correspondence with Dolley, trying to buffer any abuse of her husband, reminding the First Lady of their friendship. Clara had spent her first few months in Paris laid up with a bad knee, Ruth chattily reported, but her own health was "better than I expected, it has supported a vast deal of fatigue of every kind—if we can serve our country & do anything which may add to the honor & prosperity of the present Administration we shall esteem ourselves most happy." It wasn't a subtle message—we're working hard here, the diplomat's wife was telling the president through his own wife, don't blame my husband for Napoleon's perfidy.

The indirect communication went in the other direction as well. When Madison wanted to slap Barlow's hand for divulging the state of his negotiations to a friend who leaked it to the press, Dolley, apologizing for "aught that give you pain," delivered the unofficial message to the envoy's wife. "I am preparing you for the disapprobation expressed with Mr. Barlow's having told the state of his negotiation to Mr. Granger who directly gave it circulation & a place in the newspapers," she gently chided, "all this is from the people, not from the Cabinet—yet you know everything vibrates there." Dolley soothed the sting of those words with pages of friendly gossip, both political and personal. Her sister Lucy, the widow of George Steptoe Washington, had married Judge Todd on March 30, 1812, in the first wedding at the presidential mansion; she was grateful for the items sent from Paris, though they were too expensive, "the dresses and every other article indeed is beautiful"; she would not be able to send the portraits of herself and Madison Ruth had requested, since Gilbert Stuart left town "we have no painter of skill in this quarter." But all of the chitchat was background noise to the news: "Before this you know of our Embargo to be followed by War!! Yes that terrible event is at hand and yet England wants faith!"

Ruth Barlow didn't need Dolley Madison to tell her that there was grousing at home about her husband's failure to secure a treaty with France. She would not yet have received the First Lady's letter when she sent off one of her own: "Should censure fall on my husband, I hope it will not extend it to the president on his account, if not, we shall be content with consciousness of having tried to do the best to promote the interest and prosperity of the country, the honor and glory of the administration." Ruth could pour on the praise to protect Joel, but she didn't mince words about administration policy—the country, she believed, was headed in the wrong direction: "I am sorry to see such a warlike appearance in America, energy is necessary & to prepare forward often preserves peace—I hope and believe that will be the case now & that dreadful scourge to humanity still be averted from our happy country . . . though our property be taken & our flag insulted, it seems to me a small evil in comparison to war." But war was all Napoleon was thinking about, thwarting Joel Barlow's efforts to protect the peace: "Everything here is so occupied with the great projected expedition of the Emperor, that everything else seems of little consequence." Bonaparte was preparing to invade Russia, a fateful maneuver for the French army and for Joel Barlow.

Throughout the summer of 1812 the Barlows received word of the heightening hostilities at home. "War, they say, is declared against England," Ruth wrote from St. Cloud to Clara back in Paris. A letter from Eliza Parke Custis gives a sense of the pressure on Barlow: "Our country is distracted with contending parties—God grant your good husband may send us good news from France or I fear we shall have war with that nation." When Napoleon signaled he was finally ready to sign a treaty and summoned Barlow to meet him in Wilna, Lithuania, the American envoy had no choice but to go. From the outset, Ruth was uneasy. "I almost fear for your safety, we have so many reports here that I am anxious on every account." Ruth was not just concerned for her husband's safety, she had ample reason to doubt the prospects of his success. "He has to be sure been often and long put off with promises," she admitted to Dolley Madison soon after Barlow departed; "he has endeavored to parry their strokes, and thinks he shall have them at last, as every thing now coincides in our favor." Mrs. Barlow dared not say more for fear of her letter being intercepted, except that Joel harbored "high raised expectations" as he set out on his long, cold crossing of Europe. Ruth amplified that information a few days later: "He left Paris with the most flattering hopes of being able to communicate directly with the Emperor and of being able to convince him that in doing us justice he would advance his own interest and glory." That hope gave "Mr. B." courage to brave the terrible weather and treacherous roads from Berlin to Wilna.

As Barlow traveled east, Ruth sent on his coded diplomatic dispatches, along with her own words of support to "the lover of my age, the partner of my youth, of my joys and sorrows." Barlow needed all the encouragement he could get. Describing the roads to Ruth, "The mud, the true sublime, the real majesty of mud you know nothing about, having seen nothing of it either in Paris or Hartford or Maryland or Holland or any other country," the frustrated poet waxed on. "The horses legs are the ladles that stir it up, the carriage wheels whirl it over your head in a black rainbow as you move." In Poland a friend, General Wattersdorff, met up with the American envoy, which was welcome news to Ruth: "To find a friend and companion in such a place is very pleasant," she surmised in a letter to the general, teasing that he should keep a "watchful eye" on her husband "when he is in the society of those fascinating Polish beauties, those suns that shine by night." More seriously, Ruth expressed her fears: "I feel afraid you will all freeze if you do not starve—the weather here is bitter cold, 10 degrees at sunrise this morning and we have no sun. The poor army! How I feel for them, do try to get away . . . before they reach your vicinity. You will be swallowed up and not get straw to lie upon I fear." Ruth Barlow had it right.

By the time she penned those words Napoleon had snuck out of Russia by sleigh and was headed back to Paris to quell an attempted coup. The French army fled the frozen steppes in full retreat as hundreds of thousands of men and horses perished on snow-covered exit routes. Trying to outrun Russian troops in pursuit of the French, the diplomats who had assembled in Wilna, including Joel Barlow, turned back toward Paris, moving day and night by carriage in sub-zero temperatures. Stopping for a brief rest after three days on the road, Napoleon sped by them, rushing west. Barlow shot off a coded message to Ruth: "The Emperor is fleeing from assassination by his own troops." In the chaos, with temperatures so low that the carriage driver beat his passengers to keep them from freezing to death, the fifty-eight-year-old Joel Barlow contracted pneumonia. The American diplomat died near Krakow, Poland, at Christmastime 1812 having never succeeded in signing a treaty with France.

Ruth Barlow received official word of her husband's death on January 17, 1813, but by then the news had already reached her. American friends gathered around as condolences came in. In August, as Ruth was preparing to sail home, she wrote her will. In it she declared "my intention of erecting a monument over the grave of my beloved husband near Cracovia in Poland." She then stipulated instructions: "I desire that the said monument be made in a pyramidical form fifteen feet high. That it be of the marble or stone of that country, that it be built solid and plain but in all respects suitable to its objects." No such monument was ever built, but there's a plaque in the church adjoining the cemetery where the diplomat was buried, placed there by a young Polish soldier whose life Barlow saved. In the 1990s an American diplomat living in Krakow found the church and arranged to have the plaque restored. A couple of years later the organization of retired diplomats and consular officers raised the funds for an outdoor monument, finally fulfilling Ruth Barlow's wishes.

WHILE THE BARLOWS sat frustrated by Napoleon in France, Louisa and John Quincy Adams continued to succeed in establishing commercial relationships as the American representatives in St. Petersburg. But Abigail Adams wanted them back in Boston. When, soon after their arrival, the couple wrote home about the strains on their finances in the extravagant Russian capital, Abigail—who had suffered similar economic hardships when her husband was envoy in England—decided to take matters into her own hands. Without consulting her son, John Quincy Adams's mother wrote to the president of the United States asking him to recall his ambassador to Russia: "The outfit and salary allowed by Congress is altogether so inadequate to the state and manner of living required as indispensable at the court of St. Petersburg that inevitable ruin must be the consequence to himself and family." Reminding Madison that she knew what it was to sacrifice for her country, Abigail Adams pressed on, "I will allow sir that there are situations and circumstances in which a country may be placed when it becomes the duty of a good citizen to hazard not only property but even his life to save and serve it—in that school I was raised—but those days I hope have past." She feared, she said, her son would be subject to "pecuniary embarrassments which would prevent his future usefulness." The former First Lady closed this meddling missive by bestowing her blessing on the Republican president: "As this is the only opportunity I have ever had of addressing you sir permit me to say that I entertain a high respect for your person and character and to add my best wishes for the success and prosperity of your administration." (The once ardent Federalist Abigail Adams had, in fact, supported Madison's election, telling her daughter Nabby Smith that she judged him "a moral man unexceptionable in private life" and, since her party had no chance of winning, "the best and least exceptionable on the other side is a desirable object.")

President Madison wasted no time replying to the formidable Mrs. Adams from his home at Montpelier. He hadn't heard that Adams wanted to come home, he said, but because of her letter he had told "the Secretary of State to let him understand that as it was not the purpose of the Executive to subject him to the personal sacrifices which he finds unavoidable, he will not in retiring from them, impair the sentiments which led to his appointment." In other words,

Adams would suffer no repercussions if he decided to come home. Graciously, the president signed off: "Be pleased, Madame, to accept my acknowledgements for the gratifying expressions with which you have favored me and to be assured of my high esteem and very respectful consideration." Madison then transmitted to Ambassador Adams papers for his resignation with the bulletin that his "highly respectable mother" had requested his return. But the president hoped the "peculiar urgency manifested in the letter of Mrs. Adams was rather hers, than yours." He suspected correctly that Abigail's letter was the work of the mother, not the son; President Madison needed his envoy in St. Petersburg and feared what message it might send to Adams's friend the czar if he suddenly departed.

But domestic politics soon trumped concerns about foreign potentates and an opening on the Supreme Court changed the president's mind. The death of a man from Massachusetts, Justice William Cushing, meant that Madison needed to shore up support in New England, a region in full revolt against his policies. Ideal solution: appoint Bostonian John Quincy Adams, loyal to Madison but still a New Englander of perfect pedigree. Abigail was ecstatic. Crowing to Louisa, "An appointment so honorably made, so unanimously concurred in and so universally accepted," she cheered, "cannot fail to excite in this breast the most pleasant sensations." To her son, Abigail made the case for his acceptance of the appointment: in addition to his service to the public in a nonpartisan position he would be able to guide his boys' schooling and care for his elderly parents. She was certain "that after mature reflection you will resign yourself to the call of your country, and hold the office of Justice with an honest heart, and a steady hand." John Quincy's mother needed him nearby—her daughter Nabby was terribly sick and she feared it was "one of the most dreaded of all complaints," breast cancer. Waiting to hear what her son would do, Abigail Adams couldn't get information fast enough. She wrote to Louisa's mother in Washington asking if she thought it would be proper to poke around and find out if a ship had been ordered to bring the family home. But

John Quincy Adams had neither a desire to serve on the Supreme Court nor an urgent wish to leave St. Petersburg and he had an excuse to stay put that Abigail couldn't argue with: Louisa was pregnant.

Instead of blowing up at his mother for interfering in his life, John told her that he understood "your letter to the President was written from the tenderest and most affectionate concern for myself and my family." But they were managing, he assured her, to handle their finances, and so he had informed President Madison that "peculiar circumstances" would keep him in Russia for at least another year. (When word of Adams's refusal reached Washington, the politicking for the bench began in earnest as Dolley Madison told her friend Ruth Barlow, "The judges are not yet made—Mr. Duvall is thought of for Maryland . . . Mr. Adams having declined to return or accept." These women were forever worrying the politics.) Louisa's pregnancy was actually her third in Russia; she had suffered two miscarriages. But by the time her husband used it as a pretext to do what he wanted to do, she was well along with this baby. In fact, her condition had already been detected at court.

One night at the palace in January 1811, when the czar assigned one of his officials to act as Mrs. Adams's guardian throughout the evening, "my astonishment and embarrassment was painful, for I had no idea that my delicate situation had been observed by anyone and it put me sadly to the blush." Alexander tried to convince Louisa to take a seat on the dais "by the Empress who sat on an elevated seat attended by her ladies. I thankfully declined the honor—when he insisted and said don't you know that no one says nay to the Emperor. I laughed and replied 'but *I* am a republican.' He smiled and went on his way." She didn't want to be the center of attention but this court life could be tricky.

With a baby on the way and the long winter upon them, "we all pined for home." Louisa missed her children and she was apprehensive about this one: "To give birth to another child in a strange land after all I had suffered was a cause of incessant fear and anxiety."

And then—"a new anxiety"; there were "rumors of war between Russia and France." Still, the entertainments continued, though the French were "a little down." There was the event at the home of Baroness Strogonoff whose husband was ambassador to Naples, "but he would not take her with him, she is too eccentric and might have brought trouble on him." There was "a party at Madame Lessep's . . . a very sensible woman." But sensible, Louisa wryly noted, would only take a woman so far. "The maxim of men that 'pretty is better than good' is almost universally adopted by them where money does not bias the taste." There were balls with suppers at three in the morning and "a craps table for the elderly." And there was the night when her dinner partners almost sent her into a rage: "What on earth is so disgusting as two old men chuckling over their past follies and vices!"

Once spring came Louisa kept close to home: "My situation precludes me from entering into the dissipations of the day." Now the couple could expect mail after telling Abigail that they had not "received any letters from America for six months, the Baltic was not clear of ice so that vessels could get up." But when letters did arrive they brought only bad news. Louisa's sister Nancy Hellen had died in childbirth, losing the baby as well, terrifying her pregnant sister who had such a hard history with her own deliveries: "The fright produced alarming consequences and a premature birth was threatened with dangerous symptoms for some hours." As she recovered, Louisa "received letters from our children . . . they allayed my fears and assisted my recovery."

Before the baby was born, the Adams entourage was forced to move again since the house they were renting had been sold, and they found a pleasant place near the czar's summer palace on Apothecary Island. Ambassador John Quincy Adams was in a reflective mood, writing on his fourteenth wedding anniversary at the end of July that he enjoyed "a portion of felicity resulting from this relation in society greater than falls to the generality of mankind, and far beyond anything that I have been conscious of deserving." It's not the "effusion of sentiment" that Abigail Adams kept wanting from her husband when they were separated for years, and it probably would have made Louisa at least cock an eyebrow, but it was John Quincy's way of saying he loved her. He then did go on, of course, to cite the problems that had arisen over the years—she was sick much of the time, they disagreed about "domestic economy" and the education of the children, and their tempers were both "quick and irascible," but all in all, he concluded, it was a good match. Louisa too seemed to be in a somewhat satisfied state that summer. "I go down to the end of the garden, have a chair on the bank of the river with Charles and we catch fish not worth eating," the very pregnant Louisa wrote in July. "It is an indolent sort of amusement that just suits me for I *do not think*—when I look forward I tremble." But a couple of weeks later, on August 12, 1811, she trumpeted with glee, "My child, a daughter, the first that I was ever blessed with was born at half past seven o'clock . . . my sister went and announced her birth to her father and he soon came in to bless and kiss his babe." A girl—Louisa Adams was thrilled. So was John Quincy, who beamed to his mother, "I think this will convince you that the climate of St. Petersburg is *not* too cold to produce an American." When the baby was about three weeks old, Louisa joyously inscribed, "my lovely little babe was christened . . . and she was named after *me* by her father's special desire contrary to my wish." The Adamses decided it was the better part of wisdom, as good republicans, not to have the emperor stand as godfather. For a few months Louisa knew true happiness with her beautiful baby girl. "O she grows lovely. Such a pair of Eyes!! I fear I love her too well."

But then a courier delivered devastating news from home: "A letter full of woe announcing my mother's death and that of my brother-in-law." Louisa's mother, Catherine Johnson, had died on September 29 from a fever that ravaged Washington, taking her daughter Caroline's husband as well. A letter from Abigail Adams also informed them of the deaths within twenty-four hours of her sister and soul mate, Mary Cranch, and Mary's husband, Richard, custodians of young George Adams. The grim missive added a bulletin on what Louisa described as her sister-in-law's "dangerous and hopeless illness." In October Nabby Smith had undergone a mastectomy. She was conscious while she endured the twenty-five-minute surgery. Abigail Adams declared her daughter a "heroine," and concluded "she is doing as well as could be expected after an operation in which the whole breast is taken off." Though Louisa saw the disease as "hopeless," Nabby's mother clung to the belief that her daughter would fully recover. Abigail had originally been willing to buy the diagnosis of Boston doctors who thought it was not cancer. Nabby, suspecting the doctors were wrong, had consulted her parents' old friend Benjamin Rush, still the nation's foremost doctor, who had recommended the surgery. Rush had also been pestering John Adams and Thomas Jefferson to put aside their political differences and resume their old friendship through the mails. The doctor finally effected the rapprochement in late 1811, when Jefferson said he would agree to a correspondence but that "from this fusion of mutual affections, Mrs. Adams is, of course, separated." The former president was still smarting from his exchange with Abigail.

That terrible winter when Nabby Adams tried to recuperate in Quincy, in St. Petersburg, with the thermometer at "thirty two and a quarter below zero," Louisa mourned her mother: "After ten years of poverty, dependence and severe suffering which at the great distance it was so utterly out of my power to mitigate or assuage." And then there was more to mourn: "My lovely beautiful babe is very, very ill." That was February 1812 and Louisa was filled with foreboding: "Everyone who sees her stops her in the street and they all say 'she is born for heaven.'" Came summer, French forces marched toward Russia, America declared war on Great Britain, and little Louisa grew sicker. Her mother and aunt took the baby to the country hoping the change of air would help, but they soon returned with the infant "in convulsions." The baby's father described them as "so severe that the sight of them would have wrung compassion from a heart of marble." On September 15, 1812, John Quincy Adams sadly chronicled, "at twenty five minutes past one this morning expired my daughter Louisa Catherine, as lovely an infant as ever breathed the air of heaven." The baby's heartbroken mother entered only one line in her own diary: "My child gone to heaven." A few days later, John wrote to his mother about the loss of his baby girl "with the finest pair of black eyes you ever saw." It was then Abigail's sad task to tell baby Louisa's big brothers. George and John had never met this little sister who had so delighted their parents.

"My heart is buried in my Louisa's grave and my greatest longing is to be laid beside her." Louisa blamed herself for the baby's death—convinced that she had weaned little Louisa too soon, even though the doctor had insisted on it. She missed her children in America more than ever, and wished she could cry on her mother-in-law's shoulder: "In Mrs. Adams I should have found a comforter, a friend who would pity sufferings which *she* would have understood." Abigail Adams too had lost a thirteen-month-old baby girl. Sitting down to write her daughter-in-law, Abigail remembered her baby Susannah's death: "Forty years has not obliterated from my mind the anguish of my soul upon the occasion. . . . Let us with gratitude bless our preserver that we have yet so many blessings left us. Such I hope will prove to you, and to their father [of] your surviving children who most earnestly long for your return to your native country." But with war on both continents, travel was not possible. And soon John Quincy Adams's diplomatic services in St. Petersburg would be essential. "We behold here," Louisa registered in astonishment, "the Emperor of France, after sixteen years of the most unheard of successes, in the short space of one month, plunged into the horrors of extreme distress, flying for his life." With the routing of Napoleon's army in Russia, the victorious Czar Alexander was ready to flex his newfound power. He offered to mediate the war between Britain and the United States. President Madison accepted and dispatched two emissaries—Secretary of the Treasury Albert Gallatin and Senator James Bayard—to join John Quincy Adams in St. Petersburg to negotiate terms for peace.

THE DEMANDS ON AMERICA'S DIPLOMATS stationed abroad were the result of the war fever at home that President Madison could no longer stave off. Settlers in the West were itching to fight England; those in the South had Spain in their crosshairs. Thomas Jefferson had tried to claim the Spanish possessions along the Gulf of Mexico, called West Florida, as part of the Louisiana Purchase, but Spain insisted that it had not ceded that separately administered area. After years of talk, in 1810 the American settlers rebelled against their Spanish rulers and were expected to join their area to the United States. But the West Floridians decided instead to form an independent republic, captured the Spanish headquarters in Baton Rouge, and briefly flew their own flag. President Madison quickly issued a proclamation annexing the territory to the United States and, after token resistance, the Republic of West Florida succumbed. Though Spain did not recognize the annexation, it was a done deal, leaving Spanish rule nowhere east of the Mississippi, except for Mobile, a small strip along the Gulf of Mexico to the east, plus the current state of Florida. Some American settlers wanted to grab those outposts as well, but Madison wasn't ready to take on the Spanish when he was already at swords' points with the British and failing to reach an accommodation with the French.

Tensions in the U.S. Congress grew tauter, as no policy short of war succeeded in stopping the British from harassing American ships at sea and aiding the Indians hassling American settlers in the West. Madison kept trying various kinds of economic sanctions, infuriating his opponents. One, the always volatile John Randolph let loose with such scathing remarks against an 1811 version of trade restrictions and one of its sponsors, John Eppes, that an outraged Eppes challenged his fellow Virginian to a duel. This was the second of Thomas Jefferson's sons-in-law to demand John Randolph's presence on the dueling grounds. Dolley Madison, well aware that a killing over the unpopular law would inflame passions even more, intervened and somehow managed to convince the duelists to stand down. "Everybody is astonished at a conclusion so contrary to custom," the French minister explained to Paris, "and all the credit of the affair remained Mrs. Madison's."

The First Lady was unable to work the same magic on Secretary of State Robert Smith. No longer willing to put up with Smith's lack of diplomatic skills and open hostility to his foreign policy, Madison replaced him with James Monroe. Nonetheless, the Madisons wanted to stay in the good graces of Robert Smith and his powerful brother in Congress, Samuel Smith. So Dolley pulled out the stops—bringing both of her sisters along to call on the Smith family. But this time Mrs. Madison's charm didn't work. The Smith brothers would become sworn enemies of the Madison administration. To find out exactly what they were up to, Dolley dispatched her cousin, the president's secretary Edward Coles, to Baltimore to see what he could learn. He related that though he had been well received by all branches of the Smith family, "The Smiths are said not directly to vent their spleen, but to spur on their relations & friends, many of whom are extremely abusive of the President & Col. Monroe." With this piece of useful but worrisome intelligence to relay to the president, Dolley concluded the correspondence by supporting Madison's choice of James Monroe: "I exult in my heart at the full indemnification we have for all their malice in Col. Monroe's talents and virtue."

Dolley Madison had not always been so fond of the new secretary of state, who ran for Congress against Madison back in 1788 and had allowed himself to be put forward for president by John Randolph in 1808. As that campaign heated up, John Quincy Adams had noted in his diary that he had heard Mrs. Madison "spoke very slightingly of Mr. Monroe." She had pointedly omitted Madison's fellow Virginian from the entertainments at Montpelier that year. But now an ally of her husband's, Monroe was in the First Lady's good graces, as he had been at various points earlier in his career. And Monroe was working hard to placate the War Hawks. One of them, freshman congressman William Lowndes of South Carolina, was married to Elizabeth Pinckney, daughter of Thomas Pinckney, the former governor of South Carolina and envoy to Spain and England, and the niece of Charles Cotesworth Pinckney. Lowndes wrote regularly to his wife about the other members of his "mess," the slang term for the boardinghouse, especially fellow South Carolinian John Calhoun and Speaker Henry Clay. "Mr. Monroe supped with us last night," Lowndes told Elizabeth and, in answer to her grandmother, the redoubtable Rebecca Motte, who had inquired about the price of rice futures, "expressed the opinion that until war shall be actually declared, flour and rice will sell higher than if war were not expected." Everyone believed war was inevitable, including Dolley: "*I* have no doubt but that Congress will be called before November." A special session, she stated with certainty, would be summoned to declare war against Britain.

Her sister Lucy prayed she was wrong, "I am sorry indeed our affairs over the water should wear so unfavorable an aspect—but still hope we shall not be reduced to war—fighting is as much my aversion as it ever was Jeffersons." Placing herself in the same league as the former president, Lucy also offered an analysis of the next year's election: "You despair too soon about our ticket," scolded this widow of a congressman, "no doubt twill come out [a] thumping prize." Dolley wasn't so sure. "The intrigue for P[resident] and Vice P[resident] go on," she told her sister Anna at the end of the year. Robert Smith had distributed a venom-filled diatribe against administration policies, provoking even the good-natured Dolley: "You ask me if we laughed over the Smith Pamphlet. Mr. M did, but I did not—It was too impertinent to excite any other feeling in me but anger." With Smith drumming up opposition and other factions forming inside the Republican party, Dolley couldn't predict what might happen.

Still, the First Family was managing to have a good time. "We have had plays here for some time. M. and myself have been 3 or 4 times," Dolley enthused to Anna. "The city is gayer than I ever knew it in summer." The Madisons had taken the new French minister with them to the theater and enjoyed an "elegant" party "on the queen's birth night" at the British ambassador's. The prospect of war with one or the other of these nations didn't stop their ambassadors from socializing. "As our mess is certainly the strongest war mess in Congress," William Lowndes told his wife, "we excite, I believe, not a little surprise and perhaps some suspicions by our attending the parties of Mr. Foster." The entire mess, "male and female," had been to the Queen's birth night at the British ambassador's, then these War Hawks "committed the yet more unpardonable offense of inviting him to dinner, and I dare say some of the papers will consider this as an overt act of treason." In part, the Republican Lowndes was trying to show how broad-minded he was to his staunchly Federalist wife. It was the Federalists who decided to stay home as the election heated up, briefly boycotting the First Lady's "squeezes." But members of the president's own party disturbed Dolley more: "Electioneering yet," she fretted to her sister in March 1812, "DeWitt, etc, etc, & The Smiths & I know not who all, intend to break us down." DeWitt Clinton, nephew of the sitting vice president, was leading a Republican revolt against Madison. A week later Dolley issued another bulletin: "The vice p lies dangerously ill—Electioneering for his office goes on beyond all description. The world seems to be running mad, what with one thing & another." But the First Lady could privately show smug satisfaction about one thing—the snubbing of her receptions by the opposition party had backfired into Republican support for the Madisons, forcing the Federalists to shift their tactics: "Last *night* & the *night* before, our rooms were crowded with Republicans, & such a rallying of our party has alarmed them into a *return*. They came in a large party last night also & are continually calling." As sweet as that triumph might be, the reality remained stark—the nation was on the brink: "The war business goes on slowly—but I fear twill be sure."

Abigail Adams too saw war as "inevitable" unless England ended "her injurious conduct," and Rosalie Calvert agreed that "our poor President Madison is at the end of his maneuvers." Predictably pessimistic, she wrote to her sister in the spring of 1812, "He doesn't know where to turn anymore and loses supporters every day." Rosalie's letter, which included the announcement that "our family has increased again by a daughter who is doing very well . . . I hope, however, that we won't have any more now," could not be mailed for more than a year because of the renewed embargo. Unable to sell their tobacco "at a tolerable price" due to the inability to ship it, the Calverts were "living a very retired life at present." "We have cut back on all possible expenses," Rosalie disclosed to her father in Belgium when she sent a letter informing him of the birth of her latest child. (Henry Stier advised her it was "time to rest on your laurels" and stop having children. That had also been his recommendation after the last baby: "Tell your husband to spare you a little in the future." Childbirth could be dangerous.) Rosalie was also having difficulty finding a wise investment for her father's money in the unstable economic situation. Nothing seemed certain in the country as the election of 1812 got under way. Vice President George Clinton died in April. In mid-May the Republican congressional caucus chose James Madison and Elbridge Gerry for president and vice president. Later that month a breakaway group of Republicans in New York nominated De Witt Clinton to challenge Madison. And all the while the Congress was debating war.

"John Randolph has been firing away at the House this morning against the declaration of War, but we suppose it will have little effect," Dolley Madison wrote to Anna in May. Dolley might well have witnessed the debate, since she and the other women of Washington were fixtures at the Capitol, taking in arguments in Congress and the Supreme Court, a practice that John Randolph found unseemly. The real purpose of this letter to her sister, however, was not to provide information but to press for the vote of Congressman Richard Cutts, Anna's husband, who was at home in Massachusetts. "If Mr. Cutts does not come it will be a disadvantage to him as well as to his party";

Dolley advised that Cutts needed to rush to the capital "to give his vote for War." He needn't have hurried. The debate droned on—in that era unlimited debates, or filibusters, were permitted in the House of Representatives—until one of the supporters of the war threw a brass spittoon across the chamber. The clatter (and the contents?) so surprised the speaker that he momentarily stopped talking and the filibuster was declared over. The House, with no Federalist votes in favor and fifteen Republicans in opposition, adopted the war resolution on June 4. The Senate followed suit a couple of weeks later by a vote of 19–13, and President Madison formally announced the declaration of war against Great Britain on June 19, 1812. Unbeknownst to him, the British parliament, under pressure from manufacturers who wanted to sell their goods in America, had just rescinded the "Orders in Council," the measures that had virtually shut down U.S. shipping. Had communication been faster, war would have been averted. It took until August for the message to reach Washington. "The Orders in Council are removed & *negotiation* must follow," Dolley Madison told a friend; "every disposition to meet an honorable peace is *here*." But Madison didn't know how Britain had responded to the U.S. declaration of war, making immediate negotiation impossible. The official documents took weeks, sometimes months, to make their way across the ocean, though the vessels that carried them were supposed to have diplomatic immunity from any interference.

Rosalie Calvert thought the British would make short shrift of her adopted country: "The English can, with some fishing line, take all our frigates," she wrote with some exasperation. "But what I fear infinitely more is that it could produce a civil war—[something] much more to be feared than the English. In Baltimore the mob already governs the city, has demolished one house and is threatening others. This same mob only needs a leader like Burr, for example, to come to Washington, throw our poor President out the window and take the government." (The Baltimore mob had destroyed the house of a newspaper editor who had written an antiwar editorial. When he moved, that house was also mobbed, and when the police took him to jail for safekeeping the rowdies took down the jail.) What Rosalie probably did not know as she wrote those words was that Aaron Burr, five years after escaping to Europe, had just returned to America.

ONCE THE DISGRACED former vice president failed to find backing in England for his scheme of empire, Aaron Burr headed for France in 1809, angling for Napoleon's support. (He was essentially driven out of England for failure to comply with the laws requiring the registration of aliens. This man, who had fought in the American Revolution, claimed that he had been born a British citizen and that could not be taken away from him.) Burr sailed first to Sweden and then made his way down through Germany to Paris. Along the way he visited anyone who would take him in, including Rosalie Calvert's sister Isabelle van Havre. "I am vexed that you didn't write me any more about Colonel Burr's visit to you," Rosalie pouted when she learned about it. "You say he has the air of a rogue. He is certainly not a man one can esteem, but he does have some superior talents, and I wouldn't be surprised to see him at the head of the government in a few years."

But Aaron Burr's talents weren't working for him in France. Bonaparte would have nothing to do with the outcast American, who found himself poverty-stricken in Paris and desperate to go home. It took years for the fugitive from justice to convince the government to grant him a passport, and more years to book safe passage. Burr arrived in New York on June 8, 1812, more interested in making money after his years of privation than in taking over the government. And he was most interested in seeing his daughter and adored grandson. Those long-cherished hopes were soon shattered by a letter from his son-in-law, Joseph Alston, now the governor of South Carolina, with the dreadful news that little Aaron Burr Alston was dead: "He who was to have transmitted down the mingled blood of Theodosia and myself—he who was to have redeemed all your glory, and shed new lustre upon our families—that boy, at once our happiness and our pride, is taken from us—is dead." The ten-year-old, his parents' only child, had succumbed to some sort of fever. His mother, of course, was devastated: "Theodosia has endured all that a human being could endure; but her admirable mind will triumph. She supports herself in a manner worthy of your daughter." Alston knew that the sight of her father would be the best medicine for Theodosia. "My present wish is that Theodosia should join you, with or without me, as soon as possible." The governor served as brigadier-general of the state militia and wasn't sure what his duties would be "if the war be seriously carried on," but he knew his always sickly wife would be better off in the company of her long-lost father.

Theodosia wasn't well enough to travel until December, when Burr sent his friend Timothy Green to escort her to New York. "Alston seemed rather hurt that you should conceive it necessary to send a person here, as he or one of his brothers would attend Mrs. Alston to New-York," Green confided after he had visited with the governor in Columbia, the state capital. "He said that he was inclined to charter a vessel to take her on. I informed him that I should return to Charleston, where I should remain a day or two, and then proceed to Georgetown (S.C.) and wait his arrival."

Two weeks later, Green communicated an update: "I have engaged a passage to New-York for your daughter in a pilot-boat that has been out privateering, but has come in here, and is refitting merely to get to New-York. My only fears are that Governor Alston may think the mode of conveyance too undignified, and object to it; but Mrs. Alston is fully bent on going." (A "privateer" attacked British ships with U.S. government approval. In this case the guns were all under wraps.) They would leave in about eight days and Burr, his friend prepared him, should not be surprised to see how feeble and emaciated his daughter had become. Joseph Alston went to the port city of Georgetown, South Carolina, to see his wife off on December 31. He would never see her again.

After two weeks, when Alston hadn't heard from Theodosia, not knowing what else to do, he frantically wrote to his phantom wife: "Another mail, and still no letter! I hear, too, rumors of a gale off Cape Hatteras the beginning of the month! The state of my mind is dreadful. Let no man, wretched as he may be, presume to think himself beyond the reach of another blow. . . . All that I have left of heart is yours. All my prayers are for your safety and well-being." By the next week Alston was forced to deal with the fact that she was most likely gone. "Forebodings! wretched, heart-rending forebodings distract my mind. I may no longer have a wife; and yet my impatient restlessness addresses her a letter. To-morrow will be three weeks since our separation, and not yet one line. Gracious God! for what am I reserved?" The same day, Alston, desperate to take some action, addressed a somewhat accusatory letter to his father-in-law: "Tomorrow will be three weeks since, in obedience to your wishes, Theodosia left me. It is three weeks, and not yet one line from her. . . . Gracious God! Is my wife, too, taken from me? I do not know why I write, but I feel that I am miserable."

Letters from Burr to Alston crossed in the mails. Answering anguished questions, the son-in-law drew a detailed picture of the circumstances of Theodosia's departure: "I parted with our Theo. near the bar about noon on Thursday, the last of December. The wind was moderate and fair. She was in the pilot-boat-built schooner *Patriot*, Captain Overstocks, with an experienced New-York pilot, Coon, as sailing-master. This vessel, the same which had been sent by government last summer in pursuit of Commodore Rodgers's squadron, had been selected as one which, from her reputed excellence and swiftness in sailing, would ensure a passage of not more than five or six days. From that moment I have heard nothing of the schooner nor my wife. . . . I have in vain endeavored to build upon the hope of long passage. Thirty days are decisive. My wife is either captured or lost. . . . A short time since, and the idea of capture would have been the source of painful, terrible apprehension; it now furnishes me the only ray of comfort, or rather of hope, that I have. Each mail is anticipated with impatient, yet fearful and appalling anxiety."

No one knows what happened to the highly talented and once beautiful Theodosia Burr Alston. The idea that this "most accomplished woman of her time" had been captured by pirates caught the imaginations of nineteenth-century novelists, and several deathbed confessions by ancient sailors lent some credence to the theory. One old pirate claimed to have actually laid the plank that Theodosia then walked, all dressed in white, into the stormy sea. Another had his victim shouting from the end of the plank, "Vengeance is mine, saith the Lord." Yet another pictured her bobbing up from the water and waving gracefully before going under. The mystery of Theodosia Burr Alston's disappearance captivated the country. People named their children after her, including the silent movie star Theda Bara whose real name was Theodosia Burr Goodman. And conspiracy theories emerged surrounding the portrait of a beautiful woman in white said to have come from a pirate ship off the coast of North Carolina. Aaron Burr never bought into these fantasies: "Were she alive, all the prisons in the world could not keep her from her father. When I realized the truth of her death, the world became a blank to me, and life then lost all its value." The true story is likely to be one told by a British admiral to Alston family friend Thomas Pinckney. Because the English were patrolling the American coast during the War of 1812, Governor Alston had given the *Patriot's* captain a letter requesting safe passage for his ship, with an explanation of Theodosia's reasons for traveling. The admiral in charge, who told the tale to Pinckney, honored the request and let the *Patriot* proceed. But a spectacular storm blew up that night off Cape Hatteras and the admiral assumed that the ship had foundered, everyone lost. It isn't as romantic an ending as walking the plank, but somewhat more probable.

THE BRITISH ADMIRAL who granted passage to Theodosia Alston's ship commanded part of a flotilla that blockaded the entire eastern seaboard. "A fleet of two English ships of 74 cannon and six frigates close the entry to the Chesapeake and Delaware and do not allow the smallest boat to pass," Rosalie Stier Calvert advised her brother as the war heated up. "Meanwhile the country is torn apart by numerous factions and in Congress there is open talk of dissolving the union of the states." New England was in an uproar over the war, with the governors of Massachusetts and Connecticut refusing to send their militias into battle. The West took the opposite stance— demanding retribution against the British for backing Indian raids, especially after the 1811 Battle of Tippecanoe, when William Henry Harrison attacked the stronghold of Tecumseh's brother. Following that rout, Dolley Madison tried a charm offensive on the leaders of several tribes, telling a friend, "A few days ago we had 29 Indians to dinner with us, attended by 5 interpreters and the Heads of Departments."

The American army attempted to cut off British supply lines by attacking Canada. The maneuver resulted in spectacular failure. At the end of August the president and his wife received "the melancholy tidings that Gen. Hull had surrendered Detroit, *himself* & the whole army to the British." Outraged, Dolley asked her cousin, "Do you not tremble with resentment at this treacherous act?" Hull's surrender of the Northwest army was not only treacherous to the country but dangerous to James Madison's chances for reelection as well. The Federalists had decided to join the breakaway Republicans in nominating De Witt Clinton for president and Philadelphian Jared Ingersoll for vice president. Clinton managed to run as an antiwar candidate in the North and a supporter of a better-managed war in the South. Dolley Madison, highly suspicious of her husband's opponent, tried to keep track of his comings and goings. "It is said that the Queen at the Palace was heard to ask what that fellow wanted here," a Federalist congressman gossiped to his wife after DeWitt Clinton showed up at the Capitol one day.

The seemingly indefatigable Dolley also continued to wage her social campaign, particularly with the new congressmen from the West and South and with the press. "Yesterday the first drawing-room of the season was held," young Sarah Gales Seaton wrote to her family in North Carolina in October 1812. Sarah was the sister of Joseph Gales, publisher of the *National Intelligencer,* and her husband, William Seaton, had just gone into business with him. "I have not yet been presented to her majesty, and it not being etiquette to appear in public until that ceremony be performed," she stayed home. This "Republican Court" had its rules after all. Soon Sarah was a regular at the executive mansion and, like so many others, devoted to Dolley Madison: "Tis not her form, tis not her face, it is the woman altogether, whom I should wish you to see." But it was an election year and Dolley was once again a target: "Mrs. Madison has acted with singular discreetness during a very embarrassing season," Pennsylvania Congressman Jonathan Roberts approvingly noted to his brother. "By her deportment in her own house you cannot discover who is her husband's friends or foes." It was an "embarrassing season" because the opposition and their press were again spreading stories of Dolley's alleged infidelities. Even Federalist Charles Carroll bristled that "the attack on Mrs. Madison is very reprehensible." Now the nation knew Dolley Madison, and wasn't ready to credit the stories. She had done such a good job in her husband's first term, a Federalist senator from Kentucky joked that Mrs. Madison was "a very good president and must not be turned out."

Dolley Madison's old friend from Philadelphia Sally McKean, who was married to the Marquis de Yrujo, the longtime Spanish ambassador to the United States, made a trip through Baltimore in the summer of 1812 when the presidential campaign was in high gear. The marquis and marquise were on their way back to Spain from a posting in Brazil and Sally had "prevailed on the marquis to return by the way of my dear native country." Though she had wanted to write to Dolley the minute she arrived, she waited until the "state of affairs . . . took a decisive turn, lest some exalted patriot might suspect our innocent correspondence treasonable under existing circumstances." Now that war had been declared, the "decisive turn" had been taken, and the wife of the ambassador felt free to write a wonderful, long newsy letter to her dear friend the First Lady. Dolley's son Payne had dutifully tried to call on the Marquise de Yrujo in Baltimore, but had missed her: "I shall make an attempt to see him today and intend to ask him if he remembers when he was a little fellow, his pulling off Gen. Van Courtland's wig at the very moment he was making me a flourishing compliment." Proving she was the same old catty Sally, she continued: "I find Madame Bonaparte a good deal changed, she is not by a good deal so pretty as she was;" that was one among the many changes, "among others that Mrs. Law—is Miss Custis." Sally McKean Yrujo still could bite. But for Dolley she had nothing but praise: "They tell me here in answer to a thousand enquiries I have made about you—that you never looked so well in your life—and that you give and have given universal satisfaction to all your friends and visitors, which is indeed a very difficult matter to please everybody, but you always possessed so much goodness and sweetness of manner as had made everybody your friends." Dolley Madison had a true gift for people, a gift that James Madison would need desperately as he ran for reelection.

Campaigning for her husband, the First Lady insisted that she had only one concern, that she was "anxious for the fate of the war, *only*—knowing that if success crowned our arms, prosperity and happiness would attend our country," she added to a friend with some relief. "The disgraceful conduct of Hull has been repaired and the Brave Harrison will soon finish a contest forced upon us." William Henry Harrison would take charge in the West. In going to the voters, the president could point to that change in command plus some significant American victories against the vaunted Royal Navy. As commander of the U.S.S. *United States*, Stephen Decatur actually seized a British ship and hauled it like a trophy into the harbor at Newport, making him a national hero. Decatur's wife, Susan, had tried to keep him out of the war. She had privately appealed to Dolley Madison, pleading her husband's illness. When Decatur found out he was understandably furious: "My husband has never thought himself too unwell for service, nor ever wished for any indulgence and was extremely mortified that I should have suffered my fears to have magnified what he considered a trifling indisposition into a serious disease," Susan backpedaled frantically. "If he had thought himself too much indisposed to go to sea, he would have applied for a furlough. The unfavorable impression, which, he apprehended, my request might have made upon Mr. Madison, and the Secretary of the Navy, was not from the report of his ill health, but from a belief that he wished to screen himself from service upon so slight an indisposition." Sometimes the women got caught in their meddling. But Susan Decatur obviously believed Dolley Madison could keep her husband from harm's way. Instead, Decatur lustily joined the fray and claimed his prize.

Aided by other naval victories, James Madison easily won the Electoral College, though he received only fifty percent of the popular vote. De Witt Clinton took New York, New Jersey, most of the Middle Atlantic votes, and all of New England except Vermont. Madison won Pennsylvania plus the West and the South, including the brand-new state of Louisiana. Analyzing the election later in the century, politician and historian James G. Blaine determined that "Mrs. Madison saved the administration of her husband," concluding unequivocally: "But for her De Witt Clinton would have been chosen President in 1812." Dolley had done it again, but the Presidentess would face a tough term ahead with the nation at war.

CHAPTER FIVE

THE SECOND TERM OF JAMES MADISON AND "THE BRAVEST AMERICAN SOLDIER"

1813–1817

LOUISA CATHERINE ADAMS
Hulton Archive/Getty Images

IT MIGHT HAVE BEEN wartime when James Madison took his second oath of office, but the revelry went right on. Madison once again delivered an inaugural address in a voice "so low, and the audience so very great, that scarcely a word could be distinguished," and then "the little man was accompanied on his return to the palace by the multitude; for every creature that could afford twenty five cents for hack-hire was present." It was the first presidential inauguration for Sarah Gales Seaton, the wife of the new publisher of the *National Intelligencer*, and she didn't want her family in North Carolina to miss a minute of it: "The major part of the respectable citizens offered their congratulations, ate his ice-creams and bonbons, drank his Madeira, made their bow and retired, leaving him fatigued beyond measure with the incessant bending to which his politeness urged him." Sarah Seaton then passed on to her parents news that had only recently arrived from Europe: "Your good friend Joel Barlow is dead . . . the place and circumstances of his death seemed a fitting close to his volcanic and eccentric career."

The death of the American ambassador to France was a reminder, if it was needed, that the United States had pressing problems with that country as well as war with England. Still, an inaugural ball gathered "a most lively assemblage of the lovely ones of our District," according to the next day's *National Intelligencer*. To Dolley Madison it was important that the show go on, to keep up the appearance of normalcy even as the British raided nearby cities from their ships in the Chesapeake Bay. "Mrs. Madison called on me last week, and very politely invited me to attend the drawing-room of Wednesday, and 'not to desert the standard altogether,'" Sarah Seaton revealed in early March. A polite invitation from the First Lady served as a summons. Dolley was gathering her troops around her to keep the partisans partying as a diversion from their criticisms of "Mr. Madison's War." A longtime member of Dolley's team was the wife of the secretary of the treasury, Hannah Gallatin, who contributed her own entertainments, including the "most profuse ball ever given in Washington" at the New Year. "Ladies of fifty years of age were decked with lace and ribbons, wreaths of roses and gold leaves in their false hair, wreaths of jasmine across their bosom, and no kerchiefs," Sarah Seaton clucked to her mother, "though the splendid dress of these antiquated dames of the *beau monde* adds to the general grandeur, it certainly only tends to make the contrast still more striking between them and the young and beautiful." Of course Betsy Bonaparte with "the most transcendently beautiful back and shoulders that ever were seen" stood out as "a model of fashion, and many of our belles strive to imitate her." The older women not only dressed immodestly in Sarah's view, their makeup also shocked her. "Mrs. Monroe paints very much, and has, besides an appearance of youth which would induce a stranger to suppose her age to be thirty." That comment would have probably pleased Mrs. Monroe.

Elizabeth Kortright Monroe, wife of the new secretary of state, shared some history with the reigning "Queen Dolley" when she arrived on the Washington scene. The two women were the same age, both were forty-four at the beginning of 1813, and the Madison and Monroe couples had at times been close. But the men had been competitors almost as often as they were collaborators, making friendship complicated, to say the least. Still, Monroe was eager to serve in Madison's cabinet, and he and Elizabeth set up house at 2017 I Street, west of the president's house and a good distance from the legislators living atop Capitol Hill. The British minister was surprised to see that the couple entertained "very sparingly, which does not fail to be commented on in a place where good dinners produce as much effect as in any part of the world." It was true then, as Dolley Madison knew, and is true now, that dinner party diplomacy often is more effective than that waged in official meetings. Maybe the Monroes were just slighting the British. When Mary Crowninshield, wife of an American politician, went to the secretary of state's home, she told her mother it was "the most stylish dinner I have been at." Given to much delicious detail, Mrs. Crowninshield described the evening: "The plates were handsome china, the forks silver, and so heavy I could hardly lift them to my mouth," and then there was the hostess, "a very elegant woman. She was dressed in a very fine muslin worked in front and lined with pink, and a black velvet turban close and spangled."

Washington had more than parties to worry about as Madison began his second term—the city was awash with rumors that the British were coming. After almost a year of a declared war—when Rosalie Calvert had found that "the moderation of the English is surprising. We have already taken three of their frigates, there is nothing to prevent their reducing all our ports to ashes (for there is no one to defend them) and still they are content to blockade us"—it suddenly seemed real in 1813. And President Madison thought he needed to make some changes in command. He asked Secretary of the Navy Paul Hamilton to resign, something the secretary was prepared for because, according to a newspaper report, Mrs. Hamilton had noticed "the great attention paid her by Mrs. Madison." The *New England Palladium* claimed that the First Lady who "moves many things" employed her skills at paying "more than common attention" to the women in the family of a man about to get the ax. Dolley was trying to soften the blow. Replacing both the secretary of the navy and the secretary of war did nothing to stop the enemy. With Napoleon in disgrace after his Russian campaign, the British could now afford to concentrate on America. The Royal Navy attacked Havre de Grace, Maryland, on May 3, 1813, under the command of Rear Admiral Sir George Cockburn, who put out the word that he would soon "make his bow" in Dolley Madison's drawing room. "I do not tremble at this, but feel *affronted*," an indignant Dolley fumed to her cousin Edward Coles, her husband's secretary, who was sick in Philadelphia. She had taken over Coles's secretarial duties and assured him that "Mr. M. can do very well without a secretary until your health is re-established." Having put her cousin at ease about his future, the First Lady continued: "& now, if I could, I would describe to you the fears & alarms that circulate around me. For the last week all the City & G[eorge]town (except the Cabinet) have expected a visit from the enemy & were not lacking in their expressions of terror & reproach." Reproach because the city was not well defended. That was changing, "we are making considerable efforts for defense," and she thought the preparations were going well. "In my eyes as I have always been an advocate for fighting when *assailed*, though *a Quaker*, I therefore keep the old Tunisian saber within my reach." It was brave talk in a scary situation: "One of our Generals has discovered a plan of the British. It is to land as many *rogues* as they can about 14 miles below Alexandria in the night, who may arrive before day & set fire to the offices & President's House when, if opposed, they are to surrender themselves as prisoners." Despite those dire warnings, Dolley refused to be cowed. The night before she had hosted "a large party" where she sent Coles's respects to the Monroes.

As the spring of 1813 turned to summer, and the British stepped up their attacks in the area, alarm spread among the women of Washington: "Your fears, my dear mother, were not entirely without foundation, though we laughed you out of them when they were mentioned." Sarah Seaton's mother had balked at her daughter moving from North Carolina to Washington, fearing a British invasion "and consequent cruelty." Though the maternal uneasiness had seemed silly at the time, now Sarah wasn't so sure: "You will see by the *Federal Republican* that the plan might be carried into execution . . . of seizing the President and Secretaries . . . and rendering this nation a laughing stock to every other in the world." William Smith, Nabby Adams's husband, who had been elected to Congress as a Federalist from New York, gave a grim report to his daughter Caroline: "The British have landed from 1500 to 2000 regular troops below Norfolk . . . and attending frigates, sloops, and schooners threaten the destruction of that important city. Our great folk here of course are not on a bed of roses." If Washington was worried the British might come north, South Carolina Congressman William Lowndes thought they might go south. "They have lately landed a considerable force in the neighborhood of Norfolk," he reported with some alarm to his wife back in the state. "I really do not see why they might not land one near forts Moultrie or Johnson," two South Carolina redoubts.

Margaret Bayard Smith had hoped her nieces might come for the summer, but "it is now out of the question while the British are such near neighbors and continue to menace us. Until the late alarm I have never been able to realize our being in a state of war." But men were signing up for the militia and "our little army is full of ardor and enthusiasm." Margaret was sure that "every precaution has been taken to ensure the safety of the city." What she feared most was a slave uprising: "We have however counted on the possibility of danger and Mr. S. has procured pistols, etc. etc. sufficient for our defense." Whites lived in terror that slaves would for good reason escape to side with the British and rise up against their oppressors.

Sarah Seaton and her children were staying in the country with Margaret Smith where Mrs. Henry Clay and others would join them if danger struck. Sarah's husband William Seaton, and his business partner, her brother Joseph Gales, had volunteered for service and were encamped on the outskirts of Washington. The men returned to the city regularly to put out the newspaper and the record of congressional debates because their friends thought "the proper and continual direction of the public record printed in their office is of infinitely more importance than any individual exertion they could possibly make in the camp." Though the Americans staved off the British at Norfolk, the enemy had overrun Hampton, Virginia, on June 25, plundering the town and raping its women. A newspaper report that women were "abused in the most shameful manner" sent shivers through the countryside. Though Dolley Madison's cousin Sarah Coles claimed that the attack had "turned our young men into heroes," it was too close for comfort for Sarah Seaton. She could not be as sanguine as her hostess, Mrs. Smith: "You will see that Congress has reported that we are in a securely defended position, nevertheless it is not to be expected that our fears can be so easily calmed after an excessive fright." She trusted that she and the children were safe out in the country; it was the men she fretted about, though her brother "assures us most solemnly that he does not believe they will dare attempt to land or pass the numerous and brave force of volunteers and regulars who are assembled, and positively believes that there will be no fighting." Joseph Gales was right, for the time being, and Washington relaxed its vigilance.

It was the only time that Dolley Madison stopped entertaining. Her shut-down drawing room had nothing to do with preparations for war; quite the contrary, that was the time to "show the standard." The "squeezes" at the executive mansion were called off because President Madison had contracted "bilious fever," probably malaria. Concern about the war had kept the couple in mosquito-infested

Washington into the summer and the president became deathly ill. While "rumor with her hundred tongues had circulated at least a hundred reports" about Madison, according to Dolley's cousin, the First Lady "nursed him night & day—sometimes in despair" for three weeks. By early July, Madison was out of the woods and Dolley could admit, "Now that I see he will get well I feel as if I should die myself, with fatigue." The couple retreated to Montpelier, where Mrs. Madison spent her time worrying about congressional approval of the commission assigned to negotiate peace.

In response to Czar Alexander's offer to mediate the war between England and the United States, President Madison had named a three-man team: Federalist Senator James Bayard and Republican Secretary of the Treasury Albert Gallatin would join John Quincy Adams in St. Petersburg. That decision caused James Monroe to answer Abigail Adams's inquiry as to whether "there is a probability of Mr. Adams's return the ensuing season, and whether any method may be devised for him and his family to get back to America with safety during the war." The secretary of state somewhat gingerly informed envoy Adams's mother that her son would be staying abroad: "It is impossible to state the precise time when your son will return to the U States. He is appointed in the negotiation with G Britain, which is to be commenced at St. Petersburg, under the mediation of the Emperor of Russia. His service in that negotiation is considered of high importance to his country." When Abigail Adams learned of the honor accorded her son, she dropped all efforts to bring him home, instead informing the secretary of state that his news had caused "many reflections in my mind—but with regard to the path of duty before me, I have not any hesitation." Abigail explained that she had been "early instructed to relinquish all personal considerations and enjoyments to the calls of my country" and had with "a young family and residing at the seat of war" submitted to years of separation during the Revolution "from my protector, the friend of my youth, my companion and the husband of my choice." That she had then suffered "the painful separation from my eldest son who was honored with an embassy to Holland by President Washington." Recently, "having advanced many years toward the close of life and knowing that Mr. Adams had a young family to educate and provide for (I need not say to you sir that this is not to be done by a foreign embassy!) I confess it was with still greater and increased reluctance that I consented to a second separation when President Madison honored him with the embassy to St. Petersburg." But now, "do I fully and willingly relinquish him to his country upon an occasion so highly important, and so pregnant with consequences to this nation, fervently praying that he may be an instrument in the hand of providence to restore peace upon a just and honorable basis between the contending nations." Abigail told her sister Elizabeth that she prayed for peace and hoped "my Dear son may be an instrument in the hand of providence for accomplishing it." But she also backed the war: "I am one of those who believe in the rightness and justice of the present war with Great Britain. It was become necessary to preserve that independence and to defend it as the former war was to obtain it." To her son, Abigail exulted, "It had been my constant and daily petition to heaven for you that you might be made an instrument in the hand of providence of much good to your native lands," if he could bring about a cessation of hostilities. "I should say with Simeon mine eyes have seen thy salvation." John Quincy Adams had the blessing of his sixty-eight-year-old mother. But Albert Gallatin did not have the approval of the U.S. Congress.

The country remained deeply divided over the war, still smarted from the lack of trade, and now faced dwindling domestic shipping due to the tightening British blockade. Waterways remained a primary means of transportation and with water traffic closed off, the terrible roads couldn't handle the increase in vehicles on land. So shortages and high prices exacerbated the general unhappiness. The Madison administration needed Russia to come through as a peace-broker; so before Congress approved his nominees, the president dispatched Bayard and Gallatin to Russia, along with Gallatin's son James and Dolley's son Payne Todd to act as secretaries. "I am most anxiously preparing Payne for his voyage to Russia," Dolley dashed off the news to a friend. Her anxiety stemmed from her son's "reluctance to leave America." (The doting mother was probably beginning to suspect what turned out to be true—that her happy-go-lucky son would never amount to anything.) The party of would-be peace commissioners left in May 1813 in order to reach Russia before winter, with some Federalist skepticism about their intentions. "I have just learned that a cartel ship is to sail to carry ministers to St. Petersburg who are going to negotiate with England under the auspices of Alexander," Rosalie Calvert rejoiced to her brother in April. She was pleased that the ship could take her letter, but she hadn't much hope for anything else: "I don't think our President was sincere in sending a minister to Russia; perhaps it was only a ruse to obtain money." The cost of the war combined with the loss of tariff revenues from the lack of trade plus the demise of the Bank of the United States meant the country was hurting for cash. Albert Gallatin, the secretary of the treasury, despite his efforts to raise revenue, was being blamed for the deficit. So when the Senate received the nominations for the peace commissioners after the men had already departed for Russia, opposition lawmakers vented their dislike of the Swiss-born treasury secretary. "You will see that prejudice exists as strongly here against foreigners as anywhere," Sarah Seaton huffed to her English parents in July 1813, "the Senate refusing to confirm Mr. Gallatin's appointment." First, the lawmakers demanded, Gallatin would have to resign his cabinet post, then they would decide whether to confirm him. Madison, who was just beginning to recover from his life-threatening illness, saw this for what it was—a direct challenge to his executive authority and a move to get Gallatin out of the government altogether.

"Every art had been employed to defeat the mission, to ruin the Administration, and to depreciate Mr. Gallatin," Hannah Gallatin's friend A. J. Dallas told her after her husband's rejection, "the political mischief that has been done and will be done is incalculable." Mrs. Gallatin, who was in New York with her family, was a woman of strong and stridently expressed political views. The president needed to assure her that Gallatin had his support, and Madison needed her assurance that he still had *her* support, given this insult to her husband. Dolley Madison took on the job of placating her. She sent a letter by their mutual friend John Jacob Astor: "You have heard no doubt, of the illness of my husband but can have no idea of its extent, and the despair in which I attended his bed for nearly five weeks!" Having, she hoped, evoked some sympathy, Dolley claimed "party spirit" had contributed to the president's suffering: "Nothing however has borne so hard as the conduct of the Senate in regard to Mr. Gallatin—Mr. A. will tell you many particulars that *I aught not to write,* of the desertion of some whose support we had a right to expect & of the *maneuvering* of others, always hostile to superior merit." If it came down to a choice of the peace mission or the treasury, the president wasn't sure which Gallatin preferred. That was a little dicey even for Dolley to ask directly. She turned over the task to the ubiquitous Mr. Astor, who put the question to Hannah. "Mr. Madison is at a loss how to *act* to please Mr. Gallatin best. Mrs. M had a very long conversation with me today in confidence on this subject, wishing to know whether I thought Mr. Gallatin would prefer a confirmation of the nomination or remain in the Department . . . Mrs. M wishes very much your wishes on the subject." (Astor apparently had no problem at all dealing with women as sources of power. The year before he had written to Dolley, "He well remembers Mrs. Madison's assurances that all Mr. Astor's ships should arrive.")

Hannah Gallatin quickly dispelled the Madisons' apprehensions. Though she was "all anxiety to hear of the safe arrival of our dear *voyagers*" and feeling guilty about not accompanying her husband, she did not seem concerned about the Senate. "His enemies have triumphed over him in his absence, but that is a trifle, he is much happier than they are for he has a self-approving conscience . . . and if he is the means of restoring peace to our beloved country, that will be sufficient reward to him." A couple of weeks later the Madisons with a "crowd of company" were at Montpelier and the peace commissioners had arrived safely in Gothenburg, but Dolley hoped for "their safe & early return, when you will find your dear husband standing higher than ever in his country's estimation & attachment; for Mr. Madison says, that though his enemies *imagine* they have prevailed in a *degree* against him, their machinations will treble his friends & show him to the world as he really is, one of the best, as well as one of the greatest men." Dolley added, as usual, some news of friends and neighbors: "I expect Mrs. Randolph with her father to visit us in a few days—she is miserable at parting with Mr. R. who leaves for the army." And the French minister "tells a foolish story about Mrs. Barlow's being on the eve of marriage with some young French man, but I will not believe it." (It wasn't true.)

By the time Bayard and Gallatin arrived in St. Petersburg in July, the British had already turned down the czar's mediation offer. As the envoys waited to see what would happen next, Dolley Madison tried to convince Hannah Gallatin and her daughter to come stay with her at the president's house "until the arrival of your dear husband, who will bring in his hand my son." But the delegation would not return any time soon; instead the men cooled their heels in Russia for several months while the various governments negotiated about negotiations. Ambassador to Russia John Quincy Adams and Mrs. Adams played hosts to their fellow citizens, something Louisa seemed to enjoy more than John, noting in her journal, "I miss them most unaccountably" after they left. Perhaps the outings with the Americans helped get her still troubled mind off the loss of her baby girl. By that time Louisa was not the only Adams woman mourning the death of a daughter.

In July 1813, as the Americans were traveling to St. Petersburg, a cancer-ridden Abigail Adams Smith insisted on making a painful pilgrimage from her husband's home in western New York to her parents' home in Massachusetts. Abigail Adams had not expected to be able to see her daughter to comfort her. "Your dear and only sister," she lamented to John Quincy "is a patient sufferer under severe and afflicting pain." The agonized mother moaned to her son, "My heart bleeds—I cannot get to her, nor she to me." But ten days later Abigail told her old friend Mercy Warren that her grandson had written "that it is his mother's most earnest wish to be brought to Quincy, and that although for six weeks she has not been able to get across her room, yet in compliance with her desire he has undertaken to journey with her by slow degrees and, if possible, get her here. . . . I hope the journey and the change of air, the society of her family and friends will have a favorable effect." More than two miserable weeks over three hundred jolting miles by sheer force of will, Nabby traveled home to die. On the road she turned forty-eight years old, and on her birthday her mother wrote to John Quincy, "I fear I shall have one of the most distressing and trying scenes of my life to go through." Once Abigail saw her daughter, she knew she was right. "How she got here is a marvel to me," was all she could say. Nabby's son John, daughter Caroline, and sister-in-law Nancy made the trek with her. Her son William, still in St. Petersburg as John Quincy's secretary, could not be there. Her husband, Congressman William Smith, joined them from Washington about a week later.

After two weeks in Quincy, weeks when her horrendous suffering was only somewhat alleviated by opium, Nabby Smith declared that the time had come. She gathered the family around, called for a hymnal, and requested that all sing together "Longing for Heaven." The crushed little choir wept through the opening lines:

> *O could I soar to worlds above*
> *That blessed state of peace and love!*
> *How gladly would I mount and fly*
> *On angels' wings to joys on high!*

A few hours later Abigail Adams Smith died of breast cancer. "The wound which has lacerated my bosom cannot be healed," cried her mother, Abigail Smith Adams. She poured out her heart to her son: "To me the loss is irreparable." And to Louisa: "Bitter is the loss of a sweet infant" was the somewhat unfeeling message, "but how much more increased are the pangs which rent the Heart of a Mother when called to part with the Head of a family, in the midst of her days, and usefulness?" Still, even as she wept, Abigail assured her son that she counted her blessings: "One of the first of these is the life, health and cheerfulness of your father." And to her old friend Mercy Warren, she extolled the virtues of Nabby's daughter Caroline: "All that I can wish for, she is."

John Adams too felt the loss keenly. Having renewed his correspondence with Thomas Jefferson, he was midletter about arcane ideas of language and politics when he stopped and then started again a couple of days later: "Your friend, my only daughter, expired yesterday morning in the arms of her husband, her son, her daughter, her father and mother, her husband's two sisters and two of her nieces." Benjamin Rush, the doctor who signed the Declaration of Independence, who advised that Nabby Smith endure a mastectomy, who had been the intellectual touchstone as well as the physician of choice for most of the Founders and their families, had died just a few months earlier, but not before he had successfully reunited Adams and Jefferson. As to Jefferson's insistence that he would renew correspondence only with Mr. Adams, not Mrs. Adams, unsurprisingly Abigail herself, presumably unaware of Jefferson's dictum, had taken up her pen to add a P.S. to one of her husband's letters: "I have been looking for some time for a space in my good husband's letters to add the regards of an old friend, which are still cherished and preserved through all the changes and vicissitudes which have taken place since we first became acquainted." She scribbled those lines as her dying daughter was on the road to Quincy. In the same way that she had mended fences with Mercy Warren, she was clearly ready to do so with Thomas Jefferson, a friend she had once described as the "one of the choice ones of the Earth." And Jefferson was ready to respond in kind, answering her before he received John Adams's letter about their daughter's death, explaining that he had been very busy but now would take time to ask: "How you do, how you have done? And to express the interest I take in whatever affects your happiness." And then, endearingly, he engaged in the grandparents' competition: "I have compared notes with Mr. Adams on the score of progeny, and find I am ahead of him. . . . I have 10 1/2 grandchildren and 2 3/4 great grandchildren; and these fractions will ere long become units." Of course almost all of those progeny—all but one of the grandchildren—were Martha's children and grandchildren. And, almost forty-one years old, she was pregnant again. He couldn't know as he sent off that letter to Abigail that she was "in great affliction for the loss of my dear and only daughter, Mrs. Smith."

That's how Abigail Adams answered Thomas Jefferson's question of "How you do, how you have done?" She described Nabby's illness and death with the understanding that "You sir, who have been called to separations of a similar kind can sympathize with your bereaved Friend." It had been nine years since their touchy correspondence following the death of Jefferson's own daughter, Maria. Now, in response to "the assurance you gave me that you took an interest in what ever affected my happiness," Abigail quoted a poem:

> "'Grief has changed me since you saw me last,
> And careful hours, with time's deformed hand
> Hath written strange defections o'er my face.'"

"But," she continued, "although time has changed the outward form, and political 'back wounding calumny' for a period interrupted the friendly intercourse and harmony which subsisted, it is again renewed." They could be friends again, and she was pleased. John Adams sent off several more lengthy letters on philosophy and religion before Jefferson responded with his own tomelike treatise, only at the end referring to the news of Nabby's death. On that subject, he said simply, "I am silent. I know the depth of the affliction it has caused and can sympathize with it the more sensibly. . . . I have ever found time and silence the only medicine, and these but assuage, they never can suppress, the deep-drawn sigh which recollection for ever brings up, until recollection and life are extinguished altogether."

WHILE THE OLDER MEMBERS of the Revolutionary generation pored over the past, their younger compatriots were caught up in the present. With President Madison's health restored, the First Family returned to Washington from Montpelier in the fall of 1813, and with war on, Dolley threw herself more than ever into her work—helping with patronage and pardons and entertaining, entertaining, entertaining. Planning to visit the capital for some fun, Elizabeth Bonaparte wrote from Baltimore asking if Mrs. Madison needed anything from the stores there: "There are in the shops in Baltimore French gloves, fashions, etc." Dolley, while first assuring Mme. Bonaparte that "such is the interest you excite in all who know you, that I trust your time here will glide happily on," eagerly accepted the offer; "I will avail myself of your taste, in case you meet with anything elegant in the form of a turban."

The First Lady no longer had to place orders for the executive mansion—it was finished and something to behold. "The President's house is a perfect palace," reported young Elbridge Gerry, the son of the vice president, when he visited. "On the side opposite to the entrance are doors opening to four rooms. The corner is the dining room. . . . This is furnished in the most elegant manner. . . . At the head of the room, General Washington is represented as large as life. This room opens by a single door into Mrs. Madison's sitting-room . . . this is furnished equally as well. . . . This room, the same way, enters into the drawing-room, which is an immense and magnificent room, in an oval form. . . . A door opens at each end, one into the hall, and opposite one into the terrace. . . . The windows are nearly the height of the room, and have superb red silk velvet curtains which cost $4.00 a yard . . . these three rooms are all open on levee nights." The biggest "levee" of all, on New Year's Day, drew "*every*body, affected or disaffected towards the government." Sarah Gales Seaton regaled her family with her account: "The Marine Band, stationed in the ante-room, continued playing in spite of the crowd pressing in on their very heads." It was so hot that the ladies' makeup ran: "the rouge which some of our fashionables had unfortunately laid on with an unsparing hand, and which assimilating with the pearl powder, dust and perspiration, made them altogether unlovely to soul and eye." Not Dolley, however: "Her majesty's appearance was truly regal—dressed in a robe of pink satin, trimmed elaborately with ermine, a white velvet and satin turban, with nodding ostrich plumes and a crescent in front, gold chain and clasps around the waist and wrists. . . . I cannot conceive a female better calculated to dignify the station which she occupies in society than Mrs. Madison—amiable in private life and affable in public, she is admired and esteemed by the rich and beloved by the poor. . . . Her frank cordiality to all guests is in contrast to the manner of the president. . . . Being so low of stature, he was in imminent danger of being confounded with the plebeian crowd, and was pushed and jostled about like a common citizen. But not so with her ladyship! The towering feathers and excessive throng distinctly point out her station wherever she moved."

The British might be threatening, but the capital was determinedly festive. "We have ladies from almost every state in the union & the city was never known so thronged with strangers," Dolley marveled to Martha Jefferson Randolph in early January. Martha had just had another baby girl and the First Lady was inviting teenager Ellen Randolph to town for a chance to get away from baby watching at Monticello: "It is a pleasing and instructive scene for the young and gay." Margaret Bayard Smith agreed that Washington was "more and more the resort of strangers from every part of the union." One congressional wife who joined her husband in 1814, Elizabeth Pinckney Lowndes, was welcomed warmly by Secretary of State Monroe and his wife, greeting the now grown woman they had known as a little girl in London when her father was posted there. Then, as now, the capital provided, as Margaret Smith noted, "peculiar facilities for forming acquaintances, for a stranger cannot be long here, before it is generally known. The House of Representatives is the lounging place of both sexes, where acquaintance is as easily made as at public amusements. . . . The debates in Congress have this winter been very attractive to the ladies." Women were flocking to the Capitol, where Margaret Smith admitted, "curiosity led me against my judgment to join the female crowd who throng the [Supreme] court room. A place in which I think women have no business. The effect of female admiration and attention has been very obvious." One day, a lawyer had finished his argument "when Mrs. Madison and a train of ladies entered. He recommenced, went over the same ground, using fewer arguments, but scattering more flowers." Even so, Margaret observed approvingly, "The women here are taking a station in society which is not known elsewhere. On every public occasion, a launch, an oration, an inauguration, in the court, in the representative hall, as well as the drawing room, they are treated with marked distinction."

Women certainly felt free to go to the top with their concerns. In April, Ruth Barlow, back from France but in New York, asked Dolley Madison to intervene on behalf of a "young artillery officer" who had been court-martialed for fighting with infantry officers. It was all politics, Ruth protested, because her friend was "a brave Republican and friend to government, his opponents Federalists & enemies to government." She wanted the president to intervene to serve the "cause of justice at the same time relieving the distress of a respectable family, good friends to government." Ruth had told Dolley in December that she would spend the winter in New York at the home of Robert Fulton and his wife because "Kalorama would recall too painful ideas." She was trying to figure out what to do with her life, but in the interim she, like everyone else, wanted a favor from Dolley. Even the vice president asked the First Lady to intervene for a friend complaining that his small fishing boat was "restrained by the embargo law so as to be useless to their needy owners."

The embargo continued to rankle at home, but the news from Europe "of the Allies' entry into Paris and the restoration of the

Bourbons" greatly cheered Rosalie Calvert. The British had defeated Napoleon, who was exiled to the island of Elba, and the French monarchy had reclaimed the throne. Rosalie was "sure that our imbecile government will now make peace with England, since it is impossible for them to continue the war without money, without credit, without soldiers or shops. It must be hoped that everything will return to normal, as undoubtedly already has in Europe." That was the hope of many in America, as the country took in what was happening in Europe. Dolley Madison's cousin Sally Coles wrote that Thomas Jefferson had paid her a visit "and gave us a very interesting account of the Bourbons. . . . He says the King is scarcely one degree removed from idiotism . . . his wife was a *great drunkard,* but for the honor of France died some years ago. The King's brother is the greatest *Gamester* in the world and has very little more understanding than his August Majesty, the King." After offering her opinions on Napoleon and "the poor Empress," Sally was tickled: "I cannot forebear smiling when I look back on all I have written about Kings and Emperors, but who is it that does not feel interested in this great and surprising revolution, so important to our own country. May it give us the blessings of Peace." Napoleon's demise also brought hope to Betsy Bonaparte. Finally, she thought, she could go to Paris! "The obstacles which the Emperor Napoleon opposed to my continual desire of residing in Paris, have ceased with his power," she cheered to Dolley Madison, in a request that the First Lady intercede with friends to permit Betsy to sail with them. The bold young woman didn't want to ask herself, for fear of rejection; she also begged Dolley to keep her request a secret in case the answer was no: "The public are so malicious & so much pleased when people meet with disappointment that I wish to avoid gratifying them again at my expense." For all her brazenness, Betsy Bonaparte had been stung by gossip. Dolley did ask her friends the Eustises to allow Betsy "to sail under your wing. You know, she is good, interesting & unfortunate," but by the time they were ready to sail Napoleon had returned to power.

Instead of bringing peace, events in Europe brought the British navy off America's coast reinforcements of freshly victorious troops. "The English are going to send a considerable force here," Rosalie worried to her sister in June. "Their ships are already in our Patuxent [River]. They have burned several houses and tobacco warehouses. I don't know how it will all end." But the powers-that-were in Washington, especially the secretary of war, General John Armstrong, remained convinced that the capital city was too inconsequential for the British to bother attacking; the important port of Baltimore would be the target, they argued. Underscoring the insistence on normalcy, Dolley Madison held her annual Fourth of July bash, attended by a young visitor from New England, identified by nineteenth-century social historian Anne Wharton only as "Miss Brown." The fifteen-year-old girl left valuable impressions of the federal city in the summer of 1814, including those of her July 4 hostess: "Her hair hung in ringlets on each side of her face, surmounted by the snowy folds of her unvarying turban, ornamented on one side by a few heads of green wheat. She may have worn jewels, but if she did, they were so eclipsed by her inherent charms as to be unnoticed." Like any tourist today, Miss Brown took in the sights: "I explored with some young friends the intricacies of the Capitol, often pausing to admire its many architectural beauties. . . . There were two magnificent wings of the Capitol connected by a long, unpainted wooden shed. Passing over a mile of rough road, bordered here and there by Congress boarding-houses, with veritable swamps between, you came to the President's house—beautiful with architecture, upholstery, gilding and paintings, set down in the midst of rough, unornamented grounds. Then another stretch of comparative wilderness till you came to Georgetown. Almost everyone of distinction drove four horses, and these fine equipages on these wretched roads, with their elegant occupants, formed no trifling part of the contrasts." No wonder the war planners thought Washington wasn't worth the enemy's attention. But of course they were wrong.

In late June the young men who had volunteered for the army

were called to action. Sarah Seaton received a firsthand account from her brother, who returned from a "really dangerous expedition, without any other injury than excessive weariness, after being exposed to the fire of the British on an open plain, where the balls whistled round his ears for the first time." The men had gone to check on enemy movements, but Sarah believed that her brother and husband would not be called up again "as Gen. Armstrong has issued orders for the return of those who are at Benedict." The British had landed at Benedict, Maryland, as reported in the newspaper Joseph Gales and William Seaton published, the *National Intelligencer,* which fluctuated between sounding the alarm about the British at Washington's doorstep, and reassuring the populace that all was well. Regardless of what they printed, the brothers-in-law thought it wise to take their families home to Raleigh for safety. The president pushed his feuding cabinet members to prepare a defense of the city, but the secretary of war continued to ridicule the idea of a British attack. Even the First Lady began to have her doubts about their security, admitting in late July, "We have been in state of perturbation here, for a long time. The depredations of the Enemy approaching within 20 miles of the City . . . making incessant difficulties for the Government. Such a place as this has become I cannot describe it. I wish (for my own part) that *we were* at Philadelphia." Dolley was venting to Hannah Gallatin about threats from the locals "if Mr. M. attempts to move from *this House,* in case of attack, they will *stop him* & that he shall *fall with it.* I am not the least alarmed at these things, but entirely disgusted & determined to stay with him." Dolley's great-niece repeated a family story that one furious woman "drove to Mrs. Madison's door, and standing up in her carriage, loosened her beautiful hair, which was celebrated for its length, praying that she might have the privilege of parting with it, for the purpose of hanging Mr. Madison." Washingtonians, Dolley knew, were understandably upset: "Our preparations for defense, by some means or other, are constantly retarded." But she was sure the "small force the British have on the Bay" would never venture closer than their current twenty-three-mile distance.

A couple of weeks later, Dolley was full of bravado when she wrote to her son Payne Todd, who was in Europe with the negotiators: "The British on our shores are stealing & destroying private property, rarely coming to battle, but when they do, are always beaten. . . . If the War should last 6 months longer the U.S. will conquer her Enemies." Despite the brave words, Dolley remained infinitely practical, asking Hannah Gallatin "in case of reinforcement of the British and their coming here, whether you have an active agent to take care of your furniture." She apologized for rushing, but "we have a large party to dine & they are now collecting." No amount of alarm could cancel Dolley Madison's dinners. When word reached Washington that the "small force" of the British had been supplemented by thousands of fresh troops, and were heading north from Benedict, Maryland, it was too late to mount a meaningful defense.

On Thursday, August 18, Dolley Madison's friend Anna Thornton wrote half a line in her journal: "Our troops marched over the Eastern Branch." The Americans had crossed what is now called the Anacostia River to confront the enemy if necessary. Two days later the *National Intelligencer* ran an edict from the mayor: "Every man, exempt from militia duty, who is able to carry a musket, will immediately enroll himself in the ward in which he resides and when enough are assembled, choose necessary officers for patrolling the city and preserving order." The newspaper surmised that for the British unloading at Benedict, "the general idea is that Washington is their object." But the editors, at the urging of the administration, steadfastly refused to print "an abundance of absurd and contradictory rumors." On Monday the twenty-second "a general removal from the city and Georgetown took place," according to Margaret Bayard Smith, and Mrs. Thornton took note that "the President went to camp this evening with Mr. Armstrong, etc." The high officials of government, completely in the dark about British intentions, were trying to garner information, leaving Dolley to prepare for a dinner party even as British rear admiral Cockburn sent "word to Mrs. Madison that unless she left, the house would be burned over her head."

The dinner party on Tuesday, August 23, was Dolley's way of carrying on as if nothing were happening. But her guests were not so ready to join in the pretense. "In the present state of alarm and bustle of preparation, for the worst that may happen," Eleanor Jones regretted that day, "I imagine it will be mutually convenient to dispense with the enjoyment of your hospitality today." Mrs. Jones's husband, the secretary of the navy, was "deeply engaged in dispatching the Marines and attending to other public duties." Eleanor was "busy packing up ready for flight, but in the event of necessity we know not where to go, nor have we any means yet prepared for the conveyance of our effects." The *National Intelligencer* revealed that day that the British force numbered in the thousands and that the Americans, under the command of Captain Joshua Barney, had blown up their own flotilla of ships and boats to try to thwart enemy advancement. Barney and his sailors dragged naval cannons to support the militia at Bladensburg, Maryland, where they would meet the enemy marching on the now panicked capital city. The tourist Miss Brown remembered: "The public officials began packing up their valuable papers to be removed to places of safety. Now all is hurry and panic, armies gathering, troops moving in all directions, the citizens trying to secure such things as were most valuable and most easily transportable, and flying from their homes to the country."

Only President Madison seemed unconcerned, writing from Bladensburg to Dolley back at the executive mansion: "I have passed the forenoon among the troops, who are in high spirits & make a good appearance. The reports as to the enemy have varied every hour. The last & probably truest information is that they are not very strong, and are without cavalry and artillery, and of course that they are not in a condition to strike at Washington." He was still trying to get information and hoped to be with her that evening.

Dolley's pregnant sister Anna Cutts was nowhere near as calm: "My Sister—Tell me for gods sake where you are and what [you are] going to do. . . . We can hear nothing but is horrible here. I know not who to send this to—and will say but little." And that night Margaret Smith's family was roused "by a loud knocking"; it was a friend with the urgent warning "'the enemy are advancing, our own troops are giving way on all sides and are retreating to the city. Go, for God's sake go.' He spoke in a voice of agony and then flew to his horse and was out of sight in a moment." Margaret and her family quickly packed up for nearby Brookville, Maryland. Anna Thornton stayed home, disgusted with the incompetence of the military commanders: "The troops were marched off their legs, were even late in the day in various parts of the City & were hastily gathered together to meet a regular force, who though likewise fatigued by a long and forced march, had a regular plan . . . it is the general opinion that if the force we had though inexperienced had been judiciously arranged the enemy might have been cut off or taken."

The First Lady, almost alone at the executive mansion, sat down to write her sister in Kentucky: "My husband left me yesterday morning to join Gen. Winder. He inquired anxiously whether I had the courage, or firmness to remain in the President's house until his return, on the morrow, or succeeding day. And on my assurance that I had no fear but for him and the success of our army, he left me, beseeching me to take care of myself and of the Cabinet papers, public and private." She had since received two letters from him "written with pencil." The second letter "is alarming because he desires I should be ready at a moment's warning to enter my carriage and leave the city; that the enemy seemed stronger than had been reported and that it might happen that they would reach the city, with intention to destroy it. I am accordingly ready; I have pressed as many Cabinet papers into trunks as to fill one carriage; our private property must be sacrificed, as it is impossible to procure wagons for its transportation. I am determined not to go myself until I see Mr. Madison safe, and he can accompany me, as I hear of much hostility toward him. Disaffection stalks around us. My friends and acquaintances are all gone, even Col C. with his hundred men, who were stationed as a guard in the enclosure." The men assigned to protect her had abandoned her. Her servant, "French John," inherited from Elizabeth Merry, "offers to spike the cannon at the gate, and to lay a train of powder which would blow up the British, should they enter the house. To the last proposition I positively object, without being able, however, to make him understand why all advantages in war may not be taken."

When Dolley received the newspaper the next day, August 24, 1814, she might have been cheered by the editors' optimism: "We feel assured that the number and bravery of our men will afford complete protection to the city." But that same edition of the *National Intelligencer* carried the order from the mayor that "all able-bodied citizens remaining here, and all free men of color, are required to convene tomorrow morning at the Capitol" to proceed to Bladensburg "to throw up a breastwork" to defend the city. "No accounts at ten this morning of the course of the enemy," Anna Thornton warily wrote that morning, "almost all our acquaintance gone out of town. Nearly all the moveable property taken away—offices shut up & all business at a stand [still]." General Armstrong called on Dolley Madison, still insisting that Washington was not in danger as she stood guard and continued her letter to Lucy: "Wednesday morning, twelve o'clock. Since sunrise I have been turning my spy glass in every direction and watching with unwearied anxiety, hoping to discern the approach of my dear husband and his friends, but, alas, I can descry only groups of military wandering in all directions, as if there was a lack of arms, or of spirit to fight for their own firesides!"

About one o'clock in the afternoon the British routed the Americans at Bladensburg, eleven miles from the president's house. A couple of hours later, according to Paul Jennings, Madison's valet, a messenger "galloped up to the house, waving his hat, and cried, 'Clear out, clear out! General Armstrong has ordered a retreat!'" Only after receiving that command would Dolley Madison leave her post: "Will you believe it my Sister? We have had a battle or skirmish near Bladensburg, and I am still here within the sound of the cannon! Mr. Madison comes not; may God protect him! Two messengers covered with dust come to bid me fly; but I wait for him. At this late hour a wagon has been procured, I have had it filled with the plate and most valuable portable articles belonging to the house, whether it will reach its destination, the Bank of Maryland, or fall into the hands of British soldiery, events must determine." A friend had come "to hasten my departure and is in a very bad humor with me because I insist on waiting until the large picture of Gen. Washington is secured, and it requires to be unscrewed from the wall. This process was found too tedious for these perilous moments; I have ordered the frame to be broken, and the canvas taken out. It is done, and the precious portrait placed in the hands of two gentlemen of New York for the sake of keeping. And now, dear sister, I must leave this house, or the retreating army will make me a prisoner in it, by filling up the road I am directed to take. When I shall again write you, or where I shall be tomorrow, I cannot tell!!" It was the act of Dolley Madison's that would be the most remembered—saving George Washington's portrait from British desecration. But at that moment she had no idea whether the portrait, the papers, or she would survive.

"All then was confusion," the valet, Paul Jennings, who later remembered that Mrs. Madison "caught up what silver she could crowd into her old-fashioned reticule and then jumped into the chariot," along with her servant Sukey, her pregnant sister Anna, and Anna's husband and children. Dolley later told a friend that she also grabbed the red velvet curtains she so loved as she reluctantly abandoned her mansion: "I confess that I was so unfeminine as to be free from fear, and willing to remain in the *Castle*! If I could have had a cannon through every window; but alas! Those who should have placed them there fled before me, and my whole heart mourned for my country!" At the Thornton household a few blocks away, "We heard rumors that the armies had engaged & expected to hear the cannon etc. but heard nothing," Anna recounted later that day. "At last saw a man riding as hard as possible toward the president's house. We went up soon after & found that Mrs. M. was gone. We sat down to dinner but I could eat nothing and we dilly dallied till we saw our retreating army come up the avenue. We then hastened away, and were escorted out of town by our defeated troops, Gen. Washington's picture and a cart load of goods from the president's house in company." The "two gentlemen from New York" had escaped with Washington's portrait and some silver urns and were headed out of town. The Thorntons ended up at the home of Martha Washington's granddaughter Martha Peters, in Georgetown, and "there witnessed the conflagration of our poor undefended & devoted city."

The British stormed into town about the time the sun was setting and headed first for the Capitol. After a mock vote they piled the furniture in the House of Representatives into a bonfire and put to the flame that symbol of American democracy. They then marched down Pennsylvania Avenue, stopping on the way at Mrs. Suter's boardinghouse. Only the elderly proprietor and a female servant were there as the British general, Robert Ross, announced that he had come "Madam, to sup with you." When she protested that she had no food, Ross demanded that she have his dinner waiting when he returned from his rampage. When they reached the executive mansion, the troops found "a dinner table spread, and covers laid for forty guests. Several kinds of wine in handsome cut glass decanters were cooling on the sideboard," marveled one of the English soldiers. Dolley Madison had prepared a meal for her husband's return, expecting him to bring his cabinet and his generals for "an elegant and substantial repast." Another British soldier somewhat guiltily recalled that they "speedily consumed" the meal "and drank some very good wine" and then set on fire the house that Dolley Madison had labored so lovingly to make an elegant bastion of executive authority.

Taking with them a portrait of Dolley Madison, not George Washington, the marauders moved next door to the treasury building, torched it and ambled back to Mrs. Suter's, where the officers sat down to her quickly devised dinner. Admiral Cockburn, the cocky commander who had threatened Dolley Madison, insisted that the candles be extinguished because he "preferred the light of the burning palace and Treasury." Before calling it a night, the admiral had one more target in his sights—the offices of the *National Intelligencer*. He planned to burn the building in retaliation for the anti-English stance of the newspaper, but two women of the neighborhood convinced him that a fire would consume all of the nearby houses. He listened to their pleas, vowed to return in the morning to destroy the presses, and retired to a brothel for the rest of the night.

Dolley Madison could see the flames from the plantation in Virginia where she had finally settled for the night, after several confusing hours. James had in fact returned to the executive mansion about an hour after she fled. He stayed there for a while and then left as the British closed in, with Dolley still desperately looking for him. She finally made her way over jammed roads to the Little Falls bridge, where she crossed the Potomac and headed to the home of a friend about ten miles away from the city. Madison, the subject of much derision for having deserted the battlefield, continued to wander in an effort to learn something of the enemy's movements. He stopped for a while at a home in Falls Church, Virginia, packed with refugees. One of them, a little girl of seven, had been rushed from her Washington home clutching her tea set. She later remembered the night: "At first I thought the world must be on fire—such a flame I have never since seen. We were told the British had taken Washington and [were] burning it up. . . . I was told not to cry."

The next day, August 25, when Mrs. Madison arrived at Wiley's Tavern—the prearranged meeting place with Madison—she was stopped by the landlady angry about the war: "Your husband has got mine out fighting and damn you, you shant stay in my house; so get out!" The other women there joined in the chant, trying to expel the First Lady, so gracious to all at her own home. Only when a terrible storm blew up did her inn-mates relent and allow her shelter while she waited for her husband. The storm, with its hurricane-force winds and deluge of rain, did almost as much damage as the British. But the enemy was back at it the following morning, ready to destroy all the public buildings, starting with the War Department. When the redcoats reached the Patent Office, Anna Thornton's husband stopped them: "They were on the point of setting it on fire & he represented to the officer . . . that it was the Museum of Arts & that it would be a loss to all the world." All the drawings and models of inventions inside belonged to the people, not the government, Thornton insisted, and the British were staying away from private property except the offices of the *National Intelligencer,* which, true to his word, Cockburn destroyed. Remarkably the newspaper was up and running five days later. The storm put out most of the fires, and Anna Thornton thought it was "almost miraculous that the whole place was not consumed," but that "it is feared that very little property had been saved out of the President's House." The city was so badly damaged that Margaret Bayard Smith thought it would never revive. On that melancholy Thursday she wailed, "Oh my sister how gloomy is the scene. I do not suppose government will ever return to Washington. All those whose property was invested in that place will be reduced to poverty." Margaret determined to use her letter to her sister as a journal to record the days ahead. She was eager to get back to town to try to protect her property but, especially since she was pregnant, her husband worried that "although troops when under their officers might behave well, yet small parties or drunken soldiers might alarm or injure me." Dispirited and distressed with the "dispreparation of our troops" she was saddened that "we shall learn the dreadful, horrid trade of war. And they will make us a martial people, for never, never will Americans give up their liberty."

What Margaret didn't know was that the British had abandoned Washington, leaving their dead and wounded behind. The fury of the storm plus an accident at an ammunition depot that killed a couple dozen of their soldiers, combined with rumors that the Americans were regrouping twelve thousand strong, had the effect of spooking the troops. They withdrew to their ships, preparing to fight another day. Dolley Madison, following her husband's direction, had disguised herself as a farmwife and was going deeper into the Virginia countryside when she heard the news and turned back toward Washington. The president kept trying to communicate with her, writing her on Saturday, August 27, that the secretary of state had reported that the enemy was gone from Washington and "advising our immediate return," though he didn't know where they would "hide their heads" when they got there. Anna Thornton noted that Madison had returned and even with "heavy cannonading" not far from town "we slept pretty well not withstanding." The British fleet had been briefly bombarded as the ships moved in on Alexandria, Virginia, causing the president to warn his wife that Washington might again be thrown "into alarm, and you may be again compelled to retire from it, which I find would have a disagreeable effect." That letter never reached Dolley, who was on her way back to the capital as Madison took heat for what the city saw as his cowardice. So did James Blake, "our stupid mayor . . . he ran away in the hour of danger," fumed Anna Thornton.

Dolley Madison, still in disguise, returned that Sunday, August 28. In order to convince someone to carry her by boat across the Potomac—the bridges had been burned—she revealed who she was. The return to her city, the place where she reigned, made her angry and afraid: "I cannot tell you what I felt on re-entering it—such destruction—such confusion. The fleet full in view and in the act of robbing Alexandria! The citizens expecting *another visit*—and at night the rockets were seen flying near us," she later described the scene to her friend Mary Latrobe. The First Lady went immediately to her sister's house, where Anna Thornton and Margaret Smith visited her. "She was very violent against the English," reported Mrs. Thornton, who thought Dolley would do better to "attribute the loss of her palace to the right cause viz want of proper defense in time."

When Margaret Smith came back into the city, she found her own home untouched except for some trees felled by the storm, but: "the poor Capitol! Nothing but its blackened walls remained!" The same was true at the president's house. "Who would have thought that this mass so solid, so magnificent, so grand, which seemed built for generations to come, should by the hands of a few men and in the space of a few hours be thus irreparably destroyed. Oh vanity of human hopes!" When Margaret stopped to see Dolley, she found her "much depressed, she could scarcely speak without tears." Everyone was understandably furious with General Armstrong; "I was assured that had he passed through the city the day after the engagement, he would have been torn to pieces." Even as they feared another invasion, the women were trading stories of what had happened over the last few days. Margaret Smith had heard Admiral Cockburn ordered his men to burn anything valuable in the president's house, but he took as a souvenir "a cushion off Mrs. M's chair . . . adding pleasantries too vulgar for me to repeat." Rosalie Calvert, whose house was right at the battlefield, breathlessly dashed off a note to her sister: "I am sure that you have heard the news of the battle of Bladensburg where the English defeated the American troops with Madison 'not at their head, but at their rear.'" It had been a scary time for her: "I saw several cannonballs with my own eyes." What would happen next, she did not know.

Now that Madison was finally trying to defend Washington against a British return, Margaret Smith reported resistance on the part of the local men: "'They now,' they said 'had neither their honor or property to loose. All they valued was gone.'" Would the British return? "What will be our fate I know not. The citizens who remained are now moving out and all seem more alarmed than before." Raids from the British ships still ransacked Alexandria, "taking in plunder," according to Anna Thornton, but she was well protected because the Madisons were living next door at Anna Cutts's house with a "nightly guard of 50 militia men." Reports from the countryside of British pillaging from Washington to Benedict added to the sense of terror and despair. Many families, especially the poor, were left without food and some without homes. In just a few days' time, however, Margaret Smith could say, "Citizens have returned and are slowly and despondently resuming business, but society and individuals have received a shock it will require a long time to recover from." The secretary of war, General Armstrong, was forced to resign, with James Monroe assuming that post in addition to his State Department duties. The president summoned a special session of Congress to convene September 19. Dr. Thornton, superintendent of the Patent Office, was asked to clear the models of inventions out of the building so the legislators could meet there. The Congress came to the burned-out and broken-down town to decide, among other matters, whether Washington would remain the capital city.

"They talk," William Lowndes confided in his wife, "of moving the seat of government, at least for a time; an attempt at least will be made to move it, and its success is not improbable." News that the capital might be moved had spread around the country, even before survivors in Washington could get word of their well-being to friends and relatives. Abigail Adams wrote to her son-in-law, who was serving in Congress, asking him to check on other family members, adding, "I perceive the apple of discord is thrown out in Congress, and the removal of the seat of government proposed." Philadelphia was pushing hard to reclaim the title of capital, and New Hampshire senator Jeremiah Mason told his wife that the proposal was gaining strength, but "the discussion has created a most violent excitement among the people of this district and vicinity. The derangement occasioned by the visit of the enemy to this place is much greater than I had supposed." The Federalist politician added that the administration was "universally condemned" for the lack of defense. "Poor Mrs. Madison, it is said, shows the most sensibility on the subject. In her flight from the enemy, she was not only without assistance or consolation from the inhabitants, but treated with abuse. The President left her to shift for herself. . . . The disgraceful and distressing stories told are innumerable." When the stories reached Hannah Gallatin, she felt for her old ally. "What would I give my dear friend could I enjoy the happiness of an hour's conversation with you, it would be worth all the letters I could write. How often do I think of you, & how much have I felt for you, what trials you have passed through. . . . I hope you may never witness such scenes again." Dolley Madison must have hated being the object of pity.

ADDING TO THE FIRST Lady's miseries was concern about her son. Payne Todd had gone to St. Petersburg as secretary to the peace delegation, but the British rejected the Russian mediation offer, leaving the negotiators at loose ends. All of 1814, their families in America kept expecting them to come home, but information moved slowly from the frozen north of Europe. "What can be the cause that we can neither see nor hear from our beloved friends," a frantic Hannah Gallatin asked her friend Dolley Madison in January 1814. Hannah's son too had gone along with her husband, Albert Gallatin, as part of the team and she had no idea where they were. "This state of uncertainly is too dreadful. What does the President think." The president didn't know what to think. He had just received word from the British that they were ready for direct negotiations, expected to take place in the city of Gothenburg, Sweden. But Madison omitted Gallatin from the list of negotiators, thinking he was already headed home. At the end of January a relieved Dolley had heard from Payne: "He says—'If you should see Mrs. Gallatin, or the families, of any of our party, inform them that we are all perfectly well.' . . . He says also 'That our friend' (meaning your estimable Husband) 'does not care for machinations &c &c.' . . . Be consoled then, my precious friend in the knowledge, that your Husband & son are safe & well. Mr. Madison has looked with anxiety & impatience for Mr. Gs arrival, & does not at this moment give up the hope of seeing him notwithstanding the uncertainty expressed in his letter to you—but for this hope, Mr. M would have taken advantage of his talents, to form the new treaty; & will yet propose him to the Senate, if he should hear that Mr. G. will pass the winter in Europe."

Madison did hear that Gallatin was still in Europe and took "advantage of his talents," appointing him to the peace commission.

This time the Senate readily concurred. But Hannah hoped the slowness of communication would, for once, work in her favor: "My prayers night and day are that he will have left Europe before the news of his new appointment can possibly reach him. If the President should know or hear any thing further about him, you will I know have the goodness to communicate it to me." Hannah was miserable not knowing what was going on, but at least she had a good friend in the First Lady, who was equally anxious for information. When the president received word that Gallatin knew of his appointment, Dolley immediately relayed the information: "Mr. M. *thinks* the *Ministers* are *now all together* in Gothenburg—I grieve for your disappointment—your long & anxious trials—yet I trust, your fortitude my beloved, will support you a little longer—It may be, that your good Husband, will have sailed for America before Mr. M's letters could reach him—still it is not probable. The Negotiations will not last more than a month, when the chance for propitious Gales will be augmented & July or August will bring back your happiness." Dolley could not have been further off the mark. The five ministers—Speaker Henry Clay and the new minister to Sweden, Jonathan Russell, had been added to the trio of James Bayard, Albert Gallatin, and John Quincy Adams—were not all together, and the negotiations, once they finally began, would last a good deal longer than a month. Sorry to have to impart such unwelcome news to Hannah Gallatin, Dolley was also upset on her own behalf. She had learned that her son was no longer with Hannah's husband: "I am distressed at Payne's leaving Mr. Gallatin—What could have led him to do so? nothing but anxiety to get home I hope." Young Payne Todd had taken off for Paris and had no intention of going home. He was having too good a time.

What Dolley Madison couldn't know as she attempted to reassure Hannah Gallatin about her husband's return by summer was that John Quincy Adams was still trapped in icy waters on his way to Sweden. He had left St. Petersburg at the end of April, expecting to sail from the port of Reval (now Tallinn, the capital of Estonia) in a day or two. But the frozen harbor held him hostage in the town for three weeks. "I arrived here about 11 o'clock on Sunday morning, amidst the hurly burly of rejoicings for Paris and the downfall of Bonaparte," he told Louisa, who was back in St. Petersburg with little Charles. "The merry bells were ringing all their most laughing feasts." Showing more humor and affability than he normally did (he ended this letter with "a kiss for Charles—as for you—as the song says, 'that fruit must be gathered from the tree.'"), John Quincy wrote to Louisa almost daily during his tenure as a peace commissioner, giving a blow-by-blow account of his travels, his amusements, and eventually of how the negotiations proceeded. And, like his father before him, who had made the mistake of praising the French women to his wife struggling in America during the Revolution, Adams reported, "I am told that Reval is famous for the beauty of the women. . . . I saw at the ball a very good proportion of samples." Just what a wife waiting at home wants to hear. On her end, Louisa announced, "We are rejoicing at the reappointment of Mr. Gallatin to whom I beg you will present my best respects." It was easier for Louisa Adams to get news in Russia than for Hannah Gallatin in America.

After a week in Reval, John was going stir-crazy. "I went last evening to the Theatre, to see the *Surfs Family,* announced as a *Lyric Opera.* . . . It was a foolish and servile imitation of *Nina,* about three times as long, and the music not half so good." A couple of days later he admitted to missing his six-year-old son: "Not an hour has passed away since I left him but I have longed to have him with me, and felt the pain of the separation from him." From what she was hearing, Louisa thought the separation would not last long. "It is reported here that you will shortly return on many accounts. I trust this is not true, but for my own sake I should certainly not be sorry for it. We are overwhelmed with bad news and I almost rejoice that you are out of the reaches of it." The war was not going well in America, and Louisa thought the peace mission was doomed. John too was discouraged, having heard "that the British Government had come to the positive Resolution not to treat with America at Gothenburg. . . . If so, my voyage to Sweden is more abundantly useless than I have always supposed it would be." At that moment the voyage itself was problematic. The ship finally sailed, was hit by ice, and returned to the harbor after a couple of days. And the winds were all blowing in the wrong direction.

After three long weeks in Reval, John Quincy Adams again set off for Sweden, shivering in single-digit temperatures as the ship dodged ice floes. In Stockholm he learned "Mr. Gallatin and Mr. Bayard are still in England, and incline not to go to Gothenburg at all, but elsewhere; or to stay where they are." At least he wasn't late to the negotiating table. Back in St. Petersburg, Louisa had expected different news. "Mr. Gallatin, and Mr. Bayard will most likely be in Gothenburg before you arrive there, and something decisive will be arranged concerning the time of your absence or return. If anything can be done there to promote the interests of our country, I should be the last to regret our separation." Louisa Adams might have been intimidated by her mother-in-law, but she was just as staunch a patriot. Still, she was worried. "God bless you and protect you where ever you are. May he turn the hearts of our enemies and grant us a solid and permanent peace. Our prospects are very gloomy and I fear there is not much to hope." Her husband had been gone a month and he hadn't even reached his destination, much less started haggling with the British. In fact he didn't even know what his destination would be. "The proposal has been made, somewhere, to remove the seat of negotiations to Holland." Adams suspected, correctly, that the British were stalling. In St. Petersburg Louisa heard that England would insist on territorial concessions. "The general opinion here is that there will be no peace and if England is as hostile as her little representative we have certainly but little to hope. Any place is better than Gothenburg and it is of little consequence where provided the negotiations terminate happily." She was trying to jolly John out of what she could see was his pique over the relocation of the peace conference, so she chattily filled him in on their move to the country ("Charles has already derived benefit from air and exercise and takes milk from the cow every morning. He has a lake, a spade, and a wheel-barrow") and the comings and goings of their friends and neighbors ("the unfortunate circumstance of Brown's death has opened the mouths of every body against him. She is left with 7 children and pregnant, totally unprovided for").

In her letters, Louisa would muse on human nature in ways she probably wouldn't have in person with her stern husband. "You will I know laugh at this, and call me romantic but I believe contrary to the usual system of philosophers, that we come into the world with germs of character, which even the best education cannot eradicate, nor all the worldly experience that can be heaped upon us totally destroy. I know that I am singular in my opinions upon most subjects but my observations on my own children have contributed very much to strengthen my conviction." For his part, John was more open about his feelings in writing. "In the affection of those who truly love, there is a favor of sentiment when they are separated from each other, more glowing, more unmingled and more anxious, than while being together it has the continual opportunity of manifesting itself by acts of kindness," and more amusing about his activities, like his evening watching tightrope walkers at the French theater: "They actually fall from the rope four or five times every evening; and they are in continual danger of breaking their necks—It is said that among the amusements of the Ancient Romans, there was nothing that gave the people so much delight as to see the Gladiator die.—My nerves are not strung to the Roman Standard." But politics made up the meat of both John and Louisa's letters—that's what they were concerned about. And, working his way through a stack of American newspapers, Adams was disgusted with "the nauseating bickerings of party spirit." Sound familiar?

John Quincy Adams arrived in Amsterdam on June 19, 1814, and learned that his fellow Americans were still spread around Europe; the British commissioners were nowhere in sight. He couldn't deny his discouragement: "As I approach the term of my journey, the prospect darkens and thickens—The effort to be of good cheer becomes more laborious." Louisa too saw little bright light; she had heard that the venue for the talks had changed again "and that you are now to go to Ghent in Flanders. I do not think these changes wear a friendly aspect and I much fear from what I can gather that the mission will be dragged on for some months without producing any thing decisive." Rumors were flying that the Americans weren't getting along, when the Americans hadn't even reached their destination. But Louisa didn't know that; she wasn't at all sure where her husband was. If it were true that he was headed for Ghent, however, she had a shopping list. "Should you really go to Ghent I shall commission you to purchase me some lace as it is a very cheap article in that part of the country and I believe table linen is to be had there at small expense of the best kind." When she did hear from her husband, Louisa had her own views about why the British weren't proceeding with the negotiations: "It is the dire necessity of acknowledging our power as a nation that rankles in their hearts and mortifies their pride so bitterly but peace, or war, disasters, or good fortune, they must one day or other be brought to it." Louisa Adams understood what was at stake—America's place in the community of nations, something she had worked to promote in Germany and Russia. What John was hearing from home, once he arrived in Ghent, did nothing to convince either of them that the British would have to acknowledge American power any time soon. The war was dragging on—"We have General Andrew Jackson's official report of his victory over the Creek Indians on the 17th of March," that was the good news; the bad news: "It seems to be supposed that an attack upon Washington itself or upon Baltimore is intended."

Albert Gallatin, who had traveled to London seeking information, wrote discouraging words to his wife as well, and she repeated them far and wide. An upset Dolley Madison told Hannah that people were talking "about your having received a letter from Mr. G. full of alarming information, such, as his having no prospect of making peace & urging you for your personal safety to quit N. York & reside in Philadelphia—It had a distressing effect on our loan & threw many into consternation for a while but we were able to contradict & soften consequences." Message sent: keep your mouth shut. But Dolley managed to blunt the blow with chatty gossip—her sister Anna was "very *large* & complaining" in her pregnancy, Mrs. Clay was preparing a garden for her husband ("They will elect him again in Kentucky")—and to make common cause with Hannah about their sons. "I was rejoiced at your last letter containing the account of my precious Payne's going to France from England—I have written him . . . to return only with Mr. Gallatin & James—be that when it may—I hope we shall see our sons highly benefited by their tour." "Precious Payne" couldn't be pried out of Paris, though he was supposed to join the commission as "a gentilhomme d'Ambassade, quite independent in his movements," John Adams joked to Louisa in mid-July, "very naturally thinking Paris a more agreeable residence than Ghent." A week later, when all members of the American delegation had finally assembled in Flanders except the First Lady's son, still in Paris, Adams added another wry note, "Mr. Todd stays there a little longer—He finds his knowledge of French not sufficiently perfect, and had taken a maitresse de langue, to give him the last polish—A very virtuous and beautiful young woman, who teaches the language to gentlemen, without scandal; her reputation being perfectly unimpeachable." The Americans didn't need Payne Todd for the negotiations to get under way—they needed the British.

Adams assumed the enemy was waiting to see how they did on the ground in America before emissaries would be dispatched to Ghent, and Louisa saw the British as suddenly standoffish in St. Petersburg. "The English here appear to have their heads quite turned and I feel almost afraid to meet any of them," but the rest of official society continued to welcome her. She regaled John with an evening of theater and entertainment at the palace, "My *terrors* at the idea of going alone to Court were great, but the polite attention I received from the members of the Corps Diplomatique, gave me a degree of fortitude and I hope I got through without disgracing you. On the whole I never was at a more charming party in my life." She had enjoyed a good evening but life was not easy on her own. When a friend, Captain Bates, reported that he had never seen her husband in such good spirits, she jabbed at John: "What being on Earth is so wretched as a Woman without her Husband, more especially in a foreign Country, without knowing the Language of those who surround her; at first it was dreadful, I am now becoming more reconciled to it, and perhaps in time *I shall like it*." Fair warning. When Adams received that letter three weeks later, he fell all over himself to explain. "I hope you do not think that the good spirits which Captain Bates ascribes to me arose from any forgetfulness or unconcern for you. That you are reconciling yourself to the inconveniences and troubles of a separation from me, cannot give me pain; on the contrary, I hear it with pleasure; because present or absent the first wish of my heart is that you should enjoy life in cheerfulness and conform. But I should deeply lament if the time should ever come that you would *like* to live absent from me. I certainly never shall *like* to live absent from you." Another three weeks, and she replied: "Really Mon Ami, I think you cannot complain as you acknowledge that you received pleasure from the information that I was becoming more contented with my situation. As to my wishes, had they not been cruelly disappointed we should not now be writing upon the subject of our separation, and I should never even in jest have hinted that I could live happily without you."

Among her other concerns, Louisa wasn't sure what to do about living arrangements. Adams was not being paid anything extra for his service as negotiator and was, as always, instructing frugality. "I am informed that your stay is likely to be prolonged, I wish I could ascertain this fact correctly, I should be induced to change my abode, for a much smaller residence." It was all so uncertain, and so unpromising. "All the late letters from England assure us there is to be no accommodation between the two Countries this year." And soon Louisa Adams would have more cause for unhappiness. A year earlier, her sister, the flirtatious Kitty Johnson, had found herself pregnant by John Quincy's nephew and secretary, William Smith. The couple had hastily married in early 1813, but their baby died. The next year another baby, Caroline Amelia, was born. Now, with John Quincy Adams gone from his post, William Smith had no job, so the family was reluctantly returning to America. They left Russia with their four-month-old at the end of July. "My spirits were so much depressed at the parting with my sister and her dear Babe and the house is so dull and gloomy without them that I roam about like a spirit without knowing what to do with myself or on what to fix my attention." Louisa was really alone, except for Charles. But she continued to swim in the social whirl. At court in early August, "The Empress . . . expressed much sorrow at the bad prospect of affairs but told me that notwithstanding appearances she hoped we should soon make a good Peace." The American consul had not attended that night's fete, so "poor I became the only representative of America (not so bad neither considering how we go on in Canada, an old woman or a child would answer the purpose)." Clearly the reports from the war zones across the sea, including British victories in Canada, were making it hard to be a proud American.

Finally, at the beginning of August, the British commissioners showed up in Ghent—more than three months after John Quincy Adams had left his wife and son in St. Petersburg. On August 8 the two sides held the first meeting, and Adams cautioned his wife: "You will now, my Dearest Friend receive in the most exclusive confidence whatever I shall write you on this subject—Say not a word of it to any human being, until the result shall be publicly known." He was trusting her with state secrets. And Louisa Adams often knew more than President James Madison, given the slowness of communication. The president, as always, used Dolley to try to garner information, hoping that maybe Hannah Gallatin had heard from her husband: "Is there hope of their return soon? or can the expectation of peace be cherished still? In case of peace would you like to be in Europe, as Minister?" Madison didn't want to put Gallatin's name forward as an ambassador if he didn't want the job. "The question you put to me about going to Europe, I can only answer for myself, as far as I can judge thus hastily I think it would not be disagreeable to me, but I cannot answer for my husband. I think he is at this moment on his passage home." Instead, Albert Gallatin was sitting down with the British to bargain for peace.

The first issue facing the negotiators was where they would meet—the British proposed their quarters, the Americans theirs; the decision was made to gather at a hotel the first day and then alternate between the two countries' headquarters. But the place the Americans had rented had its problems, according to Adams: "The house was *haunted*, and its ill fame in this respect was so notorious that the servants and the children of our party were very seriously alarmed before, and when we first came in—The perturbed Spirits have all forsaken the house since we entered it, and we hope they are *laid* for ever." As the talks got under way, the gentlemen were all very friendly, but the conversations weren't going anywhere. "I was delighted to hear you were so much pleased with your initiation, owing to the amiability of your companions," Louisa sighed, "but am very sorry that your absence is likely to be prolonged; but as I have often said if peace should really be the consequence, I should not repine at passing the whole of the ensuing winter alone." Rumors of planned British attacks on America pushed Adams past discouragement: "It is impossible that the summer should pass over without bringing intelligence which will make our hearts ache; though I hope and trust that nothing will or can happen, that will break the Spirit of our Nation." He couldn't know that the British were that day in the Patuxent River, staging their attack on Washington.

"Since I wrote you last we have neither seen nor heard of the British Commissioners," a bemused Adams reported in mid-August. "The conferences have now been ten days suspended, and I may say to you it is by no means clear that they will be resumed." It was such a roller-coaster. One day it would seem that all deals were off: "We are in hourly expectation of receiving the reply of the British Plenipotentiaries to our note in answer to theirs and we already know that it will contain a refusal to continue the negotiation." Another day, they were back on again: "Yesterday we received the reply to our note, but it does not, as I expected it would, terminate our business here," he was surprised to say in early September. "It presents even a possibility of further negotiation, but in a manner so ambiguous and equivocal, that I cannot foresee the result of our next note to them—Nor can I indeed precisely judge what that will be, as it is not yet prepared."

This was incredibly sensitive stuff. "We are surrounded by so many commercial spies," markets would move up and down, fortunes could be made or lost, depending on the outcome at Ghent: "As the commerce of all Europe will be profoundly affected by its issue, there are in every commercial city persons eager to seize upon its incidents for purposes of private speculation." Everyone was trying to find out what was going on: "I have had many letters of solicitation for information. . . . I have declined giving information of any kind respecting the negotiation to any person in Europe, excepting yourself and Mr. Crawford [the American envoy to France]." She was his trusted confidante. But when he reiterated the caution "let me again remind you of the request that you would disclose to no human being a word of what I write you concerning what is passing here," Louisa chose to be insulted: "You appear to be under great anxiety about my discretion, and I am very uneasy likewise because every thing that you write me is known before your letters arrive not from your letters but from England. . . . Should this letter reach you and you should have to remain I wish you to tell me nothing whatever concerning the business and only to mention the time of your return when it is *positively* fixed." She was afraid he would blame her for news spreading about what was happening at Ghent. More than a month later when he received that poutily penned note, Adams tried to fix it. There had been evidence, he told her, that Americans close to the commissioners were speculating in the commodities markets based on what was happening at the negotiating table, that's why he had repeated his warning. "I was further induced to it because you had written me that Master Charles had assumed a sort of privilege of reading all my letters, and although it did not apprehend that he would engage in any profound project . . . upon the Exchange, by means of *his* correspondence with Ghent, it occurred to me that an indiscretion on his part might be possible." He firmly restated his "unqualified confidence in you, I trust that all my subsequent as well as my preceding letters have given you the most unequivocal proofs.—I shall continue to give them notwithstanding your intimation of a wish that I would withhold them, because I take pleasure in giving those proofs, and because I know that the confidence will be safely reposed." Arguments over the miles and months were hard to tamp down, but he needed her as his sounding board, and used his letters as an escape valve, which he would continue to do.

In addition to the continued uncertainty about the outcome of their months in Ghent, starchy John Quincy Adams was not enjoying the company of his fellow Americans. "I know one gentleman, who says, 'as to the note for the Plenipotentiaries, I can take that up, after I have been to the play'—and I have heard of another who prepares himself for diplomatic musing by six hours of relaxation at the card table; and there might in the reveries of fancy be imagined a third, who adjourns from the meeting of the delegation, to be punctual to the meeting with a fair Delilah." His compatriots didn't seem too keen on Adams either: "It happens sometimes . . . that I have views of the subject in discussion not acceptable to some of my colleagues, and not deemed important by others.—There is much more verbal criticism, used with me too, than with any other member of the mission." As to the British negotiators—they just weren't very smart. "They are certainly not mean men, who have been opposed to us; but for extent and copiousness of information, for sagacity and shrewdness of comprehension, for vivacity of intellect, and fertility of resource, there is certainly not among them a man equal to Mr. Gallatin." With the Crown's top diplomats busy at the Congress of

Vienna, the men in Ghent had no authority. Every exchange had to go back to London for consideration, which frustrated the Americans and prolonged the proceedings.

And then there were the rumors about a large British expedition headed for America: "Lord Hill has the command of it; and at a dinner last week, promised the company that he would humble the Yankees, and reduce them immediately to submission." Lord Rowland Hill had led the British to glorious victories over Napoleon's armies, but Louisa refused to be cowed by him: "As for my Lord Hill. He may have the *elements* to contend with before he meets the Yankees. I hope that notwithstanding his great force, he may find the Yankees able and willing to teach him the lesson of humility. . . . Englishmen give one a pretty just idea of what man would be, without . . . restraints." This from a woman born and raised in England. The same reports had reached Washington, and Congressman William Lowndes, who shared Louisa's view about the elements, feared for his family at home in South Carolina: "It is commonly supposed here that Lord Hill will attack either the Southern ports or Louisiana. . . . If they were to attack Charleston and take it, their European troops would suffer more in the first summer than from the severest European campaign, yet our calculation should be that they will attack it." He added pessimistically to Elizabeth, "We do not hear at this place a whisper of peace." A week later he had sunnier news: "The negotiations at Ghent have not been broken off. Lord Hill will not be in America this winter. I feel less anxiety from the expectation of an attack on South Carolina than I have done." That must have been a relief to his wife, who was there without him. Louisa Adams was also relieved at what she read in a newspaper report: "The *Conservateur* of today announces the postponement of the departure of Lord Hill, and his troops, but expressly says, 'not on account of any thing done at Ghent.'" Lord Hill never did fight against the United States, but the paper was right, it wasn't because of progress at Ghent. That same day, Adams expected another rejection of the latest proposal. "It will be like the last . . . scolding like an old woman; (pardon me, dear Louisa, you know our bargain is that you will always be young, to me) insulting in one paragraph and complaisant in another."

By the end of September the news of the attack on Washington had still not reached the peacemakers, but they were expecting something any minute: "If they get the news of their troops having taken Washington or Baltimore before they transmit to us their next note they may perhaps undertake to dismiss us.—If not they may prepare for us materials for another note." By the end of October the whole of Europe knew that the U.S. capital had been burned: "The news of the destruction of Washington makes much noise here and they seem to think as you say that all America is destroyed. Everybody looks at one with so much sorrow and compassion that I hate to stir," a dejected Louisa wrote from St. Petersburg, "you would suppose that we had not a chance left of ever again becoming a nation." And at the negotiating table the calculations had shifted: "Since the late news from America, they have totally changed their grounds, they now come forward with new inadmissible pretensions. . . . While they are sporting with us here, they are continually sending reinforcements, and new expeditions to America—I do not, and will not believe that the Spirit of my Countrymen will be subdued by any thing that the British forces can accomplish, but they must go through the trial, and be prepared at least for another year of desolating war." That sad statement came as the New England states had decided they had had enough of a war they had opposed from the beginning. They voted to meet in Hartford, Connecticut, in a secret convention, with talk of secession heavy in the air.

The lack of progress at Ghent, the stories swirling about the Hartford Convention, the grinding on of the war—all were taking their toll on the spirit of John Quincy Adams's countrymen, and countrywomen. One of Thomas Jefferson's oldest friends, Eliza Trist, sounded so despondent in a letter he received in December that she elicited this teasing reply: "I think while you were writing it the candle must have burnt blue, and that a priest or some other conjurer should have been called in to exorcise your room. To be serious, however, your view of things is more gloomy than necessary." He then proceeded to predict to her exactly what would happen. There would be peace, he believed, as soon as the British negotiators could find out what "the Convention of Hartford will do. When they shall see, as they will see, that nothing is done there, they will let go their hold, and we shall have peace on the *status ante bellum.*" Unbeknownst to him, Jefferson wrote those words the day after the peace treaty was signed, and it essentially did what he supposed it would—returned the two countries to the state of play before the war.

After the burning of Washington the British had not scored any major victories; the prospect of prolonging a war no one really wanted made no sense. And the tide of public opinion was running against the British. "I am not surprised that you should have been so much affected by the vandalism at Washington," John Quincy Adams sympathized with his wife. "The disgust which you observe that the conduct of the British there, gave at St. Petersburg, has been generally felt throughout Europe. The whole transaction has done more injury to them than to us—especially as Baltimore, Plattsburg, Lake Champlain and Fort Erie have since retrieved part of our loss of character, while they have tended to aggravate their disgrace—By this time I believe that even your *compassionating* friends in Russia begin to suspect that all America is not yet conquered—We have yet much to endure and go through but I trust we shall triumph at the last." By the end of November, Adams for the first time saw glimmers of peace: "The British Government have withdrawn just so much of their inadmissible demands, as would avoid the immediate rupture of the Negotiations," he informed Louisa. "We have been here five months, enduring everything, rather than break off, while a possibility of peace remained." A few days later: "They have rejected without exception everything that we had demanded on the part of the United States—But they have abandoned every thing important that was inadmissible, of their own demands. . . . They have given up without qualification all demand for a cession of Territory . . . it is evident that the British Government are now sensible of the difficulty and danger to themselves of continuing the War. . . . For the first time I now entertain a hope, that the British Government is inclined to conclude the Peace—We are now in sight of Port—Oh! That we may reach it in safety!" And then they did. And, as Thomas Jefferson had surmised, after more than two years of war, no one won anything.

John Quincy Adams did not know how the public would react: "You must expect that we shall all be censured and reproached for it, and none with more bitterness than your nearest friend—We shall however have the conscious satisfaction of having surrendered no right of the nation—of having secured every important interest, of having yielded nothing, which could possibly have been maintained, and of redeeming our Union from a situation of unparalleled danger and deep distress—I am also well assured that our enemies, whom peace will I fear not make sincerely our friends, will give as little satisfaction to their nation by the treaty, as we shall to ours . . . neither party will have cause to exult." The issues of neutral shipping rights and impressment—the two issues cited as causes of war—were not addressed in the treaty, but they were essentially moot, given the downfall of Napoleon. So John Quincy Adams's determination to stay in Ghent no matter how bleak success might seem, paid off. "On Saturday last: the 25th of December, the Emperor Alexander's birth day, a Treaty of Peace and Amity was signed by the British and American Plenipotentiaries in this city," he trumpeted to Louisa. "The secret was kept I believe as faithfully as any such secret can be."

Now there was the question of what next. Adams was hoping for the embassy in London, and he had "written to the Secretary of State, that I shall go to Paris and there wait for the president's orders. Whether he returns the intention of sending me to England or not, I have definitively requested to be recalled from the Russian Mission." Instead of returning to Louisa, he was off to Paris! First he would copy documents and convey the terms of the treaty to European capitals. Adams sent papers to the America consul in Russia, telling him to impart them to the czar's government: "He is also at liberty to communicate them to you, and you may give him and others whom you please the information, that the hostilities are to cease as soon as possible *after the ratification in America*." Now it was time for Louisa to leave Russia. "The Peace will doubtless enable you to part with mutual looks and feelings of kindness from our English friends and acquaintances—If there has been no sympathy during the war between their joys and sorrows and ours, there will it is hoped, henceforth be no opposition between them—Indeed although the peace is not what I should have wished, and although it may acquire no credit in our country to those who made it, I consider the day on which I signed it, as the happiest of my life, because it was the day on which I had my share in restoring Peace to the world." Abigail Adams's prayer that her son might be an "instrument in the hand of providence" had been answered, and Louisa Adams's insistence that Britain "acknowledge our power as a nation" had been met.

WHILE THE NEGOTIATORS wrangled in Europe, Americans had come together after the dispiriting burning of the capital. A few weeks after the British victory in Bladensburg and humiliation of Washington and Alexandria, the enemy mounted a large-scale attack on Baltimore, but failed to take the city. When day broke and young lawyer Frances Scott Key saw the enormous American flag made by Mary Young Pickersgill still flying over Fort McHenry guarding Baltimore harbor, he was inspired to write the poem that we know as "The Star-Spangled Banner." Then the Royal Navy chugged out of the Chesapeake, out to the Atlantic, where reinforcements from England joined the fleet in Jamaica and moved around to the Gulf of Mexico, preparing to take New Orleans. The British believed that cosmopolitan city would welcome its "liberation" from America and assist the invaders in taking the Mississippi River Valley all the way to Canada. The United States, squeezed by the British on the west and north and by the Spanish on the south, would never, in the eyes of the enemy, amount to anything more than a third-rate power. But the British had it wrong.

It was an understandable mistake about New Orleans. Why would such a city feel any allegiance to America? On the last count, in 1810, the population of just over seventeen thousand made New Orleans the nation's seventh largest city, but only a small percentage was of the Anglo-American descent of most of the country. The rest were French, Spanish, Portuguese, German, Italian, Irish, free people of color, slaves, and white, black, and mixed race immigrants from Haiti. The language spoken was French. And the restrictions on trade had hit the port city particularly hard—filling its warehouses with sugar and cotton begging to go to market. But the burning of Washington had outraged New Orleanians along with everyone else, and no one lost any love for the English. The city started preparing for invasion soon after news of Washington's fate reached them. Louise Livingston, wife of prominent lawyer Edward Livingston, wrote in October to her sister-in-law in New York: "The people seem disposed to defend themselves. A committee has been named to provide means of resistance. Your brother is president of it."

Edward Livingston was already in charge of the defense committee when his old friend Andrew Jackson arrived in New Orleans on December 2, 1814, fresh from defeating the Creek Indians in Alabama and the British in Florida. Jackson had been promoted from a colonel in the Tennessee militia to a major-general in the United States Army as a result of his victory over the Creeks, telling his wife, Rachel, now that he was such an exalted officer she "must appear elegant and plain, not extravagant—but in such style as strangers expect to see you." If he was puffed up with his title, at least he was able to deliver the goods as a master of military strategy. Jackson also harbored a lifelong hatred of the British. The redcoats had held him captive as a young boy during the Revolutionary War and he blamed them for the deaths in his family. To his wife, Jackson made no bones about his feelings—"I owe to Britain a debt of retaliatory vengeance," he seethed, as he summoned that passion to mobilize the citizens of the Crescent City, who seemed willing, if not particularly able, to defend themselves.

In New Orleans General Jackson was met by William C. C. Claiborne, who had been elected governor of the new state of Louisiana, as well as Edward Livingston. When Jackson addressed the crowd that quickly gathered under the balcony of the house he would use as headquarters, it was Livingston who translated the call to arms—"cease all differences and divisions and unite with me in patriotic resolve to save this city"—into the French everyone could understand. Jackson then went to dinner at Livingston's home, somewhat to the displeasure of the lady of the house. Louise D'Avezac Livingston, having fled with her family from Haiti, had become a central figure in the Creole life of the city. That night she had planned one of her elegant dinners and feared that her sophisticated friends would not take well to the inclusion of an American from the wilds of Tennessee. When the general turned out to be a perfect gentleman, the surprised Creoles declared Jackson "a prince." Jackson inspired such enthusiasm that "the ladies formed committees to provide all that was necessary for the wounded and to care for them," and men started pouring into the city from bayou backcountry, rifles at the ready. For news, everyone would stop by the Livingston household, knowing Edward had the job of the general's aide-de-camp. His son Lewis also enlisted with Jackson, and wrote to his aunt in New York: "Great bustle but little alarm now prevail in town. We daily expect the enemy to make an attack upon this place. We are ready, however, to receive them."

The braggadocio of the young man was not shared by the women of the city. Unaware that the negotiators were near agreement at Ghent, as the British sailed through the Gulf of Mexico to the mouth of the Mississippi. Word spread that the sailors had been promised "beauty and booty" in New Orleans, and the whole country by now knew that the women of Hampton, Virginia, had been raped by rampaging members of the Royal Navy, while their officers looked the other way. This time the officers brought their own women along, expecting to enjoy the entertainments of New Orleans. The wives made merry on the ships off Louisiana's shore as the city prepared for battle. Andrew Jackson staged a grand public ceremony on the square that is now named for him, with all the men in the militias of the nearby states as well as Louisiana lined up at St. Louis Cathedral "decorated with bouquets" made by the women, whose blood must have run cold as Jackson stirred them to battle an enemy "marked by cruelty, lust, and horrors unknown to civilized nations." Among those signed up to fight—the Baratarian pirates, led by Jean Lafitte and his brothers. Jackson had been loath to accept the services of the "hellish banditti," though he readily enrolled regiments of free blacks, but the locals had convinced him that the pirates' knowledge, manpower, and ammunition would be extremely valuable. Edward Livingston so trusted them that he had assigned one of the Lafittes to bring Louise and their young daughter Cora out of the city, if it came to that.

The British off the coast of Louisiana had defeated the great armies of Napoleon; they had every reason to believe they could best the motley ménage of Tennessee backwoodsmen, pirates, Creole merchants and lawyers, and local militias. So did some of the women of New Orleans. Though they participated in the preparations, sewing silk banners and flags, and making clothes for the troops, many wept in the streets as the Americans marched off to meet the enemy south of the city. Jackson told Livingston to assure the women that the British would never take New Orleans as long as he "held the command," but still the commander was criticized for not evacuating the women and children. A prominent Creole, Bernard de Marigny, scoffed at that idea, proudly proclaiming: "No lady fled from the city. Fly? That thought never came to the mind of Louisiana ladies," instead, he insisted, if the enemy had attacked, "more than one young lady would have assumed an Amazon costume and taken the lance."

The first major engagement, on December 23, essentially ended in a draw. The wounded were brought back to the city to be nursed by nuns and free women of color in the hospitals and convents, and by other women in their homes. For unexplained reasons, Edward Livingston asked General Jackson if he could bring a British officer of "interesting appearance" to his home, where the young man was nursed back to health by Louise. When the Englishman regained consciousness he found himself "in an Elysium, with beautiful women waiting on him." After hearing of some conspiracy among the prisoners, Jackson ordered that they all be sent back to the camp hospital— all except Louise Livingston's captive. She "went to General Jackson and asked permission to retain the wounded officer, notwithstanding the order. It was the return she 'desired for the services of entire family'—her husband, stepson, two brothers, and brother-in-law were all engaged in active service." Mrs. Livingston won that argument. She also prevailed on the men to let her go get a look at the battlefield.

The battles raged on until early January, with neither side knowing that a peace treaty had been signed in Ghent. Welcome reinforcements of two thousand Kentucky militia arrived on the fourth, so scantily dressed that a subscription drive was launched to raise money to buy warm fabrics. The women of the city used the material to whip up more than a thousand cloaks and another thousand pairs of pants, plus waistcoats and shirts by the hundreds, all in the matter of a week. Even with the influx of men, it was still a life-and-death situation. In a book about Louise Livingston her great-niece wrote, "Crowds of women and children came to the house for safety." But the Livingstons felt anything but safe. On January 6, Edward Livingston wrote a goodbye letter to his sister, telling her that they might never meet again: "We trust in God that we shall be able to defend our firesides and every one capable of bearing arms is in the field . . . the service is dangerous and we have lost many respectable citizens but the survivors are animated with a glorious spirit, and if we fail, the enemy will not find us an easy conquest." He then told her goodbye, instructing her to tell all "my relations to whom I cannot write, that I love them very affectionately." He expected to die.

The whole country waited to hear what was happening in New Orleans. On January 8 "an account of the English having destroyed our little flotilla on Lake Pontchartrain" reached Washington, William Lowndes told Elizabeth, "this success will enable them to get within a couple of miles of the city conveniently and safely, but the difficulties of marching from the lake to the river are such as to afford a reasonable hope that they may be repelled." The terrified women and children of New Orleans joined the Ursuline nuns throughout the night of the seventh of January and into the morning of the eighth, gathering in the chapel of Our Lady of Consolation at the Ursuline convent, to beg for their protection before the statue of Our Lady of Prompt Succor. The next morning—the feast of Saint Victoria, the nuns happily realized—a courier rushed into the chapel during mass with the triumphant news: "Victory is ours!" The British commander, Lieutenant General Sir Edward Michael Packenham, who had bragged that he would have Christmas dinner in New Orleans and perhaps stay for carnival had been killed; the British had borne a devastating and decisive defeat. Rejoicing that "Louisiana is still American," Louise Livingston described it in detail to her sister-in-law a few days later: "We killed eight hundred of the English and took five hundred prisoners, besides having five hundred wounded sent to our hospitals, among whom are twenty-five officers of mark. Their loss is said to be about twenty-five hundred men." Louise's numbers were exaggerated, but the British casualties did come to more than two thousand dead, wounded, missing or taken prisoner, compared to only seventy-one American casualties: "There never was a more glorious victory, nor one that cost less blood. Not a single father of a family was killed, and the joy of the people, thanks be to God is unalloyed by private sorrow." Her husband and stepson were still at camp and Louise would "not dwell on all I have endured during the four different engagements of anxiety and terror. Such feelings cannot be described. The battleground is only a league from the city, and I could not only hear the booming of the cannon, as the house shook each time, but every musket could be heard also. All I can say, dear sister, is that people do not often die of it, however great the anguish of such hours." She would survive. And Louise

Livingston gloated that her English patient was a prisoner though he "came to conquer."

Other wounded soldiers were in the care of the Ursulines, who converted schoolrooms into hospital wards for both the victors and the vanquished. One of the nuns remembered that the care of her community "was so highly appreciated by their patients, that British veterans were seen to weep like children when obliged to leave with their officers;" and the militia men from Kentucky and Tennessee for years sent large baskets "filled with bacon, fruit, etc. as tokens of gratitude to their Ursuline Mothers." General Jackson also showed his gratitude on a visit to the convent to thank the nuns for their prayers and, according to the Ursuline archives, the religious "in their turn were happy to offer him their felicitations and to be able to contribute to the expense of a banquet which was given in honor of the illustrious General."

The illustrious general had led the army back into the city "amidst the acclamations of an immense multitude of old men, women, and children, the only ones who did not share in the dangers of the field," Edward Livingston's son Lewis told his aunt in a letter that went on to describe the only-in-New Orleans ceremony that took place at the cathedral a couple of weeks after the final battle. "On the public square, facing the building was erected a triumphal arch . . . nearest to the arch were to be seen eighteen young ladies, dressed in the same apparel and each representing one of the States. In the middle of the arch there were two little children, standing on two thrones . . . each held a crown in her hand: General Jackson easily found out who they were for; his modesty suffered but he was obliged to submit. He passed through the arch and was crowned, amidst the huzzahs of the Americans and the acclamations of the French who did not cease to repeat, 'Vive Jackson! Vive notre General!'" An eight-year-old girl was chosen to read the congratulatory speech to Andrew Jackson, who halted the procession to thank the young women and then continued on his flower-strewn path into the cathedral for the hymn of thanks and praise, the *Te Deum*. The battle was won, the curfew was lifted, the kaleidoscope of a city celebrated as one.

It took a while for the news to reach the nation's capital. "In twenty four hours, dearest mother, we shall hear whether the British are repulsed from the shores of the Mississippi, or in possession of New Orleans," Sarah Seaton worried on January 11, "the general opinion here is that nothing short of a miracle can save that devoted city." A few days later Dolley Madison fretted to Hannah Gallatin, "The fate of N. Orleans will be known to day—on which so much depends." But then the official report on the great victory came from Louisa Adams's brother, Thomas Johnson, the postmaster of New Orleans. He sent it to *Mrs.* Madison: "Madam, the American army in Louisiana has gained immortal glory. It has made a defense against the most valiant and fortunate troops of Europe, excited to desperation by resistance, and staking its all of reputation on the die, unsurpassed in the annals of military warfare. . . . The 8th of January will form an epoch in the history of the republic." He wrote on January 19 when the remaining British were still huddled at the mouth of the Mississippi but midway through the letter, Johnson had a fresh report: "12 o'clock—Intelligence has at this moment been received from General Jackson that the British have evacuated the country. The rear of their army completed the retreat to their shipping last night. . . . The city is in a ferment of delight. The country is saved, the enemy vanquished, and hardly a widow or an orphan whose tears damp the general joy. All is exultation and jubilee." Thomas Johnson, who had gotten his job through the First Lady's efforts, concluded by offering "my congratulations on this auspicious termination of our trials and tribulations" to Dolley Madison. It was welcome news indeed. "We are all rejoicing over the good news from New Orleans," reported Margaret Bayard Smith, still angry over the outrageous handling of the defense of Washington. "Oh, if we had had a Jackson, we should not have exhibited such a shameful sight." Sarah Seaton hailed the triumph as "the most decided victory over our enemies that ever was obtained by America."

A few weeks later the great news from New Orleans was topped by even better news—a peace treaty had been signed. The Christmas Eve pact finally reached America on February 13 and word quickly spread around the country. In Boston, "We heard the bell of the Old South, and of the Federal Street Church, begin to ring and we thought it was a fire," sixteen-year-old Susan Quincy wrote in her diary. When a friend burst in shouting that the bells were ringing for peace, her father, Josiah Quincy, rushed out and "soon confirmed the joyful news and said the whole town was in an uproar, cannons firing, drums beating, bells ringing." The family went out in their sleigh to find a city filled with people, "gentlemen shaking hands and congratulating each other, ladies and women running wildly about . . . flags were generally displayed, and even suspended across the streets. The joy of the poorer classes of society who had suffered most from the war was very touching. . . . The gentlemen of Boston decided to defer the public celebration until official intelligence from Washington could be received." Intelligence from Washington awaited the delivery of the treaty itself, which happened the next day. A carriage bearing it, accompanied by excited crowds, rushed to the Madisons' temporary home, Octagon House. The president and his cabinet brought the document to the second floor, where Dolley's cousin Sally Coles spied them. She went to the head of the stairs, "crying out, 'Peace! Peace!' and told John Freeman (the butler) to serve out wine liberally to the servants and others. I played the President's March on the violin," remembered Madison's valet, Paul Jennings, years later. "John and some others were drunk for two days, and such a joyful time was never seen in Washington." As the president perused the Treaty of Ghent, the public crowded into Octagon House to celebrate, with Dolley Madison welcoming "gentlemen of the most opposite politics," according to the *National Intelligencer*. Former enemies congratulated each other with "elated spirits." The center of attraction in the midst of all this exuberance "was Mrs. Madison herself." By just looking at her anyone could see "that all uncertainty was at an end." Soon the whole country was jubilant: "Now gladdens the hearts of millions," Nelly Custis Lewis rejoiced to a friend about the news of peace. Though the treaty didn't address the issues that actually caused the war—impressment and harassment of shipping—the pact, combined with the victory at New Orleans, was enough for the country to hold its head high. "The time of making it is more fortunate than the peace itself," William Lowndes analyzed the document to his wife, "the best effect of the war is the deep impression which our enemy must feel, that on our own soil we are unassailable." And, as Rosalie Calvert could be counted on to note, the administration was in no position to reject the Treaty of Ghent: "If our envoys had not signed the peace when they did, our government would not have been able to continue for six months," she told her father. The treasury had been unable to pay "the last dividends on the public bonds."

THEIR EFFORTS TO ACHIEVE peace finally realized, two of the Ghent commissioners went their separate ways—Jonathan Russell retuned to his post in Sweden; James Bayard turned down the offer of Russia, became deathly ill in Europe, and died a few days after arriving in America. The third, Albert Gallatin, had accepted the job as envoy to France, Henry Clay and John Quincy Adams were assigned to negotiate a commercial treaty with England. Adams had received unofficial word that the coveted appointment to the Court of St. James's would be his, but he felt it unwise to arrive in London without his credentialing documents, so he decided to wait in Paris until they arrived. He summoned Louisa to deal first with their possessions accumulated over six years in St. Petersburg, then to arrange transportation for herself and seven-year-old Charles and meet him in the French capital, "where I shall be impatiently waiting for you." It was quite an assignment. More than twenty years later, when Louisa had become an advocate for women's rights, she described her adventures in order to "show that many undertakings which appear very difficult and arduous to my sex, are by no means so trying as imagination forever depicts them." She wanted to dispute "the fancied weakness of feminine imbecility."

After selling some of their things and shipping the rest to England, in the dead of winter, February 12, 1815, Louisa Catherine Adams left St. Petersburg "in the company with my son Charles between 7 and 8 years of age; a French nurse, who entered my service on that day, and two men servants." The women and Charles would ride in a carriage placed on runners; the men followed in a hooded sled. Soon all of their provisions froze in the bitter weather, "even the Madeira wine had become ice." But when they reached Riga, now in Latvia, then part of Russia, a couple of days later, it was a thaw that gave them trouble—forcing them to rerig the carriage and abandon the sled. The diplomat's wife was wined and dined by all the "distinguished persons in town" for four or five days before hitting the road again. As they made their way across what is modern-day Latvia "once or twice the carriage sunk so deep in the snow . . . that we had to ring up the inhabitants, who came out in numbers with shovels and pickaxes to dig us out." Loud carriage bells were essential. As she journeyed west, European nobility at every stop invited Louisa to stay at their estates, but she insisted on pressing on as fast as she could, stopping at the best inns she could find. At one, in Mittau, then the capital of a region of Latvia, the innkeeper warned her that "last night a dreadful murder had been committed on the very road which I was about to take," and that one of her men servants was "known to be a desperate villain, of the very worst character; and that he did not consider my life safe with him." With that cheery news to digest, Louisa got back in her carriage to travel on. Soon they were lost, "until eleven o'clock at night, we were jolted over hills, through swamps, and holes, and into valleys, into which no carriage had surely ever passed before; and my whole heart was filled with unspeakable terrors for the safety of my child." But the "villain" behaved very admirably and found the help of a local man who led them to the road and safety.

More adventures, over the not-so-soundly frozen Vistula River, on across war-scarred Europe with its "silent houses half burnt, a very thin population; women unprotected, and that dreary look of forlorn desertion . . . announcing devastation and despair," caused Louisa to contemplate the "fearful remnants of men's fiery and vindictive passions." But on she drove to Konigsberg, in what was then Prussia, where she made "some trifling purchases of amber, and should have gone to the theatre if I had not been unprotected by a gentleman." Very different from her husband's travels a year earlier. When a wheel on the carriage "fell to pieces" they were forced to spend the night in "little more than a hovel" presided over by a "dirty, ugly and ill natured" woman and some "surly, ill looking men." Louisa "had my little boy's bed brought in, and while he slept soundly my woman and I sat up, neither of us feeling very secure in the agreeable nest into which we had fallen." As unpleasant as it might have been, the folks at the "hovel" fashioned a crude new wheel and the party was once again on its way. "The desolation of this spot was unutterably dismal," she remembered about the city of Kustrin, where everyone talked about "The Cossack! The dire Cossacks! Were the perpetual theme, and the cheeks of the women blanched at the very name." In this part of Prussia, the men of Louisa's friend the czar were the enemy, the exiled Napoleon, the hero. And then "after an absence of fourteen years, I entered Berlin with the pleasant recollections of the past; and youth seemed again to be decked with rosy smiles, and glad anticipations." Berlin had been the city of her new marriage; a place where she had enjoyed her first successes in diplomatic circles, but suffered the sadness of her many miscarriages before the birth there of her son George. Taken altogether, Louisa realized the irony in her happy recollections: "Memory; how ineffably beautiful is thy power!" Visits with old friends, despite many tales of the hardships endured during the long wars, meant she "left the city of Berlin for the last time with feelings both of gratitude and regret. There I had felt *at home* . . . in Petersburg for five long years I had lived a *stranger* to all, but the kind regards of the imperial family; and I quitted its gaudy loneliness without a sigh, except that which was wafted to the tomb of my lovely Babe."

Back on the road, where Louisa put on her "military cap and tall feather" because "I had been told that anything that *looked* military escaped from insult." She arrived at a town in Prussia (whose name she couldn't remember) where "a rumor had arrived of the return of Napoleon to France." Though she believed the rumor was ridiculous because the deposed emperor was "*known* to be very safe at Elba" it reminded her of a Russian woman who had insisted on reading cards to tell her fortune just before she left the country: "She said that I was perfectly delighted to quit Petersburg...that when I had achieved about half of my journey, I should be much alarmed by a great change in the political world, in consequence of some extra-ordinary movement of a great man which would produce utter con-sternation, and set all Europe into a fresh commotion." Louisa recalled that she laughed and thanked the woman but dismissed her predictions "as it was a time of peace, and we were all very merry at the skill with which she had strung together so many improbabili-ties." Now, as she wended her way west "whenever we stopped to change horses, we heard of the return of Napoleon; and . . . we found it was received with less doubt, and the measures were already sup-posed to be adopted for calling the disbanded troops together." And, if Louisa needed any reminder of what that meant, it was at hand as they crossed a battlefield "over which was scattered remnants of clothes; old boots in pieces; and an immense quantity of bones . . . in that plain ten thousand men had been slain. Conceive my horror at the sight of such a butchery!"

In fact, Napoleon *had* escaped from Elba on February 26, 1815, and the Bourbon monarch, Louis XVIII, was trying to assemble the army to stop Bonaparte's progress toward Paris. The men Lou-isa Adams had hired as servants "began to grow uneasy, and fre-quently talked about conscripts, and renewal of wars, for which neither appeared to have any taste." In Frankfurt, the men "requested to speak to me, and informed me . . . that they must quit my service, and preferred to remain at Frankfurt . . . as there they would be likely to meet with opportunities of service." If they went on with her to Paris, as they had promised, the men feared they would be drafted into the army. What was Louisa to do? *"Here was a situation:* I could not compel them to stay; no bribe could induce them to go on in their state of panic." Her husband had provided her with letters of credit that she could present at banks all along her journey, so she called on "my banker," who advised her to stay in the city for a few days while he tried to "make arrangements for me." But Louisa Adams knew enough of the world to understand that she should move while all was still unsettled: "At present the panic itself would prove advantageous; as it would require time to ascertain events, before the governments could take decisive measures." If she waited, borders could close. The banker agreed but advised that she take a more circuitous route to Paris than planned, and then left to find "some person to go with me . . . he returned in short time with a boy of fourteen, the only creature he could find willing to go." No one knew what was going on politically, and everyone had a different story. At her first stop after Frankfurt, the "master of the inn came in and informed me that Napoleon had been taken, and that he had been tried immediately and *Shot*. He said the news might be relied on, as it had just arrived at the Palace." Napoleon, of course, was hearty, healthy, and ready to retake France. And the false report that he had been killed apparently didn't enjoy widespread circulation because troops were gathering, and instead of preparing to defend the reigning king, they were signing up on the side of the deposed emperor.

The emperor's return meant the wars would resume and "wagons of every description full of soldiers, were continually rushing towards the frontier, roaring national songs, and apparently in great glee at the idea of a renewal of hostilities," Louisa observed with horror. "What a mere animal man may become!" As her trusty little troupe traveled on, the possibility of conflict grew more real.

Reaching the Rhine River at Strasburg, in Alsace, Louisa "was questioned, and troubled; and after some delay permitted to cross, which we accomplished with success, and landed in safety Here again I was stopped; my passports demanded, my baggage taken off, etc. The Officer in command, recommended to me an excellent hotel, and politely told me he would wait on me there." Just being the wife of an American diplomat wasn't going to be enough to get her through to Paris; Mrs. Adams would be questioned by the authorities to determine whether she would be allowed to proceed. She wisely consulted the hotel owner on what the local constabulary would be looking for. He advised her how best to present her documents and it worked. The officer "informed me that my baggage would be allowed to pass, and that my passports would be endorsed etc. and returned to me in proper form. He said the country was in a very unsettled state, and that it would require great prudence and caution in the pursuit of my journey to Paris." The hotel owner then found her "a most respectable looking person" to accompany them on the road. Still, with the warnings of the officer and the unknown ahead, Louisa looked for something to fortify her: "I had been a year absent from my husband, and five years and a half from my two sons; and the hope of soon again embracing them, gave me strength to sustain the fatigue and excitement to which I was necessarily exposed."

Riding on with some trepidation—the group now consisted of Louisa, her seven-year-old son, the French nurse, the fourteen-year-old, and Dupin, the respectable-looking person who joined them in Strasburg—they stopped the first night at "a miserable place" with "several very surly looking men" and "Charles seemed very much frightened as these men asked him several questions, and I was obliged to tell them the child was too sleepy to talk." Keeping guard over her little boy all night, Louisa heard the excited voices of men in the inn discussing Napoleon's return and their boasts of what would happen to "the horrible Cossacks." And she was riding in a Russian carriage! As they crossed into France they found troops "mustering to express their delight at the return of the Emperor." Louisa was determined to get to Paris before the army could organize, but an hour out of Epernay, in the Champagne region (after an excellent bottle of the local bubbly), "we suddenly found ourselves in the midst of the Imperial Guards, who were on their way to meet the Emperor. The first notice I had of my danger, was hearing the most horrid curses, and dreadful language from a number of women, who appeared to be following the troops. . . . Presently I heard these wretches cry out, 'tear them out of the carriage; they are Russians, take them out, kill them.' At this moment a party of the soldiers seized hold of the horses, and turned their guns against the drivers. I sat in agony of apprehension, but had presence of mind enough to take out my passports." A general rode up to the carriage and examined the documents "and he called out that I was an American lady, going to meet her husband in Paris. At which the soldiers shouted 'vive les Americains' and desired that I should cry 'vive Napoleon!' which I did waving my handkerchief; they repeated their first cry adding 'ils sont nos amis.'" Friends or not, "a number of soldiers were ordered to march before the horses, and if we attempted to push on out of a walk, the order was to fire on us directly." The general warned her that "my situation was a very precarious one; the army was totally undisciplined; that they would not obey a single order; that I must appear perfectly easy and unconcerned; and whenever they shouted I must repeat the Vive's." Louisa's perfect French, the general said, would "contribute much to my safety, as no one would believe me to be a foreigner." And she was proud that she showed "no evidence of fear or trepidation; yet my heart might have been heard to beat, as its compulsive throbbings heaved against my side." She had Charles to think of: "My poor boy seemed to be absolutely petrified, and sat by my side like a marble statue." No wonder! "In this way we journeyed; the soldiers presenting their bayonets at my people with loud and brutal threats every half hour. The road lined on each side for miles with intoxicated men, ripe for every species of villainy, shouting and vociferating 'a bas Louis dix-huit! Vive Napoleon!' till the whole welkin rang with the screech, worse than the midnight owls' most dire alarm to the startled ear."

At midnight they arrived at an inn, where the general, with some effort, prevailed on the landlady to take in the foreigners. "Soldiers were crowding into the house all night, drinking, and making the most uproarious noises." But Charles managed to fall asleep. His nurse, however, "really appeared to have lost her senses. She clasped her hands continually, while tears rolled down her cheeks, crying out that she was lost! For the Revolution was begun again, and this was only the beginning of its horrors." And soldiers attacked the fourteen-year-old boy "with a bayonet and forced him to burn his military Prussian cap; and it was with great difficulty that his life was saved by the dexterity of the Landlady." Pushing on the next day, they reached Chatillon, where some passengers "informed me that I had better not go on to Paris, as there were forty thousand men before the gates; and a battle was expected to take place. This news startled me very much, but on cool reflection, I thought it best to persevere." Louisa was convinced that her husband would come to meet her if there were real danger, "or by some means have conveyed intelligence to guide my course," though she knew he might not have heard of her change of route since Strasburg. Dupin agreed that they should press on toward Paris and told her "that in consequence of my being almost the only traveler on the road going towards Paris, that a whisper was abroad that I was one of Napoleon's sisters going to meet him; and that this idea was so favorable to the promotion of my success that *he* was *very mysterious* and only shrugged and smiled at the suggestion." Two more harrowing days on the road and they "arrived in perfect safety and without molestation at the gates of Paris; and descended at eleven o'clock at the Hotel du Nord Rue de Richelieu. Mr. Adams had not returned from the theatre; but he soon came in, and I was once more happy to find myself under the protection of a husband, who was perfectly astonished at my adventures, as everything in Paris was quiet, and it had never occurred to him that it would have been otherwise in any other part of the country." Imagine—she had traveled all that way, survived all those terrors finally to reach her destination, ready to fly into the arms of her husband, and he was at the theater! John Quincy Adams's recording of the events that same day is slightly different. After first noting that he had called on "Mr. Gallatin and also Mr. Bayard but he was asleep and I could not see him," and then critiquing his night at the Théâtre de Variété: "All the performances at the theatre are examples of low and vulgar humor." He then added, "When I returned home I expected to have found my wife's carriage in the yard, and was disappointed; but had scarcely got into my chamber when she arrived. It was eleven in the evening—she and Charles are both well and I was delighted after an absence of eleven months to meet them again. They have been exactly forty days in coming from St. Petersburg." That was it.

Louisa Adams throughout her harrowing journey had been convinced that her husband would be aware of their plight and finding a way to protect them. Instead because Napoleon's escape had ignited the countryside but left Paris nonplussed he was blissfully oblivious. "A moral is contained in this lesson. If my sex act with persevering discretion, they may from their very *weakness* be secured from danger, and find friends and protectors; and that under all circumstances, we must never desert ourselves. I was fortunately neither young nor beautiful; a fact in itself calculated to prove my safeguard; and I had others under my protection to whom the example of fortitude was essential; and above all the object which drew me on, was the reunion with my beloved husband." There were those who would argue that forty-year-old Louisa Catherine Adams was indeed beautiful when she made her own triumphal entry into Paris on March 23, 1815, three days after Napoleon made his.

Louisa Adams was not only reunited with her husband, but also with her sister Kitty and baby Caroline. The Smith family had missed the boat in Amsterdam, where they had expected to sail to America, and gone, at John's invitation, to Ghent. Now they were in

Paris, along with Dolley Madison's son Payne Todd. William Smith was hoping for the commission as secretary to the British mission, but he received no word from the State Department, and the family finally went to America, docking in the spring of 1815. It turned out that Smith did have the London job, but learned of it too late. Even before they left Europe, Kitty started badgering Dolley Madison: "I have written this letter for you alone. And hope my dear Madam you will extend your Patronage to me and my Husband when we return for we shall return to nothing." In fact, Smith did return to nothing, and Kitty wrote more and more frantic letters to Dolley as the couple sank into poverty and lost their baby girl to measles.

When John Quincy Adams's official papers came through naming him as ambassador to Great Britain, he and Louisa and Charles headed to London. They arrived on May 25 and found George and John waiting for them. It had been almost six years since the parents had seen their sons, since Charles had seen his brothers. The joyous reunion began what was one of the most pleasant times in Louisa Adams's life. The nephew sent as secretary this time, John Smith, turned out to be far more diligent than his brother Billy. John got the job after his grandmother, Abigail Adams, of course, sent him to Dolley Madison: "John Adams Smith, has written to me: to request of the president, the appointment, if he should deem it proper to grant it to him. . . . Mr. Smith who will have the honor to deliver you this letter, has been educated to the Bar, is a young gentleman of correct principles, and by no means addicted to dissipation."

One of John Quincy's first tasks as ambassador must have seemed like déjà vu. He joined Gallatin and Clay to negotiate a commercial treaty—and the British named their Ghent commissioners as well. Dolley Madison told Hannah Gallatin that news, quoting a letter from her son: "They have had several meetings, & the project on a treaty has been given by our Ministers who await a counter project. . . . A disadvantageous Treaty will not be signed—though I apprehend there is not much room to hope for a happy settlement of the question of Impressment. The existence of this Negotiation is not made public here. It is best, therefore, not to mention it until one of our Ministers shall write." Poor Hannah Gallatin had been expecting her husband to show up any minute for more than a year, but now she would have to wait longer. The treaty was successfully concluded and ratified on July 3, 1815, and Gallatin went home just long enough to settle his affairs, collect his wife, and return to Europe as ambassador to France. Henry Clay returned to the political wars of Washington.

THE NATION'S CAPITAL was still struggling to recover from the British attack. "I went to look at the ruins of the President's House," Virginia lawyer William Wirt sadly told his wife. "The rooms which you saw so richly furnished, exhibited nothing but unroofed naked walls, cracked, defaced and blackened with fire." In the spring of 1815, Harriott Pinckney Horry, the sister of Charles Cotesworth and Thomas Pinckney, kept a journal of her trip north from South Carolina with her niece Eliza Pinckney. When they reached Washington in June, they "went to see the ruins of the President's house, the Capitol and Navy Yard. . . . The walls of the buildings appear good and they are beginning to repair them, it being now fixed that the seat of government is to remain here." Goods were scarce and expensive. "We can hardly creep on with the greatest economy & self denial," Anna Maria Thornton complained, "almost every article is trebled in price." But, burned and broke, Washington was determined to be the "phoenix on the Potomac" and it had won the battle against other cities trying to capture the title of capital. The fact that the city had suffered so added weight to its claim, as Rosalie Calvert saw it: "The burning of the public buildings in Washington is the best thing that has happened in a long time, as far as we are concerned, since this has finally settled the question of whether the seat of government would stay here. In the future they will no longer keep trying to change it."

One of the generals in the fight for Washington was Dolley

Madison, who, now that peace was at hand, enjoyed enormous popularity. The stories of her heroism—saving the government papers and the portrait of George Washington—had taken on the aura of legend, and she came to serve as the symbol of American resilience. One historian summed up the general attitude in his description of the First Lady: "Next to Joshua Barney she was the bravest American soldier." When soldiers were released from the army after the war, they marched past the Pennsylvania Avenue house the Madisons had moved to in the fall of 1815 to salute Mrs. Madison—giving her three cheers and receiving a gracious greeting. Children gathered at the window to watch the First Lady feed her parrot. "She as well as her pet was very engaging," remembered one of those children many years later. But Dolley did more than play with parrots and smile at soldiers. Seeing the tremendous need in the capital after the invasion, she worked with the women of the city to establish the Washington Female Orphan Asylum.

"The Ladies of the county of Washington and neighborhood are requested to meet at the Hall of Representatives, this day, at 11 o'clock, A.M. for the purpose of joining an association to provide an asylum for destitute orphans," read the announcement in the *National Intelligencer*. "It is hoped that the Ladies will shew the interest they take in the fate of those destitute and forsaken children, by their zeal and humanity in endeavoring to supply them, as far as is in their power, the place of deceased parents." Reminding its readers that the future could not be known, the newspaper reflected that it might be "our own descendants" who benefited from the asylum. "It is therefore hoped, that there will be a full and punctual attendance; particularly by those ladies who have already subscribed to this institution." Mrs. Madison, who was elected "First Directress," paid her twenty-dollar subscription, donated thirty-five more, plus a cow, and an offer to cut patterns for clothes.

On November 27 the *National Intelligencer* reported that the society had purchased a house for the orphans at the corner of Pennsylvania Avenue and Tenth Street. The women drew up a constitution delineating the duties of the society's officers: "The First Directress shall preside at all meetings both of the Society and Trustees—preserve order—state questions for discussion and declare the decision; in all equal divisions she shall have the casting vote." That would be Dolley Madison's job, in addition to taking "an active superintendence" of the society. The Second Directress was Marcia Van Ness, a wealthy local woman who had thought up the idea of the society but understood the value of putting Dolley Madison out front. The secretary would be responsible for collecting dues, recording the proceedings, and keeping the accounts. Margaret Bayard Smith would take that assignment. The "governess" they would hire "must be a woman of pious character and capable of teaching to read and sew." Constitution drawn, the ladies then petitioned Congress, which was meeting temporarily in a building across the street from the Capitol, for incorporation and for some land: "A number of females in the City of Washington and its vicinity have associated for the purpose of protecting, relieving and instructing female orphans, and, if the funds of the Society should become sufficient, of extending the same benefits to male orphans and other destitute children." A house had been procured "and several destitute female orphans, who might have been suffering all the miseries of want, especially at this season of the year, and exposed to vice, are now comfortably situated under the protection and care of your petitioners." The girls were training to be "useful members of society." The women coyly claimed there was no need for them to make their case to the Congress: "Your petitioners would deem it a want of respect to so enlightened a body to urge all the arguments and motives in favor of relief for those destitute and friendless infants." But the body was not at all enlightened. The Senate voted no on the petition to incorporate—some voted against Madison, some voted against women, some voted against corporations. But the women continued to serve the orphans and persisted in their pursuit of incorporation and eventually won approval more than a decade later, having begun a long history of the local women of Washington working with political wives to provide social services.

While creating a home for orphaned little girls, Dolley Madison also had to start all over again fashioning a suitable house for the president. It was back to the task of collecting furniture. Everything was secondhand, even the china, and Dolley readily accepted donations from friends and relatives, and asked them to shop for her. Nothing matched, as the disgruntled wife of Navy Secretary Crowninshield noted, complaining that she was served on "saucers instead of plates—very common ones, like your old china cup—all put on the same one waiter." Even if Mrs. Madison was making do, she was determined to keep up her entertainments. "Our house is crowded with company—in truth ever since the peace my brain has been turned with noise & bustle. Such over flowing rooms I never saw before," Dolley told Hannah Gallatin as she asked her to look for furniture. "There is every reason to expect a crowded and interesting winter, as it will be the first meeting of Congress since the peace," Sarah Seaton cheerily conveyed. "Mr. Jefferson's granddaughter, Miss Randolph, will lead the van in accomplishments and beauty." Young Ellen Randolph, Martha's daughter, earned her sojourn in Washington by translating an important diplomatic document. The State Department had received a communication in Spanish that no one could read, so Madison sent it off to Thomas Jefferson, an accomplished linguist. According to Sarah Seaton's account, Jefferson handed the job to Ellen "for her morning task, and long before the appointed hour she placed in his hands an elegant and correct translation . . . it paved the way for Miss Randolph. She will stay with Mrs. Madison, and will no doubt be very attractive to the various well-informed visitors at the palace." But the big attraction of the season was not the granddaughter of the ex-president; it was the hero of New Orleans.

"General Jackson's visit here has excited a great commotion. Dinners, plays, balls, throughout the District," Sarah excitedly told her family. "I wish much that some little aerial machine . . . could be invented that you could take wing and remain a day, or an hour even, with us." Everyone was thrilled to meet the "distinguished warrior," but "on Mrs. Jackson's arrival a dilemma was presented, and a grand debate ensued as to whether the ladies would visit her." It was a foreshadowing of the abuse that would be heaped on Rachel Donelson Jackson when her husband ran for president and it stemmed from the fact that she had not been divorced from her first husband when she married Andrew. The Jacksons insisted that it was an honest mistake, that they believed Rachel's husband, Lewis Robards, had filed the papers. But he charged her with adultery and seeded scandalous stories that would sprout up for the rest of her life. The women of Washington were atwitter about how to handle it. Even when they decided to call on Rachel, they criticized her: "Mrs. Jackson is a totally uninformed woman in mind and manners, but extremely civil, in her way." Apparently Jackson's attempts to school Rachel as "a Major General's lady" didn't take. Dolley Madison, of course, entertained the couple in the best style she could muster. And even if her house was not anything elegant to behold, the First Lady made sure that her person was. Mrs. Crowninshield sent descriptions of Dolley's costume home to her mother: "She was dressed in a white cambric gown, buttoned all the way up in front, a little strip of work along the button-holes, but ruffled around the bottom . . . She looked very well indeed." That was daytime attire. A few weeks later at a ball where all the women were decked out in new dresses: "Mrs. Madison's is a sky-blue striped velvet—a frock— fine, elegant lace around the neck." And on New Year's Day 1816, "Mrs. Madison was dressed in a yellow satin embroidered all over with sprigs of butterflies, not two alike." Getting a good look at what Dolley was wearing wasn't easy: "Such a crowd I never was in. It took us ten minutes to push and shove ourselves through the dining room." Everyone was thronging to the First Lady's "squeeze," ready for the social season to go into full gear, even if the capital was in ruins. Despite her cramped quarters, Mrs. Madison found ways to glamorize her receptions. Since she had no good lights for her rented house, she assigned black servants to stand in the windows holding torches, creating a stir on the street and prompting snide remarks about her "barbarous grandeur."

With the end of war, and the beginnings of prosperity, even Rosalie Calvert stopped grousing about the government. She was able to ship her father his tobacco and to buy shares in the newly established Second Bank of the United States. And, to her relief, the second exile of Napoleon meant peace and security in Europe. Since her family had gone back to Belgium she and her husband had been the custodians of her father's extremely valuable art collection. A descendant of Rubens, Stier hid his paintings in America to protect them from Napoleon, who plundered Europe to fill the Louvre. Many of Rosalie's letters show how nerve-wracking it was for her to be saddled with the responsibility for the art; she kept the paintings crated up and hidden away. Now Henry Stier was reclaiming his collection, which involved an arduous packing job for Rosalie, who was pregnant with her ninth child. Before shipping the artworks, the Calverts decided to display them for the first time, inviting America's foremost artists along with the public for a five-day exhibit. Members of Congress and diplomats joined the likes of Rembrandt Peale in the trek to Bladensburg to see the old Flemish masters. Sarah Seaton called the show of "some of the finest paintings ever in America" a treat. And the new British ambassador's wife recorded in her journal that "everybody flocked to see them, a collection of pictures being almost unheard of in the United States."

The country might still be unsophisticated but it had gained self-confidence and stature by hanging together and driving foreigners from its soil. The "era of good feeling" took hold in the election year of 1816, and following in the example of Washington and Jefferson, Madison decided to retire after two terms. His chosen successor would be his secretary of state and fellow Virginian James Monroe, though he stayed officially neutral. In early March Dolley wrote to her cousin Edward Coles, who was traveling to New Orleans, "most of the politicians are busy forming the next president. Me & mine still adhere to Colo. M[onroe] as the best deserving on every point. Mr. Crawford has many friends & few open enemies—Colo. M many of the last description. Gov. Tompkins too, divides the republican interest but, I think, however the storm may rage for a time our estimable countryman will gain the prize." "Mr. Crawford" was former Georgia senator William H. Crawford, who had served as Madison's ambassador to France and as secretary of war and of the treasury. Daniel D. Tompkins was the governor of New York and represented a faction of the Republican Party fed up with Virginia's dominance.

"The election of the next President is a subject so interesting to everybody that even the most idle and indifferent think and talk a good deal about it," Ellen Randolph, enjoying her stay in the city, wrote home to her grandfather, Thomas Jefferson. "The merits of the candidates are discussed, and even the ladies of their families come in for their full share of praise or blame. Mrs. Monroe has made herself very unpopular by taking no pains to conceal her aversion to society, and her unwillingness to be intruded on by visitors." Elizabeth Monroe was no Dolley Madison, who would be an impossible act to follow. While Ellen was enjoying Dolley's hospitality, Jefferson was missing his granddaughter's company, "When are you coming home?" He pleaded with the not quite twenty-year-old, "The void you have left at our fireside is sensibly felt by us all." Jefferson was close to all his grandchildren, but Ellen held a special place. "I was thrown most into companionship with him," she told one of her grandfather's biographers. "I used to follow him about, and draw as near to him as I could." Ellen had no desire to go back to the country; she was enjoying quite the season in Washington. "We count one hundred young ladies in the city—not 10 of them belong to the place—some of them are really fine & handsome," Dolley tried to entice Ned Coles to come home. "Our Virginia Belles for instance, Miss Randolph & Misses Barbour & Robertson—We have also an unusual number of young men from every direction—in short, we never had so busy a winter because the city was never before so full of respectable strangers . . . This is Drawing Room evening—& we have such throngs, you never saw." A reception honoring the new British ambassador was especially memorable, hosting the returned peace commissioners along with the Supreme Court, the cabinet, Congress, and the diplomatic corps. Dolley Madison, dressed "in rose-colored satin, and white velvet train . . . lined with lavender satin and edged with a ruching of lace," was, as always, at the center of it all, causing the new arrival, Sir Charles Bagot, to declare, "Mrs. Madison looked every inch a queen."

Ellen Randolph's time in the capital introduced her to the wider world. Abigail Adams told Thomas Jefferson she had heard about "your granddaughter, Miss Ellen Randolph, whose praises are in the mouths of all our northern travelers, who have been so happy to become acquainted with her." The travelers also brought "such delightful accounts of Monticello and its inhabitants" that she wished she could visit them, "but I am so far down hill, that I must only think of those pleasures which are past. Amongst which, and not the least is my early acquaintance with, and the continued friendship of the philosopher of Monticello." She had truly made amends. So had Thomas Jefferson. His granddaughter "is justly sensible of, and flattered by your kind notice of her," he told his old correspondent, "and could I, in the spirit of your wish, count backwards a score of years, it would not be long before Ellen and myself would pay our homage personally in Quincy. But those 20 years, alas! Where are they?" He signed himself "your affectionate and respectful friend." That must have been a relief to both of them.

The election of 1816 was the least contested since George Washington left office. Monroe supporters appealed to William Crawford to wait his turn in deference to "the last of the Revolutionary generation to offer for the presidency," and the Georgian never actively pursued the nomination, though his name was put forward in the congressional caucus. Monroe won that vote and chose New York's Tompkins as his running mate. That was the only real election. The

Federalists were so downtrodden and demoralized after rebelling in Hartford and opposing a war that had ended with the country feeling confident and cohesive that they didn't stand a chance. They put up Rufus King as a sacrificial lamb, and he was predictably trounced by an Electoral College vote of 183 for Monroe to 34 for King. A new president had been elected and now it was time for Washington to say goodbye to James and Dolley Madison. So many people gave them farewell parties, the couple remained in Washington a full month after Monroe's inauguration to fit them all in. At a ball in Georgetown dedicated to *Mrs.* Madison, Dolley's portrait dominated the scene, accompanied by a song of praise:

> *The power divine,* when Time begun
> *Bade charming WOMAN and the SUN*
> *Illumine the Terrestrial Ball*
> *A charming WOMAN* still *we find,*
> *Like the bright SUN, cheers all Mankind*
> *And like IT, is admired by all!*

The Federalist newspaper, the *Portfolio,* recalled the words of Jefferson's first inaugural address: "We are all federalists, we are all republicans." He had said it, but "Mrs. Madison reduced this liberal sentiment to a practice. . . . Like a summer's sun she rose in our political horizon, gloriously, and she sunk, benignly." The wife of the Swedish ambassador told Mrs. Madison she was "loved by all your country men and country women" with "friends among both parties."

With the encomiums coming in from all quarters, perhaps the most meaningful to Dolley was a letter from her old friend Eliza Collins Lee, written the day of Monroe's inauguration, reminding her, "on this day eight years ago I wrote . . . to congratulate you on the joyful event that placed you in the highest station our country can bestow. I then enjoyed the proudest feelings—that my friend—the friend of my youth, who never had forsaken me, should be thus distinguished and so peculiarly fitted to fill it. How much greater cause have I to congratulate you, at this period for having so filled it as to render yourself more enviable this day, than your successor." Eliza knew that Dolley must have some concerns about the days ahead, as she comforted her: "Talents such as yours were never intended to remain inactive—on retiring from public life, you will form a more fortunate arrangement of your time, be able to display them in the more noble and interesting walks of life. I remember at this moment in my last conversation with my venerable Uncle Parrish, your father's friend, he said of you 'She will hold out to the end, she was a dutiful daughter and never turned her back on an old friend, and was charitable to the poor.' Thus the blessing of this good old man went with you, better even, we are taught to believe, than the sounding trumpet of fame!" And so Dolley Madison, who had done so much to build the capital city and then rebuild it, retired to Montpelier. But she returned as a widow twenty years later and provided again such an overarching presence that Daniel Webster declared her "the only permanent power in Washington—all others are transient."

CHAPTER SIX

THE PRESIDENCY OF JAMES MONROE AND SOME CHARACTERS TO CONTEMPLATE

1817–1825

ELIZABETH KORTRIGHT MONROE
The Granger Collection, New York

WITH THE INDEPENDENCE of the United States of America secure and the country's place in the world recognized, the inauguration of James Monroe signaled a time of settling down, of coming together to consolidate the considerable achievements of the young nation. The ceremony for the man dubbed "the last of the cocked hats" because of his revolutionary-era garb and his war-time service, seemed more of an ending than a beginning, but it did break precedent. It was the first outdoor oath-taking ritual for the chief executive. Rather than repeat the fights of the last inaugural over who would sit where, with the ladies pushing the senators out of their seats, the ceremonies were moved outside. Since they then took place in March, not January, the prospect of freezing was not quite so daunting as it is today and Monroe was in luck. The new president "was fortunate in being able to deliver his inaugural address from the unfinished portico of the Capitol amid balmy breezes," historian Anne Wharton tells us. Then the fifth president with his wife and daughters received visitors at home before attending the inaugural ball. One journal described the occasion as "simple, but grand, animating and impressive." None of the excitement or drama that surrounded Dolley Madison's debut as First Lady attached itself to Elizabeth Monroe's ascension. And none of the crisis atmosphere of the Madison presidency plagued his successor.

Balmy breezes accompanied the first few years of Monroe's term as well, christened the "era of good feeling" by the Boston newspaper *Columbian Sentinel* when the president followed George Washington's example and made a tour of the northern and eastern states. No battles with Britain or France threatened the peace and, "The animosities between Federalists and Democrats are almost gone," Rosalie Calvert acknowledged to her brother. To her sister she added, "We learned our strength during the recent war which, although it was disastrous, made us realize the immense resources the United States possesses." Though Andrew Jackson was waging war on the Seminoles, other Indian tribes were handing over their land to the federal government with scarcely a protest. (One notable voice was raised against the Cherokees ceding any more land. It came from a legendary "beloved woman" Nancy Ward, or Nanye'hi, whose attempt to convince the tribal Council failed.) The question of slavery was simmering but not yet boiling. The one note of discord in this happy harmony was sounded by the women of Washington. As Ellen Randolph had told her grandfather, Elizabeth Monroe's refusal to pay calls insulted and incensed her fellow females. "Although they have lived 7 years in W[ashington] both Mr. and Mrs. Monroe are perfect strangers not only to me but all the citizens," Margaret Smith fumed to her sister, "Few persons are admitted to the great house and not a single lady has as yet seen Mrs. Monroe, Mrs. Cutts excepted, and a committee from the Orphan Asylum." Elizabeth Monroe apparently understood that she had certain obligations to the Orphan Asylum but Dolley Madison's sister Anna Cutts was the only one of Margaret's friends invited to the inner sanctum. It was the cause of crisis Cabinet meetings, summons to the secretary of state, and grousing gossip gaggles.

The affable, accommodating, and heroic Dolley Madison had been replaced by a woman who had grown up in a decidedly different environment from the Quaker girl whose mother ran a boarding house in Philadelphia and whose winning southern ways welcomed all. The new First Lady's experiences during her more than thirty-year marriage to James Monroe made for a marked, much more formal, shift in the Washington social scene. The couple met when the twenty-seven-year-old Monroe was a member of the Continental Congress in New York and the seventeen-year-old Elizabeth Kortright, the daughter of a once wealthy merchant, was dazzling all his colleagues. After an evening at the theater, a friend wrote to Monroe that the Kortright sisters "made so brilliant and lovely an appearance as to depopulate all the other boxes of all the genteel male people therein." She was a catch and Congressman Monroe preened proudly over wooing and winning the young beauty. He couldn't wait for his friend James Madison to meet his intended: "If you will visit this place shortly I will present you to a young lady who will be adopted a citizen of Virginia in the course of this week."

After the wedding in early 1786 Monroe "decamped for Long Island with the little smiling Venus in his Arms," gossiped a friend, "we have not yet seen him in town." The marriage meant Monroe would abandon his plan of visiting Thomas Jefferson in Paris: "Having formed an attachment to this young lady (a Miss Kortright, the daughter of a gentleman of respectable character and connections in this state though injured in his fortunes by the late war) I have found that I must relinquish all other objects not connected to her." As it turned out, James Monroe would have plenty of opportunities to see

Paris with his "young lady." But soon after their marriage the couple made their home in the far more prosaic Fredericksburg, Virginia. By the end of the year, the New York maiden had married, settled in the Virginia countryside, and become a mother. Again, James Monroe happily passed on the news to Thomas Jefferson: "Mrs. Monroe hath added a daughter to our society who though noisy, contributes greatly to its amusement."

Elizabeth and baby Eliza often accompanied lawyer Monroe as he argued cases in various northern Virginia towns. Once, when traveling alone, James wrote the only letter between the Monroes that has survived. Family tradition claims that the bereft widower burned all their correspondence after Elizabeth died. Whether or not that's true—and it probably is given how often the surviving member of a couple destroyed anything intimate—all of their letters, with the exception of this one, are gone. After expressing "the utmost anxiety to know that yourself & our little Eliza are well," Monroe moved on to practical matters. The furniture they had ordered in New York had not been shipped and "Mr. Madison writes me some time will yet elapse before our furniture will reach Fredericksburg." James Madison was helping James Monroe with his furniture in 1787, but by 1788 the two men were running against each other for Congress. Their disagreement was philosophical—Monroe objected to the new Constitution "fathered" by Madison—not personal, but campaigns have a way of turning personal. Remarkably, through the years, the men were able to renew their friendship after each breach.

In the next election, Monroe went to the Senate, bringing his wife and baby with him to Philadelphia, where Elizabeth could occasionally see her New York family. On recess trips back to Virginia, Monroe practiced law, sometimes dropping his family off at Monticello while he was on the road. "Mr. Monroe is gone to Williamsburg to stay two or three weeks, and has left his lady here. She is a charming woman," not quite thirteen year old Polly Jefferson wrote to her father the secretary of state in the summer of 1791. From Philadelphia the following year, Jefferson guessed to his daughter Martha that

Mrs. Monroe would leave town in about a month, "she will probably do it with more pleasure than heretofore; as I think she begins to tire of the town and feel a relish for scenes of more tranquility." Clearly, Mrs. Monroe had not been so pleased to head back to sleepy Fredericksburg, Virginia, in the past. Soon this city girl would leave the Old Dominion behind as she and seven-year-old Eliza went off to the Old World with her husband, the new Minister to France.

It was a touchy time for the two countries because Americans were taking sides in the French Revolution and its subsequent reign of terror. Some, mainly the Republicans, continued to support the cause of the Revolution and republicanism; others, mainly Federalists, repudiated the violence and the government responsible for it. The more extreme Federalists, like Alexander Hamilton, hoped for the return of the French monarchy. As American ambassador in Paris, Federalist Gouverneur Morris took such a strong position against the revolutionary regime that France asked the United States to recall him. President Washington decided that a pro-French Republican, but a fellow Virginian whom he knew well, James Monroe, should succeed Morris. When the family arrived in Paris in the summer of 1794, Robespierre had just been guillotined; the government was uncertain whether to accept this new American envoy, and a party hosted by the Monroes at their new Paris home drew not one guest. Still, the ambassador arranged to free all American prisoners from French jails, and Mrs. Monroe bravely took action that resulted in the release of the most famous prisoner of them all.

Monroe had managed, he related in his autobiography, to get his hands on one of the few carriages in the beleaguered city, and had it fixed up regally, with servants in full livery: "In this carriage Mrs. Monroe drove directly to the prison." The rare sight of an elegant equipage drew a crowd: "Inquiry was made, whose carriage was it? The answer given was, that of the American Minister. Who is in it? His wife. What brought her here? To see Madame Lafayette." The wife of the great celebrity of the American Revolution, the Marquise de Lafayette, was not only held prisoner, she was almost certainly under a death sentence. When her mother and grandmother were summoned from the same jail, as she was that day, they had been taken directly to the guillotine and beheaded. The Marquise assumed that her hour had come but "on hearing that the wife of the American Minister had called with the most friendly motives to see her, she became frantic, and in that state they met. . . . The report of the interview spread through Paris and had the happiest effect." The Monroes had gambled on public opinion, using it to create sympathy for the release of Lafayette's wife, and their gamble paid off. After the Marquise was freed, Monroe obtained passports for the family to leave France. The only boy, George Washington Lafayette, would go to America and live with Eliza and Alexander Hamilton. The two girls, Virginie and Anastasie, would go with their mother to join their father, a prisoner of Austria. Though an enemy to the radicals who had seized power in Paris, the popular democrat Lafayette was also considered dangerous by the monarchs of Europe who colluded to hold him captive. Adrienne de Lafayette insisted on sharing the foul prison cell, along with their daughters, living there for almost two years. Her letters from captivity so enraged the public in America and much of Europe that the Austrians eventually agreed to Lafayette's release. Given the tense times in Paris, that trip to the prison was a gutsy move for Elizabeth Monroe and she was soon besieged by the families of other French inmates asking for help.

The American envoy's protestations of friendship and the couple's appreciation of all things French eventually won them the respect and recognition of the government. The Monroes moved into an elegant home, enrolled Eliza in a fancy school where she made a lifelong friendship with Hortense the daughter of Josephine, Napoleon's wife, and enjoyed the pleasures of Paris where Elizabeth was admired as "la belle Americaine." But Monroe was too friendly with the ruling regime for the tastes of the American government, and President Washington soon replaced him with Charles Cotesworth Pinckney. The family stayed in Europe for a few months waiting for better seagoing weather, befriended the Pinckneys and then sailed home. Back in Virginia, James Monroe's old friend and sparring partner, James Madison, introduced them to his wife, Dolley, who sent preserves and pickles to help tide them over until the next season's crops came in. One Virginia friend judged that post-Paris, Elizabeth Monroe was the "very model of a perfect matron" even if she still carried a "little too much of New York."

At the end of 1799 Monroe was elected governor of Virginia, the same year that Elizabeth finally carried another pregnancy to term. James Spence Monroe was born in May, so-named, according to his father, because "his mother is an old fashioned woman & chose . . . to follow the old fashioned track of calling him after his father." When the baby died sixteen months later, both parents were bereft. "I cannot give you an idea of the effect this event has produced on my family," Monroe lamented to Madison the day after the baby's death, "Many things have occurred my friend, in these late years that abated my sensibility to the affairs of this world, but this has roused me beyond what I thought it was possible I could be." The little boy's mother took many months to recover.

Among the affairs of this world Monroe was dealing with was a slave uprising in Richmond planned by a blacksmith named Gabriel with the help of his brothers and his wife, Nanny. The plot to kill all whites except Methodists, Quakers, and Frenchmen was revealed by two slaves who refused to murder their masters. As Monroe organized the militia to quell the attack of hundreds, perhaps thousands, of slaves armed with weapons forged from farm tools, a driving rainstorm did his job for him, thwarting the slaves' march on Richmond. Whites demanded retribution, threatening the entire black population, while the governor kept vigil by his dying baby boy. Fending off the calls for black blood, Monroe was forced to confront his views about the institution of slavery. His conclusion that blacks should be repatriated to Africa resulted years later in the founding of Liberia, whose capital city still bears his name.

With the election of 1800, and the victory of his old friend Thomas Jefferson and the Republican Party, James Monroe was once again summoned into service for his country, assigned to return to France to aid Robert Livingston in what would become the Louisiana Purchase. On his way to New York, he stopped in Washington where he told New York Congressman Samuel Mitchill "that Mrs. Monroe would accompany him. He appears to have fine conjugal feelings and thought it too hard to cross the ocean without this amiable consort. Accordingly he takes her with him." A couple of days later, apparently after asking around about "one of our Manhattan girls," Mitchill had this report on Elizabeth Kortright Monroe for his wife: "She is commended exceedingly by those who know her, as a charming and amiable woman." And as James and Elizabeth and their now sixteen-year-old daughter Eliza pulled out of New York harbor on March 8, 1803, a new baby, not quite one-year-old Maria Hester Monroe, completed the family group. Though the Monroes were forced to sell their china and silver to the Madisons to pay for the passage, Elizabeth wasted no time re-filling her cupboards—Europe provided prime shopping opportunities not only for household items but also for expensive gowns and jewelry.

Eliza comfortably re-enrolled in school in St. Germaine, but her friend Hortense was no longer there. She had married Napoleon's brother and was soon crowned Queen of Holland. Unhappily for the family, the tour in Paris would be brief, since the Louisiana Purchase was accomplished almost immediately after James Monroe arrived on the scene. French mission accomplished, the Monroes were off to London where they had the bad luck to arrive just as President Jefferson was lobbing etiquette insults at British Ambassador Anthony Merry's wife in Washington. The British were rude to the American in return, and Monroe complained that they did not treat him with "the respect due to the office I held, to the government and country I represented." It was a common complaint of Americans, who thought the United States was not being taken seriously enough abroad. In retaliation for the treatment of Elizabeth Merry, no one would accept the Monroes' dinner invitations. They must have pined for Paris where a friend wrote them, "I often hear Mrs. Monroe's name mentioned with respect and admiration by the ladies of Paris." It was all in all unpleasant in London. "The moisture of the climate and smoke have given us all colds," James griped, and his wife was "attended with a stricture of the breast, which is an additional reason for us to get home as soon as possible." Not only was the family miserable, Monroe's attempts at reaching an agreement to stop British impressment were also unsuccessful, so much so that Jefferson refused even to submit to the Senate the treaty Monroe negotiated. When the family returned to America in 1807, James Monroe was not happy with his president or his party.

Opponents of Thomas Jefferson, John Randolph chief among them, mounted a presidential campaign for James Monroe as an alternative to James Madison in 1808. Competing conventions in Richmond each nominated one of the Virginians, but when the Congressional Caucus threw its support to Madison, Monroe's candidacy fizzled, adding yet another disappointment. But one bright spot shone on the family—Eliza married Virginia lawyer and judge George Hay in October, a man three years older than her mother. And the Jefferson family was working hard at healing any rift. Martha Randolph wrote her father that she was on the lookout for the Monroes arrival in the county: "Eliza is to be married as soon as they come up." The next year Hortensia Hay was born, making Elizabeth a grandmother at 41 and Maria Hester an aunt at age seven. The little girl seemed to take after her stylish mother, as "an account of little Maria Monroe" by a family friend illustrates. "She was dressed in a short frock, that reached half way between her knees and ankles—under which she displayed a pair of loose pantaloons, wide enough for the foot to pass through with ease, frilled round with the same stuff as her frock and pantaloons." This was written by a man! He continued, "The little monkey did not fail to evince the advantages of her dress. She had a small spaniel dog with whom she was constantly engaged in a trial of skill—and the general opinion seemed to be that she turned and twisted about more than the spaniel." A cute little girl, a new baby granddaughter, and before long Monroe was able make the assessment to a friend that "Neither of us have escaped our afflictions of a public nature—but both have been happy in domestic life." But another stint as governor of Virginia didn't seem to satisfy James Monroe's ambitions, and he readily quit the job to take the post of secretary of state to his old friend and sometime foe James Madison.

Leaving his home, the Highlands, under the management of his daughter Eliza, Monroe moved to Washington with Elizabeth and Maria Hester into the job of secretary of state, which had become the stepping-stone to the presidency, and it worked. After he was elected president in December of 1816, but before he took office, James Monroe's wife's standoffishness made her attention seem more valuable than Dolley Madison's welcome to all. "With Mrs. Monroe I am really in love," Margaret Smith announced in late 1816, "She is charming and very beautiful. She did me *the honor* of asking to be introduced to me and saying 'she regretted very much she was out when I called,' etc. and though we do not believe all these kind of things it is gratifying to the vanity to hear them. It would not however have flattered me half so much from Mrs. Madison as from her." Once she was First Lady, however, in an effort to restore some pre–Dolley Madison formality and because she was often ill, Elizabeth Monroe stopped calling and stopped receiving calls. The town was up in arms.

"Entertaining has not yet begun in Washington," Rosalie Calvert said with some astonishment at the beginning of the social season, "Up to now Mrs. Monroe has been confined to her room. Some say it is because her health does not permit her to receive company; others say it is because her house is still not furnished." Not only were the women accustomed to Dolley Madison's whirl of sociability, they were eager to see the newly reoccupied executive mansion, now painted white to cover the damage done by the British. Finally, at the 1817 New Year's drawing room, the doors to the mansion were thrown open. Freshman Congressman Louis McLane described the event to his wife, Kitty, at home in Delaware: "The splendor of this scene could not easily be surpassed, and it fully gratified the curiosity of all. . . . The large hall into which was the entrance was the space for sauntering, and lounging. . . . Immediately back of the hall were four rooms magnificently furnished. . . . The taste and splendor of Europe have contributed to decorate and enrich these rooms, and have given them a splendor which is really astonishing." Elizabeth Monroe had turned the president's house into a regal establishment to suit her queenly style. Though one guest did note "the frugality of Congress has prevented them from finishing the principle reception-room of the building." For the occasion, the First Lady dressed "in white and gold made in the highest style of fashion," Louisa Adams reported, "and moved not like a Queen (for that is an unpardonable word in this country) but like a goddess."

Rosalie Calvert joined the New Year's mob scene because she was introducing her daughter Caroline to society. "There was such a crowd in the room where Mrs. Monroe was that we could hardly move, either forward or backward. She received us very graciously." To give Caroline a head start among the debutantes, Rosalie asked her sister to send the very latest European fashions. For herself she requested "a complete dress outfit topped off with a matching bonnet or turban for paying my first visit to *our court,* as I am on very good terms with Mrs. Monroe." She was one of the few. Though the First Lady made clear she would not call on the wives of new arrivals—after all, she had refused to do so as the wife of the secretary of state—she decided to appease the women of Washington by asking Louisa Adams to play the part of Dolley Madison, to greet every newcomer to town. Soon after the New Year's party, Elizabeth Monroe summoned Louisa to her chambers. "It was to inform her that the ladies had taken offence at her not paying them the first visit," John Quincy Adams faithfully recounted the meeting in his diary, "All ladies arriving here as strangers it seems expect to be visited by the wives of the heads of departments, and even by the president's wife—Mrs. Madison subjected herself to this torture, which she felt very severely but from which having begun the practice, she never found an opportunity of receding from it. Mrs. Monroe neither pays nor returns any visits—My wife returns all visits but adopts the principle of not visiting first every stranger who arrives, and this is what the ladies have taken in dudgeon."

Louisa Adams told Elizabeth Monroe that she would not change her calling customs, regardless of the "dudgeon." The situation was completely unacceptable to "the ladies" though they could still enjoy the regular entertainments of the French and British ambassadors, who "each give an assembly on a regular day once a week, and you are invited to come there for the season," Rosalie Calvert explained to her sister, who was curious about the coming-out customs in the American capital, "there is dancing and these parties are very pleasant. In addition, there is a public ball each fortnight." (Those embassy soirees shocked Congressman McLane. Most women "put on some apology for a covering of the bosom" but two "defied all such useless drapery." Mrs. McLane decided to accompany her husband to Washington for the next Congress.) And, try as she might to eliminate them, the First Lady found that she had to continue the large receptions at the executive mansion. "One always finds all the Ambassadors there with their wives, secretaries, etc., consuls, all the foreigners who are in Washington, a large number of members of Congress and sometimes the residents of Washington and Georgetown with their families," Rosalie described the scene. "During Mrs. Madison's reign everybody went, even the shoemakers and their wives, but things are better managed now and one meets the best of society there."

Rosalie Calvert was in a decided minority in her views. "Do you know? or do not know my beloved Dolley that your absence from this City is more and more lamented," Eliza Lee asked the former First Lady, "the urbanity, benevolence, and cheerfulness that was defused through the circles over which you presided will be long sought for in vain." For her part, Dolley, out of the action in the Virginia countryside, missed her friends in Washington, especially her sister Anna Cutts, "I am . . . [a] poor dull creature, & at such a distance that I must submit & live along as well as I can detached from others—but while I do live I shall be your affectionate & anxious sister—& friend in all cares." She was taking care of her aging mother-in-law, working on her husband's papers, preparing them for publication, and of course entertaining whatever travelers stopped by Montpelier. To add some variety to the table she asked the French ambassador's wife for some dishes, and received the reply: "I will send you the recipes that you desired for the French salad and the fish, as soon as I can get them from our old cook."

While Dolley Madison continued to supply "harvest home" meals, the friendly tone she set at the executive mansion had vanished: "It is said that the dinner parties of Mrs. Monroe will be very select," Sarah Seaton huffed, "Mrs. Hay, daughter of Mrs. Monroe, returns the visits paid to her mother, making assurances in the most pointedly polite manner, that Mrs. Monroe will be happy to see her friends morning or evening, but that her health is totally inadequate to visiting at present." Nobody could stand Mrs. Hay. She had been in school with Europe's elites and it had gone to her head. When the president asked her to do him a favor and accept an invitation to a ball given by the French ambassador, she first set down rules for the secretary of state to convey to the envoy: "Her object was to desire me to inform Mr. Hyde de Neuville, that she would, at the request of her father, though she said it was much against her own inclination, go to the ball next Monday; but it was upon conditions. . . . that it should leave her position with respect to the ladies of the foreign ministers precisely where it was. That she would afterwards neither visit them, nor receive visits from them, nor accept of any invitations to their parties. . . . That Mr. de Neuville might write to his own government, whatever he pleased upon the subject but that if an account of the ball was to be published in the newspapers here, her name should not be mentioned as having been present." Charming. Even Louisa Adams, who defended the Monroes' social stand, had to admit that Eliza Hay could be tough to take. "This woman is made up of so many great and little qualities, is so full of agreeables and disagreeables, so accomplished and so ill bred, has so much sense and so little judgment, she is so proud, and so mean . . . no reputation is safe in her hands, and I *never* since the first moment of my acquaintance with her have heard her speak well of any human being." Louisa recounted the whole flap about "first visits" to her mother-in-law, who was of the opinion that a "council of ladies" should decide the issue. But Abigail Adams viewed the customs of the first family with amazement, "in my day, if so much style, pomp and etiquette had been assumed, the cry of monarchy, monarchy would have resounded from Georgia to Maine."

THOUGH ABIGAIL ADAMS could still be counted on for tart observation, she was greatly enjoying the return of her son's family from Europe. When the boys alighted from the stagecoach in Quincy in the summer of 1817, "The first who sprang out was John, who with his former ardor was round my neck in a moment. George followed half crazy calling out 'O Grandmother—o grandmother,'" she delightedly told a friend. The not quite seventy-three-year-old Abigail had also developed a newfound respect for her daughter-in-law after Louisa's travails in Europe, particularly her harrowing trip from Russia to France. "I have really acquired the reputation of a heroine at a very cheap rate," Louisa joked, but she was grateful for Abigail's apology when she "told me she was worried she had not better understood my character." The two women became companionable for the first time, sitting together with the dog, Satan, in Abigail's bedroom. And when she moved to Washington, leaving her boys in school in Boston, once again under their grandmother's eye, Louisa entertained her mother-in-law with gossipy letters. A month's summer vacation in Quincy in 1818 provided another pleasant interlude for the three generations. But that fall, soon after Louisa and John Quincy returned to Washington, they received word that Abigail was dangerously ill with typhoid fever.

With her usual collection of friends and relatives surrounding her and alert to the end, Abigail Adams died on October 28. Secretary of State Adams noted it four days later when the news reached him: "My mother was an angel upon earth," he wrote dismally in his diary. "She has been to me more than a mother. She has been a Spirit from above watching over me for good and contributing by my mere consciousness of her existence to the comfort of my life. That consciousness is gone and without her that world feels to me like a solitude. Oh! What must it be to my father, and how will he support life without her who has been to him its charm?" John Adams had anticipated the "appalling event," as his son Thomas termed it, in a letter to Thomas Jefferson: "The dear partner of my life for fifty four years as a wife and for many years more as a lover, now lies in extremis." So Jefferson was prepared when he read "the public papers" announcing the death of the nation's second First Lady. "I know well, and feel what you have lost, what you have suffered, are suffering, and have yet to endure. . . . it is of some comfort to us both that the term is not very distant at which we are to deposit . . . our sorrows and suffering bodies and to ascend in essence to an ecstatic meeting with the friends we have loved and lost and whom we shall still love and never lose again. God bless you and support you under your heavy affliction." Those words were a great comfort to eighty-three-year-old John Adams who had managed to walk in his wife's funeral procession: "I believe in God and in his wisdom and benevolence, and I cannot conceive that such a Being could make such a species as the human merely to live and die on this Earth." And so these men of the Enlightenment, one of them once virulently attacked as an atheist, comforted each other on the loss of Abigail Adams.

To amuse old John Adams, Louisa Adams kept a journal of her comings and goings in Washington for him to read aloud back in Quincy. "The Supreme Court is now quite the fashion and is thronged with ladies every day . . . the gentlemen knowing the fondness our sex have for talking mean to do all in their power to gratify them." Both the Congress and the court met in the Capitol, and one day in the courtroom after listening to a lawyer whose "oratory is of the modern theatrical school and consists chiefly of whispered breathings and burst of vehemence," the ladies moved on to the House "where we were entertained with a very different style of oratory which I denominate the hum drum as it produced on my ear something like the effect of the cotton spinning wheel which is not dull enough to set you to sleep but sufficiently monotonous to weary your spirits."

Congress, the Court, and calling by day, balls, dinners, and drawing rooms at night made up the schedule during a Congressional session. Elizabeth Monroe presided over it all in her distant and queenly fashion. "Her costume consisted of a white gown of India mull, embroidered with gold, her hair was braided with pearls and adorned with a lovely diadem of gold set with pearls," Swedish Baron Axel Klinkowstrom sized up Elizabeth Monroe in 1819. "She seemed to be between thirty and forty years old, medium sized, her face set off to advantage by her beautiful hair." The fifty-year-old Mrs. Monroe would have loved to read that! These social events were the places to exchange information, as well as win over allies. At dinner with the French minister, Louisa Adams learned that "the Spanish Treaty was completed. At which I was much rejoiced knowing how Mr. A. had labored to get anything like so an amicable arrangement between the two countries." Louisa had heard before her husband did that the pact he had negotiated with Spain was a done deal—it turned over Florida to the United States. A few days later, at a Washington's Birthday Ball, she was told that her husband had negotiated the "best treaty this country had ever made and it would pass the Senate with éclat." In fact it did—the Adams-Onis Treaty was ratified on February 25, 1819.

"The social season is coming to an end along with the session of Congress," Rosalie Calvert reported to her father in the middle of March. The season "was quite lively this winter and Washington quite splendid. Caroline has gone to thirteen dancing parties, not to mention the dinners, the tea parties, and the assemblies at the President's every fortnight. . . . There was something every day during December, January and February, and sometimes two assemblies on the same evening." And her daughter Caroline was a hit: "she has been much sought after this winter. Her gowns have been quite the most beautiful in Washington, except for those of Mrs. Bagot and Mrs. Monroe's daughter." She also enjoyed concerts and "a good company of actors" currently performing. "There is great deal of diversity in Washington society," Rosalie observed; and she was pleased to tell her father that she and her husband were right at the top of the heap: "Yesterday we dined at the President's House. I have never seen anything as splendid as the table—a superb gilt plateau in the center with gilt baskets filled with artificial flowers. All of the serving dishes were solid silver the dessertspoons and forks and knives were silver-gilt. The plates were fine French porcelain." And to her sister Rosalie added, "Mrs. Monroe gave me the most flattering reception; she does the honors with much grace and dignity. She is a charming woman, much superior to the last President's wife." Mrs. Calvert was about the only person in Washington who didn't miss Dolley Madison.

Rosalie Stier Calvert had been in America for twenty-five years. She was sixteen years old when she arrived; she was now a matron of forty-one. She had borne nine children, managed her family's money, and supervised a large plantation, but her letters still reveal a certain defensiveness about her adopted land. She was eager to tell her sophisticated European family about the amusements that had come to the capital—in addition to the theatre, "there is also a circus where the performance is extremely good and with beautiful horses. [This season] there were about a dozen concerts, recitations, etc . . . we have every kind of social activity here except gambling parties, and I am very pleased about that. Sometimes at balls there are four or five gaming tables for the men, but none of the women play." She was also pleased that the blatant marital infidelity her brother-in-law must have described in Europe was not the norm in America: "I must admit that we don't have husbands here who are as complacent as those you describe. That style will not catch on here, I think. I expect you will laugh at us when I tell you that it is really a pleasure to see how attentive husbands are to their wives in Washington society and with what courtesy and affection they treat them in public. Perhaps in some instances this is only for appearances and not at all sincere, but it is nevertheless agreeable to see. For a married woman to have a 'gallant' –that is not done and would not be tolerated. She would be banished from society." That cultural difference separating the New World from the Old seems to have been there from the beginning.

Fortunately for Rosalie, the social season ended just in time to plant her kitchen garden and get back to the work of the plantation. In those years Congress generally adjourned in March, and the new Congress, the one elected the year before, convened in December. When the Sixteenth Congress met in 1819 one major issue confronted the lawmakers: "Hear much of the Missouri question," Louisa Adams wrote to Founding Father John Adams. "Should like to know your opinion of the right of Congress to stop the progress of slavery as this is a strongly disputed point. We shall hear much of this this winter." The nation-threatening question of slavery had come to Congress in a way that could not be avoided. As new states joined the union, some came in as slave states, others as free. Since Monroe's election Indiana and Illinois had entered as free states, Mississippi as a slave state and Alabama was about to join as a slave state as well. That made the numbers equal—eleven free states, eleven slave states. But the Missouri Territory was petitioning for statehood. Earlier that year the House of Representatives, but not the Senate, had passed amendments to the Missouri bill requiring freedom for all slaves born there at the age of twenty-five and forbidding the importation of slaves as requirements for statehood. Now, as Louisa Adams had said, the Missouri question was once again before the Congress.

THOUGH THE IMPORTATION OF SLAVES had been outlawed in 1808, smuggling was rampant. In March 1819 Congress voted to pay rewards to informants reporting smugglers and to return smuggled slaves to Africa. It was not much, but it was a beginning. And it came at a time when the country was once again clamoring for greater liberties. The economic panic of 1819 led non-property-holding men to demand the vote so they could elect politicians who would pay attention to them. And here and there a woman's voice calling for more political power could be heard as well. Hannah Mather Crocker published her *Observations on the Real Rights of Women* in 1818 following in a long line of Massachusetts "female scribblers." The oldest of that group, Hannah Adams, was still publishing as well, having come out with her *Dictionary of All Religions and Religious Denominations* in 1817.

In her time Hannah Adams was the most celebrated woman writer in the country. Though she was of a distinguished family, her father failed in business and Hannah was forced to earn a living. She became the first American author to support herself by her writing. In order to protect her income she asked her friend, Congressman Fisher Ames, to introduce the first copyright bill into the Congress in 1790. She took the highly unusual step of publishing under her own name in the eighteenth century, when she produced several histories, including religious histories. She started in 1784 with *An Alphabetical Compendium of the Various Sects Which have Appeared from the Beginning of the Christian Era to the Present Day,* quite an undertaking. Then it was *A View of Religions* in 1791 and *A Summary History of New England* in 1799. An attempt to sell an abridged version of her New England history as a school text resulted in a legal dispute with a competitive author, which she eventually won. By the time Louisa Adams met her husband's distant cousin in 1806, Miss Adams "was one of the most remarkable women of the age. The world was to her a vacuum." The cantankerous author, "peculiar in her appearance, her manners, her conversation," kept churning out her volumes. Her *History of the Jews* came out in 1812, followed by her *Dictionary.* She had set the stage for other women writers, and Hannah Mather Crocker was happy to step onto it.

Hannah Crocker first produced *A Series of Letters on Free Masonry,* in 1815 and then her *Observations on the Real Rights of Women.* One of her assertions in that tome: "Women have an equal right, with the other sex, to form societies for promoting religious, charitable and benevolent purposes." Of course women had been doing that for quite some time. But they were branching out. In 1819 Rebecca Gratz had been long prominent in Philadelphia society and active in relief agencies when she established the Female Hebrew Benevolent Society. "The ladies of the Hebrew Congregation of Philadelphia, sensible to the calls which have occasionally been made on their small society and desirous of rendering themselves useful to their indigent sisters of the house of Israel, agree to establish a charitable society," read the preamble to the constitution written by the organization's secretary, Rebecca Gratz, who has been described as "the foremost American Jewish woman of the nineteenth century." In addition to her brilliance, beauty, and benevolent works—she went on to found the Jewish Foster Home and Orphan Asylum and the Hebrew Sunday School Society of Philadelphia—she stirred romantic souls as the supposed model for Rebecca of York in Sir Walter Scott's *Ivanhoe*.

Rebecca's father Michael Gratz, and her mother Miriam's father Joseph Simon, had each emigrated from Germany before the American Revolution. A supporter of the Patriot cause, Gratz and his brother Barnard first grew wealthy as importers and then, with the pre-Revolutionary boycotts of British goods, shifted their sights to internal manufactures and land speculation. Along with Gratz's father-in-law they became suppliers to settlers moving west, and went into the fur trade as they pushed to the frontier. Simon also manufactured rifles for the Continental army. Called "the merchant prince of Philadelphia," Michael Gratz and his family, though German, became stalwarts in the Sephardic Mikveh Israel synagogue, the only Jewish place of worship in Philadelphia. Jews from Spain, Portugal, and Italy had been the first of the religion to come to America, and by the end of the eighteenth century they had established congregations along the Atlantic seaboard in Newport, Rhode Island, New York, Philadelphia, Richmond, Charleston, and Savannah. Rebecca, born in 1781, the seventh of twelve Gratz children, grew up with a strong sense of Jewish identity even as the family mixed and mingled with all the leading Philadelphia families.

Along with her sister Richea and mother Miriam, in 1801 Rebecca Gratz joined other well-off women to form "The Female Association for the Relief of Women and Children in Reduced Circumstances." The twenty-year-old served as first secretary, a job that might have been expected to go to one of the older, married women. The treasurer, on the other hand, "must be chosen from among the UNMARRIED LADIES," in order to protect the association from a treasurer's husband trying to get his hands on its assets. While working with the women helping their less fortunate sisters—they started a soup kitchen in 1803—Rebecca also socialized with a group of young men who produced the *Port Folio,* a weekly literary magazine representing Federalist political views. And the Gratz household evolved into a social and intellectual salon for many of the writers and artists of the day, including Washington Irving and Thomas Sully. It was Rebecca's friendships with these talented young men that gave rise to the *Ivanhoe* story.

One of the men she kept company with at the time was Samuel Erving, one of the *Port Folio* writers. According to the legend, Rebecca and Samuel were madly in love but she rebuffed his advances because he was Christian, and she would not marry outside her faith. But, goes the tale, Rebecca remained true to Samuel throughout her long and unmarried life (other versions have her friend Charles Fenno or politician Henry Clay as the rejected Christian lover). When Erving died, his granddaughter told a Gratz biographer, Rebecca went to his house "and remained an hour. When she came out, she left three white roses on his breast and her miniature on his heart." Washington Irving is credited with telling this story to Walter Scott, who then incorporated into *Ivanhoe* a Rebecca refusing to marry her Christian love. Scott is then supposed to have sent the novel to Irving with the query: "How do you like your Rebecca? Does the Rebecca I have pictured compare well with the pattern given?" Though there's no written evidence of the Scott question, the story spread quickly that the popular novel's heroine was right there in Philadelphia, and Rebecca Gratz did nothing to discourage it.

Soon after the book came out she asked her sister-in-law, "have you received Ivanhoe? When you read it tell me what you think of my namesake Rebecca." When Maria Gratz apparently answered that she admired the character, Rebecca continued the conversation: "Ivanhoe's . . . prejudice was a characteristic of the age he lived in—he fought for Rebecca, though he despised her race—the veil that is drawn over his feelings was necessary to the fable, and the beautiful sensibility of hers, so regulated, yet so intense might show the triumph of faith over human affection. I have dwelt on this character as we sometimes do on an exquisite painting until the canvas seems to breathe and we believe it is life." While she was alive Rebecca Gratz achieved some notoriety as a result of the *Ivanhoe* story and countless romantic renderings have been repeated in articles, books, and plays over the years, including some by members of her own family.

But it doesn't take a tale of unconsummated love to illustrate Rebecca's faithfulness to her religion—her works do that. She played an active part in every attempt to better the lives of poor people in Philadelphia: she helped establish the Fuel Society and Sewing Society; she worked to found the Philadelphia Orphan Asylum in 1815, again taking on the job of secretary, this time for forty years. When the orphanage burned in 1822, she undertook to replace it in heartbreaking circumstances—twenty three of the 106 children perished: "Poor little souls—how sad their fate!" she lamented to her sister-in-law, "One would scarcely think it possible such a total destruction could take place in so rapid a manner there was not an article of anything saved, except what was round the bodies of those who escaped . . . the whole state takes an interest in our misfortune." She would have to convince the public to trust the orphanage again, and send more donations: "A great deal of occupation has devolved on me in consequence of that unfortunate accident," she admitted to a friend, "with thanking great and small, distant and present donors, providing for the family, and legislating about the new Asylum, I have not been a very companionable character to any one above the rank of poor orphans and their concerns." And she was doing this while building up the Female Hebrew Benevolent Society and running a Jewish Sunday School in her home.

Rebecca had taken care of both her mother and father as they became sick and died. She also left Philadelphia periodically to tend to a sister in childbirth or a sister's children. Three of her sisters married, and they all married Jewish men. Two of her brothers married; and though Rebecca disapproved of the fact that their wives were not Jewish, she became quite close to one of her sisters-in-law. Her three remaining brothers and her sister Sarah, along with Rebecca, never married and all lived together. When Sarah, who shared the caretaking duties, died in 1817, Rebecca became more religious, studying Judaism herself and deciding that it was time her nieces and nephews learn the principles of the faith. At her request, her brothers hired a Hebrew teacher: "A young gentleman of good education in the sacred language lately arrived here who was desirous of opening a school in a congregation," Rebecca explained to a friend, "I proposed an afternoon class at our house and myself as scholar." That home school formed a framework for Jewish education in America; Rebecca Gratz used what she learned there twenty years later when she and the other women of the Female Hebrew Benevolent Society succeeded in establishing the first Hebrew Sunday School in America. And Jewish women in Savannah, New York, and Charleston used Rebecca's lesson plans to set up schools in their cities as well. Though serving as secretary of every other organization she helped found, Rebecca Gratz chose the presidency this time around, heading the school where Jewish women taught children of immigrants the tenets of their faith, marking the first time that Jewish women taught religion in public. After the Hebrew School's "founder and first directress" died, Mikveh Israel's rabbi declared in his eulogy, "The Sunday School founded by Rebecca Gratz became the mold for all others elsewhere."

But before Rebecca had the opportunity to open the Hebrew School for strangers' children, she first had to worry about those in her own family. Her sister Rachel died in 1823, leaving six living children who moved in with the Gratz family. "These precious children are the objects of my constant and tenderest concern, they have given me a deep interest in life—which the many & severe trials it has pleased heaven to visit upon me, might otherwise have made a weary pilgrimage," Rebecca sighed to her sister-in-law, "but I dare not complain—and feel that I ought not, whilst . . . so many important duties still remain to be done." One of those duties was taken on by her brothers, with her keen interest—the establishment of a school for the deaf in Philadelphia. Jacob Gratz spent three weeks in the state capital in Harrisburg, "his object to obtain a charter & endowment for the Deaf & Dumb Institution and has a prospect of succeeding," Rebecca enthused, "the bill now proposed gives $8000 per year for five years, by which time we hope the good resulting will induce future legislators to continue it." And so future legislators have—The Pennsylvania School for the Deaf is still chartered by the state. The commitment of the Gratz family to children in need did not end there. Rebecca would go on to found one more major social service agency—the Jewish Foster Home and Orphan Asylum.

Worried that even non-sectarian orphanages came with a heavy dose of Christian doctrine, the founder of the Hebrew School started militating for a separate space for Jewish orphans. In order to drum up donations for the project, she was encouraged by a fellow supporter to write a letter for the Jewish magazine, *The Occident,* firmly associating her revered name to the cause. She initially refused the request altogether, thinking it would be unseemly to attract such attention to herself. Still pressed, she determined to write the rallying cry but under the pseudonym *"a daughter in Israel."* Rebecca Gratz was seventy-four years old when the first Jewish orphanage in the country opened in 1855, accepting children from all over the United States and Canada. Once again she assumed the job of secretary, while still serving on the boards of the Female Hebrew Benevolent Society and the Philadelphia Orphan Asylum and still heading her most influential institution—the Hebrew Sunday School.

SOCIAL SERVICE CONCERNS were on the minds of the women of Washington along with their sisters around the country. When the founder of education for the deaf in America, Thomas Hopkins Gallaudet, came to town with his sister, they visited Margaret Bayard Smith and "calculated the expense of a soup-house we want to establish." And Louisa Adams was now a trustee of the Orphan Asylum, though she found the institution struggling against "two giant evils: poverty and ridicule. And the best and most laudable intentions of the society are cramped by the difficulties of the times." The financial panic of 1819 had increased the need and decreased the resources for all endeavors to help the poor. And it was hard for the ladies to devote much time to the orphaned children since they were engaged in a presidential campaign. Even though James Monroe had only held office for a couple of years and everyone expected him to run for a second term, his cabinet members, plus the speaker of the house, were already running hard to succeed him. The Federalist Party was essentially defunct on a national level, so the nomination for the Republican Party was crucial, though the process for choosing the nominee was unclear. The congressional caucus had served as the party convention, but critics who cried cronyism were trying to do the caucus in. One thing was certain, however: most of the men critical to the selection of the party standard-bearer were in Washington—so that's where the protracted campaign was waged. The candidates called on the congressmen, the candidates' wives called on the congressmen's wives. And the candidate couples vied with each other to provide the best entertainments.

As the Sixteenth Congress convened in December 1819, Louisa

Adams, the wife of presidential candidate John Quincy Adams, confided to her father-in-law, "It is the first Tuesday and opens my campaign having given a general invitation for every Tuesday during the winter. This plan makes some noise and creates jealousy . . . My evenings are called sociables. I wish they may prove so." Louisa had found a way to make a distinctive mark on the social scene. If the drawing rooms at the executive mansion were stiff and formal, the ones at her house would be fun. But it would take her a while to convince the still surly Washingtonians to accept her invitations. The women had decided to boycott the First Lady and the wife of the secretary of state because of their policies of not calling on newcomers. "The drawing room of the President was opened last night to a 'beggarly row of empty chairs.' Only five females attended three of whom were foreigners," Sarah Seaton gloated, "Mrs. Adams, the previous week, *invited* a large party, which we attended, at which there were not more than three ladies." The boycott could not be ignored. President Monroe summoned his cabinet to discuss the etiquette wars.

"We had this day at the president's the meeting to consider the important question of etiquette in visiting," the secretary of state sarcastically recorded on December 20. Senators were complaining that cabinet members weren't paying proper respect to them, and their wives echoed the criticism. Adams proposed "to separate entirely the official character from the practice of personal visiting, to pay no visits but for sake of friendship or acquaintances, and then without enquiring which is first, or which last and that their wives should practice the same." Secretary of the Treasury William Crawford and Secretary of War John Calhoun, both rivals for the presidency, said they agreed with him, "but their wives have made it a point to visit first those of all members of congress, and they would not alter that rule. My wife has followed the same rule for the ladies that I have for the men, and as this has brought us into disgrace with all the members of congress who have wives here, and with many others." Adams knew what these potential opponents were up to, they were using their wives to woo members of Congress, especially

Crawford with his "steady eye upon the caucus, insists upon adhering to this system, though it gives offence to all the stranger ladies who come here without happening to be the wives of congressmen—and are therefore not honored with Mrs. Crawford's visits."

Now it was Louisa Adams's turn to be in a dudgeon. "The etiquette question has become of so much importance as to be an object of state. This I know you will scarcely believe," she fussed to her father-in-law. "Being continually told that I cannot by the Constitution have any share in the public honors of my husband, it is certainly very flattering to me that people should insist upon becoming acquainted with, and *force* me even against my will to visit them . . . I am now more resolved than ever to defend *myself* and maintain my rights and privileges as a common citizen and private individual. And if any gentleman in the United States will prove to me that he insists upon his wife's visiting every stranger who may happen to visit the city where she dwells, I will give up my argument."

Fortunately for Louisa, her second "sociable" had gone very well. The Washington women ended their boycott so she could succeed as a hostess—but not without some concessions on her part: "This evening was expected to show whether I was to fall or to stand for the remainder of the winter. . . . There is something so insupportable in the idea of being put as it were upon a trial, that I felt my spirits sink and was much more ready to cry than to laugh when my company arrived . . . it is a very painful thing for me to be dragged into public notice and made an object of debate in every company, but these are the penalties I must pay for being the wife of a man of superior talents." These were high stakes and she knew it. "It is understood," she ruefully wrote, "that a man who is ambitious to become president of the United States, must make his wife visit the ladies of the Members of Congress first; otherwise he is totally inefficient to fill so high an office." There it was—right out on the table—if her husband wanted to be president, she had to play her part. This a full five years before the presidential election. And when Louisa saw that even Elizabeth Lowndes who had "visited me in the most friendly manner all the summer during the absence of her husband, but has now dropped my acquaintance on the score of etiquette," she realized she would have to succumb.

The next day the wife of the secretary of state went in search of congressional wives who had already called on her: "After traveling through this spacious city for two hours and stopping at nine or ten boarding houses was obliged to return home fretted and fatigued to death and almost unfitted by my anxiety to return the civilities shown me and the ill success of my efforts for which I shall never have the least credit." But the following day, Christmas Eve, she reported with relief: "Rode out again today in search of the ladies and proved successful. They were however not at home and I left cards and cards of invitation." Perfect—the credit without the visit. And soon the ladies were readily accepting her invitations to the Tuesday night "sociables."

"I can easily believe that the etiquette question has become an object of state," former President John Adams wisely acknowledged to his daughter-in-law. Given the intensity of the argument over etiquette, it's hard to believe there was an actual crisis facing the country—the question of slavery. "The interests are becoming very deep to the two great sections of the Union. May the next year prove propitious and seal more solidly the confederacy," Louisa Adams prayed on New Year's Eve 1819. She outlined the hope of a solution: "They have endeavored to unite Maine and Missouri in the question." Missouri was pushing for statehood and representatives of the northern states were trying to attach restrictions on slavery as a condition for admission to the union. "Much is expected on this subject and as passion and interest are the spurs we must anticipate a long and sharp debate."

It was a debate that captivated the city. "Our Vice-President was so gallant that he admitted ladies in the senate chamber," Margaret Smith gushed to her sister, "their numbers were so great for some days, that they not only filled these and all other seats that at last they got literally on the floor." His "gallant" move proved embarrassing for Vice President Daniel Tompkins: "The Senate Chamber in which they now admit ladies on the floor, has been occupied quite early everyday," Louisa Adams amusedly recounted, "However as the grave fathers of the Senate are supposed to be *old enough* to set a good example for the lower house, it has been thought by the public rather indecorous and the respectable ladies of Washington can now only get admittance through the medium of a Senator. As however ladies of a very public character did get in and take seats on either hand of the Vice President he has been subjected to some jest for having been thus supported." That must have given old John Adams a good laugh. (This came on top of "a lady of ill fame" showing up at the president's New Year's party.)

The House of Representatives had also allowed ladies on the floor where they flocked to hear the orator Henry Clay. When the floor space filled, the overflow women took seats in the galleries where, according to Margaret Bayard Smith, they received much attention, including a steady supply of snacks sent by the gentlemen below. "They tied them up in handkerchiefs, to which was fixed a note indicating for whom it was designed and then fastened to a long pole. This was taken on the floor of the house and handed up to the ladies who sat in the front of the gallery. I imagine there were near a 100 ladies there, so that these presentations were frequent and quite amusing, even in the midst of Mr. C's speech."

In the Senate, it was William Pinkney of Maryland whose speeches drew the crowds, including Louisa Adams: "The room was so thronged with ladies the Senators could scarcely keep their proper seats; and after having waited some time in longing expectation, he appeared in all the elegance of dress, with his hair nicely oiled and curled 'shedding odors round.'" To Louisa it was all show, no substance: "a tax was laid on poor common sense." But it was important that Louisa not give a hint of that opinion publicly, "Even my countenance was watched at the Senate during Mr. Pinkney's speech as I was afterwards informed by some of the gentlemen." Everyone was examining Louisa Adams's facial expressions to try to detect what her husband, the presidential candidate, might think.

It's amazing that anyone could even see Louisa Adams. "There have been not less than a hundred ladies on the floor of the Senate every day on which it was anticipated that Mr. Pinkney would speak," Sarah Seaton told of a rebellion among the members, "The Senators (some of them) frowned indignantly, and were heard to mutter audibly, 'Too many women here for business to be transacted properly!'" She herself had so many friends in the Senate that she expected to retain floor privileges even after the Vice President imposed restrictions. "The excitement during this protracted debate has been intense. The galleries are now crowded with colored persons almost to the exclusion of whites . . . They know it to be a question of servitude or freedom, and imagine that the result will immediately affect their condition." The Missouri question was about more than statehood, it was also about presidential politics: "This subject being made subservient to political views, and having in perspective the presidential election, is bandied from one to the other speaker alternately." The debate was fierce and angry, both inside and outside the Capitol, and the possibility of compromise often looked bleak. "We hear of nothing but Missouri and the ladies now decline that the very word gives them a headache," Louisa Adams sighed in mid-February, "I wish it may not end by giving a pain much more insupportable the *heartache.*" But on March 3 she reported, "The famous question was decided this morning."

The Missouri Compromise had passed Congress—Maine would be admitted as a free state, Missouri a slave state, and slavery would be outlawed in the lands of the Louisiana Purchase north of latitude 36 degrees 30'. It took some parliamentary sleight of hand for Speaker Henry Clay to get the measure through the House of Representatives, which infuriated Louisa: "If this is the vaunted superiority of our Government and the purity of our elective institutions, I do not think we have much to be proud of, and morality and religion are of little use if they cannot teach us to discern the difference between right and wrong." To her slavery was "a gross political inconsistency with all our boasted institutions, liberty and so forth, it is so palpable a stain that the veryest dunce can see it and understand it . . . I see too much, and was certainly never intended by nature to enjoy the Machiavellianism which is performing around me." But for the moment the national reckoning over slavery was postponed. A few days later, Congress passed a law allowing the Missouri Territory to draft a state constitution, and a few days after that on March 15, 1820, Maine joined the union as the twenty-third state.

With a sigh of relief the city changed the subject. "Maria Monroe is to be married on Tuesday to her cousin, young Gouverneur," Sarah Seaton announced. The president's younger daughter, Maria Hester Monroe, was marrying her father's secretary Samuel Gouverneur, in the first wedding of a presidential offspring at the executive mansion. "The New York style was adopted at Maria Monroe's wedding. Only the attendants, the relations and a few old friends of the bride and groom witnessed the ceremony." The Washington women were insulted that they were excluded from the nuptials. "In all things which do not concern the public I am very much inclined to do as I please and I think the President should do so too," Louisa Adams defended the Monroes, and then dutifully went off to the drawing room where the bride and groom were presented to society. "The bride was attended by her bridesmaids 7 in number all very pretty girls . . . The Speaker was in high spirits and came and spoke very graciously to me . . . we meet but to *war* and each of us are ready with a jest on all occasions." Henry Clay charmed her with his "generous and good" heart despite his "neglected education, vicious habits, and bad company, united to overweening ambition." Louisa could sound very much like her mother-in-law. But soon the wedding festivities were supplanted by tragedies.

First, Floride Calhoun, the well-liked wife of the secretary of war, lost her baby. The ladies had rallied round: "I walked over to Mrs. Calhoun's to offer to assist in nursing her child," Louisa wrote in mid-March. Margaret Smith "went into the city and offered my services, and stayed 2 days and sat up one night. . . . I never in my life witnessed such attentions . . . The President called every day, and his daughter Mrs. Hay, although in the midst of bridal festivities came . . . Mrs. Adams in the like manner and 20 others would attend." It was not just rank, but affection, Margaret insisted, after "an unusually long train of carriages" wound their way to the baby's burial. Then a much more shocking death shook the city—the hero of the War of 1812 and the Barbary Wars, the husband of one of the most popular women in town, Stephen Decatur, was killed in a duel.

"My blood ran cold as I heard it and Mr. A immediately went off to see him and to offer every assistance in his power," Louisa Adams reacted to the news that Decatur had been shot, "I followed and when I got there was informed that there were faint hopes of his life. The whole town was in a state of agitation." The feud between Stephen Decatur and Commodore James Barron had been long simmering. Barron commanded the *Chesapeake* back in 1807, when he ignominiously surrendered to the British ship *Leopard* and Decatur sat on the panel that court-martialed him. When Barron applied to re-enter the navy after the War of 1812, Decatur opposed him with language that eventually led to the duel. Louisa Adams looked on Barron with disdain, "What this man has gained by destroying a fellow creature with a view to fetch a broken reputation I cannot understand." Sarah Seaton agreed that Barron "will be an object of execration to his enemies, and scarcely of pity to his friends." Sarah wrote six days after the duel when everyone was worried about Susan Decatur who "never saw her husband, even after his death. She still lies in a lethargic stupor . . . no child, no relative except her father, an old man, what must be her situation when her sense of feeling shall return with all its poignancy." To Margaret Smith "Commodore Decatur's death was a striking and melancholy event." But Louisa Adams wasn't melancholy, she was mad: "Mr. A. was anxious to have some law passed with a view to check this fatal practice, but the people of our country still seem to possess a little of their aboriginal barbarism." Given that she thought dueling should be outlawed, Louisa disapproved of the great parade at Decatur's funeral: "Surely this man threw his life away, and his example ought to be held up as a warning to others that they may avoid his fate."

Uncharacteristically, Rosalie Calvert never weighed in on the Decatur duel. She was in mourning herself. "Pity, my dear Sister, your poor friend—in one week I have just lost two of my children." Her nine-year-old boy, Henri, and three year old girl Amelie both died in February of symptoms that were probably diphtheria. "These two children were so promising. They were always in the best of health and were so lovable and engaging, and I had such expectations for them," Rosalie cried, "out of nine children to have lost four—was there ever such misfortune?" Later that year, in an effort to recover, the miserable mother and her husband took a sightseeing tour in the north. Her spirits and her health briefly improved. But then, in March 1821, at the age of forty-three, Rosalie Stier Calvert died, "after an illness of four months confined to the bed the whole time and suffering much pain," her husband told his absent in-laws. Congestive heart failure probably caused her death. Daughter Caroline took up the story, "She was buried with her four children on an eminence not far from the house, and my father has ordered a beautiful white marble tombstone, which is nearly finished. On the head of the panel . . . my mother ascending to heaven on a cloud, and a little higher, four angels, her children, are stretching out their arms to receive her into the Celestial City."

The sense of common grief that had settled over Washington with the death of Stephen Decatur was short-lived as the congressional session dragged on well beyond its usual March farewell. In April the congressional caucus met to pick candidates for that year's election, but the smoke-filled room selection process had fallen into disrepute, and some state legislatures had already re-nominated President Monroe. "The Caucus very unpopular," Louisa Adams predicted a couple of days before the meeting. "There were not more than forty members who attended," she rejoiced the day after the event. "Caucusing is at last deemed unconstitutional. I congratulate the country at large on this occasion." Still the session dragged on, with Louisa forced to keep entertaining, though by the end of April she complained, "it is scarcely possible to get provisions." Food suppliers weren't used to capital parties extending into late spring. The drawing rooms at the president's house shut down altogether because Elizabeth Monroe was sick all spring. (Historians are not sure what ailment afflicted Mrs. Monroe; but some have speculated that it was epilepsy.) But with the nicer weather, there were some pleasant outings—fishing excursions, trips to the falls, and calls in the country, "went to see Mrs. Harrison Smith who lives about four miles and a half from the city." Louisa bought Stephen Decatur's horses, making such calls a little easier.

At the end of the session, in early June, the wife of the secretary of state went to a meeting of the trustees of the Orphan Asylum and learned that a long congressional session left more in its wake than testy tempers. One of the trustees warned that more space for orphans would soon be needed, "Congress having left many females in such difficulties as to make it probable they would beg our assistance." Mrs. Adams asked for an explanation and received the answer: "the session had been very long, the *fathers* of the nation had left forty cases to be provided for by the public and that our institution was the most likely to be called upon to maintain this illicit progeny." Congress wouldn't incorporate the Orphan Asylum but the members were busy producing "orphans." Can you imagine what would happen today if forty women showed up pregnant at the end of a congressional session, while the members went home to their wives? It would produce a world-class scandal. As it was, Louisa Adams simply reacted with a sarcastic suggestion! "I recommended a petition to Congress next session for that *great* and *moral* body to establish a foundling institution and should certainly move that the two additional dollars a day which they have given themselves as an increase in pay may be appropriated as a fund toward the support of the institution." Later that year, Louisa did in fact lobby members of Congress for the society. At a large party

"I begged Mr. Tracy to aid and assist as much as possible in getting the Orphan Asylum incorporated and he promised to exert himself with the committee." Albert Tracy of New York chaired the Committee on Expenditures in the Department of the Treasury.

While Louisa Adams worried about the orphans of the district, she also had her own children and surrogate children to attend to. Her sons (Louisa described them to her father-in-law, "George appears to be as eccentric as ever and John as wild") usually spent their school holidays in Washington and Mary Hellen, her sister Nancy's child, lived with her. Mary's brother Johnson was often there as well along with other nieces and nephews who paid long visits to their prominent aunt and uncle. When Louisa's brother's daughter, Fanny Johnson, came to stay for a while, she almost caused a duel between two would-be swains. Fanny was quite "the coquette" in Louisa's view and always caused problems. "When young people get together it is scarcely possible to keep order . . . My sons are ardent admirers of the sex, and the charms of Fanny are too striking to escape their observation." (In the end, however, it was Mary Hellen that John Adams II married.) As Mary grew older and started going to all the balls with John Quincy and Louisa, she created something of a problem for them since protocol called for the secretary of state to leave the event first, but she wanted to dance the night away.

The advent of the new congressional session meant another season of socializing. "Sent out cards of invitation for a dinner on Thursday. Thus the routine begins for the next four months and evening and morning will be fully occupied," Louisa sighed in November. "The roads are in such a state in consequence of what are called repairs that I fear there will be plenty of work for the surgeons. 28 visits yesterday." Soon after Congress returned, the ticket of James Monroe and Daniel Tompkins was reelected without opposition; the collapse of the Federalist Party was complete. Monroe received every electoral vote except one—Federalist holdout William Plummer of New Hampshire cast his ballot for John Quincy Adams. It was a sign that the election of 1824 was now under way and what masqueraded as teas, dinners, balls, receptions, card parties, and calls would actually be campaign events. Louisa Adams added a new room to her house for entertaining, and routinely hosted dinners for twenty and occasional balls for hundreds. With Elizabeth Monroe's health restored, the drawing rooms at the president's house were again a regular feature of capital life, Louisa told her father-in-law, adding: "On these occasions we all endeavor to look well but even when looking our best . . . certain of being always eclipsed by the Sovereign Lady of the mansion."

"The city is unusually gay and crowded with agreeable and distinguished visitors," Sarah Seaton cheerily observed in February 1821; the new British Ambassador Canning's "initiatory ball seemed to rouse the emulation of his neighbors and we have had a succession of fetes." And the George Washington Birthday ball "was brilliant. The contrast between the plain attire of President Monroe and Mr. Adams, and the splendid uniforms of the diplomatic corps was very striking." Louisa Adams hated that ball—it was "excessively warm" and "insupportably vulgar" and "the race to supper" was such that the British ambassador "must have thought the house was on fire and I was endeavoring to escape with all my might." Earlier that afternoon Louisa had hosted dinner for about twenty politicians and then "went to dress for the ball, the consequence of which was that the candles in the room were not lighted and I never thought about it until I heard the excellencies tumbling over the chairs in total darkness." When John Quincy stormed into her room, furious, "I was seized with such a convulsive fit of laughter that I could scarcely stand." She then apologized to the gentlemen, assuring them "it would give me much more real pleasure to *enlighten them* than to plunge them in greater darkness than was natural to them." Louisa thought members of Congress spent a good deal of time in the dark. One day in February she "paid several visits in the morning and finding the House insupportably dull went to the circus at which I laughed most heartily, the performances being altogether absurd and as usual exaggerated. They however appear to fascinate our very wise Members of Congress." A couple of weeks later, at the close of the congressional session, she listened to "one or two speeches which betrayed strong indications of *spirit* . . . one of these disordered gentlemen . . . was shortly after altogether incapacitated to discharge his great duties toward his constituents." At least it was a short session, adjourning in time for James Monroe's second inaugural.

The president "arrived safe and sound . . . though looking frightened to death and considerably agitated and went through the ceremony with a great deal of dignity," Louisa Adams reported with some relief that she had gotten there early because the crowd was immense. Then it was on to the drawing room and the "in the evening at Mrs. Monroe's request I went to the ball expressly to meet her. She looked more beautiful than I ever saw her and I thought acquitted herself remarkably well . . . and I only wish should it be my fate to exhibit under the same circumstances that I may perform my part as well." Louisa knew she might be next in the First Lady spotlight, "It is a most awful trial and much, much more to be dreaded than to be desired. The eye of the public is already on me and although I endeavor to give them as little opportunity of attacking me as possible . . . yet I cannot escape and my very dear five hundred friends begin to think my manners too generally *courtly* . . . and that I am not choice enough in the selection of my company."

It would be a rough road ahead, but Louisa thought she had one advantage going for her: "I am a very good diplomat. You may laugh but it is so," she boasted to her affectionate father-in-law. The wife of the secretary of state tried to use her diplomatic talents to secure a job for her brother-in-law, John Quincy's no good nephew: "I applied to the president for a place for William Smith which he gave me a very formal promise the night of the Inauguration to do as soon as he possibly could." Just as her mother-in-law Abigail Adams had tried to convince her husband to find a position for Billy Smith's father, Louisa worked to no avail on her husband, so she went directly to the president. It was harder to wire a patronage post with Dolley Madison no longer on the scene. Despite her boldness in approaching

President Monroe, as Louisa Adams contemplated her future she concluded, "Excepting having conquered in some measure the natural timidity of my character I am precisely the Louisa Johnson I was when I married Mr. Adams. The same romantic enthusiastic foolish animal as unfit for real life as I was then and as conscious of all my defects which as I rise become more striking."

LOUISA CATHERINE JOHNSON ADAMS, as always, sold herself short. A "traveled lady," by her own telling, a sophisticated and savvy woman, a voracious reader, visitors to the capital city sought her out. After one of her many parties, she had this tidbit for John Adams: "Had some conversation with Miss Wright, she is remarkably tall, not handsome, but has an intelligent and expressive countenance . . . and appears to have a cultivated and powerful mind." The young Scottish writer, Frances Wright, and her sister Camilla passed through Washington on a tour of America, and Louisa found it "curious to see two young ladies, the eldest not three and twenty crossing the ocean without a protector and traveling perfectly unattended in a foreign country. But these I suppose are old and vulgar prejudices, not at all calculated for these enlightened times; so I wonder, and admire." Fanny Wright would challenge just about every prejudice imaginable in the course of her life, as she went on to found a commune in Tennessee where she promoted free love and miscegenation with the slaves she had freed. She also made her mark as an abolitionist and militant for the rights of women. But at the time of her first trip to America, a country that had fascinated her since early childhood, Fanny Wright was seen as something of a prodigy for her work as a poet, author, and playwright. Her play, *Altorf,* garnered positive reviews, if not financial success, after performances in New York and Philadelphia. Though the critics assumed the author was a man, word leaked out, encouraged by Fanny, that she was the play's creator.

In still small town Washington, Fanny Wright was introduced

to most of the key players in government; Henry Clay announced on the House floor that the chamber was graced by a "distinguished foreign lady." The capital city also gave the young Scotswoman a close up look at slavery, and though she and her sister sailed back to England as ardent Yankee fans, the visit planted the seeds of Fanny's activism. The next year she published *Views of Society and Manners in America,* in praise of her New World discovery. It drew the attention of Jeremy Bentham and the Marquis de Lafayette and paved the way for her return to the United States a few years later. Though the book sang an encomium to the country, Fanny Wright condemned the sin of slavery ("The sight of slavery is revolting everywhere, but to inhale the impure breath of its pestilence in the free winds of America is odious beyond all that the imagination can conceive"), the excesses of the press ("Were a foreigner, immediately upon land-ing, to take up a newspaper . . . he might suppose that the whole political machine was about to fall to pieces"), and, while cheering the "improvement of female education," Wright believed American women needed more exercise. ("In her struggles for liberty much of her virtue emanated from the wives and daughters of the Senators and soldiers, and to preserve to her sons the energy of freemen and patriots she must strengthen that energy in her daughters.") When she settled in America, she worked to change what she could, editing a weekly newspaper and thundering from the lecterns of the lecture halls, in a highly unusual move for a woman. It was not just that she spoke to mixed audiences, it was what she said that was shocking: "Until women assume the place in society which good sense and good feeling alike, assign to them, human improvement must ad-vance but feebly. It is in vain that we would circumscribe the power of one half of our race, and that half by far the most important and influential."

The radical writer joined the mainstream when she argued for better education for women. And while she was thinking and talk-ing there were more and more women in the country actually doing the work of teaching girls. During Fanny Wright's initial visit to

America, Emma Hart Willard opened the first school of higher education for girls. It still operates, under her name, in Troy, New York. Emma Hart began teaching as a seventeen year old and at age twenty was recruited to run the "girls' academy" in Middlebury, Vermont. There she met and married widower John Willard, whose son studied at Middlebury College. Emma devoured her stepson's books and determined to devise an advanced curriculum for young women. She started by setting up a classroom in her home and drafting *A Plan for Improving Female Education*. Mrs. Willard intended to establish a public institution, supported by the state, in the same way that men's schools were; she sent her document to all the men she thought could help and the Governor of New York, DeWitt Clinton, responded favorably, proposing to take the idea to the state legislature. Favorable comment also came from presidents James Monroe, Thomas Jefferson, and John Adams, who wrote her, "The female moiety of mankind deserve as much honor, esteem and respect as the male . . . I rejoice that the experiment has been made under the legislature of New York."

Emma Willard traveled to Albany to lobby individual legislators and, with the support of the governor, opened a school in Waterford, New York, but the state legislature refused to fund it. She was preparing to close down altogether when the Troy Common Council coughed up four thousand dollars. The Troy Female Seminary opened in September 1821 and attracted young women from around the country, as Emma Willard's *Plan* circulated, even enjoying publication in Europe. Soon her students became teachers themselves, taking Mrs. Willard's curriculum, carrying her course of study over the miles. She sent one "young lady about to leave me to take charge of a female academy" off with a poem: "Go, in the name of God. Prosper, and prove a pillar in the cause of woman." At the end of her long career— she published several books while running the school—Emma Willard considered what she had wrought: "I was engaged in teaching thirty years, and have had under my charge as nearly as I can calculate, 5000 pupils, of whom as many as one in ten . . . have been teachers; and of these teachers, I think more than half have been those whom I have educated without present pay—their bills to be refunded from their earnings." By supporting the young women while they were studying, Emma Hart Willard guaranteed her legacy.

While Emma Willard worked with the power brokers of New York, Rose Philippine Duchesne and her tiny troupe of French nuns in 1818 founded in a log cabin the first free school west of the Mississippi. Though the cabin no longer stands, the school in St. Charles, Missouri, flourishes today. The frontier town of St. Charles was quite a shock to Philippine Duchesne who had grown up in a wealthy family in Grenoble, France, and joined the convent when she was eighteen. The French Revolution dispersed her religious community, causing her and some other nuns to band together with a new order, The Religious of the Sacred Heart of Jesus, founded in 1800 by Madeleine Sophie Barat. Mother Duchesne was convinced she had a calling to teach and preach to the Indians in America, and tried to persuade her superior to allow her to travel to the New World. Mother Barat finally relented when William DuBourg, Bishop of Louisiana and the Floridas, went hat in hand to Europe begging for help evangelizing the French and Indian children of his diocese.

At Easter time in 1818, the forty-eight-year-old Mother Duchesne and four other religious left a cosmopolitan life in France for the wilds of North America. After a more than a two month voyage aboard the *Rebecca*, which featured storms, pirates, and sailors spooked by a comet, the women arrived in New Orleans, where the Ursuline nuns took them in and begged them to stay, but the intrepid group of Frenchwomen boarded the steamboat *Franklin* in the heat of July and headed up the Mississippi to St. Louis. There the prominent French families were eager for the nuns to start a school for their girls, but the bishop had other ideas. He managed to alienate the local families and to thwart Philippine Duchesne's desire to work in the Indian missions by dispatching the nuns to the one horse town of St. Charles. Mother Duchesne wrote Mother Barat that DuBourg predicted the outpost would some day "become one of the most important cities of North America, as it is situated on the Missouri River."

Though not happy about it, the women conscientiously obeyed the prelate and through "many halts and detours" made it to St. Charles, where Philippine was at once dubious of the bishop's belief that the village "will become a great commercial link between the United States and China." Her skepticism was well placed, and though she conceded that DuBourg looked "far into the future," for the present the nuns would be faced with primitive living conditions. "There is no market. The gift of a pound of butter and a dozen eggs is like a fortune received . . . During the hunting season, which we are in now, we can procure venison and ducks, but in the spring and summer one can get only salted fish and meat. Many of the cows are almost dry." To her sister she added, "the only edible oil to be had here is bear grease and it is disgusting." Though Mother Barat had sent DuBourg money for the nuns, he wasn't turning it over. Even so the women managed to open the free school for poor children only a few weeks after they arrived, and a boarding school to support the free school a few weeks after that. "In our free school we now have twenty two children, and in proportion to the population this equals a school of one hundred in France," Philippine wrote in October, "Some of the boarding pupils have more dresses than underclothes or handkerchiefs . . . They scorn black shoes and must have pink or blue, yellow or green ones, and the rest to match."

Much to her sorrow, Mother Duchesne had no "savages" to teach. There was one girl who was a "*half-breed . . . against this race there is not the same prejudice as there is against Negroes and mulattoes.*" The bishop would not allow them to admit "colored people" to the school for fear of driving off the whites, so Philippine set aside one day a week to teach those children. Even so, wealthy white families didn't want to send their children to St. Charles because they saw it for what it was—a backwater, not the gateway to the west. Without girls from St. Louis, the boarding school failed and Philippine was forced to start over the next year in the more hospitable town of Florissant. More schools followed in Louisiana and Missouri, including St. Louis, where the nuns also established a Mother House for the expanding Sacred Heart order, as more women signed up to provide girls on the American frontier with a fine French education.

At age seventy-one, Mother Duchesne fulfilled her dream of missionary work with the Indians. She joined other nuns and priests in Sugar Creek, Kansas, in an effort to educate the Potawatomi. But the language was too difficult for her to learn (she had had a very hard time with English), so she spent most of her time praying for the success of the mission, earning her the Indian name, Kwah-kah-kum-ad, "The Woman who Always Prays." Kansas proved too hard for the old nun's health, so Philippine had no choice but to retreat to St. Charles: "For thirty eight years my great desire was to work among the savages . . . Then after one year of uselessness at the Indian mission, I came back here by order of my Superior General, without accomplishing anything," she summed up sadly. "It seems to me that in leaving the Indians I left my real element, and now I can only yearn for that land from which there will be no departure. God knows why I was recalled, and that is enough." She felt she was a failure, but Sacred Heart schools soon covered the continent, and her example earned her sainthood. Pope John Paul II canonized Rose Philippine Duchesne in 1988.

As a new immigrant from France, Philippine Duchesne, arriving in Missouri just as its contentious statehood quest was hotly debated, was shocked by prejudice against blacks in the land of the free. In 1821, a Second Missouri Compromise had to be hammered out because the constitution drawn up by the territory had excluded "free Negroes and mulattos" from the state, an obviously unacceptable condition to congressmen from northern states. Missouri was admitted as the twenty-fourth state on the condition that it not infringe on the privileges of any U.S. citizen. But the attempt at exclusion underlined the hostility toward free blacks, and as the nineteenth century moved into its second decade, the cause of colonization became somewhat fashionable. Embraced by President Monroe and his mentor Thomas Jefferson, in addition to Henry Clay and Daniel Webster, the American Colonization Society sought to repatriate blacks to Africa, and settled on land in West Africa for that purpose, naming it Liberia. Shiploads of free blacks did migrate but many more preferred to stay in what was now their home. A vigorous self-help movement started among African Americans to better their lives.

As early as 1790, blacks in Newport, Rhode Island, a port of entry for slaves, formed the Free African Union Society. A few years later, in Philadelphia, the Female Benevolent Society of St. Thomas's African Episcopal Church provided help to dues-paying members. In 1808, the African Benevolent Society organized to raise money for a school in Newport. Membership was open to any "person of color, whether male or female," but only men could vote or hold office. So the next year the women formed their own Female Society and made a contribution to the school, authorizing "ten dollars be taken out of our treasury . . . and we hope it may be acceptable as a widows' mite." In Salem, Massachusetts, the Colored Female Religious and Moral Society came together in 1818 "for the benefit of the sick and destitute" with dues of a penny a week. The constitution warned "if any member commit any scandalous sin, or walk unruly, and after proper reproof continue manifestly impenitent, she shall be excluded from us." The Daughters of Africa, a group of almost 200 Philadelphia women, made a mutual assistance pact in 1821 and left meticulous records: "Hannah Morris Treasurer Please to Pay E. Griffith for Leah Gibson, a sick member, $1.50 cent." The African-American female self-help organizations sprouted in cities both north and south during the 1820's and, as education improved, some literary groups came together in the next decade, along with female antislavery societies.

White women were beginning to speak for the abolitionist cause, and black women were speaking for themselves. In 1821, the *Franklin Herald* of Greenfield, Massachusetts, ran the obituary of "Mrs. Lucy Prince, a woman of color," taken from the Bennington *Vermont Ga-*

zette: "In this remarkable woman there was an assemblage of qualities rarely to be found among her sex. Her volubility was exceeded
by none, and in general the fluency of her speech was not destitute
of instruction and education." It was an altogether unusual story to
read in the newspaper. An obituary of a woman was rare enough, but
of a ninety-seven-year-old African-American woman? Lucy had been
brought to America as a slave almost a century earlier. Still a child,
she went to a family in Deerfield, Massachusetts, where as a young
woman she witnessed the last Indian raid in 1746 and composed a
poem, the first known poetry of an African American, *The Bars
Fight,* to commemorate it. It's not known whether the poem was
written down or simply recited in the oral tradition of a "singer of
history," but it survives today as an accounting of what happened to
the good folk of Deerfield, including:

> *Eunice Allen see the Indians coming*
> *And hoped to save herself by running;*
> *And had not her petticoats stopped her,*
> *The awful creatures had not cotched her,*
> *Nor tommyhawked her on the head,*
> *And left her on the ground for dead.*

Lucy Terry seems to have been well known as a storyteller and
talker in early Deerfield. In 1757, she married a free black man, Abijah Prince and their sons served in the Revolutionary War. The family moved to Vermont in 1785, and that's where Lucy's oratorical
talents first became useful, in representing her family's interest before the governor and several councilors in a dispute with a neighbor.
The council sided with Lucy Terry Prince. Then she took on Wil-
liams College. When her son was rejected because he was black his
mother, according to a nineteenth-century history, "argued the case
in a '3-hour speech' before the trustees." The college's records don't
document the event, but would they? One college history does include the story of Lucy Prince's ultimately unsuccessful appearance.

Records are missing as well from the other oratorical feat attributed to Lucy Terry Prince—her argument of a property claim before Supreme Court Justice Samuel Chase. The justice praised her performance, saying she "made a better argument than he had ever heard from a lawyer in Vermont." Lucy's death occasioned a eulogy by a Vermont preacher, printed along with her obituary, which attacked the recent Missouri compromise, and condemned slavery.

With the United States free from outside threats, the internal division over slavery grew more distinct. Leading the charge to abolish the "peculiar institution" as human bondage was euphemistically called, were the country's Quakers. Raised in a Quaker community in Massachusetts, Lucretia Coffin grew up to be a teacher, and then, in 1821, a preacher, a privilege granted to women in her religion. Married to James Mott in 1811, she and her husband moved to Philadelphia ten years later, where she started sermonizing against slavery, organizing antislavery societies, and boycotting goods produced by slaves. Her preaching became famous as she traveled to nearby states spreading the message of abolition and repentance. While she worked to free slaves, Mott repeatedly suffered sex discrimination, with some antislavery groups denying her the right to participate, others the right to speak, leading her eventually to the cause of women's suffrage, where she worked with Elizabeth Cady Stanton, a former student of Emma Willard. Though the evolution and activism took place over many decades, for Lucretia Mott it was a direct line—Quakerism led to abolition led to women's suffrage and the meeting in Seneca Falls in 1848 with its "Declaration of Sentiments," stating, "We hold these truths to be self-evident: that all men and women are created equal."

Deliberately mimicking the Declaration of Independence, which charged the British with multiple abuses, the Seneca Falls declaration cited the crimes of man against woman, including: "He has never permitted her to exercise her inalienable right to the elective franchise. He has compelled her to submit to laws, in the formation of which she had no voice." Lucretia Mott had first raised her voice as a Quaker preacher in 1821; it took until 1920 for that voice and those of the other women who started their public careers battling against slavery and ended them fighting for women's suffrage to be heard by the men who amended the constitution.

ℰDUCATORS, REFORMERS, AND RELIGIOUS revivalists all made their way to Washington, as well as the rest of the country, but then as now, both men and women in the federal city were absorbed with politics. "The present incumbent is treated with very little ceremony, while casting about for his successor." Sarah Seaton joked to her family in 1822 that one wag had proposed that "'a committee be appointed to wait on the President and ask him to have the goodness to resign, inasmuch as gentlemen were in a hurry and did not like to wait.'" Everyone wanted to know which candidate Sarah's husband and brother, the editors of the *Intelligencer* would endorse: "Encompassed as they are by friends in the shape of presidential candidates, the choice will be unpleasant, come when it may, and they feel no anxiety to anticipate the free and full expression of the Republican majority." A newspaper backing Secretary of War John Calhoun for president, the *Washington Republican* was trying "to get Mr. Crawford out of the Cabinet," according to Margaret Bayard Smith. "The discussion is kindling personal feelings, and the friends of these gentlemen will I fear be made hostile to each other."

More than two years before the election Margaret bemoaned the fact that a revivalist preacher was captivating the capital "*This,* and the Presidential election are the two animating principles at present in our city society." Secretary of the Treasury William Crawford of Georgia could split the southern vote with South Carolinian Calhoun, whose chances had already been dealt a blow when his home state legislature in late 1821 nominated Congressman William Lowndes for president. On hearing the news, the powerful congressman teased his wife: "I hope you have not set your mind too strongly on being President's lady. While you wish only a larger fence for the poultry yard, and a pond for the ducks I may be able to gratify you, but this business of making a President, either of myself or another, I have no cunning at."

Other state legislatures soon got into the act nominating their favorite sons—in 1822 Tennessee went for General Andrew Jackson who was elected to the senate that year, and Kentucky gave the nod to House Speaker Henry Clay. The plethora of candidates crowding the capital was creating chaos, complained William Lowndes: "We live in a terrible confusion. I thought when I first came here the question was confined to Mr. Crawford and Mr. Adams." Now everyone seemed to be running, including himself. Responding to his state legislature, Lowndes pompously insisted that he had never campaigned for president: "It is not in my opinion an office to be either solicited or declined." John Quincy Adams often issued similar statements, thinking it proper for the people to ask him to be their president rather than the other way around.

During the summer of 1822, when Louisa Adams was in Philadelphia nursing her sick brother, she visited with some Adams supporters who confided that her husband's "aristocratic hauteur, and learned arrogance" were turning people off. She thought John Quincy should come to Philadelphia to dispel that image, telling him he should "show yourself if only for a week," in other words, to campaign. He said no but she persisted, "Do for once gratify me," she begged, "and if harm come of it I promise never to advise you again." He adamantly refused to show "how much I long to be president," even as he complained, "I have not . . . one member of any one State Legislature disposed to caucus for me." Candidates had to be much more subtle than today's office-seekers, using surrogates, especially their wives, to do their heavy lifting. And in that department, Adams and Calhoun had a decided advantage. Congressman McLane told his wife that William Crawford's wife and daughter "were never designed to the wife and daughter of a president," and another Crawford guest found his hostess "without any of the airs and graces which seem appropriate to the wife of a president." Mrs. John Quincy Adams possessed those graces and then some.

With the Congress back in town in December 1822, when Louisa Adams revived her journal for her father-in-law, she thought "the intriguing for the Presidency will . . . make it interesting." Having spent much of the last winter sick in bed, this winter she renewed her "Tuesday campaign" with vigor. "My Tuesday evenings appear to have some attractions; at least they afford the probable certainty of giving opportunity for amusement throughout the winter and in this consists the charm." Politicians could count on seeing each other at the Adams's, where Louisa might sing for them or hire musicians (the Marine Band cost "five dollars to each performer plus wine and supper"), or feature a lecture in order to provide some amusement. After one of these events she would casually report, "had a party of 100 persons . . . altogether the evening was pleasant." "In the evening we had a party of one hundred and thirty odd persons all very sociable and good humored. The young ladies danced, played and sang and were very merry." Mrs. Adams would play her part, "I am very willing to show that I am the public *servant* but I will never be the *public slave.*"

All of these men running for president while constantly rubbing elbows not to mention rubbing egos made for an interesting social life: "To get through a dinner without clashing in some way or other in these boisterous times is a difficult matter. All are partisans and each warm for his friend though perhaps not an enemy to his opponent, but it is hard with interests so divided to steer clear of offence. We found in this instance wine maketh the heart glad and none were inclined to wrath." Somewhat disingenuously, Louisa griped, "If Mr. A instead of keeping me back when I was a young woman had urged me forward in the world I should have better understood the maneuvering part of my situation. But instead of this I find myself almost a stranger to the little arts and intrigues of the world in which I move." That self-deprecating statement was not even close to reality. In fact

Louisa had become quite popular: "Received a note from a milliner requesting I would go and look at her things. This is a thing that has happened several times, am I so much in vogue?" she laughed.

As the New Year dawned Louisa Adams was ready to do battle: "If the weather of today is ominous of the storms of the ensuing year we must not expect much quiet. Let it come: I will not flinch, be the end what it may." Bring it on. Louisa seemed to be thoroughly enjoying the game. Her sons were all in town over the Christmas holidays and the entire family, including her niece Mary Hellen, was invited to dinner at the executive mansion, where Louisa found the First Lady "handsomer than ever and in fine health." Her health too was "unusually good" and her spirits "proportionally high." Good thing, because the entertainment had to have been onerous. "Had a party of upwards two hundred and fifty two, ladies being a much larger proportion than we have had this winter," she breezily recounted, and among the guests was "the *Washington Republican,* a violent partisan of Mr. Calhoun." It was all out war with the Calhouns who held up their end of the entertainment madness. "In the evening went to a ball at Mr. Calhoun's which was so crowded it was scarcely possible to breathe . . . Mr. Clay was at Mr. Calhoun's and seemed to be desirous of making his attentions very public." That must have set the gossips buzzing.

When Louisa Adams put on a party for the newlywed secretary at the French Embassy, she added her special flair: "As the bride has no bridesmaids, I invited four young ladies and had them dressed alike. They presented her with a bouquet on her entrance, afterwards formed themselves into a cotillion and then did the honors of the supper . . . it had the effect of novelty and pleased." Floride Calhoun took up the challenge and threw her own party for the bride and groom, and though Louisa Adams stayed home, she had the satisfaction of hearing that the ball "was a gaudy imitation of the simple compliment I had offered and according to account, ill conducted and ill managed." Score one for Mrs. Adams.

Louisa had to admit that things were going well. Her parties were all-too well attended, even an ardent supporter of one her husband's opponents "gave me a hint that he would like an invitation to my Tuesdays and I gave it to him." With some surprise she told old John Adams, "this winter we are all the fashion." Still it was hard "to be an object of attention to the busy censorious multitude, whose praise is tinctured by envy, and whose approval is embittered by irony." As the object of attention, Louisa had to worry about her clothes and she wryly noted, "If we trace the course of human nature we shall find that even minds of superior order are caught by the tinsel trappings of outward splendor . . . beauty always appears to advantage here." These were her reflections after a ball at the British ambassador's where her dress was a success. "I generally cut out and fix my own clothes, this occasion brought out a gown which I have had seven years and which I have never made up, and taking some trimmings from one nearly worn out I put the materials together and produced a dress so splendid that it created great admiration." Another triumph.

Susanna Crawford tried to compete as well, sending out more than six hundred invitations to a ball that "was handsome, everything in profusion, but I know not why it was dull and uncomfortable and we left it before ten o'clock, believing it to be at least twelve." The ungracious assessment was followed by Louisa's not-to-be-believed assertion: "I will never condescend to court popularity and I will preserve my independence." That from a woman who was entertaining hundreds weekly and rejoicing that her "evenings keep up their reputation." Congressmen usually jammed all the balls, but one was sparsely attended—the annual gala commemorating George Washington's Birthday. Since it wasn't thrown by someone running for president, the politicians were less interested. Mrs. Adams was of the opinion that the turnout was an insult to the Father of the Country, "the events of the Revolution and the brilliant part he took in it . . . should be cherished by the present generation and handed down to posterity as a shield to our institutions." Louisa understood the true value of patriotic exercises, but her mother-in-law must have been rolling in her grave. Abigail Adams had been so furious when the people of Philadelphia celebrated George Washington's birthday, taking it as a slap in the face to the President John Adams.

Louisa Adams constantly used social events to size up her husband's opposition, and she was amused at Henry Clay's charm offensive. After the party for the bride and groom, where he seemed "inclined to play the courtier," at another event Clay "took an opportunity of assuring me that it was his wish to be on terms of friendship with me and my family." Louisa couldn't figure out what her husband's potential rival was up to. "I always mistrust those sudden changes and though I do not interfere in politics, it is difficult for me to avoid knowing transactions which are talked of by everyone and which places a man in the light of a decided enemy to my husband. How much direction and discernment it requires to be the wife of a great man." She was wondering just how to deal with Clay's newfound friendliness. Louisa didn't want to offend the speaker, but she also didn't want to give "an appearance of fawning and intrigue which is despicable to the soul of a proud and virtuous woman." This woman who didn't interfere in politics then reported on a visit to her sister's where a cousin from Frederick, Maryland, was visiting. Louisa dropped by to talk up her husband's candidacy: "As my connections in this state are of the most respectable and distinguished I am solicitous to secure them in his interest. Maryland, it is said will be his." With that bit of work accomplished, Mrs. Adams was quick to disabuse her father-in-law of her own interest in the presidency, "For myself I have no ambition beyond my present situation; the exchange to a more elevated station must put me in prison." John Adams must have read that with some skepticism.

The congressional session proved dull, so social life took up more of the city's attention, along with weekly attendance at church services. More religious denominations were building churches all the time, and Louisa sampled different sects, hoping to hear a good preacher, though generally she joined in the rituals held in the Capitol. But she never seemed to like them much. One Sunday she heard a fine sermon at St. John's Episcopal Church, but "the young men went to the Capitol and heard a violent and threatening sermon from Mr. McHaoame, full of bitter denunciations and punishment having little hope for either sinner or penitent." The other diversion of that winter was the influx of diplomats from the newly independent nations of South America. The United States recognized the revolutionary governments, whose representatives caused new etiquette issues in the diplomatic corps, which the secretary of state had to handle.

A dinner for ambassadors at the Adams home was negotiated ahead of time with the British envoy, who demanded the seat of honor at Louisa's right, though the newest member of the corps, the Mexican ambassador should have been awarded that place. The newcomer sat on Louisa's left, speaking not a word of English, and clearly miserable in his new assignment. To the polite question of whether he had yet been around the city, the ambassador replied through an interpreter "he had been round what would be a City when our grandchildren were grown." The capital of the United States still struggled with its somewhat primitive appearance. But Louisa was delighted that "several weddings are likely to take place among the Corps Diplomatique and our Ladies, a sign that our foreign relations are on a peaceable footing." (Other liaisons of a less legal nature also titillated the locals. "The reports about Mrs. Decatur and Mr. Canning still continue, and their conduct the evening I spent there is enough to authorize the general rumors." The very married British Ambassador Canning seemed to have taken up with the grieving widow Susan Decatur.)

It would be an early adjournment for the lame duck Congress; the members elected in 1822 would take their seats the following December. So everyone crowded into the last drawing room at the president's house on February 19, 1823. Despite the crush, "it was however very pleasant and our *Queen,* as a Lady from New York said, looked very beautiful." About a week later Louisa held "my last open day and we had a great crowd, almost all strangers. The party as usual was very gay and everybody was pleased and good humored."

The next day brought "morning visitors in abundance" And then, on March 1, it all stopped. "This is the close of the session and the close of my journal, for now we plunge not into dreary but a sort of waking vacancy, something between life and death, which produces much the same effect as the sleep procured by opiates, full of visions seen too indistinctly to excite attention or to live in memory." Louisa Adams knew that when the new Congress convened in the fall, the campaign for president would be in full swing.

"This session begins with me pretty much as I suppose it will pass in Congress," Louisa Adams prophesied on November 30, "that is to say with chills and fevers alternately low and high and at all times very unequal to labor in my fatiguing vocation . . . during this tremendous struggle for the presidential election." Her "fatiguing vocation?" See to it that her husband would be elected president of the United States. It was back to the drawing rooms, where a somewhat different cast of characters appeared on the guest list with this new Eighteenth Congress. William Lowndes, the highly influential Chairman of the Ways and Means Committee, had died, and William Crawford, secretary of the treasury, had suffered a paralytic stroke. Both men had been presidential contenders. Lowndes, along with his wife Elizabeth, and twelve year old daughter Rebecca, set sail for Europe in an effort to improve his health. Six days into the voyage, he died. A burial at sea followed, and according to a fellow passenger, "Mrs. Lowndes and her daughter were in their stateroom, and I believe they were not aware for some days of his body having been buried in the ocean, as we thought it too trying a scene for her to witness." Rebecca Lowndes remembered it differently. She and her mother were below deck when they heard the body plunge into the sea and "To her dying day. . . . recalled with awe that solemn sound, and the scream of her mother who instantly recognized its import." News of Lowndes death reached Washington in early 1823, when Louisa Adams mourned, "His talents, his moral worth and his mild and persuasive abilities having ranked him very high in the estimation of his countrymen . . . From my heart I pity his poor wife whose situation under such circumstances must have been inexpressibly distressing for under the appearance of coldness of character she possesses much real sensibility." Elizabeth Lowndes made a quick turnaround once she arrived in France, after she was embraced by the American community and General Lafayette she quickly headed home.

Lowndes was dead, Crawford was sick, but another contender for the presidency joined Washington society that December: General Andrew Jackson had been elected to the Senate from Tennessee. Now all of the key candidates were in the capital and the politicking picked up steam. On December 2, James Monroe delivered to congress the message for which his presidency is most remembered. The Monroe Doctrine warned Europe against interfering in the affairs of the Western Hemisphere, bluntly asserting that the American continents were no longer subject to colonization. Louisa Adams barely mentioned the brash doctrine, largely her husband's product, to her father-in-law: "The president's message went in today but I have heard nothing about it." She was much more concerned about the fact that, for the first time, a foreign diplomat, Prussian Ambassador Frederick Greuhm, died in this country and no one knew what the proper protocol surrounding his funeral should be. It still was a very new nation, having to figure out everything as it happened. But the main thing the city was figuring out was who would be the next president. And by the third day of the session, Louisa's campaign was in high gear: "My whole morning was occupied with visits and writing cards of invitation. We have had forty or more Members of Congress already here and all who call I invite to my evenings. If I can help it I will invite only those who call, lest it should be said I am courting them to further any political purpose." As if the city didn't know what she was up to.

The rounds of calls and balls started up even more frenetically than the previous winter, with the president's house off the circuit because Elizabeth Monroe was sick. "Everyday brings forth a new rumor, not one of which can be believed or relied on," Louisa fretted,

"The caucusing is eternal." "Mr. C[alhoun] and A[dams] seem not such good friends as they were," William Crawford supporter Margaret Bayard Smith told a friend that December, when her candidate was still terribly sick. "You have no conception of the attentions with which the winning, courtly Mr. Clay and the interesting agreeable Mr. Calhoun ply the new and old members here." Sarah Seaton added her analysis, "Mr. Adams moves either to the right or left, but keeps an undeviating course regardless of the opinion or friend or foe. . . . General Jackson . . . is, indeed, a polished and perfect courtier in female society, and polite to all." Notwithstanding Jackson's politeness, social events were testy. In mid-December, Louisa hosted a dinner party that included both Clay and Calhoun: "This was what we call a snarling dinner composed of such opposite materials it was not possible to prevent sharp speeches."

Given that atmosphere all the women needed some diversion. They found it in Daniel Webster's speech on Greek independence from the Ottoman Empire. Massachusetts sent the great orator to Congress that year, and everyone wanted to hear him. "Mr. Webster is about to make a great display about the Greeks and a great stir is made about it," Louisa Adams announced right after Christmas. "I shall certainly try to hear it," Margaret Smith added. Sarah Seaton was also gearing up for the moment: "We are prepared for an unusual display of eloquence from Mr. Webster, and other conspicuous members, on the subject of the Greeks." But before Webster could deliver his great declamation, another event eclipsed it: on January 8, the anniversary of the Battle of New Orleans, John Quincy and Louisa Adams were throwing a ball in honor of Andrew Jackson. The town buzzed with anticipation.

"Much talk about the ball and a great deal of nonsense in the newspapers," Louisa kept her father-in-law in the loop, after initially telling him: "I objected much to the plan but was overpowered by John's arguments and the thing was settled," she sighed. She and her husband had been that night to a ball for General Edmund Gaines, the new commander of the Eastern Department of the Army and a decorated veteran of the War of 1812, who bragged that his wife "had written the accounts of his campaigns with infinitely more accuracy in all their details than he or his aides could do," causing Louisa to crack, "America is doubly blessed in having possessed of generals in petticoats as well as generals in breeches." But now it was another general who would occupy Mrs. Adams for the next few weeks—her husband's rival for the presidency, General Jackson. Adams had convinced his wife that a showy event flattering Jackson might persuade "Old Hickory" to run with Adams for vice president instead of against him for president. With little time to prepare, Louisa frantically pulled it together. "This day like many others was passed in running about the town to carry invitations," she complained on December 27. There were so many people invited "we have been obliged to order pillars to be placed in our rooms to support the ceilings, to conceal which I must make some sort of ornament and this of itself will occasion more talk than I like . . . I must take my chance and brave it as well as I can." Her sister came over to help make flowers but in early January she learned that "we must make all the laurel wreaths ourselves. I worked very hard . . . in preparing them besides receiving visits which crowd in such manners that I really fear for the house." More flower making, more invitation delivering, more people demanding invitations, and finally the day arrived.

One wag wrote a long poem published in the *Washington Republican* listing all the families rushing to the ball with the refrain:

> *Belles and matrons, maids and madames,*
> *All are gone to Mrs. Adams'.*

John Quincy's niece, Abigail, was there and remembered the floor of the ballroom decorated with chalk "spread-eagles, flags and the motto 'Welcome to the hero of New Orleans.'" Louisa had commented on the chalk floor decoration she had seen the year before at a ball at the British ambassador's, so she took the idea and adapted it to celebrate Jackson's feat. The other decorations were even more intricate, according to Louisa herself: "Busy all the morning in fixing the laurel wreaths which John under my direction hung . . . these wreaths were intermixed with roses and arranged in festoons in the center of which was placed a small variegated lamp. Chandeliers to match were suspended from the ceiling in the center of the rooms and garlands were hung from the pillars within so as to fasten them up which had altogether a beautiful effect." She took the doors off all the rooms on the first floor, which added more space and "looked very showy." Louisa, too, looked pretty showy, wearing steel lamé with cut steel "ornaments for head, throat, and arms . . . producing a dazzling effect."

At seven-thirty the guests began to arrive and "Mr. Adams and I took our stations near the door that we might be seen by our guests and be at the same time ready to receive the general to whom the fete was given. He arrived at nine o'clock and I took him round the rooms and introduced him to the ladies and gentlemen whom we passed." When supper was announced, Louisa again took Jackson's arm and "led him to the top of the table . . . the general drank my health and professed to be much gratified by the compliment." When the party moved into the ballroom and Louisa finally sat down, "one of the lamps fell upon my head and ran all down my back and shoulders. This gave rise to a good joke and it was said that I was already anointed with the sacred oil and that it was certainly ominous. I observed that the only certain thing I knew was that my gown was spoilt." Everyone stayed until about one-thirty "all in good humor and more contented than common with their entertainment. To have got so well through this business is a matter of gratulation to us all." Louisa Adams wasn't the only one who thought her ball was a success: "It really was a brilliant party & admirably well arranged," a friend told Dolley Madison. "The ladies climbed the chairs and benches to see Gen[era]l Jackson & Mrs. Adams very gracefully took his arm & walked through the apartment with him, which gratified the general curiosity. It is said there were 1400 cards issued,

& about 800 supposed to be present." The "Adams Ball" was talked about for years to come.

LOUISA ADAMS SOON made a friend among the new congressional wives. Edward Livingston had been elected from Louisiana and his wife, the beautiful Creole Louise D'Avezac Livingston, soon charmed Washington, just as she had New Orleans. Louise Livingston's impressions of the city were not as kind as the city's impression of her: "Washington is certainly the dullest-looking town I have ever seen. It is neither a village nor a city, but unites the inconveniences of both without the advantages of either," she told her sister-in-law. "There are elements here to form a very good society, but dispersed on so large a space that people are seldom brought together, except in immensely crowded assemblies, where it matters little whether a man is a fool or not, provided he can fight his way through." Louise had recently been to one of those crowded assemblies, this one at the executive mansion. Elizabeth Monroe's health had improved, she looked "more beautiful than any woman of her age I ever saw," and she was dutifully holding her "drawing rooms." After relating her initial impressions, Louise got down to the real news: "The canvass for the presidency is carried on with great ardor by all the parties. I have been very graciously received by the ladies whose husbands are foremost on the list of candidates—Mrs. Adams, Mrs. Calhoun, and Mrs. Crawford. This is the best time for the wife of a member of Congress to visit the seat of government—she is sure of the most flattering reception."

Louise Livingston would probably have received a flattering reception under any circumstances. She was not only well-read and interesting, she was different from most of the women in town. Born in 1781 into a wealthy French family on the island of Saint-Domingue, now Haiti, she was married off at the age of thirteen to a landholding French officer, had three children who died as infants, and was widowed at age sixteen. After two brothers were killed in the Haitian Revolution, in 1800 the family arranged for Louise and her little sister Aglae, along with their grandmother, a young aunt, and some cousins to escape to America. A lifeboat sent out by a British frigate offshore picked them up on the beach after a night hiding in the jungle, clutching the jewelry they planned to sell. Shots fired by revolutionaries from shore killed the grandmother and a slave who was going with them, but the rest made it to the ship. They sailed to Jamaica, and then transferred to a small, crowded, fever-ridden schooner to New Orleans. The French city, just changing to American hands, took in the D'Avezac family. At first the young women lived off the money from selling their jewelry; when that ran out they went to work as seamstresses. At night they would put their work aside and go with the rest of the city to the Creole balls; at one of those festive dances Louise D'Avezac met the American, Edward Livingston.

Livingston had gone to New Orleans to start life anew after a scandal happened on his watch as mayor of New York. A talented lawyer, he soon was assisting the newly American city adapt to the legal codes, and attracting a steady clientele. When he married Louise in the summer of 1805, many members of the D'Avezac family moved in to what became a lively Creole household. A year later the couple's only child, Coralie, was born. With Edward often away fighting a protracted legal battle over a large parcel of land, Louise sent scores of letters combining witty local stories, passionate love sentiments, and practical business matters. She always watched out for his interests: "There is a movement afoot to organize a lawyer's society . . . P. intrigues and wants to be its president. W . . . nominates you for the position. The lawyers are divided and the public laughs." She also guarded her own interests. When he would go home to New York—to "America"—she felt quite foreign: "You were deprived for so long of the company of attractive American women that they must now exercise a powerful charm on you . . . the very language they speak, your own native tongue," she worried. She told

Edward to avoid temptation by remembering his own wife, "knows how to love me better and it is she who deserves to be loved." She was also determined to provide a fine education for their little girl. When Cora was not yet four her mother ordered:

A good French grammar . . .

A geography book and geographical dictionary . . .

An abbreviated account of the arts and sciences in general. . . .

A concise abbreviated account of ancient and modern history, suitable for the youngest children.

A little treatise on rhetoric and, finally, the dictionary of the Academie.

Edward Livingston sought Louise's guidance in all his work. "Why are you not with me?" he asked when dealing with a tricky issue, "in cases where I doubt before I decide, I am never quite sure my decision is right until you have approved it." She was especially helpful in his great work, the production of a model Penal Code, and she was delighted when it was well received: "The notice taken of the Code in the Senate gratified equally your daughter and myself."

Over the years Louise and Cora began to spend some time in New York, in the city and at Edward's sister Janet Montgomery's estate in the Hudson River valley. By the time Louise and seventeen-year-old Cora set up housekeeping with Edward in the capital city, the Creole girl had become a sophisticated middle-age matron, and soon her "*salon* became famous in Washington just as it had been in New Orleans," according to social historian Mary Caroline Crawford.

Though the Livingstons forged an allegiance to Andrew Jackson during the Battle of New Orleans, Louise Livingston and Louisa Adams shared a love of books and each other's company. After Adams was elected president, the two women became especially close. Then, when Jackson won the White House, Louise insisted to her husband that he lobby for a high position in the new government: "I have never heard you speak of a quiet and insignificant role. It is not one which suits you, and if I may say so without too much pride, it is not one which suits the man who was the choice of my judgment and of my heart. . . . for you, for your glory, and for your renown, I admit that my ambition is without limit." Instead Edward Livingston went to the Senate, but was, a couple of years later, appointed Jackson's secretary of state, and from there went on to serve as ambassador to France. When the choice of Livingston as ambassador was announced, irascible John Randolph paid one of his few compliments, urging Livingston to accept the post: "In Mrs. Livingston . . . you have a most able coadjutor. *Dowdies*, dowdies won't do for European courts, Paris especially . . . It is the very place for her. There she would dazzle and charm, and surely the salons of Paris must have far greater attractions for her than the yahoos of Washington." The Livingstons did go to Paris, bringing Cora and her husband along. They eventually retired to Montgomery Place, which Louise Livingston turned into a garden showplace of its own, studied by horticulturalists, while buying up land to preserve the Hudson River Valley as industrialization encroached. Louise D'Avezac Livingston, the teenage refugee from Haiti, ended life as an early advocate of conservation.

ALL OF THOSE EVENTS in Louise Livingston's life would come later. For now, like the rest of Washington, she was enmeshed in a heated campaign for president. On February 14, 1824, only sixty six of 216 members of congress showed up for what's come to be called the "rump caucus" and nominated William Crawford, whose health was improving. The next day, politicians meeting in Boston made John Quincy Adams their standard-bearer for president, and the other New England states soon followed suit. Henry Clay had long since been endorsed by the Kentucky legislature, and Andrew Jackson by Tennessee, and then, in March, by politicians in Pennsylvania as well; there were now at least four men running for president. John Calhoun grudgingly conceded that he didn't have enough support to compete, and settled instead on campaigning for vice president. "Mr. Calhoun has removed to his house on the hills behind Georgetown and will live I suspect quite retired the rest of the season," was the judgment of Margaret Bayard Smith. "He does not look well and feels very deeply the disappointment of his ambition." Margaret Smith had just acquired William Crawford as a neighbor, and quickly switched her support to him.

After almost a quarter of a century in the capital, Margaret was reflecting on the transient nature of city, something that's saddened many residents since. "Had the intimate acquaintances I formed when I first came been continued, twenty years would have ripened them into friendship." Many of her friends had moved, of course, and those in the diplomatic corps were regularly re-assigned, and "some have been estranged by differing and conflicting politics. For instance Mr. Calhoun's family. You have no idea . . . of the embittered and violent spirit engendered by the presidential question." Margaret Smith was able to remove herself to some degree from the battles around her, by pursuing her own career. That year she published her first novel, the two volume *A Winter in Washington* or *Memoirs of the Seymour Family*, the next year her popular *What Is Gentility* was published.

Louisa Adams was also able to briefly escape the "violent spirit" of the presidential election but only because she was terribly sick. She had been periodically plagued by erysipelas, a painful skin infection that caused high fevers and vomiting as well as ugly eruptions on her face. A bout of the infection that summer sent her to a spa in Pennsylvania to bathe in the mineral waters. John Quincy Adams professed he was "deeply affected at parting with her." But soon he was distracted, along with the rest of the nation. At the suggestion of President Monroe, and with the official invitation of the United States Congress, the great hero of the Revolution, the Marquis de Lafayette, arrived in New York in August, and the whole country was ready to put on an extravaganza of welcome. Excitement had started building as early as January when the congressional resolution inviting the French general was introduced. Dolley Madison's friend Phoebe Morris asked her, "What do you think of the probability of having the Marquis de Lafayette for a visitor. For surely he will go to Montpelier, should he visit the United States." And once the heralded patriot was on these shores presentations, plays, and pageants greeted him wherever he traveled as he stood and received curious Americans by the thousands.

To avoid scandal, Lafayette's young friend Fanny Wright did not travel with him, but she and her sister followed on a few days later, or arrived ahead of him and waited for him and his son and secretary. A couple of years earlier, Louisa Adams had heard that "the Marquis de Lafayette is about to marry the celebrated Miss Wright whose travels in this country have made such a flattering impression. Almost every great man seems to be doomed to commit some great folly; I suppose to put him on a level with the rest of the world." Lafayette, whose wife had died seventeen years earlier, hadn't committed that "folly," nor, much to the relief of his daughters and daughter-in-law, had he taken Fanny up on her suggestion that he adopt her to keep tongues from wagging. So when Fanny and Camilla Wright docked in New York a few weeks after the general, it was with the status of "friends."

From the over-the-top festivities in New York—at one ball decorated with fake clouds and a huge transparency of his home in France, Lafayette's picture was painted on everything in sight: fans, gloves, hats, handkerchiefs—the official entourage went on to Albany, then up to Boston for a visit with John Adams and more dramatic displays, back to New York, down to Philadelphia, where Independence Hall was restored in his honor, south to Baltimore and on to the nation's capital. "You will see, dear mother, that Lafayette is expected on the first; and nothing is heard but drumming, nothing seen but regiments from one end of the District to the other," Sarah Seaton excitedly reported in September. Her husband was on the arrangements committee and he had let her in on some of their "very magnificent plans . . . as yet secrets of state." One idea: "throw a treble arch over the central dome of the Capitol, containing three rows of colored lamps of primary colors, to represent a rainbow. It will require about six thousand lamps." It was the old dome of the Capitol, not the soaring capstone we see today, but still quite an undertaking.

After the great personage had come and gone, Sarah breathlessly provided a detailed account of the visit. Her job had been "to superintend the dress and decoration of twenty five young ladies representing the states and District, and procure appropriate wreaths, scarves, and Lafayette gloves and flags for the occasion." At the ball, "I was presented to Lafayette, once by mine host, once by my husband. On both occasions my hands were most affectionately pressed, though I had my suspicions that my second introduction was like unto the first in the Veteran's eyes, it being next to an impossibility that he should recognize all the ladies with whom he was compelled to shake hands, amounting to thousands during his triumphal tour."

Thomas Jefferson wanted his old friend to hurry on to his mountaintop. "You mention the return of Miss Wright to America, accompanied by her sister . . . herself and her companion will nowhere find a welcome more hearty than with Mrs. Randolph, and all the inhabitants of Monticello." That might be an inducement to Lafayette. Poor Martha Randolph would somehow have to put together a grand welcome, as she was used to doing. One Jefferson biographer unearthed a friend's query to Martha: "What was the largest number of persons for whom she had been called upon unexpectedly to prepare accommodations for the night, and she replied *fifty*!" And with no money. Jefferson's public service and profligate entertaining had left him broke. The Congress bought his library after the British burned the first Library of Congress, and that was a help but the family was struggling. Still, the visit of Lafayette was something special. Martha's son, Jefferson Randolph, recorded the meeting of the two revolutionaries: "As they approached each other, their uncertain gait quickened itself into a shuffling run, and exclaiming, 'Ah, Jefferson!' 'Ah, Lafayette!' they burst into tears as they fell into each other's arms." President James Monroe and former President James Madison were on hand for the official ceremonies at the University of Virginia, and then Madison wrote Dolley that the Frenchman was headed her way next.

"He will have with him besides his son & secretary the 2 councilors, and such of the Company of Orange meeting & conducting him as may choose to stop at Montpelier. The Miss Wrights are expected here tomorrow." He was having trouble learning "whether the Miss Wrights will precede or accompany or follow the General." When the visit was over Dolley didn't mention "the Miss Wrights" in a report to her brother-in-law: "We have lately had a visit from Gen. Lafayette & family of a few days—the former, you know, was an old friend of Mr. M——s I was charmed with his society—& never witnessed so much enthusiasm as his appearance occasioned here and at our court house, where hundreds of both sexes collected together, to hail & welcome him." Then Lafayette's entourage returned to Washington, where the city was reacting to the surprising results of the presidential election.

Throughout November the popular votes trickled in, ending with a Jackson victory, but Adams's support in the New England states meant the Electoral College outcome could be a different story. On December 1 when the electoral votes were tallied, no candidate held a majority. The results—Andrew Jackson 99, John Quincy Adams 84, William Crawford 41 and Henry Clay 37—meant the election would go to the House of Representatives, with Henry Clay dropping off as low man. When Lafayette passed back through the city, the candidates were campaigning furiously with the Congress, even as they socialized at the same events honoring Lafayette. "We are boarding at the same house as the nation's guest, Lafayette. I am delighted with him. All the attentions, all the parties he goes to never appear to have any effect on him." Rachel Jackson wrote to a friend in Nashville soon after her twenty-seven-day trip to Washington. Her husband, the winner in the popular vote for president and the leader in the electoral college, was equally excited to meet Lafayette whom he had seen "on the field of battle; the one a boy of twelve, the Marquis twenty three. He wears a wig and is a little inclined to corpulency." And Sarah Seaton swooned, "Last evening we had the high gratification of entertaining and welcoming Lafayette in our own house, being the only private individuals so honored as yet." More than 300 people shoved their way into the Seaton home, "The leader of the Marine Band came up in the morning and requested to play for us in the evening, which added much to the enjoyment . . . Mr. J.Q. Adams and family seemed to enjoy themselves as much as our other friends." The Seatons had battled with Adams over a report in the *Intelligencer*, but that didn't stop the families from inviting each other to their balls. "No individual could have had more enjoyment, or been treated with more attentive politeness by the master of the feast than I at Mr. Adams's ball," Sarah had written earlier.

On January 1, 1825, the Congress honored Lafayette at a banquet attended by all the candidates. Then, on the tenth anniversary of the Battle of New Orleans, one year after Louisa Adams's great triumph, Commanding General of the Army Jacob Brown and his wife invited in the warring camps. "The whole city was invited to celebrate the anniversary of Jackson's victory; and I wish it may not be the only victory at which he may have an opportunity of rejoicing, though Mr. Crawford's friends are still sanguine rather than despairing. Much depends on Mr. Clay, and he is scarcely to be depended on." Sarah went on to describe the ball at Calhoun's the week before where she was standing with Adams when Clay "passed in high glee" saying the dancers were in his way. "'O,' says J.Q. 'that is very unkind; you who get out of everybody else's way, you know.' This dry joke, so evidently alluding to his exclusion from the House of Representatives, was received as merrily as it was given, and they both 'laughed long and loud.'" Sarah joked that she had introduced one Jacksonite to Rachel Jackson at the ball, and he accused her of trying to change his mind. Poor Mrs. Jackson was not having any fun at all: "To tell you of this city, I would not do justice to the subject. The extravagance is in dressing and running to parties," she clucked to a friend in Tennessee, "Oh, my dear friend, how shall I get through this bustle. There are not less than from fifty to one hundred persons calling in a day."

As the time approached for the House to meet and vote on February 9, the calls became constant. "Mrs. Adams came to see me this morning," Sarah Seaton said with some amusement. "They are all very courteous just now; but should Mrs. A. be Presidentess . . . she perhaps will not forget that her husband was foiled in combat with us." John Quincy Adams's fight with the *Intelligencer* was some cause for worry if he won. "You do not know how acceptable the news from Washington is to us—a far off," Dolley Madison wrote to her niece Mary Cutts, "In two weeks more you will make a new president and go to the Coronation; in the mean time people will think freely and act under some restraint." Dolley knew that the uncertainty would cause people to behave rather than risk making enemies.

Margaret Bayard Smith had moved into the Crawfords' house in the city for the duration. William Crawford's health was still an issue, and "His friends in Congress are very desirous that he should give a Grand Ball and invite all Congress and all the citizens and strangers and think, seeing with their own eye, they might perhaps believe that he is no longer a sick man." A social occasion would fix everything! Mrs. Crawford had her doubts, and worried about the effect of "lights, noise, a crowd and the atmosphere of a crowded room might have." Susanna Crawford knew better the true state of her husband's health. But she sallied forth to carry the standard. At the theatre one night she was "ably supported" by the politicians in attendance. Margaret thought Crawford's friends would "adhere to him faithfully. Whether they will succeed in their endeavors is doubtful. Folks here generally consider Gen. J[ackson] as having a better chance."

Finally the day of the vote arrived, and Margaret Bayard Smith was privy to inside information as she had been back in 1800 when the House was deadlocked over the election of Thomas Jefferson versus Aaron Burr. Then she was a new bride, espousing her husband's Republican views in the face of her Federalist family; then the primitive Capitol just under construction served as a reminder that this was a newborn nation; now the Capitol represented the survival and success of a country, if not mature, at least secure. As with that election twenty five years before, a snowstorm was raging when the Congress gathered on February 9, 1825. First, the Senate, accompanied by General Lafayette, joined the House for the official count of the Electoral College vote; then the Senators and Lafayette filed out, leaving the House to do the work of electing the next president. The candidates' counts showed that no one had locked up the majority of states and the voting might go on for days, just as it had the only other time the presidency was decided by the House of Representatives. But after one ballot, much to everyone's surprise, John Quincy Adams was chosen. Henry Clay, the powerful and persuasive speaker of the house, had thrown his support to Adams, adding the states of Kentucky, Ohio, Missouri, and probably Louisiana to the six New England states in Adams's corner. Then Clay worked over wavering congressmen from states where the members were split—some for one candidate, some for another. As a result of Clay's strong-arming, John Quincy Adams won on the first ballot in the House of Representatives. When Adams then appointed Henry Clay as his secretary of state, the supporters of Andrew Jackson, the winner of the popular vote and the plurality in the Electoral College, charged Adams and Clay with having negotiated a "corrupt bargain." No one knows whether there was, in fact, a quid pro quo, but the suspicion haunted the rest of Henry Clay's political life.

William Crawford's hopes had rested on a deadlock—no majority for either Adams or Jackson, with supporters of each turning to him as the compromise. Crawford's supporter Margaret Smith felt betrayed by the first ballot outcome: "promises had been pledged,— that three states that voted for [Adams] first would come over to Mr. C. on the second—and that on each succeeding ballot, his course would have gained strength . . . it was likewise supposed that when

Jackson's friends lost hope of success, they would prefer C. to A."
Margaret admitted that she never thought the plan would work, but
still, since she was living with the Crawfords, she was outraged that
members had succumbed to pressure and voted for Adams. The vote
of one member was particularly crucial. Stephen Van Rensselaer,
who was pledged to Crawford, voted for Adams, delivering the split
New York delegation to the secretary of state. Spectators in the gallery, Fanny Wright among them, could watch as various Crawford
supporters sidled up to Van Rensselaer and urged him to hold firm.
"Some one said," Margaret Smith reported, "his wife had written to
him on the subject and that she ruled him with an iron rod." When
Margaret countered that she knew Mrs. Van Rensselaer to be "a very
mild woman," she was told, "'you are mistaken, madam . . . he refers
to her on all occasions.'"

As disappointed as she was, Mrs. Smith was grateful that the
whole thing had gone off without a hitch. "In one ward of the city . . .
an effigy of Mr. Adams had been prepared and had it not been a
stormy day, his opponents among the lower citizens would have
burnt it. This would have excited his friends, (particularly the Negroes, who when they heard of his election were the only persons
who expressed their joy by Hurrahs) some riot might have taken
place." She was more than relieved, Margaret Bayard Smith was
proud: "How admirable are our institutions. . . . In Washington on
the 9th of February not a sign of military power was visible and even
the civil magistrates had nothing to do." That peaceful transfer of
power we take so for granted, was always a wondrous thing.

That night, President and Mrs. Monroe threw open the doors of
their last drawing room. The First Lady wore "superb black velvet,
neck and arms bare and beautifully formed, her hair in puffs and
dressed high on the head, and ornamented with white ostrich plumes;
round her neck an elegant pearl necklace." Elizabeth Kortright Monroe would go out in style. Both John Quincy Adams and Andrew
Jackson were there, Margaret Bayard Smith was not, but she received
a full report: "'Mr. Adams was not more attended to than usual,

scarcely as much so as General Jackson.' 'I am pleased to hear that,' said I, 'it is honorable to human nature.' 'But it was not very honorable to see *Clay*, walking about with exultation and a smiling face, with a fashionable *belle* hanging on each arm,—the villain! He looked as proud and happy as if he had done a noble action by selling himself to Adams and securing his election.'" It was going to be a rough four years for Adams—the public thought the election had been stolen from them; the politicians would never forgive Henry Clay. Margaret Bayard Smith resolved to "resume my books and pen without any wandering thoughts."

"The city is thronged with strangers, and *Yankees* swarm like the locusts of Egypt in our houses, our beds, and our kneading-troughs!" Sarah Seaton exclaimed in late February. It was the end of the "Virginia Dynasty," for the first time since John Adams left office, the second time in American history, a man who was not from Virginia would be president. Now John Quincy and Louisa Adams were preparing for the inauguration: "Their last drawing room for the season was on Monday last, which we all attended, immediately after ascertaining our triumphant election . . . The great Hal, as the Kentuckians style Mr. Clay, is not our friend and probably never will be, but his friends are peculiarly ours, so that we shall have a smooth path for the next four years, as Mr. Adams is evidently in a conciliatory mood. . . . They have tried, and found it rather inconvenient to do without the *Intelligencer*, which will probably hold the same place in relation to the administration as heretofore." The politicians might not like it, but they knew they needed the newspapers, they couldn't ignore the press.

When Inauguration Day, March 4, 1825, dawned, Louisa Adams, who had done so much to contribute to her husband's success, was sick in bed. She wasn't there when John Quincy Adams stood in the House of Representatives, the Chamber where he was elected, and took the oath of office from Chief Justice John Marshall. She didn't hear the new president declare his political creed that "the will of the people is the source and the happiness of the people the end of all legitimate government upon earth." The new First Lady roused herself to host a large reception that afternoon, as always steadfast to the role she played so well. Had she not called and charmed and conspired, John Quincy Adams might never have been elected president.

But this moment in history—this moment when the era of the founding generation ended would have happened under any circumstances. None of John Quincy Adams's opponents had been Revolutionary War leaders like Washington and Monroe; writers of the Declaration of Independence like Jefferson and Adams; or of the Constitution like Washington and Madison. None of them had been grown men for the events that gave birth to the United States of America. They had witnessed them as children; they knew the stories of their valiant mothers, their courageous fathers. It would now be up to a new generation to carry the ideals of the founding documents on into the next centuries. And it would take the women to make that happen—to push and prod the country toward a more perfect union, to create the institutions that would shape our nation. As they did so, they would build on the foundation left by the women who had come before them, the founding mothers who knew they would some day entrust the American experiment to their children. As Abigail Adams wrote when she left public office: "I leave to time the unfolding of a drama. I leave to posterity to reflect upon the times past; and I leave them characters to contemplate."

RECIPES

AMERICAN COOKERY

by Amelia Simmons

INDIAN SLAPJACK

One quart of milk, 1 pint of Indian meal, 4 eggs, 4 spoons of flour, little salt, beat together, baked on gridles, or fry in a dry pan, or baked in a pan which has been rub'd with suet, lard or butter.

COOKIES

One pound sugar boiled slowly in half pint water, seum well and cool, add two tea spoons pearl ash dissolved in milk, then two and a half pounds flour, rub in 4 ounces butter, and two large spoons of finely powdered coriander seed, wet with above; make roles half an inch thick and cut to the shape you please; bake fifteen or twenty minutes in a slack oven—good three weeks.

HOUSEKEEPING BOOK

by Nelly Custis Lewis

FOR WORMS. MRS G WN.

1 oz seeds of wormseed,
Half an oz rhubarb,
1 tablespoon small cloves of garlic

Put the ingredients into a pint bottle. Fill it with best wine or whiskey, let it stand a few days, shaking it well, then strain it. For a child of 5 years a small teaspoonful, less for younger children.

For Lumps or Swelling in the Breast

For lumps, or Swelling in the breast, nothing is so good as the white of raw eggs, spread on linen, and applied wet to the place. It must be frequently moistened in the egg.

Potato Fritters

Beat the yolks of 6 eggs very light, add to them a quart of milk, boil as many Irish potatoes as will make a quart, skin & beat them very fine, put them into the milk & eggs, & thicken with flour, the thickness of common fritter batter, beat all 'till very light. Fry in lard as common fritters.

Baked Wine Custards

The yolks of 9 eggs, beat them a little light, add half a pint of wine, sweeten'd to your taste, add a little beaten mace or cinnamon, put it into cups & grate nutmeg over it, & bake it. Put water in the oven before you put your cups in.

To Preserve Pears

To ev'ry lb. of Pears, 1 lb. of sugar beaten & sifted, put your sugar into your preserving pan, & add as much water as will be sufficient to cover your parts, let it boil, then put in your pears, & stew them gently until they are done, & of a pretty pink color, then take out your fruit & let the syrup boil until it is as thick as you like, then pour it over the fruit & let it stand until cold.

RECIPES

OYSTER SOUP

Take 2 quarts of Oysters, drain them in a cullender, take the liquor, put it in a stew pan with a few slips of bacon, when the Bacon is done, put in the Oysters, a bunch of sweet herbs, a pint of milk, or half a pint of cream, a spoonful of butter rolled in flour, season to your taste.

CABBAGE PUDDING

Take a bit of stale bread & grate it, 2 or 3 slices of Bacon, also of veal of any cold meat, chop it fine, sweet herbs sliced fine, a large onion, yolks of 3 eggs, pepper & salt, of boiled cabbage a large bit chopped up with it. Beat all well together, take a large Cabbage, cut a hole at the end, where the stalk was, get out all the inside, then put in the above ingredients, tie up the cabbage in a napkin, let it boil for three hours.

DOLLEY MADISON RECIPES

From the *President's Cookbook, Practical Recipes from George Washington to the Present* by Poppy Cannon & Patricia Brooks, Funk & Wagnalls, 1968.

Interesting little fact: During Madison's Presidency, the White House food bills were high, sometimes as much as $50.00/day. That $50.00 seems even higher when one learns that a whole turkey cost as little as $.75.

DOLLEY MADISON'S LAYER CAKE

Apparently, Lucia B. Cutts, niece of Dolley, wrote that her aunt "delighted in company and her table fairly groaned with the abundance of dishes." This recipe for layer cake was a Madison specialty, frequently served to guests.

8 Egg Whites
Butter
Sugar
Milk
Cornstarch
Flour
Vanilla

Beat the whites of 8 eggs until stiff and in peaks. Set aside. Cream
1 cup butter with 2½ cups sugar. Add 1 cup milk slowly, mixing well.
Add ¾ cup cornstarch and 3 cups sifted flour to the butter—egg
mixture. Mix well and add 2½ teaspoons vanilla. Fold in the egg
whites carefully. Bake in 4 layer pans, well greased. Bake in a
medium 350 degree oven for 30 to 35 mins. Or until the cake springs
back when touched lightly. Cool on racks and frost with Dolley's
Caramel.

CAST OF CHARACTERS

FIRST LADIES

Martha Dandridge Custis Washington
Abigail Smith Adams
Dorothea (Dolley) Payne Todd Madison
Elizabeth Kortright Monroe
Louisa Catherine Johnson Adams

REFORMERS, EDUCATORS, AND EXPLORERS

Sophia Browning Bell
Joanna Bethune
Mary Billings
Rose Philippine Duchesne
Catherine (Katy) Ferguson
Isabella Graham
Rebecca Gratz
Elizabeth (Eliza) Schuyler Hamilton
Dorothea (Dolley) Payne Todd Madison
Lucretia Coffin Mott
Sacagawea
Elizabeth Bayley Seton
Alethia Browning Tanner
Emma Hart Willard
Ursuline Nuns of New Orleans
Daughters of Africa of Philadelphia

WRITERS AND TALKERS

Hannah Adams
Hannah Mather Crocker
Hannah Foster
Judith Sargent Murray
Lucy Terry Prince
Margaret Bayard Smith
Susanna Rowson
Mercy Otis Warren

PRESIDENTS

George Washington—husband of Martha Dandridge Custis
Washington, grandfather of Elizabeth (Eliza) Parke Custis
Law, Martha Parke Custis Peters, and Eleanor (Nelly) Parke
Custis Lewis

John Adams—husband of Abigail Smith Adams, father of Abigail
Adams Smith, father-in-law of Louisa Catherine Johnson
Adams

Thomas Jefferson—husband of Martha Wayles Skelton Jefferson,
father of Martha Jefferson Randolph and Maria Jefferson
Eppes, grandfather of Ellen Wayles Randolph Coolidge,
owner and probably lover of Sally Hemings

James Madison—husband of Dorothea (Dolley) Payne Todd
Madison, brother-in-law of Anna Payne Cutts and Lucy Payne
Washington Todd

James Monroe—husband of Elizabeth Kortright Monroe, father
of Elizabeth (Eliza) Monroe Hay and Maria Hester Monroe
Gouverneur

John Quincy Adams—husband of Louisa Catherine Johnson
Adams, son of Abigail Smith Adams, brother of Abigail
Adams Smith, brother-in-law of Catherine Johnson Smith

Andrew Jackson—husband of Rachel Donelson Jackson

SOLDIERS AND STATESMEN

Joseph Alston—husband of Theodosia Burr Alston

Joel Barlow—husband of Ruth Baldwin Barlow

James Bayard—cousin of Margaret Bayard Smith

Napoleon Bonaparte—brother-in-law of Elizabeth (Betsy) Patterson Bonaparte

Aaron Burr—father of Theodosia Burr Alston

John Calhoun—husband of Floride Bonneau Colhoun Calhoun

William Charles Cole Claiborne—husband of Elizabeth Lewis Claiborne, Clarissa Duralde Claiborne, and Suzette Bosque Claiborne

William Crawford—husband of Susanna Gerardine Crawford

Benjamin Crowninshield—husband of Mary Boardman Crowninshield

Richard Cutts—husband of Anna Payne Cutts, brother-in-law of Dorothea (Dolley) Payne Todd Madison

Stephen Decatur—husband of Susan Wheeler Decatur

John Eppes—husband of Maria Jefferson Eppes

Albert Gallatin—husband of Hannah Nicholson Gallatin

Alexander Hamilton—husband of Elizabeth (Eliza) Schuyler Hamilton

Benjamin Henry Latrobe—husband of Mary Elizabeth Hazlehurst Latrobe

Edward Livingston—husband of Louise D'Avezac Livingston, father of Cora Livingston Barton

William Lowndes—husband of Elizabeth Pinckney Lowndes

Marquis de Lafayette—husband of Adrienne de Noailles de Lafayette

Marquis de Yrujo—husband of Sally McKean Yrujo

John Marshall—husband of Mary Amber (Polly) Marshall

Anthony Merry—husband of Elizabeth Death Merry

Harrison Gray Otis—husband of Sally Foster Otis

Charles Cotesworth Pinckney—husband of Mary Stead Pinckney, uncle of Elizabeth Pinckney Lowndes

Thomas Pinckney—father of Elizabeth Pinckney Lowndes,
    brother-in-law of Mary Stead Pinckney
John Randolph—cousin of Martha Jefferson Randolph and Maria
    Jefferson Eppes

PLAYERS IN THE NEW CAPITAL

George Calvert—husband of Rosalie Stier Calvert
William Seaton—husband of Sarah Gales Seaton
William Thornton—husband of Anna Maria Brodeau Thornton
Samuel Harrison Smith—husband of Margaret Bayard Smith
Thomas Law—husband of Elizabeth (Eliza) Parke Custis Law
Thomas Peters—husband of Martha Parke Custis Peters

NOTES

INTRODUCTION

xv "He well remembers": John Jacob Astor to Dolley Payne Madison, November 29, 1812, Dolley Madison Digital Edition.

xv "Lowndes cannot escape": in Ravenal, Harriott Rutledge, *Life and Times of William Lowndes of South Carolina, 1782–1822,* Houghton, Mifflin and Company, Boston & New York, 1901, p. 61.

xvii On his way to Ghent: John Quincy Adams to Louisa Catherine Adams, Courtesy Massachusetts Historical Society.

xvii "There is so much": John Quincy Adams to Louisa Catherine Adams, May 9, 1814, Adams Papers courtesy Massachusetts Historical Society.

xviii "I have the extreme": John Marshall to Mary Ambler Marshall, January 2, 1803, *My Dearest Polly, Letters of Chief Justice Marshall to His Wife, with their Background, Political and Domestic, 1779–1831,* Frances Norton Mason, Garrett & Massie, Incorporated, Richmond, Virginia, p. 153.

xviii "Yet the hope": Ravenal, p. 138.

xviii "facts or opinions": Ibid.

xviii "had a distressing": Dolley Payne Madison to Hannah Gallatin, July 28, 1814, edited by David B. Mattern and Holly C. Shulman, *The Selected Letters of Dolley Payne Madison,* University of Virginia Press, Charlottesville, 2003. p. 189.

xix "By her deportment": Historical Society of Pennsylvania, quoted in Arneiff, p. 110.

xx "There cannot be": Abigail Adams to Louisa Catherine Adams, January 19, 1806, in Levin. Phyllis Lee, *Abigail Adams, A Biography*, Thomas Dunne Books, New York, 2001. p. 411.

1790 Census numbers from Bureau of the Census, *A Century of Population Growth,* U.S. Government Printing Office, Washington, D.C., 1909, pp. 96–110, in Berkin, Carol, and Mary Beth Norton, *Women of America, A History,* Houghton Mifflin Company, Boston, 1979, 28, 2000. Census numbers from U.S. Census Bureau, telephonic and electronic inquiries to Robert Bernstein, Public Information Office.

And that first accounting of the nation revealed that almost one-quarter of the population—twenty-four percent—was held in bondage: *Recollections of the Early Republic,* ed. Joyce Appleby, Northeastern University Press, Boston, 1997, p. xi.

xxii "To Congress, lo!": "The Freedom of Election. A New Song, *Centinel of Freedom,* Newark, N.J., October 18, 1797, in Rosemary Zagarri, "The Rights of Man and Woman in Post-Revolutionary America," *The William and Mary Quarterly,* 3rd ser., vol. 55, no. 2, April 1998, p. 220.

xxii Almost all Americans—ninety percent—worked on farms in 1790: Appleby, ed. *Recollections of the Early Republic,* p. xviii.

CHAPTER ONE

2   **"A Philadelphia Woman"**: Drinker, Elizabeth, December 27, 1899, *The Diary of Elizabeth Drinker,* ed. Elaine Forman Crane, Boston, 1991, vol. II, pp. 1250-5, quoted in Simon P. Newman, *Parades and the Politics of the Street,* Philadelphia, 1997, p. 69.

2   **"a time for intrigue"**: Abigail Adams to William Smith, December 25, 1799., Smith-Townsend papers, courtesy of the Massachussetts Historical Society.

2   **"The calamitous tidings"**: Judith Sargent Murray to Esther Sargent Ellery, December 23, 1799, Smith Bonnie Hurd, *The Letters I Left Behind, Judith Sargent Murray Papers, Letter Book 10,* Judith Sargent Murray Society, Salem, MA, 2005, p. 377.

2   **"The bells commenced"**: Ibid.

3   **"It is difficult"**: Henrietta Liston to James Jackson, December 19, 1799, *Women's Letters, America from the Revolutionary War to the Present,* edited by USA Grunwald and Stephen J. Adler, The Dial Press, New York, 2005, p. 89.

3   **"He stood the barrier"**: Ibid

3   **"The city, indeed"**: Isabella Graham to Dr. Marshall, March 3, 1800, *The Power of Faith, Exemplified in the Life and Writings of the Late Mrs. Isabella Graham,* Joanna Bethune, ed., New York, 1843, reprinted by IndyPublish.com, Boston, p. 95.

3   **"And waft his spirit"**: *Funeral Music, for 22d February, 1800,* published according to Act of Congress, provided by the Mount Vernon Ladies' Association.

4   **"Before my eyes"**: Harrison Gray Otis to Sally Foster Otis, 1765–1848, Houghton Mifflin Company, Boston, 1969, December 26, 1799, in Morison, Samuel Eliot, *Harrison Gray Otis, The Urbane Federalist,* p. 141.

4   **"Orations, prayers"**: John Adams to Thomas Jefferson, September 3, 1816, Cappon, Lester J. *The Adams-Jefferson Letters, The Complete Correspondence Between Thomas Jefferson and Abigail and John Adams,* The University of North Carolina Press, Chapel Hill, 1959, p. 488.

4   **"cast into the background"**: Ibid., p. 488.

4   **"All business in Congress"**: Abigail Adams to William Smith, December 25, 1799, Smith-Townsend Papers.

4   **She announced in the newspapers that women visitors would not be welcome at her receptions unless they donned mourning clothes:** *Gazette of the United States,* December 20, 1799, *Parades,* p. 69.

4   **"the president by"**: *The Centinel of Liberty, and George-Town and Washington Advertiser,* December 31, 1799, American Antiquarian Society, 2004, vol. IV, iss. 63, p. 3.

5   **"defended our mothers"**: A Society of Females to Martha Washington, February, 14, 1800, *Worthy Partner, The Papers of Martha Washington,* compiled by Joseph E. Fields, Greenwood Press, Westport, CT., 1994, p. 351.

5   **(Descriptions of Martha Washington in the time after GW's death come from many sources, primarily, Patricia Brady, *Martha Washington, An American Life,* Viking, NY, 2005, and Helen Bryan, *Martha Washington, First Lady of Liberty,* John Wiley & Sons, Inc., NY, 2002).**

5   **"had not been able"**: Abigail Adams to Mary Cranch, January 7, 1800 in *New Letters of Abigail Adams, 1788–1801,* edited by Stewart Mitchell, Houghton Mifflin Company, Boston, 1947, p. 227.

5   **"assent to the"**: John Adams to Martha Washington, December 27, 1799, *Worthy Partner,* p. 328.

5   **"never to oppose"**: Martha Washington to John Adams, December 31, 1799, ibid. p. 332.

5   **"I cannot say"**: Ibid.

5 **"pass a secret vote"**: Entry for January 6, 1800, *Diary of Mrs. William Thornton, 1800–1863,* Columbia Historical Society, 1907, p. 92.

6 **"To no one"**: Abigail Adams to Mary Cranch, January 28, 1800, *New Letters,* p. 228–29.

6 **"at no time"**: Ibid.

7 **"my mother with her"**: John Quincy Adams to Joseph Sturuf, March 1846, *The Adams Papers*: Adams Family Correspondence, 1963, Butterfield, L. H. Harvard University Press, Atheneun, New York, 1965, vol. 1, p. 223n.

9 **"My friendship for him"**: Abigail Adams to John Adams, January 15, 1797 (electronic edition), *Adams Family Papers: An Electronic Archive,* Massachusetts Historical Society. http://www.masshist.org/digitaladams/.

9 **"subtle intriguer"**: Abigail Adams to John Adams, December 31, 1796, ibid.

9 **"look at every word"**: Abigail Adams to John Adams, February 20, 1796, ibid.

9 **"A woman *can*"**: John Adams to Abigail Adams, March 1, 1796, ibid.

9 **"I never wanted"**: John Adams to Abigail Adams, March 22, 1797, ibid.

9 **"I must entreat"**: John Adams to Abigail Adams, March 27, 1797, ibid.

9 **"I pray you"**: John Adams to Abigail Adams, April 1, 1797, ibid.

9 **"I will not live"**: John Adams to Abigail Adams, April 3, 1797, ibid.

9 **"You, I must"**: Ibid.

9 **"The times are critical"**: John Adams to Abigail Adams, April 6, 1797, ibid.

9 **"We must resign"**: John Adams to Abigail Adams, April 11, 1797, ibid.

10 **"It seems to me"**: John Adams to Abigail Adams, April 24, 1797, ibid.

10 **"You and I are now"**: John Adams to Abigail Adams, May 4, 1797, ibid.

10 **"I hope the burden"**: John Adams to Abigail Adams, May 4, 1797, ibid.

10 **"that I may"**: Abigail Adams to Mary Cranch, April 30, 1797, *New Letters,* p. 88.

11 **"lovely babe"**: Ibid. p. 89.

11 **"the most valuable"**: *The Works of John Adams,* III, 530, in McCullough, David, *John Adams,* Simon & Schuster, New York, 2001, p. 530.

11 **"prove himself"**: Ibid.

11 **"Yesterday being Monday"**: Abigail Adams to Mary Cranch, May 5, 1797, *New Letters,* 1947, p. 90.

11 **"splendid misery"**: Ibid.

11 **"The ladies of"**: Abigail Adams to Mary Cranch, ibid. p. 91.

12 **"hawks eyes"**: Sally McKean to Dolley Payne Madison, August 3, 1797, in *Selected Letters,* p. 32.

12 **"set up for"**: Ibid.

12 **"for she is not"**: Ibid.

12 **"effectual measures of defense"**: *The Works of John Adams,* in McCullough, *John Adams,* p. 484.

12 **"Bache opened"**: Abigail Adams to Mary Cranch, May 24, 1797, *New in Letters,* p. 92.

13 **"tomorrow we are"**: Ibid. p. 91.

13 **"For the love I"**: Abigail Adams to John Quincy Adams, May 20, 1796, in Levin, p. 323.

13 **"perfectly natural"**: John Quincy Adams to Abigail Adams, February 8, 1797, quoted in Levin, p. 324.

13 **"the tastes and"**: Ibid.

13 **"goodness of heart"**: Ibid.

13 **"an amiable"**: Abigail Adams to Mary Cranch, October 31, 1797, *New in Letters,* p. 110.

13 **"negotiate a"**: Ibid.

14 **"These salaries are"**: Abigail Adams to Mary Cranch, June 8, 1797, *New in Letters,* p. 97.

14 **"The mischief of"**: Ibid.

14 **"an honest man"**: Abigail Adams to Mary Cranch, June 23, 1797, *New in Letters*, p. 99.

14 **"The task of"**: Ibid.

14 **"From every side"**: Abigail Adams to Mary Cranch, July 6, 1797, *New in Letters,* p. 101.

14 **"The threatened invasion"**: Abigail Adams to Mary Cranch, January 5, 1798, *New in Letters,* p. 123.

16 **"French and English"**: Mary Stead Pinckney to Margaret Izard Manigault, August 1, 1796, *The Correspondence of Mary Stead Pinckney Covering the Period of the French Mission, 1796–1798,* compiled by Elizabeth F. Mallin, unpublished manuscript, The South Carolina Library, Columbia, S.C. 1977, p. 20.

16 **"bid the future"**: Mary Stead Pinckney to Margaret Izard Manigault, September 16, 1796, ibid. p. 24.

16 **"a man of a"**: Mary Stead Pinckney to Margaret Izard Manigault, November 14, 1796, ibid. p. 29.

16 **"would be as cool"**: Mary Stead Pinckney to Margaret Izard Manigault, November 16, 1797, *Letter-book of Mary Stead Pinckney, November 14th, 1796 to August 29th, 1797,* The Grolier Club, NY, 1946, p. 12.

16 **"two ladies of"**: Ibid. p. 14.

16 **"still more immense"**: Ibid.

17 **"The successes"**: Mary Stead Pinckney to Alice DeLancey Izard, November 18, 1796, ibid., pp.19–20.

17 **"The Pope has"**: Ibid.

17 **"Corsica is evacuated"**: Ibid.

17 **"will not receive"**: Mary Stead Pinckney to Elizabeth Stead Izard, December 11, 1797, ibid. p. 23.

17 **"should unintentionally give"**: Ibid. p. 24.

17 **"our dress and"**: Ibid. p. 25.

17 **"strongly recommended"**: Ibid.

17 **"who have"**: Ibid. p. 26.

17 **"if chased"**: Ibid.

17 **"living in the"**: Ibid., p. 27.

17 **"leave Paris with"**: Ibid.

17 **"Very gay"**: Mary Stead Pinckney to Margaret Izard Manigault, December 13, 1796, ibid. p. 30.

18 **"amuse a stranger"**: Ibid. p. 33.

18 **"sometimes she"**: Ibid. p. 31.

18 **"almost continually in"**: Ibid. p. 32.

18 **"Mrs. Monroe . . . was"**: Ibid. p. 33.

18 **"I think it"**: Ibid. p. 34.

18 **"The French nation"**: Mary Stead Pinckney to Alice DeLancey Izard, December 18, 1796, ibid. p. 40.

18 **"I am extremely"**: Ibid. p. 41.

19 **"The French I believe"**: Mary Stead Pinckney to Margaret Izard Manigault, December 30, 1796, in *Correspondence*, p. 48.

19 **"venture to foretell"**: Mary Stead Pinckney to Elizabeth Stead Izard, January 6, 1797, *Letter-book,* p. 42.

19 **"I wish I had"**: Mary Stead Pinckney to Margaret Izard Manigault, January 11, 1797, ibid. pp. 50–1.

19 **"very pleasantly"**: Ibid. pp. 50–1.

19 **"with my family"**: Ibid. pp. 50–1.

19 **"the fatal month"**: Mary Stead Pinckney to Rebecca Izard, January 11, 1797, ibid. p. 53.

19 **"kind of a scare crow"**: Mary Stead Pinckney to Margaret Izard Manigault, January 21, 1797, précis, in *Correspondence*, p. 60.

19 **"first thought"**: Mary Stead Pinckney to Margaret Izard Manigault, February 13, 1797, ibid. pp. 62–3.

19 **"to see my"**: Ibid., pp. 62–3.

19 **"I thought if"**: Ibid. p. 63.

19 **"There does not seem"**: Mary Stead Pinckney to Margaret Izard, Manigault, March 16, 1797, *Letter-book*, p. 61.

19 **"Perhaps my mind"**: Ibid.

20 **"within 8 posts"**: Mary Stead Pinckney to Margaret Izard Manigault, April 21, 1797, in *Correspondence*, p. 71.

20 **"The splendor"**: Mary Stead Pinckney to Margaret Izard Manigault, May 23, 1797, ibid. p. 77.

20 **"though we had"**: Ibid. p. 80.

20 **"weary of being"**: Ibid. p. 84.

20 **"All of Europe"**: Mary Stead Pinckney to Margaret Izard Manigault, June 11, 1797, ibid. p. 86.

20 **"Two large dishes"**: Mary Stead Pinckney to Alice DeLancey Izard, June 22, 1797, *Letter-book,* p. 74.

21 **"I have heard"**: Mary Stead Pinckney to Margaret Izard Manigault, July 13, 1797, *Correspondence*, p. 87.

21 **"the westerly wind"**: Mary Stead Pinckney to Margaret Izard Manigault, August 11, 1797, ibid., p. 88.

21 **"our poor Rhode Island"**: Mary Stead Pinckney to Eliza Izard, August 23, 1797, *Letter-book,* pp. 77–8.

21 **"You must not"**: Ibid.

21 **"General Marshall"**: Mary Stead Pinckney to Margaret Izard Manigault, September 8, 1797, in *Correspondence,* p. 98.

22 **Lock of Hair Story:** (The John Marshall House, http://www.apva.org/marshall/justice/polly.php).

22 **"sound and safe"**: Mason, Frances Norton, *My Dearest Polly, Letters of Chief Justice John Marshall to His Wife, with Their Background, Political and Domestic, 1779–1831,* Garrett & Massie, Inc., Richmond, VA, 1961, p. 43.

22 **"regretted the adoption"**: Ibid.

22 **"regretted its rejection"**: Ibid.

22 **"Do tell me"**: John Marshall to Mary Ambler Marshall, June 24, 1797, ibid. pp. 90–1.

22 **"while I am gone"**: Ibid.

22 **"It is be happy"**: Ibid.

22 **"the delight of"**: John Marshall to Mary Ambler Marshall, July 10, 1797, ibid. pp. 96–7.

23 **"we contemplated"**: Ibid.

23 **"return until"**: John Marshall to Mary Ambler Marshall, September 9, 1797, ibid. p. 109.

23 **"General P. and"**: Mary Stead Pinckney to Margaret Izard Manigault, October 5, 1797, *Correspondence*, p. 102.

23 **"Was this love"**: Mary Stead Pinckney to Margaret Izard Manigault, October 22, 1797, ibid., p. 107.

23 **"there are but"**: Mary Stead Pinckney to Margaret Izard Manigault, November 5, 1797, ibid., p. 112.

24 **"How much time!"**: John Marshall to Mary Ambler Marshall, November 27, 1797, in Mason, p. 112.

24 **"Paris presents"**: Ibid.

24 **"I now have"**: Ibid.

24 **"No! No! Not a sixpence"**: Quoted in McCullough.

24 **"Millions for defense"**: Mary Stead Pinckney to Margaret Izard Manigault, January 19, 1798, in *Correspondence*, p. 114.

24 **"I love my country"**: Ibid.

24 **"We dread the future"**: Mary Stead Pinckney to Margaret Izard Manigault, February 5, 1798, ibid. p. 119.

24 **"deep melancholy from which"**: Quoted in Mason, *My Dearest Polly*, p. 113.

24 **"Our envoys"**: Abigail Adams to William Smith, February 22, 1798, in McCullough, p. 494.

24 **"In short they"**: Abigail Adams to Mary Cranch, January 20, 1798, *New Letters*, p. 125.

25 **"The president of"**: Abigail Adams to Mary Cranch, February 15, 1798, ibid. p. 133.

25 **"But the propriety"**: Ibid.

25 **"they now have"**: Abigail Adams to Mary Cranch, February 28, 1798, ibid. p. 137.

25 **"The difficulties of"**: Mary Stead Pinckney to Margaret Izard Manigault, March 9, 1798, *Correspondence*, p. 122.

25 **"I fear"**: Abigail Adams to Mary Cranch, February 28, 1798, *New Letters*, p. 140.

25 **"Ministers can never"**: Abigail Adams to Mary Cranch, March 20, 1798, ibid. p. 146.

26 **"to calumniate the"**: Abigail Adams to Mary Cranch, ibid. p. 147.

26 **"struck dumb"**: Abigail Adams to Mary Cranch, April 4, 1798, ibid. p. 152.

26 **"The common people"**: Abigail Adams to Mary Cranch, April 13, 1798, ibid. p. 156.

26 **The lyrics were far from subtle**: *Immortal patriots rise once more/Defend your rights—defend your shore* (in Waldstreicher, David, *In the Midst of Perpetual Fetes, The Making of American Nationalism, 1776–1820*, UNC Press, Chapel Hill, 1997, p. 319).

26 **"Wherever I passed"**: Abigail Adams to Mary Cranch, April 28, 1798, ibid. p. 167.

26 **"in short we"**: Ibid.

27 **"I feel ministers"**: Waldstreicher, p. 150.

27 **"Politics and party"**: Thomas Jefferson to Martha Jefferson Randolph, May 17, 1798, *The Family Letters of Thomas Jefferson*, University of Missouri Press, Columbia, MO, 1966, p. 162.

27 **"He has been"**: Mary Stead Pinckney to Margaret Izard Manigault, April 15, 1798, *Correspondence*, p. 123.

27 **"If he is not"**: Ibid.

27 **"You may easily"**: Abigail Adams to Mary Cranch, June 13, 1798, *New Letters*, p. 192.

27 **"an immense concourse of citizens"**: Mason, p. 118.

27 **"I believe they"**: Abigail Adams to Mary Cranch, June 19, 1798, *New Letters*, p. 194.

27 **"France can pour"**: Abigail Adams to William Shaw, June 2, 1798, in Levin, p. 344.

27 **"her depravity of"**: Ibid.

28 **"Congress would"**: Abigail Adams to Mary Cranch, July 17, 1798, *New Letters*, p. 207.

28 **"Mrs. President"**: Anthony, Carl Sferrazza, *First Ladies, The Saga of the Presidents' Wives and Their Power, 1789–1961*, William Morrow, New York, 1990, p. 63.

28 **"My tears"**: Mary Stead Pinckney to Margaret Izard Manigault, October 15, 1798, *Correspondence*, p. 128.

28 **"it will not be"**: Ibid.

28 **"You should know":** Thomas Jefferson to Martha Jefferson Randolph, May 17, 1798, *Family Letters,* p. 162.

28 **"I am becoming":** Eleanor Parke Custis to Elizabeth Bordley, May 14, 1798, *George Washington's Beautiful Nelly, The Letters of Eleanor Parke Custis Lewis to Elizabeh Bordley Gibson, 1794–1851,* University of South Carolina Press, 1991, p. 52.

28 **Women like Nelly were expected to show up at patriotic events decked out in their party colors to encourage the men to rally round the Federalist flag:** David Waldstreicher, "Federalism, The Styles of Politics, and the Politics of Style," in *Federalists Reconsidered,* University of Virginia Press, Charlottesville, 1998, p. 114.

29 **At elaborate ceremonies throughout the summer of 1798, as men formed militias to protect the homeland, female Patriots presented flags emblazoned with the company insignia, often embroidered by one of the women:** Branson, Susan, *These Fiery Frenchified Dames,* University of Pennsylvania Press, 2001, pp. 83–4.

29 **"Our love can":** *Federalists Reconsidered,* p. 114.

29 **"bearded or":** *Porcupine's Gazette,* November 3, 1798, in Branson, p. 97.

29 **"Even they are":** "Adams and Liberty": *Country Porcupine,* October 23–24, 1798, Branson, p. 84.

29 **"alien enemies":** The Alien Enemies Act, July 6, 1798, ibid. 1:577, in Levin, p. 350.

29 **"shall write":** The Sedition Act, July 14, 1798, ibid. 1:596–7, in Levin, p. 350.

30 **"will provoke":** Abigail Adams to Mary Cranch, April 21, 1798, *New Letters,* p. 159.

30 **"nothing will":** Abigail Adams to Mary Cranch, April 26, 1798, ibid. p. 165.

30 **"I wish the laws":** Abigail Adams to Mary Cranch, May 26, 1798, ibid. p. 179.

30 **"dilly dallying":** Abigail Adams to Mary Cranch, June 19, 1798, ibid. p. 193, in Lynne, *A Life of Abigail Adams, Dearest Friend,* Simon & Schuster, New York, 1981.

30 **"were shaved":** Abigail Adams to John Quincy Adams, December 2, 1798, Withey, p. 257.

30 **"weak as they are":** Ibid.

30 **By July 1798, Abigail had been preparing a surprise for her husband for months. She decided to build a major addition to the house in Quincy without telling him! She cooked up the scheme with her cousin Cotton Tufts, who was overseeing the construction. He would enclose his updates and bills in Mary Cranch's letters, because when Abigail had found John opening a missive from her sister, she testily made him promise not to do it again:** Abigail Adams to Mary Cranch, March 14, 1798, *New Letters,* p. 145.

30 **"without Mr. Adams":** Abigail Adams to Mary Cranch, April 22, 1798, ibid. p. 160.

31 **"master of the":** Abigail Adams to Mary Cranch, July 3, 1798, ibid. p. 199.

31 **"The President":** Ibid.

31 **"Her destiny":** John Adams to George Washington, October 9, 1798, in Levin, p. 355.

31 **When the First Couple learned that fifty children had been left without parents, they anonymously sent five hundred dollars for the orphans' care:** Bober, Natalie S., *Abigail Adams, Witness to a Revolution,* Aladdin Paperbacks, NY, 1995, p. 190.

31 **"If I had":** John Adams to Abigail Adams, November 12, 1798, The Massachusetts Historical Society electronic edition.

31 **"The House of Representatives":** John Adams to Abigail Adams, December 14, 1798, ibid.

31 **"the dangerous Vice":** Ibid.

31 **"The republican":** Thomas Jefferson to Martha Jefferson Randolph, December 27, 1798, in Betts, p. 169.

32 **"I want"**: Abigail Adams to John Adams, December 15, 1798, ibid.

32 **"the two strongest"**: Abigail Adams to John Adams, December 21, 1798, ibid.

32 **"With my family"**: John Adams to Abigail Adams, December 17, 1798, ibid.

32 **"You have the"**: Abigail Adams to John Adams, December 28, 1798, ibid.

32 **"talkative wife"**: Abigail Adams to John Adams, December 23, 1798, ibid.

33 **"I have not"**: Abigail Adams to John Adams, January 13, 1799, ibid.

33 **"I would not"**: Ibid.

33 **"You used to"**: Abigail Adams to John Adams, January 18, 1799, ibid.

33 **"I shall get more"**: Ibid.

33 **"entitled to"**: Abigail Adams to William Shaw, December 23, 1799, in Levin, p. 363.

33 **"Whoever questions"**: Abigail Adams to John Adams, January 1, 1799, Massachusetts Historical Society electronic edition.

34 **"though I thought"**: Ibid.

34 **"I wish some"**: John Adams to Abigail Adams, February 4, 1899, ibid.

34 **"Oh how they"**: John Adams to Abigail Adams, February 25, 1899, ibid.

34 **"That ought to"**: Ibid.

34 **"This was pretty saucy"**: Abigail Adams to John Adams, February 27–28, 1899, ibid.

34 **"pacific"**: Ibid.

34 **"Pray am I?"**: Ibid.

35 **"I have not any"**: Abigail Adams to John Adams, March 3, 1899, ibid.

35 **"which has agitated"**: Abigail Adams to William Shaw, March 9, 1799, in Levin, p. 371.

35 **"Are there any"**: Ibid.

35 **"to have the public"**: Abigail Adams to John Adams, March 9, 1899, ibid.

35 **"I never pretended"**: Ibid.

35 **Abigail took to hiding state papers from him, for fear that he would act impetuously:** Ferling, John, *Adams vs. Jefferson,* Oxford University Press, NY, 2004, p. 122.

36 **"rake, buck, blood and beast"**: John Adams to Abigail Adams, October 12, 1799, Massachusetts Historical Society electronic edition.

36 **"I renounce him"**: John Adams to Abigail Adams, October 12, 1799, Massachusetts Historical Society electronic edition.

36 **"To go from"**: Ibid.

36 **"An election is"**: John Adams to Abigail Adams, October 25, 1799, ibid.

36 **"the next winter"**: Ibid.

36 **"adjusting for some late importations"**: Abigail Adams to Mary Cranch, November 15, 1799, *New Letters,* p. 214.

36 **"I expect it"**: Abigail Adams to Mary Cranch, November 26, 1799, ibid., p. 217.

37 **"but it would"**: Abigail Adams to Mary Cranch, December 4, 1799, ibid., p. 218.

37 **"full and unqualified"**: Abigail Adams to Mary Cranch, December 11, 1799, ibid., p. 221.

37 **"Mrs. Bingham is"**: John Marshall to Mary Ambler Marshall, July 14, 1797, in Mason, p. 100.

37 **"was everyday walking with her mother"**: Harrison Gray Otis to Sally F. Otis, January 18, 1800, in Morison, p. 136.

37 **"I have been regaled"**: Ibid.

38 **"She has all"**: Abigail Adams to Mary Cranch, November 15, 1799, *New Letters,* p. 214.

38 **"leaders of the fashion"**: Abigail Adams to Mary Cranch, March 5, 1800, ibid. p. 242.

38 **"or the modest woman"**: Ibid.

38 **"nursing mothers"**: Ibid.

38 **"this is much more"**: Abigail Adams to Mary Cranch, December 4, 1799, ibid. p. 218.

38 **"Our Washington is no more!"**: Mason, p. 136.

38 **"all in mourning"**: Abigail Adams to Mary Cranch, December 30, 1799, ibid. p. 225.

38 **"Their caps were"**: Ibid.

38 **"they intended shining"**: Abigail Adams to Mary Cranch, December 30, 1799, ibid. p. 225.

38 **"Congress Ladies"**: Abigail Adams to Mary Cranch, January 30, 1800, ibid. p. 231.

38 **"they do not"**: Ibid.

38 **"I have changed"**: Thomas Jefferson to Martha Jefferson Randolph, February 11, 1800, in Betts, p. 183.

38 **"abandoning the rich"**: Ibid.

39 **"frequent popular elections"**: Abigail Adams to Mary Cranch, March 5, 1800, *New Letters*, p. 237.

39 **"corrupt and destroy"**: Ibid.

39 **"A whole year we shall"**: Ibid. p. 252.

39 **"between Adams"**: Callendar, James, *The Prospect Before Us,* in Levin, p. 380.

39 **"It is like"**: Abigail Adams to Mary Cranch, February 27, 1800, *New Letters,* p. 234.

39 **"The houses which are"**: Ibid.

40 **"None in the world"**: Abigail Adams to Mary Cranch, April 26, 1800, ibid. p. 247.

40 **"More pleasure"**: Ibid.

40 **"I acted"**: Abigail Adams to John Adams, May 22, 1800, Massachusetts Historical Society electronic edition.

40 **"admired, and regretted, etc."**: Ibid.

40 **"The establishment"**: John Adams to Abigail Adams, June 13, 1800, ibid.

40 **"The President intends"**: *Diary of Mrs. William Thornton,* June 3–5, 1800, Columbia Historical Society of Washington, D.C., pp. 151–52.

41 **"You as a widow"**: John Marshall to Martha Jefferson Randolph, August 20, 1800, in Mason, p. 143.

41 **"One of the most"**: Brodie, Fawn, *Thomas Jefferson, An Intimate History,* W.W. Norton & Co., Inc., NY, 1974, p. 325.

41 **"If this is true"**: John Adams to William Tudor, December 13, 1800, in McCullough, p. 544.

41 **"General Pinckney"**: Ibid.

41 **Abigail had been right to distrust the man she once called as ambitious as Julius Caesar.** Abigail Adams to John Adams, December 31, 1796, Massachusetts Historical Society electronic edition.

42 **"great intrinsic defects"**: McCullough, p. 549.

42 **"ensure the choice"**: John Adams to Abigail Adams, November 15, 1800, Massachusetts Historical Society electronic edition.

42 **"services to a"**: Abigail Adams to John Quincy Adams, September 1, 1800, Bober, p. 197.

42 **"May none but"**: John Adams to Abigail Adams, November 2, 1800, Massachusetts Historical Society electronic edition.

42 **"fit and proper"**: Ibid.

42 **"Sally was with him"**: Abigail Adams to Mary Cranch, November 10, 1800, *New Letters*, p. 255.

42 **"an unknown"**: Ibid.

42 **"nothing but"**: Abigail Adams to Abigail Adams Smith, November 27, 1800, in Levin, p. 388.

42 **city**: Ibid.

43 **"a new country"**: Ibid.

43 **"the very dirtiest hole I ever saw"**: Ibid.

43 **"in a beautiful"**: Ibid.

43 **"the great unfinished audience room"**: Ibid.

43 **"I had much rather"**: Abigail Adams to Mary Cranch, November 21, 1800, ibid., pp. 257–60.

43 **"I am determined"**: Abigail Adams to Abigail Adams Smith, November 27, 1800, in Levin, p. 388.

43 **"situation is beautiful"**: Abigail Adams to Abigail Adams Smith, November 21, 1800, in Levin, p. 389.

43 **"the ladies from"**: quoted in Randolph, Sarah, *The Domestic Life of Thomas Jefferson,* University of Virginia Press, Charlottesville, 1978, reprint of 1871, p. 266.

43 **"Mrs. A is a"**: Thornton, November 19, 1800, p. 213.

43 **"There were a"**: Thornton, November 22, 1800, p. 214.

43 **"The ladies are"**: Roof, Katherine Metcalf, *Colonel William Smith and Lady, The Romance of Washington's Aide and Young Abigail Adams,* Houghton Mifflin, Boston, 1929, p. 257.

44 **"He was no"**: Abigail Adams to Mary Cranch December, 8, 1800, *New Letters,* p. 262.

44 **"with more skill"**: Abigail Adams to Thomas B. Adams, November 13, 1800, in Ferling, p. 131.

44 **"northern men"**: Abigail Adams to Thomas B. Adams, November 13, 1800, in Levin, p. 387.

44 **"lover's vows"**: Ibid.

44 **"I wish for"**: Abigail Adams to Mary Cranch, January 15, 1801, *New Letters,* p. 263.

44 **"I do not"**: Ibid.

45 **"choose to converse"**: Notes of a conversation between Abigail Adams and Thomas Jefferson, January 1801, in McCullough, p. 559.

45 **"but he believes"**: Abigail Adams to Mary Cranch, February 7, 1801, *New Letters,* pp. 265–66.

45 **"What a lesson"**: Ibid.

45 **"frequent elections"**: Ibid.

45 **"the fate of"**: Ibid

46 **"told her that"**: Carl Sferrazza, *First Ladies, The Saga of the Presidents' Wives and Their Power 1789–1961,* William Morrow, New York, 1990, p. 71.

46 **"well resorted tavern"**: George Washington to Mary Ball Washington, February 17, 1787, Bryan, Helen, *Martha Washington, First Lady of Liberty,* NY, John Wiley & Sons, 2002, p. 280.

46 **"received us"**: Sally F. Otis to Mary Foster Apthorp, January 13, 1801, in Morison, pp. 147–48.

46 **"I believe"**: Thomas Jefferson to Martha Jefferson Randolph, February 5, 1801, in Betts, p. 196.

47 **"Crowds of anxious"**: Smith, Margaret Bayard, *The First Forty Years of Washington Society, in the Family Letters of Margaret Bayard Smith,* T. Fisher Unwin, London, 1906, p. 22.

47 **"was shabby"**: Harrison Gray Otis to Sally F. Otis, February 15, 1801, in Morison, p. 150.

47 **"the People's Choice"**: Thomas Jefferson to Maria Jefferson Eppes, February 15, 1801, in Betts, p. 198.

47 **"after 4 days"**: Ibid.

47 **"The balloting"**: Smith, p. 24.

47 **"In a room"**: Ibid.

47 His choice was Jefferson. Without Nicholson, Maryland could have easily gone for Burr, and history might be quite different: Ferling, p. 187.

47 "It was for her country!": Smith, p. 24.

48 "wish me a good journey": Abigail Adams to Thomas B. Adams, February 3, 1801, in McCullough, p. 559.

48 "violent snow storm": Abigail Adams to John Adams, February 13, 1801, Massachusetts Historical Society electronic edition.

48 "The election will be": John Adams to Abigail Adams, February 16, 1801, ibid.

48 "The assembled crowds": Smith, p. 25.

48 "I want to see": Abigail Adams to John Adams, February 21, 1801, Massachusetts Historical Society electronic edition.

49 "Having effected this": Abigail Adams to John Adams, February 19, 1801, ibid.

49 "accustomed to get": Abigail Adams to William Shaw, February 14, 1801, Shaw Family Papers, Library of Congress, quoted in Bober, Natalie, *Abigail Adams, Witness to a Revolution,* Aladdin Paperbacks, NY, 1995, p. 201.

50 "Invitations in the form": *The Power of Faith, Exemplified in the Life and Writings of the Late Mrs. Isabella Graham,* 1843, IndyPublish.com, Boston, MA, p. 85.

50 "some of the": *Power,* p. 100.

50 "distant parts of the city": Ibid.

50 Running soup kitchens became the job of other clients: Scott, Anne Firor, *Making the Invisible Woman Visible,* University of Illinois Press, Urbana, 1984, p. 265.

50 Soon providing food, fuel, and clothes to about 150 widows and more than 400 children, the welfare organization stood as the first of several charities Graham and her colleagues created, including the Society for the Promotion of Industry among the Poor: Ginzberg, Lori D., *Women and the Work of Benevolence, Morality, Politics and Class in the 19th Century United States,* Yale University Press, New Haven, CT, 1990, p. 73.

50 After enlisting thirty women to sign a petition to the mayor and city council in support of that organization, Isabella successfully lobbied the state legislature to pony up five hundred dollars a year to employ women as seamstresses, weavers, and tailors: Burrows, Edwin G., and Mike Wallace, *Gotham, A History of New York City to 1898,* Oxford University Press, NY, 1999, p. 382.

50 "The poor increase fast": *Power,* p. 86.

51 "The men could not": *Power,* p. 140.

51 "painful banter": Ibid.

51 "Its fame is spread": Ibid.

52 Within a few weeks she had enrolled fifty students: Boylan, Anne M., *The Origins of Women's Activism,* UNC Press, Chapel Hill, 2002, p. 99.

52 "state prisoner": Martha Washington to Fanny Bassett Washington, October 23, 1789, in Fields, *Worthy Partner,* p. 220.

52 "prospered beyond": *Power,* p. 140.

52 "sold my mother": Tappan, Lewis, "Catherine Ferguson," *American Missionary* 8, no. 10 (August 1854): pp. 85–6, annotated clipping in Lewis Tappan's journal for July 1, 1853–April 18, 1855, p. 299 in *The Papers of Lewis Tappan, 1809–1903,* microfilm, reel 2, fr. 238, Manuscript Division, Library of Congress, Washington, D.C., all rights reserved. On website AARDOC, African American Religion: A Documentary History Project, http://www.amherst.edu/~aardoc/Ferguson_1.html

52 It's possible that as a teenager Katy worked for Isabella Graham, who may have been the person who set the young slave free.: Ibid.

52 "a benevolent lady": Lossing, Benson J. *Our Countrymen or Brief Memoirs of Eminent*

Americans, Lippincott, Grambo & Co., Philadelphia, PA, 1855, p. 404, on http://book.google.com/books

53 **"did not live long":** Mott, Abigail, *Narratives of Colored Americans,* William Wood and Co., NY, 1875, 69, property of the University of North Carolina at Chapel Hill, from electronic edition funded by the National Endowment for the Humanities, http://docsouth.unc/mott/mott.html

53 **"nicer provisions of the":** Ibid.

53 **"none to care":** Ibid.

53 somehow the former slave took charge of forty-eight kids, both black and white, either placing them with other people or taking them in herself. In about 1793, when she realized how little the children knew about religion, she set up Katy Ferguson's School for the Poor in New York City: *Gotham,* p. 384.

53 **"sometimes the sainted":** Lossing, p. 404.

54 As well as running her school, working with *Boston Weekly Magazine,* and engaging in social activism, Rowson published prolifically—eight novels, seven plays, six textbooks, two poetry collections, magazine pieces, and song lyrics: Weil, Dorothy, *In Defense of Women, Susanna Rowson, 1762–1824,* Pennsylvania State University Press, University Park, PA, 1976, p. 1.

54 (She composed songs and poems for special occasions. Among them: the dirge for George Washington's funeral and a celebratory rhyme for John Adams's birthday: Weil, p. 177, n19.

54 Only Federalists were honored by Susanna's pen, she had no words of praise for Thomas Jefferson.) In her work she found ways to look at the role of women in the world and the role of the world toward women. Rowson's geography textbooks, for instance, rebuked some countries—Egypt, Turkey, Tibet—for their treatment of females. "Susanna Rowson: Early American Geography Educator," Ben A. Smith and James W. Vining, *The Social Studies Journal,* vol. 89, iss. 6, 1998, p. 267.

54 And her plays directly addressed women in the audience about their position in society. In the epilogue to her popular production *Slaves in Algiers,* the lead actress-playwright came onstage to ask the Philadelphia audience, "Well, Ladies, tell me—how d'ye like my play?"
Did they think:

> Women were born for universal sway,
> Men to adore, be silent and obey.
> Or:
> To bind the truant, that's inclined to roam,
> Good humor makes a paradise at home.
> To raise the fall'n—to pity and forgive,
> This is our noblest, best prerogative.
> By these pursuing nature's gentle plan,
> We hold in silken chains the lordly tyrant man.: Branson, Susan,
> *These Fiery Frenchified Dames,* University of Pennsylvania Press,
> Philadelphia, 2001, pp. 114–15.

54 **"whole tribe":** Branson, p. 116.

55 Soon she published an American edition of her English novel with the title *Charlotte Temple,* which reigned as the bestselling book in this country until Harriet Beecher Stowe wrote *Uncle Tom's Cabin* more than fifty years later, giving it the longest popular run of any American novel: Matthews, Glenna, *The Rise of Public Woman, Woman's Power and Woman's Place in the United States, 1630–1970,* Oxford University Press, NY, 1992, p. 76.

55   Because she didn't own the copyright to her work, its huge success didn't do much for the Rowson family pocketbook, so gambling that the 1796 opening of a new theater in Boston—where plays had been banned by the Puritans until 1793—would allow for some financial stability, the couple moved back to the state where Susanna had grown up, hoping for receptive audiences: American Passages, A Literary Survey, Unit 4 Spirit of Nationalism: Authors, http://www.learner.org/ameripass/unit04/authors-8.html

55   "amiable lady": Eliza Southgate to Robert Southgate, February 13, 1798, in *American Women Writers to 1800,* Oxford University Press, NY, 1996, p. 55.

55   "all her scholars": Ibid.

56   "This morning I": Salmon, Marilynn, "The Limits of Independence, 1760–1800, in *No Small Courage,* ed. Nancy Cott, Oxford University Press, NY, 2000, p. 155.

56   "It would be": Weil, p. 37.

56   "Female Biography": Weil, p. 47.

56   "weaker sex": Ibid.

56   "perhaps through": Ibid.

56   "the doctrine": Weil, p.164.

56   "although by": Ibid.

56   "a pretty formidable": Ibid.

57   "fallen woman": Rowson, Susanna, *Charlotte Temple: a Tale of Truth,* College and University Press, New Haven, CT, 1964, p. 104.

57   "Surely when we reflect": Ibid.

57   "I say, dear Madam": Ibid.

57   "sales exceed": Weil, p. 171, n21.

57   The *Washington Household Account* books include an entry of a payment "for a book called Charlotte (by Mrs. Rowson) for Mrs. Washington": Weil, p. 172, n25.

57   As the novel became an integral part of the nation's culture, a cult grew up about the title character, with readers coloring in her illustrations in the book: Matthews, p. 76.

58   "female stranger": Foster, Hannah W., *The Coquette,* ed., and with an introduction by Cathy N. Davidson, Oxford University Press, NY, 1986, p. vii.

58   "excite curiosity": Ibid.

59   "Why then should": Foster, p. 44.

59   The 1790 population of four million people could choose from fewer than one hundred newspapers; twenty years later the number of newspapers had more than tripled as the population doubled: Appleby, Joyce, *Recollections of the Early Republic,* Northeastern University Press, Boston, MA, 1997, p. xiv.

59   And magazines designed explicitly for women, with articles often written by women, started filling the stacks in the 1790s. (The first American cookbook was also published. In 1796, *American Cookery,* by Amelia Simmons, An American Orphan, finally provided U.S. cooks with recipes using New World ingredients like cornmeal. The word "cookie," taken from the Dutch *koekje,* appeared for the first time in Amelia Simmons's book: Simmons, Amelia, *The First American Cookbook, A Facsimile of "American Cookery," 1796,* essay by Mary Tolford Wilson, Dover Publications, Inc., NY, 1958, p. xvi.

59   Recognizable to readers of women's magazines today, the eighteenth-century versions featured fiction, poems, and advice on such subjects as how to have a happy marriage, but they also served as platforms for and against women's rights: Branson, pp. 22–7.

59   "Desultory Thoughts upon the Utility of Encouraging a Degree of Self-Complacency, Especially in Female Bosoms." Writing as "Constantia" in

The Gentleman and Lady's Town and Country Magazine, she argued "to teach young minds to aspire ought to be the ground work of education": *The Selected Writings of Judith Sargent Murray,* ed. Sharon M. Harris, Oxford University Press, Inc., p. 45.

60   **"throw herself"**: Ibid., pp. 47–8.

60   **"As their years increase,"** *Selected Writings of Judith Sargent Murray,* NY, 1995, p. 7.

60   **"domestic duties"**: Ibid.

60   **"while we are"**: Ibid.

60   **"that a candidate"**: Ibid.

61   **"the indifference"**: *The Letters I Left Behind, Judith Sargent Murray Papers, Letter Book 10,* transcribed and introduced by Bonnie Hurd Smith, Judith Sargent Murray Society, Salem, MA, 2005, p. 346.

61   **"Mutual esteem"**: *The Gleaner,* no. XII, *Massachusetts Magazine,* April 1793, 208, in Smith, p. 349.

61   **"distinguish myself"**: Smith, p. 431.

61   **"we entered your"**: Judith Sargent Murray to John Adams, November 1, 1796, in Smith, p. 77.

61   **"Deign, honored"**: Judith Sargent Murray to George Washington, November 1796, in Smith, p. 82.

61   **"Our illustrious"**: Judith Sargent Murray to Mrs. J, a friend, January 4, 1797, in Smith, p. 92.

62   **Her dozens of letters and ads**: Smith, p. 367.

62   **"I may be accused"**: *The Gleaner,* vol. II, 188, in Smith, p. 369.

62   **"an enjoyment so richly zested"**: Smith, p. 370.

62   **"Accept, illustrious Chief"**: Judith Sargent Murrary to George Washington, August 13, 1798, in Smith, p. 230.

62   **"Had the new theory"**: Kirkland, *An Oration, Delivered at the Request of the Society of Phi Beta Kappa, in the Chapel of Harvard College, on the Day of their Anniversary, July 19, 1798,* Boston, 1798, 11, in Zaguirre, p. 227.

62   **"illiberal and tyrannical"**: Ibid. p. 227.

62   **"Every man"**: Ogden, John Cosens, *The Female Guide: or Thoughts on the Educations of That Sex, Accommodated to the State of Society, Manners and Government in the United States,* Concord, NH, 1793, p. 26 in Zaguirre, p. 218.

CHAPTER TWO

64   **"man of the people"**: Ferling, John, *Adams vs. Jefferson,* Oxford University Press, NY, 2004, p. 201.

65   **"by the representatives"**: Margaret Bayard Smith to Susan B. Smith, March 4, 1801, *Forty Years,* p. 25.

65   **"Seismic shifts of this kind"**: Margaret Bayard Smith to Susan B. Smith, March 4, 1801, *Forty Years,* p. 25.

65   **"Revolution of 1800"**: Ibid. p. 26.

66   **"delivered"**: Ibid.

66   **"in so low a tone"**: Ibid.

66   **"We are all"**: Ibid.

66   **"for a moment"**: Margaret Bayard Smith, p. 12.

66   **"Mr. Claiborne"**: Margaret Bayard Smith to Susan B. Smith, March, 4, 1801, *40 Years,* p. 26.

67   **As Abigail Adams had noted . . . the federal government . . . "removed"**

to the capital . . . One hundred and nine buildings were considered "permanent," ready to house the three hundred government employees who settled there, joining the population of some three thousand already scattered about the neighborhood: Young, James Sterling, *The Washington Community, 1800–1828,* Columbia University Press, NY, p. 22, and Allgor, *Perfect Union,* p. 46.

67   **A carriage ride from Georgetown to the Capitol, with a stop at the White House in between, took three hours round-trip:** Young, p. 76. Much of the information on early D.C. comes from this book and from Margaret Bayard Smith.

67   **"in the gayest":** Margaret Bayard Smith, *40 Years,* pp. 13–14.

68   **"even women":** Ibid.

68   **"we want":** Ellet, Elizabeth, *The Court Circles of the Republic Arnopress,* New York, 1975, reprint of 1869, publication of the Hartford Publishing, Co., Hartford, p. 49–50.

68   **"far from pleasant":** Albert Gallatin to Hannah N. Gallatin, January 15, 1801, in Allgor, Catherine, *A Perfect Union, Dolley Madison and the Creation of the American Nation,* Henry Holt & Co., NY, 2006, p. 42.

68   **"one tailor":** Ibid., p. 42.

68   **In another couple of years other "amenities" such as bookstores, taverns, and, of course, a liquor store had cropped up as well:** Young, p. 71.

68   **"Without hardly any":** Albert Gallatin to Hannah N. Gallatin, January 22, 1801, in Allgor, *Perfect Union,* p. 42.

68   **"soothe and calm":** Norton, Mary Beth, *Liberty's Daughters,* Cornell University Press, Ithaca, NY, 1980, p. 190–91.

68   **"They have obtained":** Ibid.

69   **"I have ever":** Allgor, Catherine, *Parlor Politics, in which the Ladies of Washington Help Build a City and a Government,* University of Virginia Press, Charlottesville, 2000, p. 22.

69   **When the widower:** Randolph, p. 282.

69   **"She came upon our":** Anthony Morris to Anna Payne, June 26, 1837, *Selected Letters,* University of Virginia Press, 2003, p. 13.

70   **"not been insensible to your charms":** William W. Wilkins to Dolley Payne Todd, August 22, 1794 *Selected Letters,* p. 29.

70   **"Dolley Payne Todd":** Dolley Payne Madison to Eliza Collins Lee, September 16, 1794.

70   **"Evening, Dolley Madison!":** Ibid. p. 31.

70   **"It is marvelous":** Quoted in *Selected Letters,* p. 19.

71   **"Mrs. Madison's stay":** Thomas Jefferson to Martha Jefferson Randolph, in Betts, May 28, 1801, p. 202.

71   **"awkward":** Ibid.

71   **"It would make":** Thomas Jefferson to Maria J. Eppes, May 28, 1801, ibid. p. 203.

71   **"Capt. Lewis and myself":** Thomas Jefferson to Martha Jefferson Randolph, ibid. p. 202.

71   **"Thomas Jefferson begs":** Thomas Jefferson to Dolley Payne Madison, May 27, 1801, *Memoirs and Letters of Dolley Madison, Wife of James Madison, President of the United States,* Kennikat Press, Port Washington, NY, 1971, p. 28.

71   **"She has good humor":** Margaret Bayard Smith to Susan B. Smith, May 26, 1801, *40 Years,* p. 28.

72   **"I look in vain":** Margaret Bayard Smith to Bayard Family, October 5, 1800, in Fredrika J. Teute, "Roman Matron on the Banks of Tiber Creek: Margaret Bayard

Smith and the Politicization of Spheres in the Nation's Capitol, *Republic for the Ages, The United States Capitol and the Political Culture of the Early Republic,* U.S. Capitol Historical Society, 1999, p. 89.

72 "ladies of the": Ibid.

72 **the Merry Wives of Windsor and were a more than welcome addition to the bleak little capital:** Allgor, *Perfect Union,* p. 50.

72 "The appointment": Appleby, Joyce, *Inheriting the Revolution,* Cambridge, Belknap Press, 2000, p. 31.

73 **Jefferson family lore:** Brodie, p. 168.

73 "When at last": Randolph, Sarah N., *The Domestic Life of Thomas Jefferson,* University of Virginia Press, Charlottesville, 1978, reprint of 1871 edition published by Harper, NY, p. 63.

73 **His oldest daughter went along. Jefferson enrolled Martha, called Patsy, in a course of study that he deemed inappropriate for a girl anyplace but in America, where mothers would need to raise virtuous sons as citizens:** Langhorne, Elizabeth, *Monticello, A Family Story,* Algonquin Books, Chapel Hill, 1987, p. 27.

74 "from 3 to 4": Thomas Jefferson to Martha Jefferson, November 28, 1783, in Randolph, p. 69.

74 "I do not wish": Thomas Jefferson to Martha Jefferson, December 22, 1783, ibid. p. 71.

74 "never to say": Thomas Jefferson to Martha Jefferson, December 11, 1783, ibid., p. 70.

74 "It is impossible": Elizabeth Eppes to Thomas Jefferson, October 13, 1784, in Brodie, p. 190–91.

74 "Life is scarcely": Elizabeth Eppes to Thomas Jefferson, ibid.

74 "as many dolls": Thomas Jefferson to Mary Jefferson, September 20, 1785, in Randolph, p. 103.

74 "Dear Papa—I want": Mary Jefferson to Thomas Jefferson, ca. September 13, 1785, in Betts, p. 29.

75 "I don't want": Mary Jefferson to Thomas Jefferson, ca. May 22, 1786, ibid. p. 31.

75 "Dear Papa—I should": Mary Jefferson to Thomas Jefferson, ca. March 31, 1787, ibid. p. 36.

75 "We have made": Elizabeth Eppes to Thomas Jefferson, March 1787, in Randolph, p. 124.

75 "The children will": Elizabeth Eppes to Thomas Jefferson, May 7, 1787, ibid. p. 125.

75 "It would reconcile": Abigail Adams to Thomas Jefferson, June 26, 1787, Cappon Lester J., *The Adams-Jefferson Letters,* University of North Carolina Press, Chapel Hill, 1959, p. 178.

75 "But of this": Abigail Adams to Thomas Jefferson, June 27, 1787, ibid. p. 179.

75 "She told me": Abigail Adams to Thomas Jefferson, June 6, 1787, ibid. p. 183.

76 "The girl she": Ibid.

76 **"It is well known," the *Richmond Recorder* trumpeted on September 1, 1802 . . . Her name is SALLY":** James T. Callendar, *The Richmond Recorder,* September 1, 1802, in *Sally Hemings and Thomas Jefferson, History, Memory and Civic Culture,* University of Virginia Press, Charlottesville, 1999, appendix b, p. 259.

77 "There is not": Ibid.

77 "Dusky Sally": Philadelphia *Port Folio,* October 2, 1802, in Brodie, *Thomas Jefferson, An Intimate History,* pp. 354–55.

78 "mighty near white": *Memoirs of a Monticello Slave,* Charlottesville, 1951, 13, in *Sally Hemings and Thomas Jefferson,* p. 109, n3.

78 **In an 1830 census . . . the government listed the youngest Hemings son as a white man:** Brodie, p. 469.

78 **"resembled Mr. Jefferson"**: Henry S. Randall to James Parton, June 1, 1868, quoting Thomas Jefferson Randolph, in Brodie, Appendix III, p. 494.

78 **"a gentleman"**: Ibid.

78 **"the likeness"**: Ibid.

79 **"have been very"**: Ibid. p. 248.

79 Martha **"took the"**: Lewis, Jan Ellen, "The White Jeffersons," *Sally Hemings and Thomas Jefferson,* p. 146.

79 **"I am all"**: Langhorne, *Elizabeth, Monticello, A Family Story,* Algonquin Books of Chapel Hill, 1989, p. 37.

80 **"The first sensations"**: Martha Jefferson Randolph to Thomas Jefferson, received July 1, 1798, in Betts, p. 166.

80 **"Mrs. Madison"**: Martha Jefferson Randolph to Thomas Jefferson, October 29, 1802, in Betts, p. 238.

80 **"neither of us"**: Ibid.

80 **"She is really"**: Margaret Bayard Smith to Susan Bayard Smith, December 26, 1802, *40 Years,* p. 34.

81 **"numberless"**: Thomas Jefferson to Anne Cary Randolph, February 1, 1803, in Betts, p. 243.

81 **"I felt"**: Thomas Jefferson to Martha Jefferson Randolph, January 1, 1803, in Betts, p. 242.

81 **"They seem inclined"**: Louisa Catherine Adams to Abigail Adams. December 7, 1803, unpublished letter, courtesy of Massachusetts Historical Society, II 4859.1

82 **"They plan on"**: Rosalie Stier Calvert to Mme. H. J. Stier, December 12, 1803, *Mistress of Riversdale, The Plantation Letters of Rosalie Stier Calvert, 1795–1821,* Johns Hopkins University Press, Baltimore, 1991, p. 70.

82 **"take Mrs. Merry"**: Much of the information about the Merry Affair comes from two books by Catherine Allgor, *A Perfect Union, Dolley Madison and the Creation of the American Nation,* Henry Holt, NY, 2006, and *Parlor Politics, In Which the Ladies of Washington Help Build a City and a Government,* University of Virginia Press, Charlottesville, 2000.

82 **"this will be the cause of war!"**: Ibid.

82 **"playing a game"**: Wharton, Anne Hollingsworth, *Social Life in the Early Republic,* Corner House Publishers, Williamstown, MA, reprinted 1970, first printed 1902, p. 103.

83 **"instead of conducting"**: Rosalie Stier Calvert to Mme. H. J. Stier, December 12, 1803, *Mistress,* p. 70.

83 **"At public ceremonies"**: Jefferson, Thomas, *Writings,* "A Memorandum (Rules of Etiquette)," The Library of America, NY, 1984, p. 705.

84 **"that Mrs. Merry"**: Thomas Jefferson to James Monroe, January 1804, in Foley, John Pl., ed., *The Jefferson Cyclopedia,* NY, 1967, vol. 2, p. 549, in *Mistress,* 71n.

84 **"virago"**: Allgor, *Perfect Union,* p. 94.

84 **"disturbed our harmony extremely"**: Ibid.

84 **"themselves into Coventry"**: Ibid.

84 **"large, tall, well-made" and "rather masculine"**: Margaret Bayard Smith to Jane Kirkpatrick, January 1, *40 Years,* p. 46.

84 **"her dress attracted"**: Margaret Bayard Smith to Jane Kirkpatrick, ibid.

84 **"Her hair bound"**: Margaret Bayard Smith to Jane Kirkpatrick, ibid.

84 **"bare bosom"**: Rosalie Calvert to Mme. H. J. Stier, March 2, 1804, *Mistress,* p. 77.

84 **"Mrs. Merry, the new"**: Ibid.

84 **"She is said"**: Margaret Bayard Smith to Jane Kirkpatrick, January 23, 1804, *40 Years,* p. 46.

84 **"An Englishwoman"**: Aaron Burr to Theodosia Burr Alston, January 17, 1804,

Correspondence of Aaron Burr and His Daughter Theodosia, Covici-Friede, NY, 1929, pp. 147–48.

84 **"always riding on":** Dolley Payne Madison to Anna Cutts, May 25, 1804, *Selected Letters,* p. 57.

85 **"questions of etiquette":** Thomas Jefferson to Martha Jefferson Randolph, January 23, 1804, in Betts, p. 255.

85 **"acquiesce in":** Ibid.

85 **"acquisition of Louisiana":** Ibid.

85 **Between 1790 and 1800, the populations of Kentucky and Tennessee grew by three hundred percent and Ohio followed close behind:** Fleming, Thomas, *The Louisiana Purchase,* John Wiley & Sons, Inc., Hoboken, NJ, 2003, p. 16.

86 **To pay for:** Fleming, p. 82.

87 **"beautiful women and fashionable men":** Hatfield, Joseph T. *William Claiborne, Jeffersonian Centurion in the American Southwest,* University of Southwest Louisiana, Lafayette, 1976, p. 112.

87 **"strangers to":** Hunt, Louise Livingston, *Memoir of Mrs. Edward Livingston,* Harper & Brothers, NY, 1886, p. 24.

87 **As the city grew, they cared, as well, for other women in need—chaperoning and housing the *filles à la cassette,* the marriageable women sent by the French government as mates for the colony's large population of men:** Hosmer, James K., *The History of the Louisiana Purchase,* D. Appleton and Co., NY, 1902, p. 15.

88 **"My ladies, the need":** Heaney, O.S.U., Sister Jane Frances, *A Century of Pioneering, A History of the Ursuline Nuns of New Orleans, 1727–1827,* Ursuline Sisters of New Orleans, New Orleans, LA, 1993, p. 206 (much of the information about the Ursulines is taken from this book).

88 **The city turned out to say farewell: former students and slaves assembled at the convent; a crowd including city officials escorted them mournfully to the dock:** Hosmer, p. 163.

88 **Rumors about what would happen to the nuns spread as far as Paris, where one newspaper printed the fiction that the U.S. had announced that the state would eventually seize Ursuline property:** Ibid., p. 219.

88 **"that they would":** W.C.C. Claiborne to James Madison, December 27, 1803, ibid. p. 222.

88 **"seventy-three boarders":** Ibid. p. 221.

88 **Even so, the nuns worried what their place would be in the new secular society, writing twice to President Jefferson to enlist him in an effort guaranteeing their property rights:** Ibid. p. 222.

89 **"the wholesome":** Thomas Jefferson to Sister Therese de St. Xavier Farjon, 1804, ibid. p. 224.

89 **"you Sister and":** W.C.C. Claiborne to the Superior of the Convent of St. Ursula, October 6, 1804, *Interim Appointment, WCC Claiborne Letter Book, 1804–1805,* LSU Press, Baton Rouge, LA, 2002, p. 31.

90 **A Georgetown ball drew even more happy revelers assembled to praise the president for his remarkable coup:** Fleming, Thomas, *Duel, Alexander Hamilton, Aaron Burr and the Future of America,* Basic Books, NY, 1999, pp. 143–44.

90 **"dined and danced together":** Rosalie Stier Calvert to Mme. H. J. Stier, August 20, 1805, *Mistress,* p. 126.

90 **"Jerome Bonaparte":** Aaron Burr to Theodosia Burr Alston, January 3, 1804, in Van Doren, p. 144.

90 **"There are various":** Ibid.

90 **"I hated":** Elizabeth Patterson Bonaparte to William Patterson, December 4, 1829, in Didier, see citation later, p. 230.

91 **"Whatever clothes":** *Duel,* p. 130.

91 **"wears dresses":** Rosalie Stier Calvert to Mme. H. J. Stier, March 2, 1804, *Mistress,* p. 77.

91 **"so transparent":** Ibid. p. 78.

91 **"Mobs of boys":** Margaret Bayard Smith to Jane Bayard Kirkpatrick, January 23, 1804, *40 Years,* pp. 46–7.

91 **"Her back, her":** Ibid.

91 **For the next:** Ibid.

91 **"with taste and":** Aaron Burr to Theodosia Burr Alston, January 17, 1804, in Van Doren, p. 147.

91 **setting more tongues:** *Duel,* p. 131.

91 **"Madame Bonaparte":** Louisa Catherine Adams to Abigail Adams, February 11, 1804, unpublished letters, Massachusetts Historical Society, II 4888.1.

91 **"we lived in":** Louisa Catherine Adams, *Adventures of a Nobody,* Adams Papers, Massachusetts Historical Society, transcribed by Ann Charnley.

92 **Betsy and Jerome accepted the invitation to the country estate of Alexander and Eliza Hamilton:** Chernow, Ron, *Alexander Hamilton,* The Penguin Press, NY, 2004, p. 693.

92 **"For reasons unknown":** Aaron Burr to Theodosia Burr Alston, May 8, 1804, in Van Doren, p. 161.

92 **"She has chosen":** Louisa Catherine Adams to John Quincy Adams, June 14, 1805, Adams Papers, II 4934.2, Massachusetts Historical Society.

92 **"Miss Patterson . . . member of the imperial family":** Didier, Eugene Lemoine, *The Life and Letters of Madame Bonaparte,* 2005, Adamant Media Corporation Elibron Classics Replica Edition of 1879 edition, Sampson Low, Martston, Searle and Rivington, London, p. 37. Most of the information on Elizabeth Patterson Bonaparte after she left America comes from this book and *Betsy Bonaparte, The Belle of Baltimore,* by Clause Bourguignon-Frasseto, translation by Elborg Forster, Maryland Historical Society, Baltimore, 1988, 2003.

93 **Prime Minister Pitt:** Didier, p. 40.

93 **The next day's London newspapers:** Bourguignon-Frasseto, p. 64.

93 **"try and sound":** Elizabeth Patterson Bonaparte to William Patterson, August 14, 1805, in Didier, p. 41.

93 **"any member of his family":** Ibid. p. 20n.

94 **"dilatoriness of business":** Thomas Jefferson to Maria Jefferson Eppes, November 11, 1803, in Betts, p. 249.

94 **"good spirits":** Ibid.

94 **"delivery of New Orleans":** Thomas Jefferson to Maria Jefferson Eppes, December 26, 1803, ibid. p. 250.

94 **"meet and adjourn":** Ibid.

94 **"on your account":** Ibid.

94 **"Some female friend":** Ibid.

94 **"scientific aid":** Ibid.

94 **"amidst the noises":** Martha Jefferson Randolph to Thomas Jefferson, January 14, 1804.

94 **"Maria's spirits":** Ibid.

94 **"her mind":** Martha Jefferson Randolph to Thomas Jefferson, January 14, 1804.

95 **"A thousand joys":** Thomas Jefferson to Maria Jefferson Eppes, February 26, 1804, ibid. p. 250.

95 **"I rejoice":** ibid. p. 258.

95 **"terrible anxiety":** March 3, 1804, ibid. p. 238.

95 **"God bless":** Ibid.

95 **"blessing of us all":** Ibid.

95 **"She is extremely":** J. Eppes to Thomas Jefferson, March 23, 1804, Langhorne, *Monticello*, p. 129.

95 **"the sherry":** Ibid. p. 128.

95 **"spirits and confidence":** Ibid. p. 129.

95 **"my daughter":** Ibid. p. 130.

95 **"This morning":** Jefferson Memorandum Book, April 17, 1804, in *Monticello*, p. 130.

95 **"Bible in his hands":** Randolph, p. 300.

95 **"Oh my daughter":** *Monticello*, p. 130.

96 **"This is among":** Dolley Madison, to Anna Cutts, April 26, 1804, in *Selected Letters*, p. 53.

96 **"A girl so young":** Ibid.

96 **"She was his":** Louisa Catherine Adams to John Adams, April 17, 1804, unpublished, Massachusetts Historical Society II, 4911.1.

96 **"sorrow over":** Ibid.

96 **"feelings of mutual sympathy":** Abigail Adams to Thomas Jefferson, May 20, 1804, Cappon, p. 269.

96 **"tasted the bitter cup":** Ibid.

96 **"who once took":** Ibid.

96 **"lessen mutual esteem":** Thomas Jefferson to Abigail Adams, June 13, 1804, in Cappon, p. 270.

96 **"never stood":** Ibid.

96 **"some one of":** Ibid.

97 **"keep down all":** Ibid.

97 **"I did consider":** Ibid.

97 **"They were from":** Ibid.

97 **"The Constitution empowers":** Abigail Adams to Thomas Jefferson, July 7, 1804, Cappon, pp. 271–74.

97 **"in the last days":** Ibid.

97 **"at the time":** Ibid.

97 **"One of the first":** Ibid.

97 **"the lowest":** Ibid.

98 **"the serpent you":** Ibid.

98 **"There is one":** Ibid.

98 **"no eye but":** Ibid.

98 **"told some useful":** Thomas Jefferson to Abigail Adams, July 22, 1904, in Cappon, pp. 274–76.

98 **"to a beggar":** Ibid.

98 **"I discharged every":** Ibid.

98 **"I declare":** Ibid.

99 **"If a Chief":** Abigail Adams to Thomas Jefferson, August 18, 1804, in Cappon, pp. 276–78.

99 **"That some restraint":** Ibid.

99 **"the sword and":** Ibid.

99 **"Soon after my":** Ibid.

99 **"As soon as":** Ibid.

99 **"With pleasure":** Ibid.

99 **"written to you":** Ibid.

99 **"It would have"**: Thomas Jefferson to Abigail Adams, September 11, 1804, in Cappon, pp. 278–80.

100 **"The Executive"**: Ibid.

100 **"While we deny"**: Ibid.

100 **"I hope you"**: Ibid.

100 **"Pardon me Sir"**: Abigail Adams to Thomas Jefferson, October 25, 1804, in Cappon, pp. 281–82.

100 **"be considered an"**: Ibid.

100 **"I will not sir"**: Ibid.

101 **"I have no"**: in Cappon, p. 282.

101 **"My Story"**: Adams, Louisa Catherine, "My Story, Record of a Life," courtesy Massachusetts Historical Society, transcript p. 52.

101 **"Conceive my dear sons"**: Ibid.

101 **"forfeited all"**: Ibid.

102 **"Adventures of a Nobody"**: Adams, Louisa Catherine, "The Adventures of a Nobody," courtesy Massachusetts Historical Society, unnumbered transcript, p. 13.

102 **"It is forty three"**: Ibid.

102 **"no longer sage"**: "My Story," p. 3.

102 **"utter ignorance of"**: Ibid. p. 6.

102 **"I became serious"**: Ibid. pp. 6–7.

102 **"My father was"**: Ibid. p. 8.

102 **"My mother's"**: Ibid. p. 22.

102 **"Never did man"**: Ibid. pp. 34–5.

103 **"live among republicans"**: Ibid. pp. 34–5.

103 **"His devotions were"**: Ibid. p. 42.

103 **"was a great favorite"**: Ibid.

103 **"had a prejudice"**: Ibid.

103 **"He recommended to"**: Ibid. p. 47.

104 **"Consider untoward events"**: Shepherd, Jack, *Cannibals of the Heart, A Personal Biography of Louisa Catherine and John Quincy Adams,* McGraw Hill, NY, 1980, p. 72.

104 **"*suffering* with dignity"**: Ibid.

104 **"our nuptials"**: "My Story," p. 50.

104 **"concealed with"**: Ibid. p. 51.

104 **"procure him"**: Ibid.

104 **"At this moment"**: Ibid.

104 **"to give each"**: Ibid.

104 **"When I arose"**: Ibid. p. 53.

105 **"without a female"**: "The Adventures of a Nobody," unnumbered transcript, p. 4.

105 **"entirely occupied"**: Ibid.

105 **"a Belle"**: Ibid.

105 **"Remember I was"**: Ibid. p. 17.

105 **"make me a"**: Ibid. p. 35.

105 **"smiled at"**: Ibid. p. 35.

105 **"he said I"**: Ibid. p. 35.

105 **"being more than"**: Ibid. p. 63.

106 **"look quite beautiful"**: Ibid.

106 **"He took a towel"**: Ibid.

106 **"everlasting teasing"**: Ibid. pp. 74–5.

106 **"I walked boldly"**: Ibid.

106 **"we returned home"**: Ibid.

106 **"much affected"**: Ibid. p. 62.

106   **"I was a *Mother*"**: Ibid. p. 85.

107   **"My only consolation"**: Ibid. pp. 87–8.

107   **"Mrs. Adams is"**: Abigail Adams to John Quincy Adams, September 23, 1801, in Levin, p. 396.

107   **"We had never"**: "Adventures of a Nobody," p. 88.

107   **"the celebrated"**: Ibid. p. 89.

108   **"We were all Federalists"**: William Parker Cutler and Julia Perkins Cutler, eds, *Life, Journals and Correspondence of Rev. Manasseh Cutler, LLD,* 2 vols, Robert Clarke, Cincinnati, OH, 1888, 2:56–8, in Brady, Patricia, *Martha Washington, An American Life,* Viking, 2005, p. 227.

108   **"the greatest misfortune"**: Ibid.

108   **"She was the"**: *The New England Pledium,* Bryan, Helen, *Martha Washington, First Lady of Liberty,* John Wiley & Sons, Inc., NY, 2002, p. 380.

108   **"They lived an"**: Ibid.

108   **"constantly shrieking"**: Shepherd, *Cannibals,* p. 107.

108   **"Suffering and sorrow"**: Ibid.

108   **"Under such circumstance"**: Ibid. p. 92.

108   **"completely disagreeable"**: "Adventures of a Nobody," p. 93.

108   **"I have many"**: Ibid.

109   **"added a weight"**: Shepherd, *Cannibals,* p. 108.

109   **"spoilt child of indulgence"**: "Adventures of a Nobody," in Levin, p. 92.

109   **"gazed at"**: Ibid. pp. 398–99.

109   **"It was lucky"**: Ibid.

109   **"the old gentleman"**: Shepherd, *Cannibals,* p. 108.

109   **All twenty of**: Nagel, Paul C., *The Adams Women, Abigail and Louisa Adams, Their Sisters and Daughters,* Harvard University Press, Cambridge, 1987, p. 176.

110   **"open just wide"**: Louisa Catherine Adams, pp. 34–35.

110   **"the highest honors"**: Shepherd, *Cannibals,* p. 112.

110   **"We frequented the"**: Louisa Catherine Adams, p. 46.

110   **"a coldness of"**: Abigail Adams to John Quincy Adams, March 24, 1806, in Levin, p. 410.

110   **"While conversing he"**: Louisa Catherine Adams, pp. 46–47.

111   **"won golden opinions"**: Louisa Catherine Adams, p. 47.

111   **"Or to charge upon"**: Ibid.

111   **"cracker in his jacket"**: Abigail Adams to Louisa Catherine Adams, December 8, 1804, in Levin, p. 410.

111   **"the cut of his coat"**: Ibid.

111   **"In a democratic"**: Louisa Catherine Adams, p. 52.

111   **"an unruly crowd"**: Louisa Catherine Adams, p. 51.

111   **"Tom Jefferson"**: Louisa Catherine Adams, p. 51.

112   **"that the People"**: Ibid.

112   **"I do not think"**: Louisa Catherine Adams to John Quincy Adams, April 17, 1804, Adams Papers unpublished, unedited transcripts provided courtesy of the Massachusetts Historical Society.

112   **"He says you"**: Louisa Catherine Adams to John Quincy Adams, May 20, 1804, Adams Papers, II 4932.1, Massachusetts Historical Society.

112   **"He understands the"**: Louisa Catherine Adams to John Quincy Adams, June 10, 1804, Adams Papers, II 4932.1, Massachusetts Historical Society.

112   **"Poor little fellow"**: Louisa Catherine Adams to John Adams, October 1, 1804, Adams Papers, II 4974.1, Massachusetts Historical Society.

112   **"Life is not"**: Louisa Catherine Adams to John Quincy Adams, August 12, 1804, Adams Papers, II 49454.1, Massachusetts Historical Society.

112 **"something will arise":** Louisa Catherine Adams to John Quincy Adams, May 20, 1804, Adams Papers, II 4923.1, Massachusetts Historical Society.

113 **"He is grown":** Louisa Catherine Adams to John Quincy Adams, July 4, 1804, Adams Papers, II 4941.1, Massachusetts Historical Society.

113 **"a company of":** Louisa Catherine Adams to John Quincy Adams, September 4, 1804, II 4965.1, Massachusetts Historical Society.

113 **"even the *clerks*":** Louisa Catherine Adams to John Quincy Adams, September 16, 1804, II 4969.1, Massachusetts Historical Society.

113 **"the president":** Louisa Catherine Adams to John Quincy Adams, October 18, 1804, Adams Papers, II 4979.1, Massachusetts Historical Society.

113 **From Quincy, Louisa had received letters from her mother-in-law:** in Withey, p. 290.

113 **"his manners are":** Louisa Adams to Abigail Adams, November 27, 1804, Adams Papers, II 4994. 1, Massachusetts Historical Society.

114 **"decided on their":** Aaron Burr to Theodosia Burr Alston, February 16, 1804, in Van Doren, p. 153.

114 **"Hamilton is intriguing":** Ibid.

114 **"wicked enough":** Alexander Hamilton to Gouvernour Morris, December 24, 1800, in Chernow, Ron, *Alexander Hamilton,* Penguin Press, NY, 2004, p. 633.

114 **"The election is lost":** Aaron Burr to Theodosia Burr Alston, May 1, 1804, in Van Doren, p. 160.

115 **"when she met":** Robert Troup, in Chernow, p. 654.

115 **"injure any person":** Aaron Burr to Theodosia Burr Alston, July 7, 1804, in Van Doren, pp. 169–70.

115 **"of my female":** Ibid.

115 **"debts and no":** Ibid.

116 **"Adieu. Adieu":** Ibid.

116 **"love for you":** Alexander Hamilton to Elizabeth Schuyler Hamilton, July 7, 1804, Desmond, Alice Curtis, *Alexander Hamilton's Wife, A Romance of the Hudson,* Dodd, Mead & Co., NY, 1952, p. 239, and Chernow, p. 709.

116 **"Nor can I":** Ibid.

116 **"Adieu, best of wives":** Ibid.

117 **"frantic grief":** Chernow, p. 706.

117 **"weeping her heart":** Ibid.

117 **"I have the":** Angelica Church to Philip Schuyler, July 11, 1804, in *Women's Letters,* pp. 104–5.

117 **"My dear sister":** Ibid.

117 **"You have heard":** Dolley Payne Madison to Anna Cutts, July 16, 1804, in *Selected Letters,* p. 59.

117 **"His loss must":** Louisa Catherine Adams to John Adams, July 20, 1804, Adams Papers, II 4946. 1, Massachusetts Historical Society.

117 **"America has just had":** Rosalie Stier Calvert to Mme. H. J. Stier, July 30, 1804, *Mistress,* p. 92.

117 **"The city of New York":** Ibid.

117 **"Hang Burr!":** handbills posted around New York.

118 **"I shall journey":** Aaron Burr to Theodosia Burr Alston, July 20, 1804, in Van Doren, pp. 171–72.

118 **"I absent myself":** Aaron Burr to Theodosia Burr Alston, August 3, 1804, ibid. p. 173.

118 **"Those who wish":** Ibid.

118 **"If any male":** Aaron Burr to Theodosia Burr Alston, August 11, 1804, ibid. p. 174.

118 **"Mr. R. King":** Aaron Burr to Theodosia Burr Alston, August 28, 1804, ibid. p. 175.

118 **"which shall have"**: Aaron Burr to Theodosia Burr Alston, December 4, 1804, ibid. p. 198.

118 **"You shall have"**: Ibid.

119 **"Everybody is flocking"**: Rosalie Stier Calvert to Isabelle van Havre, February 18, 1805, *Mistress*, p. 112.

119 **"everybody seemed to"**: Louisa Catherine Adams, Adventures of a nobody, Adams Papers, Massachusetts Historical Society, transcribed by Ann Charnley, p. 58.

119 **"attended by so"**: Wharton, Social Life, p. 124.

120 **"we were quite"**: Ibid. p. 61.

120 **"both useful and"**: Aaron Burr to Theodosia Burr Alston, March 10, 1805, in Van Doren, p. 204.

120 **"occasionally on my"**: Ibid.

CHAPTER THREE

121 **"I see by"**: Rosalie Stier Calvert to Mme. H. J. Stier, August 20, 1805, *Mistress*, p. 125.

121 **"Here we talk"**: Ibid.

122 **"astonishment"**: Margaret Bayard Smith to Mary Kirkpatrick, February 9, 1808, in *40 Years*, p. 52.

122 **"They looked and looked"**: Ibid.

122 **"America displeases me"**: Rosalie Stier Calvert to Charles Stier, *Mistress*, p. 2.

122 **"In the large"**: Rosalie Stier Calvert to Isabelle van Havre, August 8, 1805, ibid., pp. 124–25.

122 **"People think only"**: Mme. H. J. Stier to Rosalie Stier Calvert, November 10, 1804, ibid., p. 115.

122 **"You are mistaken"**: Rosalie Stier Calvert to Mme H. J. Stier, June 13, 1805, ibid., p. 120.

122 **"I find that"**: Ibid.

122 **"The more I contemplate"**: Ibid.

123 **"Everything here is improving"**: Rosalie Stier Calvert to Mme. H. J. Stier, June 21, 1805, ibid., p. 123.

123 **"It certainly has"**: Ibid.

123 **"the education"**: Rosalie Stier Calvert to Mme. H. J. Stier, May 10, 1805.

123 **"cause me a"**: Ibid.

123 **"Tommy Jeff"**: Ibid.

123 **"the Democratic party"**: Rosalie Stier Calvert to Isbelle van Havre, August 8, 1805, ibid., p. 124.

123 **(The women were treated to special souvenirs from the journey when it was finally over)**: Allgor, *Perfect Union*, pp. 55–6.

123 **"We have just heard"**: Thomas Jefferson to Martha Jefferson Randolph, June 24, 1805, in Betts, p. 273.

124 **"who wintered"**: Ibid.

124 **Much of the information for this section comes from three sources:** *The Lewis and Clark Journals, An American Epic of Discovery,* University of Nebraska Press, Lincoln, 2003; Howard, Harold P., *Sacajawea,* University of Oklahoma Press, Norman, 1971; and Ambrose, Stephen E., *Undaunted Courage, Meriwether Lewis, Thomas Jefferson and the Opening of the American West,* Simon & Schuster, NY, 1996.

124 **"Her labor was"**: Meriwether Lewis, February 11, 1805, in *Journals*, p. 100.

124 **"never failed to"**: Ibid.

124 **medical uses of wild plants made her legendary**: Ambrose, p. 23.

125   **"Her labor soon":** *Journals,* April 9, 1805, p. 113.

125   **"and she procured":** Ibid.

125   **"brought me a":** *Journal,* April 30, 1805, p. 122.

125   **"white apple":** Ambrose, p. 222.

125   **"by 4 o'clock":** *Journal,* May 16, 1805, p. 133.

125   **"The Indian woman":** Ibid.

126   **"Sacagawea . . . after our interpreter, the Snake woman":** *Journal,* May 20, 1805, p. 134.

126   **"the Indian woman":** *Journal,* June 16, 1805, p. 162.

126   **"the poor object":** Ibid.

126   **"for a friendly":** Ibid.

126   **"The Indian woman very":** *Journal,* ibid., p. 163.

126   **"scrambled up":** *Journal,* July 29, 1805, pp. 170–71.

127   **"I was fearful":** Ibid.

127   **"refreshed them with":** Ibid.

127   **"This piece of":** *Journal,* July 22, 1805, pp. 184–85.

127   **"If we do not":** *Journal,* July 27, 1805, p. 193.

127   **"If she has enough":** *Journal,* July 28, 1805, p. 194.

128   **"recognized the":** *Journal,* August 7, 1805, p. 201.

128   **"painted their":** *Journal,* August 13, 1805, pp. 208–11.

128   **"we met a":** Ibid.

128   **"Both parties":** Ibid.

128   **"all the women":** Ibid.

128   **"She instantly":** Howard, p. 57.

129   **"The meeting of":** Ibid., August 17, 1805, p. 221.

129   **"A woman with":** *Journal,* January 1, 1805, p. 263.

129   **"The sight of":** Ibid., October 19, 1805, pp. 267–68.

129   **"Great joy":** Ibid., November 7, 1805, p. 283.

130   **"a robe of":** Ibid., November 20, 1805.

130   **"Both Capt. Lewis":** Ibid.

130   **Poor Sacagawea had to give up her beautiful blue belt so one of the men could have the fur. She ended up with a blue cloth coat out of the deal:** Ambrose, p. 315.

130   **"Janey in favor":** *Journal,* November 24, 1805, p. 292.

130   **"revived the spirits":** Ibid., December 3, 1805, p. 296.

130   **"broke two shank":** Ibid.

130   **"cheerful all the":** Ibid. December 25, 1805, p. 302.

130   **"two dozen white":** Ibid.

130   **"the Indian woman":** Ibid.

130   **"canoes and 12 men":** Ibid. January 1, 1806, p. 312.

130   **"very impatient":** Ibid.

131   **So the translation train geared up again as Sacagawea forged friendships in the various tribes and discovered shortcuts for the journey:** Howard, p. 98, and Ambrose, pp. 358–59.

131   **"Sacagawea gathered":** *Journal,* May 16, 1806, p. 379.

131   **"several of":** Ibid., May 14, 1806, p. 378.

131   **"was attacked with":** Ibid., May 22, 1806, p. 381.

131   **"free of fever":** Ibid., May 28, 1806, p. 384.

131   **"the Indian woman":** Ibid., July 6, 1806, p. 425.

131   **"informed me":** Ibid.

132   **"The Indian woman":** Ibid., July 13, 1806, p. 427.

132   **"pursuers whose":** Ibid., July 14, 1806, July 17, 1806, p. 428.

132   **"took our leave":** Ibid., August 17, 1806, p. 441.

132   "to take his": Ibid., August 17, 1806, p. 441.

132   "in one year": Ibid.

132   "Your woman, who": William Clark to Toussaint Charbonneau, August 20, 1806: in Howard, p. 141.

133   "whose mother was": Ibid, p. 171.

133   "his wife, an Indian": Ibid, p.157.

133   "wife of Charbonneau, a Snake squaw": Ibid, p. 160.

133   "the best woman": Ibid.

133   "she left a fine": Ibid.

133   **The little girl, Lizette, joined her brother as a ward of William Clark:** Ibid. p. 161, and Ambrose, p. 448.

134   **the Wind River Reservation in Wyoming: "Sacajawea, Died April 9, 1884. A Guide with the Lewis and Clark Expedition, 1805–1806":** Howard, p. 191.

134   "heads of departments": Richard, Jeffrey H., *Mercy Otis Warren,* Twayne Publishers, NY, 1995, p. 125; much of the information for this section comes from this book and from Zagarri, Rosemary, *A Woman's Dilemma, Mercy Otis Warren and the American Revolution,* Harlan Davidson, Inc., Wheeling, IL, 1995, and Brown, Alice, *Mercy Warren,* in the series *Women of Colonial and Revolutionary Times,* Charles Scribner's Sons, NY, 1896. In Washington to subscribe to her magnum opus: *The History of the Rise, Progress and Termination of the American Revolution. Interspersed with Biographical, Political and Moral Observations.*

135   "I should belie": Zagarri, p.126.

136   "Female genius": Ibid., p. 138.

136   "Why do my": Ibid., p. 134.

136   "in this Commercial": Richards, p. 126.

136   "disappointed patriot": Morison, p. 207.

136   "She assures me": Ibid.

137   "had not yet": Zagarri, p. 148.

137   "a *gentleman*": Ibid.

137   "plain in person": Warren, Mrs. Mercy Otis, *History of the Rise, Progress and Termination of the American Revolution Interspersed with Biographical, Political and Moral Observations,* edited and annotated by Lester H. Cohen, Liberty Fund, Indianapolis, IN, 1994, vol. 1, p. 160, originally printed by Manning and Loring, for E. Larkin, No. 47, Cornhill, Boston, 1805.

137   "a bold genius": Ibid.

137   "barbarous abuse": Ibid., vol. I, p. 297.

137   "gave a glorious": Ibid., vol. II, p. 449.

137   "gaieties of the city": Ibid.

137   "they visited": Ibid.

137   "conduct": Ibid.

138   "exposed them": Ibid.

138   "attack and defeat": Ibid., vol. II, p. 638.

138   "In this lady's": Ibid.

138   "was blended that": Ibid.

138   "circumstance could": Ibid.

138   "a man of": *History,* vol. II, p. 488.

138   "indecisive": Ibid.

138   "never discovered": Ibid.

138   "was doubted by": *History,* vol. II, p. 424.

138   "the address": Ibid.

139   "Mr. Adams was": *History,* vol. II, pp. 675–77.

139   "A partiality": Ibid.

139 **"a large portion"**: Ibid.

139 **"forgotten the principles"**: Ibid.

139 **"and much ambition"**: Ibid.

139 **"endowed with"**: Ibid.

139 **"honest indignation"**: Ibid.

139 **"beclouded by a"**: Ibid.

139 **"with more pleasure"**: Ibid.

139 **"notwithstanding any"**: Ibid.

139 **"The faithful historian"**: Brown, p. 222.

139 **"I hope Mrs. Warren"**: John Adams to Mercy Otis Warren, August 19, 1782, quoted by Warren to Adams in her letter to him August 27, 1808, "Correspondence between John Adams and Mercy Warren," *Collections of the Massachusetts Historical Society,* vol. IV–fifth series, published by the Society, Boston, 1878, p. 490.

139 **"The recollection of"**: Mercy Otis Warren to Abigail Adams, December 28, 1806—the letter is dated 07 but from the context that is impossible, Adams Papers, courtesy Massachusetts Historical Society.

140 **"I may censure"**: Ibid.

140 **"Should I ask"**: Ibid.

140 **"May I ask"**: Abigail Adams to Mercy Otis Warren, March 9, 1807, Adams Papers, courtesy Massachusetts Historical Society.

140 **"He is now"**: Mercy Otis Warren to Abigail Adams, July 11, 1807, Adams Papers, courtesy Massachusetts Historical Society.

141 **"Be it so"**: John Adams to Mercy Otis Warren, July 20, 1807, ibid., p. 358.

141 **"in the spirit"**: Mercy Otis Warren to John Adams, July 28, 1807, ibid., p. 360.

141 **"inaccuracies"**: Ibid.

141 **"confute the"**: Ibid.

141 **"angry and indigested"**: Ibid.

141 **"This may be"**: Ibid., p. 360.

141 **"enroll her name"**: John Adams to Mercy Otis Warren, August 1807, ibid.

141 **"'But Mrs. Warren's"**: John Adams to Mercy Otis Warren, August 1807, ibid., p. 478–89.

142 **"Yet, as an old"**: Mercy Otis Warren to John Adams, August 27, 1807, ibid., pp. 490–91.

142 **"History is"**: John Adams to Elbridge Gerry, April 17, 1813, in Richards, p. 147.

142 **"celebrated by"**: Richards, pp. 53–4.

142 **"a share,"**: Brown, p. 240.

143 **Mercy Otis Warren asked John Adams to testify that she, in fact, had written the now-celebrated play. He readily complied:** Zagarri, p. 159.

143 **"by far the"**: Peacock, Virginia Tatnall, *Famous American Belles of the Nineteenth Century,* J. B. Lippincott Co., NY, 1900.

143 **Much of the information for this section comes from Cote, Richard N., *Theodosia Burr Alston: Portrait of a Prodigy,* Corinthian Books, Mt. Pleasant, SC, 2003; Isenberg, Nancy, *Fallen Founder, the Life of Aaron Burr,* Viking, NY, 2007, and Melton, Jr., Buckner F., *Aaron Burr, Conspiracy to Treason,* John Wiley & Sons, Inc., NY, 2002.**

144 **"Is it, in my"**: Crawford, Mary Caroline, *Romantic Days in the Early Republic,* Grosset & Dunlap, Inc., NY, 1912, p. 318.

144 **"Is it owing"**: Aaron Burr to Theodosia Prevost Burr, February 16, 1793, in Cote, p. 68.

144 **Aaron Burr kept a portrait of Mary Wollstonecraft with him throughout his life:** Ibid., p. 69.

144 **"performance above your years"**: Aaron Burr to Theodosia Burr, February 13,

1794, in Van Doren, p. 20, and the rest from letters throughout the early 1790s in the same volume, pp. 3–20.

144 **"My little daughter"**: Richard N., *Theodosia Burr Alston: Portrait of a Prodigy,* Corinthian Books, Mt. Pleasant, S.C., 2003, p. 80.

144 **"your manners"**: Aaron Burr to Theodosia Burr, August 4, 1794, in Van Doren, p. 25.

145 **He never let up on the little girl: practice Greek verbs, play the harp, study arithmetic, pay the help, date your letters, stand up straight, don't eat dessert:** Ibid., pp. 25–42.

145 **"wit, sprightliness"**: Aaron Burr to Theodosia Burr, January 16, 1797, in Van Doren, p. 43.

145 **"The happiness"**: Aaron Burr to Theodosia Burr, January 4, 1799, ibid., pp. 46–47.

145 **"It is for"**: Ibid.

145 **Gracing Theodosia's parlor were the men we know as the Founding Fathers—Washington, Adams, Jefferson, Madison, and even Hamilton:** Cote, p. 99.

145 **"You must bring"**: Peacock, p. 30.

145 **"we shall all up"**: Ibid.

145 **Even when her father was away Theodosia entertained illustrious guests, including a then-famous Mohawk chieftain, William Brant Thayendanegea:** Cote, pp. 100–03.

145 **"elegant without"**: Cote, p. 104.

145 **"dances with"**: Ibid.

145 **"her reading has"**: Ibid.

146 **"the opinion of"**: Joseph Alston to Theodosia Burr, December 28, 1800, in Cote, pp. 115–18.

146 **"I give you"**: Ibid., p. 119.

146 **"No Charleston"**: Ibid.

147 **"The only solid"**: Aaron Burr to Theodosia Burr Alston, April 8, 1801, in Van Doren, p. 60.

147 **"and the certainty"**: Ibid.

147 **"nothing but *matrimony*"**: Aaron Burr to Theodosia Burr Alston, April 11, 1801, ibid., p. 61.

147 **"She was, you know"**: Aaron Burr to Theodosia Burr Alston, April 28, 1801, ibid., p. 66.

147 **"I want your"**: Ibid.

147 **"My only friends"**: Theodosia Burr Alston to Frederick Prevost, June 6, 1801, in Cote, p. 132.

148 **"It would have"**: Aaron Burr to Theodosia Burr Alston, November 3, 1801, in Van Doren, p. 69.

148 **"My friend Mrs. Madison"**: Theodosia Burr Alston to Frederick Prevost, October 10, 1801, in Cote, p. 150.

148 **"lawful"**: Ibid.

148 **"The house is"**: Ibid., October 10, 1801, in Cote, p. 150.

148 **Read the newspapers:** Aaron Burr to Theodosia Burr Alston, November 26, 1801, and December 8, 1801, in Van Doren, pp. 74–75.

148 **"You must walk"**: Aaron Burr to Theodosia Burr Alston, January 16, 1802, ibid., p. 78.

148 **"Get a very"**: Ibid.

148 **"The judiciary"**: Aaron Burr to Theodosia Burr Alston, February 27, 1802, ibid., p. 87.

148 **"Anna Payne":** Aaron Burr to Theodosia Burr Alston, February 2, 1802, ibid., p. 80.

149 **"The stage was":** Aaron Burr to Theodosia Burr Alston, May 3, 1802, ibid., pp. 97–98.

149 **"you are *well*":** Ibid.

149 **"Every woman":** Theodosia Burr Alston to Joseph Alston, June 28, 1802, in Cote, p. 159.

149 **"possess a magic":** Theodosia Burr Alston to Joseph Alston, September 9, 1802, in Cote, p. 162.

150 **"It little concerns":** Ibid

150 **"It keeps you":** Ibid.

150 **"You must summon":** Theodosia Burr Alston to Joseph Alston, October 30, 1802, ibid., p. 163.

150 **"the trouble of":** Theodosia Burr Alston to Aaron Burr, March 17, 1803, in Van Doren, p. 104.

150 **"Would to God":** Aaron Burr to Theodosia Burr Alston, June 11, 1803, ibid., p. 116.

150 **"still pretty":** Theodosia Burr Alston to Aaron Burr, October 16, 1803, ibid., 129.

150 **"unfortunate":** Ibid.

150 **"drank tea with":** Ibid.

150 **"Mr. Alston appears":** Theodosia Burr Alston to Aaron Burr, October 2, 1803, ibid., p. 130.

151 **"unpleasant":** Theodosia Burr Alston to Aaron Burr, October 10, 1803, ibid., p. 131.

151 **"frets the boy":** Ibid.

151 **"We travel in":** Ibid.

151 **"He may read":** Aaron Burr to Theodosia Burr Alston, January 17, 1804, ibid., p. 147.

151 **"Both parties":** Aaron Burr to Theodosia Burr Alston, April 4, 1804, ibid., p. 159.

151 **"lost by a":** Aaron Burr to Theodosia Burr Alston, May 1, 1804, ibid., p. 160.

151 **"laughed an hour":** Aaron Burr to Theodosia Burr Alston, June 24, 1804, ibid., p. 165.

151 **"I have called":** Aaron Burr to Joseph Alston, July 10, 1804, in Cote, p. 175.

151 **"all that is":** Ibid.

152 **"It is indispensable":** Ibid.

152 **"If you would":** Ibid.

152 **"It is a fact":** Aaron Burr to Theodosia Burr Alston, September 26, 1804, ibid., p. 188.

152 **"I have invitations":** Cote, p. 196.

152 **"effect a separation":** Ibid.

152 **"great ambition":** Ibid.

153 **"hear of me":** Aaron Burr to Theodosia Burr Alston, February 10, 1805, in Van Doren, pp. 203–04.

153 **"other particulars":** Ibid.

153 **"properly speaking":** Aaron Burr to Theodosia Burr Alston, April 30, 1805, ibid., p. 209.

153 **"house of some":** Aaron Burr to Theodosia Burr Alston, May 25, 1805, ibid., p. 211. This letter is dated May 25 but is written over several months, recounting Burr's travels throughout the summer.

153 **"always met a most":** Ibid.

153 **"rich in beauty":** Ibid.

153 **"Fair, pale, with":** Ibid.

154 **"congratulating me on":** Ibid., p. 212.

154 **"We conversed":** Ibid. p. 212.

154 **"All was gaiety":** Ibid.

154 **"repast of wine":** Ibid.

154 **"received with distinction":** Ibid.

154 **"On the map":** Ibid., pp. 214–15.

154 **"Something whispers"**: Theodosia Burr Alston to Joseph Alston, August 6, 1805, in Cote, pp. 198–201.

155 **"May heaven prosper"**: Ibid.

155 **"Do not be"**: Ibid.

155 **"British ships and forces?"**: *Gazette of the United States,* August 2, 1805, Melton, p. 87.

155 **"interrupted the dancing"**: Cote, p. 221.

156 **"Nor does it"**: Rosalie Stier Calvert to Mme. H. J. Stier, January 19, 1807, *Mistress,* p. 156.

156 **"I suppose you"**: Dolley Payne Madison to Anna Cutts, March 27, 1807, *Selected Letters,* p. 81.

157 **"That is all"**: Ibid.

157 **"I am to be"**: Aaron Burr to Theodosia Burr Alston, March 27, 1807, in Van Doren, p. 216.

157 **"Was there in Greece"**: Aaron Burr to Theodosia Burr Alston, April 26, 1807, ibid., pp. 216–17.

157 **"The democratic papers"**: Aaron Burr to Theodosia Burr Alston, May 15, 1807, ibid., p. 217.

157 **"Nothing is left"**: Ibid.

157 **"From all appearances"**: Rosalie Stier Calvert to Jean Michel van Havre, April 25, 1807, *Mistress,* p. 164.

157 **"It is the general"**: Dolley Payne Madison to Anna Cutts, July 18, 1807, *Selected Letters,* p. 82.

158 **"I beg and expect"**: Aaron Burr to Theodosia Burr Alston, June 24, 1807, in Van Doren, p. 221.

158 **"quite a polite"**: Aaron Burr to Theodosia Burr Alston, July 3, 1807, ibid., p. 222.

158 **"Very well, sir"**: Ibid., p. 222.

158 **"If you come"**: Aaron Burr to Theodosia Burr Alston, July 6, 1807, ibid., p. 223.

158 **"Remember, no"**: Ibid., p. 223.

159 **"Beautiful, intelligent"**: Cote, p. 243.

159 **"idolatrous"**: Peacock, p. 34.

159 **"Nor can he"**: Ibid.

159 **"Colonel Burr would be"**: Isenberg, p. 356.

159 **"We therefore find"**: Cote, p. 243.

159 **"The knowledge of"**: Ibid. p. 244.

159 **"Since my residence"**: Ibid.

160 **"Sometimes feminine"**: Aaron Burr to Theodosia Burr Alston, 1807–08, in Van Doren, p. 229.

160 **On June 7, 1808, the night before he left New York, under the alias of G. H. Edwards, Theodosia, or "Mary Ann Edwards," secretly met with her father for the last time. She was to tell the New York newspapers that he had headed by land to Canada**: Isenberg, p. 371.

160 **"Jeremy Bentham"**: Theodosia Burr Alston to Aaron Burr, December 5, 1808, in Van Doren, p. 268.

160 **"The world begins"**: Theodosia Burr Alston to Aaron Burr, September 30, 1808, in Van Doren, p. 247.

160 **"No doubt there"**: Theodosia Burr Alston to Aaron Burr, October 31, 1808, ibid., pp. 251–57.

160 **"Where are you"**: Ibid.

160 **"I would to"**: Ibid.

160 **"Thank God, I"**: Theodosia Burr Alston to Aaron Burr, December 5, 1808, in Van Doren, p. 270.

160 Much of the background for this section comes from biographies of Alexander Hamilton: Hamilton, Allan McLane, *The Intimate Life of Alexander Hamilton,* Charles Scribner's Sons, NY, 1910; Brookhiser, Richard, *Alexander Hamilton, American,* Simon & Schuster, NY, 1999; Randall, Willard Sterne, *Alexander Hamilton, A Life,* HarperCollins, NY, 2003; Chernow, Ron, *Alexander Hamilton,* The Penguin Press, NY, 2004.

161 . . . rushing to burn the wheat fields of her country home before the enemy could harvest the crop: Zall, P. M., *Founding Mothers,* Heritage Books, Washington, DC, 1991, p. 159.

162 "the morning you": Thomas Jefferson to Angelica Schuyler Church, February 21, 1788, Electronic Text Center, University of Virginia Library.

162 "Major Pinckney's": *Adams Papers,* Massachusetts Historical Society, p. 37.

162 "caused much scandal": Ibid.

162 "Probably her own": *Last Will and Testament of Alexander Hamilton,* July 9, 1804, Papers of Alexander Hamilton, in Chernow, p. 695.

163 "It had long before": Bethune, The Rev. George W., *Memoirs of Mrs. Joanna Bethune,* Harper & Brothers, NY, 1862, p. 78.

164 "the young daughters": Matthews, Joanna, *A Short History of the Orphan Asylum Society in the City of New York, Founded 1806,* Anson D.F. Randolph and Co., NY, 1893, p. 10.

164 "before many years": Ibid.

164 "Mrs. Hamilton, widow of": Ibid.

164 "promoters of the": Ibid.

164 "God himself": Ibid. p. 12.

164 "a respectable physician": Ibid. pp. 14–5.

164 "at the expiration": Ibid.

165 "shall be managed": *An Act to incorporate the Orphan Asylum Society in the City of New York. Passed April 7, 1807,* ibid. pp. 16–7.

165 "any loss": Ibid.

165 "In any time": Bethune, p. 96.

166 "might become vagrants": *Short History,* p. 28.

166 "Arrangements made": Thomas Jefferson to Martha Jefferson Randolpoh, May 6, 1805, in Betts, p. 270.

166 "a fashionable wig": Martha Jefferson Randolph to Thomas Jefferson, October 26, 1805, in Betts, p. 280.

166 "If Mrs. Randolph": Dolley Payne Madison to James Madison, January 26, 1805, *Selected Letters,* p. 66.

166 "a commission from": Dolley Payne Madison to James Madison, October 30, 1805, *Selected Letters,* p. 68.

166 "Mrs. Randolph is": James Madison to Dolley Payne Madison, October 30, 1805, *Selected Letters,* p. 76.

166 "Mrs. Randolph": Louisa Catherine Adams to Abigail Adams, December 6, 1805, Adams Papers, II 5063.1–2, Massachusetts Historical Society.

167 the resident, Mrs. Merry, should call on her first: Wharton, *Social Life,* p. 114.

167 "Mrs. Randolph is": Louisa Catherine Adams to Abigail Adams, January 6, 1806, Adams Papers, II 5074.2, Massachusetts Historical Society.

167 "expects to be": Ibid.

167 "after the baby": Lousia Catherine Adams, "Adventures," Adams Papers, Massachusetts Historical Society.

167 "nor a servant": Ibid.

167 "Mrs. Randolph": Margaret Bayard Smith to Mrs. Kirkpatrick, May 4, 1806, *40 Years,* p. 50.

167 **"While I sat"**: Ibid.

168 **"Mrs. Randolph was"**: "Adventures," Charnley transcription, p. 53.

168 **"Who is that"**: Wister, Mrs. O. J., *Worthy Women of Our First Century*, J. B. Lippincott & Co., Philadelphia, 1877, pp. 40–1; Holloway, Laura C., *Ladies of the White House,* Bradley & Co., Philadelphia, 1881, p. 155; Sweetser, Kate Dickinson, *Famous Girls of the White House,* Thomas Y. Crowell Co., NY, 1930, p. 79.

168 **"Don't you know?"**: Ibid.

168 **"unusually intimate"**: Dolley Payne Madison to Anna Cutts, *Selected Letters*, June 4, 1805, p. 61.

168 **"Mrs. Merry's airs"**: Ibid.

168 **"This *Lady* of"**: Louisa Catherine Adams, Adventures, p. 79–80.

168 **"this was the"**: Ibid.

169 **"she never took"**: Ibid. p. 42.

169 **"to play chess"**: Ibid. p. 79.

169 **"We saw Mrs. Merry"**: Adams, Louisa, Adventures, Adams Papers, Massachusetts Historical Society, Charnley transcription.

169 **"I think her"**: Nellie Custis Lewis to Elizabeth Bordley Gibson, March 23, 1806, *George Washington's Beautiful Nelly, The letters of Eleanor Parke Custis Lewis to Elizabeth Bodley Gibson,* 1794–1851, ed. by Patricia Brady, University of South Carolina Press, Columbia, 1991, p. 67.

169 **"one who knew:"** Ibid.

169 **"Mr. Merry did"**: Rosalie Stier Calvert to Isabelle van Havre, January, 1806, *Mistress*, p. 138.

169 **"In short, it"**: Ibid.

169 **"they have been"**: Rosalie Stier Calvert to Mme. H. J. Stier, May 22, 1806, *Mistress,* p. 144.

169 **"the Americans will"**: Louisa Catherine Adams to John Quincy Adams, May 18, 1806, *Adams Papers*, II 5124.2, Massachusetts Historical Society.

169 **"a vast addition"**: Dolley Payne Madison to Anna Cutts, May 22, 1805, *Selected Letters*, p. 60.

169 **"good natured"**: Ibid.

169 **"I never visit"**: Ibid.

169 **"very well"**: Ibid.

170 **"whipped his wife"**: *Social Life in the Early Republic*, Anne Hollingsworth Wharton, Corner House Publishers, MA, 1970, p. 148.

170 **"Don't breathe"**: Ibid.

170 **"the poor woman's"**: Ibid.

170 **"There has been"**: Rosalie Stier Calvert to Mme. H. J. Stier, June 21, 1805, *Mistress,* p. 122–23.

170 **"even though his wife"**: Ibid.

170 **"These kinds of"**: Ibid.

170 **"the French minister"**: Louisa Catherine Adams, "Adventures," Adams Papers, Massachusetts Historical Society, Charnley transcription. Louisa Catherine Adams, p. 53.

170 **"poor vulgar"**: Ibid.

170 **"Mr. Jefferson's"**: Charnley transcript.

170 **"all the scandalous"**: Ibid.

171 **"eccentric"**: Wharton, *Social Life,* p. 68.

171 **"Since childhood"**: Rosalie Stier Calvert to Isabelle van Havre, February 18, 1805, *Mistress,* p. 111.

171 **"She never cared"**: Ibid.

171 **"Never were two"**: Ibid.

171   "eloped with": Faux, William, *Memorable Days in America, The City of Washington*, Junior League of Washington, ed. Thomas Froncek, Alfred Knopf, NY, 1977, p. 72.

171   "the fashionable talk": Dolley Payne Madison to Anna Cutts, May 8, 1804, *Selected Letters*, p. 54.

171   "in colors that": *City of Washington*, p. 72.

172   "He has very": Louisa Catherine Adams to John Quincy Adams, May 13, 1804, Adams Papers, II 4919.2, Massachusetts Historical Society.

172   "This is setting": Ibid.

172   "disagreement in disposition": *City of Washington*, p. 72.

172   "no elopement took place": Ibid.

172   "All of our": Rosalie Stier Calvert to Isabelle van Havre, November 11, 1806, *Mistress*, p. 150.

172   "better classes": Rosalie Stier Calvert to Isabelle van Havre, February 11, 1805, *Mistress*, p. 111.

172   "buy a small": Ibid.

172   "in her tastes": Ibid.

172   "too much activity": Rosalie Stier Calvert to Isabelle van Havre, January 1806, *Mistress*, p. 137.

172   "false alarm": Ibid.

172   "quite frail": Ibid.

173   "I hourly feel": Louisa Catherine Adams to Abigail Adams, December 6, 1805, Adams Papers, II 5063.1–2, Massachusetts Historical Society.

173   "Kiss my darling": Ibid.

173   "Having been": Louisa Catherine Adams to Abigail Adams, January 6, 1806, Adams Papers, II 5074.1, Massachusetts Historical Society.

173   "There cannot be": Abigails Adams to Louisa Catherine Adams, January 16, 1806, in Levin, p. 411.

173   "I should suppose": Ibid.

173   "and know how": Ibid.

173   "I did not feel": Louisa Catherine Adams to Abigail Adams, May 11, 1806, Adams Papers, II 5120.1–3, Massachusetts Historical Society.

174   "given a harshness": Ibid.

174   "I fear my": Ibid.

175   "forward to his": Louisa Catherine Adams to John Quincy Adams, Adams Papers, II 5127.1, Massachusetts Historical Society.

175   "even my approaching": Ibid.

175   "a long mile": Adventures, p. 82.

175   "gave birth": Ibid.

175   "Her child": Diary of John Quincy Adams, June 29–30, 1806, Adams Papers, digital edition. Massachusetts Historical Society.

175   "Her letter": Ibid.

175   "for having preserved": John Quincy Adams to Louisa Catherine Adams, Adams Papers, II 5140.1, Massachusetts Historical Society.

175   "the last dispatches": Louisa Catherine Adams to John Quincy Adams, May 18, 1806, Adams Papers, II 5124.1, Massachusetts Historical Society.

176   "John Randolph": Louisa Catherine Adams to John Quincy Adams, June 29, 1806, Adams Papers, II 5139.1, Massachusetts Historical Society.

176   "Self and family": Louisa Catherine Adams to John Quincy Adams, June 15, 1806, Adams Papers, II 5134.2, Massachusetts Historical Society.

176   "John is at Quincy": Louisa Catherine Adams to John Quincy Adams, January 1, 1807, Adams Papers, II 5187.2, Massachusetts Historical Society.

176 **"I am reconciled"**: Ibid.

176 **"Your mother says"**: Louisa Catherine Adams to John Quincy Adams, January 21, 1807, Adams Papers, II 5200.2, Massachusetts Historical Society.

176 **"Your father"**: Louisa Catherine Adams to John Quincy Adams, February 15, 1807, Adams Papers, II 5217.1, Massachusetts Historical Society.

176 *"certain friend of"*: Ibid.

177 **"always kind"**: *Adventures, p. 90.*

177 **"by the Otis"**: Ibid. p. 104.

177 **"told him to"**: Ibid.

177 **"he brought my"**: Ibid. p. 108.

177 **"Congress should not"**: "Adventures," 1807, Charnley p. 110. p. 89.

177 **"Mr. Randolph has"**: Louisa Catherine Adams to Abigail Adams, November 11, 1807, Adams Papers, II 5247.1, Massachusetts Historical Society.

177 **"affair of the Leopard"**: Ibid.

178 **"This fracas"**: Rosalie Stier Calvert to Mme. H. J. Stier, mid-July 1807, *Mistress,* p. 171.

178 **"Good-bye too"**: Ibid.

178 **"We are making"**: Thomas Jefferson to Martha Jefferson Randolph, July 27, 1807, in Betts, p. 311.

178 **"the war-fever is"**: Ibid.

178 **"We hear of nothing"**: Louisa Catherine Adams to Mary Cranch, December 13, 1807, Adams Papers, II 5251.1, Massachusetts Historical Society.

179 **"The ladies say"**: Ellen Wayles Randolph to Thomas Jefferson, January 29, 1808, in Betts, p. 324.

179 **"and that principle"**: Thomas Jefferson to Ellen Wayles Randolph, February 23, 1808, in Betts, p. 329.

179 **Martha Randolph . . . actually wove 157 yards of homespun**: Betts, p. 334.

179 **"if the embargo"**: Thomas Jefferson to Martha Jefferson Randolph, February 6, 1808, in Betts, p. 327.

179 **"This year is"**: Rosalie Stier Calvert to Mme. H. J. Stier, January 1, 1808, *Mistress,* p. 181.

179 **"The cry for war"**: Louisa Catherine Adams to Abigail Adams, January 24, 1808, Adams Papers, II 5272.1–2, Massachusetts Historical Society.

179 **"Parties are becoming"**: Ibid.

179 **"our situation here"**: Ibid.

179 **"the embargo"**: Roof, Katherine Metcalf, *Colonel William Smith and Lady, the Romance of Washington's Aide and Young Abigail Adams,* Houghton Mifflin, Boston, 1929, p. 280.

180 **"Upon every occasion"**: Ibid. p. 281.

180 **"The eastern"**: Rosalie Stier Calvert to Mme. H. J. Stier, May 5, 1808, *Mistress,* p. 184.

180 **"The farmers and planters"**: Ibid.

180 **"staggered my belief"**: Nagel, Paul C., *John Quincy Adams, A Public Life, A Private Life,* Harvard University Press, Cambridge, 1997, p. 178.

180 **"a true American"**: in Roof, p. 285–6.

180 **"Jefferson is definitely"**: Rosalie Stier Calvert to Mme. H. J. Stier, May 12, 1808, *Mistress,* pp. 189–90.

180 **"Mr. Madison I think"**: in Roof, p. 292.

181 **"All doubt of"**: Thomas Jefferson to Martha Jefferson Randolph, June 21, 1808, in Betts, p. 345.

181 **"Your friend"**: Samuel Mitchill to Catherine Mitchill, November 23, 1807, Allgor, Catherine, *A Perfect Union,* Henry Holt & Co., NY, 2006, p. 122.

181 **"The Secretary"**: Ibid.

181 **"succor on his side"**: Ibid.

181 **"The President"**: Dolley Payne Madison to Anna Cutts, August 28, 1808, *Selected Letters*, p. 87.

181 **"the evading it"**: Ibid.

181 **"The embargo"**: Roof, p. 286.

181 **"and hopes its her last"**: Ibid.

181 **"As the *period*"**: Martha Jefferson Randolph to Thomas Jefferson, February 17, 1809, in Betts, p. 382.

182 **"that the evening"**: Ibid.

182 **"was beaten by"**: Anthony, *First Ladies*, p. 81.

182 **"with Madison"**: Rosalie Stier Calvert to Isabelle van Havre, December 3, 1808, *Mistress*, p. 194.

CHAPTER FOUR

Books for this section are: Catherine Allgor, *A Perfect Union;* Allgor, *Parlor Politics;* Paul M. Zall, *Dolley Madison;* Cutts, *Memoirs and Letters of Dolley Madison,* first issued 1886, reissued 1971 (Port Washington, NY: Kennikat Press, 1971); Katharine Anthony, *Dolly Madison, Her Life and Times* (New York: Doubleday & Co., 1949); Carl Anthony, *First Ladies;* and Arnett, Ethel Stephens, *Mrs. James Madison, The Incomparable Dolley* (Greensboro, NC: Piedmont Press, 1972).

183 **"peculiarly fitted to"**: Eliza Collins Lee to Dolley Payne Madison, March 2, 1809, *Selected Letters*, p. 107.

184 **"She really in manners"**: Margaret Bayard Smith to Susan Bayard Smith, March 1809, *40 Years*, pp. 58–62.

185 **That affability would**: Allgor, *Perfect Union*, p. 144.

185 **Jefferson had shored**: Louisa Catherine Adams, Adventures, Massachusetts Historical Society, p. 113.

186 **"2 dozen very elegant"**: Benjamin Henry Latrobe to Dolley Payne Madison, March 22, 1809, *Selected Letters*, p. 112.

186 **Latrobe began a report**: Benjamin Henry Latrobe to Dolley Payne Madison, April 21, 1809, *Selected Letters*, p. 115.

186 **Included in the purchases**: Hunt-Jones, Conover, *Dolley and the "great little Madison,"* American Institute of Architects, Washington, 1977, p. 29.

187 **When Jefferson was president**: Martha Randolph to Dolley Payne Madison, January 15, 1808, *Selected Letters*, p. 83.

187 **"I cannot express the gratitude"**: Martha Randolph to Dolley Payne Madison, February 10, 1808, *Selected Letters*, p. 84.

188 **"In expectation that under"**: George Watterston to Dolley Payne Madison, March 10, 1809, *Selected Letters*, p. 109.

188 **"muff and tippet"**: John Jacob Astor to Dolley Payne Madison, February 11, 1811, in the *Dolley Madison Digital Edition,* Holly C. Shulman, Charlottesville, University of Virginia Press, Rotunda, 2004, http://rotunda.upress.virginia.edu/dmde/DPI.

188 **"the unintentional breach"**: Jane O'Bryan to Dolley Payne Madison, January 27, 1811, *Selected Letters*, pp. 134–35.

188 **"a daughter whose soul"**: Theodosia Burr Alston to Dolley Payne Madison, June 24, 1809, Dolley Madison Digital Edition.

189 **"Everybody loves Mrs. Madison"**: Anthony, Carl, p. 83.

189 **"Queen of Hearts"**: Ibid. p. 84.

189 **"more like a harvest"**: Cannon, Poppy, and Patricia Brooks, *The President's Cookbook,* Funk & Wagnalls, NY, 1968, p. 79.

189 **"as easy as if"**: Elbridge Gerry to Ann Gerry, June 2, 1813, and May 29, 1811, in Allgor, *Perfect Union,* p. 183.

190 **Dolley Madison's dinners:** Sarah Gales Seaton in Cannon, *Cookbook,* p. 82.

190 **"She makes herself"**: Catharine Akerly Mitchill to Margaretta Akerly Miller, January 2, 1811, in Allgor, *Perfect Union,* p. 190.

190 **"Dolley Madison adopted"**: Anthony, p. 195.

190 **"Invitations" took the form:** Young, *Washington Community,* p. 171.

191 **"Now let us put"**: Rosalie Stier Calvert to Henry Stier, April 1, 1809, *Mistress,* p. 201.

191 **"This country has reached"**: Rosalie Stier Calvert to Charles J. Stier, April 1, 1809, *Mistress,* p. 203.

191 **"now comes the"**: Rosalie Stier Calvert to Henry Stier, July 29, 1809, *Mistress,* p. 207.

192 **"All of the"**: Ibid. June 9, 1809, *Mistress,* p. 206.

192 **Dolley Madison was full:** http://inventors.about.com/library/inventors/blkeis.htm.

192 **"Commercial obstacles . . ."**: Rosalie Stier Calvert to Charles J. Stier, September 1, 1809, *Mistress,* p. 208.

192 **"One day it"**: Rosalie Stier Calvert to Henry Stier, November 11, 1809, *Mistress,* p. 212.

193 **"I don't know, dear Father"**: Ibid. November 10, 1810, *Mistress,* p. 230.

193 **"I must confess"**: Rosalie Stier Calvert to Isabelle van Havre, July 15, 1811, *Mistress,* p. 239.

193 **"It often makes"**: Rosalie Stier Calvert to Charles J. Stier, April 11, 1811, *Mistress,* p. 236.

193 **"I agree with"**: Rosalie Stier Calvert to Isabelle van Havre, October 30, 1809, *Mistress,* p. 211.

194 **"that another little brother"**: Isabelle van Havre to Rosalie Stier Calvert, undated 1812, *Mistress,* p. 233.

194 **"As you know"**: Rosalie Stier Calvert to Isabelle van Havre, August 12, 1810, *Mistress,* p. 224.

195 **"immense and costly"**: *40 Years,* p. 68.

195 **"excepting the hours"**:Ibid., p. 70.

195 **"Oh ye whose envenomed"**: Ibid., p. 76.

195 **"he is truly a philosopher"**: Ibid., p. 79.

195 **"'Oh,' said she laughing"**: Ibid., p. 81.

195 **"all plain country people"**: Ibid., p. 82.

196 **"a most excellent Virginia"**: Ibid., p. 83.

196 **Margaret Smith enjoyed:** Ibid., pp. 82–3.

196 **"have talked of"**: Louisa Adams to John Quincy Adams, March 1, 1809 (dated 1808 but that's impossible, she wasn't in Boston then), Adams Papers, II 5284.1.

196 **"I sensibly feel"**: Louisa Adams to Dolley Payne Madison, July 24, 09, Dolley Madison Digital Edition.

197 **"lest I should excite"**: Louisa Adams, "Adventures," p. 132.

197 **"was always very"**: Ibid. p. 90.

197 **"if domestic separation"**: Ibid. p. 133.

197 **Having left his own mother:** Ibid. p. 163.

197 **"His father scorns"**: Ibid. p. 129.

197 **"No substitute on the"**: Ibid. p. 25.

197 **"I begin to think"**: Abigail Adams to Abigail Adams Smith, late 1808 or early 1809, in Roof, p. 295.

198 **"This separation from"**: Abigail Adams to Caroline Smith, 1809, in Roof, p. 300.

198   **"Adieu to America":** Louisa Adams, p. 132.
198   **"I had passed":** Ibid., p. 133.
198   **"vessel rolling and":** Ibid., p. 134.
198   **"as usual I":** Ibid., p. 133.
199   **It was exquisite:** Ibid., p. 139.
199   **The women got:** Ibid., p. 141.
200   **"And thus ended":** Ibid., pp. 144–45.
200   **That of the Corps:** Ibid., p. 147.
200   **The American was:** Ibid., p. 149.
200   **"what would have":** Ibid.
201   **The toddler led:** Ibid., p. 150.
201   **"a lady who had":** Ibid., p. 151.
201   **Louisa Adams stewed:** Ibid., p. 162.
201   **Even so, with:** Shepherd, p. 153.
202   **"who always had":** Louisa Adams, p. 163.
202   **"so charmed with":** Louisa Adams, p. 166.
202   **"what weight and":** Abigail Adams to Catherine Johnson, September 13, 1810, in Levin, p. 440.
202   **"The distinction paid":** Louisa Adams, p. 174.
203   **So the ladies:** Ibid., pp. 176–68.
203   **"I observed that it":** Ibid., p. 177.
203   **"makes ruin stare":** Shepherd, p. 149.
203   **"All well":** Louisa Adams, p. 168.
204   **"A splendid bridge":** Rosalie Stier Calvert to Isabelle van Havre, July 15, 1811, *Mistress,* p. 240.
204   **"He tells me":** Francis Scott Key to Dolley Payne Madison, March 30, 1810, Dolley Madison Digital Edition.
205   **When she reopened:** *FreeBlacks and Slaves, 1790–1861,* copyrighted, http://media .wiley.com/product_data/excerpt/83/04714025/0471402583.pdf.
205   **The well-educated:** Much of the information for this section comes from Feeney, Leonard, *Mother Seton,* The Ravengate Press, Cambridge, MA, 1999, first published 1938; Edward T. James, editor, *Notable American Women, A Biographical Dictionary,* The Belknap Press, Harvard University, Cambridge, MA, 1971; "Biography of St. Elizabeth Ann Seton," http://www.emmitsburg.net/setonshrine/bio.htm.
205   **"my own home at 20":** Briggs, Kenneth A., "For Mother Seton, Sainthood Crowns Career in Church, *New York Times,* December 13, 1974, p. 47.
206   **"began jumping away":** Feeney, p. 72.
206   **"My husband on":** Ibid., p. 74.
206   **"at no loss":** Ibid., p. 76.
206   **"a sensation of":** "Mother Seton Began Her Charities Here," *New York Times,* July 26, 1931.
207   **She wrote to her friends:** Feeney, p. 127.
207   **"If you could":** Ibid., p. 141.
208   **"would prefer before":** Ibid., p. 172.
210   **"I never will":** Dwight, Margaret Van Horn, *A Journey to Ohio in 1810,* University of Nebraska Press, Lincoln, 1991, first published 1913, p. 5.
211   **"If we drown":** Ibid., p. 8.
211   **"5 or 600 miles":** Ibid., p. 12.
211   **"I believe at":** Ibid., p. 16.
211   **"In the middle":** Ibid., p. 18.
211   **"as we see":** Ibid., p. 21.
212   **"If I were going":** Ibid., p. 23.

212 **She was young:** Ibid., p. 30.

212 **"it is not a":** Ibid., p. 32.

212 **"I have a":** Ibid., p. 33.

212 **"we have nothing":** Ibid., p. 35.

212 **"the reason so":** Ibid., p. 37.

213 **"he intended no":** Ibid., p. 40.

213 **"the landlord was":** Ibid., p. 41.

213 **"From what I":** Ibid., p. 47.

213 **"Rejoice with me":** Ibid., p. 52.

213 **"worn out my":** Ibid., p. 61.

213 **"not to run":** Ibid., p. 62.

213 **"Saturday—PM—Warren":** Ibid., p. 63.

213 **"I have a":** Ibid., p. 64.

214 **Soon Clay was on:** Allgor, *Parlor Politics*, p. 82.

215 **"I have never":** Dolley Payne Madison to Ruth Baldwin Barlow, November 15, 1811, Baldwin Family Papers, Huntington Library.

215 **"I have formed":** Margaret Bayard Smith to Mrs. Kirkpatrick, early 1811, *40 Years*, pp. 84–85.

215 **"Mrs. Clay and her":** Margaret Bayard Smith to Mrs. Kirkpatrick, Summer 1811, *40 Years*, p. 87.

216 **"are troublesome and difficult":** Dolley Payne Madison to James Taylor, November 10, 1810, *Selected Letters*, p. 133.

216 **"but as *people*":** Dolley Payne Madison to John G. Jackson, April 10, 1811, *Selected Letters*, p. 138.

216 **"*some very wicked*":** Dolley Payne Madison to James Taylor, March 13, 1811, *Selected Letters*, p. 137.

216 **"one of the":** Dall, Caroline H., *The Romance of the Association: or One Last Glimpse of Charlotte Temple and Eliza Wharton, A Curiosity of Literature and Life*, Press of John Wilson and Son, Cambridge, 1875, p. 78, google.com/books.

217 **"the only American":** Douty, Esther M., *Hasty Pudding and Barbary Pirates, A Life of Joel Barlow*, The Westminster Press, Philadelphia, 1975, p. 103.

218 **"I do not":** Ruth Barlow to Abraham Baldwin, June 19, 1795, in Baldwin Family Papers, Huntington Library.

219 **The Barlows had:** Ruth Barlow to Clara Baldwin, January 7, 1810, Baldwin Family Papers, Huntington Library.

219 **"uncommonly gay this":** Ibid., March 10, 1810.

219 **"popped in . . . without the":** Ibid., February 7, 1810.

219 **"Mme. Bonaparte was there":** Ibid., February 10, 1810.

219 **"handsome and disposed":** Ibid.

219 **"Mrs. Madison is gay":** Ibid., July 1, 1810.

219 **"You must not":** Ibid., March 10, 1810.

219 **"before you put":** Ibid., February 7, 1810.

220 **"We think it":** Ibid., March 10, 1810.

220 **"the folly of":** Ibid., April 9, 1810.

220 **"more fortunate in":** Ibid., June 10, 1810.

220 **"one of the finest":** Ibid., July 17, 1810.

220 **"This will reach you":** Rosalie Stier Calvert to Isabelle van Havre, July 15, 1811, *Mistress*, p. 240.

220 **"could manage it":** Rosalie Stier Calvert to Isabelle van Havre, December 12, 1811, *Mistress*, p. 242.

220 **"I will ask":** Dolley Payne Madison to Ruth Baldwin, November 15, 1811, *Selected Letters*, p. 151.

220   **"Never a poor"**: Clara Baldwin to Dolley Payne Madison, January 1, 1812, *Selected Letters*, p. 115.

221   **"The president may"**: Joel Barlow to Dolley Payne Madison, December 21, 1811, *Selected Lettters*, p. 152.

221   **"I have got"**: Ibid.

222   **"better than I expected"**: Ruth Barlow to Dolley Payne Madison, March 4, 1812, *Selected Letters*, p. 156.

222   **"Before this you"**: Dolley Payne Madison to Ruth Barlow, April 20, 1812, Baldwin Family Papers, Huntington Library.

223   **"Everything here is"**: Ruth Barlow to Dolley Payne Madison, April 15, 1812, Dolley Madison Digital Edition.

223   **"War, they say, is declared against England"**: Ruth Barlow to Clara Baldwin, July 25, 1812, Baldwin Family Papers, Huntington Library.

223   **"Our country is"**: Eliza Parker Custis to Ruth Barlow, August 15, 1812, Baldwin Family Papers, Huntington Library.

223   **"I almost fear"**: Ruth Barlow to Joel Barlow, November 5, 1812, Baldwin Family Papers, Huntington Library.

224   **"high raised expectations"**: Ruth Barlow to Dolley Payne Madison, November 10, 1812, Dolley Madison Digital Edition.

224   **That hope gave "Mr. B." courage**: Ibid., November 25, 1812.

224   **"the lover of"**: Ruth Barlow to Joel Barlow, November 12, 1812, Baldwin Family Papers, Huntington Library.

224   **"The horses legs"**: In Douty, 130.

224   **"I feel afraid"**: Ruth Barlow to General Wattersdorff, December 13, 1812, Baldwin Family Papers, Huntington Library.

225   **"The Emperor is"**: Douty, 133.

225   **"I desire that"**: Will of Ruth Baldwin Barlow, August 24, 1813, Baldwin Family Papers, Huntington Library.

226   **"As this is"**: Abigail Adams to James Madison, August 1, 1810, Adams Papers, Massachusetts Historical Society.

226   **"a moral man"**: Abigail Adams to Abigail Adams Smith, March 18, 1808, in Levin, p. 430.

227   **"Be pleased, Madame, to"**: James Madison to Abigail Adams, August 15, 1810, Adams Papers, Massachusetts Historical Society.

227   **"peculiar urgency manifested"**: James Madison to John Quincy Adams, October 10, 1810, in Levin, p. 442.

227   **"An appointment so"**: Abigail Adams to Louisa Adams, March 4, 1811, in Levin, p. 445.

227   **"that after mature"**: Abigail Adams to John Quincy Adams, March 4, 1811, in Levin, p. 446.

227   **"one of the most"**: Abigail Adams to Elizabeth Shaw Peabody, July 10, 1811, in Levin, p. 448.

227   **She wrote to Louisa's mother in Washington**: Levin, p. 447.

228   **"your letter to"**: John Quincy Adams to Abigail Adams, June 30, 1811, in Levin, p. 447.

228   **"peculiar circumstances"**: Nagel, Paul C., *John Quincy Adams: A Public Life, A Private Life,* Harvard University Press, Cambridge, MA, 1999. *John Quincy Adams,* p. 198.

228   **"The judges are"**: Dolley Payne Madison to Ruth Barlow, November 15, 1811, *Selected Lettters*, p. 150.

228   **"by the Empress"**: Louisa Catherine Adams, p. 181.

228   **"To give birth"**: Ibid. p. 183.

229 **"a new anxiety," there were "rumors":** Ibid. p. 184.

229 **"a little down":** Ibid. p. 185.

229 **"but he would":** Ibid. p. 179.

229 **"The maxim of":** Ibid. p. 184.

229 **"a craps table":** Ibid. p. 185.

229 **"What on earth is":** Ibid. p. 186.

229 **"My situation precludes":** Ibid. p. 188.

229 **"received any letters":** Abigail Adams to William Smith, in Roof, p. 306.

229 **"The fright produced":** Louisa Catherine Adams, p. 189.

229 **"received letters from":** Ibid.

230 **"quick and irascible":** John Quincy Adams Diary, July 26, 1811.

230 **"I think this":** Nagel, p. 201.

230 **"my lovely little":** Louisa Catherine Adams, pp. 192–93.

230 **"O she grows":** Ibid. p. 196.

231 **"dangerous and hopeless illness":** Ibid. p. 198.

231 **"heroine":** Abigail Adams to John Quincy Adams, November 17, 1811, in Levin, pp. 448–50.

231 **"from this fusion of":** Thomas Jefferson to Benjamin Rush, December 5, 1811, in Randolph, p. 352.

231 **"in convulsions":** Louisa Catherine Adams, p. 198.

231 **"so severe that the":** Shepherd, p. 163.

232 **"My child gone to":** Louisa Catherine Adams, p. 198.

232 **"with the finest":** John Quincy Adams to Abigail Adams, September 21, 1812, in Levin, p. 453.

232 **"My heart is":** Louisa Adams Journal, November 6, 1812.

232 **"in Mrs. Adams I":** Louisa Adams Journal, October 25, 1812.

232 **"Forty years has not":** Abigail Adams to Louisa Adams, January 20, 1813, in Levin, p. 454.

234 **"Everybody is astonished":** In Arnett, Ethel Stephens, *Mrs. James Madison, the Incomparable Dolley,* Piedmont Press, Greensboro, NC, 1972, p. 103.

234 **"The Smiths are":** Edward Coles to Dolley Payne Madison, June 10, 1811, *Selected Letters,* p. 142.

234 **"spoke very slightingly":** John Quincy Adams Diary, March 13, 1806, Massachusetts Historical Society, digital.

235 **"expressed the opinion":** William Lowndes to Elizabeth Pinckney Lowndes, December 7, 1811, in Ravenal, Mrs. St. Julien, *Life and Times of William Lowndes of South Carolina 1782–1822,* Houghton, Mifflin & Co., Cambridge, 1901, p. 90.

235 **"*I have no*":** Dolley Payne Madison to Edward Coles, June 15, 1811, *Selected Letters,* p. 144.

235 **"You despair too":** Lucy Payne Washington to Dolley Payne Madison, July 1811, *Selected Letters,* pp. 146–47.

235 **"The intrigue for":** Dolley Payne Madison to Anna Cutts, November 22, 1811, *Selected Letters,* p. 154.

236 **"The city is":** Dolley Payne Madison to Anna Cutts, July 15, 1811, *Selected Letters,* p. 148.

236 **"elegant" party "on the queen's birth night":** Dolley Payne Madison to Anna Cutts, December 22, 1811, *Selected Letters,* p. 154.

236 **"committed the yet":** William Lowndes to Elizabeth Pinckney Lowndes, February 9, 1812, in Ravenal, pp. 100–01.

236 **"DeWitt, etc, etc, ":** Dolley Payne Madison to Anna Cutts, March 20, 1812, *Selected Letters,* p. 157.

236 **"The vice p lies":** Ibid., p. 158.

236 **"The war business"**: Dolley Payne Madison to Anna Cutts, March 27, 1812, *Selected Letters*, p. 158.

237 **"her injurious conduct"**: Levin, p. 451.

237 **"our family has"**: Rosalie Stier Calvert to Isabelle van Havre, March or April 1812, *Mistress*, p. 245.

237 **"time to rest"**: Henry Stier to Rosalie Stier Calvert, January 3, 1813, *Mistress*, p. 252.

237 **"Tell your husband to"**: Henry Stier to Rosalie Stier Calvert, March 3, 1810, *Mistress*, p. 253.

238 **"to give his"**: Dolley Payne Madison to Anna Cutts, May 1812, *Selected Letters*, pp. 165–66.

238 **"every disposition to"**: Dolley Payne Madison to Phoebe P. Morris, August 16, 1814, *Selected Letters*, p. 171.

238 **"But what I fear"**: Rosalie Stier Calvert to Henry Stier, June 1812, *Mistress*, pp. 251–52.

239 **"You say he"**: Rosalie Stier Calvert to Isabelle van Havre, March or April 1812, *Mistress*, p. 245.

240 **"My present wish"**: Joseph Alston to Aaron Burr, July 26, 1812, Davis, Matthew L., in *Memoirs of Aaron Burr, Complete with Miscellaneous Selections from His Letters,* New York, 1836, FullBooks.com.

240 **"He said that"**: Timothy Green to Aaron Burr, December 7, 1812, in Davis.

240 **"I have engaged"**: Timothy Green to Aaron Burr, December 22, 1812, in Davis.

241 **"Another mail, and!"**: Joseph Alston to Theodosia Burr Alston, January 15, 1813, in Davis.

241 **"Forebodings! wretched, heart-rending"**: Joseph Alston to Theodosia Burr Alston, January 19, 1813, in Davis.

241 **"To-morrow will be"**: Joseph Alston to Aaron Burr, January 19, 1813, in Davis.

241 **"I parted with."**: Joseph Alston to Aaron Burr, January 31, 1813, in Davis.

242 **"Were she alive,"**: Cote, Richard N., *Theodosia Burr Alston: Portrait of a Prodigy,* Corinthian Books, Mount Pleasant, S.C., 2003, p. 271.

243 **"Meanwhile the country"**: Rosalie Stier Calvert to Charles J. Stier, February 24, 1813, *Mistress*, p. 253.

243 **"A few days"**: Dolley Payne Madison to Phoebe P. Morris, August 16, 1812, *Selected Letters*, p. 171.

243 **"Do you not"**: Dolley Payne Madison to Edward Coles, August 31, 1812, *Selected Letters*, p. 172.

243 **"It is said"**: Abijah Bigelow to his wife, in *Perfect Union*, p. 277.

244 **"I have not"**: Sarah Gales Seaton, October 1812, Seaton, Josephine, *William Winston Seaton of the National Intelligencer: A Biographical Sketch with Passing Notices of His Associates and Friends,* James R. Osgood & Co., Boston, 1871, Legacy Reprint Series, p. 83.

244 **"Tis not her"**: Sarah Gales Seaton, November 12, 1812, in Seaton, p. 85.

244 **"By her deportment in her own house"**: Historical Society of Pennsylvania, in Arnett, p. 110.

244 **"the attack on"**: Ibid.

244 **"a very good"**: Anthony, p. 87.

245 **"They tell me"**: Sally McKean Yrujo to Dolley Payne Madison, June 20, 1812, *Selected Letters*, pp. 166–68.

245 **"The disgraceful conduct"**: Dolley Payne Madison to Phoebe P. Morris, October 17, 1812, *Selected Letters*, p. 173.

246 **"If he had"**: Susan Wheeler Decatur to Dolley Payne Madison, March 8, 1811, Dolley Madison Digital Edition.

246 **"But for her"**: Arnett, p. 111.

247 **"so low"**: Seaton, Josephine, *William Winston Seaton of the National Intelligencer: A Biographical Sketch with Passing Notices of His Associates and Friends,* James R. Osgood and Co., Boston, 1871, Legacy Reprint Series, SGS, April 5, 1813, p. 99.

247 **"the little man"**: Ibid.

248 **"The major part"**: Ibid.

248 **"Your good friend"**: Ibid.

248 **"a most lively"**: Arnett, pp. 180–81.

248 **"Mrs. Madison called"**: Sarah Gales Seaton, March 5, 1813, p. 98.

248 **"most profuse ball"**: Sarah Gales Seaton, January 2, 1813, pp. 90–91.

248 **"Ladies of fifty years"**: Ibid.

248 **"though the splendid"**: Ibid.

248 **"the most transcendently"**: Ibid.

248 **"a model of"**: Ibid.

249 **"Mrs. Monroe paints"**: Ibid.

249 **"very sparingly"**: Augustus Foster to the Foreign Minister, April 24, 1812, in Ammon, Harry, *James Monroe, The Quest for National Identity,* American Political Biography Press, Newtown, CT, 1971, pp. 290–91.

249 **"the most stylish"**: Ibid

249 **"The plates were"**: Ibid.

249 **"she was dressed"**: Ibid.

249 **"the moderation of"**: Rosalie Stier Calvert to Charles J. Stier, February 24, 1813.

250 **"the great attention"**: *New England Palladium,* January 19, 1813, in *Perfect Union,* p. 294.

250 **"moves many things"**: Ibid.

250 **"more than common"**: Ibid.

250 **"I do not"**: Dolley Payne Madison to Edward Coles, May 13, 1813, *Selected Letters,* p. 176.

250 **"Mr. M. can"**: Ibid.

250 **"for the last"**: Ibid.

250 **"we are making"**: Ibid.

250 **"In my eyes"**: Ibid.

250 **"One of our"**: Ibid.

251 **"a large party"**: Ibid.

251 **"Your fears"**: Sarah Gales Seaton, March 1813, in Seaton, p. 109.

251 **"and consequent cruelty"**: Ibid.

251 **"You will see"**: Ibid.

251 **"Our great folk"**: William S. Smith to Caroline Smith, June 25, 1813, in Roof, p. 315.

251 **"Until the late"**: Margaret Bayard Smith to Mrs. Kirkpatrick, July 20, 1813, *40 Years,* pp. 87–88.

251 **"our little army"**: Ibid.

251 **"every precaution has"**: Ibid.

251 **"We have however"**: Ibid.

252 **"the proper"**: Sarah Gales Seaton, July 22, 1813, in Seaton, p. 111.

252 **"abused in the"**: Allgor, *Perfect Union,* p. 306.

252 **"turned our young"**: Sarah Coles to Dolley Payne Madison, July 19, 1813, *Selected Letters,* p. 178.

252 **"You will see"**: Sarah Gales Seaton, July 20, 1813, in Seaton, p. 110.

252 **"assures us most"**: Ibid.

253 **"rumor with her"**: Sarah Coles to Dolley Payne Madison, July 19, 1813.

253 **"nursed him night"**: Dolley Payne Madison to Edward Coles, July 2, 1813, *Selected Letters,* p. 177.

253 **"Now that I"**: Ibid.

253 **"there is a"**: Abigail Adams to James Monroe, April 3, 1813, in Levin, p. 456.

253 **"his service in"**: James Monroe to Abigail Adams, April 10, 1813, courtesy of the Massachusetts Historical Society.

253 **"many reflections"**: Abigail Adams to James Monroe, April 10, 1813, courtesy of the Massachusetts Historical Society.

253 **"early instructed"**: Ibid.

253 **"a young family"**: Ibid.

253 **"from my protector"**: Ibid.

253 **"the painful separation"**: Ibid.

254 **"having advanced many"**: Ibid.

254 **"do I fully"**: Ibid.

254 **"my Dear son"**: Abigail Adams to Elizabeth Peabody, June 26, 1813, in Gelles, Edith Bgelles, Portia, *The World of Abigail Adams,* Indiana University Press, 1992, p. 128.

254 **"It was become"**: Ibid.

254 **"It had been"**: Abigail Adams to John Quincy Adams to John Quincy Adams, April 23, 1813, in Levin, p. 457.

254 **"I should say"**: Ibid.

254 **"I am most"**: Dolley Payne Madison to Phoebe Morris, April 24, 1813, *Selected Letters,* p. 175.

255 **"reluctance to leave"**: Dolley Payne Madison to Edward Coles, May 13, 1813, *Selected Letters,* p. 176.

255 **"I have just"**: Rosalie Stier Calvert to Charles J. Stier, April 11, 1813, *Mistress,* p. 255.

255 **"I don't think"**: Ibid.

255 **"You will see"**: Sarah Gales Seaton, July 1813, in Seaton, p. 112.

255 **"Every art had"**: A. J. Dallas to Hannah Gallatin, July 22, 1813, in Adams, Henry, *The Life of Albert Gallatin,* B. Lippincott & Co., Philadelphia, 1879, p. 488, digitized by Google.

255 **"the political mischief:"** Ibid.

256 **"You have heard"**: Dolley Payne Madison to Hannah N. Gallatin, July 29, 1813, *Selected Letters,* p. 179.

256 **"Nothing however"**: Ibid.

256 **"Mr. Madison is"**: J. J. Astor to Hannah N. Gallatin, in Arnett, p. 215.

256 **"He well remembers"**: J. J. Astor to Dolley Payne Madison, November 29, 1812, Dolley Madison Digital Edition.

256 **"all anxiety to"**: Hannah N. Gallatin to Dolley Payne Madison, August 15, 1813, *Selected Letters,* pp. 180–81.

256 **"His enemies have"**: Ibid.

257 **"their safe & early"**: Dolley Payne Madison to Hannah N. Gallatin, August 30, 1813, *Selected Letters,* p. 181.

257 **"I expect Mrs. Randolph"**: Ibid.

257 **"tells a foolish"**: Ibid.

257 **"until the arrival"**: Dolley Payne Madison to Hannah N. Gallatin, November 12, 1813, Dolley Madison Digital Edition.

257 **"I miss them"**: Louisa Catherine Adams, post-January 25, 1814, courtesy of the Massachusetts Historical Society.

257 **"Your dear"**: Abigail Adams to John Quincy Adams, July 1, 1813, in Gelles, p. 167.

257 **"is a patient"**: Ibid.

257 **"My heart bleeds"**: Abigail Adams to John Quincy Adams, July 1, 1813, in Gelles, p. 167.

258 **"that it is his"**: Abigail Adams to Mercy Otis Warren, July 11, 1813, in Roof, p. 316.

258 **"I fear I"**: Abigail Adams to John Quincy Adams, July 14, 1813, in Gelles, p. 168.

258 **"How she got"**: Nagel, *Adams Women*, p. 145.

258 *On angels' wings to joys on high!:* Ibid.

258 **"The wound"**: Abigail Adams to John Quincy Adams, October 22, 1813, in Gelles, p. 168.

258 **"To me the loss"**: Abigail Adams to John Quincy Adams, September 13, 1813, in Gelles, p. 168.

258 **"Bitter is the"**: Abigail Adams to Louisa Catherine Adams, December 6, 1813, in Gelles, p. 170.

258 **"but how much"**: Ibid.

259 **"One of the first"**: Abigail Adams to John Quincy Adams, October 22, 1813, in Gelles, p. 171.

259 **"All that I"**: Abigail Adams to Mercy Otis Warren, September 13, 1813, in Gelles, p. 171.

259 **"Your friend"**: John Adams to Thomas Jefferson, August 16, 1813, in Cappon, p. 366.

259 **"one of the choice ones"**: Bober, *Abigail Adams*, p. 134.

259 **"How you do"**: Thomas Jefferson to Abigail Adams, August 22, 1813.

260 **"I have compared"**: Ibid.

260 **"in great affliction"**: Abigail Adams to Thomas Jefferson, September 20, 1813, in Cappon, pp. 377–78.

260 **"How you do"**: Ibid.

260 **"You sir"**: Ibid.

260 **"the assurance"**: Ibid.

260 *"Grief has changed"*: Ibid.

260 **"But . . . although"**: Ibid.

260 **"I know the"**: Thomas Jefferson to John Adams, October 12, 1813, in Cappon.

261 **"There are in"**: Elizabeth P. Bonaparte to Dolley Payne Madison, November 22, 1813, Dolley Madison Digital Edition.

261 **"such is the interest"**: Dolley Payne Madison to Elizabeth P. Bonaparte, November 24, 1813, Dolley Madison Digital Edition.

261 **"I will avail"**: Ibid.

261 **"The President's"**: Anthony, Katharine, p. 215.

261 **"The windows are"**: Ibid.

261 *"everybody, affected"*: Sarah Gales Seaton, January 2, 1814, in Seaton, pp. 112–13.

262 **"The Marine Band"**: Ibid.

262 **"the rouge which"**: Ibid.

262 **"Her majesty's appearance"**: Ibid.

262 **"We have ladies"**: Dolley Payne Madison to Martha Jefferson Randolph, January 9, 1814, *Selected Letters*, p. 183.

262 **"It is a pleasing"**: Ibid.

262 **"more and more"**: Margaret Bayard Smith to Mrs. Kirkpatrick, March 13, 1814, *40 Years*, pp. 94–97.

262 **"peculiar facilities":** Ibid.

263 **"The effect":** Ibid.

263 **"He recommended":** Ibid.

263 **"On every public":** Ibid.

263 **"a brave Republican":** Ruth B. Barlow to Dolley Payne Madison, April 8, 1814, Dolley Madison Digital Edition.

263 **"cause of justice":** Ibid.

263 **"Kalorama would":** Ruth B. Barlow to Dolley Payne Madison, December 16, 1813, Dolley Madison Digital Edition.

263 **"restrained by the:"** Elbridge Gerry to Dolley Payne Madison, March 3, 1814, Dolley Madison Digital Edition.

263 **"of the Allies'":** Rosalie Stier Calvert to Isabelle van Havre, May 24, 1814, *Mistress,* p. 266.

264 **"It must be":** Rosalie Stier Calvert to Henry J. Stier, June 10, 1814, *Mistress,* p. 267.

264 **"The King's brother":** Sarah Coles to Dolley Payne Madison, June 28, 1814, *Selected Letters,* p. 187.

264 **"the poor Empress":** Ibid.

264 **"May it give":** Ibid.

264 **"The obstacles which":** Elizabeth P. Bonaparte to Dolley Payne Madison, December 29, 1814, Dolley Madison Digital Edition.

264 **"The public are":** Ibid.

264 **"You know":** Dolley Payne Madison to Caroline Langdon Eustis, January 1, 1815, Dolley Madison Digital Edition.

265 **"The English are":** Rosalie Stier Calvert to Isabelle van Havre, June 24, 1814, *Mistress,* p. 271.

265 **"I don't know":** Ibid.

265 **"She may have":** Wharton, p. 163.

265 **"Almost everyone of":** Ibid., pp. 161–62.

266 **"really dangerous expedition":** Sarah Gales Seaton, June 27, 1814, in Seaton, p. 114.

266 **"as Gen. Armstrong":** Ibid.

266 **"I wish":** in Cutts, pp. 99–100.

266 **"if Mr. M.":** Ibid.

266 **"I am not":** Ibid.

266 **"loosened her beautiful":** Ibid.

266 **"Our preparations for":** Ibid.

266 **"small force the":** Ibid.

267 **"The British on":** Dolley Payne Madison to John Payne Todd, August 6, 1814, *Selected Letters,* p. 190.

267 **"in case of":** Dolley Payne Madison to Hannah N. Gallatin, August 1814, *Selected Letters,* p. 192.

267 **"we have a large":** Ibid.

267 **"Our troops marched":** Thornton, Anna, *Diary of Mrs. William Thornton. Capture of Washington by the British,* Columbia Historical Society of Washington, D.C., p. 173.

267 **"Every man":** Arnett, p. 219.

267 **"the general idea":** Ibid.

267 **"an abundance of":** Ibid.

267 **"a general removal":** Margaret Bayard Smith to Mrs. Kirkpatrick, August 1814, *40 Years,* p. 98.

267 "the President went": Allgor, *Perfect Union,* p. 311.

268 "word to Mrs. Madison": Ibid.

268 "In the present": Eleanor Young Jones to Dolley Payne Madison, August 23, 1814, Dolley Madison Digital Edition.

268 "I imagine it": Ibid.

268 "deeply engaged": Ibid.

268 "busy packing": Ibid.

268 The *National Intelligencer* revealed that day that the British force numbered in the thousands and that the Americans, under the command of Captain Joshua Barney, had blown up their own flotilla of ships and boats to try to thwart enemy advancement: Arnett, p. 220.

268 "Now all is": Wharton, p. 163.

268 "The last & probably": James Madison to Dolley Payne Madison, August 23, 1814, *Selected Letters,* p. 192.

269 "I know not": Anna P. Cutts to Dolley Payne Madison, August 23, 1814, *Selected Letters,* p. 194.

269 "by a loud": Margaret Bayard Smith, p. 99.

269 " 'He spoke in": Ibid.

269 "The troops were": Thornton, p. 174.

269 "And on my": Dolley Payne Madison to Lucy Payne Todd, August 23, 1814, *Selected Letters,* p. 193.

269 "written with pencil": Ibid.

270 "My friends": Ibid.

270 "To the last": Ibid.

270 "We feel assured": Arnett, p. 221.

270 "all able-bodied": Ibid.

270 "to throw up": Ibid.

270 "No accounts at": Thornton, pp. 174–75.

270 "Nearly all": Ibid.

270 "Since sunrise": Dolley Payne Madison to Lucy Payne Todd, August 23, 1814, *Selected Letters,* p. 193.

270 "galloped up to": Jennings, Paul, *A Colored Man's Reminiscences of James Madison,* James Madison University, p. 9, in Herrick, Carole L., *August 24, 1814, Washington in Flames,* Higher Education Publications, Falls Church, VA, 2005, p. 78.

271 "When I shall": Dolley Payne Madison to Lucy Payne Todd, August 24, 1814, *Selected Letters,* pp. 193–94.

271 "All then was": Jennings, in Herrick, p. 80.

271 "caught up what": Ibid.

271 "Those who should": Dolley Payne Madison to Mary Elizabeth Latrobe, December 3, 1814, in Anthony, p. 230.

271 "We heard": Thornton, p. 175.

272 "there witnessed": Ibid.

272 "Madam, to sup": Arnett, p. 225.

272 "a dinner table": Ibid.

272 "an elegant and": Ibid.

272 "speedily consumed": Herrick, p. 98.

272 "and drank some": Ibid.

273 "preferred the light": Arnett, p. 227.

273 "We were told": Herrick, p. 106.

273 "Your husband": In Allgor, p. 317.

274 **"They were on"**: Thornton, August 25, 1814, p. 175.

274 **"almost miraculous"**: Ibid.

274 **"it is feared"**: Ibid.

274 **"All those whose"**: Margaret Bayard Smith to Mrs. Kirkpatrick, August 25, 1814, *40 Years*, p. 101.

274 **"although troops when"**: Ibid., pp. 103–04.

274 **"disprepartion of our"**: Ibid.

274 **"And they will"**: Ibid.

275 **"advising our immediate"**: James Madison to Dolley Payne Madison, August 27, 1814, *Selected Letters*, p. 194.

275 **"hide their heads"**: Ibid.

275 **"heavy cannonading"**: Thornton, August 27, 1814, p. 177.

275 **"we slept pretty"**: Ibid.

275 **"into alarm"**: James Madison to Dolley Payne Madison, August 28, 1814, *Selected Letters*, p. 195.

275 **"our stupid mayor"**: In Thornton, August 27, 1814, p. 177.

275 **"The citizens expecting"**: Dolley Payne Madison to Mary Elizabeth Latrobe, December 3, 1814, in Anthony, p. 230.

275 **"She was very"**: Thornton, August 28, 1814, p. 178.

275 **"attribute the loss"**: Ibid.

275 **"the poor Capitol!"**: Ibid.

276 **"Oh vanity of!"**: Margaret Bayard Smith to Mrs. Kirkpatrick, August 30, 1814, *40 Years*, pp. 109–10.

276 **"much depressed"**: Ibid.

276 **"I was assured"**: Ibid., p. 115.

276 **"a cushion off"**: Ibid., p. 112.

276 **"I am sure"**: Rosalie Stier Calvert to Isabelle van Havre, August 30, 1814, *Mistress*, p. 271.

276 **"I saw several"**: Ibid.

276 **"All they"**: Margaret Bayard Smith to Mrs. Kirkpatrick, August 30, 1814, *40 Years*, p. 114.

276 **"The citizens"**: Ibid.

276 **"taking in plunder"**: In Thornton, September 3, 1814, p. 180.

276 **"nightly guard"**: Ibid.

276 **"Citizens have"**: Margaret Bayard Smith, September 11, 1814, p. 119.

277 **"They talk"**: William Lowndes to Elizabeth P. Lowndes, September 25, 1814, in Ravenal, p. 136.

277 **"of moving"**: Ibid.

277 **"I perceive the"**: Abigail Adams to William S. Smith, October 1, 1814, in Roof, p. 321.

277 **"the discussion"**: Jeremiah Mason to Mary Means Mason, October 6, 1814, Dolley Madison Digital Edition.

277 **"universally condemned"**: Ibid.

277 **"The disgraceful"**: Ibid.

277 **"What would I"**: Hannah Gallatin to Dolley Payne Madison, January 18, 1815, Dolley Madison Digital Edition.

278 **"What can be"**: Hannah Gallatin to Dolley Payne Madison, January 14, 1814, Dolley Madison Digital Edition.

278 **"What does the"**: Ibid.

278 **"Be consoled then"**: Dolley Payne Madison to Hannah N. Gallatin, January 21, 1814, Dolley Madison Digital Edition.

278 **"advantage of his talents"**: Hannah N. Gallatin to Dolley Payne Madison, May 15, 1814, Dolley Madison Digital Edition.

279 **"If the President"**: Ibid.

279 **"The Negotiations"**: Dolley Payne Madison to Hannah N. Gallatin, May 22, 1814, Dolley Madison Digital Edition.

279 **"nothing but anxiety"**: Ibid.

280 **"I arrived here"**: John Quincy Adams to Louisa Catherine Adams, May 3, 1814, Adams Papers, Massachusetts Historical Society, transcription by Heather Gilbert.

280 **"The merry bells"**: Ibid.

280 **"a kiss for"**: John Quincy Adams to Louisa Catherine Adams, May 7, 1814, Adams Papers, Massachusetts Historical Society, Heather Gilbert.

280 **"I am told that"**: Ibid.

280 **"We are rejoicing"**: Louisa Catherine Adams to John Quincy Adams, May 8, 1814, Adams Papers, Massachusetts Historical Society, Heather Gilbert.

280 **"I went last"**: John Quincy Adams to Louisa Catherine Adams, May 9, 1814, Adams Papers.

280 **"Not an hour"**: John Quincy Adams to Louisa Catherine Adams, May 13, 1814, Adams Papers.

280 **"We are overwhelmed"**: Louisa Catherine Adams to John Quincy Adams, May 19, 1814, Adams Papers.

281 **"If so, my"**: Ibid.

281 **"Mr. Gallatin and"**: John Quincy Adams to Louisa Catherine Adams, May 26, 1814, end of May 19 letter.

281 **"If anything"**: Louisa Catherine Adams to John Quincy Adams, May 27, 1814.

281 **"Our prospects"**: Louisa Catherine Adams to John Quincy Adams, May 28, 1814.

281 **"The proposal"**: John Quincy Adams to Louisa Catherine Adams, May 31, 1814.

281 **"Any place"**: Louisa Catherine Adams to John Quincy Adams, June 10, 1814.

282 **"He has a lake"**: Louisa Catherine Adams to John Quincy Adams, June 13, 1814.

282 **"She is left"**: Ibid.

282 **"I know that"**: Louisa Catherine Adams to John Quincy Adams, June 10, 1814.

282 **"In the affection"**: John Quincy Adams to Louisa Catherine Adams, June 14, 1814, continuation of letter begun June 12.

282 **"My nerves"**: John Quincy Adams to Louisa Catherine Adams, July 15, 1814.

282 **"the nauseating"**: John Quincy Adams to Louisa Catherine Adams, June 15, 1814, continuation of letter begun June 12.

283 **"The effort"**: John Quincy Adams to Louisa Catherine Adams, June 19, 1814, continuation of letter begun June 12.

283 **"I do not"**: Louisa Catherine Adams to John Quincy Adams, June 24, 1814.

283 **"Should you really"**: Ibid.

283 **"It is the"**: Louisa Catherine Adams to John Quincy Adams, June 24, 1814, no. 13.

283 **"We have General"**: Ibid.

283 **"It seems to"**: Ibid.

283 **"about your having"**: Dolley Payne Madison to Hannah N. Gallatin, July 28, 1814, Dolley Madison Digital Edition.

284 **"very *large* & complaining"**: Ibid.

284 **"They will elect"**: Ibid.

284 **"I was rejoiced"**: Ibid.

284 **"a gentilhomme"**: John Quincy Adams to Louisa Catherine Adams, July 12, 1814, Adams Papers.

284 "very naturally thinking": Ibid.

284 "Mr. Todd stays": Ibid.

284 "The English": Louisa Catherine Adams to John Quincy Adams, July 12, 1814.

284 "On the whole": Louisa Catherine Adams to John Quincy Adams, July 8, 1814, in letter begun July 6.

285 "What being on": Louisa Catherine Adams to John Quincy Adams, July 19, 1814.

285 "I certainly": John Quincy Adams to Louisa Catherine Adams, August 12, 1814.

285 "As to my": Louisa Catherine Adams to John Quincy Adams, September 4, 1814.

285 "I am informed": Louisa Catherine Adams to John Quincy Adams, July 15, 1814.

285 "All the late": Ibid.

286 "My spirits": Louisa Catherine Adams to John Quincy Adams, August 7, 1814.

286 "The Empress": Ibid.

286 "poor I became": Ibid.

286 "You will now": John Quincy Adams to Louisa Catherine Adams, August 9, 1814, Adams Papers.

286 "In case of peace": Dolley Payne Madison to Hannah N. Gallatin, August 8, 1814, Dolley Madison Digital Edition.

286 "The question you": Hannah N. Gallatin to Dolley Payne Madison, August 9, 1814, Dolley Madison Digital Edition.

287 "The perturbed": August 12, 1814.

287 "I was delighted": Louisa Catherine Adams to John Quincy Adams, August 15, 1814.

287 "but am very": Ibid.

287 "It is impossible": John Quincy Adams to Louisa Catherine Adams, August 16, 1814.

287 "Since I wrote": John Quincy Adams to Louisa Catherine Adams, August 19, 1814.

287 "The conferences": Ibid.

287 "We are in": John Quincy Adams to Louisa Catherine Adams, August 30, 1814.

288 "Yesterday we received": John Quincy Adams to Louisa Catherine Adams, September 6, 1814.

288 "Nor can I": Ibid.

288 "We are surrounded": Ibid.

288 "As the commerce": Ibid.

288 "I have had": Ibid.

288 "let me again": Ibid.

288 "You appear to": Louisa Catherine Adams to John Quincy Adams, September 30, 1814.

289 "I was further": John Quincy Adams to Louisa Catherine Adams, November 4, 1814.

289 "—I shall continue": Ibid.

289 "I know one": John Quincy Adams to Louisa Catherine Adams, September 23, 1814.

289 "There is much": John Quincy Adams to Louisa Catherine Adams, September 27, 1814.

289 "They are certainly": John Quincy Adams to Louisa Catherine Adams, September 9, 1814.

290 "Lord Hill has": John Quincy Adams to Louisa Catherine Adams, August 16, 1814.

290 "I hope that": Louisa Catherine Adams to John Quincy Adams, September 10, 1814.

290 **"It is commonly"**: William Lowndes to Elizabeth P. Lowndes, October 16, 1814, in Ravenal, p. 138.

290 **"We do not hear"**: Ibid.

290 **"I feel less"**: William Lowndes to Elizabeth P. Lowndes, October 23, 1814, in Ravenal, p. 139.

290 **"The *Conservateur* of"**: Louisa Catherine Adams to John Quincy Adams, September 13, 1814.

290 **"It will be like"**: John Quincy Adams to Louisa Catherine Adams, September 13, 1814.

291 **"If not they"**: John Quincy Adams to Louisa Catherine Adams, September 30, 1814.

291 **"Everybody looks at"**: Louisa Catherine Adams to John Quincy Adams, October 25, 1814.

291 **"you would suppose"**: Ibid.

291 **"—I do not"**: John Quincy Adams to Louisa Catherine Adams, October 25, 1814.

291 **"To be serious"**: Thomas Jefferson to Eliza House Trist, December 26, 1814, in Randolph, pp. 359–60.

292 **"When they shall"**: Ibid.

292 **"—We have yet"**: John Quincy Adams to Louisa Catherine Adams, November 22, 1814.

292 **"The British Government"**: Ibid.

292 **"We have been"**: Ibid.

293 **"Oh! That we"**: Ibid.

293 **"I am also"**: John Quincy Adams to Louisa Catherine Adams, December 23, 1814.

293 **"On Saturday last"**: John Quincy Adams to Louisa Catherine Adams, December 27, 1814.

293 **"The secret was"**: Ibid.

293 **"Whether he returns"**: Ibid.

294 **"He is also at"**: John Quincy Adams to Louisa Catherine Adams, December 30, 1814.

294 **"—Indeed although"**: Ibid.

294 **"instrument in the"**: Ibid.

294 **"acknowledge our power"**: Ibid.

295 **"Your brother is"**: Louise Livingston to Janet Montgomery, October 25, 1814, courtesy of the Historic Hudson Valley Library.

295 **"must appear elegant"**: Andrew Jackson to Rachel Jackson, August 10, 1814, in Remini, Robert V., *The Battle of New Orleans, Andrew Jackson and America's First Military Victory,* Penguin Books, New York, 1999, p. 15.

295 **"I owe to"**: Ibid.

296 **"cease all differences"**: Remini, p. 43.

296 **"a prince"**: Hunt, Louise Livingston, *Memoir of Mrs. Edward Livingston with Letters Hitherto Unpublished,* Harper & Brothers, New York, 1886, p. 53.

296 **"the ladies formed"**: Remini, p. 45.

296 **"We are ready"**: Lewis Livingston to Janet Montgomery, December 16, 1814, in Hunt, Charles Havens, *Life of Edward Livingston,* D. Appleton and Co., New York, 1864, Legacy Reprint Series, p. 198.

296 **"beauty and booty"**: Remini, pp. 59–60.

297 **"decorated with bouquets"**: Ibid.

297 **"marked by cruelty"**: Ibid.

297 **"held the command"**: Ibid.

297   **"That thought never"**: Remini, p. 71.

297   **"more than one"**: Ibid.

298   **"interesting appearance"**: Hunt, Louise, pp. 54–55.

298   **"in an Elysium"**: Ibid.

298   **"It was the"**: Ibid.

298   **The battles raged on until early January. . . . The women of the city used the material to whip up more than a thousand cloaks and another thousand pairs of pants, plus waistcoats and shirts by the hundreds, all in the matter of a week**: Remini, p. 123.

298   **"Crowds of women"**: Hunt, p. 56.

298   **"We trust in God"**: Edward Livingston to Janet Montgomery, January 6, 1815, courtesy of the Historic Hudson Valley Library.

298   **"my relations to"**: Ibid.

298   **"an account of"**: William Lowndes to Elizabeth P. Lowndes, January 8, 1815, in Ravenal, pp. 145–46.

299   **"this success will"**: Ibid.

299   **"Victory is ours!"**: Heaney, Sister Jane Frances, *A Century of Pioneering, A History of Ursuline Nuns in New Orleans, 1727–1827*, 1993, p. 238.

299   **"Louisiana is still"**: Louise Livingston to Janet Montogmery, January 12, 1815, in Hunt, pp. 59–60.

299   **"We killed eight"**: Ibid.

299   **"There never was"**: Ibid.

299   **"All I can say"**: Ibid.

300   **"came to conquer"**: Ibid.

300   **"was so highly"**: Heaney, pp. 238–39.

300   **"filled with bacon"**: Ibid.

300   **"in their turn"**: Heaney, p. 239.

300   **"amidst the acclamations"**: Lewis Livingston to Janet Montgomery, February 2, 1815, in Hunt, Charles, p. 202.

300   **"'Vive Jackson!'"**: Ibid.

301   **"In twenty four hours"**: Sarah Gales Seaton, January 11, 1815, in Seaton, pp. 124–25.

301   **"the general opinion"**: Ibid.

301   **"The fate of"**: Dolley Payne Madison to Hannah N. Gallatin, January 14, 1815, Dolley Madison Digital Edition.

301   **"The 8th of January"**: Thomas Johnson to Dolley Madison, January 19, 1815, in Anthony, Katharine, pp. 240–41.

301   **"All is exultation"**: Ibid.

301   **"my congratulations"**: Ibid.

301   **"We are all"**: in Anthony, p. 238.

301   **"Oh, if we"**: Ibid.

301   **"the most decided"**: Sarah Gales Seaton, February 4, 1815, in Seaton, p. 126.

302   **"We heard the"**: M. A. DeWolfe Howe, ed: *The Articulate Sisters, Passages from Journals and Letters of the Daughters of President Josiah Quincy of Harvard University*, Harvard University Press, Cambridge, MA, 1946, pp. 12–13.

302   **"soon confirmed"**: Ibid.

302   **"The gentlemen of"**: Ibid.

302   **"I played the"**: in Arnett, p. 192.

302   **"John and some"**: Ibid.

302   **"gentlemen of the most opposite politics," according to the *National Intelligencer:*** Allgor, *Perfect Union*, p. 333.

302 "elated spirits": Ibid.

302 "was Mrs. Madison": Ibid.

302 "that all uncertainty": Ibid.

303 "Now gladdens": E. Custis Lewis to Elizabeth Bordley, March 1, 1815, in Brady, Patricia, ed., *George Washington's Beautiful Nellie*, University of South Carolina Press, Columbia, 1991, p. 77.

303 "The time": William Lowndes to Elizabeth P. Lowndes, February 17, 1815, in Ravenal, p. 147.

303 "the best effect": Ibid.

303 "If our envoys": Rosalie Stier Calvert to Henry J. Stier, March 20, 1815, *Mistress*, p. 279.

303 "the last": Ibid.

303 "where I shall": Nagel, *John Quincy Adams*, p. 222.

303 "show that many": *Narrative of a Journey from Russia to France,* unpublished, Adams Papers, courtesy of the Massachusetts Historical Society, p. 1.

304 "the fancied": Ibid.

304 "in the company": Ibid., p. 2.

304 "even the Madeira": Ibid.

304 "once or twice": Ibid.

304 "last night a": Ibid., p. 4.

304 "known to be": Ibid., p. 5.

304 "until eleven": Ibid., pp. 6–7.

305 "silent houses": Ibid., p. 11.

305 "some trifling purchases": Ibid., p. 12.

305 "fell to pieces": Ibid.

305 "little more": Ibid., p. 13.

305 "dirty, ugly and ill": Ibid.

305 "surly, ill looking": Ibid.

305 "had my little": Ibid.

305 "The desolation": Ibid., p. 14.

305 "The Cossack!": Ibid.

305 "after an absence": Ibid., p. 15.

305 "Memory": Ibid.

305 "There I had felt": Ibid., pp. 20–21.

306 "military cap": Ibid.

306 "I had been": Ibid.

306 "a rumor had": Ibid., p. 21.

306 "*known* to be": Ibid., p. 16.

306 "She said that": Ibid.

306 "as it was a": Ibid., p. 17.

306 "whenever we": Ibid., p. 22.

306 "over which was": Ibid.

306 "began to grow uneasy": Ibid., p. 23.

306 "requested to speak": Ibid., p. 24.

307 "*Here was a situation*": Ibid.

307 "make arrangements": Ibid., p. 24.

307 "At present the": Ibid.

307 "some person to": Ibid., p. 25.

307 "He said the": Ibid., p. 26.

307 "wagons of every": Ibid.

307 "What a mere": Ibid.

308 "The Officer in": Ibid., p. 27.

308 **"He said the"**: Ibid., pp. 27–28.

308 **"a most respectable"**: Ibid., p. 29.

308 **"I had been"**: Ibid.

308 **"Charles seemed"**: Ibid., p. 29.

308 **"the horrible Cossacks"**: Ibid., p. 30.

308 **"mustering to express"**: Ibid., p. 31.

309 **"I sat in agony"**: Ibid.

309 **"At which the soldiers"**: Ibid.

309 **"a number of"**: Ibid., p. 32.

309 **"my situation"**: Ibid.

309 **"contribute much"**: Ibid.

309 **"no evidence"**: Ibid.

309 **"My poor boy"**: Ibid.

310 **"'Vive Napoleon!'"**: Ibid.

310 **"Soldiers were"**: Ibid., p. 33.

310 **"For the Revolution"**: Ibid., p. 34.

310 **"with a bayonet"**: Ibid.

310 **"This news"**: Ibid., p. 35.

310 **"or by some means"**: Ibid.

310 **"that in consequence"**: Ibid.

310 **"arrived in perfect"**: Ibid.

311 **"Mr. Gallatin"**: John Quincy Adams, *Diary,* March 23, 1815, Massachusetts Historical Society, Digital.

311 **"All the performances"**: Ibid.

311 **"They have been"**: Ibid.

311 **"I was fortunately"**: Ibid., p. 37.

312 **"And hope my"**: Catherine Johnson Smith to Dolley Payne Madison, December 25, 1814, Dolley Madison Digital Edition.

312 **"John Adams Smith"**: Abigail Adams to Dolley Payne Madison, May 14, 1815, Dolley Madison Digital Edition.

313 **"The existence of"**: Dolley Payne Madison to Hannah N. Gallatin, August 12, 1814, Dolley Madison Digital Edition.

313 **"I went to look"**: Hunt-Jones, p. 50.

313 **"The rooms"**: Ibid.

313 **"went to see"**: Horry, Harriott Pinckney, *Journal 1815,* unpublished, courtesy of the South Carolina Historical Society, June 6, 1815, p. 16.

313 **"We can hardly"**: Zall, p. 57.

313 **"almost every"**: Ibid.

313 **"In the future"**: Rosalie Stier Calvert to Isabelle van Havre, May 6, 1815, *Mistress,* p. 282.

314 **"Next to Joshua"**: Hurd, Charles, *Washington Cavalcade,* in Arnett, p. 250.

314 **"She as well"**: Anthony, p. 243.

314 **"The Ladies of"**: *National Intelligencer,* October 10, 1815, in Arnett, p. 260.

314 **"It is hoped"**: Ibid.

314 **"our own descendants"**: Ibid.

314 **"It is therefore"**: Ibid.

314 **"First Directress"**: The Constitution of the Washington Orphan Asylum Society, December 1815, Dolley Madison Digital Edition.

315 **"must be a"**: Ibid.

315 **"A number of"**: The Washington Orphan Asylum Society to Congress, December 18, 1815, Dolley Madison Digital Edition.

315 **"and several destitute"**: Ibid.

315 **"useful members of society"**: Ibid.

315 **"Your petitioners"**: Ibid.

316 **"saucers instead of"**: Hunt-Jones, p. 55.

316 **"Such over flowing"**: Dolley Payne Madison to Hannah N. Gallatin, March 5, 1815, Dolley Madison Digital Edition.

316 **"There is every"**: Sarah Gales Seaton, November 1815, in Seaton, pp. 126–27.

316 **"Mr. Jefferson's"**: Ibid.

316 **"She will stay"**: Ibid.

316 **"General Jackson's"**: Sarah Gales Seaton, November 1815, in Seaton, pp. 131–32.

317 **"I wish much"**: Ibid.

317 **"on Mrs. Jackson's"**: Ibid.

317 **"Mrs. Jackson is"**: Ibid.

317 **"She was dressed"**: Anthony, Katharine, p. 236.

317 **"Mrs. Madison's"**: Ibid.

317 **"Mrs. Madison was"**: Ibid.

317 **"It took us"**: Arnett, p. 197.

318 **"barbarous grandeur"**: Anthony, p. 244.

318 **"some of the"**: Sarah Gales Seaton, May 1816, in Seaton, pp. 134–35.

318 **"everybody flocked"**: "Exile in Yankeeland: The Journal of Mary Bagot, 1816–1819, quoted in *Mistress,* p. 296n.

319 **"Gov. Tompkins"**: Dolley Payne Madison to Edward Coles, March 6, 1816, Dolley Madison Digital Edition.

319 **"The election"**: Ellen Randolph to Thomas Jefferson, March 19, 1816, in Betts, p. 413.

319 **"Mrs. Monroe"**: Ibid.

319 **"When are"**: Thomas Jefferson to Ellen Randolph, March 14, 1816, in Betts, pp. 412–13.

319 **"The void you"**: Ibid.

319 **"I was thrown"**: Randolph, p. 344.

319 **"I used to"**: Ibid.

319 **"We count one"**: Dolley Payne Madison to Edward Coles, March 6, 1816, Dolley Madison Digital Edition.

319 **"Our Virginia Belles"**: Ibid.

320 **"in rose-colored"**: in Arnett, p. 200.

320 **"Mrs. Madison"**: in Cutts, p. 140.

320 **"your granddaughter"**: Abigail Adams to Thomas Jefferson, January, 15, 1816, in Cappon, p. 500.

320 **"such delightful"**: Ibid.

320 **"but I am"**: Ibid.

320 **"is justly sensible"**: Thomas Jefferson to Abigail Adams, January 11, 1817, in Cappon, p. 504.

320 **"and could I"**: Ibid.

320 **"your affectionate"**: Ibid.

320 **"the last of the"**: Ammon, p. 355.

321 *And like IT, is admired by all!*: in Arnett, p. 201.

321 **"We are all"**: in Zall, p. 61.

321 **"Mrs. Madison"**: Ibid.

321 **"loved by all"**: Allgor, *Perfect Union,* pp. 340–41.

321 **"friends among"**: Ibid.

322 **"How much greater"**: Eliza Collins Lee to Dolley Payne Madison, March 4, 1817, Dolley Madison Digital Edition.

322 **"Thus the blessing":** Ibid.

322 **"the only permanent":** in Allgor, *Perfect Union,* p. 83.

CHAPTER SIX

323 **"the last of":** Crawford, Mary Caroline, *Romantic Days in the Early Republic,* Grosset & Dunlap, Inc., NY, 1912, p. 196.

324 **"was fortunate in":** Wharton, p. 184.

324 **"simple, but grand":** Wharton, p. 184

324 **"era of good":** *Columbian Sentinel,* Schlesinger, *Almanac,* p. 206.

324 **"The animosities":** February 12, 1817, Rosalie Stier Calvert to Charles J Stier, in *Mistress,* p. 315.

324 **"We learned":** Rosalie Stier Calvert to Isabelle van Havre, January 8, 1818, *Mistress,* p. 332.

324 **"beloved woman" Nancy Ward, or Nanye'hi, whose attempt to convince the tribal Council failed:** *Notable American Women, 1607–1950,* ed. Edward T. James, Janet Wilson James, Paul S. Boyer, Belknap Press of Harvard University Press, Cambridge, 1971, III: p. 542.

324 **"Although they":** Margaret Bayard Smith to Mrs. Kirkpatrick, November 23, 1817, *40 Years,* p. 141.

324 **"Few persons":** Ibid.

325 **"made so brilliant":** William Grayson to Monroe, November 28, 1785, in materials provided by Daniel Preston, The Papers of James Monroe, University of Mary Washington.

325 **"If you will":** Wootton, James E., *Elizabeth Kortright Monroe, 1768–1830,* Ash-Lawn Highland, the home of James Monroe, Charlottesville, 1987, p. 6.

325 **"decamped for":** Stephen M. Mitchell to William S. Johnson, February 21, 1786, in Preston materials.

325 **"we have not":** Ibid.

325 **"Having formed an":** James Monroe to Thomas Jefferson, May 1786, in Cunningham, Noble E. Jr., *Jefferson and Monroe, Constant Friendship and Respect,* Thomas Jefferson Foundation, Monticello Monograph Series, University of North Carolina Press, Chapel Hill, 2003, p. 22.

326 **"Mrs. Monroe hath":** in Wootton, p. 7.

326 **"the utmost anxiety":** James Monroe to Elizabeth Kortright Monroe, April 13, 1787, in Preston materials.

326 **"Mr. Madison":** Ibid.

326 **"She is a charming":** Martha Jefferson to Thomas Jefferson, July 10, 1791, Betts, p. 87.

327 **"she will probably":** Thomas Jefferson to Martha Jefferson Randolph, March 22, 1792, Betts, p. 96.

327 **"In this carriage":** quoted in Ammon, Harry, *James Monroe, The Quest for National Identity,* American Political Biography Press, Newtown, CT, 1971, p. 137–8.

327 **"To see Madame":** Ibid.

328 **"on hearing that":** Ibid.

329 **"very model":** William Wirt to Mrs. Mary Ellis, April 12, 1797 in Ammon, p. 163.

329 **"little too much":** Ibid.

329 **"his mother is":** James Monroe to Janet Montgomery, May 6, 1800, in Preston materials.

329 **"I cannot give":** Ibid.

329 **"Many things have"**: James Monroe to James Madison, November, 29, 1800, in Preston materials.

330 **"Accordingly he takes"**: Samuel L. Mitchill to Catherine Ackerly Mitchill, February 9, 1803, in Preston materials.

330 **"one of our"**: Samuel L Mitchell to Catherine Ackerly Mitchill, February 11, 1803, in Preston.

330 **"She is commended"**: Ibid.

330 **"the respect due"**: James Monroe to James Madison, March, 3, 1803, in Ammon, p. 229.

330 **"I often hear"**: George Sullivan to James Monroe, May 5, 1806, in Preston materials.

331 **"The moisture of"**: James Monroe to Joseph Jones, March, 12, 1804 in Preston materials.

331 **"attended with"**: Ibid.

331 **"Eliza is to be"**: Martha Jefferson Randolph to Thomas Jefferson, June 23, 1808, in Betts, p. 346.

331 **"an account of"**: St. George Tucker to Anne Frances Bland, December 18, 1807, in Wharton, p. 136.

331 **"She was dressed"**: Ibid.

331 **"The little monkey"**: Ibid.

332 **"Neither of us"**: James Monroe to Charles F. Mercer, November 18, 1811, in Preston materials.

332 **"With Mrs. Monroe"**: Margaret Bayard Smith to Mrs. Kirkpatrick, December 5, 1816, *40 Years,* p. 134.

332 **"It would not"**: Ibid.

332 **"Entertaining has not"**: Rosalie Stier Calvert to Isabelle van Havre, December 30, 1817, *Mistress,* p. 329.

332 **"Some say it"**: Ibid.

332 **"The splendor of"**: Cunningham, Noble E., Jr. *The Presidency of James Monroe,* University of Kansas Press, Lawrence, 1971, p. 139.

333 **"the frugality"**: Holloway, Laura C. *The Ladies of the White House,* U.S. Publishing Company, NY, 1870, p. 241.

333 **"in white and"**: Louisa Catherine Adams to John Adams, January 1, 1818, in Preston materials.

333 **"and moved not"**: Ibid.

333 **"She received us"**: Rosalie Stier Calvert to Isabelle van Havre, January 8, 1818, *Mistress,* p. 331.

333 **"a complete dress"**: Rosalie Stier Calvert to Isabelle van Havre, May 12, 1817, p. 320.

333 **"It was to"**: John Quincy Adams Diary, January 22, 1818, Massachusetts Historical Society, Digital Edition.

333 **"Mrs. Monroe"**: Ibid.

334 **"each give an"**: in Cunningham, p. 139.

334 **"In addition"**: Ibid.

334 **"put on some"**: Ibid.

334 **"defied all such"**: Ibid.

334 **"One always finds"**: Rosalie Stier Calvert to Isabelle van Havre, April 26, 1818, *Mistress,* p. 334.

334 **"During Mrs. Madison's"**: Ibid.

334 **"Do you know?"**: Eliza Collins Lee to Dolley Payne Madison, March 30, 1819, Dolley Madison Digital Edition.

334 **"the urbanity"**: Ibid.

334 **"I am . . . [a]"**: Dolley Payne Madison to Anna Cutts [ca. 23 July 1818], Dolley Madison Digital Edition.

335 **"I will send"**: Anne Marguerite-Henriette Hyde de Neuville to Dolley Payne Madison, October 22, 1818, Dolley Madison Digital Edition.

335 **"It is said"**: John Quincy Adams Diary, December 12, 1818, Massachusetts Historical Society, Digital Edition.

335 **"Mrs. Hay, daughter"**: Ibid.

335 **"Her object was"**: John Quincy Adams Diary, December 12, 1818, Massachusetts Historical Society, Digital Edition.

335 **"This woman is"**: Louisa Catherine Adams Journal, March 7, 1820, unpublished, courtesy of Massachusetts Historical Society.

336 **"in my day"**: Abigail Adams to Louisa Catherine Adams, January 24, 1818, in Withey, p. 313.

336 **"The first"**: Abigail Adams to Harriet Welsh, August 18, 1817, in Withey, p. 311.

336 **"I have really"**: in Nagel, *Women,* p. 193.

336 **"told me she"**: in Shepherd, *Cannibals,* p. 196.

337 **"My mother was"**: John Quincy Adams Diary, November 1, 1818, Massachusetts Historical Society, Digital Edition.

337 **"Oh! What must"**: Ibid.

337 **"appalling event"**: Thomas Boylston Adams to John Quincy Adams, November 13, 1818, in Levin, p. 487.

337 **"The dear partner"**: John Adams to Thomas Jefferson, October 10, 1815, in Cappon, p. 529.

337 **"God bless you"**: Thomas Jefferson to John Adams, November 13, 1818, in Cappon, p. 529.

337 **"I believe in"**: John Adams to Thomas Jefferson, December 8, 1818, in Cappon.

337 **"The Supreme Court"**: Louisa Catherine Adams, February 23, 1819, in Cappon.

337 **"oratory is of"**: Louisa Catherine Adams Journal, February 11, 1819, in Cappon.

338 **"where we were"**: Ibid.

338 **"Her costume"**: Louisa Catherine Adams, February 20, 1819, in Cappon.

338 **"She seemed to"**: Ibid.

338 **"the Spanish Treaty"**: Ibid.

338 **"best treaty"**: Louisa Catherine Adams, February 22, 1819, in Cappon.

338 **"The social season"**: Rosalie Stier Calvert to Henry J Stier, March 13, 1819, *Mistress,* p. 342–3.

338 **"was quite lively"**: Ibid.

338 **"she has been"**: Ibid.

339 **"a good company"**: Ibid.

339 **"There is great"**: Ibid.

339 **"The plates were"**: Ibid.

339 **"She is a charming"**: Rosalie Stier Calvert to Isabelle van Havre, March 25, 1819, *Mistress,* p. 348.

339 **"Sometimes at balls"**: Ibid. p. 345–348.

340 **"She would be"**: Rosalie Stier Calvert to Jean Michel van Havre, January 10, 1819, *Mistress,* p. 339.

340 **"Hear much of"**: Louisa Catherine Adams to John Adams, Journal, December 13, 1819.

340 **"Should like to"**: Ibid.

341 **"Women have an"**: in Anthony, C. p. 73.

341 Osterweis, Rollin G., *Rebecca Gratz, A Study in Charm,* G.P. Putnam's Sons, NY, 1935; *Letters of Rebecca Gratz,* ed with an introduction and notes by Rabbi David Philipson, D.D., The Jewish Publication Society of America, 1929; Ashton, Dianne,

Women and Judaism in Antebellum America, Wayne State University Press, Detroit, 1997 and the online Jewish Women's Archive, http://jwa.org.

342 **"The ladies of"**: Ashton, p. 13.

342 **"the foremost American"**: Ibid.

342 **"the merchant prince"**: in Osterweis, p. 63.

343 **"The Female Association"**: in Ashton, p. 63.

343 **"must be chosen"**: Ibid.

343 **"When she came"**: in, Osterweis, p. 123.

343 **"How do you?"**: Crawford, *Romantic Days*, p. 72.

344 **"When you read"**: Rebecca Gratz to Maria Gist Gratz, April 4, 1820, in Philipson, p. 29.

344 **"I have dwelt"**: Rebecca Gratz to Maria Gist Gratz, May 10, 1820, in Philipson, p. 32.

344 **"Poor little souls"**: Rebecca Gratz to Maria Gist Gratz, February 9, 1822, in Philipson, p. 55.

344 **"One would scarcely"**: Ibid.

344 **"A great deal"**: Rebecca Gratz to Maria Fenno Hoffman, March, 24, 1822, in Osterweis, p. 175.

345 **"with thanking great"**: Ibid.

345 **"A young gentleman"**: Rebecca Gratz to Maria Fenno Hoffman, March 9. 1818, in Osterweis, p. 183.

345 **"I proposed an"**: Ibid.

346 **"founder and first directress"**: in Osterweis, p. 190.

346 **"The Sunday School"**: Ibid.

346 **"These precious children"**: Rebecca Gratz to Maria Gist Gratz, December 13, 1824, Philipson, p. 71

346 **"but I dare"**: Ibid.

346 **"his object to"**: Rebecca Gratz to Maria Gist Gratz, January 21, 1821, Philipson, p. 44.

346 **"the bill now"**: Ibid.

346 *"a daughter in Israel"*: http://jwa.org.

347 **"calculated the expense"**: Margaret Bayard Smith to Anna Maria Smith, November 15, 1819, in letter started on November 12, *40 Years,* p. 144.

347 **"And the best"**: Louisa Catherine Adams, December 7, 1819.

348 **"I wish they"**: Louisa Catherine Adams, December 14, 1819.

348 **"The drawing room"**: Sarah Gales Seaton, December 1819, Seaton, p. 144.

348 **"Mrs. Adams"**: Ibid.

348 **"We had this"**: John Quincy Adams Diary, December 20, 1819, Massachusetts Historical Society Digital Edition.

348 **"to separate entirely"**: Ibid.

348 **"My wife has"**: Ibid.

349 **"steady eye upon"**: Ibid.

349 **"The etiquette question"**: Louisa Catherine Adams, December 21, 1819.

349 **"Being continually told"**: Ibid.

349 **"This evening was"**: Ibid.

349 **"It is understood"**: Ibid, December 22, 1819.

349 **"that a man"**: Ibid.

349 **"After traveling through"**: Ibid, December 23, 1819.

350 **"Rode out again"**: Ibid, December 24, 1819.

350 **"I can easily"**: John Adams to Louisa Catherine Adams, January 13, 1820, in Allgor, *Parlor Politics*, p. 153.

350 **"May the next"**: Louisa Catherine Adams, January 31, 1819.

350 "They have endeavored": Ibid.

350 "Much is expected": Louisa Catherine Adams, January 8, 1820.

350 "Our Vice-President": Margaret Bayard Smith to Mrs. Kirkpatrick, January 30, 1820.

350 "their numbers were": Ibid.

351 "As however ladies": Louisa Catherine Adams, January 20, 1820.

351 "a lady of ill fame": Ibid, January 24, 1820.

351 "I imagine there": Margaret Bayard Smith to Anna Maria Smith, January, 1819, p. 146–7.

351 "The room was": Louisa Catherine Adams, January 21, 1820.

351 "a tax was": Ibid.

351 "Even my countenance": Louisa Catherine Adams, January 29, 1820.

352 "There have been": Sarah Gales Seaton February, 1820, p. 145–147.

352 "The Senators": Ibid.

352 "The galleries are": Ibid.

352 "This subject": Ibid.

352 "We hear of": Louisa Catherine Adams, February 15, 1820.

352 "I wish it": Ibid.

352 "The famous question": Ibid, March 3, 1820.

352 "If this is": Ibid, March 3, 1820.

353 "a gross political": Ibid, March 4, 1820.

353 "Maria Monroe": Sarah Gales Seaton, February 2, 1820, p. 148.

353 "Only the attendants": Ibid., March 28, 1820, p. 148.

353 "In all things": Louisa Catherine Adams, March 10, 1820.

353 "The bride was": Louisa Catherine Adams, March 13, 1820.

353 "generous and good": Ibid.

353 "neglected education": Ibid.

353 "I walked over": Margaret Bayard Smith to Mrs. Kirkpatrick, April 23, 1820, p. 149–50.

354 "went into the": Ibid.

354 "an unusually long": Ibid.

354 "My blood ran": Louisa Catherine Adams, March 22, 1820.

354 "The whole town": Ibid.

354 When Barron applied to re-enter the navy after the War of 1812, Decatur opposed him with language that eventually led to the duel: McCarty, Clara S., *Duels in Virginia and Nearby Bladensburg,* The Dietz Press, Richmond, 1976, p. 41–43.

354 "What this man": Sarah Gales Seaton, March 28, 1820, p. 149.

354 "will be an": Ibid.

354 "She still lies": Ibid.

354 "Commodore Decatur's": Margaret Bayard Smith to Mrs. Kirkpatrick, April 23, 1820, p. 150.

354 "Mr. A. was": Louisa Catherine Adams, March 23, 1820.

355 "Surely this man": Ibid, March 24, 1820.

355 "Pity, my dear": Rosalie Stier Calvert to Isabelle van Havre, February 29, 1820, p. 357.

355 "They were always?" Ibid.

355 "after an illness": George Calvert to Henry J Stier, March 18, 1821, p. 366.

355 "On the head": Caroline Calvert to Charles J. Stier, February 27, 1821, p. 368.

355 "The Caucus": Louisa Catherine Adams, April 9, 1820.

355 "There were not": Ibid.

356 "Caucusing is at": Ibid.

356 **"it is scarcely":** Ibid, April 27, 1820.
356 **"went to see":** Ibid, April 28, 1820.
356 **"Congress having left":** Ibid, June 6, 1820.
356 **"the session had":** Ibid.
356 **"I recommended a":** Ibid.
357 **"I begged Mr.":** Ibid, December 19, 1820.
357 **Louisa deemed George "eccentric" and John "wild":** Ibid.
357 **"the coquette":** Ibid.
357 **"When young people":** Ibid.
357 **"Thus the routine":** Ibid, November 17, 1820.
357 **"The roads are":** Ibid.
358 **"On these occasions":** Ibid, February 21, 1821.
358 **"The city is":** Sarah Gales Seaton, February, 1821, Seaton, p. 152–3.
358 **"initiatory ball seemed":** Ibid.
358 **"The contrast between":** Ibid.
358 **"excessively warm":** Louisa Catherine Adams, February 22, 1821.
358 **"insupportable vulgar":** Ibid.
358 **"the race to supper":** Ibid.
358 **"must have thought":** Ibid.
358 **"went to dress":** Ibid.
358 **"I was seized":** Ibid.
358 **"it would give":** Ibid.
359 **"one or two":** Ibid, March 3, 1820.
359 **"arrived safe and":** Louisa Catherine Adams, March 5, 1821.
359 **"in the evening":** Ibid.
359 **"The eye of":** Ibid.
359 **"You may laugh but it is so":** Ibid.
359 **"I applied to":** Ibid, March 12, 1821.
360 **"The same romantic":** Ibid, March 15, 1821.
360 **"Had some":** Ibid, April 25, 1820.
360 **"But these I":** Ibid.
361 **"distinguished foreign lady":** Eckhardt, Celia Morris, *Fanny Wright, Rebel in America,* Harvard University Press, Cambridge, 1984, p. 40.
361 **"It is in vain":** Fanny Wright, *Course of Popular Lectures, 1829,* http:/www.spartacus .schoolnet.co.uk/Rewright.htm.
362 **"The female moiety":** Lutz, Alma, *Emma Willard, Pioneer Educator of American Women,* Beacon Press, Boston, 1964, p. 29.
362 **"young lady about":** Lutz, p. 48.
362 **"Prosper, and":** Ibid.
362 **"I was engaged":** http://www.emma.troy.ny.us/about/history/ehwillard/ehwillard .php.
363 **"become one of":** Rose Philippine Duchesne to Madeleine Sophie Barat, August 22, 1818 in Callan, Louise, RSCJ, *Philippine Duchesne, Frontier Missionary of the Sacred Heart,* The Newman Press, Westminster, M.D., 1965, p. 179–180.
364 **"many halts":** Rose Philippine Duchesne to Madeleine Sophie Barat, September 12, 1818, in Callan, p. 194.
364 **"will become a":** Ibid.
364 **"far into the":** Rose Philippine Duchesne to Madeleine Sophie Barat, 1818, in Callan, p. 198.
364 **"Many of the cows":** Ibid.
364 **"the only edible":** Ibid. www.kofc2951.org/koc/rose.html.

364 **"In our free":** Rose Philippine Duchesne to Madeleine Sophie Barat, October 1818, in Callan, p. 197.

364 **"Some of the":** Ibid.

364 **"savages":** Ibid.

364 *"half-breed . . . ":* Ibid.

364 **"colored people":** Ibid.

365 **"God knows why":** www.kofc2952.org/koc/rose.html

366 A few years later, in Philadelphia the Female Benevolent Society of St. Thomas' African Episcopal Church provided help to dues-paying members: Dorsey, Bruce, *Reforming Men and Women: Gender in the Antebellum City,* The Cornell University Press, 2002, p. 28.

366 **"In 1808 the African Benevolent Society formed to raise money for a school in Newport. Membership was open to any "person of color, whether male or female":** *We Are Your Sisters, Black Women in the Nineteenth Century,* ed. Dorothy Sterling, W.W. Norton & Co., New York, 1984, p. 107.

366 **"ten dollars be":** in Sterling, p. 108.

366 **"for the benefit":** Ibid, p. 109.

366 **"if any member":** Ibid.

366 **"Hannah Morris Treasurer":** Ibid, p. 106.

366 **"Mrs. Lucy Prince":** Proper, David R., *Lucy Terry Prince, Singer of History,* Pocumtuck Valley Memorial Assn, Deerfield, MA, 1997, p. 6.

367 **"Her volubility was":** Ibid.

367 *The Bars Fight:* in Proper, p. 19.

367 **"argued the case":** Ibid., 30.

368 **"made a better":** Ibid., p. 32.

368 **"Declaration of Sentiments":** *History of Woman's Suffrage,* vol. 1, by Elizabeth Cady Stanton, Susan B. Anthony and Matilda Joslyn Gage, 1887, About.Com: Women's History.

368 **"We hold these":** Ibid.

368 **"He has compelled":** Ibid.

369 **"The present incumbent":** Sarah Gales Seaton, 1822, Seaton, p. 155.

369 **"a committee be":** Ibid.

369 **"Encompassed as they":** Ibid.

369 **"The discussion is":** Margaret Bayard Smith to Mrs. Kirkpatrick, October, 12, 1822, *Forty Years,* p. 160–161.

369 *"This,* and the":** Ibid.

369 **"While you wish":** William Lowndes to Elizabeth P Lowndes, January 6, 1822, Ravenal, p. 230.

370 **"I thought when":** Ibid.

370 **"It is not":** Ibid.

370 **"aristocratic hauteur":** Nagel, *John Quincy Adams,* p. 282.

370 **"show yourself if":** in Shepherd, *Cannibals,* p. 226.

370 **"Do for once":** Louisa Catherine Adams to John Quincy Adams, June 28, 1822, in Allgor, *Parlor Politics,* p. 166.

370 **"and if harm":** Ibid.

370 **"how much I":** John Quincy Adams to Louisa Catherine Adams, July 15, 1822, Ibid.

370 **"I have not":** in Shepherd, *Cannibals,* p. 22.

370 **"were never designed":** Louis McLane to Kitty McLane, January 4, 1822, in *Parlor Politics,* p. 172.

370 **"without any of":** William Cabell Rives to Judith Walker Rives, December 17, 1823.

371 **"the intriguing for"**: Louisa Catherine Adams, December 1, 1822.

371 **"Tuesday campaign"**: Ibid., December 12, 1822.

371 **"My Tuesday evenings"**: Ibid.

371 **"five dollars to"**: Ibid., February 20, 1823.

371 **"had a party"**: Louisa Catherine Adams, December 10, 1822.

371 **"In the evening"**: Ibid., December 24, 1822.

371 **"I am very"**: Ibid., December 11, 1822.

371 **"We found in"**: Ibid., December 19. 1822.

371 **"But instead of"**: Ibid., December 12, 1822.

372 **"This is a"**: Ibid., December 14, 1822.

372 **"Let it come"**: Ibid., January 1, 1823.

372 **"handsomer than ever"**: Ibid., January 6, 1823.

372 **"unusually good"**: Ibid.

372 **"proportionally high"**: Ibid.

372 **"Had a party"**: Ibid., January 14, 1823.

372 **"the *Washington Republican*"**: Ibid.

372 **"In the evening"**: Ibid., January 24, 1823.

372 **"They presented her"**: Ibid., February 4, 1823.

372 **"was a gaudy"**: Ibid., February 13, 1823.

373 **"gave me a"**: Ibid., January 23, 1823.

373 **"this winter we"**: Ibid., February 3, 1823.

373 **"to be an"**: Ibid., February 8, 1823.

373 **"If we trace"**: Ibid., January 19, 1823.

373 **"I generally cut"**: Ibid.

373 **"was handsome"**: Ibid., February 21, 1823.

373 **"I will never"**: Ibid.

373 **"evenings keep up"**: Ibid., January 28, 1823.

373 **"the events of"**: Ibid., February 22, 1823.

374 **"inclined to play"**: Ibid., February 3, 1823.

374 **"took an opportunity"**: Ibid., February 10, 1823.

374 **"How much direction"**: Ibid., February 7, 1823.

374 **"an appearance of"**: Ibid.

374 **"Maryland, it is"**: Ibid., February 19, 1823.

374 **"For myself I"**: Ibid.

374 **"the young men"**: Ibid., December 29, 1822.

375 **"he had been"**: Ibid., February 27, 1823.

375 **"several weddings are"**: Ibid., February 21, 1823.

375 **"The reports about"**: Ibid., December 9, 1823.

375 **"it was however"**: Ibid., February 19, 1823.

375 **"The party as"**: Ibid., February 25, 1823.

376 **"morning visitors in"**: Ibid., February 26, 1823.

376 **"This is the"**: Ibid., March 1, 1823.

376 **"This session begins"**: Ibid., November 30, 1823.

376 **"that is to say"**: Ibid.

376 **"fatiguing vocation?"**: in Ravenal, p. 233.

376 **"Mrs. Lowndes and"**: Ibid.

376 **"To her dying"**: Ibid.

376 **"His talents"**: Louisa Catherine Adams, January 19, 1823.

377 **"The president's message"**: Ibid., December 2, 1823.

377 **"If I can"**: Ibid., December 3, 1823.

377 **"Everyday brings forth"**: Ibid., December 13, 1823.

378 **"The caucusing is"**: Ibid., December 4, 1823.

378 **"Mr. C[alhoun]"**: Margaret Bayard Smith to Mrs. Boyd, December 19, 1823, *40 Years,* p. 163.

378 **"You have no"**: Sarah Gales Seaton, December 1823, Seaton, p. 159–161.

378 **"Mr. Adams moves"**: Ibid.

378 **"This was what"**: Louisa Catherine Adams, December 19, 1823.

378 **"Mr. Webster is"**: Ibid, December 26, 1823.

378 **"I shall certainly"**: Margaret Bayard Smith to Mrs. Boyd, December 19, 1823, *40 Years,* p. 162.

378 **"We are prepared"**: Sarah Gales Seaton, December 1823, in Seaton, p. 159.

378 **"Much talk about"**: Louisa Catherine Adams, January 4, 1824.

378 **"I objected much"**: Ibid., December 20, 1823.

379 **"had written the"**: Ibid.

379 **"America is doubly"**: Ibid.

379 **"This day like"**: Ibid, December 27, 1823.

379 **"we have been"**: Ibid.

379 **"I worked very"**: Ibid., January 2, 1824.

379 *Belles and matrons:* John T. Agg in Wharton, p. 214, or John Ogg in Allgor, *Parlor Politics,* p. 179.

379 **"spread-eagles"**: in Wharton, p. 212.

380 **"Chandeliers to match"**: Louisa Catherine Adams, January 8, 1824.

380 **"looked very showy"**: Ibid.

380 **"ornaments for head"**: Allgor, *Parlor Politics,* p. 180.

380 **"He arrived at"**: Louisa Catherine Adams, January 8, 1824.

380 **"led him to"**: Ibid.

380 **"one of the"**: Ibid.

380 **"To have got"**: Ibid.

380 **"It is said"**: Phoebe Morris to Dolley Payne Madison, January 19, 1824, *Selected Letters,* p. 252.

381 **"Washington is certainly"**: Louise D'Avezac Livingston to Janet Montgomery, February 16, 1824, in Hunt, p. 74–75.

381 **"There are elements"**: Ibid.

381 **"more beautiful than"**: Ibid.

381 **"drawing rooms"**: Ibid.

381 **"This is the"**: Ibid.

382 **"The lawyers are"**: Louise D'Avezac Livingston to Edward Livingston, April 28, 1808, unpublished, Princeton University Archives, courtesy of Historic Hudson Valley.

382 **"you were deprived"**: Louisa D'Avezac Livingston to Edward Livingston, June 1, 1808.

383 **"knows how to"**: Ibid.

383 **"A little treatise"**: Louise D'Avezac Livingston to Edward Livingston, January 16, 1810.

383 **"Why are you"**: Edward Livingston to Louise D'Avezac Livingston, in Hunt, p. 89.

383 **"in cases where"**: Ibid.

383 **"the notice taken"**: Louise D'Avezac Livingston to Edward Livingston in Hunt, p. 87.

383 *"salon* became famous"**: in Crawford, Romantic Days, p. 394.

384 **"It is not one"**: Louise D'Avezac Livingston to Edward Livingston, December 23, 1828, Princeton University Archives, courtesy of Historic Hudson Valley.

384 **"There she would"**: in Wharton, p. 191.

385 **"Mr. Calhoun has"**: Margaret Bayard Smith to Mrs. Samuel Boyd, April 11, 1824, *40 Years,* p. 164.

385 **"He does not"**: Ibid.

385 **"Had the intimate"**: Margaret Bayard Smith to Mrs. Kirkpatrick, June 28, 1824, *40 Years,* p. 165.

385 **"You have no"**: Ibid.

385 **"deeply affected at"**: in Nagel, *John Quincy Adams,* p. 290.

386 **"For surely he"**: Phoebe Morris to Dolley Payne Madison, January 19, 1824, *Select Letters,* p. 251.

386 **"Almost every great"**: Louisa Catherine Adams, December 7, 1822.

386 **From the over-the-top festivities in New York:** in Eckhardt, p. 73.

386 **"You will see"**: Sarah Gales Seaton, September 1824, Seaton, p. 163–4.

386 **"very magnificent plans"**: Ibid.

387 **"It will require"**: Ibid.

387 **"to superintend the"**: Ibid., p. 167–8.

387 **"I was presented"**: Ibid.

387 **"You mention the"**: in Randolph, pp. 389–90.

387 **"what was the"**: in Randolph, p. 403.

387 **"As they approached"**: in Randolph, p. 390.

388 **"whether the Miss"**: James Madison to Dolley Payne Madison, November 5, 1824, *Select Letters,* p. 256.

388 **"We have lately"**: Ibid, November 27, 1824.

388 **"All the attentions"**: in Wharton, p. 200.

389 **"on the field"**: Ibid.

389 **"Last evening we"**: Sarah Gales Seaton, December 16, 1824, Seaton, p. 170.

389 **"The leader of"**: Ibid.

389 **"No individual could"**: Ibid., October 1824.

389 **"The whole city"**: Ibid., p. 172.

389 **"passed in high"**: Ibid.

389 **"This dry joke"**: Ibid.

389 **"The extravagance is"**: in Wharton, p. 200.

390 **"There are not"**: Ibid.

390 **"Mrs. Adams came"**: Sarah Gales Seaton, January 1825, Seaton, p. 172.

390 **"They are all"**: Ibid.

390 **"You do not"**: Dolley Payne Madison to Mary E.E. Cutts, January 22, 1825, Dolley Madison Digital Edition.

390 **"in two weeks"**: Ibid.

390 **"His friends in"**: Margaret Bayard Smith to Mrs. Boyd, January 14, 1825.

390 **"lights, noise"**: Ibid.

390 **"ably supported"**: Ibid.

390 **"Folks here generally"**: Ibid.

391 **"promises had been"**: Margaret Bayard Smith Notebook, February 1825, *40 Years,* p. 182 following.

392 **"Some one said"**: Ibid.

392 **"his wife had"**: Ibid.

392 **"a very mild"**: Ibid.

392 **"This would have"**: Ibid.

392 **"superb black velvet"**: Minnigerode, Meade, *Some American Ladies: Seven Informal Biographies,* Curtis Publishing Company, December 1925, p. 173.

393 **"He looked as"**: Margaret Bayard Smith Notebook, *40 Years,* February 1825, p. 183.

393 **"resume my books"**: Margaret Bayard Smith to Mrs. Boyd, January 14, 1825, Ibid., p. 180.

393 **"The city is"**: Sarah Gales Seaton, February 24, 1825.

393 **"Their last drawing"**: Ibid.

393 **"the will of"**: in Nagel, *John Quincy Adams,* p. 298–99.

394 **"I leave to"**: Abigail Adams to Thomas Boylston Adams, November 13, 1800, in Levin, p. 387.

Photograph Credits

INDEX

BOOKS BY
COKIE ROBERTS

ISBN 978-0-06-078235-1

ISBN 978-0-06-009026-5

ISBN 978-0-06-095954-8

ISBN 978-0-06-174195-1